Carlo Vessella
Sophisticated Speakers

Trends in Classics – Supplementary Volumes

Edited by
Franco Montanari and Antonios Rengakos

Scientific Committee
Alberto Bernabé · Margarethe Billerbeck
Claude Calame · Jonas Grethlein · Philip R. Hardie
Stephen J. Harrison · Stephen Hinds · Richard Hunter
Christina Kraus · Giuseppe Mastromarco · Gregory Nagy
Theodore D. Papanghelis · Giusto Picone · Kurt Raaflaub
Tim Whitmarsh · Bernhard Zimmermann

Volume 55

Carlo Vessella
Sophisticated Speakers

Atticistic pronunciation in the Atticist lexica

DE GRUYTER

ISBN 978-3-11-068517-6
e-ISBN (PDF) 978-3-11-043229-9
e-ISBN (EPUB) 978-3-11-043240-4
ISSN 1868-4785

Library of Congress Cataloging-in-Publication Data
A CIP catalog record for this book has been applied for at the Library of Congress.

Bibliographic information published by the Deutsche Nationalbibliothek
The Deutsche Nationalbibliothek lists this publication in the Deutsche Nationalbibliografie;
detailed bibliographic data are available in the Internet at http://dnb.dnb.de.

© 2019 Walter de Gruyter GmbH, Berlin/Boston
This volume is text- and page-identical with the hardback published in 2018.
Logo: Christopher Schneider, Laufen
Printing: CPI books GmbH, Leck
♾ Printed on acid-free paper
Printed in Germany

www.degruyter.com

To all those who could not pay for their education.

Foreword

Ancient Greek lexicography is a notoriously intricate field, and the reconstruction of ancient Greek phonology possibly poses more questions than it answers regarding the interpretation of ancient scholarship on spelling and pronunciation. The scope of this book is, fortunately, limited to a specific intersection of two areas, the prescriptive Atticist lexica composed in the 2nd and 3rd centuries AD, and the pronunciation that the readers of the lexica thought to be the most fitting for the educated speaker. Unfortunately, the study of the intersection of the two fields can often be many times more complicated than the study of each field in their own right. Consequently, many times the thread I was trying to follow lead to speculative areas of phonological reconstruction, and even more shadowy paths in the jungle of ancient lexicography: I hope at least that the following pages will serve the purpose of stimulating fresh discussion on what the Atticist lexica had to say to their audiences.

The discussions of Atticism and phonological problems have been purposefully separated from the commentary to the individual entries in the Atticist lexica. The reader can refer to the first six chapters for the discussion of the general problems concerning Atticism and the pronunciation of Greek. Alternatively, the reader will have the chance to jump directly to the second half of this book and use it as a commentary to the text of the Atticist lexica. The indexes and concordances at the end of the book enable the reader to find the most relevant technical terms of ancient Greek scholarship pertaining to the Atticist lexica and related texts, the ancient Greek terms used, and the authors and the passages referenced within this book.

This work would not have been possible without the support of the Foundation Hardt, the Center for Hellenic Studies, the Onassis Foundation, and the opportunity to stay in academia by teaching at the University of Glasgow and then at Harvard. To my *alma mater* La Sapienza, in Rome, I owe the opportunity of having had access to affordable education and a PhD programme in the first place, and to have met the inspiring teacher who would become my supervisor, Albio Cesare Cassio. To him I wish to give my deepest thanks for having made this work possible.

Sophisticated Speakers was born in Italian many years ago, as a PhD dissertation with the hellenising title *Le prescrizioni ortoepiche dei lessicografi atticisti* (Rome). Many people have followed the evolution of this book: Claudia A. Ciancaglini, Daniela Colomo, Emanuele Dettori, Julián Méndez Dosuna, Gregory Nagy, Michele Napolitano, Marden Nichols, Niall Strawson, Olga Tribulato have read and given insightful help throughout the process. Geoff Horrocks,

Philomen Probert and Andreas Willi have enabled further studies and discussion of my work in Cambridge and Oxford, as have Julián Méndez Dosuna in Salamanca, Marina Passalacqua in Rome, and Stephanos Matthaios and Antonios Rengakos in Thessaloniki. I am extremely thankful to all of them, as I am to my family and friends who have supported, and still support me in these years of academic wanderings.

Thessaloniki, 9 October 2017

Contents

I	**Atticist lexica and atticising pronunciation** — 1
1	Atticism and pronunciation — 1
2	Literary evidence for atticising pronunciation — 6
3	Lexica and higher education — 12
4	Descriptive and prescriptive Atticist lexicography — 14
5	The corpus — 17
5.1	*Antiatticista* — 17
5.2	Aelius Dionysius and Pausanias — 18
5.3	Phrynichus — 19
5.4	Moeris — 20
5.5	Philemon — 21
5.6	Philetaerus — 22
5.7	Herennius Philo / Ammonius — 23
5.8	Pollux — 24
5.9	Atticist lexica on papyrus — 25
6	Descriptions of pronunciation in the lexica — 26
6.1	Orthoepic prescriptions — 27
6.2	Technical terms — 28
6.3	Orthography and orthoepy — 32
7	Reconstructing the phonology of Greek in the second century AD — 34
8	Sound changes and the lexica: habits to unlearn — 38
9	Note on transcriptions — 39
II	**Vowel timbre** — 40
1	Timbre and spelling: evidence from inscriptions and papyri — 40
2	Front unrounded vowels — 45
2.1	The digraph ⟨ει⟩ — 46
2.1.1	The raising of /eː$_2$/ from Classical Attic to the 2nd century AD — 46
2.1.2	The digraph ⟨ει⟩ in the lexica — 49
2.2	The digraph ⟨αι⟩ — 50
2.2.1	The monophthongisation /ai/ > /ɛː$_3$/ — 50
2.2.2	⟨αι⟩ in the lexica — 53
2.3	The letter ⟨η⟩ — 54
2.3.1	The four alternative spellings for ⟨η⟩ in inscriptions and papyri — 54
2.3.2	⟨η⟩ in the lexica — 57

3	The monophthongisation /oi/ > /y/ —— 58
3.1	⟨ου⟩ ~ ⟨υ⟩ in inscriptions and papyri —— 58
3.2	⟨ου⟩ ~ ⟨υ⟩ in the Atticist lexica —— 59
4	Unrounding /y/ > /i/ —— 60
5	Diphthongs with long first element —— 61
6	⟨α⟩ ~ ⟨ε⟩ after a high vowel —— 63

III	**Vowel quantity: variations in spelling** —— 64
1	Spelling vowels, marking vowels —— 64
2	Grammarians, lexicographers and the chronology of isochrony —— 64
3	Dating isochrony —— 67
3.1	The role of the accent in the establishing of isochrony —— 68
3.2	Isochrony does not imply the merger of ⟨η⟩ and /i(:)/ —— 70
4	Spelling variations in inscriptions and papyri as evidence for isochrony —— 72
4.1	⟨o⟩ ~ ⟨ω⟩ —— 73
4.2	⟨η⟩ ~ ⟨ε⟩ —— 74
4.3	⟨η⟩ for short /i/ —— 75
4.4	⟨αι⟩ ~ ⟨ε⟩ —— 75
4.5	⟨ει⟩ for short /i/ —— 76
4.6	⟨ει⟩ ~ ⟨ε⟩ —— 77
4.7	⟨ου⟩ for short /y/ —— 77
4.8	⟨ου⟩ for short /u/ or /w/ —— 78
5	Spelling variations in the Atticist lexica —— 78
5.1	⟨o⟩ ~ ⟨ω⟩ —— 78
5.2	⟨η⟩ ~ ⟨ε⟩ —— 79
5.3	⟨αι⟩ ~ ⟨ε⟩ —— 80
5.4	⟨ει⟩ for short /i/ —— 80
5.5	⟨ει⟩ ~ ⟨ε⟩ —— 81
5.6	⟨ου⟩ for short /y/ —— 81

IV	**Prosodies** —— 82
1	Accents, breathings, quantity marks —— 82
2	Lectures without lectional signs —— 83
3	Lectional signs in inscriptions and papyri —— 88
4	*Dichrona* in orthoepic prescriptions —— 88
4.1	A —— 90
4.2	I —— 92
4.3	Y —— 93
5	The attribution of long vowels to Attic —— 93

6	Accentuation —— 95	
6.1	Accent types and accent changes —— 95	
6.2	Accent prescriptions in the lexica —— 96	
7	Breathings —— 101	
7.1	Initial aspiration and psilosis in Greek —— 101	
7.2	Initial aspirations in the lexica —— 101	
V	**Degemination —— 104**	
1	Degemination in Greek —— 104	
2	Degemination in inscriptions and papyri —— 107	
2.1	Degemination in Attic inscriptions of the archaic and classical periods —— 107	
2.2	Degemination in Hellenistic inscriptions and papyri —— 109	
2.3	Degemination in papyri of the Roman period —— 111	
3	Geminates in Greek loanwords in Latin —— 112	
4	Geminates in Latin loanwords in Greek —— 113	
5	The geminate ⟨ζ⟩ —— 114	
6	Degemination in the Atticist lexica —— 116	
VI	**Conclusions. Traits of atticising pronunciation —— 119**	
VII	**Lemmata and glosses —— 122**	

ἄ, ᾶ ἄ —— 122
ἄγανος —— 122
ἀγνοία —— 124
ἀγοράζειν —— 125
ἀγροῖκος —— 125
ἀγυιᾶ —— 126
ἀδολέσχης —— 129
ἀείτης —— 130
ἄθρους —— 131
ἄθυρμα —— 132
αἱματοπώτης —— 132
αἴτιαι —— 132
αἰώρα —— 134
ἄκρατον —— 136
ἀκταινοῦν —— 137
Ἀλαείς —— 138
ἀληθές —— 138
ἁλιέα —— 139

ἅλις —— 139
ἁλμυρός —— 139
ἀλοᾶν —— 141
ἀλύειν —— 141
ἁλυκός —— 142
ἅλυϲιϲ —— 142
ἅμαξα —— 143
ἀμίϲ —— 143
ἀμνός —— 144
ἀμπίϲχεϲ, ἀμπίϲχου —— 144
ἀμφορέα —— 144
ἀμῶϲ —— 146
ἀνάθημα —— 146
ἄναντεϲ —— 148
ἀναπηρία —— 148
ἀνάπλεωϲ —— 149
ἀναριχᾶϲθαι —— 149
ἀνεῖν —— 151
ἀνίλλειν —— 152
ἀντήλιοϲ —— 153
ἀνύειν —— 154
ἀνυπόδητοϲ —— 155
ἀξιόχρεωϲ —— 157
ἄπαν —— 157
ἀπαντικρύ —— 158
ἀπέδραν —— 158
ἀπέρατοϲ —— 161
ἀπέϲβηϲε —— 162
ἄπεφθοϲ —— 163
ἀπηδέϲ —— 165
ἀπηθεῖν —— 165
ἀπηλιώτηϲ —— 165
ἀπηχία —— 166
ἀποκτινύναι —— 166
ἀποχρῆ —— 166
ἆρα —— 167
ἄρκυεϲ —— 168
ἁρπαγή —— 168
ἄρχων —— 170
ἀϲμενώτεροϲ —— 170

ἀςφόδελος —— 171
ἀτεχνῶς —— 172
Ἀτρέα —— 172
ἄττα —— 172
αὐτοχειρίᾳ —— 173
ἀφοῦ —— 174
ἀχρεῖος —— 174
βαδίζειν —— 176
βιβλία —— 178
βοϊκός —— 179
βότρυς —— 179
βύβλινος —— 181
γέλοιος —— 181
γενέςθαι —— 182
γήϊνος —— 183
γρῦ —— 183
γρυλίζειν —— 184
γρυμεῖα —— 185
δανείζειν —— 186
δένδρα —— 187
δεξαμενή —— 188
διέτης —— 188
Διονυςεῖον —— 189
δόχμη —— 190
δύςερως —— 190
δύω —— 192
ἐβουλόμην —— 193
ἔγγεια —— 195
Ἐλαία —— 197
ἔπηλις —— 198
ἐπιμέλου —— 198
ἐπιτάδε —— 198
ἔπτυςχλοι —— 199
εὔκλεια —— 199
εὑρέ —— 199
εὕρεμα —— 199
εὐφυᾶ —— 200
ἑωθώς —— 201
ἦδος —— 201
ἡδύνω —— 202

ἠθάς —— 202
ἤμελλον —— 203
ἡμίςεια —— 203
ἡμωδία —— 204
ἤνυςτρον —— 204
Θαλῆς —— 205
θεῶςαι —— 205
Θηςέῳ —— 206
ἱερεία —— 207
ἱκετεία —— 208
ἱππέα —— 209
ἱππέας —— 209
ἰςότης —— 209
καρίς —— 211
κατάγειος —— 211
κάταντες —— 212
κεχρίςθαι —— 212
κλῆςαι —— 213
κνημίς —— 214
κυδώνιον —— 215
κυνηγεττεῖν —— 216
κυνοκέφαλλος —— 216
λαγώς —— 218
λῆμα —— 219
λητουργεῖν —— 220
λιπόνεως —— 220
μᾶζα —— 221
μανός —— 222
μάντεων —— 224
μιαρός —— 225
μόλυβδος —— 228
μυελός —— 228
μύςταξ —— 229
νεαλές —— 229
νεώς —— 230
νῆςτις —— 230
νόμος —— 230
ξῆναι —— 232
ξυάλη —— 233
ξυρεῖν —— 234

ξυρόν —— 234
οἰνοπώτης —— 235
ὀπτάνιον —— 235
ὄστρια —— 236
ὄφλειν —— 237
πάπυρος —— 237
πελαργός —— 238
πένταχα —— 239
πινακίς —— 239
πνῖγος —— 239
πρωπέρυσι —— 240
πύελος —— 241
πυθοῦ —— 243
πῶμα —— 245
ῥαφανίς —— 246
ῥοίδιον —— 246
σάκκος —— 247
σίαλον —— 249
στάχυς —— 249
σύνθημα —— 249
τητινός —— 249
τιμώρια —— 250
τριπλᾶ —— 250
ὑάλινος —— 251
ὕαλος —— 251
ὑδαρές —— 251
ὑδροπωτεῖν —— 251
ὑδροπώτης —— 251
ὑγίεια —— 251
υἱέος —— 252
φαρμακός —— 253
φιάλη —— 254
φιλόγελως —— 254
φρούριον —— 254
χαμᾶζε —— 254
χρέως —— 255
χρυσᾶ —— 256
χρυσόκερως —— 257
ψίαθος —— 257
ψιμύθιον —— 257

ψύα —— 258
ᾤδηκεν —— 260
ὦ τάν —— 260

VIII **Concordances and indexes** —— 263
Phonological traits involved in Atticist prescriptions —— 263
Technical terms employed in the glosses —— 269

IX **Abbreviations and bibliography** —— 278
1 Abbreviations; Atticist lexica —— 278
2 Bibliography —— 279

Index locorum —— 295

Index of Authors —— 312

Index of Subjects —— 313

Index of lemmata and glosses —— 314

Index of Greek technical terms and other notable words —— 319

I Atticist lexica and atticising pronunciation

1 Atticism and pronunciation

This book argues that the Atticist lexica written between the 2nd and 3rd centuries AD contain prescriptions about the pronunciation of Greek. Such prescriptions reflect what the educated elites of the imperial period thought to be the correct pronunciation of Greek: the same individuals who thought there was a pure variety of Greek to write – the Atticists – also thought that there was a pure pronunciation of Greek one should adopt in speaking. All the entries[1] that may contain relevant information on the special pronunciation of the Atticists in the 2nd and 3rd centuries AD are collected and discussed in the second half of this book, in an attempt at defining the standard of pronunciation associated with 2nd century linguistic purism.

The inquiry of this work walks a fine line between problems of spelling and pronunciation. Discussion of orthographical problems began with Alexandrian scholarship, and gradually evolved into an autonomous branch of grammatical tradition: by the 2nd century AD Herodian would provide a systematic discussion of orthography in his lost περὶ ὀρθογραφίας[2]. As all discussions of alternative spellings, ancient discussions of orthography may provide indirect information on the pronunciation of Greek. If a full a theoretical discussion becomes necessary to discuss whether one should write μῖμος or μεῖμος, ἔμπορος or ἔνπορος[3], we may reasonably suppose that one and the same pronunciation corresponded to both alternative spellings, not differently that when an explanation is needed to prescribe whether one should write *it's* or *its*, *bear* or *bare* in English. This book, however, bases on a corpus of prescriptions from the Atticist lexica that have a focus on pronunciation: exclusively, or in support of a specific spelling[4].

A very clear example of the information on pronunciation that can be found in the Atticist lexica is a gloss like the following – the Atticist Phrynichus included it in the *Ecloga*, a short Greek lexicon he composed towards the end of the 2nd century AD:

---

[1] When necessary, I will make a distinction between entries, lemmata, glosses: an entry is a lemma and its gloss. Most times however, I will just use gloss as a synonym of entry.
[2] On ancient orthography see Valente 2015b.
[3] Examples from Johannes Charax, περὶ ὀρθογραφίας (6th century AD), a work that continues Herodian's doctrine (dicussed in Valente 2015b: 964–9).
[4] Together with information on word-choice and correct usage, information on orthography must have been one of the reasons why the lexica were copied and used through Byzantine times.

(1) πελαργός· οἱ ἀμαθεῖς ἐκτείνουσι τὸ α, δέον cυcτέλλειν· Πελαργός γὰρ οὐδὲν ἄλλο ἢ Ἐρετριακῶς Πελαςγός.

πελαργός: the ignorant lengthen the *alpha*, whereas it needs to be short. Πελαργός is nothing else but the Eretrian for Πελαςγός.

Phryn. *Ecl.* 80

The gloss to πελαργός raises a number of questions. Why would a lexicographer care about the length of a vowel that is never accented? Why would a lexicographer care about the length of a vowel that is entirely indifferent for the scansion of a word? Note that (a) the scansion of *pe.lār.gós* does not change if the second syllable has a short vowel, and that (b) the length of the *alpha* is not relevant here for the purpose of accentuation.

These are not the only questions that a gloss like text (1) evokes. We may also ask ourselves to what extent, in the late 2nd century AD, were speakers of Greek used to an artificial pronunciation (πελᾱργός is not etymological), and what were the ideas about literacy and education that prompted the lexicographer to label as ἀμαθεῖς, 'ignorant' those who pronounced πελᾰργός and not πελᾱργός.

Atticistic Greek literature played with a distant Greek past, both mythical and historical – from Homer to the feats of Marathon and the political struggles of Demosthenes – conjuring a fictional world that D. Russell felicitously called 'Sophistopolis'[5]. This attitude is no less apparent in the linguistic choices of the Atticists[6]. Choices in lexicon, syntax or morphology aim at reproducing the style of 5th century Attic in works of the imperial period. The three aspects have been studied together to appraise the language of the Atticists at least since W. Schmid's *Der Atticismus* (Schmid 1887–1897): its five volumes contain detailed information on how the authors who strived to imitate classic Attic usage deviated from the model in word-choice, syntax, or morphology, but there is no mention at all of the way Greek was pronounced.

The same aspects considered by Schmid are still the main features that modern scholarship on Atticism takes into consideration when examining the style of Atticist writers[7]. There are certainly very good reasons to privilege these aspects

---

5 Russell 1983: 21 ff.
6 In addition to the general introduction to the Second Sophistic in Whitmarsh (2005), see also Anderson (1993: 101–133) on reenactments of the Greek past in imperial Greek oratory, Whitmarsh (2001) on imperial Greek literature and 2013: 86–112 on various instances of fictional past.
7 Swain 1996, Whitmarsh 2005: 41–54, Kim 2010 – and it has lead to somewhat inaccurate generalisations as Arnott's (1989: 374) statement that "the Atticists were not concerned with prosody".

of Atticism. Possibly the most important such reason is that ancient literature is known to us only in written form, to which we may add that writers of the imperial period certainly composed their works knowing that they would circulate mostly in writing. The Atticists themselves where concerned with word-choice. This trend is apparent in ancient Greek scholarship beginning as early as Aristophanes of Byzantium's περὶ τῶν ὑποπτευομένων μὴ εἰρῆϲθαι τοῖϲ παλαιοῖϲ, one of the first works to draw a line between contemporary usage and the language of Classical Attic literature[8]. Closer to the chronological scope of this book, the problem of word choice is explicitly addressed in Greek literature: the most outstanding example possibly being some of Lucian's parodies of Atticism, e. g. the *Lexiphanes, Pseudologista, Pro lapsu inter salutandum*, to mention but some[9].

But oratory – despite hard copies of speeches that could be purchased on the book market – was still performed orally. The remarks on the oral delivery of individual speakers as we read them in ancient literary criticism might have to do not only with the tone of the orators' voice or their style: they can actually refer to their accent, i.e. to the pronunciation they consciously adopted – or failed to adopt. Therefore, just as we see that imperial Greek literature tries to recreate forms and subjects of a Classical past, we may legitimately ask ourselves whether orators, and whoever read literature aloud, would not try to adopt a special pronunciation of Greek.

The anonymous treatise *On Rhetoric*, a work post-dating the late 2nd century AD[10], still rejects bad habits in composition as appalling to the hearers, and not the readers:

(2) αἱ καινοτομίαι τῶν ϲυντάξεων καὶ τῶν ἐγκλίϲεων καὶ τῶν διαθέϲεων καὶ αἱ περὶ τοὺϲ χρόνουϲ μεταλλάξειϲ καταϲείουϲι τὰ τοῦ ἀκροατοῦ ὦτα.

The innovations in word order, inflection, mood, and the changes in rhythm shake the ears of the audience.

Anon. Rhet. Spengel 1853 [I] 322.27–9

Flavius Philostratus uses exactly the same definition in his praise of an orator (Quirinus of Nicomedia),

(3) ἐρρωμένοϲ μὴν καὶ ϲφοδρὸϲ καὶ καταϲεῖϲαι δεινὸϲ ἀκροατοῦ ὦτα, καὶ γὰρ δὴ καὶ ἀπεϲχεδίαζεν.

---
8 Valente 2013: 159.
9 We can add the *Soloecista* (Luc. 18) to the list – even if possibly spurious, the work shares the same ideology as the other ones quoted.
10 It quotes Hermogenes of Tarsus (who lived between the 2nd and 3rd centuries AD) and Longinus (213–273 AD).

He was vigorous and energetic, and was skilled in startling into attention the ears of his audience.[11]

Philostrat. *VS* 621

Correct pronunciation of Greek was certainly part of the good delivery of any orator who could claim to have received respectable training. In this respect, Philostratus' remarks on Pausanias of Caesarea are of the greatest interest:

(4) ὁ δὲ Παυσανίας ἐπαιδεύθη μὲν ὑπὸ Ἡρώδου καὶ τῶν τοῦ Κλεψυδρίου μετεχόντων εἷς ἐγένετο, οὓς ἐκάλουν οἱ πολλοὶ διψῶντας, ἐς πολλὰ δὲ ἀναφέρων τῶν Ἡρώδου πλεονεκτημάτων καὶ μάλιστα τὸ αὐτοσχεδιάζειν ἀπήγγελλε δὲ αὐτὰ παχείᾳ τῇ γλώττῃ καὶ ὡς Καππαδόκαις ξύνηθες, ξυγκρούων μὲν τὰ σύμφωνα τῶν ϲτοιχείων, ϲυϲτέλλων δὲ τὰ μηκυνόμενα καὶ μηκύνων τὰ βραχέα, ὅθεν ἐκάλουν αὐτὸν οἱ πολλοὶ μάγειρον πολυτελῆ ὄψα πονήρως ἀρτύοντα.

[Pausanias] was educated by Herodes, and was one of the members of the Clepsydrion, who were vulgarly called "the thirsty ones." But though he inherited many of the peculiar excellences of Herodes, and especially his skill in extempore oratory, yet he used to deliver his declamations with a coarse and heavy accent, as is the way with the Cappadocians. He would make his consonants collide, would shorten the long syllables and lengthen the short. Hence he was commonly spoken of as a cook who spoiled expensive delicacies in the preparation.

Philostrat. *VS* 594

Philostratus' remarks reveal that a non-standard accent could seriously impair the effectiveness of otherwise excellent rhetorical training; its negative impact on the overall appreciation of a rhetor could counteract one's training in the most prestigious rhetorical milieus of the time, and rhetorical skills equal to those of a celebrated teacher like Herodes Atticus. In the centuries of the Roman Empire "an ability to use the classical language (rather like the use of 'BBC English' until very recently) came to be regarded as a conspicuous and exclusive badge of class membership" (Horrocks 2010: 135). The simile is particularly felicitous: as BBC English is distinctive also because of its specific phonological traits, we may expect atticising Greek too to be characterised by a special phonology, and this is indeed recorded in literary sources of the period.

Recreating the usage of Classical Attic could be relatively easy in writing: a written copy of Demosthenes is helpful for imitating the orator's word-choice, syntax, or morphology, all of them bestowed with the mark of good Attic usage. But how could good Attic pronunciation be imitated? Hearing Demosthenes again was certainly not an option. Audiences of imperial times would have to invent their own criteria of linguistic purity to judge what should be

---

[11] The translations of all passages from Philostratus' *Lives of the Sophists* are by Wright (1921).

the purest accent, in a time when the number of speakers of Greek as a second language was high, and Greek itself was undergoing major sound changes. Also in this respect, Philostratus' description of Pausanias' delivery is revealing: his accent is described as 'Cappadocian', and he is said to 'make his consonants collide, [...] shorten the long syllables and lengthen the short.' Philostratus uses the same terminology that grammar handbooks of his time would use to describe the quantities of syllables and vowels[12]. Although it is impossible to reconstruct further the details of the speech of Pausanias, it is interesting that if we turn at the atticist lexica, we find the highest number of prescriptions on pronunciation precisely when long and short vowels are concerned.

Rhythm played a role in the appreciation of literary prose at least during Hellenism, especially the type that the Atticist contributed to obliterate, and labelled as 'Asianic' (Hutchinson 2015: 788). We should not be surprised, therefore, to hear of clashing long and short quantities and of speech rhythm in early accounts of oratory of the imperial times, Atticistic or not: at least the correct distribution of quantities was a factor in the appraisal of diction[13].

Playing on the conventional label of 'Second Sophistic', this work aims at describing the speech habits of the 'sophisticated speakers', the educated who consciously adopted a special pronunciation of Greek. It investigates the ideas concerning 'correct pronunciation' that were current among the Atticists in the 2nd century AD, and considers how they relate to the phonology of Greek reconstructed for the same period. In order to do this, this book analyses a specific kind of technical texts, the prescriptive Atticist lexica. These are word lists composed in the same period when Philostratus wrote his judgement on Pausanias, and they are a by-product of the same rhetorical training that Pausanias had received. The entries of such lexica prescribe correct linguistic usage contrasting 'correct Attic' forms to others that are not acceptable in correct writing, and – as I argue in this book – correct speaking.

---

12 Some examples are collected by Rothe (1989: 158–9), who supports the view that Philostratus is referring to syllables when he writes 'cυcτέλλων δὲ τὰ μηκυνόμενα καὶ μηκύνων τὰ βραχέα', even though he mixes terminology that normally refers to vowels only with terminology that refers to syllables. There is no need to imagine that Philostratus wanted to be impeccably accurate in the description of Pausanias' accent: but it is important that the wrong distribution of quantity should be the most noticeable trait of a less than accurate accent.

13 Whether quantitative patterns of short and long syllables were heard, and critically appreciated in terms of rhythmical prose is more controversial: Usher 2010: 94–5 argues that rhythm is only a rudimentary trait in most Greek prose; cf. Hunter 1983: 85 on Longus; Winterbottom 2011: 263–4 on Hellenistic rhythmical prose, the Atticist reaction to it, and accentual/metrical patterns in Cicero; Hutchinson 2015 on Appian, bibliography on Greek rhythmical prose in fn. 1 (cf. also Usher 2010: 82); an overview in also in Valiavitcharska 2013: 23–46.

This chapter serves as an introduction to the question of a 'received pronunciation of Attic Greek' in the late 2nd century AD and the role of the lexica in its prescription. Four chapters follow it, each one addressing a different set phonological changes that affect imperial Greek and are detectable in the Atticist lexica. I decided to keep the matter organised around the same ideas with which the lexicographers were working – changes that affect vowel timbre (chapter II), or quantity (chapter III), when they are also related to changes in spelling; changes that affect vowel quantity, the type and position of the accent, or initial aspiration, i.e. what ancient scholarship would label as προσῳδίαι in the broadest sense (chapter IV); the spelling of geminate consonants (chapter V).

The second part of the book presents the all the entries in the lexica that touch on the pronunciation of Greek, and comments on them individually. The entries are presented in alphabetical order. Again, I avoided grouping them according to modern categories which were absent at the time of their composition. Many of them involve more than one trait of ancient Greek phonology, and it seemed to me that organising them by the phonological traits involved would impose a modern view on texts that were not originally conceived to form a systematic discussion of individual points of Greek pronunciation. The concordances and indexes at the end of the volume provide an overview of the phonological traits implied in each entry and the technical terms that are used to describe them.

2 Literary evidence for atticising pronunciation[14]

The observation on the accent of Pausanias of Caesarea (text n.(4) above) is not the only remark on a speakers' accent that Philostratus makes in his writings. In his biography of Apollonius of Tyana – another Cappadocian –, Philostratus (VA 1.7) says that he had a surprising command of Attic: ἡ γλῶττα Ἀττικῶς εἶχεν, οὐδ' ἀπήχθη τὴν φωνὴν ὑπὸ τοῦ ἔθνους "his language (γλῶττα) was Attic, and was not strayed off in the pronunciation (τὴν φωνήν) by his nationality" (text n. (5) below).

Janse (2002: 354–7) pairs these examples with other passages in which speakers from Cappadocia are criticised for their language, arguing that they at-

---

14 James (2008), a paper read at the 139th APA (now SCS) conference (Chicago, 2008), discusses much of the evidence presented in this paragraph, and reaches very similar conclusions to mine in so far the similarities between the pronunciation of the sophists and the phonology of Attic inscriptions of the 2nd century AD is concerned. I am deeply grateful to the author for having given me a copy of his paper, unpublished to date.

test to ancient criticism of the Cappadocian accent in particular[15]. One of these reveals an association between local accent and education still apparent in the 4th century AD: nearly two centuries after the blossoming of pagan atticising oratory, Gregorius of Nazianzus tries to fight the bias against his regional accent, and the lack of education traditionally associated with it (ἀπαιδευςίαν δὲ οὐκ ἐγκαλέςεις ἢ ὅτι τραχύ ςοι δοκῶ καὶ ἄγροικον φθέγγεςθαι; *PG* 36.224, Janse 2002: 356).

The retention of a regional accent as a mark of ἀπαιδευςία is indicative of the expected role of higher rhetorical education. The absence a regional accent was the desired outcome of rhetorical training, that distinguished the most accomplished orators: this is apparent if one reads both passages quoted at the beginning of this section in their context. In the *Life of Apollonius*, command of Attic is part of the description of Apollonius' childhood, and Philostratus presents it as if it were the attribute of an *enfant prodige* – Apollonius could speak Attic even *before* moving on to higher education with a rhetor:

> (5) προϊὼν δὲ ἐς ἡλικίαν, ἐν ᾗ γράμματα, μνήμης τε ἰςχὺν ἐδήλου καὶ μελέτης κράτος, καὶ ἡ γλῶττα Ἀττικῶς εἶχεν, οὐδ' ἀπήχθη τὴν φωνὴν ὑπὸ τοῦ ἔθνους, ὀφθαλμοί τε πάντες ἐς αὐτὸν ἐφέροντο, καὶ γὰρ περίβλεπτος ἦν τὴν ὥραν. γεγονότα δὲ αὐτὸν ἔτη τεςςαρεςκαίδεκα ἄγει ἐς Ταρςοὺς ὁ πατὴρ παρ' Εὐθύδημον τὸν ἐκ Φοινίκης. ὁ δὲ Εὐθύδημος ῥήτωρ τε ἀγαθὸς ἦν καὶ ἐπαίδευε τοῦτον...
>
> When he reached an age to study literature, he showed a retentive memory and a power of application; his Greek was of the Attic kind and his accent unaffected by the region. All eyes were turned to him, so conspicuous was his youthful bloom. When he reached fourteen his father took him to Tarsus to study with Euthydemus of Phoenicia. Euthydemus was a good orator and began to teach him...[16]
>
> Philostrat. *VA* 1.7

The same is true of Pausanias of Caesarea. Philostratus spells out clearly that his defect of pronunciation contrasted with the training he had received from Herodes Atticus – Pausanias was 'a cook awfully concocting luxury delicacies (μάγειρον πολυτελῆ ὄψα πονήρως ἀρτύοντα)'.

Philostratus clearly traces the origin of linguistic proficiency to rhetorical training. We have seen that Apollonius of Tyana was portentous in mastering

---

[15] An epigram attributed to Lucian attests a bias against Cappadocia: θᾶττον ἔην λευκοὺς κόρακας πτηνάς τε χελώνας / εὑρεῖν ἢ δόκιμον ῥήτορα Καππαδόκην (*AP* 11.436). The extent to which such a remark refers to accent is questionable. Not being δόκιμος can reflect bad word-choice, or just be a convenient way of generally saying that people from Cappadocia did not normally have access to the same education as the author of the epigram, who apparently values their own much more than that of the Cappadocian orators.

[16] Transl. C.P. Jones, Loeb Classical Library 16, Cambridge, MA – London, 2005.

Attic without substantial training. In an anecdote on Herodes Atticus, Philostratus tells his readers that Herodes met a certain Heracles or Agathion, a shepherd dwelling in the Attic countryside, of god-like proportions and worshipped by the locals. Among the qualities of this portent, Philostratus mentions his flawless mastery of Attic.

(6) "τὴν δὲ δὴ γλῶτταν" ἔφη ὁ Ἡρώδης "πῶς ἐπαιδεύθης καὶ ὑπὸ τίνων; οὐ γάρ μοι τῶν ἀπαιδεύτων φαίνῃ." καὶ ὁ Ἀγαθίων "ἡ μεσογεία" ἔφη "τῆς Ἀττικῆς ἀγαθὸν διδασκαλεῖον ἀνδρὶ βουλομένῳ διαλέγεσθαι, οἱ μὲν γὰρ ἐν τῷ ἄστει Ἀθηναῖοι μισθοῦ δεχόμενοι Θρᾴκια καὶ Ποντικὰ μειράκια καὶ ἐξ ἄλλων ἐθνῶν βαρβάρων ξυνερρυηκότα παραφθείρονται παρ' αὐτῶν τὴν φωνὴν μᾶλλον ἢ ξυμβάλλονταί τι αὐτοῖς ἐς εὐγλωττίαν, ἡ μεσογεία δὲ ἄμικτος βαρβάροις οὖσα ὑγιαίνει αὐτοῖς ἡ φωνὴ καὶ ἡ γλῶττα τὴν ἄκραν Ἀτθίδα ἀποψάλλει."

"And what about your speech?" asked Herodes. "How were you educated, and by whom? For you do not seem to be an uneducated man". "The interior of Attica educated me," Agathion replied, "a good school for a man who wishes to be able to converse. For the Athenians in the city admit as hirelings youths who come in like a flood from Thrace and the Pontus and from other barbarian peoples, and their own speech deteriorates from the influence of these barbarians to a greater extent than they can contribute to the improvement of the speech of the newcomers. But the central district is untainted by barbarians, and hence its language remains uncorrupted and its dialect sounds the purest strain of Atthis".

Philostrat. *VS* 553

In order to evaluate this evidence, understanding technical terminology is crucial. Terms like γλῶττα, φωνή or ἀποψάλλειν can refer to the accent of a speaker, or more broadly to word-choice. The correct words may resonate, or it could actually be the correct sounds of Attic that resonate. ἀποψάλλειν is a metaphor, the verb originally refers to the plucking of a lyre's strings. Although it must remain speculative (the metaphor can be applied happily to word-choice too), the verb does suggest a connection with sound, and it may refer to the actual pronunciation of Attic.

It is interesting that Herodes thinks immediately of training and education as the only means through which one could achieve linguistic proficiency. He asks 'τὴν δὲ δὴ γλῶτταν πῶς ἐπαιδεύθης καὶ ὑπὸ τίνων;' 'how were you educated in the language, and by whom?'. The plural τίνων implies a number of tutors, and so possibly the whole curriculum of education from the elementary school master to the higher rhetorical training[17].

---

[17] Teaching of literature followed training in writing, and was the responsibility of a γραμματικός (cf. Marrou 1965: 244, on the semantic evolution of γραμματικός to the modern sense of 'grammarian' see Cribriore 1996: 9). Rhetorical training was a prerogative of higher education, and would take place under the guidance of a ῥήτωρ or σοφιστής. On the ancient curriculum

The same approach to Attic proficiency as a result of training is apparent in another passage of Philostratus, this time from the *Heroicus*. A Phoenician man and a vinedresser have this dialogue somewhere outside Elaus (in Chersonesus, modern Crimea). The Phoenician is surprised by the vinedresser's proficiency and inquires:

> (7) Φοῖνιξ – τὴν δὲ φωνήν, ἀμπελουργέ, πῶς ἐπαιδεύθης; οὐ γάρ μοι τῶν ἀπαιδεύτων φαίνῃ. Ἀμπελουργός – ἐν ἄστει, ξένε, τὸ πρῶτον ἐτρίβομεν τοῦ βίου διδασκάλοις χρώμενοι καὶ φιλοσοφοῦντες.
>
> [Phoenician:] Where did you learn to speak, vinedresser? You seem to be quite well educated. [Vinedresser:] I spent the first part of my life in town, attending lectures and studying philosophy[18].
>
> Philostrat. *Heroicus* 4.5–6 [132 K.]

The setting here is different: in Attica the countryside may be regarded as more conservative and therefore purer, as opposed to the mingled ethnic and linguistic society of the city, but the *Heroicus* is set in the outskirts of the Greek-speaking world. In that remote region, it is the city that provides the highest standard in education[19]. Philostratus also writes that higher education enhances Greekness: in Smyrna, Polemon's school attracted 'pure Greekness' from other parts of the world:

> (8) νεότητος αὐτῇ ἐπιρρεούσης ἐξ ἠπείρων τε καὶ νήσων οὐκ ἀκολάστου καὶ ξυγκλύδος, ἀλλ' ἐξειλεγμένης τε καὶ καθαρᾶς[20] Ἑλλάδος.
>
> Since the youth flowed into her from both continents and the islands; nor were they a dissolute and promiscuous rabble, but select and genuinely Hellenic.
>
> Philostrat. *VS* 531

Cappadocian is not the only accent that imperial audiences would detect. Just like Apollonius of Tyana, other speakers were praised for mastering a Greek without accent, despite being native speakers of other languages. For instance

---

see Marrou 1965: 218–64 (esp. 243), 356–74, Cribiore 1996, Morgan 1998 and 2007, Too – Livingstone 1998, Too 2001. On rhetoric in the 2nd century AD see Goldhill 2001b, Whitmarsh 2005. Virtually all the teachers would be Greek speakers, also in Roman households: Lucian's *De mercede conductis* offers abundant sharp criticism of highly specialised Greek rhetors reduced to a state of semi-slavery in affluent Roman households (later reconsidered, possibly for political and personal reasons, in the *Apologia*).

18 Transl. J.S. Rusten (Loeb Classical Library 521, Cambridge, MA, 2014).
19 Morgan 1998: 159, 163 ascribes to bigger, highly hellenised cities the teaching of grammar.
20 καθαρᾶς Kayser: καθαρῶς Cobet.

Favorinus, yet another sophist whose native language was not Greek, received praise for his mastery of Greek. Born in Arelates, in Roman Gaul, Favorinus

(9) ὡς παράδοξα ἐπεχρηςμῴδει τῷ ἑαυτοῦ βίῳ τρία ταῦτα· Γαλάτης ὢν ἑλληνίζειν, εὐνοῦχος ὢν μοιχείας κρίνεςθαι, βαςιλεῖ διαφέρεςθαι καὶ ζῆν.

used to say in the ambiguous style of an oracle, that there were in the story of his life these three paradoxes: Though he was a Gaul he led the life of a Hellene; a eunuch, he had been tried for adultery; he had quarrelled with an Emperor and was still alive.

Philostrat. VS 489

A similar case is that of Aelian, who mastered an Attic like the Athenians of the interior of Attica, despite being a Roman[21]:

(10) Αἰλιανὸς δὲ Ῥωμαῖος μὲν ἦν, ἡττίκιζε δέ, ὥςπερ οἱ ἐν τῇ μεςογείᾳ Ἀθηναῖοι. ἐπαίνου μοι δοκεῖ ἄξιος ὁ ἀνὴρ οὗτος, πρῶτον μέν, ἐπειδὴ καθαρὰν φωνὴν ἐξεπόνηςε πόλιν οἰκῶν ἑτέρᾳ φωνῇ χρωμένην, ἔπειθ', ὅτι προςρηθεὶς ςοφιςτὴς ὑπὸ τῶν χαριζομένων τὰ τοιαῦτα οὐκ ἐπίςτευςεν, οὐδὲ ἐκολάκευςε τὴν ἑαυτοῦ γνώμην, οὐδὲ ἐπήρθη ὑπὸ τοῦ ὀνόματος οὕτω μεγάλου ὄντος, ἀλλ' ἑαυτὸν εὖ διαςκεψάμενος ὡς μελέτῃ οὐκ ἐπιτήδειον τῷ ξυγγράφειν ἐπέθετο καὶ ἐθαυμάςθη ἐκ τούτου.

Aelian was a Roman, but he wrote Attic as correctly as the Athenians in the interior of Attica. This man in my opinion is worthy of all praise, in the first place because by hard work he achieved purity of speech though he lived in a city which employed another language; secondly because, though he received the title of sophist at the hands of those who award that honour, he did not trust to their decision, but neither flattered his own intelligence nor was puffed up by this appellation, exalted though it was, but after taking careful stock of his own abilities, he saw that they were not suited to declamation, and so he applied himself to writing history and won admiration in this field.

Philostrat. VS 624

The verb 'ἡττίκιζε' can hardly refer to Aelian's style: in his works, Aelian deviates in places form classical usage, and includes some Latinisms[22]: as James (2008)

---

[21] Cf. also Aspasius of Ravenna (VS 627–628) who was educated by his father Demetrianus in the Italian city of Ravenna, and was to become Caracalla's (or Alexander Severus') secretary *ab epistulis graecis* and the only sophist of Western descent to hold the chair of rhetoric in Rome (Rothe 1989: 269). Nothing is said of his mother tongue. He may have been born in a Greek speaking family, or be yet another speaker of Latin who had received training in the Greek language. On the quarrel beween Aspasius and Philostratus of Lemnos cf. Bowersock 1969: 92. On Romans imitating Greek accent, see Adams 2003: 108–10, and pp. 9–14 on Greek learning among the Roman elites.

[22] In word order especially, cf. Wilson 1997: 14–15 and Schmid 1893: 314 on word order, Schmid 1893: 259 on ἑαυτὸν ἀθροίζειν = *se colligere*. On textual criticism of Aelian's works and its consequences on the appraisal of his language, cf. Guillén 2005.

remarks, it is more likely that the verb here refers to correct pronunciation[23]. For the same reason, and also because it is contrasted with the ἄλλη φωνή, the foreign language of the Romans, καθαρὰ φωνή here may have more to do with pronunciation than with the correct selection of words (the usual meaning of καθαρός in Philostratus)[24].

Education imparted by Greek rhetors, and in the Greek language, was a key component in the upbringing of the ruling class of Rome[25]. Greek grammarians, rhetoricians, sophists, and the lexicographers themselves turned their attention to Rome, as the Romans too were increasingly seeking Greek education, much to the dismay of the Greeks (or speakers of Greek) who had to renounce their engagements with higher education to become elementary school teachers in Roman households[26].

There is evidence that rhetorical education paid attention to correct pronunciation also in Roman rhetorical education. Even though in Roman rhetorical theory 'barbarism' can mean simply bad word-choice[27], the term may also refer to the bad pronunciation of a word. Quintilian discusses whether barbarism exists in writing only or also in speech (*Inst.* 1.5.6). He lists examples of barbarisms in spoken language (*Inst.* 1.5.10–13) and admits the difficulty of representing non-standard pronunciation in a written discussion of the language (*Inst.* 1.5.17). Such care for good pronunciation is reflected in Quintilian's recommendation that Roman youths begin their education with instruction in Greek, but that Latin be introduced early enough. The benefit of introducing Latin early is precisely to allow the correct mastering of Latin phonology:

---

23 Wilson 1997: 4.
24 A single slip in word-choice can lead to an accusation of 'barbarism', cf. the beginning of Lucian's *Pseudologista* (Luc. *Pseudol.* 1): ἀλλ' ὅτι μὲν ἠγνόεις τοὔνομα τὴν ἀποφράδα παντί που δῆλον. πῶς γὰρ ἂν ᾐτιῶ βάρβαρον εἶναί με τὴν φωνὴν ἐπ' αὐτῷ, εἰπόντα ὑπὲρ σοῦ ὡς ἀποφράδι ὅμοιος εἴης τὸν γὰρ τρόπον σου νὴ Δία μέμνημαι εἰκάσας τῇ τοιαύτῃ ἡμέρᾳ, εἰ μὴ καὶ παντάπασιν ἀνήκοος ἦσθα τοῦ ὀνόματος; ("That you did not know the word nefandous is surely clear to everyone. When I had said of you that you were like a nefandous day—for I well remember comparing your character to a day of that kind—how could you, with reference to that word, have made the stricture that I was barbarous in my speech, unless you were wholly unacquainted with it?", transl. Harmon 1936).
25 On the relations between power and education in the Roman Empire cf. McNelis 2007: 295–6.
26 If their expertise was even recognised, and they were not just allowed into the household as showpieces of the landlord's opulence, as Lucian satirised in one of his opuscles (*On Service in a Rich Household / De mercede conductis potentium familiaribus*). On Greek rhetors in Rome cf. Connolly (2007 and 2001: 344–6, with a discussion of Lucian, *Merc. Cond.* 25).
27 Quintilian (*Inst.* 1.5.8) gives examples of single words that have to be considered barbarisms.

> (11) *non tamen hoc adeo superstitiose fieri uelim, ut diu tantum Graece loquatur aut discat, sicut plerisque moris est. hoc enim accidunt et oris plurima uitia in peregrinum sonum corrupti et sermonis; cui cum Graecae figurae assidua consuetudine haeserunt, in diuersa quoque loquendi ratione pertinacissime durant.*
>
> However, I do not want a fetish to be made of this, so that [the student] spends a long time speaking and learning nothing but Greek, as is commonly done. This gives rise to many faults both of pronunciation (owing to the distortion of the mouth produced by forming foreign sounds) and of language, because the Greek idioms stick in the mind through continual usage and persist obstinately even in speaking the other tongue.
>
> Quint. *Inst.* 1.1.13

The concern that a Roman student would not acquire a good accent in Latin because the teaching was imparted in Greek (and quite possibly by a Greek), reveals that the Romans too had idealised a special accent as characteristic of the educated.

In the light of this passage, one may look at another observation earlier in the *Institutio Oratoria* (1.1.4–5), that the nurses should speak a pure variety of the language: if education should start in Greek, it implies that the nurses should speak a variety of Greek with a socially acceptable accent. Ideally, the statement implies that the nurses had received higher education – Quintilian is obviously aware of the absurdity of such a pretension (*ne sit uitiosus sermo nutricibus, quas si fieri posset sapientes Chrysippus optauit, Inst.* 1.1.4).

Correct pronunciation was therefore a priority in the educational system at the time when Philostratus, Lucian, and Quintilian were writing. In what follows we are going to see how Atticist lexicography fulfilled a need to provide indications as to the best accent to use while speaking Greek.

3 Lexica and higher education

The Atticist lexica were composed for an audience of highly educated purists. As the title of one of Phrynichus' works suggests, coφιcτικὴ προπαραcκευή / *Praeparatio Sophistica*, 'the preparation of the Sophist', lexica would be consulted by orators who had undergone the full school curriculum, and had received higher education[28].

Because of their nature of scholarly works designed for an educated audience, the transmission of Atticist lexica on papyrus is much scantier than that

---

[28] If we understand coφιcτήc, *sophist*, as denoting the accomplished orator, and not just an educated individual.

of school excercises of a more elementary kind. Lexica are of course scholarly work, and not school excercises, despite serving a similar function as school teaching in reinforcing the linguistic practice of the Koine and 'strengthen the correct daily usage of Greek'[29]. Rather than in the smaller centres of Egypt, which yield the majority of school excercises on papyrus, lexica must have been used in the bigger hellenised cities of the Empire, and in Rome, where the teaching of Greek rhetoric had a tradition tracing back to the Republic and continuing well into the imperial period[30].

Atticist Lexica were meant as scholarly aids for the correct use of a variety of Greek (classical Attic), which possibly was on many occasions unintelligible to speakers of the Koine, be they native speakers or learners of (Koine) Greek[31]. In this respect, they have something in common with the teaching of Greek *as a foreign language*[32]. Their tradition traces back to Hellenism and Alexandrian scholarship, beginning perhaps with Philetas (340–285 BC). It is a work of Aristophanes of Byzantium (257–180 BC), περὶ τῶν ὑποπτευομένων μὴ εἰρῆςθαι τοῖς παλαιοῖς, which for the first time hints at a distinction between a contemporary usage and one of more ancient authors. The work of Aristophanes was still influential on imperial atticist lexicography (it is one of the sources of the *Antiatticista*, for instance). When – starting with Dionysius of Halicarnassus (1st century BC – 1st century AD) –, Atticism defines a canon of authors whose usage should be used as a model for good writing in Greek, lexicography turns to the compilation of works supporting the usage found in the texts of the canon in contrast to other varieties of Greek[33].

Some, like the works of Phrynichus and Pollux, are dedicated to the Emperor himself, or his entourage. Phrynichus dedicated the *Ecloga* to the imperial secretary Cornelianus, and the *Praeparatio Sophistica* to the Emperor Commodus – albeit reserving the right to dedicate most of the individual books to other friends and colleagues, as Photius (*Bibl.* 158) diligently reports. Photius' list of dedicatees of the *Praeparatio Sophistica* (he names nine of them) provides an in-

---

29 Cribiore 2001: 210, 214.
30 Connolly 2007; Morgan 2007: 309.
31 'There is no evidence [...] that formal grammar was used to teach non-speakers to speak' (Morgan 1998: 167). The view is contested by Cribiore (2001), who argues that exercises in grammar are part of the basic teaching of the language.
32 In the 4th century AD, Timaeus compiled a lexicon to Plato, with the goal of explaining words which were obscure *also* for the Greeks, but in the first place were obscure for the Romans (*Lex. Plat., praef.* 7-11 ἐξέλεξα τὰ παρὰ τῷ φιλοσόφῳ γλωσσηματικῶς ἢ κατὰ συνήθειαν Ἀττικὴν εἰρημένα, οὐχ ὑμῖν μόνοις τοῖς Ῥωμαίοις ὄντ' ἀσαφῆ, ἀλλὰ καὶ τῶν Ἑλλήνων τοῖς πλείστοις).
33 See the various groups of speakers addressed in Pollux' *Onomasticon* (Matthaios 2013 and 2015, § 5.9).

teresting picture of the imperial court and the scholars orbiting around it: it is possible that some of them were native speakers of Latin rather than Greek, and at least one can be identified with a rhetor who would go on to be a Roman senator, and then a *consul suffectus*[34].

Atticist lexicography, despite surviving in the work of authors that are likely to originate from the Eastern, Greek speaking, Roman Empire, must have had a strong Roman component, and indeed an early one. The first occurrence of the notion of 'Atticism' goes back to Republican Rome, not to the Greek-speaking Empire[35]. During the reign of Hadrian, Julius Vestinus, the imperial secretary[36], Philostratus of Tyrus, Valerius Pollio[37] and his son Valerius Diodorus, had composed lexica of the ten Attic orators, possibly of the same kind as the one composed in the same period and milieu by Valerius Harpocration[38].

Glosses on pronunciation contained in the lexica must therefore address an audience of the most sophisticated kind. They contain information on the speech habits that Atticist lexicographers would regard as characterising of the most polished variety of Greek.

4 Descriptive and prescriptive Atticist lexicography

The earliest λέξεις Ἀττικαί, lexica concerned with the usage of Attic authors, are attested as early as the 3rd century BC, with the work of Philemon of Aexone, a contemporary of Callimachus[39]; they may have been only collections of special usages or special vocabulary that could be found in authors of the Classical period.

---

[34] Ti. Claudius Aristocles of Pergamum, apart from Herodes Atticus, 'the only other sophist in the *Lives* [Philostrat. *VS* 567–8] to have reached the consulate or indeed to have been elevated to senatorial rank' (Bowie 1982: 49); Schmid, *RE* II 937; Bowie, *N. Pauly* I 1111, The other dedicatees of the *Praeparatio Sophistica*, Julianus, Tiberinus, Menophilus, Rufinus, Rheginus, Basileides, and Menodorus (to whom Phrynichus dedicated 22 of the books Photius could read), are otherwise unknown. The identification of Julianus with the lexicographer whose works Photius comments in *Bibl.* 150 is unlikely (Gudeman, *RE* X, 10, *s.v.* Iulianos (2)).
[35] Cf. Connolly 2007, Kim 2010: 472–4, Horrocks 2010: 126.
[36] *IG* XIV 1085 = *CIG* III 5900, *Su.* o 835. Vestinus was the author of lexica, possibly of the descriptive kind, to Demosthenes, Thucydides, and the canon of ten Attic orators.
[37] On Pollio's συναγωγὴ Ἀττικῶν λέξεων see Photius *Bibl.* 149.
[38] Degani 1995: 516, 518.
[39] The fullest discussion of Philemon of Aexone work is still Weber (1888); cf. also Degani (1995: 509). Philemon of Aexone's work is transmitted in indirect quotations in Athenaeus and Ammonius (Matthaios, *N. Pauly* IX 786).

Early Atticist lexica are concerned with the definition of difficult words contained in the canon of Attic authors, as it was taking shape over the centuries. Attic oratory seems to have been an early focus of interest, and the lexica were designed to clarify the meaning of words referring to every day life or aspects of politics, law, judicial procedure in 5th and 4th century Athens[40].

In the 2nd century AD, this descriptive sort of lexicon is still represented by the work of Harpocration on the ten Attic orators[41]. Yet in the same period a new genre of lexicography emerges. This later generation of lexica is peculiar, for the first time in the history of ancient Greek lexicography, in that it produced works that are overtly *prescriptive* and not descriptive. The earliest examples of prescriptive Atticist lexicography date from the 2nd century AD[42], and its latest seem not to be later than the 3rd century[43]. They answer the challenge expressed in ps.-Aristides' *Ars Rhetorica* (2.10.1 Spengel) μήτε ὀνόματι μήτε ῥήματι χρῆσθαι ἄλλως πλὴν τοῖς ἐκ τῶν βιβλίων[44]. As I hope to show in this book, this strand of Atticist lexicography also provides its readers with useful information about the best pronunciation to adopt in combination with a pure atticising style.

The attitude towards language is not the only thing that changed over time. The canon of authors itself expanded, at least in the work of some of the lexicographers, to include a larger number of Attic authors. In addition to the orators, 2nd and 3rd-century lexica usually include the tragic poets and the playwrights of Old Comedy. The canon of Attic authors, however, was fluid: not all the lexica based on the same group of authors, and usages that one lexicographer deems as illegitimate may be perfectly acceptable for another who drew on a different choice of authors. This trait is so salient of one lexicon that it won it the name of *Antiatticista* among modern editors (cf. below §5.1): not because it does not reflect atticist principles of acceptable *vs.* non acceptable usages, but because it includes, as evidence that some words are indeed acceptable, authors that are not part of the canon of most other Atticist lexica.

---

40 Alpers 1990: 20–1.
41 λέξεις τῶν δέκα ῥητόρων, cf. Dickey 2007: 94.
42 A precursor could be the λέξεις Ἀττικαί of Irenaeus (Degani 1995: 519).
43 The dating of Moeris is debated, but a composition date in the 3rd century is likely. The only prescriptive lexicon of a later date is that of Oros, possibly composed in the 5th century AD, cf. Alpers 1981: 91–2.
44 On the prescriptive character of Atticist lexicography see Serrano Aybar 1977 and Kim 2010: 472, 476–8; Degani 1995 provides an overview of Greek lexicography, with a discussion of Atticist and imperial lexicography on pp. 514–21; cf. also Tosi 2015: 632–3, a short overview of Atticist lexica (not including Moeris); general considerations on some of the Atticist lexica in Strobel 2005 and 2009.

Analysing the material included in the lexica, as they are available today in modern print editions, can be a very challenging task. The textual history of the lexica is a particularly complex one. Unlike works of literature, they are susceptible of being continuously adapted during their transmission. The reasons are quite easy to understand: works of literature needed to be preserved, but a lexicon could be improved to become more accessible, or to include more glosses.

Lexica were frequently epitomised: some of the works that we know to have been originally published in tens of books have reached us only as collections of few hundred entries (Phrynichus' *Praeparatio Sophistica* is an example, cf. below 5.3), some others clearly look like abridgments, but we have no information on their original scope (this is the case with the *Antiatticista*, cf. below §5.1).

Most importantly, lexica tend to be the compilations of material coming from pre-existing lexica. The filiation between texts is often very intricate, and heavily characterised by cross-contamination between different branches of the same tradition, or sharing of the same sources – any introduction to a recent edition of a lexicon will show quite clearly how complicated these relations can be, see for instance the textual story of the cυναγωγὴ λέξεων χρηcίμων, an early Byzantine lexicon[45]. The same procedure of expansion and contamination is common to lexicography as a genre, if we may say so, and it is quite likely that the state of affairs should not be different for Atticist lexicographers of the imperial time[46].

Not all lexica are transmitted in full, or under the name of their authors. Two of them are the work of Phrynichus, the *Training of the Sophist* (cοφιcτικὴ προπαραcκευή, *Praeparatio Sophistica*, fragmentary) and the *Selection of Attic verbs and nouns* (ἐκλογὴ Ἀττικῶν ῥημάτων καὶ ὀνομάτων, *Ecloga*, surviving in full). Another one is a lexicon ascribed to an otherwise unknown Moeris and a fragmentary lexicon transmitted under the name of Philemon. The φιλέταιροc (*Philetaerus*) is a lexicon transmitted under the name of Herodian, but it must be at least one century later than Herodian's time (cf. §5.6 below). The *Antiatticista* is – despite the name – an anonymous Atticist lexicon.

The works of Aelius Dionysius and Pausanias, despite their impact on ancient grammar and philology, are only known by indirect quotations, mostly in Eustathius' commentary on Homer. The lexicon transmitted under the name

---

45 Cunningham 2003: 13–61.
46 Alpers (1990) provides as very clear introductory overview of the textual problems of Greek lexicography, especially byzantine. Contemporary lexicography is no way simpler when it comes to the merging of the sources and interdependencies: the history of the various redactions of the Greek-English dictionary by Liddell, Scott, and Jones is itself an excellent example of what happens in the transmission of lexica.

of Ammonius is a later reworking of a 2nd century AD lexicon; because of the textual history of the work and its synonymical character, it is included in the corpus only as a secondary source (see § 5.7 below).

5 The corpus

The following paragraphs provide some information on the lexica which constitute the corpus of glosses discussed in this book. Degani (1995) and Dickey (2007) provide very useful overviews on Greek lexicography, and further bibliography. Abbreviations of the lexica are listed at the end of the volume, before the general bibliography.

5.1 *Antiatticista*

The *Antiatticista* is a list of 841 glosses preserved in only one manuscript (Paris. Coislin. 345), a collection of grammatical works consisting for the greatest part of lexica[47]: the manuscript is one of the extant copies of Moeris' lexicon, and the only known copy of Phyrnichus' *Praeparatio Sophistica* (cf. §§ 5.3 and 5.4 below).

In its surviving shape, the *Antiatticista* is an abridgment of a lost longer lexicon[48], which becomes more and more radical as we progress in the alphabetical series (Valente 2015a: 7 fn. 27). The authorship of the lexicon is unknown. The work should date to a period after Herennius, or possibly Aelius Dionysius and Herodian (cf. §§ 5.2, 5.7 below): it is not always clear, however, whether the mutual resemblance of some entries proves that the *Antiatticista* depends on Herennius (or Aelius or Herodian), or just that these authors were using one or more common sources[49]; so far, the most convincing relation between the *Antiatticista* and any other Atticist lexicon remains that with Phrynichus' *Ecloga*, which Latte (1915: 378–383) showed to engage directly with glosses of

---

[47] Known as *Lexica Segueriana* after Pierre Séguier (1588–1672), who came into possession of the manuscript (Cassio 2012: 252).
[48] Drawing heavily on Aristophanes' of Byzantium περὶ τῶν ὑποπτευομένων μὴ εἰρῆcθαι τοῖc παλαιοῖc, see Latte (1915); Slater (1986: 5–27); Tosi (1997); Cassio (2012: 252).
[49] Valente (2015a: 38 ff., 52 ff., 59) suggests a date after the work of Herennius (if not Ael. D. or Herodian) a *terminus post quem*, and before the composition of the second book of Phrynichus' *Ecloga*.

the anonymous lexicon[50]. A *terminus post quem* must therefore be the composition of the second book of the *Ecloga* (Valente 2015a: 52–55, 59).

The manuscript transmits the lexicon with the generic title 'ἄλλος ἀλφάβητος': D. Ruhnken gave it the name *Antiatticista* in preparation for an edition which never saw the light[51]. In what follows I will use *Antiatticista* in reference to both the lexicon and its author.

The name *Antiatticista* is a fortunate one: although in many respects this work aligns with Atticism, and gives the same sort of prescriptions that are usual in the Atticist lexica, the lexicon is at the same time a *pamphlet* against stricter Atticistic purism. It includes a wider selection of authors than that of other Atticist lexica, and it supports usage of words condemned by stricter atticists with examples a wider canon of authors, which includes post-classical Attic writers and even non-Attic ones[52]. Most glosses of the *Antiatticista* address lexical problems. The few that may refer to prosody[53], are discussed here (e.g. *Antiatt.* μ 37 μύcτακα· βραχέωc, → μύcταξ).

5.2 Aelius Dionysius and Pausanias

Aelius Dionysius of Halicarnassus[54] lived during Emperor Hadrian's times (*Su.* δ 1174)[55]. He wrote five books of Ἀττικῶν ὀνομάτων λόγοι, surviving only through indirect quotations in later grammarians and lexicographers. Several glosses of Phrynichus' *Ecloga* depend on Aelius' lexicon[56].

---

50 Cf. also the discussion in Fischer 1974: 39–41. Latte argued that Phrynichus responded to glosses of the *Antiatticista* in the second book of the *Ecloga*. Fischer (1974: 41, fn. 19) is less confident that the dependence should be limited to the second book only, and suggests that both books of the *Ecloga* engage with the *Antiatticista* (some objections in Slater 1977: 259, there is evidence that Phrynichus responded to friends and colleagues in different books of the *Ecloga* and of the *PS*).
51 Cassio 2012: 252; Valente 2015a: 3.
52 Cassio 2012 examines the glosses of the *Antiatticista* which support Koine usages with examples from Sicilian authors; cf. also Latte 1915: 383; Degani 1995: 520; Dickey 2007: 97–8.
53 Cf. Tosi 1997: 172–4 on *Antiatt.* η 5 (ἥδιον ~ ἥδιον).
54 It is likely that Aelius Dionysius can be identified with Aelius 'ὁ Μουcικόc', and with the grammarian Dionysius quoted in some scholia to Euripides, cf. Montanari in *N. Pauly* I 638–9.
55 On Aelius Dionysius and Pausanias see Erbse 1950; Degani 1995: 519; Dickey 2007: 99.
56 Fischer 1974: 41–3.

A contemporary of Aelius Dionysius, Pausanias too lived under Hadrian[57]. A scholion to Thucydides[58] is the only source for the title of his work, Ἀττικῶν ὀνομάτων cυναγωγή. Moeris and Photius[59] must have relied on the lexicon, and it was still available to Eustathius in the 12th century AD. The surviving fragments from the two lexica suggest that the lexicon of Aelius Dionysius contained more information of a grammatical kind, whereas entries from the lexicon of Pausanias deal more often with *realia* and Attic local traditions[60]. Together with Pausanias', Aelius' lexicon was known to Photius (*Bibl.* 152–153)[61]; Eustathius is our main source for the fragments of both lexica, uses them in strict conjunction (ἄλλος, ἕτερος are common designations for either lexicographer[62]), some glosses are also transmitted in the expansions of the cυναγωγὴ λέξεων χρηcίμων, cf. Cunnigham 2003: 53): we owe the glosses as we read them to Erbse (1950). Fragments of dubious attribution are preceded by *, here and in Erbse's edition.

5.3 Phrynichus

The two lexicographical works of Phrynichus Arabius represent the most intransigent wing of Atticism[63]. The lexicographer lived under the emperors Marcus Aurelius and Commodus[64]. Only one manuscript transmits his major achievement, the *Training of the Sophist*, coφιcτικὴ προπαραcκευή (*Praeparatio Sophistica*), and in a radically abridged version (edited by de Borries 1911). The work originally comprised 37 books[65]. We can still read Phrynichus' *Selection of Attic verbs and nouns*, ἐκλογὴ Ἀττικῶν ῥημάτων καὶ ὀνομάτων (*Ecloga*) in a more

---

[57] Wendel *RE* XVIII,4 2406–16; Matthaios in *N. Pauly s.v.* Pausanias [9], IX 449. Wright (1921: XXXIX) argues that Pausanias might be the sophist from Caesarea whose life is told by Philostratus, *VS* 593–594, the same person who could not make a distinction between long and short sounds in his speech (cf. n. (4)).
[58] Sch. Thuc. 6.27.1 (M).
[59] Hansen 1998: 46–7, Erbse 1950: 59, Theodoridis 1982: LXXIII.
[60] Such trends of either lexicon were identified by Wentzel (1895: 396); Erbse lists them again (1950: 20).
[61] Cf. Wentzel 1895. According to Wentzel Aelius Dionysius was the only source for glosses on Thucydides in Photius (Wentzel 1895: 384).
[62] Erbse 1950: 18–19.
[63] On Phrynichus see Degani 1995: 519, Dickey 2007: 96–7.
[64] Photius, *Bibl.* 158.
[65] The *Suda* mentions 47 or 74 books (*Su.* φ 764 Φρύνιχος, Βιθυνός, cοφιcτής. Ἀττικιcτὴν ὑπ' Ἀττικῶν ὀνομάτων βιβλία β', Τιθεμένων cυναγωγήν, cοφιcτικῆc παραcκευῆc βιβλία μζ', οἱ δὲ οδ'), Photius (*Bibl.* 158) knew of 37 books, of which he could read only 36.

or less intact version, in two books, and two epitomes: a new edition of the *Ecloga* and its two epitomes has been prepared by Fisher (1974); there are two nineteenth-century commented editions of the work, by Lobeck (1820) and Rutherford (1881).

Phrynichus' work is surely dated to the end of the 2nd century AD. The identity of the dedicatee of the *Ecloga*, Cornelianus, is uncertain[66], and the dispute with Julius Pollux (on account of which the *Ecloga* is dated to year 178 AD) is possibly only a modern speculation[67]. Even though an exact dating of the *Ecloga* is not possible, a likely period for its publication is the early 160s[68].

5.4 Moeris

We do not know anything of the Moeris who wrote the Atticist lexicon, known as λέξεις Ἀττικῶν κατὰ στοιχεῖον or ἀττικιστής[69]. Because it relies on Phrynichus[70], it should be dated between the end of the 2nd and the beginning of the 3rd century AD[71], even if it is difficult to ascertain the *terminus ante quem* of its composition[72].

The importance of this lexicon depends on the fact that it is one of the few Atticist lexica preserved in its entirety, whereas works still available, for instance, to Photius (Aelius Dionysius' and Pausanias' lexica, the unabridged *Praeparatio Sophistica*) are now partially or totally lost. It survives in 15 manuscripts, dating fom the 10th to the 17th centuries AD[73]. Moeris' entries are extremely bare, most

---

66 According to Argyle (1989: 526–7) Cornelianus is the author of the *Philetaerus* (cf. § 5.6). The imperial secretary Cornelianus cannot be the friend to whom Fronto addressed a letter in 146 AD (*ad Amic.* 1.1 – cf. Champlin 1980: 29–30; *Oxford Classical Dictionary s.v.* Phrynichus Arabius), since a consequence of this would be that the Cornelianus who was Commodus' secretary *ab epistulis* should have been 50 or 60 years old in AD 178, too old for the average age of this charge, which stands normally between 35 and 40 (Argyle 1989: 530).
67 Naechster (1908) had put forward the hypothesis that Pollux's *Onomasticon* contains in its tenth book the replies to a dispute with Phrynichus. Fischer (1974: 44) rejects Naechster's idea, since some of the alleged replies by Phrynichus are actually taken from the *Antiatticista*; more evidence against Naechster's reconstruction in Tosi 2013.
68 Swain 1996: 53 fn. 43; and also fnn. 46 and 48.
69 Photius *Bibl.* 157: Μοίριδος Ἀττικιστής· κατὰ στοιχεῖον δὲ καὶ τοῦτο πονημάτιον.
70 Disputed by Fischer (1974: 43) but confirmed by Alpers (1981: 108 fn. 35) and Hansen (1998: 36–40).
71 Dihle 1989: 266; Swain 1996: 51.
72 Degani 1995: 520 fn. 58, Dickey 2007: 98.
73 The most ancient is the Paris. Coislin. 345, the same (and only) manuscript of the *Antiatticista* and of Phrynichus' *Praeparatio Sophistica*; see Hansen 1998: 10 and 14–19.

times merely attaching Ἀττικοί to one term and Ἕλληνες to its gloss; a much fewer number of terms are qualified by κοινόν or cυνήθεια[74]. Even in its simplicity, Moeris' lexicon is especially rich in information about word prosody (there is quite a number of glosses contrasting μακρῶc ~ βραχέωc, ὀξυτόνωc ~ περιcπωμένωc etc.).

5.5 Philemon

We owe a treatise περὶ Ἀττικῆc ἀντιλογίαc τῆc ἐν ταῖc λέξεcιν to Philemon, who lived around the end of the 2nd century AD[75]. The work's title is mentioned only by Choeroboscus. The *termini* for the dating of Philemon, according to Cohn, come from a passage by Porphyrius[76], who mentions him along with Alexander Κοτιαεύc, *grammaticus* of Marcus Aurelius' family[77]. Philemon seems to have corrected a statement of Alexander, and this would be a *terminus post quem* for his dating. Philemon shows great consideration towards his opponent. According to Cohn (1898: 366), this is explained because the two Atticists were almost contemporaries, and this makes a dating to the late 2nd century AD the most likely option.

There are two versions of Philemon's lexicon, one preserved in cod. Vindobonensis Phil. gr. 172 (edited by Reitzenstein 1896: 392–6, who did not recognise the authorship of the lexicon), and another in cod. Laurentianus 91 super. 10, edited by L. Cohn (1898), the only manuscript that bears the superscription Φιλήμονοc[78] at the beginning of the lexicon. Incidentally, the Laurentianus is also one of the manuscripts transmitting Moeris, which immediately precedes the lexicon of Philemon.

The prescriptions of this lexicon fall mainly into two classes: some are lexical, i.e. they prescribe correct terms, synonyms to be preferred to other words, probably in current usage, often clearly more recent (μίνθαν· οὐχ ἡδύοcμον Philem. 395.20 R.), some more glosses, on the other hand, concern morphology (in

---

[74] These categories are one of the most fascinating features of Moeris' lexicon, which allows for an appraisal of the relationship between literary Attic and current usage in the 2nd century AD (cf. Maidhof 1912).
[75] Wendel *RE* XIX,2 2151–2; Degani 1995: 520, Dickey 2007: 98–9.
[76] *Quaest. hom. ad Il.* 8.286 Schrader.
[77] F. Montanari, *N. Pauly* I 485.
[78] Cf. Cohn 1898; the version of the *Laurentianus* is shorter but richer than the one in the *Vindoboniensis*, and appears to be closer to the source employed by Thomas Magister.

many cases, verbal voice, as θερεύϲομαι· οὐ θερεύϲω Philem. 394.34 R.[79]). Yet among Philemon's glosses trasmitted by the codices Parisinus and Laurentianus there can be found some fifty that deal with problems more directly related to pronunciation (place of the accent, vowel quality and quantity).

Philemon's fragments are quoted from Reitzenstein's edition of the cod. Vindobonensis (Reitzestein 1896: 392–6) and Cohn's edition of the cod. Laurentianus (Cohn 1898: 354–8). A lexicon transmitted in the codex Parisinus 2616, circulating under the name of Philemon, and including only lemmata beginning with letters from α to δ was edited by F. Osann (1821: 285–301), but the work is a 16th-century forgery[80].

5.6 Philetaerus

The *Philetaerus* attributed to Herodian is a reworking of Atticist material, mostly from Herodian, and therefore originating in the 2nd century AD. The version still available to us must be dated between the 2nd and 5th centuries AD[81]. Similar material is included in the περὶ ζητουμένων λέξεων attributed to Herodian and in an epitome ἐκ τοῦ Ἡρωδιανοῦ (Dain 1954: 30–1), transmitted together with the *Philetaerus* in the codex that has the fullest version of the glossary (*Vat. gr.* 2226). A shorter version of the *Philetaerus* and a rielaboration of the περὶ ζητουμένων λέξεων are transmitted in the codex *Vindobonensis phil. gr.* 172, edited by Criscuolo (1972).

A dating of the *Philetaerus* to the end of the 2nd century AD has been proposed on the basis of parallel glosses in Phrynichus' *Ecloga*[82]. The attribution to Cornelianus, the dedicatee of the *Ecloga*[83], has been rejected[84].

---

[79] Instances in which the usage of passive voice is reproached are rather frequent, cf. e.g. Philem. ἡττήϲομαί ϲου· οὐκ ἡττηθήϲομαι 394.18 R. This must reflect an ongoing and inexorable change in Greek, that would lead to the merger of the passive and the middle voice (cf. Horrocks 2010: 130).
[80] By Jacobus Diassorinus (Cohn 1888b: 133–43), see Barber (2015: 240 fn. 12) for a brief overview, and Degani (1995: 520, 526); on the dependence of the lexicon edited by Osann on Hesychius and other Byzantine sources, cf. Lehrs (1873: 164–90).
[81] Dain 1954: 15 (possibly the 3rd, but perhaps as late as the 5th century AD); Degani 519–20 (*ca.* 300 AD); Dickey 2007: 77, 2014: 341 (2nd–4th century AD).
[82] Phryn. *Ecl.* 231, 197, 371 ~ *Philet.* 121 and 146; the dependency is rejected by Fischer (1974: 43), based on Cohn (1888: 412); Hansen (1998: 52) follows Dain in dating the lexicon to the period between the 2nd and 4th centuries AD (the original version dating to the 2nd century AD, and its reworking to the 3rd or 4th centuries AD).

5.7 Herennius Philo / Ammonius

A lexicon ascribed to Ammonius bases on material dating to the 2nd century AD, even though, in the form it has reached us, the text must be a reworking of the 4th century AD[85]. Strictly speaking, the lexicon is not a prescriptive but a synonymic one. Eustathius quotes some of the lemmata, ascribing them to a treatise περὶ διαφόρων σημαινομένων by Herennius Philo of Byblos, who lived between the 1st and 2nd centuries AD[86]. It is this correspondence of glosses that points to a dating to the 2nd century AD for the core of the lexicon ascribed to Ammonius.

The lexicon cannot however have been written earlier than the 2nd century AD, since it quotes Heraclides Milesius (who lived around 100 AD) as a contemporary author[87], and among the grammarians indirectly quoted in the lexicon the most ancient is Herodianus. Three names are associated with the lexicon: Ἑρέννιος (or Ἐράνιος), Πτολεμαῖος and Ἀμμώνιος. Ptolemy (of Ascalona) cannot be the author of the lexicon, since he is quoted in one of the entries[88], and no grammarian Ammonius is known to have lived in the times when the lexicon was compiled[89]. This leads to the consequence that Herennius is the author of the lexicon[90], and Ammonius a later editor[91].

There is an account of a grammarian Ammonius who could have written a treatise περὶ τῶν διαφόρων σημαινομένων or περὶ διαφορᾶς σημασίας, later ascribed to Herennius Philo of Byblos[92]. Nickau supports the attribution of the lex-

---

[83] Argyle (1989: 526–7), based on two entries of the *Ecloga* where Phrynichus seems to be correcting Cornelianus' usage (Phryn. *Ecl.* 231 and 371, similar to *Philet.* 121 and 146).
[84] Alpers (1998: 103–8); Dyck (1993: 791); Valente (2015a: 55–6, fn. 327).
[85] For the identification of Ammonius with the 4th-century teacher of Socrates of Costantinople see Palmieri 1988: 63 and Nickau 2000; cf. also Degani 1995: 522 with fn. 65; Dickey 2007: 94–6.
[86] Cf. Gudeman *RE* VIII 650ff. s.v. Herennios, esp. 652: it is likely that Herennius' ἀκμή is to be placed between years 79 and 100 AD, and that he was old by Emperor Hadrian's times (117–138 AD).
[87] Nickau (1966: LXVI); on Heraclides cf. *N. Pauly* V 378. Heraclides Milesius is quoted in gloss 436 as "ὁ ἡμέτερος".
[88] Amm. 436 σταφυλὴν ὀξυτονητέον† ὡς ἀλυκὴν καὶ σταφύλην βαρυτόνως ὡς Μελίτην διαφέρειν φησὶ Πτολεμαῖος ὁ Ἀσκαλωνίτης κτλ.
[89] Nickau 1966: LXVI–LXVII.
[90] Nickau is more favourable to an attribution to Herennius, whose obscure name was neglected in favour of Ammonius' or Ptolemy's, who lived when the lexicon was composed (Gudeman *RE* sv *Herennios* (2) col. 650f.) and seems to have been working on synonyms (*FHG* Herennii fr. 15a, 19, *Etymologicum Genuinum* in *Et.Gud.* 306.16 d2); *EM* 227.52); but cf. Palmieri 1988: 65–70.
[91] Wendel, *RE* XV,2: 2507; Hansen 1998: 36; cf. Nickau 2000 for 4th-century interpolations in Ammonius.
[92] Nickau 1966: LXVI.

icon to Herennius (1966: LXVII): Ammonius' name (as Ptolemy's and Heranius Philo's, the alleged authors of similar lexica) must have replaced Herennius' in times when the life and work of the latter were forgotten.

The glosses in Ammonius' synonmical lexicon are sometimes difficult to evaluate. It is unquestionable that an entry like Amm. 165, contrasting ἐλέατροc and ἐδέατροc, is contrasting two items that are similar enough in sound and meaning to be confused by some: but such an entry cannot be taken as evidence of an incipient merger of the sounds represented by ⟨λ⟩ and ⟨δ⟩. It is however difficult to know how much entries like Amm. 273 κλῆμα ~ κλίμα or Amm. 300 λητουργεῖν ~ λιτουργεῖν owe to the merger of the sounds written by ⟨η⟩ and ⟨ι⟩[93].

I have taken such entries into consideration when they are matched by explicit prescriptions in the Atticist lexica (cf. e.g. Moer. λ 8, *Philet.* 142 → λῆμα ~ λῆμμα). The original core of the lexicon, ascribed to Herennius, must date to the same time as the stricter Atticists that constitute our corpus. This book takes into account the glosses of Herennius (Palmieri 1988) when they match glosses found also in other Atticists, and with their variants as they appear in the version of the lexicon ascribed to Ammonius (Nickau 1966).

5.8 Pollux

Ioulios Poludeukes, best known by his Roman name Julius Pollux, was born in Naucratis (the exact date is uncertain). He was educated in Athens under the guidance of Hadrian the Rhetor (Philostratus, *VS* 585–590) and was elected to the chair of rhetoric at Athens around the beginning of Commodus' reign, i.e. in the early 80s of the 2nd century AD[94].

Julius Pollux' *Onomasticon* shares more traits with descriptive, rather than prescriptive lexica[95]. *Onomastica* are a special kind of lexica, on the opposite side of the spectrum from prescriptive lexica. They can be described as having

---

[93] The textual typology of 'synonymic lexicon' prevents us to draw sure conclusions about the terms paired and contrasted in each lemma. For instance, a gloss such as Heren. 107 κατοίκιcιc καὶ κατοίκηcιc διαφέρει for instance does not necessarily contrast two homophones – it is more likely that it is concerned only about two competing formations from quite similar verbs, κατοικέω and κατοικίζω. It would be far-fetched to look at such a gloss as a proof of that the vowels spelt ⟨η⟩ and ⟨ι⟩ had the same sound.

[94] Philostratus includes Pollux in his *Lives* (*VS* 592–4); cf. also *Su.* π 1951. Bibliography in Matthaios 2013: 68 fn. 1.

[95] Dickey 2007: 96; Tosi 2013. The comparison in Strobel (2005, 2009) does not clearly point out this difference with the other lexica.

a 'positive' rather than a 'negative' approach: they usually lack the prescriptive structure 'say *x*, not *y*', and group together items with similar or identical meaning, not always contrasting two variants of the same word. Hence another possible definition of this kind of work, as having a 'horizontal onomastic' structure: they expand on a given meaning, rather than listing different entries in a 'vertical lexicographic' fashion[96]. This is of course only a general trend: Pollux does identify different groups of speakers and their uses of the language, and for this reason his *Onomasticon* is a valuable witness for the variability of Greek in the 2nd century AD[97]. However, precisely because Pollux' work is structured as a list of words grouped by semantic areas, it more often provides information on the belonging of a word to a specific literary genre, author, or sociolect that it contrasts an acceptable and an unacceptable usage[98] – than it mentions variants of the same word which may differ only for their pronunciation. In this respect, the *Onomasticon* provides very little information.

Explicit prescriptions as the ones common in the works of Phrynichus or Moeris are much harder to find in the *Onomasticon*. Only a few times does Pollux employ explicitly an prescriptive phrasing[99]; one of the group of speakers that he sometimes mentions, the ἰδιῶται, apparently refers to those who are not trained in the correct usage of Atticising Greek (they are therefore opposed to the Ἀττικοί); but, as is the case with most of the prescriptions of the *Onomasticon*, Pollux rejects a lexical item, not a special pronunciation.

5.9 Atticist lexica on papyrus

Esposito (2009), expanding on the pioneering work of Naoumides (1969), lists twenty-two lexica on papyrus. Of these lexica, twelve date to the second or be-

---

[96] Tosi 2015: 623–5.
[97] Matthaios (2013) offers a detailed study of the groups of speakers to which the *Onomasticon* attributes different usages. He identifies five of them: οἱ νῦν, οἱ πολλοί, οἱ ἰδιῶται, οἱ ποιηταί, οἱ παλαιοί.
[98] "[Pollux'] spracherklärende Vorgehensweise offenbart sich in dem Versuch, die jeweilige Wortbedeutung in den verschiedenen Nuancierungen, in denen ein Ausdruck bei unterschiedlichen Autoren und sprachlichen Ebenen Anwendung fand, möglichst exakt und differenziert wiederzugeben. In diesem Aspekt unterscheidet sich das Onomastikon wesentlich von den Lexika präskriptiver Art, die den Sprachgebrauch aus dem zeitlich unspezifischen Gegensatz zwischen Erlaubtem und nicht Erlaubtem betrachten. In den historisch angelegten Artikeln zeigt sich Pollux' sprachhistorische Interesse", Matthaios 2013: 126.
[99] Cf. e.g. 'οὐκ ἂν εἴποις' (Poll. 3.78), ῥητέον (*passim*, yet never applied to pronunciation), παραφυλακτέον (of grammatical gender, 1.162).

tween the second and third century AD. None of them is, however, an Atticist lexicon. The only instance of an Atticist lexicon on papyrus (P.Oxy. 1803) dates to the sixth century AD.

Not many people in the smaller towns of Egypt would go on to rhetorical training, after receiving the rudiments of writing and reading. Therefore school exercises on papyrus outnumber by far the lexica (Morgan 2007: 310, the school exercises are listed and studied in Cribiore 1996). This also supports the view that texts as the lexica, which are less represented in papyri than school exercises, belonged to the later stage of rhetorical training.

Bilingual papyri containing glossaries and 'manuels de conversation' (Cavenaile (1958: nn. 275–281) in Latin and Greek are more similar to the later texts transmitted as *Hermeneumata Pseudodositheana*[100]. The information one can gather from the crude spellings of Latin and Greek that abound in some of this texts provides an interesting insight in the language of the less educated in the later imperial period.

6 Descriptions of pronunciation in the lexica

The entries in Atticist lexica are not homogeneous. The vast majority contrast two lexical items, as e.g. Phrynichus, *Ecloga* 384, δροπακίζειν ἀδόκιμον, ἀρχαῖον δὲ τὸ παρατίλλεςθαι ἢ πιττοῦςθαι. There are some entries, however, that contrast two spellings of the same word, e.g. Moer. λ 25 λητουργεῖν διὰ τοῦ η Ἀττικοί· διὰ δὲ τῆς ει διφθόγγου Ἕλληνες. [...], and some prescribe their pronunciation, e.g. Philem. 355 Ἀτρέα, ὡς βασιλέα, τὸ α μακρόν. Whereas the gloss of Moeris contrasting λητουργεῖν and λειτουργεῖν could theoretically refer to spelling only and not pronunciation, is it very unlikely that the gloss in Philemon meant to contrast the spellings Ἀτρέᾰ and Ἀτρέᾱ.

An entry like Phryn. *Ecl.* 80 (text (1) above) makes it clear that the lexicographer was addressing pronunciation: he uses a verb that means 'to lengthen', ἐκτείνω, and refers it to a letter that can spell either a long or a short vowel and a syllable that would not show quantity in any other way that pronunciation (the length of the *alpha* of πελαργός does not affect the scansion or the accent).

---

100 Cf. Dickey 2012b.

6.1 Orthoepic prescriptions

Orthoepy and *orthoepic* are calques on Greek ὀρθοέπεια. The term has a long story, tracing back at least to Democritus and Plato, and its early meaning had more to do with the relation between names and their signifieds (ὀρθότης τῶν ὀνομάτων)[101]. The use of ὀρθοεπεῖν to refer to the sounds (φθόγγοι) of the language, and not to word-choice is attested at least as early as the 1ˢᵗ century AD, when Dionysius of Halicarnassus wrote[102]

> (12) Ῥωμαῖοι δὲ φωνὴν μὲν οὔτ' ἄκρως βάρβαρον οὔτ' ἀπηρτισμένως Ἑλλάδα φθέγγονται, μικτὴν δέ τινα ἐξ ἀμφοῖν, ἧς ἐστιν ἡ πλείων Αἰολίς, τοῦτο μόνον ἀπολαύcαντες ἐκ τῶν πολλῶν ἐπιμιξιῶν, τὸ μὴ πᾶσι τοῖς φθόγγοις ὀρθοεπεῖν.
>
> The language spoken by the Romans is neither utterly barbarous nor absolutely Greek, but a mixture, as it were, of both, the greater part of which is Aeolic; and the only disadvantage they have experienced from their intermingling with these various nations is that they do not pronounce all their sounds properly.
> D. Hal. *Ant. Rom.* 1.90.1[103]

At the end of the first century AD, Quintilian gives a definition of ὀρθοέπεια as the accurate articulation of words, and the definition itself of correct pronunciation. Following his considerations on the difficulty of addressing in writing the problems of pronunciation (*Inst.* 1.5.17), he writes

> (13) *et illa per sonos accidunt, quae demonstrari scripto non possunt, uitia oris et linguae:* ἰωτακιcμοὺc *et* λαμβδακιcμοὺc *et* ἰcχνότητας *et* πλατειαcμοὺc *feliciores fingendis nominibus Graeci uocant, sicut* κοιλοcτομίαν, *cum uox quasi in recessu oris auditur. sunt etiam proprii quidam et inenarrabiles soni, quibus nonnunquam nationes reprehendimus. remotis igitur omnibus, de quibus supra dixi, uitiis erit illa quae uocatur* ὀρθοέπεια, *id est emendata cum suauitate uocum explanatio: nam sic accipi potest recta.*
>
> There are accidental features of pronunciation, which cannot be shown in writing, being faults of the mouth and the tongue. The Greeks, who are more fertile than we are in inventing names, call them *iotacisms*, *lambdacisms*, *ischnotētes* and *plateiasmoi*, and also *koilostomia*, when the voice seems to come from the back of the mouth. There are also certain special, indescribable sounds, by which we sometimes recognise particular nations.
> If all these faults which I have described have been removed, we have what is called Orthoepy, "rightness of speech," that is to say, a correct and agreeable articulation of

---

101 Cf. Corradi 2006.
102 According to the *Suda* (π 3038), Ptolemy of Ascalona was the author of a treatise περὶ ἑλληνιcμοῦ καὶ ὀρθοεπείας. The contents and approach of the work are unknown, but given its pairing with ἑλληνιcμός, ὀρθοέπεια here may have to do more with linguistic correctness connected with word choice than with the mere relation between names and their signifieds.
103 Transl. E. Cary (Loeb Classical Library 319, Cambridge, MA – London, 1937).

words: this is what "right" pronunciation can be taken to mean.

Quintilian, *Inst.* 1.5.32–33[104]

In this book I will call *prescriptions* all those glosses which explicitly recommend a word or phrase, e.g. Phryn. *Ecl.* 41 cκίμπους λέγε, ἀλλὰ μὴ κράββατος· μιαρὸν γάρ. I will call *orthoepic* prescriptions all those entries prescribing the pronunciation of a word, e.g. *Philet.* 252 γενέcθαι λαβέcθαι παροξυτόνωc μᾶλλον προ{c}ενεκτέον or Phryn. *Ecl.* 346 Διονυcεῖον· ἀπαίδευτον οὕτω λέγειν, δέον βραχύνειν τὴν ci cυλλαβὴν· οἱ γὰρ ἐκτείνοντεc παρὰ τὴν Ἀττικῶν διάλεκτον λέγουcιν. [...][105].

6.2 Technical terms

The lexica do not always adopt consistent terminology in the wording of orthoepic prescriptions: their identification depends greatly on the interpretation of the technical terms that the lexicographers employed. Atticist lexica do not describe (or prescribe) pronunciation in a specialised way.

The exact nature of an entry, whether it is orthographic or orthoepic, or both, can be particularly hard to determine, especially when radical abridgements have taken place, or when the entries are limited to basic constrasts as is often the case with most entries in Moeris, whose wording is reduced to *x* Ἀττικοί· *y* Ἕλληνεc.

The terminology that can be associated with pronunciation is of different kinds, and not all of them are equally specialised. In fact, some of them show little or no specialisation at all. General verbs of saying, as λέγω, φημί 'say', for instance, can be associated with anything that goes from word-choice to spelling, to the distribution of vowel quantities in a word.

Some more specialised terminology includes the following (a table of the occurrences of these terms is available at the end of the volume):

(i) verbs meaning 'pronounce', προφέρω and ἐκφέρω, and προφορά 'pronunciation';

(ii) terminology referring to the προcῳδίαι: to vowel length (as μηκύνω, ἐκτείνω, μακρὸν ποιῶ, βραχύνω, cυcτέλλω, μακρόc, βραχύc, etc.), to the nature

---

104 Transl. D.A. Russell (Loeb Classical Library 124, Cambridge, MA, 2002).
105 Bossi–Tosi (1979–1980: 13–20) suggest a grouping of glosses according to their types, but pronunciation is not among the criteria they use for their classification.

and position of the accent (as ὀξυτονῶ, βαρυτονῶ, περιcπῶ, προπεριcπῶ, etc.), to the nature of the breathing (as δαcέωc, ψιλῶc, etc.);

(iii) ἀναγιγνώcκειν 'to read', occurring twice in our corpus, in association with the position of the accent (cf. chap. IV, § 2).

One may object that even technical terms are sometimes used ambiguously, and with good reason. This is the case with the following two entries, both from Phrynichus:

> (14) ἀφηλικέcτεροι· [...] πλὴν κατὰ cύγκριcιν ἡ λέξιc προφέρεται καὶ ἐν ὑπερθέcει, ἀφηλικέcτατοc καὶ ἀφηλικέcτατοι. οἱ δὲ ἀπολελυμένωc λέγοντεc ἀφῆλιξ, ἀφήλικεc ἀμαθέcτατοι.
>
> ἀφηλικέcτεροι: ... apart from [its use] in comparison, the word is pronounced also as a superlative, ἀφηλικέcτατοc and ἀφηλικέcτατοι. Those who say as absolutes ἀφῆλιξ, ἀφήλικεc are most ignorant.
>
> Phryn. *PS* 1.1–6

> (15) cκίμπουc λέγε, ἀλλὰ μὴ κράββατοc· μιαρὸν γάρ.
>
> Say cκίμπουc, but not κράββατοc: for it is repulsive.
>
> Phryn. *Ecl.* 41

Here προφέρω and λέγω clearly oppose different words and do not refer to pronunciation in any special way. On the contrary, they seem to be rather general terms to prescribe 'correct' usage.

Also verbs of reading, despite the centrality of pronunciation in the act of reading itself (cf. §2), may be used generically to refer to word-choice or word-division, as in

> (16) ...οὐχ ὑφ᾽ ἓν "τὰ cίγματα τῶν ἀcπίδων" ἀναγνωcτέον, ἀλλὰ διcυλλάβωc μὲν "τὰ cῖγμα"
>
> ...one should not read as one 'τὰ cίγματα τῶν ἀcπίδων', but as two syllables 'τὰ cῖγμα'.
>
> Ael. D. c 15

or they may even refer to choices in textual criticism, as in

> (17) ἠκηκόει· τὸ δὲ ἠκηκόειν οὕτωc διὰ τοῦ η Φρύνιχοc ἀναγιγνώcκει.
>
> ἠκηκόει: Phrynichus reads ἠκηκόειν like this, with the ⟨η⟩.
>
> Phryn. fr. *28 (=sch. Ar. *Pac.* 618)

Similarly, verbs addressing pronunciation as 'lengthen' and 'shorten' can be used alongside γράφω 'write':

(18) αἱματοπώτης· οἱ Ἀττικοὶ μηκύνοντες τὸ ο προφέρουςιν τὴν λέξιν, ὥςπερ καὶ τὸ οἰνοπώτης καὶ ὑδροπώτης, ἐπεὶ καὶ τὸ πόμα οἱ μὲν ἄλλοι διὰ βραχέος τοῦ ο γράφουςιν, Ἀττικοὶ δὲ ἐπεκτείνοντες.

αἱματοπώτης: the Attic [writers/speakers] pronounce the word lengthening the *o*, like οἰνοπώτης and ὑδροπώτης, because the others write also πόμα with a short *o*, but the Attic [speakers/writers] lengthen it.

Ael. D. α 53

The definition of *omega* as the result of lengthening can be explained in three ways: (a) as a mere school definition: the letter *omega* is the 'long' or 'lengthened' counterpart of *omicron*, and the glosses do not refer to anything but the spelling; (b) the technical terms are related to ancient theories of derivation (πάθη), that describe *omega* as the result of the lengthening of *omicron* to clarify the relation between similar or etymologically related words; (c) the technical terms actually allude to a long vowel corresponding in pronunciation to the letter *omega*.

None of the three explanations needs to be false: (a) became certainly true at a later period, and is one of the reasons why the material of Atticist lexica survived in later lexicography and in later orthographical treatises; (b) is part of the usual grammatical description of similar or related words, and is common in later *etymologica*; (c) is supported by the use of the verb προφέρω[106] and by positive evidence of speakers (mis)pronouncing quantities, as the description of Pausanias' speech (n. (4) above), and the indictment of the ἀμαθεῖς of Phryn. *Ecl.* 80 →πελαργός (= n. (1) above). If such prescriptions actually recommended a special pronunciation, and not just a spelling, proficient speakers of Attic would have made clear in their speech too that they used αἱματοπώτης and not αἱματοπότης.

In a world where written texts came without reading marks (cf. chap. IV, § 2), prosody was described (or prescribed) mostly through specialised vocabulary. We are particularly lucky to have a clear example of this practice in P. Oxy. 1012, an erudite commentary to literary works. The papyrus dates from the beginning of the 3rd century AD[107] and shows many affinities with Atticist lexicography of the same – or immediately later – period[108], which however is only attested in later

---

[106] Which however is not *per se* unambiguous, and can be used to describe usage in general, as in Phryn. *PS* 1.4 ἡ λέξις προφέρεται καὶ ἐν ὑπερθέσει, ἀφηλικέστατος καὶ ἀφηλικέστατοι.
[107] The *recto* of the papyrus contains a document dating from 204–205 AD, and the handwriting does not seem much later than that date (Hunt 1910 = P.Oxy. VII: 84)
[108] Erbì 2006: 145. On the development from commentaries and scholia to lexica, cf. Arrighetti 1987: 200–1 (with fn. 108).

manuscript tradition on codex: it provides us with direct insight into the usual layout that erudite works, including the lexica, may have had during the first phase of their textual tradition – on papyrus.

One of the most remarkable among the preserved portions of the text discusses the accent of αγροικοc, αληθεc, αχρειον (the three prescriptions survive in the lexica, cf. Amm. 6 → ἀγροῖκοc, Amm. 26 → ἀληθέc, *Philet.* 241 → ἀχρεῖοc). The papyrus has only one instance of an accent[109], which, however, does not happen to be written in a discussion of accentual differences.

I reproduce here this fragment of the papyrus, keeping the reading and the word-spacing of the modern editor, yet without introducing accents and breathings, i.e. preserving in this respect the original layout of the work[110]:

(19) [. . . . . . .]ον αγροικοc προcπερι|[cπωμενω]c οι ελληνεc τον ιδιω|[την ομοι]ωc αληθεc   ομοιωc και |[διτταc] δυναμειc εχει παρα τοιc |[αττικοι]c τω δε τονω διαcτελλεται |[το cημ]αινομενον οταν μεν > |[γαρ cυγ]κατατιθηται τοιc υπο τινοc | λεγομενοιc αληθεc ερει ωc cαφεc | οταν δε κατ ερωτηcιν προφερ||¹⁰ητ[α]ι τοτε τοξυτατονωc την πρω|[την ε]ξοιcει cυλλαβην αληθεc |[ωc ελη]θεc οι γε μην ελληνc|[ομοι]ωc ειωθαcιν λεγειν αληθεc|[ωc cα]φεc   αχρειον   και τουτο |[φαcι]ν διττωc οι αττικο[ι] αχρειον |με[ν β]αρυτονωc προφερομενοι |ωc α[.]ρειον τον αχρηcτον αχρει|[ον δε] προπερ[ιcπωμενωc] τον|[. . . .]. ον οι [δε ελληνεc ομοι]ωc [

αγροικοc, properispomenon is same thing as ἰδιώτηc for the Hellenes   αληθεc   in the same way has [two] meanings for the [Atti]c speakers, and they are kept distinct by the accent: for when it is said in agreement to what is said by someone, (the speaker) will say ἀληθέc like cαφέc, when it is pronounced like a question then (the speaker) will produce the first syllable as an oxytone, ἄληθεc like ἔληθεc. The Hellenes however use to say in the same way ἀληθέc like cαφέc.   αχρειον   the Attic speakers say this one too in two ways: ἄχρειον with a retracted accent like α[.]ρειον[111], 'useless', but ἀχρεῖον, perispomenon, [...][112], and yet the Hellenes in the same way [(pronounce it)...

P.Oxy. 1012, fr. 16, col. I

The papyrus discusses accents only by comparing words with identical accentutation (ἄληθεc is accented like ἔληθεc) or by employing technical terms as ὀξυ-

---

109 fr. 13.32, on πότε, possibly to differentiate the interrogative from the indefinite adverb.
110 P.Oxy. 1012 was found together with other two lexica (P.Oxy. 1801 and 1802), and a commentary (P.Oxy. 1611, on which cf. Arrighetti 1987: 204–28). The papyrus is also very interesting in other respects: fr. F (=frr. 14 and 15) = fr. 14, shows the 'accurate' spellings of [i:] with ει (γεινεται, 19, π]ειπτειν, 23) (cf. chap. II, § 2.1), fr. 14, a fragment dealing with composition, and seemingly effects of rhythm, cf. cυγ]κρουοντα, 28, με]τροιc, 32 similar to ξυγκρούοντα of Philostratus (VS 594, ex. n. (4)), and fr. 17 opposes Ἑλληνιcμόc to Ἀττικόν.
111 The reading is uncertain here, cf. Hunt in P.Oxy. VII (1910: 101–2).
112 The gloss to ἀχρεῖον in unfortunately lost, cf. Hunt in P.Oxy. VII (1910: 102)

τόνωc[113], βαρυτόνωc, προ{c}περιcπωμένωc etc. The only diacritical sign found in this section is the *trema* (ἴδιω|[την ll. 2–3, ὕπο l. 7). The methodology is strikingly similar to what we read in some of the Attic lexica when they prescribe accentuation (cf. chap. IV, § 6.2).

Still in the only papyrus fragment which is likely to be an Atticist lexicon, P.Oxy. 1803[114], and that dates from a much later period, the sixth century AD, there is only one rough breathing and no accent marks. The breathing, moreover, is on ὑ|ποζυγίων (ll. 42–3), on a word-initial *hypsilon*, a position in which later writing practice would have the rough breathing anyway. The lectional sign occurs at line-end, and it could be there to signal that the word continued in the next line: it seems to function much more like the *trema* in P.Oxy. 1012 than as a signal of initial aspiration.

In this light, we have to think of pronunciation, not spelling, when we read an entry like this:

(20) γενέcθαι, λαβέcθαι παροξυτόνωc μᾶλλον προ{c}ενεκτέον.

γενέcθαι, λαβέcθαι should rather be pronounced as paroxytones.

Philet. 252

The flexibility with which the lexicographers combine terminology referring to pronunciation with terminology referring to reading attests to the overlapping of these two areas in the fruition of the texts. For instance, προφέρω and ἀναγιγνώcκω occur together with prescriptions about accents or quantities (Ael. D. α 53, 191, *Philet.* 252) and even involving spelling itself (Phryn. *Ecl.* 72, PS 118.3–4).

6.3 Orthography and orthoepy

Information on pronunciation in the Atticist lexica is in many ways residual. Pronunciation is sometimes inferred only through spelling, most of the times indicated with 'διὰ' and the grapheme that distinguished the recommended term (Phryn. PS 26.9–10 ἀπέcβηcε πῦρ· ὁμοίως καὶ λύχνον. διὰ τοῦ η, οὐ διὰ τοῦ ε). These entries are strictly speaking *orthographic* prescriptions. They belong to a tradition of orthographical studies that was being formalised in the same period as the lexica were composed: the first systematic orthographical treatise is a frag-

---

[113] τοξυτατονωc at l. 10 is a trivial misspelling of ὀξυτόνωc.
[114] Moeris (μ 10 cτιφρόν) glosses the same word as the beginning of this papyrus.

mentary περὶ ὀρθογραφίας by Herodian, and much of the material that it contained must have been similar to what we read in the lexica[115].

Moreover, in addition to prescriptions on how many, or which letters should be used in writing a word (ποσότης and ποιότης, 'quantity' and 'quality' in the ancient terminology of orthographical treatises[116]), also all prescriptions on accents, breathings, and the quantity of the *dichrona* become relevant to orthography: centuries later that the date of our lexica, when writing of accents and breathings became consistent, and for a few writers of our time, who provided even prose with lectional marks. The writing of such marks, however, is hardly the norm in the 2nd century AD, especially in prose texts: it is therefore unlikely that all prescriptions that have a potential bearing on the writing of lectional marks were actually conceived for the purpose writing only. Also, some orthographic prescriptions discussing competing spellings provide us with a glimpse of potentially different pronunciations, and contribute to outlining what sort of diction was expected of the educated elites in the ages of the Antonines and the Severans.

As the next chapters will show, many phonological traits that are mentioned in orthoepic prescriptions were on their way to disappear from most varieties of Greek. In the second century AD, the variety of Greek spoken in Attica had probably retained some, such as distinctive vowel length, that had been lost elsewhere and could be imitated by speakers seeking to sound more refined. But even for Attica there is evidence that such distinction would be lost by the beginning of the next century.

Glosses concerning prosody, in the broad sense that the ancient grammarians gave to the word προσῳδία, may all relate to pronunciation and not spelling: they refer to the length of the *dichrona* (Phryn. *Ecl.* 241 [ὀπτάνιον] … τῆς μὲν δευτέρας συλλαβῆς ὀξυτονουμένης, τῆς δὲ τρίτης β ρ α χ υ ν ο μ έ ν η ς, Philem. 357

---

115 On the history of ancient orthography, see Valente (2015b). On Herodian's περὶ ὀρθογραφίας, cf. Dickey 2014: 337–8 (n. 38).
116 Cf. chap. II, § 2 on ποσότης and vowel timbre, and chap. IV, § 2 on the use of lectional signs in the 2nd century AD. Sextus Empiricus offers a sketch of the technical meaning of these terms in the 2nd century AD – when he reports that *orthographia* is said to comprise three areas of investigation, ποσότης, ποιότης, μερισμός (which letter is the correct spelling of a sound, how many letters correspond to a sound, how one is supposed to divide a word into syllables): τὴν γὰρ ὀρθογραφίαν φασὶν ἐν τρισὶ κεῖσθαι τρόποις, ποσότητι ποιότητι μερισμῷ. ποσότητι μὲν οὖν, ὅταν ζητῶμεν εἰ ταῖς δοτικαῖς προσθετέον τὸ ι, καὶ εὐχάλινον καὶ εὐώδινας τῷ ι μόνον γραπτέον ἢ τῇ ει· ποιότητι δέ, ὅταν σκεπτώμεθα πότερον διὰ τοῦ ζ γραπτέον ἐστὶ τὸ ϲμιλίον καὶ τὴν Ϲμύρναν ἢ διὰ τοῦ ϲ· μερισμῷ δέ, ἐπειδὰν διαπορῶμεν περὶ τῆς ὄβριμος λέξεως, πότερόν ποτε τὸ β τῆς δευτέρας ἐστὶ συλλαβῆς ἀρχὴ ἢ τῆς προηγουμένης πέρας, καὶ ἐπὶ τοῦ Ἀριστίων ὀνόματος ποῦ τακτέον τὸ ϲ (SE *M.* 1.169–170, discussed in Valente 2015b: 956–7).

βοϊκόν· τὸ ι μακρόν), initial aspiration (Moer. α 11 ἄθυρμα δασέως Ἀττικοί· ψιλῶς Ἕλληνες), accent position and/or nature (Ael. D. χ 3 χαμᾶζε ἀεὶ ⟨προ⟩περισπᾶται, τὸ δὲ χαμᾶθεν ὡς ἐπὶ πλεῖστον, Moer. γ 4 γέλοιον βαρυτόνως Ἀττικοί· γελοῖον προπερισπωμένως Ἕλληνες). It is not rare for different kinds of description to appear together in the same gloss (cf. Phryn. *Ecl.* 241).

The distinction between pronunciation and spelling is often very blurred. Artificial pronunciations could be associated to different spellings. For instance, assuming that distinctive vowel length had been lost, one can imagine that an educated speaker could still make all *omega*s and all *epsilon-iota*s sound like long vowels. Spelling is clearly used as a means to identify a different formation in Phryn. *Ecl.* 22 πιοῦμαι σὺν τῷ υ λέγων οὐκ ὀρθῶς ἐρεῖς, where the contrast /o ~ u/ is only indicated by the presence or absence of the letter ⟨υ⟩. Such lack of distinction between spelling and sound is what Sextus Empiricus contests at *M.* 1.118, when he remarks that ου is not composed of two distinct elements (στοιχεῖα), but is a single sound.

7 Reconstructing the phonology of Greek in the second century AD

The artificial pronunciation associated with Atticism is one of the many facets of the linguistic reality of the Roman Empire. Greek was taught in a bilingual environment, and even Greek speakers would have had the Koine as their first language, and would have to learn Attic[117].

The exact phonology of each of the regional varieties of Greek in the imperial period is impossible to reconstruct. The sources are not homogenous: inscriptions tend to be more conservative than papyri, and they are not distributed evenly in the Greek speaking areas of the Empire. An overwhelming number of documents on papyrus attest to all sorts of spelling mistakes (and possibly sound changes) in Egypt, and there are virtually only inscriptions in Attica, and their spelling is generally more conservative.

In three studies based on spelling variants in Attic inscriptions of the Classical and Hellenistic period, and in Egyptian papyri, Teodorsson (1974, 1977, 1978) argued that as early as the 4th century BC there were innovative sub-standard varieties of Greek, sharing a surprising number of features with Modern Greek, especially in the vowel system. Teodorsson's hypothesis was met with criticism (Ruijgh 1978) and subsequent studies, in particular Threatte's grammar of the

---

[117] Cribiore 2001: 175–6.

Attic inscriptions (1980, 1996), have opted for a more traditional reconstruction of Attic phonology (see also Allen 1987). However, it is clear that at least since Hellenistic times there must have been lower variants of the Koine showing a different phonology from that of Classical Attic and the high register, conservative variety of the Koine that was modelled on Attic. Gignac's studies on the phonology (1976) and morphology (1981) of the Egyptian papyri of the Roman and Byzantine periods are still the most complete reference work for the sound changes in Roman Egypt, and clearly show that many of them were accomplished there at a much earlier time than Attica – some of such changes are as early as the Hellenistic period (on the phonology of Ptolemaic papyri see Mayser – Schmoll 1970).

The increasing detachment from the spoken and the literary or official variants of the Koine is normally described as *diglossia*, a state in which 'low' varieties are distinct from a 'high' one, the language of literature, official documents and formal speech. In a state of diglossia, it is quite difficult to gather information about changes in the speech of the non-educated from literary or grammatical texts, which normally describe only the high variety of the language: "neither the grammatical writings, nor the texts can ever give us an idea of the chronology of the changes in the popular language [...]. These texts do not reflect the development of popular speech, but only the development of the attitude towards the standard language and towards the constraints of written language *vis-à-vis* spoken language [...]" (Versteegh 1987: 268–9). Establishing the norm for this standard was a major problem for the Atticists: the language of Thucydides is not the same as the language of Plato or Demosthenes, and different authors had different views on which was the author who should provide the model (Horrocks 2010: 135; on Atticism and diglossia see also Kim 2010: 469–71).

The lexica attest to this state of confusion; they often draw on different groups of authors, thus defying a univocal definition of the Attic canon. Moeris for instance includes Homer and Herodotus, but not tragedy, which together with Old Comedy distinguishes Phrynichus' canon form other lexica basing mostly authors of Attic prose.

The remarks on the Attic countryside found in Philostratus *VS* 553 and 624 (n. (6) and (10) above) point to Attica as a possible source of correct pronunciation. It may be that the ideals of purity in sound associated with the Atticistic pronunciation of Greek based on a current variety of Attic: in the impossibility of hearing Lysias or Demosthenes, a viable solution could have been to imitate the pronunciation of the educated Athenians of the 2nd century AD[118].

---

[118] This is also the conclusion of James 2008.

Epigraphical evidence from Attica suggests that Attic was indeed a conservative variety of Greek in the 2nd century AD. Even the most careless Attic *ostraka* or *defixiones* present spellings that do not pre-date by more than about one and a half century changes detected in official inscriptions, notoriously more accurate and conservative, whereas the same changes are well attested in Egyptian papyri, three if not four centuries earlier (Threatte 1982: 154): it is therefore likely that Attica preserved a conservative variety of the language for a longer time that other areas of the Empire. This variety of Greek could be the model that the Atticist strived to reproduce in their speech.

Threatte's (1982) comparison of spelling interchanges in Attic and Egyptian documents can be summarised as follows (table 1)[119].

---

[119] Table adapted from James (2008). A survey of the phonological system reconstructed for Greek in the 2nd century AD can be found in Horrocks (2010: 160–72), which also includes a discussion of previous scholarship.

7 Reconstructing the phonology of Greek in the second century AD — 37

Table 1

	Egypt		Attica	
Interchange	Papyri	Inscriptions (relatively small corpus)	Inscriptions (incl. funerary monuments)	*Defixiones* (4th/3rd BC), etc.
Contrasts				
ει ~ ῑ	Very freq. from 3rd c. BC	Some parallels from 100 BC	Very rare before AD 100	Not attested in *defixiones*
η ~ ε	Very freq. from 3rd c. BC	Some parallels in Ptolemaic texts	Very rare in all periods	
ω ~ o	Very freq. from 3rd c. BC	Some evidence for clustering from 200 BC	Freq. and clustered exx. after c. AD 150; (sporadic 350 BC–AD 150)	
Vowel isochrony	Very freq. from 3rd c. BC		Attested chiefly after AD 100	
η ~ ῑ/ει	Rarely attested from 3rd c. BC; common in the Roman period		Extremely rare before c. AD 150	
αι ~ ε	Fairly common by 2nd BC	Some parallels in Ptolemaic texts	Once in 1st c. AD; common after AD 120	One 1st AD text (with clustering)
οι ~ υ	Common by 2nd/1st c. BC		Very rare even in 1st and 2nd c. AD	Not attested in *defixiones*
ιoc ~ ιc,	Common from 3rd/2nd c. BC		Common in 1st–3rd c. AD	Not attested in *defixiones*
-ία ~ -ά,	Common from 3rd/2nd c. BC		Only three cases, from 1st c. BC	Not attested in *defixiones*
Parallels				
ει ~ ῑ	Well attested from the early 3rd c. BC	Very few cases	Freq. from late 3rd BC	Parallels in *defixiones*
η ~ ει⎜_V	Most exx. from 200 BC to early Roman		Most exx. from 175 BC – AD 100	
Monophthongisation of long diphthongs	3rd BC, but common after 200 BC	Very few cases	Common after AD 203/4	
ωι ~ οι	Only before 200 BC		Attested in 4th–3rd BC	
υ ~ ι	Almost only in cases of vowel assimilation (e.g. ἥμυcυ)		Likewise, only in cases of vowel assimilation	

From the data summarised in the table above it looks like the second century AD is a turning point in the history of the Attic dialect. All the changes that make the phonology of Attic – as attested in the most conservative documents – substantially the same as the one reconstructed for Egyptian Greek date to this period.

The following chapters will compare this evidence with the prescriptions of the lexicographers. The working hypothesis is that Atticist lexica record the change of their model pronunciation, responding to a need that was felt with urgency for the first time precisely in the course of the 2nd century AD. This indirectly also proves Threatte's idea that Attic was indeed more conservative.

8 Sound changes and the lexica: habits to unlearn[120]

To isolate glosses from the lexica and read them as straightforward witnesses of linguistic change would be forcing the evidence. Atticist lexicographers were not linguists in the current sense of the word, and even if they were, they were not writing their lexica with the aim of describing language change, nor were they organising their entries according to linguistic criteria.

Therefore, the glosses under examination will be only those that either employ specialised terminology describing pronunciation, or those opposing a spelling that may depend on linguistic change (see §6.2).

In this way, we can isolate a number of glosses that can be read, in the light of modern linguistics, as reflecting to various sound changes. The most frequent changes involved are those involving the προςῳδίαι: in the corpus of the lexica there are more than eighty glosses addressing vowel quantity, almost seventy involving the nature or position of the accent, more than forty involving vowel timbre, and about twenty concerning initial aspiration. A smaller group deals with geminate consonants (a table at the end of this volume summarises the distribution of the entries in relation to each phonological trait). The next four chapters discuss these features of Greek phonology as they can be reconstructed for the 2nd century AD, and how the glosses reflect such phonological system.

---

[120] Quintilian on 'unlearning' (*dediscere*) bad habits: "*non assuescat ergo, ne dum infans quidem est, sermoni qui dediscendus sit*" (*Inst.* 1.1.5). The remark is not specific, as it may refer to any speech habit; in this passage, Quitilian is referring to the speech of the *nutrices*, the first contact of a baby with language.

9 Note on transcriptions

In this book I will use the following system to refer to sounds (phones), phonemes and spellings:

/eː/ IPA symbol between *oblique bars*: a phoneme, in this case one that *can* be realised as a mid-high front unrounded vowel, but not necessarily so.

[eː] IPA symbol between *square brackets*: a phone, in this case the mid mid-high front unrounded vowel, whatever phoneme it may stand for (e. g. /eː$_1$/ or /eː$_2$/)

⟨ει⟩ any letter or group of letters between *small angular brackets*: a spelling (when not referred to in full, in this case as *epsilon-iota*).

Transliterations of Greek (mostly used in translations) adopt a one-to-one method: each letter or diacritic mark in the Greek spelling is represented by one single Latin letter. (Partial) exceptions are p^h t^h k^h for ⟨φ θ χ⟩ and *ps* for ⟨ψ⟩; *z* and *x* transcribe ⟨ζ⟩ and ⟨ξ⟩ respectively. The rough breathing is transliterated by a superscript ^{h}, subscript *iota* by $_i$, ⟨η⟩ ⟨ω⟩ by *ē ō*.

Trascriptions between oblique bars and square brackets use the International Phonetic Alphabet (IPA)[121].

---

[121] As per the *Handbook of the International Phonetic Association* (Cambridge – New York 1999).

II Vowel timbre

1 Timbre and spelling: evidence from inscriptions and papyri

Timbre, or vowel quality, denotes the articulation place of vowel sounds. Changes in the vowel system are one of the most striking features in the transition between Ancient and Modern Greek phonology, and some of them resulted in homophones whose correct spelling was already a topic of discussion in ancient tractations of orthography.

Our main direct source of information for changes in vowel timbre are spelling variations in inscriptions and papyri. However, the chronology of such changes, both absolute and relative, is particularly difficult to understand. This depends greatly on the unevenness of our sources for phonological change: official inscriptions seem to be more conservative, documentary papyri more innovative; to the great number of Egyptian papyri corresponds a relatively little number of inscriptions from the same area, and it is therefore difficult to appreciate the diffusion of some changes in the more official varieties of the language. It is clear that the social variability of the Greek language was becoming greater over time[1]: many changes that are well attested already during Hellenism in Ptolemaic papyri were not completed in the highest varieties of Greek until a fairly late time (cf. chap. I, § 7).

In order to evaluate the references to timbre in the Atticist lexica, an overview of the changes in the vowel system of Attic and the Koine will be useful. The table below (table 2) summarises them, covering the period from the sixth century BC to the fourth century AD. Although tentative dates are given in the top row[2], the table reflects the relative rather than the absolute chronology of phonological changes, and relies on the assumption that such changes were accomplished in the same in order in all Greek speaking areas. The table does not include the diphthong ‹υυ› and those with a back second element (‹αυ ευ ᾱυ ηυ ωυ›)[3]. The diphthongs with a long first element are included (superscript) in the

---

[1] Cf. Horrocks 2010: 120, 163–5 on the directions of language change in Attica and in Egypt and on the conservatism of Attic, respectively (with a positive assessment of Teodorsson's view on innovative, popular varieties).

[2] They reflect the more conservative view of Threatte 1980 and 1982.

[3] There are no entries in the lexica that deal with these diphthongs. ‹ου› appears in the table in that it is (also) used to represent the long vowel /oː/ (although more consistently since the mid-4th century BC, cf. table 2 below). ‹υυ› had merged with /y(ː)/ by the Hellenistic period (cf. Threatte 1980: 338–44); the notion that the reduction of prevocalic ‹υυ› to ‹υ› is an Attic trait is reflected in Choeroboscus (= Herodian περὶ παθῶν *339, GG 3.2 281.4–6), who groups it together with the re-

same cells as the long vowel with which they begin[4]. The length sign in brackets (:) indicates that there existed a long and a short counterpart of the same vowel. It is followed by a question mark in the relevant column for the period when contrastive vowel length was being lost (cf. chap. III) – henceforth, I will refer to the state of affairs in which vowel quantity is not distinctive as *isochrony*.

The mid front unrounded long vowels have been numbered: in the three symbols /eː$_1$ eː$_2$ eː$_3$/ the subscript number progression reflects the relative chronology of the moment when each of these vowels became a phoneme /eː/[5]. The numbering is unrelated to the openness of each vowel: for instance, the value of inherited *ē must be /εː$_1$/ in Classical Attic, but had become /eː$_1$/ by the time the diphthong /ai/ was reduced to the simple vowel /εː$_3$/ – same degree of opening, different chronology. It is only with the establishment of isochrony that such variations in timbre become phonologically distinctive.

The table shows the vowel system of Modern Greek in the last column to the right[6].

---

duction of /ai oi/ in Attic κλάω, ποιῶ, etc. The diphthongs ‹αυ ευ ηυ ωυ› resulted in simple vowels through spirantisation of their second element. The process is a context-conditioned spirantisation of /u/: as there are no entries in the lexica that involve diphthongs with a back second element, the change is not discussed here. For the variation /aːu/ ~ /aː/ see § 5 below.

4 The representation of their first element as a long vowel is conventional (cf. Allen 1987a: 84–8); on their phonetical evolution see § 5.

5 In order to avoid longer labels as 'the more recent ē vowel' (Threatte) – here represented by /eː$_2$/.

6 On phonological changes in the vowel system of Ancient Greek through Roman times cf. Horrocks 2010: 160–70.

Table 2

	Archaic Attic Spelling*	Hellenistic Spelling	Reconstructed Phonetical Value	BC					AD			Mod. Gk
				5	4	3	2	1	1	2	3	
↓ front	ΟΙ^ΟΙ	οι	(oi)							y(:?)	y	
	Υ	υ	y(:)									
	Ι	ι	i(:)			i(:)				i(:?)	i	i
	ΕΙ^ΕΙ	ει	(ei)		e:	e:C						
			e₂:			e:V		e₁,₂:^e:		e(:?)V		
	Ε	η^ηι	ε₁:^(ε:i)							e(:?)C	e	
		ε	e							ε(:?)	ε	e
	ΑΙ^ΑΙ	αι^αι	(ai)^a:i				(ai)^a:			a(:?)^a(:?)	a	a
	Α	α	a:									
↓ back	Ο	ο	o							o(:?)	o	o
		ω^ωι	ɔ:^(ɔ:i)	o:								
			o:									
	ΟΥ	ου	(ou)	u:						u(:?)	u	u

* These are the spellings prior to the adoption of the Ionic alphabet: ⟨ε⟩ and ⟨ο⟩ appear also where later we would find ⟨η⟩ and ⟨ω⟩. I have included the reverse spellings ⟨ει⟩ and ⟨ου⟩ for the new long mid-high vowels /e: o:/, as the consistent adoption of these spellings is not dependent on the adoption of the Ionic alphabet. On the adoption of the Ionic alphabet see Threatte 1980: 26–52, and pp. 173, 238 on the reverse spellings ⟨ει⟩ and ⟨ου⟩.

The major discrepancy between Egyptian and Attic chronology regards the monophthongisation of /oi/, possibly accomplished in Egyptian Koine as early as the 1st century BC, but in Attic not until the 3rd century AD (cf. table in chap. 1, § 7). There are two main changes in vowel timbre that were accomplished in Attic at a much later time that in Egypt and possibly many other areas of the Greek speaking world: the monophthongisation of /ai/ to /ɛ:₃/ and the rising of preconsonantal /e:₁/ ⟨η⟩ to /i:/ (see §§ 2.2 and 2.3 below). The atticist lexica, not surprisingly, reflect the Attic, conservative, phonology, rather than the more innovative one.

It is likely that the Greek spoken by the less educated had already undergone a number of changes that were still under check in the pronunciation of the educated. S.-T. Teodorsson suggested a particularly early dating for a number of sound changes[7]. He assumed that they had taken place in lower varieties of Greek quite a long time before they became normal in the higher varieties of the language.

According to Teodorsson, in the 'innovative [phonological] subsystem' of popular varieties of Attic ‹ι ει η ηι υ υι› had merged to /i/ by 340 BC (distinctive vowel quantity was lost, too)[8]. The only difference between Teodorsson's reconstruction of the vowel system of Attic around 340 BC and the vowel system of Modern Greek is the phonetic value of the digraph ‹οι›, which Teodorsson reconstructs as [y], and the existence, before vowels, of an allophone [e] of the vowels written ‹ει› or ‹η›, which had otherwise raised to /i/[9].

Teodorsson dates four changes to a particularly early date: (1) the loss of distinctive vowel quantity, (2) the raising of ‹η› /ɛː/ to /i/, (3) the reduction of the diphthong ‹οι› /oi/ to the simple vowel /y/, and (4) the unrounding /y(ː)/ > /i/[10]. Even though, even according to Teodorsson, these are changes that affected only the speech of the lower classes, such an early chronology is particularly surprising when one considers that learned Greek maintained many of such distinctions until a much later period. Teodorsson's reconstruction was met with some criticism (cf. Ruijgh 1978); in later years its contribution has been revalued at least inasmuch it has urged scholarship on the phonology of Ancient Greek to consider the sociolectal landscape of Classical Greek as a complex, non-uniform entity; some groups of speakers may have adopted as soon as the late Classical period pronunciation habits that would not become standard until the late imperial times[11].

Ancient descriptions of Greek phonology reflect a conservative view closer to the conservative vowel systems reconstructed by Teodorsson, and at a much later time than the dating of Teodorsson innovative phological systems. In Roman times, Sextus Empiricus would define ‹η› as the long counterpart of ‹ε›; the two vowels have different quantities, but the same value (or 'force'):

(21) ἡ γὰρ αὐτὴ δύναμις ἐπ' ἀμφοτέρων ἐστίν, καὶ cυcταλὲν μὲν τὸ η γίνεται ε, ἐκταθὲν δὲ τὸ ε γίνεται η.

---

7 Teodorsson 1974, 1977, 1978, on Attic between 400 and 340 BC, Ptolemaic Koine, and Hellenistic Attic respectively.
8 Teodorsson 1974: 286–99; Horrocks 2010: 165.
9 Teodorsson (1974: 186, 287) describes it as 'an open allophone of [iː]'.
10 Cf. Threatte 1980: 261–7; Allen 1987b: 28; Bubeník 1989: 187; Horrocks 2010: 165.
11 Willi discusses female speech in Aristophanes (2003: 157–65, 195), including the possibility that it was a itacising varity suggested in Plato, *Crat.* 418b-d (Willi 2003: 161–2).

> Both of them have the same value, and a shortened ‹η› becomes ‹ε›, while a lengthened ‹ε› becomes ‹η›.
>
> SE, *M.* 1.115

About eight centuries after Sextus, the *Suda* still attests to a pronunciation of Greek which is more conservative than the one reconstructed by Teodorsson. Lemmata are alphabetised κατ' ἀντιστοιχείαν: the alphabetical series of the *Suda* groups together homophonous graphemes (e. g., ‹ω› follows ‹ο›), and treats diphthongs as if they were simple vowels (‹αυ› follows ‹δ› and precedes ‹ε›)[12]. The resulting series is ‹α β γ δ αι ε ζ ει η θ ι κ λ μ ν ξ ο ω π ρ σ τ οι υ φ χ ψ›. The sections containing words beginning with ‹ει η ι› come in a row, thereby proving that the merger of ‹η› with /i/ was complete, but words beginning with ‹οι υ›, are still grouped together at the end of the alphabetical series, strongly suggesting that – whereas ‹ει η ι› were pronounced /i/ – by the early Byzantine times /y/ was still the pronunciation of ‹οι υ›, or had been until a time close enough to make it still the only acceptable standard in the writing of a scholarly work like the *Suda*[13].

In the following sections we will compare the reconstructed phonology of Greek in the 2nd century AD with the glosses in the lexica that may contrast homophones. In the Atticist lexica, entries referring to vowel quality normally contrast two different spellings: no reference is made to the quality of the sounds implied in the contrast by the use of specialised terminology (as modern phonology does when, for instance, it differentiates between 'back' and 'front', 'high' or 'low' vowels) – cf. e. g. Moer. η 17 ἠμωδίαν ἐπὶ τῶν ὀδόντων διὰ τοῦ η Ἀττικοί· αἱμωδίαν Ἕλληνες. For this reason, it is always difficult to tell with certainty whether the words that are contrasted are actual homophones, or just similar enough in sound or meaning to be misused by some.

It is in this sense that the Atticist lexica are also scholarly works on orthography (ὀρθογραφία)[14]. The changes in timbre that had resulted in homophones had become the object of systematic scholarly discussion by the time of Herodian: by the 2nd century AD, orthography would comprise μερισμός, ποιότης, ποσότης, respectively rules of syllabification, disambiguation of homophone

---

[12] The names *epsilon* and *hypsilon* derive precisely from this tradition: they are the 'simple' (ψιλά) /e/ and /y/ as opposed to their digraph counterparts ‹αυ› and ‹ου›, Degani 1995: 506 fn. 2.
[13] In Teodorsson's innovative subsystem for Attic *ca.* 350 BC, ‹υ› is already pronounced /i/, but ‹ου› is still a rounded front vowel /y/ (Teodorsson 1978: 96–7); /y/ however still corresponds to ‹υ› and ‹ου› in his reconstruction of the vowel system of Ptolemaic Koine *ca.* 50 BC (Teodorsson 1977: 255). On the survival of learned pronunciations of Greek throughout antiquity, and their relation to orthography. see Teodorsson 1974: 273–81.
[14] For a full discussion see Valente 2015b.

consonants, prescriptions on digraphs. ποсότης, 'quantity', literally refers to how many letters are needed to spell a particular sound, and the surviving examples deal mainly with ⟨ευ⟩ ⟨αυ⟩ and their simple counterparts ⟨υ⟩ ⟨ε⟩, or with whether a *iota* must be spelt or not after a long vowel.

The comparison will show which contrasts are more frequent, and whether they reflect recent developments in the phonological system of the Koine.

2 Front unrounded vowels

Ancient Greek had an inherited vowel system with three grades of openness and distinctive vowel length. Including the unrounded diphthongs beginning and ending within it, the front axis of the system can be schematised like this:

/i ~ iː/
    /e ~ eː$_1$, ei ~ eː$_1$i/
        /a ~ aː, ai ~ aːi/

In Modern Greek, the vowels represented in the above diagram merged to a simple, three-degree axis, composed of /i/ ~ /e/ ~ /a/. The vowels are the result, respectively, of

/i, iː, ei, eː$_1$i, eː$_1$/   > /i/
/e, ai/   > /e/
/a, aːi/   > /a/

Some of the changes leading to the modern state of affairs had already gone through by imperial times (cf. table 2), some other had in specific areas but not yet elsewhere: these are the most interesting ones for the scope of this research – how many of them are addressed in the lexica, and why?

As we shall see in the following paragraphs, changes that must have been accomplished in all, or nearly all varieties of Greek by the beginning of the 2nd century AD include the loss of /i/ in the diphthongs with a first long element /aːi eːi ɔːi/, the monophthongisations of /ai/ to /ɛː/ and of /ei/ to /iː/ (the latter in all contexts except before non-front vowels). The changes that must have been underway in the 2nd century AD include the loss of distinctive vowel length, the merger of /oi/ and /y/, the reduction of /ei/ to /i(ː)/ before vowels, and the rising of ⟨η⟩ to /i(ː)/. None of these changes is clearly attested in official Attic inscriptions before the 3rd century AD, but there is abundant evidence for all of them in Egyptian papyri, and occasionally in inscriptions from Asia Minor.

2.1 The digraph ⟨ευ⟩

2.1.1 The raising of /eː₂/ from Classical Attic to the 2ⁿᵈ century AD

The reduction of the diphthong /ei/ to a long mid-front vowel /eː₂/ is among the oldest changes in the vowel system of Attic Greek. By the late 5ᵗʰ century BC, the digraph ⟨ευ⟩ could be used to spell not only the old diphthong but also all the instances of the vowel resulting from contractions and compensatory lengthening (e.g. the imperfect of ποιέω, ΕΠΟΙΕΙ, previously spelt ΕΠΟΙΕ). The vowel is reconstructed as /eː₂/, a close-mid unrounded front vowel distinct from both short /e/ and open-mid long /εː₁/, the reflections of inherited *e and *ē respectively[15]. It is at this point that a distinction between /eː₂/ and /εː₁/ comes into being.

In official Attic inscriptions, /eː₂/ had risen to /iː/ before consonants long before the 2ⁿᵈ century AD – in fact, by the end of the Classical period: the earliest spellings for /iː/ with ⟨ευ⟩ instead of ⟨ι⟩ date to the mid-4ᵗʰ century BC[16]. By the end of the 3ʳᵈ century BC the digraph ⟨ευ⟩ is found as a spelling for /iː/ before consonants also in official decrees[17].

The raising of /eː₂/ to /iː/ was completed later before vowels, especially non-front ones. In other words, while preconsonantal and word-final instances of ⟨ευ⟩ corresponded to /iː/, and could be confused with ⟨ι⟩ in spelling, instances of ⟨ευ⟩ before ⟨α ο ω⟩ corresponded to a mid-front vowel /eː₂/, possibly shortened before vowels[18]. Attic inscriptions show this split outcome of ⟨ευ⟩ in the high frequency of the interchange between ⟨ευ⟩ and ⟨ε⟩ before ⟨α ο(υ) ω⟩, starting as early as the mid 4ᵗʰ century BC[19].

At this stage, a long mid-front unrounded vowel could be represented only by inherited /εː₁/ ⟨η⟩, occurring almost only before consonants and in final position, and by /eː₂/ ⟨ευ⟩, occurring only before non-front vowels. The contrast in openness between open-mid /εː₁/ and close-mid /eː₂/ was no longer phonologically relevant (instances of prevocalic /εː₁/ ⟨η⟩ are relatively rare): it is therefore

---

15 The long vowel that continues inherited *ē and is the outcome of various clusters with a laryngeal.

16 Non-official, sepulchral inscriptions date the confusion of ⟨ευ⟩ and ⟨ι⟩ /iː/ as early as the mid-fourth century BC: *IG* II² 12814 τείτθη, and 6053 Ἐλευcείνιοc, dated to *ca.* 350 BC. Such misspellings are particularly relevant because they cannot be careless omissions of the first letter of the digraph ⟨ευ⟩ but they involve the intentional writing of a redundant *epsilon*.

17 Threatte 1980: 195–6.

18 Threatte 1980: 202–5. In such prevocalic, unstressed environment, the length of /eː₁,₂/ might have been neutralised; the phoneme was realised as [e], or even as a glide [e̯], which would yield [j] at a later stage; cf. Méndez Dosuna 1992: 314–6.

19 Threatte 1980: 203.

not surprising that the two vowels /ɛːₗ/ and /eː₂/ merged in prevocalic position, to yield a single phoneme /eː₁,₂/|_V (quite possibly shortened, or even reduced to a glide, in faster speech)²⁰. Attic inscriptions dating between the mid-3ʳᵈ century BC and the early 2ⁿᵈ century AD (with the highest frequency between 50 BC and AD 50)²¹, show clearly that ⟨ει⟩ and ⟨η⟩²² had become interchangeable before non-front vowels²³, and Egyptian papyri reflect the same sound change, with a similar chronology²⁴.

It is only around AD 100 that there is evidence for a pronunciation [iː] of prevocalic /eː₁,₂/²⁵. At this time, all instances of prevocalic ⟨ει⟩ corresponded to /iː/, and so did the few instances of prevocalic ⟨η⟩, whereas preconsonantal ⟨η⟩ still corresponded to a mid front vowel. The resulting vowel system can be outlined as follows:

---

20 This was already noted by Sturtevant (1940: 40). The following vowel triggered the abbreviation and the formation of a glide (Méndez Dosuna 2002: 86–7). According to Méndez Dosuna also spellings with ⟨η⟩ instead of ⟨ει⟩ imply the abbreviation of the vowel. This supports the idea that when the variation ⟨ει⟩/⟨η⟩|_V was possible, prevocalic ⟨ει⟩ and ⟨η⟩ were still spellings for a vowel [e]. In Attic inscriptions the type ⟨ηος⟩ for ⟨ειος⟩ dates to the period between 2ⁿᵈ century BC and *ca.* AD 100: "[t]he reason why these spellings with *eta* die out after *ca.* 100 AD is that change of ει to [i] also takes place in this environment by about that time" (Threatte 1980: 203; cf. also p. 206).
21 Threatte 1980: 202–5.
22 Threatte 1980: 147–57. The letter ⟨η⟩ as a spelling for prevocalic [e(ː)] appears only later on, and suggests that the phoneme /ɛː/ acquired its capacity of being shortened and perhaps of undergoing synizesis later than /eː/ (Méndez Dosuna 1992: 315).
23 There is no solid evidence in support of the idea that the pronunciation of ⟨ε⟩ before vowels was 'somewhat closer' (so Threatte 1980: 146, confuted by Méndez Dosuna 1992); from the distribution of the spelling one can only infer that the difference in opening ⟨η⟩ /ɛː₁/ ~ ⟨ει⟩ /eː₂/ was neutralised before (non-front?) vowels.
24 Gignac 1976: 241. However, in Egyptian papyri ⟨η⟩ also alternates with ⟨ει⟩, ⟨αι⟩, ⟨ε⟩, ⟨ι⟩ at times when these interchanges are not yet common in Attica.
25 Threatte 1980: 206–7. Ruijgh (1978: 85–6) rejects Teodorsson's (1974) arguments in favour of the pronunciation [i(ː)] corresponding both to ⟨η⟩ and ⟨ει⟩ as early as the 4ᵗʰ century BC. On the other hand Ruijgh wants to date the change ⟨ει⟩ [eː] > [iː] to the 2ⁿᵈ century BC, on the basis of an argument "d'ordre morphophonologique", i.e. the restitution during that period of ⟨η⟩ for more recent ⟨ει⟩ in such forms as 1ˢᵗ declension datives (e.g. τῇ βουλῇ), subjunctives (e.g. λέγῃ), augmented verbs (e.g. ἥκασα). This implies that ⟨η⟩ and ⟨ει⟩ spelt different sounds (and not a single vowel /i/ as Teodorsson suggests), but not necessarily that there was still a distinction between ⟨ει⟩ and ⟨ι⟩ (*pace* Ruijgh 1978: 85). On the contrary, the very coming into being of a pronunciation [iː] of ⟨ει⟩ could have contributed to the re-establishment of spellings with η, in paradigms that alternated ⟨η⟩ and ⟨ε⟩, and not in the lexical morphemes as in λητουργία or κλῇς (Threatte 1980: 353–4).

/iː/ ι, ει, η|_V /yː/ υ   /uː/ ου
/eː₁/ η|_C   /oː/ ω
          /aː/ α

that is to say with only one mid front vowel, /eː₁/. This vowel system allowed for a new correspondence between vowel length and tension (and consequently, openness), in which a short open mid vowel [ɛ] corresponded to the vowel spelt ⟨ε⟩ and a long close mid vowel [eː] to the vowel spelt ⟨η⟩, as the standard realisation of a contrast in quantity, indifferent to openness, /e/ ~ /eː₁/.

Summing up, by the beginning of the 2nd century AD ⟨ει⟩ was pronounced [iː] in all positions, and in all parts of the Greek-speaking world, and the pronunciation was becoming the most common also in Attica. During the same time, but probably for less than one century, ⟨ει⟩ had also been used occasionally to spell short /i/ (cf. chap. III, § 4.5): also this habit reached Attica later than other parts of the Greek world, where it is well attested throughout the Roman period[26].

When also prevocalic /eː₁,₂/ raised to /iː/ every ⟨ει⟩ was pronounced /iː/, independently from the context, and the digraph would establish itself as a convenient means to express the long vowel. This was an an opportunity for the *dichronon* ⟨ι⟩ to be not longer ambiguous: ⟨ι⟩ could be employed to write only the short vowel, and ⟨ει⟩ its long counterpart. Greek inscriptions of the Roman period seize this opportunity: in the 2nd century AD, and even more so in the 3rd, ⟨ει⟩ becomes the most frequent spelling for the long /iː/ – words like τιμή, νίκη and their derivatives appear almost constantly as ⟨τειμη⟩ ⟨νεικη⟩ etc.[27]

A possible explanation for the high frequency of ⟨ει⟩ for /iː/ in the 2nd century AD is precisely the onset of isochrony. Accuracy in spelling entailed the correct distribution of vowel quantity, and the spellings with ⟨ει⟩ have to be seen as attempts at recording it. The spelling of Latin personal names too tends to have ⟨ει⟩ for /iː/,[28] although with the usual lack of standardisation[29]. As we shall see in the next paragraph, also the Atticist lexica treat ⟨ει⟩ as a grapheme for /iː/.

---

26 Schwyzer 1898: 74–5; Crönert 1903: 24–35; Nachmanson 1903: 24, 34–7, 40–4; Rüsch 1914: 65–75; Hauser 1916: 31–2, 35–7; Mayser – Schmoll 1970: 69–70; Gignac 1976: 189.
27 On ⟨ει⟩ for /iː/ in Attic inscriptions see Threatte (1980: 198–9). A similar trend is apparent in Asia Minor: Hauser (1916: 31-2) could count about 300 instances of ⟨ει⟩ against only 7 of ⟨ι⟩ as the spelling of /iː/ in Lycian inscriptions of the 2nd century AD.
28 Cf. for instance the list of personal names with Gr. ⟨ει⟩ = Lat. ī in Eckinger 1892: 42–5. The most common rendering of Lat. ī is ⟨ει⟩: about half the instances of ⟨ι⟩ represent the vowel in Lat. -*quī*-, a cluster that might have made transcriptions with simple ⟨ι⟩ to avoid an anomalous clustering of vowel graphemes. The usual transcription of Lat. -*quī*- in Greek are κοι and κουι: κοει or κουει, even if possible, are the less attested; cf. Eckinger 1892: 122–3). According to Threatte 1980: 94 a pronunciation [kyⁱnt-] corresponds to ⟨κυιντ-⟩.

The above changes account for the interchanges involving ‹ευ› and ‹η› or ‹ι›. The variation ‹ευ› ~ ‹ε› is also quite common before non-front vowels, in Attic inscriptions and in Egyptian papyri as well, and it may suggest that /e:$_{1,2}$/ was abbreviated before the following vowel, and therefore confused with /e/. The situation is quite different when the context changes: before a consonant the interchange it is virtually not attested in Attic inscriptions after the mid-fourth century BC, and the later examples are so few that one cannot rule out unintentional omission of the *iota* as the reason for the spelling with ‹ε›. Roman and Byzantine papyri sporadically attest the interchange, which seems to be more frequent before nasals, liquids, and the sibilants. I do not have the impression that one can identify a special pattern in the examples collected by Gignac (1976: 256–9). As we shall see shortly, the lexica ignore the interchange ‹ευ› ~ ‹ε›, except when a non-front vowel follows: in such cases, there is a tendency to identify forms with the digraph as the truly Attic ones.

2.1.2 The digraph ‹ει› in the lexica

The lexica treat ‹ει› as an alternative spelling for /i:/ in virtually all contexts[30]. Phryn. *PS* 80.3–7 →κεχρίσθαι makes a distinction – διαφέρει τῇ γραφῇ – between two meanings of the same verb, by only contrasting their (allegedly different) spellings. The early date of the sound change itself explains the total lack of this sort of prescriptions. It was since long fully accomplished by the lexicographers' time, and there were no alternative pronunciations in other varieties of Greek that could contrast the general pronunciation [i:] of preconsonantal ‹ει›. The correct distribution of the spellings ‹ει› and ‹ι› is a paradigmatic example of one of the domains of ancient ὀρθογραφία, namely ποσότης (cf. chap. I, § 6.3; and § 2.2.1 below). Only two entries, →ἀείτης (Paus. α 30) and →βοϊκός (Philem. 357), may involve some interchange of preconsonantal ‹ει› and ‹ι›, but neither explicitly discusses the the spelling of the vowel, and the latter is clearly concerned with the quantity of ‹ι›.

On the contrary, vowel quantity is used to disambiguate between ‹ει› and ‹ι›, as an inherent trait of the two spellings. In the wording of some entries, ‹ει› denotes by default a long /i:/, ‹ι› its short counterpart (cf. chap. III, § 5.4).

Other entries contrast ‹ει› with ‹ε›, thereby involving at the same time a constrast in timbre and quantity. They are all instances of ‹ει› before a non-front

---

29 E. g. Τειτου *IG* II² 1077 col. I 52 (Attica, AD 209/10), Μαξειμος *IG* X 2.1 750 (Macedonia, 2nd/3rd c. AD); see Eckinger 1892: 45–6.
30 The same equivalence is also implied by some rhetoricians of this period, e. g. Hermogenes *Id.* 1.6, cf. chap. III, § 2, ex. (23).

vowel, and all of them base on metrically guaranteed variants with ⟨ε⟩ in classical Attic authors. One gloss is Ael. D. ε 85, which contrasts →ἑωθώς and εἰωθώς: it supports the forms with ⟨ε⟩ as the Attic ones, but is otherwise not prescriptive, and does not refer explicitly to either vowel timbre or quantity (it only points out that Attic authors use the word χωρὶς τοῦ ι, 'without the *iota*'). The *Antiatticista* shares the same views as Aelius Dionysius, quoting →Θησέῳ (*Antiatt.* θ 13) and →θεῶσαι, θεώσειν (*Antiatt.* θ 20) alongside the forms with ⟨ευ⟩: the sources of the *Antiatticista* are fourth-century BC Attic playwrights who must have used later Attic phonology that shortened /eː₂/ to /e/ before back vowels, and the entries of the *Antiatticista* may be reactions to other prescriptions that considered the forms with ⟨ευ⟩ the only genuinely Attic ones.

Some entries restore an earlier prevocalic ⟨ευ⟩ even where Attic had most likely already generalised ⟨ε⟩: this is the case of Phryn. *PS* 73.4–6 →ἡμίσεια, and Moer. ο 32 →ὄστρια. Other entries seem to artificially contrast the spellings ⟨ευ⟩ ~ ⟨ε⟩: they all recommend the forms with the digraph, involving a normalisation to ⟨ευ⟩ of prevocalic ⟨ε⟩. These are Phryn. *PS* 60.14, contrasting γρυμέα with a (possibly non existing) form →γρυμεία, and *Philet.* 200, contrasting →ἔγγεια with ἔγγεα (allegedly Ionic). To this group we may add Phryn. *PS* 81.11 →κατάγειον, the only entry that contrasts ⟨ευ⟩ and ⟨αυ⟩. Whereas these glosses are not enough to suggest that ⟨ευ⟩ still had an open quality before non-front vowels (see below, § 2.2.2), they do imply that the atticising pronunciation of Greek was suspicious of the vowel clusters [ea], [eo], and that there was a tendency to (hyper)correct /iː/ instances of /e/ before a non-front vowel.

2.2 The digraph ⟨αυ⟩

2.2.1 The monophthongisation /ai/ > /ɛː₃/

There are no clear instances of confusion between ⟨αυ⟩ and ⟨ε⟩ in datable Attic inscriptions before the 1st century AD, and the two spellings are carefully kept distinct in official documents[31]. In Attic, the change is attested for roughly the same period as the raising of prevocalic /eː₁,₂/ to /iː/, and is common in Attic inscriptions only after AD 120[32]. The resulting mid vowel /ɛː₃/ filled a gap in the front axis of the long-vowel system:

---

[31] Threatte 1980: 294–5. In Lycia too only one attestation can be dated before the imperial period, and after that no document can be surely dated, until the half of the 2nd century AD, when ⟨αυ⟩ alternates with ⟨ε⟩ regardless of vowel quantity (Hauser 1916: 34).

[32] Chantraine (1938) suggested that the pronunciation of ⟨αυ⟩ as short [e] is the basis of the pun in Ar. *Nu.* 872–3, where "Socrates repeats the very expression of Pheidippides, but modifies the

/iː/ ι, ει, η/_V /yː/ υ   /uː/ ου
 /eː₁/ η   /oː/ ω
  /ɛː₃/ αι
        /aː/ α

The monophthongisation of ⟨αι⟩ may have been accomplished earlier in some varieties of Greek: outside of Attica, this is one of the earliest changes in the vowel system, generally dating around the end of the 4th century BC. In Egyptian papyri of the Ptolemaic period ⟨αι⟩ alternates both with ⟨ε⟩ and ⟨α⟩ (the latter variation can depend on the mere omission of a letter)[33]. Still in the imperial period, ⟨αι⟩ ~ ⟨ε⟩ is the most common variation, second only to ⟨ει⟩ ~ ⟨ι⟩[34].

The Boeotian dialect is a quite ancient and reliable witness for the monophthongisation of ⟨αι⟩ outside Attica. The case of Boeotian is interesting because it reflects a phonological system as captured by the adoption of a new alphabet (the same Ionic alphabet adopted in Attica less than one century earlier). When the Ionic alphabet was adopted, Boeotian inscriptions started employing ⟨η⟩ where the former spelling was ⟨αι⟩. Boeotian can be considered part of a pattern of development rather than as an isolated pioneer[35], attesting the same development seen in Ptolemaic Egypt, and only much later in Attica.

By the 2nd century AD also educated speakers would pronounce ⟨αι⟩ as a single vowel. Sextus Empiricus provides evidence for this:

(22) ἐπεὶ οὖν ὁ τοῦ αι καὶ ει φθόγγος ἁπλοῦς ἐςτι καὶ μονοειδής, ἔςται καὶ ταῦτα ςτοιχεῖα. τεκμήριον δὲ τῆς ἁπλότητος καὶ μονοειδείας τὸ λεχθηςόμενον. ὁ μὲν γὰρ ςύνθετος φθόγγος οὐχ οἷος ἀπ' ἀρχῆς προςπίπτει τῇ αἰςθήςει, τοιοῦτος ἄχρι τέλους παραμένειν πέφυκεν, ἀλλὰ κατὰ παράταςιν ἑτεροιοῦται, ὁ δὲ ἁπλοῦς καὶ ὄντως τοῦ ςτοιχείου λόγον ἔχων τοὐναντίον ἀπ' ἀρχῆς μέχρι τέλους ἀμετάβολός ἐςτιν. οἷον τοῦ μὲν ρα φθόγγου ἐν παρατάςει προφερομένου, δῆλον ὡς οὐχ ὡςαύτως αὐτοῦ κατὰ τὴν πρώ-

---

pronunciation". Line 872, ἰδοὺ κρέμαιό γ' ὡς ἠλίθιον ἐφθέγξατο, would not scan as it is transmitted by the manuscripts, but would be perfectly metrical if Socrates pronounced κρέμαιο ['kremeo], as a sequence of three short syllables; Chantraine suggests that this is the meaning of 'καὶ τοῖςι χείλεςιν διερρυηκόςι', '[with lips] wide open', in the next line of the play. But the same scansion of κρέμαιο is possible also by postulating a reduction of [ajjo] to [ajo] or [ao], and the lips 'wide open' would then just refer to Pheidippides' hypoarticulation; Willi (2003: 240, fn. 46) confutes analogous attempts at using the pun on Παιονίδης in Ar. Lys. 852 as proof of the monophthongisation of /ai/.

33 Mayser – Schmoll 1970: 83, 87–9; Gignac 1976: 191–5; Teodorsson 1977: 222–3. There is no uncontroversial evidence that – since it is limited to Egyptian Koine (Consani 1993: 28) – the variation depends on Coptic influence (Teodorsson 1977: 223) and is not merely a regional variety.
34 Gignac 1976: 192, and fn. 1 and 2 to p. 193.
35 Horrocks 2010: 164.

> τὴν πρό(c)πτωcιν ἀντιλήψεται ἡ αἴcθηcιc καὶ κατὰ τὴν τελευταίαν, ἀλλὰ κατ' ἀρχὰς
> μὲν ὑπὸ τῆc ρ ἐκφωνήcεωc κινηθήcεται, μεταῦθιc δὲ ἐξαφανιcθείcηc αὐτῆc εἰλικρι-
> νοῦc τῆc τοῦ α δυνάμεωc ποιήcεται τὴν ἀντίληψιν. ὅθεν οὐκ ἂν εἴη cτοιχεῖον τὸ ρα
> καὶ πᾶν τὸ ἐοικὸc αὐτῷ. εἰ δὲ τὸν τοῦ αι φθόγγον λέγοιεν, οὐδὲν ἔcται τοιοῦτον,
> ἀλλ' οἷον ἀπ' ἀρχῆc ἐξακούεται ⟨τὸ⟩ τῆc φωνῆc ἰδίωμα, τοιοῦτον καὶ ἐπὶ τέλει, ὥcτε
> cτοιχεῖον ἔcται τὸ αι. τούτου δὲ οὕτωc ἔχοντοc, ἐπεὶ καὶ ὁ τοῦ ει φθόγγοc καὶ ὁ
> τοῦ ου μονοειδὴc καὶ ἀcύνθετοc καὶ ἀμετάβολοc ἐξ ἀρχῆc ἄχρι τέλουc λαμβάνεται,
> ἔcται καὶ οὗτοc cτοιχεῖον.
>
> Since, then, the sound of αι and of ει is simple and of one kind only, these, too, will be elements. And a proof of the simplicity of their sounds and that they are of one kind only is to be found in the following statement: the composite sound does not naturally remain to the end just the same in quality as when it first strikes the sense-organ, but is altered through its prolongation, whereas the simple sound, which really has the character of "element," is on the contrary unchanged from beginning to end. Thus, when the sound ρα is prolonged in utterance, it is plain that the sense will not perceive it alike at the first impression and at the last, but will be stirred at first by the utterance of the ρ and afterwards, when this sound has vanished, it will gain the perception of the α sound in its purity. Hence, ρα and all similar vocables will not be elements. But if they should pronounce the sound αι, the result will not be at all similar, but its peculiar tone, as heard at the beginning, is just the same at the end, so that αι will be an element. And such being the case in respect of αι, since the sound ει and the sound οι are received from beginning to end as of single quality and non-composite and unaltered, these too will be elements.
>
> SE *M*. 1.117–118[36]

Sextus does not say anything on the length of the vowel written ⟨αυ⟩, but he makes very clear that the spelling corresponded to a simple vowel in his time: that there was at least a theoretical notion of vowel quantity in the 2nd century AD is clear from a passage a few lines before our text, SE *M*. 1.115, 'καὶ cυcταλὲν μὲν τὸ η γίνεται ε, ἐκταθὲν δὲ τὸ ε γίνεται η' (text (21), discussed above in §(1)).

The vowels spelt ⟨αυ⟩ for ⟨ε⟩ could have had an open quality /ɛ(:)/, opposed to the more close /e(:)$_{1,\,2}$/. Allen (1987a: 79) believes that there was a 'new need' to express the openness of ⟨ε⟩: however, it is not necessary to assume that the short vowel ⟨ε⟩ ever had a close quality – especially when it was opposed to /e:$_2$/ ⟨ευ⟩: the most natural scenario is that ⟨ε⟩ spelt an open short vowel, opposed to its newer long, close, counterpart[37].

---

[36] Transl. R. G. Bury (Loeb Classical Library 382, Cambridge, MA – London 1949).
[37] The hypothesis that later spellings with ⟨αυ⟩ for ⟨ε⟩ responded to the need of expressing a *new* open quality of ⟨ε⟩ (Allen 1987a: 79) is not compelling – or at least, one should remark that the open timbre of ⟨ε⟩ was nothing new: what had changed was that after the monophthongisation of ⟨αυ⟩ there was now a new way of writing an open /ɛ/. Quantity would still be relevant, but its relevance secondary when compared to the new need to express timbre (openness). It is perhaps worthwhile to observe in passing that writing systems do not necessarily have separate graphe-

In a small number of instances ⟨αι⟩ alternates with ⟨η⟩ in Attic inscriptions and not, as it would be more usual, with ⟨ε⟩. At least three inscriptions datable between AD 120 and 300 have ⟨η⟩ for ⟨αι⟩, certainly implying a pronunciation [e][38], if not [eː] – if the latter were the case, the preservation of vowel length may have favoured such confusion, as the phonemes written ⟨αι⟩ and ⟨η⟩ were the only two long mid vowels on the front axis.

2.2.2 ⟨αι⟩ in the lexica

The lexicographers mention the spelling with ⟨αι⟩ in four entries only. Two of them contrast ⟨αι⟩ with ⟨ε⟩, with no mention of vowel quantity, *Ael. D. α 59 →αἰώρα and Paus. ε 31 →Ἐλαία. Two glosses contrast ⟨αι⟩ with ⟨η⟩: Moer. η 17 →ἠμωδία, that contrasts the noun with non-Attic αἱμωδία, suggests that ⟨αι⟩ was a simple mid-front vowel (and at the same time supports the idea that in the 2nd century AD also ⟨η⟩ was a mid-front vowel). The two vowels were never identical – there must have been a difference in openness that eventually prevented them from merging ($/ɛː_3 \sim eː_1/$) – but it is possible that at some point they had been similar enough to be confused by some speakers. The prescription of Phryn. fr. *341 →ξῆναι and the related glosses of the *Ecloga* and Moeris[39] point to a similar conclusion. The Atticists prescribe the aorist stem in -ηνα of verbs in -αίνω (ξαίνω, θερμαίνω etc.): they are contrasting the newer aorists in -ανα, which must have originated when the sounds represented by ⟨αι⟩ and ⟨η⟩ had become similar enough to make newer aorists in ⟨α⟩ a clearer formation.

Phrynichus' recommendation of →κατάγειον against κατάγαιον (Phryn. *PS* 81.11) is an isolated case of ⟨ει⟩ ~ ⟨αι⟩. It could imply that at least for some speakers prevocalic ⟨ει⟩ /$eː_{1,2}$/ had not merged yet with /i(ː)/. In the Atticist lexica however there is normally evidence for the merger of -ειος and -ιος (cf. § 2.1 above), and the contrast in Phryn. *PS* 81.11 may have to do more with word-formation than pronunciation.

---

mes for long and short vowels, and that the Greek alphabet has always taken much more care in expressing vowel timbre rather than quantity. From this perspective, one may even wonder whether the main advantage in introducing the graphemes ⟨η⟩ and ⟨ω⟩ was to become able to distinguish the timbres /ɛː ɔː/ from those of the new long vowels ⟨ε(ι) ο(υ)⟩/eː oː/, and not their phonemic length.

38 Εὔκηρος *IG* II² 1073.16, *ca.* AD 120, γυνηκί *IG* II² 13218.7, 2nd/3rd century AD, cτήληc (dat. plur.) *IG* III 7.16, between AD 117 and 138 (Threatte 1980: 164, 295). Cf. also Gignac 1976: 248–9.
39 Phryn. *PS* 108.10–15, *Ecl.* 15; Moer. ε 15.

2.3 The letter ⟨η⟩

2.3.1 The four alternative spellings for ⟨η⟩ in inscriptions and papyri

Variations involving ⟨η⟩ are of four types: ⟨η⟩ can alternate (1) with ⟨ει⟩ before non-front vowels, and in any position (2) with ⟨ε⟩, (3) with ⟨ι⟩, or (4) with ⟨αι⟩, although in a very small number of instances (they are discussed above, § 2.2.1)[40]. With different chronology and frequency, the four of them are found in Attic inscriptions; also Egyptian papyri show them all, and as usual, with sometimes considerably earlier dates.

Variations (1) and (4) are discussed in §§ 2.1 and 2.2 respectively. Variation (2) involves vowel isochrony, and is discussed in chap. III, §§ 4.2 and 5.2.

Variation (3), i.e. between ⟨η⟩ and ⟨ι⟩, becomes increasingly frequent in the second half of the 2nd century AD. Still, instances of such confusion are rare and often attested in documents with otherwise inaccurate orthography[41]. The variation ⟨η⟩ ~ ⟨ι⟩ does not disregard original quantities (⟨η⟩ alternates with ⟨ει⟩ in the same contexts). Instances of ⟨η⟩ replacing a short [i] are most uncommon, cf. chap. III, § 4.3).

The chronology of the sound changes underlying such variations is particularly intricate. The huge discrepancies in the data from inscriptions and papyri strongly suggests that there had been sensible differences in the completion of changes in vowel timbre (a merger of /i/ and /e(:)$_1$/) and the onset of isochrony among different groups of speakers, in different areas of the Greek-speaking world.

Egyptian papyri of the Ptolemaic period attest the variation ⟨η⟩ ~ ⟨(ε)ι⟩ at the same time as ⟨η⟩ ~ ⟨ε⟩[42]. Gignac argues that in the 2nd century AD the vowel written ⟨η⟩ acquired universally a pronunciation [i][43]: variations between ⟨η⟩ and ⟨ε⟩ take place when ⟨ει η ι⟩ already were spellings for /i/, and they occur in the same contexts where the contrast between /e/ and /i/ tended to be neutralised[44].

---

[40] The same competition between variants (2) and (3) is found in Asia Minor, cf. Nachmanson (1903: 31) and Hauser (1916: 25–7), who postulate the existence of two competing pronunciations of ⟨η⟩, [ε:] and [e:], as diatopic variants: the latter, a mid high front vowel, is the one that alternates with ⟨ι⟩, the former with ⟨ε⟩.
[41] Threatte 1980: 166; Mayser – Schmoll 1970: 51–3.
[42] Mayser – Schmoll 1970: 46–7, 51–3, Gignac 1976: 235–42, 248.
[43] Gignac 1976: 241–2.
[44] The four contexts are: before or after a nasal; before [r, l]; before a back vowel; in final position (Gignac 1976: 242, 249).

The persistence of alternations of type (1), i.e. ⟨η⟩ ~ ⟨ε⟩, also in later Roman times⁴⁵ suggests that only prevocalic /eː₁,₂/ had risen to [i]. If we consider spellings with ⟨η⟩, this applies to the (extremely rare) groups ⟨ηα ηο(υ) ηω⟩, which merged with the more common ⟨εια ειο(υ) ειω⟩, but most other occurrences of /eː₁/, i.e. most spellings that had ⟨η⟩ in any other context but before a non-front vowel, could still be realised as mid-front vowel in more conservative speech styles, and in the artificial pronunciation of the Atticists. In the lexica, ⟨η⟩ alternates with ⟨ι⟩ only when the suffixes -της and -τις are contrasted, yet otherwise it alternates with ⟨ε⟩, and in one instance with ⟨αι⟩ (cf. § 2.3.2).

A couple of marginal points on the timbre of ⟨η⟩ deserve consideration at this point. Fristly, it is well known that in Ptolemaic papyri the variations between ⟨η⟩ ~ ⟨ε⟩ are so common that the phonemes written with ⟨η⟩ and ⟨ε⟩, namely /eː₁/ and /e/, must have become identical in some varieties of the Egyptian Koine already in the Hellenistic period⁴⁶. Yet elsewhere a distinction between the two phonemes, whether based on openness or quantity, whether preserved only by some part of the population or widespread and generalised, must have been mantained long enough to prevent the merger of the two vowels in the long term. In fact, the two phonemes that apparently merge in Egypt are kept distinct in modern Greek, where /eː₁/ is continued by /i/ and /ε/ has stayed /ε/, the only mid vowel on the front axis.

Secondly – or rather, as a consequence of the situation described above – one must notice that there is no need to think that the two phonemes /eː₁/ ~ /ε/ had temporarily overlapped⁴⁷. After /eː₂/ and prevocalic /eː₁/ had merged with /iː/, and /ai/ had monophthongised to /εː₃/, the mid vowels on front axis of the Greek vowel system must have had a threefold contrast /eː₁/ ~ /ε/ ~ /εː₃/. The contrast in quantity between /eː₁/ and /ε/ must have entailed also a contrast in height, which associated the greater tension – and height – to the long vowel and the greater laxity – and openness – to the short vowel. This is why /ε/ is the most accurate phonemic representation of the short mid-front vowel spelt by *epsilon*, and later by *alpha-iota*⁴⁸.

Indeed, when quantity stopped being distinctive, /εː₃/ would merge with /ε/ ⟨ε⟩, not /e₁/ ⟨η⟩. In the isochronic vowel system the contrast /eː₁/ ~ /ε/ ~ /εː₃/ resulted in /e₁/ ~ /ε/ (the new /ε/ corresponding to ⟨ε⟩ and ⟨αι⟩): the height must have been sufficient to keep the vowels distinct. A distinction in height also ex-

---

45 Threatte 1980: 160–1.
46 Mayser – Schmoll 1970: 46–9.
47 This is found in Sturtevant (1940: 39) and repeated in Threatte (1980: 160).
48 It has been made clear since long that ancient Greek short vowels /e o/ must have been mid-low [ɛ ɔ] and not mid-high (Allen 1987a: 63, 72, 89; Méndez Dosuna 1993: 97–8).

plains why the vowels written ⟨η⟩ and ⟨ε⟩ did not eventually merge: only /e/ rose to /i/, and /ɛ/ remained the only mid front vowel, merging with /ɛ:₃/.

One can only explain the irregular behaviour of ⟨η⟩, which alternates with /ɛ(:)/ or /i(:)/ in different varieties of Greek and at different, if we assume that – even before the system became isochronic – some varieties had reduced the degrees of openness on the front axis, /i/ ~ /e₁/ ~ /ɛ/, from three to two by merging /i/ and /e₁/. These are the speakers who confuse ⟨η⟩ and ⟨(ε)ι⟩[49].

In other varieties, the front axis had kept the three height degrees, also after the vowel system had become isochronic. Speakers with poor control of distinctive wovel length could still have reduced the contrast /e:₁/ ~ /ɛ/ ~ /ɛ:₃/ to /e₁/ ~ /ɛ/, and in their pronunciation timbre and not quantity would become a distinctive trait, resulting in a front axis /i/ ~ /e₁/ ~ /ɛ/. As a consequence, whoever wished to pronounce ⟨η⟩ as a long vowel in a controlled speech utterance could make sure to lengthen the right vowel by pronouncing as long only the mid-high /e₁/, even if they would otherwise ignore distinctions in vowel quantity. And such speakers could base their pronunciation on spelling: ⟨η⟩ is a long mid-high front vowel, ⟨αι⟩ the long counterpart of ⟨ε⟩, whose property of being long one can also infer from its spelling as a diphthong.

This explains why the standard pronunciation of ⟨η⟩ the 2nd century AD among the educated was a mid front vowel [e:], distinct from ⟨ε⟩ in the first place because of its quantity[50], and but also because of its timbre. And once more, the variety spoken in Attica had mantained the older threefold distinction: there the variation between ⟨η⟩ and ⟨ε⟩ is overall more usual than the one be-

---

49 The much earlier, and seemingly itacistic, women's variety that Plato mentions in the *Cratylus* (418b–d), while it certainly proves that there was sociolectal variation in Classical Attic, is not more compelling than the reconstruction of a 'older pronunciation' *δύογος for ζύγος mentioned in the same passage; there is no evidence in Plato that Attic women consistently replaced /e:/ with /i:/ (but for a tentative phonetical interpretation, see Willi 2003: 161–2).

50 Cf. Sextus Empiricus, *M*. 1.115 (no. 0 above). Also later Latin grammarians describe ⟨ε⟩ and ⟨η⟩ as the long and short counterparts of the same sound. At least in the milieu of learned Romans of the 2nd to 4th centuries AD, *eta* was still considered a mid front vowel (Blass 1888: 36): cf. Terentianus Maurus (date uncertain, possibly writing in the late 2nd or early 3rd century AD, Beck 1993: 10), who writes "*litteram namque ε uidemus esse ad ἦτα proximam, / sicut o et ω uidentur esse uicinae sibi. / temporum momenta distant, non soni natiuitas*" (*De Syllabis* 450–2 Beck), Marius Victorinus, *Ars gramm.* 39.19–21 Keil, "*quam* [i.e. the letter ⟨e⟩] *si produxeris … ut pro e η graeca audiatur*", Ausonius, *Technopaegnion* 14.3–4 (*de litteris monosyllabis Graecis*) "*eta quod Aeolidum quodque* ⟨εἶ⟩ *ualet, hoc Latiare E / praesto quod E Latium semper breue Dorica uox ε*", Martianus Capella 3.235 Préaux, "E *autem uocalis duarum graecarum litterarum uim possidet. nam cum corripitur ε graecum est, ut ab hoc hoste, cum producitur η est, ut ab hac die. ac maxime tunc circumflexum accentum tenet.*"). Latin transcribes ⟨η⟩ in Greek loanwords with ⟨e⟩ almost consistently, transcriptions with ⟨i⟩ are exceptional (Biville 1995: 33–4, 412).

tween ⟨η⟩ and ⟨υ⟩; the latter is overall not common, if not in "fairly crude texts, which may indicate that such a pronunciation of *eta* was substandard"[51].

Learned pronunciation must have maintained a mid-front pronunciation ⟨η⟩ well into the imperial period. Note that even a late Attic metrical inscription, dated to the 3rd or 4th century AD, misspells the article ἡ with *epsilon*, but is careful enough to write it with a rough breathing, ⟨ἑ⟩[52]. The (possibly learned) Greek loanwords in the the Gothic Bible normally transcribe ⟨η⟩ with ⟨e⟩ and do not confuse it with ⟨υ⟩[53]. Also Greek loanwords in Armenian transcribe Greek ⟨η⟩ with ⟨e⟩ as late as the 5th century AD[54].

2.3.2 ⟨η⟩ in the lexica

The lexicographers contrast spellings with ⟨η⟩ and with ⟨ε⟩/⟨αι⟩, suggesting that ⟨η⟩ was still a mid front vowel (Phryn. *PS* 27.12 →ἀνυπόδητος ~ ἀνυπόδετος, Phryn. *PS* 26.9–10 →ἀπέςβηςε ~ ἀπέςβεςε, Phryn. *Ecl.* 69 →γήινος ~ γέινος, Moer. η 17 →ἡμωδία, Phryn. fr. *341 →ξῆναι). For the prescriptions opposing ⟨η⟩ and ⟨ε⟩, see chap. III, § 4.2; the only one involving ⟨αι⟩ is discussed above, § 2.2.2.

Only one entry (transmitted in two lexica) contrasts ⟨ει⟩ with ⟨η⟩, and it probably involves some form of paraetymology (Phryn. *PS* 13.4–6, *Antiatt.* α 28 →ἀναπηρία). Considering the fact that by the lexicographers' time ⟨ει⟩ was the spelling of a vowel [i:], the scarcity of prescriptions distinguishing between spellings with ⟨ει⟩ and ⟨η⟩, especially when contrasted with the number of glosses contrasting ⟨ει⟩ and ⟨ι⟩, suggests that the grapheme ⟨η⟩ did not correspond yet to [i(:)]. To this entry we might add Moer. λ 25 →λητουργεῖν, which adopts a non-standard spelling of λητουργεῖν without the subscript *iota*. It is remarkable that entries directly

---

[51] Threatte 1980: 160; cf. also p. 166 for ⟨η⟩ ~ ⟨ει⟩ and ⟨η⟩ ~ ⟨ι⟩ in Attic inscriptions.
[52] Threatte 1980: 98, n. 14.
[53] E.g *Nikaudemos* (once even spelt *Nikaudaimos*) for Νεικόδημος; ⟨ι⟩ for ⟨η⟩ is exceptional, and however ⟨e⟩ is sometimes confused with ⟨i⟩ even in Gothic forms (Beck 1973: 120). The loanwords must represent the educated pronunciation of Greek in Constantinople during the 4th century AD (Sturtevant 1940: 38).
[54] Thumb 1900: 395. Evidence for the survival of /e:$_1$/ ⟨η⟩ as [e] from Pontic (Threatte 1980: 166, repeating Sturtevant 1940: 38 and Thumb 1900: 395) must be disregarded. In this dialect, originally spoken on the Turkish coast of the Black Sea, /e/ does reflect ancient ⟨η⟩, yet such vowel is the outcome of a general process of lowering of the phoneme /i/ in non-stressed position (cf. Pontic λεχνάρι /lex'nari/ < λυχνάριον) – even when it is not the outcome of ancient /e:$_1$/, but of /e:$_2$/, /i(:)/, /y(:)/, or /oi/ – that is, the modern Greek phoneme /i/ (Thumb 1901: 149, Drettas 1997: 98–9, Horrocks 2010: 400).

contrasting ⟨ει⟩ and ⟨η⟩ only appear in later lexica[55]; no such contrast is found in the Atticist lexica of the 2nd and 3rd centuries AD.

All the glosses explicitly contrasting ⟨η⟩ and ⟨ι⟩ are in fact indictments of the masculine νήcτηc, prescribing the feminine νῆcτιc as the genuine Attic word (Moer. ν 12, Phryn. *Ecl.* 298, *PS* 91.5–6 → νῆcτιc ~ νήcτηc)[56] what is under discussion is word formation and not pronunciation. It seems therefore that the current pronunciation of ⟨η⟩ among purists was [e(ː)], not [i]. The clear impression is that the lexicographers adopted the same pronunciation as the one described by Sextus Empiricus, according to which ⟨η⟩ is nothing but the long counterpart of ⟨ε⟩ (SE *M.* 1.115, text (21) above, § 1).

3 The monophthongisation /oi/ > /y/

3.1 ⟨οι⟩ ~ ⟨υ⟩ in inscriptions and papyri

In Attica, the first clear examples of a shift [oi] > [y] cannot be dated earlier than the 2nd century AD[57]. Most texts quoted by Meisterhans–Schwyzer[58], and showing the change underway, date already to the Christian period, and as such are not included in Threatte's 1980 survey. As is the case with ⟨α⟩ for ⟨αι⟩, ⟨o⟩ for ⟨οι⟩ is not necessarily conclusive evidence of a pronunciation [oi], as it could depend on the mere omission of the *iota*.

Like many other changes in the Greek vowel system, the monophthongisation [oi] > [y] did not take place at the same time in all varieties of the language. There is evidence that [oi] had become a simple vowel in Boeotian as the early 3rd century BC[59], when spellings such as ⟨υcετη⟩ or ⟨ϝυκια⟩ become usual, with ⟨υ⟩

---

55 As e.g. λεῖμμα and λῆμμα cf. Nickau *ad* Amm. 299.
56 One gloss of Ammonius (125 δαμάληc ~ δάμαλιc) is of the same kind. Ammonius' lexicon has two more glosses contrasting ⟨η(ι)⟩ with ⟨ι⟩, Amm. 273 κλῆμα ~ κλίμα and 300 λητουργεῖν ~ λιτουργεῖν, yet neither has parallels in earlier prescriptive lexica that suggest they may be concerned with pronunciation.
57 *SEG* 21.500 ἀνυγήcεται, Threatte 1980: 337; 1982: 149. Cf. also Bubeník 1989: 187; ⟨υ⟩ for ⟨οι⟩ was not usual "nicht nur im Attischen, sondern in der Litteratursprache der Griechen überhaupt" (Meisterhans–Schwyzer 1900: 58 n. 498).
58 Meisterhans–Schwyzer (1900: 58–9 and nn. 500–3), Sturtevant 1940: 50–2.
59 Kretschmer (1901: 6) discusses the possibility that the change spread from Boeotia, but cf. Thumb 1901: 228, Schwyzer 1939: 194–6, Debrunner – Hoffmann 1953: 106, Méndez Dosuna 1988, Horrocks 2010: 163–4.

corresponding to Attic ‹ου› (οἴϲεται, οἰκία)⁶⁰. However, even in Boeotian this is the last diphthong to merge into a simple vowel⁶¹. Egyptian papyri show the variation ‹ου› ~ ‹υ› already in the 3ʳᵈ century BC, but with a sensible increase in the 1ˢᵗ century AD (Mayser–Schmoll 1970: 89–90). The interchange is most usual in Roman times (Gignac 1976: 197–9). Yet still in the Herculaneum papyri⁶² there seem to be no traces of confusion between ‹ου› and ‹υ›, nor there are in Hellenistic inscriptions, at least the ones from bigger cities⁶³. Some instances of the variant datable to the 2ⁿᵈ century AD come from smaller cities in Asia Minor, and in Lycian inscriptions there is an example dating to the 3ʳᵈ century AD⁶⁴. In Attica the monophthongisation [oi] > [y] was not usual until fairly late.

3.2 ‹ου› ~ ‹υ› in the Atticist lexica

Judging from the small number of glosses that deal with the variation ‹ου› ~ ‹υ›, it would seem that Atticist lexicographers did not notice any particular problem with these spellings. There is no orthographical discussion like the section περὶ τῆc αι διφθόγγου of *An. Ox.* 2 315–8⁶⁵ that is concerned instead with the spelling of words with ‹ου› (or ‹υ›). It is remarkable that there is an entry on →πύελοc both in Phrynichus' *Ecloga* (281) and the *Philetaerus* (78), and yet the word is only quoted for the variant ‹α› ~ ‹ε›: none of the lexica mention a problem with the spelling ‹ου› for ‹υ›, even if ποίαλοc/ποίελοc is the usual spelling for πύελοc in a good number of funerary inscriptions on sarcophagi of the imperial time⁶⁶.

Phryn. *Ecl.* 124, and Moer. ω 2 contrast →ᾤδηκεν, ᾠκοδόμηκεν, and ᾠδηκώc with οἴδηκεν, οἰκοδόμηκεν, and οἰδηκώc. One reason why these glosses contrast the unreduplicated forms of the perfect may be that the old opposition /oi/ ~ /oːi/ had shifted to a more obscure /yː/ ~ /oː/ in the pronunciation of most speak-

---

60 Thumb-Scherer 1959: 26. The great anticipation on Attic cannot be explained as the result of a need to fill an empty slot /y(ː)/ in the phonological system (*pace* Bubeník 1989: 187) – a system without a phoneme /y/ should have been much better balanced, as it opposes only front unrounded to back rounded vowel sounds. Similarities in the evolution of Boeotian and Attic are so striking that one must regard them as reflections of a single, general evolution pattern (Horrocks 2010: 164).
61 Buck 1955: § 30; and Lejeune 1972: § 243.
62 Crönert 1903: 23.
63 From Pergamum and Magnesia, see respectively Schwyzer 1898: 80; Nachmanson 1903: 44–5.
64 Hauser 1916: 37, the dating of most other instances of ‹ου› ~ ‹υ› is uncertain.
65 Part of an orthographical treatise περὶ ποcότητοc, *An. Ox.* 2 283–330.
66 Some examples (imperial, but of uncertain dating) are listed in Hauser (1916: 37).

ers. Yet the problem with the perfects beginning in ‹ου› could be morphological rather than phonological: verbs beginning with a diphthong were reduplicated more and more rarely over time, and this could be the main reason for the existence of such prescriptions.

Only one more entry in the lexica contrasts ‹ου› and ‹υ›, Phryn. *Ecl.* 268 →ψύα, and it does not mention the quantity of ‹υ›, which is attested both as short or long in classical Attic literature[67]. This is quite possibly the only instance of a prescription addressing the pronunciation of ‹ου› as a simple vowel. Phrynichus condemns the word itself (one should say νέφρον), and explicitly tells that the right variant is ψύα, not ψοία, as some – who are 'twice wrong' – say. The example is isolated, but it suggests that some speakers treated ‹υ› and ‹ου› as variants, possibly ignoring the different quantities.

It is remarkable that Atticist lexicography should ignore the monophthongisation of /oi/: it confirms that it was still limited regionally (a word like →ψύα must be a non literary term imported with a dialectal phonology), and that it was accomplished only after the period of composition of the lexica in the varieties of Greek which were the model for the artificial Atticistic pronunciation of Greek.

4 Unrounding /y/ > /i/

There is no evidence of alternations between ‹ι› and ‹υ› proving that the unrounding of /y/ to /i/ was accomplished during the Classical or the Hellenistic period. Alternations are limited to specific lexical items, and all of them can be explained as assimilations or metatheses[68].

Glosses contrasting ‹ι› and ‹υ›, point in the first place to genuine uncertainty on Classical Attic usage. All the pairs involve spellings that are well attested, and often loanwords that may have entered Greek in either shape, with an ‹ι› and with an ‹υ›.

In one case, →ἁλυκός ~ ἁλικός (Moer. α 65), word-formation could be implied. All the entries prescribing →βιβλία (Moer. β 10) and βύβλινος (Ael. D. β 19), →μόλυβδος (Ael. D. μ 24, Moer. μ 6), →ψιμύθιον (Moer. ψ 3, possibly con-

---

[67] See LSJ s.v. ψύα and commentary to →ψύα.
[68] Threatte (1980: 261–2), whose data confirm that ‹υ› /y/ > /i/ cannot be dated to the Hellenistic period (*pace* Teodorsson 1978: 97 and 1974: 294–5); the unrounding is surely attested only from the 9th and 10th centuries AD on (Browning 1983: 56–7). The contextual raising of ‹υ› and ‹η› to /i/ has been invoked to explain the variation ‹η› ~ ‹υ› in Lycia (Hauser 1916: 33), which is hard to explain unless one assumes that both graphemes corresponded to /i/ as they do in Modern Greek. Unfortunately no instance of the variation ‹η› ~ ‹υ› in Lycia can be dated.

trasting ψιμίθιον, if not ψιμούθιον) contrast competing lexical items: normally both terms are attested in papyri or inscriptions from the same periods and places, which makes it unlikely that they represent two stages in the history of the same word. All these items are borrowings: the oscillations may depend on their adaptation to Greek, and also on assimilations and dissimilation with labial consonants or the vowels.

In three cases out of four (the exception being βιβλίον and its derivatives), the vowel ascribed to Attic is ‹υ›, which happens to be the more archaic variant for speakers that had unrounded [y] to [i]. However, there are no parallel examples of the unrounding of the vowel spelt ‹ου›, which at this time had merged with [y], and it therefore difficult to confirm the assumption that the unrounding of [y] was already so widespread that the constant adoption of [y] in ambiguous cases would by itself be a mark of a more accurate speech style.

5 Diphthongs with long first element

The diphthongs formed with long vowel /aː $ɛː_1$ ɔː/ followed by /i/ or /u/ underwent different evolution patterns in later Greek. The three diphthongs with a second element /i/ eventually lost it during Hellenism, by the end of the 2nd century BC. For a limited period of time, between the 4th and the 2nd centuries BC, /$ɛː_1$i/ had a separate evolution, and it tended to be shortened to /ei/; however the original /$ɛː_1$i/ was reintroduced in most places where /$ɛː_1$/ alternated with /$ɛː_1$i/ (in particular inflectional endings) after *ca.* 200 BC[69]. By the 2nd century AD, the *iota* in these diphthongs is a mere spelling convention, but the three diphthongs had exactly the same pronunciation as the long vowel that constitutes their first element.

The outcomes of /aːu $ɛː_1$u/ in Modern Greek are the same as those of /au $ɛ_1$u/; for the three of them one must assume that the first element underwent the same changes as the simple long vowel, and the second element the same as in the diphthongs with a short first element /au eu/. Between 100 BC and AD 50, Attic inscriptions showed a tendency to drop the second element of /aːu/, whereas /au/ remained intact. The lexica do not address this change in any way, but it has some relevance for the dating of isochrony in Attic. Variations involving /aːu $ɛː_1$u ɔːu/ are not discussed in the extant lexica, except for one

---

69 Allen 1987a: 85–6; Attic inscriptions replace older ‹ηυ› with ‹ευ› by the mid-fourth century BC, especially when, as in this case, the diphthong does not belong to an inflectional morpheme, but to the lexical part of a word, see Threatte 1980: 371–2.

entry in Moeris (η 5 →ἤμελλον), where ηὐξάμην is prescribed against εὐξάμην: but both forms of the imperfect of αὐξάνω were usual in Classical Attic[70].

Attic inscriptions of the Roman period use the adscript ‹ι› inconsistently for /aː εː₁ ɔː/, sometimes introducing it after a long vowel that had never been a diphthong[71] (which is an interesting trace of attention to vowel quantity). Where the *iota* had a morphological function it was retained for longer, but long diphthongs belonging to the lexical part of a word were normally simplified earlier. This results in a higher number long diphthongs fully written at word-end. The resulting spelling could be ambiguous: words like ‹αιτιαι› could either be a nominative plural or a dative singular. Indeed, some more accurate texts – even documentary papyri like nn. 15–24 in Colomo (2017) – would consistently employ a quantity mark on the diphthong to signal its function (and its pronunciation). The habit of writing adscript *iota*s only at word end also resulted in seemingly inconsistent spellings like τῆι λητουργίαι, where the ending of the dative singular retains the *iota*, but the body of the word, λητουργι-, is spelt with the *eta* only (cf. Moer. λ 25 →λητουργεῖν).

Two glosses (Ael. D. κ 29 →κλῆcαι, attributed the 'οἱ ἀρχαῖοι', and Moer. λ 25 →λητουργεῖν, if it can be taken to be a spelling for λητουργεῖν) discuss variants with ηι or ει. If we are right in assuming that ‹η› had retained its mid-front vowel value in the speech of most speakers, and certainly of the educated, whereas preconsonantal ‹ει› corresponded to /i(ː)/ in the speech of all the population, then the difference between the two spellings may have been more sensible in the 2nd century AD.

Only Phryn. *PS* 36.5–12 →ἀδολέcχηc mentions the long diphthong ‹αι›. The gloss contrasts a spelling with or without an adscript ‹ι›, but specifies the long quantity only of the simple ‹α›. The indication of an adscript ‹ι› may signal a long [aː], precisely because the second element of the diphthong was no longer pronounced. Two glosses contrast the diphthongs ‹ωι› and ‹οι›, Phryn. *Ecl.* 124 →ᾤδηκεν, and Moer. ω 2 ᾠδηκώc (cf. § 3.2).

---

70 The variation between /aːu/ and /au/ is limited to forms of the reflexive pronoun ἑαυτός (Threatte 1980: 383, 385 on isochrony); the three diphthongs /aːu εː₁u ɔːu/ may have tended to lose their second element just like /aːu εː₁u ɔːu/ did (Allen 1987a: 87): but /ɔːu/ is virtually non existent in Classical Attic, and /εː₁u/ occurs mostly in augmented and reduplicated forms where it was replaced by /eu/ by the mid-4th century BC (Threatte 1980: 384–5), and it is therefore difficult to draw any sure conclusions.

71 Threatte 1980: 362–5 on the different degrees of inconsistency in writing ‹ι› in the various kinds of inscriptions. None of them suggests that it was actually pronounced. On intrusive ‹ι› after long ‹α η ω›, cf. Threatte 1980: 365–7.

6 ⟨α⟩ ~ ⟨ε⟩ after a high vowel

A group of glosses, attested across different lexica, contrasts the sequences ⟨ια υα⟩ with ⟨ιε υε⟩. There is no general agreement in the lexica on whether the correct Attic forms should have ⟨α⟩ or ⟨ε⟩: some forms are prescribed with ⟨α⟩ (Phryn. *Ecl.* 280 →μιαρός ~ μιερός, Moer. ς 17 cίαλος ~ cίελος, Ael. D. υ 1, Moer. υ 1, Phryn. *Ecl.* 280, Phryn. *PS* 118.15–16 ὕαλος ~ ὕελος, Ael. D. υ 1, Phryn. *PS* 118.15–16 ὑέλινα ~ ὑάλινα, Moer. φ 15, *Philet.* 81 φιάλη ~ φιέλη, Moer. ψ 1, Phryn. *Ecl.* 280 ψίαθος ~ ψίεθος), some other with ⟨ε⟩ (*Philet.* 78, Phryn. *Ecl.* 281 →πύελος ~ πύαλος, Phryn. *Ecl.* 281 μυελός ~ μυαλός)[72].

The variants with ⟨α⟩ are normally first attested in the Hellenistic period, and they are the only ones surviving in Modern Greek, whenever it continues any of the words discussed in these glosses. The fact that the variation is not limited to word containing the suffix -ελο- (cf. Phryn. *Ecl.* 280 →ψίαθος) suggests that the process involved is phonetic in nature, and is a dissimilation conditioned by the preceding vowel. In these cases processes of assimilation or dissimilation may be implied, causing the opening of /e/ when it follows a high vowel (or a palatal glide [j] or [ɥ])[73].

---

[72] Thumb 1901: 75–6.
[73] Two entries involve the cluster /ps/, and show a similar alternation of /a/ and /e/. The words in question are ψακάζω and ψάλια, Phryn. *PS* 128.9–10 ψακάζειν (Ar. *Nu.* 580) διὰ τοῦ α, οὐ διὰ τοῦ ε, Moer. ψ 8 ψάλια ἐν τῷ α Ἀττικοί, διὰ τοῦ ε Ἕλληνες. Cf. Amm. 521 ψάλιον καὶ ψέλιον διαφέρει. ψάλιον μὲν τὸ τοῦ ἵππου, ψέλιον δὲ τὸ ἄκροις βραχίοσι περιτιθέμενον κόσμιον. οἱ Δωριεῖς ψίλιον καλοῦσι τὸ ἄκρον, ὅθεν καὶ ἡμεῖς τὴν ἐπ' ἄκρων χειλέων λεγομένην προσῳδίαν "ψιλήν" ἐκαλέσαμεν, ὥς φησι Τρύφων (fr. 108 von Velsen).

III Vowel quantity: variations in spelling

1 Spelling vowels, marking vowels

A good number of entries in the lexica addresses the distribution of short and long vowels. There are two different types of entries that deal with vowel quantity: (a) entries that contrast variants spelt with different *letters*, e.g. Phryn. *PS* 118.3–4 →υἱέος· ἁμαρτάνουσιν οἱ διὰ τοῦ ω τὴν γενικὴν προφέροντες, ὡς Πηλέως, and (b) entries contrasting variants that spelling could only distinguish by the use of a *lectional mark*, e.g. Moer. π 36 →πάπυρος μακρῶς Ἀττικοί· βραχέως Ἕλληνες – only a manuscript writing ‹παπῦρος› or ‹παπὔρος› (not necessarily with the accent mark) could make the spelling unambiguous: this is always the case when the letter involved is one of the *dichrona* – ‹α ι υ› – letters that owe their name precisely to their capacity of expressing either a long or a short vowel. In this chapter I will examine first the problem of isochrony, and then the entries in the lexica that refer to alternative spellings of type (a), i.e. involving different letters. I shall deal with the (b) scenarios in the next chapter, together with accents and initial aspirations, i.e. the ancient system of *prosodiai*.

From a linguistic standpoint, however, the phenomenon that underlies both types of entries is one and the same: the distinction between long and short vowels was no longer being consistently observed in the 2nd century AD. The next paragraphs (§§ 2–3) discuss the chronology of isochrony independently of orthography – for the discussion of glosses involving *dichrona* cf. chap. IV § 4.

2 Grammarians, lexicographers and the chronology of isochrony

The conservative diction prescribed by the lexicographers paid special attention to vowel quantity. A passage from Hermogenes, περὶ ἰδέων λόγου, illustrates well some of the assumptions about the sound of speech that were current in the 2nd century AD[1].

> (23) λέξις δὲ σεμνὴ πᾶσα μὲν ἡ πλατεῖα καὶ διογκοῦσα κατὰ τὴν προφορὰν τὸ στόμα, ὥστε οἷον στομφάζειν καί, ὅπερ ἐπιτηδεύουσι τινές, τοῦτο ἀναγκάζεσθαι ποιεῖν τῇ φύσει

---

[1] Hermogenes is one of the sophists whom Philostratus included in his *Lives* (*VS* 577): his ideas on style are discussed by Rutherford (1998).

τῶν λέξεων αὐτῶν. τοιαῦται δὲ καὶ ἄλλαι μέν τινες, ἐξαιρέτως δὲ αἵ τε τῷ α καὶ τῷ ω πλείστῳ χρώμεναι, ὥς που καὶ ὁ Πλάτων τὴν οἰωνιστικήν φησιν φωνιστικὴν ὀνομάσαι τινὰς ἀποσεμνύνοντας τῷ ω. καὶ περὶ τοῦ α λέγοιτ' ἄν τι τοιοῦτον· ὁ γὰρ Θεόκριτος ἀχθόμενόν τινα πεποίηκε δωριζούσαις γυναιξὶ διὰ τὸ πλατύνειν τῷ α τὰ πλεῖστα χρωμέναις τὴν φωνήν. μάλιστα δὲ τὰ στοιχεῖα ταῦτα τὸ ω καὶ τὸ α διαίρει τε καὶ διογκοῖ τὸν λόγον, εἰ κατὰ τὰς τελευταίας συλλαβὰς εἴη τῶν λέξεων, οἷον "ὁ μὲν δὴ μέγας ἡγεμὼν ἐν οὐρανῷ Ζεύς". – δεύτεραι δὲ σεμνότητος λέξεις καὶ αἱ διὰ τοῦ ο στοιχείου κατὰ μόνας εἴς τι μακρὸν καταλήγουσαι, οἷον Ὀρόντης, καὶ αἱ ταῖς μακραῖς τε καὶ διφθόγγοις πλεονάζουσαι καὶ αἱ τὰ τελευταῖα ἐν ταύταις ἔχουσαι, πλὴν τῆς ει διφθόγγου· καὶ εἰ καθ' αὐτὸ δὲ τὸ ι τιθοῖτο, ἥκιστα σεμνὴν ποιεῖ τὴν λέξιν πλεονάσαν, συστέλλει γὰρ μᾶλλον καὶ σεσηρέναι ποιεῖ, διογκοῖ δὲ οὐδαμῶς τὸ στόμα.

The diction that is appropriate for Solemnity consists on broad sounds that make us open our mouth wide when we pronounce them. We are thus forced by the nature of the words themselves to speak broadly, which some speakers do anyway. There are other possibilities, but long *a*'s and *o*'s especially produce this effect. That is why, according to Plato (*Phdr.* 244d), some people call *oiōnistikē* (augury) *ōiōnistikē*, to make it sound more solemn by adding an extra long *o*. The same is true with long *a*. Theocritus (15.88), for example, depicts a man who is angry with women who, because they speak Doric, use lots of broad *a*'s in their speech. Long *a*'s and *o*'s elevate and broaden especially if they occur in the final syllables of the words, as in Plato when he says, *ho men dē megas hēgemōn en ouranōi Zeus*, "Zeus, the great leader in heaven" (*Phdr.* 246e). – Secondly, words that contain a short *o* and end in a long syllable, such as *Orontēs*, produce Solemnity, as do those that have a lot of long vowels and diphthongs and those that end in these, except for the diphthong *ei*. If *i*[2] is often used, it does not make the style solemn, since it contracts the mouth and makes us part our lips with our teeth closed rather than opening our mouth up.

Hermog. *Id.* 1.6.247–248 Rabe[3]

It is interesting that Hermogenes singles out long vowels as giving solemnity, and treats short vowels either – as is the case with *omicron* – as something to be counterbalanced by a long counterpart, or – as is the case with *iota* – he recommends to avoid them altogether[4]. This attention to long vowels suggests that quantity distinctions were becoming weaker even in the highest varieties of the language, and therefore had become a trait to be learnt and imitated, a

---

2 Wooten translates 'εἰ καθ' αὐτὸ δὲ τὸ ι τιθοῖτο' "if long *i* is often used", adding 'long', presumably inferring it from the context. But Hermogenes does not provide examples of the contrast ει ~ ι, and in the next paragraph moves on to turns of phrase that give solemnity to a speech. I do not think there is any compelling reason to think that he was contrasting anything else that two different quantities here, especially since ει and ι had the same sound in virtually all contexts in Hermogenes' time (cf. chap. II § 2.1 and §§ 4.5, 5.3 below).
3 Transl. C. W. Wooten, *Hermogenes' On Types of Style*, Chapel Hill – London 1987.
4 This remark of Hermogenes is also interesting in that it implies that ‹ω› is by default the short counterpart of ‹ευ›: this proves that ‹ευ› wrote the same vowel as ‹υ›, and at least in the speech of the educated, the long one as opposed to the short one. Cf. chap. II, § 2.1.

mark of social and cultural status that the educated elites were proud to show off[5].

Atticist lexicographers of the 2nd century AD were writing in the period when the distinction between long and short vowels was being lost (cf. the paragraphs below), yet the entries addressing the correct distribution of vowel quantities are about as frequent as those concerning the position of the accent: readers of Atticist lexica were determined to observe the distinction between short and long vowels. The Greek sources themselves clearly show that a distinction of quantity was still retained in the 2nd century AD – Herodian for instance may have had a clear perception of the different quantities used by the Greeks and the Romans in nearly homophonous suffixes (τὰ διὰ τοῦ αριον ὑποκοριστικὰ παρὰ τοῖς παλαιοῖς Ἕλλησι cυcτέλλει τὸ α, ἱππάριον, φυτάριον, ἡ μέντοι νῦν cυνήθεια ἀπὸ τῆς τῶν Ῥωμαίων διαλέκτου πολλὰ ἐπίcταται διὰ τοῦ αριον ἐκτεταμένα, coυδάριον λέγουcα καὶ κελλάριον, Hdn. περὶ διχρόνων *GG* 3.2 13.22–5)[6].

Variations in spelling in Attic inscriptions suggest that by the time the lexica were composed vowel length was not distinctive for a large part of the Greek speakers. Yet the lexicographers who use μακρόν and βραχύ counted on the ability of their audience to understand them. Whereas inscriptions show that an increasingly large number of people had no more awareness of which were the long and which the short vowels, remarks on vowel length like the ones we read in Hermogenes point to an audience that can recongnise and pronounce them, perhaps not always successfully, as Philostratus reports when writing on Pausanias of Caesarea (Philostrat. *VS* 594, cf. chap. I §(4)). When he describes Pausanias' pronunciation as ὡc Καππαδόκαιc cύνηθεc, Philostratus is underlining its regional character. If we judge from the inscriptions of the 2nd century AD, the struggle with quantities must have affected a much wider area than only Cappadocia. It is likely that at that time all Greek speaking areas, perhaps with the partial exception of Attica, did not make any distinction between long and short vowels, and that the uncertainties of the speakers did not depend on where they came from, but on the artificiality of the distinction itself.[7]

---

[5] One wonders whether Hermogenes is also projecting this attitude on the age of Plato, when he writes that the philosopher reported peopole as being proud of calling the art of augury φωνιcτική instead of οἰωνιcτική (a misrepresetnation of Pl. *Phdr.* 244c – d (where οἰωνιcτική is given an *ad hoc* etymology form οἰνοϊcτική, Plato's own coinage).

[6] Printed by Lentz in the text of the περὶ καθολικῆc προcῳδίαc, *GG* 3.1 534.7, and similarly in *GG* 3.1 365.12: Τὰ διὰ τοῦ ριον ὑπὲρ τρεῖc cυλλαβὰc προπαροξύνεται, ὀψάριον, οἰνάριον, ἱππάριον, φυτάριον καὶ coυδάριον, κελλάριον ἀπὸ τῆc τῶν Ῥωμαίων διαλέκτου ἐκτεταμένου τοῦ α.

[7] As Schwyzer (1898: 94) believes, considering this passage of Philostratus.

In this respect, it is worthwhile to recall the role that declamation and the reading aloud of texts had throughout the Greek and Roman world. When vowels like ⟨ε⟩ ~ ⟨η⟩ or ⟨ο⟩ ~ ⟨ω⟩ are contrasted by defining either one as 'long' or 'short', these are not just shorthand definitions overlooking the difference between spelling and phonology, but are possibly explicit indications that when a 'long letter' is seen in writing, a long vowel should match it in the delivery of the text.

3 Dating isochrony

Greek originally contrasted long and short vowels. The existence of phonologically long vowels, contrasting with short counterparts, is apparent during a long time. It is proved by compensatory lengthenings and contractions, which increase the frequency of long vowels. They even yield new ones in some dialects[8], and quantity replaces inherited ablaut in some formations[9].

It is more difficult to tell when the contrast has been lost and how. I shall henceforth use the term 'isochrony' to label the state of the phonological system when vowel quantity is no longer phonologically distinctive. The dating of isochrony is not clear, both in relative and in absolute terms[10]. Allen and Horrocks both date isochrony *after* the raising of ⟨η⟩[11] to /iː/, thereby placing it at some point in the 3rd or 4th century AD[12]. Such a relative chronology would explain why the few cases in which ⟨η⟩ replaces ⟨ι⟩ almost exclusively involve a long [iː] ⟨(ε)ι⟩. However, at least in Attic the alternation ⟨η⟩ ~ ⟨ε⟩ is more common than ⟨η⟩ ~ ⟨(ε)ι⟩ at all times, and even in Ptolemaic papyri the same two alternations ⟨η⟩ ~ ⟨ε⟩ and ⟨η⟩ ~ ⟨(ε)ι⟩ suggest that a more open and a more close pronunciation of ⟨η⟩ coexisted: this is better understood if we assume that by the time

---

8 This is the case with compensatory lengthenings and contractions that yield /aː/ in Ionic, after the original /aː/ had risen to /εː/; lengthening took place with /e/ and /o/ as well, and it produced the new long vowels /eː oː/, causing the lowering of inherited *ē *ō to /εː ɔː/ (Ruipérez 1956; Bartoněk 1966; on the low or high quality of /e o/ cf. Allen (1987a: 63–4) and (1993: 97–8)).
9 Quantity is a morphologically productive device in Ancient Greek: for instance, it replaces the original ablaut in the verbal suffix *-neu-/-nu-, represented by -vū-/-vυ- in this class of Greek nasal presents.
10 "before the end of the Hellenistic period" (Petrounias 2007: 602); "[f]or most of these developments, the crucial issue of chronology still remains to be established" (Horrocks 2010: 163).
11 Preconsonantal ⟨η⟩: the few instances of prevocalic ⟨η⟩ had already merged with ⟨ει⟩ /eː₂/ (cf. chap. II, §§ 2.1.1 and 2.3.1).
12 Allen (1987b: 26–8), Horrocks dates isochrony to "broadly the same period [as η /eː/ > /iː/]" (2010: 162).

vowel quantity was lost /eː₁,₂/ had not yet raised to /iː/ in all contexts (cf. chap. II, § 2.3).

Allen reconstructs a system that becomes asymmetric after the monophthongisation /ai/ > /ɛː₃/ with four height degrees on the front axis and only three on the back axis[13]. Symmetry on both axes would be regained with the further reduction to three of the front vowels, after the raising /iː/ > /eː₁,₂/ (cf. chap. II, § 2.1.1). The system of long vowels would then look as follows:

/iː/ ι ει η /yː/ υ (οι)   /uː/ ου
   /eː₃/ αι   /oː/ ω
            /aː/ α

perfectly matching the short vowel system on the front axis

/i/ ι /y/ υ
   /e/ ε   /o/ o
            /a/ α

The merger of the long and short vowel system was triggered by a shift of accent type: the old pitch accent turned to a stress accent, that lengthened the accented vowel, thus making it difficult for quantity to survive as a distinct segmental phonological trait[14]. Possibly the change was already on its way during the Hellenistic period, and the quantitative and isochronic vowel systems could have been coexisting and concurrent between the 4th and the 1st centuries BC[15]. Different groups of speakers may subsequently have employed vowel quantity in different ways, giving rise to the sort of confusion that Atticist prescriptions seek to contrast.

3.1 The role of the accent in the establishing of isochrony

Once a free stress accent had developed, vowel length could not remain a distinctive trait in the vowel system, but needed to become a non-distinctive trait of the accent: long quantity would become a feature of stressed vowels only[16].

---

13 Allen (1987b), and for the Koine Horrocks (2010: 160–3).
14 Allen 1987b: 28.
15 Devine – Stephens 1994: 215.
16 "It is typologically anomalous for a language with free stress accent [...] also to have distinctive vowel length; and this situation was resolved in Greek by the collapse of the two now con-

Vowel quantity cannot be used at the same time as a distinctive trait and as an accessory trait of stressed vowels: otherwise e.g. [aː] would become the realisation of /aː/ in all contexts and at the same time of stressed /a/[17].

Changes in music, versification, spelling suggest an early, already Hellenistic, onset of isochrony. Between 325–1 BC, instances of ‹ε› for /eː/, ‹η› for /e/, ‹o› for /oː/, ‹ω› for /o/, and ‹ευ› for /i/, are distributed in a way suggesting substitution of a long vowel for a short is more frequent in stressed syllables, and that the opposite substitution, i.e. spellings with short vowels replacing long ones, is more frequent in unstressed syllables[18].

Two more changes point to the establishing of a stress accent in Hellenistic times:
- the loss of ‹o› in the spelling of nouns and adjectives in -ιoc, -ιov, -αιoc, resulting in -ιc, -ιv, – αιc: the phenomenon is well explained only by the development of a stress accent, and both in Attica and in Egypt it can be dated just before the time when isochrony is attested. However, it is attested in Egypt about three centuries before it is in Attica (3rd or 2nd century BC in Egypt, 1st century AD in Attica)[19];
- the first instances of quantitative verse that takes into account the position of the accent date to Antipater of Sidon (active in the second half of the 2nd century BC) and Philip of Thessalonica (1st century AD): the phenomenon is however more evident in Roman times, in Babrius' choliambs (2nd century AD – cf. Maas 1962: §§ 19–25), and much later in Nonnus' hexameters (5th

---

gruent systems into a single system indifferent to length" (Allen 1987b: 28), basing on Jakobson ([1931] 1962: 135–6): "die monotonische Tonstufekorrelation kann nicht mit der Quantitätskorrelation der Vokale in selben phonologischen Plan koexistieren [...] Man kann folglich die Frage stellen, ob nicht aus Maßgebende Eigenschaft des Gegensatzes "monotonische Betonung–Unbetontheit" im Syntagmaphonologie die Stärke und im lexikalen Plane die Dauer fungiert".

Phonological systems with coexisting vowel quantity and stress accent normally lose one of the two traits – cf. Lahiri – Riad – Jacobs (1999: 400, 403–4) for Germanic and Romance languages. The same pattern applies to the transition from Latin to Italian, i.e. from a system with vowel length and a stress accent but conditioned by syllable structure, to one with free accent but an isochronic vowel system (Garde 1972: 101–8; 105–7; 124–7; Martinet 1977: 111; Leumann 1977: 235–8).

17 Similar phenomena are reconstructed by Chadwick (1992) for Thessalian, following the hypothesis that this dialect had developed a stress accent on the first syllable.
18 Devine – Stephens 1994: 215–23, esp. 218.
19 Threatte 1980: 400–4, 1982: 152.

century AD): exclusively accentual verse becomes common only at the time of Gregorius of Nazianzus (AD 329–389)[20].

The chronology of these changes matches Kretschmer's reconstruction, dating the change form a pitch to a stress accent to the 2nd century BC[21]: this change took place just before isochrony did, but at different times in different areas of the Greek-speaking world.

However, it is not until the 2nd century AD that Attic inscriptions begin to show clear sings of confusion between long and short vowels[22], for instance by writing ‹ει› ‹ω› for expected (short) /i/ and /o/. Yet, as is the case with many other phonological changes, regions other than Attica often attest the isochrony earlier than Attic. Egyptian documents, for instance, show a poor command of vowel length already by the mid 2nd century BC[23]. For a long time, and quite possibly still around the time when our lexica were being written, varieties of Greek with distinctive vowel quantity must have coexisted with isochronical varieties.

3.2 Isochrony does not imply the merger of ‹η› and /i(ː)/

It is not necessary to date the onset of isochrony to the 3rd century AD, following Allen's model of 'catastrophe' (Allen 1987b). In Allen's perspective a series of minor sound changes, interpreted as structural discontinuities, lead to the sudden establishing of a new phonological system[24]. Such structural discontinuites in the evolution of the Greek quantitative vowel system are:

---

20 Dihle 1954, cf. also Schwyzer 1939: 394; Gignac 1976: 326 fn. 3. Whilst Gregorius of Nazianzus certainly writes quantitative verses where the distribution of long and short syllables is irrelevant, it cannot be ruled out that Hellenistic poets preferred some positions of the accent because they had a preference for special tone patterns (Probert 2003: § 13).
21 Kretschmer 1890: 599; Schwyzer 1898: 94–7 and 1939: 393; Drerup 1929; Lejeune 1972: § 223; Bubeník 1989: 216.
22 The innovative phonological system reconstructed by Teodorsson is isochronic already by the middle of the 4th century BC, but in Teodorsson's view, the conservative system had kept the distinction of quantity until the 1st century BC (1974: 293, 1978: 96). See Ruijgh (1978) for a general criticism of Teodorsson's methodology. The conservative diction prescribed by the Atticists reflects best the chronology of Attic inscriptions, in which clear signs of isochrony are attested only in the first century AD (Threatte 1980: 385–7).
23 Mayser – Schmoll 1970: 117–9; Teodorsson 1977: 253–5.
24 The idea of 'catastrophe' contrasts the teleological concept of 'conspiracy', which considers groups of sound changes part of a coherent development aiming at a restructuration of a pho-

(i) compensatory lengthenings: the creation of new long mid vowels (‹ευ› /eː₂/) had caused crowding on the front-axis of the system;
(ii) the disappearance of diphtongs, following the monophthongisation of all diphthongs with a second element /i/ and the rephonologisation of /au eu/ in /aβ eβ/[25];
(iii) the change in the type of accent, from a pitch accent to a stress accent.

Assuming that it is necessary for all these changes to have been accomplished for phonological quantity to be lost, isochrony cannot be but later than the latest of them. The change in the type of accent, which Allen dates at a time right before the collapse of quantity distinction in the vowel system of Attic, i.e. around the 3rd century AD, may in fact have occurred long before, already in Hellenistic times, in other varieties of Greek, e.g. Egyptian Koine. Even disregarding the problems in the chronology of the change in accent type, in Allen's reconstruction isochrony must follow the reduction of /oi/ to /y/[26], the rephonologisation of /au eu/ to /aβ eβ/, and lastly the rising of ‹η› to /iː)/ (Allen 1987b: 26–7) – the *terminus post quem* for the establishment of isochrony.

However, it is not necessary for the systems of long and short vowels to have reached an identical set of timbres in order for them to merge. In particular, it not necessary for the vowel written ‹η› to have risen to /iː/ for the vowel system to become isochronic. After the onset of isochrony, a conservative variety of Attic retaining a pronunciation /e/ of ‹η›, could still contrast four degrees of height on the front axis, but only three on the back axis, as follows:

/i/ ι ει η|_V /y/ υ (οι)   /u/ ου
　　　/e₁/ η|_C   /o/ ο ω
　　　/ɛ/ ε αι
　　　　　　　　　/a/ α

---

nological system (in this case the elimination of quantity as distinctive trait in the vowel system), cf. Allen 1987b: 29–32.

25 This is a case of rephonologisation in that the phoneme */β/ deriving from the second element of the diphtong merged with /v/ and /f/ together with some allophones of the older stops /b/ and /pʰ/.

26 On the intermediate stage /ø/ see Méndez Dosuna 1988. I am not sure that Teodorsson's transcription with /ɵ/, a central rounded vowel, means anything else than /ø/, a front rounded vowel (Teodorsson 1977: 227, 251–6). Teodorsson's argument (1977: 227) shows that ‹ου› spelt at some stage a vowel more open than ‹υ›, but not that it was also a central and not a front vowel.

In this system, preconsonantal ⟨η⟩ is a mid-high front (unrounded) vowel, which has not yet merged with /i/. /i/ could be a sociolinguistic variable associated with /e/ in the realisation of the vowel spelt by *eta:* the mid vowel /e/ corresponding to ⟨η⟩ in some varieties of Greek would alternate with /i/ only in some other varieties: some speakers reduced the threefold contrast on the front axis, /i/ ~ /e₁/ ~ /ɛ/ to /i/ ~ /ɛ/, merging /i/ and /e₁/, the vowel spelt ⟨η⟩ (cf. chap. II, § 2.3.1)[27].

The contrast between ⟨η⟩ and ⟨ε⟩ would only be one in height[28], to which some speakers could also associate a contrast in quantity. The lexica treat ⟨η⟩ as a mid vowel, as the glosses dealing with ⟨ε⟩ and ⟨η⟩ show (cf. § 5.2).

It is perhaps worthwhile to note that ⟨ε⟩ and ⟨η⟩ are clearly contrasted, and consistently used, to transcribe Latin ĕ and ē in papyri teaching Latin to speakers of Greek. The same papyri also tend to mark quantities on the Latin text, showing that learners of Latin had an interest in observing the right quantities. This may depend only on the willingness to accent Latin correctly, as Latin stress is determined by vowel quantity and syllable weight, but it may also reflect the idea that correct pronunciation (of any given language) could not disregard the distinction between long and short vowels[29].

4 Spelling variations in inscriptions and papyri as evidence for isochrony

The dating of isochrony is based, at least in part, on spelling variants implying that certain changes in vowel timbre had already taken place. Only two of them are independent on changes in vowel timbre, namely the confusion between ⟨ω⟩ and ⟨ο⟩ and between ⟨η⟩ and ⟨ε⟩ (the latter however often coexisting with other variations, ⟨η⟩ ~ ⟨(ε)ι⟩, cf. § 3 and chap. II, § 2.3)[30].

Other variations imply changes in timbre, not only in vowel quantity. When ⟨ει⟩ and ⟨αι⟩ begin to spell the short vowels /i e/, such spellings imply the mono-

---

27 This is the situation in Ptolemaic papyri, cf. Mayser-Schmoll 1970: 46–53, 118.
28 A similar reconstruction explains the variations between ⟨η⟩ ~ ⟨ε⟩ in Ptolemaic papyri (Mayser – Schmoll 1970: 118).
29 Dickey 2015: 48.
30 The local alphabet of Attica did not include the letters ⟨η⟩ and ⟨ω⟩, but these were increasingly employed during the 5th century BC, even before the Ionic alphabet of Miletus would become the offical writing system of Athens (Threatte 1980: 26–51; Immerwahr 1990: 179–82). The occasional variations ⟨ο⟩ ~ ⟨ω⟩ or ⟨ε⟩ ~ ⟨η⟩ in Attic inscriptions of the 4th century BC are therefore more likely to depend on uncertainty in the usage of the new writing system (Threatte 1980: 159).

phthongisations ⟨ευ⟩ /eː/ > /iː/ and ⟨αυ⟩ /ai/ > /ɛː/, and then the loss of distinctive vowel length. The same is true for ⟨ου⟩ when it begins to spell the short vowel /y/, a monophthongisation that in Attic at least was late enough to have yielded directly a short vowel, after isochrony was already established.

Between about 100 BC and AD 50 the diphthong /aːu/ tended to be replaced by /aː/ before consonants, resulting in a variation ⟨αυ⟩ ~ ⟨α⟩. Such variation is no longer found after *ca.* AD 50, when /aːu/ merged with /au/ as a result of the loss of distinction between /aː/ and /a/ (Threatte 1980: 383).

4.1 ⟨ο⟩ ~ ⟨ω⟩

The confusion between ⟨ο⟩ and ⟨ω⟩ is particularly useful in dating the loss of distinctive vowel length in Attic. In the five centuries intervening between the introduction of the Ionic alphabet and the beginning of the 2nd century AD this variation is only sporadically attested, yet starting with the second quarter of the 2nd century AD it increases drastically[31]. This strongly suggests that vowel length was no longer distinctive by the beginning of the 2nd century AD.

Attic inscriptions are the last to show the variation ⟨ο⟩ ~ ⟨ω⟩, with the first examples dating to the 2nd century AD. Egyptian papyri show it as soon as the 3rd century BC, and even more frequently in the following centuries, especially in non-accented syllables (Mayser–Schmoll 1970: 73–6); by Roman times the confusion is common in every context (Gignac 1976: 275–7).

The Herculaneum papyri keep the two vowels distinct[32]. Nachmanson (1903: 63–4) dates the first examples of the variations ⟨ο⟩ ~ ⟨ω⟩ (and ⟨η⟩ ~ ⟨ε⟩) as early as the 2nd century BC, basing on the variation ⟨ο⟩ ~ ⟨ω⟩. Yet, like in Pergamum and in Lycia, evidence for isochrony is more abundant in Roman times[33]. Also inscriptions of Delphi show instances of ⟨ο⟩ for ⟨ω⟩ that can be dated to the 2nd century BC (Rüsch 1914: 144–7, yet basing on transcriptions that he found unreliable).

---

[31] Cf. Threatte 1980: 228, Meisterhans – Schwyzer 1900: 24–6. Although there are instances of confusion between ⟨ο⟩ and ⟨ω⟩ starting form about 300 BC, they can hardly be the result of isochrony (Threatte 1980: 161, 224; 1982: 154).

[32] Crönert 1903: 19–20. Some variations in the manuscripts of the NT have been interpreted as 'future subjunctives' (e.g. ἐκφευξώμεθα, κερδηθήϲωνται), cf. Blass – Debrunner – Funk 1961: § 28.

[33] For Pergamum see Schwyzer (1898: 95–6); for Lycia Hauser (1916: 48–9); cf. also Brixhe (1987: 47, 55–6).

4.2 ⟨η⟩ ~ ⟨ε⟩

The confusion between ⟨η⟩ and ⟨ε⟩ is also an excellent sign of isochrony. It is, of course, more problematic than the variation ⟨o⟩ ~ ⟨ω⟩ as the letter ⟨η⟩ at some point must have come to spell a high front vowel /i(:)/ (the pronunciation [i(:)] of ⟨η⟩ is ignored by the lexicographers)[34].

The persistence of the pronunciation of ⟨η⟩ as a mid front vowel /e/ must explain the instances of variation between ⟨η⟩ and ⟨ε⟩ that keep occurring in Attic inscriptions as late as the 3rd century AD[35]. Confusion between ⟨η⟩ and ⟨ε⟩ is only occasional in Attica, although attested throughout the Hellenistic and Roman periods[36] and earlier than the first traces of isochrony, which are later than AD 125–150[37].

The capacity of ⟨η⟩ to be confused with /e/ or /i/ seems to vary across the Greek speaking areas of the Empire. The Herculaneum papyri are quite accurate in preserving the distinction between ⟨η⟩ and ⟨ε⟩ (Crönert 1903: 19). In Asia Minor, the interchange between ⟨η⟩ and ⟨ε⟩ is not as well attested as the one between ⟨η⟩ and ⟨ι⟩ (Hauser 1916: 25–7; Nachmanson 1903: 31–2 for some Hellenistic examples), Egyptian papyri suggest that a pronunciation [i] coexisted with [e] already in the Ptolemaic period[38].

Greek ⟨η⟩ can represent Latin ĕ, but it also happens that Latin inscriptions have ⟨i⟩ where Greek has ⟨η⟩. The latter spelling could be evidence of the raising of the vowel represented by ⟨η⟩ to /i(:)/, but as short /i/ in Latin tended to a more open pronunciation [e] the oscillation may merely prove that both Latin ⟨i⟩ and Greek ⟨η⟩ could be used to spell a mid-close front vowel /e(:)/[39].

---

[34] Cf. chap. II, §§ 2.3.1 and 2.3.2.
[35] Threatte 1980: 163–4.
[36] This "presumably indicates that some persons mantained η as an e-vowel" (Threatte 1980: 161, cf. also pp. 160 and 163–4 nn. 35, 37–8, 50).
[37] Cf. Threatte 1980: 228, 386; Gignac 1976: 248 fn. 3.
[38] In Egyptian papyri of Roman times ⟨ε⟩ appears instead of ⟨η⟩ in the same contexts where any /i/ vowel could be replaced by /e/, which suggests that ⟨η⟩ had risen to /i/ already (Gignac 1976: 248–9) the spelling variations Ptolemaic papyri suggest that ⟨η⟩ could represent either /e/ or /i/ (cf. chap. II, § 2.3.1).
[39] cf. οὐηξιλλατίοcιν *Agora de Palmyre* 242, Annexe 21, AD 242/3, ουηξιλλοις Marek 1993, *Kat. Amastris* 5 and 111/112; cf. Eckinger (1892: 19). *vixillatio* occurs in later Latin inscriptions, but cf. the correction to *vexillatio* in *SGLIBulg* 130 (4th century AD).

4.3 ⟨η⟩ for short /i/

In Attic inscriptions spellings with ⟨η⟩ representing a short /i/ are quite rare in the Classical period and do not increase significantly in Roman times. The few examples quoted by Threatte are precisely of the same kind as the only gloss contrasting ⟨η⟩ and ⟨ι⟩ (Moer. v 12, Phryn. *Ecl.* 298 and *PS* 91.5–6 →νῆϲτιϲ ~ νήϲτηϲ): all of them involve feminine derivatives, where expected -ιϲ has been replaced by -ηϲ[40].

4.4 ⟨αι⟩ ~ ⟨ε⟩

Any confusion between ⟨αι⟩ and ⟨ε⟩ involves at the same time a change in vowel quality, i.e. the monophthongisation of ⟨αι⟩, and indifference to the original quantities. In Attica, the first instances of ⟨ε⟩ replacing ⟨αι⟩ can be dated to the 1st century AD, but are frequent only from the 2nd century AD on: the monophthongisation was probably completed by AD 125 (Threatte 1980: 294)[41]. Egyptian papyri, as usual, show innovative spellings earlier: there the confusion between ⟨αι⟩ and ⟨ε⟩ is common already from the beginning of Roman times (Gignac 1976: 193); and the two pronunciations [ai] and [e] may have coexisted already in Ptolemaic Egypt, cf. Mayser – Schmoll 1970: 83–6). Inscriptions of Lycia show ⟨αι⟩ for ⟨ε⟩ from the 2nd century AD on (Hauser 1916: 34)[42]. Rüsch (1914: 77) reports only one sure instance from Delphi, dating to the 1st century AD (Νίκαια, *SGDI* 2257.4, a manumission that has Νίκεα everywhere else)[43].

From the mid-2nd century AD on, ⟨ε⟩ may also transcribe Lat. *ae* (e.g. ἐράριον, Γνέος[44], as opposed to the learned transcriptions we find in Polybius like

---

[40] Ἐπίχαρης *IG* II² 9579 (*post* 317/6 BC) for Ἐπίχαρις, Ἡραής *IG* II² 7903a (1st century BC) for Ἡραίς. Ἡρακλεώτης *IG* II² 8548a (*in add. nova*, 2nd or 1st century BC, Threatte 1980: 168 n. 4) for Ἡρακλεῶτις may be influenced by the masculine in -της. In Roman times cηνωπεύς II² 10328 is the only example of ⟨η⟩ for short [i] not involving the suffix -ιϲ of feminines. The uncertainty regarding this suffix is not clearly accounted for (Threatte 1980: 166).
[41] There is a sensible difference between the frequency with which ⟨ε⟩ replaces ⟨αι⟩ and ⟨αι⟩ replaces ⟨ε⟩, which is much less common (cf. Threatte 1980: 295).
[42] An isolated case in the transcription of a Latin name, cαιργηου, gen. di *Sergius*, in an inscription from Nabatea dating to the 4th century AD (Le Bas – Waddington (1847–73) V, 3, 1921, quot. in Eckinger 1892: 23).
[43] Cf. also κοντοπέκτης (date uncertain, *Fouilles de Delphes* III 1.128 n. 226.4).
[44] ἐράριον *Smyrna* 386 (imperial period), *IG* XIV 911 (AD 218/9, Velitrae), *IGBulg* I² 50 (2nd/3rd c. AD, *ante* AD 212), Γνέος *IG* X,2 1 819 (Thessalonike, 2nd/3rd century AD), *Lagina* 84 (imperial),

πραιφέκτος = Lat. *praefectus*). The general outcome of the Latin diphthong is /ɛ(ː)/ – but it coexisted with a closer outcome /eː/, which however must have been marginal (cf. /e/ ~ /ɛ/ in Italian ['seːta] *seta* < sēta(m) < saetam ~ ['ljɛːta] *lieta* < lĕta(m) < laetam)⁴⁵. The transcription ⟨ε⟩ may reflect the open quality of the vowel, rather than its length.

4.5 ⟨ει⟩ for short /i/

We have seen that by the end of the 2ⁿᵈ century AD ⟨ει⟩ represented a long vowel /iː/ (cf. chap. II, § 2.1.1). When the digraph appears where we would expect the short vowel /i/, loss of distinctive quantity is probably involved.

The earliest Attic inscriptions where ⟨ει⟩ spells a short /i/ date to Roman times⁴⁶, starting with the age of Nero⁴⁷, and their number increases during the 2ⁿᵈ century AD. Even though ⟨ει⟩ is found in public as well as in private inscriptions as the spelling of a short /i/, it is rather uncommon to find it in official inscriptions even after the mid-second century AD⁴⁸: it "is normally avoided in inflectional endings […], but it occurs in the suffixes -ιος, -ιον, -ίᾱ, -ιώτης" (Threatte 1980: 200). Instances of -ειος/εια for Lat. *-ius/ia* are so common that they should be regarded as a special subset of the spellings with ⟨ει⟩ for /i/.

Outside of Attica ⟨ει⟩ could spell a short /i/ already by the end of the 3ʳᵈ century BC: this is the case of Egypt, where – however – the confusion becomes most common more or less at the same time as Attica, i.e. in Roman times⁴⁹. In Attica as well the cooccurrence of ⟨ει⟩ for short /i/ with the variants ⟨ε⟩ ~ ⟨η⟩ and ⟨ο⟩ ~ ⟨ω⟩ is more evident from the 3ʳᵈ century AD and supports the idea that at that time the vowel system of Attic Greek too had become isochronic. The data from all the Greek speaking areas of the Roman Empire, Asia Minor⁵⁰,

---

Aphrodisias 572 (imperial), Robert, *Carie* II 381.194 (AD 160/1), Dorner, *Bericht* (*DAW* 75.1) 55.141, cf. Eckinger 1892: 78–9.
45 Cf. Adams 2007: 78–82, 88, 109–10.
46 Only one not very likely instance of ⟨ει⟩ for short [i] in the 2ⁿᵈ century BC (Threatte 1980: 199).
47 Threatte 1980: 200, nn. 1 and 3, a funerary monument and a dedication, respectively; some instances also in the papyri of Herculaneum (Crönert 1903: 30).
48 Threatte 1980: 198–207, esp. 203, 303, 387.
49 Mayser – Schmoll 1970: 69–70; Gignac 1976: 190–1.
50 Inscriptions from Magnesia and Pergamum have ⟨ει⟩ for short /i/ quite often in Roman times, even though the earliest instance in Magnesia dates already to the 1ˢᵗ century BC (Nachmanson 1903: 64, Schwyzer 1898: 72–3). Inscriptions from Lycia (Hauser 1916: 30–1), present the first datable instances of ⟨ει⟩ for short [i] by the reign of Domitian (yet many inscriptions quoted by Hauser 1916 are not dated).

Egypt, Attica, all attest spellings ⟨ει⟩ for short /i/ from the beginning of the Roman empire on, and certainly before the beginning of the 2nd century AD.

4.6 ⟨ευ⟩ ~ ⟨ε⟩

For this variation, see chapter II, § 2.1.2: the interchange ⟨ευ⟩ ~ ⟨ε⟩ must have involved also timbre, and it receives no treatment in the lexica that may suggest any contrast between the sole quantities of the vowels written ⟨ευ⟩ ~ ⟨ε⟩, /eː/ ~ /e/.

4.7 ⟨ου⟩ for short /y/

The earliest example of ⟨υ⟩ for ⟨ου⟩ dates to the 2nd century AD (chap. II, § 3.1), yet the interchange does not demonstrate isochrony, as ⟨υ⟩ may spell a long vowel. There are no Attic inscriptions before the end of the same century in which ⟨ου⟩ is a spelling for short /y/[51]. The first sure example of ⟨ου⟩ for ⟨υ⟩ in an Attic inscription is Ποιανεψιῶνα in a list of ephebes dating to the middle of the 3rd century AD[52]. ⟨ου⟩ and ⟨υ⟩ alternate very frequently in Egyptian papyri from the 1st century AD on, regardless of the quantity of ⟨υ⟩[53]. The same is true for private documents and inscriptions of smaller towns in Asia Minor dating to the same period, and the confusion of ⟨ου⟩ and ⟨υ⟩ is uncommon in also inscriptions from bigger urban centres[54].

The change is apparently later than other variations in spelling that clearly suggest the loss of distinctive vowel length, such as ⟨ο⟩ ~ ⟨ω⟩ or ⟨ει⟩ for short /i/. Therefore spellings confusing ⟨ου⟩ and ⟨υ⟩ probably already ignore altogether the original long quantity of the diphthong.

---

[51] ⟨τοιχη⟩ for τύχη – along with κοιμητήριον – in *SEG* 34.252, a Christian inscription of uncertain date (Threatte 1980: 337).
[52] *IG* II² 2239.82, AD 238/9–243/4.
[53] Gignac 1976: 198–9.
[54] Schwyzer (1898: 80), does not list instances of ⟨ου⟩ ~ ⟨υ⟩ at Pergamum, but quotes οιπο (=ὑπό) in *TAM* III.1 875, an inscription dating to AD 125/6.

4.8 ‹ου› for short /u/ or /w/

There are no glosses in the Atticist lexica discussing the quantity of ‹ου›. Spellings with ‹ου› do not provide conclusive evidence for isochrony. The digraph had come to express a vowel /uː/ possibly by the end of Classical times, and certainly by the beginning of the Roman period[55], and the vowel has no short counterpart in Greek. The use of ‹ου› in loanwords to write [w] or [u], e.g. in adaptations from Latin as Λειουιανός, where it represents the glide /w/, or αὐγούστια where it represents the short Latin vowel /u/, does not necessarily attest to the completion of isochrony (*pace* Blass 1888: 34; Hauser 1916: 41). As the only way of writing a high back vowel, ‹ου› is in any case the most accurate rendering of Latin /w u uː/, even in a system that was not yet isochronic.

5 Spelling variations in the Atticist lexica

5.1 ‹ο› ~ ‹ω›

Many of the glosses concerning ‹ο› and ‹ω› deal with competing formations rather than different stages of a sound change. A good number of them discusses derivatives of πίνω (→πῶμα)[56]. There are also some nouns and adjectives in -ως following the second declension, contrasted to their more recent, analogical counterparts in -ος (*Philet.* 89 →λαγώς, Ael. D. χ 17, Moer. χ 7, Philem. 396.26 R., Phryn. *Ecl.* 371, *Philet.* 146 →χρέως, Moer. α 67 →ἀνάπλεως, Ael. D. α 151 ἀξιόχρεως, λιπόνεως). If πρωπέρυσι (Phryn. *PS* 105.9–10) is really attested in Pherecrates (fr. 196 K.–A.), it was a competing form of προπέρυσι already in classical times: the lexicographers were probably more interested in prescribing the more ancient form here than in favouring the variant with the long vowel.

An explicit reference to pronunciation can be found in Phrynichus (*PS* 118.3–4) prescribing →υἱέος instead of υἱέως. The two forms belong to two different inflection paradigms, yet what Phrynichus criticises is explicitly the pronunciation of some speakers (*PS* 118.3–4: "ἁμαρτάνουσιν οἱ διὰ τοῦ ω τὴν γενικὴν προφέροντες"). He is clearly condemning a speaking habit, recognisable precisely because some people kept ‹ο› and ‹ω› distinct in their pronunciation.

---

[55] On the chronology of the development that led to this pronunciation of ‹ου› see Allen 1987a: 76–7; the change was certainly complete by Roman times, but it is probably as early as the mid-4th century BC.
[56] Philem. 393.32 R. ἔκπωμα, Ael. D. α 53 (αἱματο-, οἰνο-, ὑδρο-)πώτης, πῶμα, Moer. υ 12 ὑδροπωτεῖν.

Aelius Dionysius (δ 31) defines →δύω as the variant 'κατὰ ἔκτασιν' of δύο. We find technical terms addressing pronunciation also in Philem. 393.32 R. ἔκπωμα· τὴν μέσην μακρὰν ποιητέον, and Ael. D. α 53 αἱματοπώτης· οἱ Ἀττικοὶ μηκύνοντες τὸ ο προφέρουσιν τὴν λέξιν [...] τὸ πόμα οἱ μὲν ἄλλοι διὰ βραχέος τοῦ ο γράφουσιν, Ἀττικοὶ δὲ ἐπεκτείνοντες (for both see →πῶμα, and cf. also chap. I, text (18)). There is at least an equivalence between the notion of long vowel and *omega*, and on the other hand, between that of short vowel and *omicron*. All the three glosses define the variants with *omega* as the outcome of lengthenings; they explicitly tell their reader which is the pronunciation associated to the correct spelling.

5.2 ⟨η⟩ ~ ⟨ε⟩

With only one exception, →νῆςτις[57] (see chap. II, § 2.3.2), the Atticist lexica contrast ⟨η⟩ only with one short vowel, ⟨ε⟩[58]. Yet we cannot find any explicit reference to the long quantity of *eta* in the surviving Atticist lexica. They normally employ the phrase 'διὰ τοῦ η' when prescribing a variant, and there is no indication like what we read in Ael. D. α 53 (→αἱματοπώτης), where *omega* is described as the outcome of a lengthening.

At least two large groups of glosses involve derivative morphology (mostly nouns in -ημα (→ἀνάθημα)[59] and verbs augmented with ἠ-[60] (→ἐβουλόμην), but also the root vowel of →ἀνυπόδητος[61], →ἀπέςβηςε[62] and →ἠθάς[63]). Only one entry, →ἤνυστρον[64], contrasts variants that are not so closely linked by a morphological pattern (even though paraetymology may be involved here).

The fact that most atticist glosses contrast ⟨η⟩ with ⟨ε⟩ seems to support anyway the view that ⟨η⟩ and ⟨ε⟩ were identical in timbre, or at least closer to each other than ⟨η⟩ and ⟨ι⟩, and is in line with the descriptions of *eta* as the long counterpart of *eta* which we read in Sextus Empiricus (*M.* 1.115 "ςυςταλὲν μὲν τὸ η

---

[57] Moer. ν 12, Phryn. *Ecl.* 298, *PS* 91.5–6.
[58] The contrast ξυάλη ~ ξυήλη involves long /aː/; see also § 2.3.2.
[59] Moer. α 57, Philem. 354 ἀνάθημα, Moer. c 21 cύνθημα, Philem. 393.22 R., Phryn. *Ecl.* 420 εὕρημα.
[60] Moer. η 5 ἤμελλον, ἠδυνάμην, ηὐξάμην, η 22 ἠδύνω, ἠπίςτω, Philem. 394.10 R. ἐβουλόμην.
[61] Moer. α 63, *Philet.* 149, Phryn. *Ecl.* 419, *PS* 27.12 ἀνυπόδητος.
[62] Phryn. *PS* 26.9–10.
[63] Ael. D. ε 10.
[64] Phryn. *Ecl.* 133 and 414.

γίνεται ε, ἐκταθὲν δὲ τὸ ε γίνεται η", text n. (21) above) and in the Roman grammatical tradition (cf. chap. II, § 2.3).

5.3 ‹αι› ~ ‹ε›

There is only one entry contrasting ‹αι› with ‹ε›, *Ael. D. α 59 → αἰώρα, and it may depend on textual variants in Sophocles. It does not mention any difference in quantity.

5.4 ‹ει› for short /i/

The Atticist lexica treat ‹ει› as a spelling for /iː/ and openly mention vowel quantity only in two instances. In both cases a non-front vowel immediately follows the digraph (Phryn. *Ecl.* 346 → Διονυcεῖον and *Ecl.* 241 → ὀπτάνιον). It is remarkable that Phrynichus does not refer his prescription only to orthography (he could have written something like Διονυcεῖον 'διὰ τῆc ει διφθόγγου' or 'διὰ τοῦ ι', cf. Phryn. *PS* 80.3–7 → κεχρίcθαι)[65]: he does not mention spelling at all, and addresses pronunciation directly, implicitly identifying long [iː] with the spelling ‹ει› and short [i] with ‹ι›. A similar distinction in length is implied by *Antiatt.* κ 71 → κυδώνιον, however without explicit mention of orthography.

Phryn. *Ecl.* 346 contrasts → Διονυcεῖον and Διονύcιον as if the only difference concerned were the length of the vowel, and not its timbre. Spellings with ‹ει› and with ‹ι› are treated as interchangeable when the only reference is to the length of the vowel, the digraph automatically implying a long vowel, the simple *iota* a short vowel[66]. This can be seen clearly in Phryn. *PS* 77.1–2 and *Ecl.* 52 → ἱκετεία (contrasted with ἱκεcία), and quite possibly in Phryn. *Ecl.* 241 → ὀπτάνιον, where the form is contrasted with ὀπτάνιον, characterised by having a short antepenultimate (τῆc τρίτηc βραχυνομένηc), as if it sufficed to specify that the ending is the short counterpart of -εῖον to imply that it is -ιον, and not, for instance, -εον. Such glosses also imply that the pronunciation of prevocalic ‹ει› was al-

---

[65] Phryn. *Ecl.* 241 contrasts μαγειρεῖον and ὀπτάνιον "with as short third syllable" (τῆc δὲ τρίτηc βραχυνομένηc). The same correspondence is implied by Ammonius (Amm. 449) cτρατεία ἐκτεταμένωc τὸ πρᾶγμα, cτρατιὰ δὲ cυνεcταλμένωc τὸ τῶν cτρατιωτῶν πλῆθοc. ἐναλλάccει δὲ πολλάκιc ἐν τῇ χρήcει (on the accent shift see Phryn. *PS* 10.9–11 → αὐτοχειρίᾳ).
[66] Note that the commentary on P.Oxy. 1012 (3rd century AD, cf. chap. I, text (19)) consistently uses ει for long /iː/.

ready /iː/, and that accurate speakers preserved a distinction in length, that other varieties of Greek were losing or had already lost in the same context.

Two glosses on ι μακρόν discuss words that we would expect to be spelt with ‹ει›, but are described as having a ‹ι› (Moer. o 32 → ὄςτρια, Philem. 357 → βοϊκός). In both cases a spelling with ‹ει› can be hypothesised, but its existence cannot be proven.

All these glosses suggest that the distribution of the suffixes -ειο- [iːo] and -ιο- [io] was problematic for a good number of speakers. The educated may have kept alive the difference between the two by preserving the different quantities of the penultimate vowel.

An entry about verbs in -ίζω in the *Philetaerus* (230) treats → δανείζειν as an exception to a rule that assigns to verbs in -ίζω a short /i/. The lexicographer does not define the difference between δανείζω and the verbs -ίζω in terms of spelling or pronunciation; perhaps the need to point out that δανείζω is exceptional is a sign that the spellings ‹ειζω› and ‹ιζω› were homophones, in which case the entry is evidence for both the raising of /eː$_2$/ and isochrony (cf. chap. III, § 5.4). The anomalous and isolated spelling of Paus. α 30 → ἀείτης, if it actually reflects the orthography of the 2nd century AD, may be an attempt at signalling in spelling the long quantity of the vowel /iː/. It confirms that the lexicographers and their readers did pronounce preconsonantal ‹ει› as a simple, long vowel.

5.5 ‹ει› ~ ‹ε›

Cf. above § 4.6 and chap. II, § 2.1.2.

5.6 ‹οι› for short /y/

The monophthongisation of /oi/ is possibly later than the establishment of isochrony. The few entries that seem to imply it do not mention explicitly any difference in quantity (some variation between short vowel and diphthong may be involved in Phryn. *Ecl.* 268 → ψύα, but Phrynichus does not dicuss it). See chap. II, § 3.

IV Prosodies

1 Accents, breathings, quantity marks

By the time of Herodian's περὶ καθολικῆς προσῳδίας, ancient Greek scholarship would label as προσῳδίαι, 'prosodies' three aspects of the language: vowel length, accentuation, initial aspiration. A common property of 'prosodies' is that they can be indicated by lectional signs in writing, in ways that are similar – or identical – to the modern editorial practice[1].

The other common property of προσῳδίαι is that they are not written consistently. Breathings and accent marks were not written consistently in Greek manuscripts until Byzantine times, and quantity marks, although they are found even in some documentary prose texts of the imperial period, gradually fall out of use. Therefore, the reader of a prose text in the 2nd century AD would expect it to be virtually free of lectional marks, or to include at the same time some accents, breathings, and even quantity marks on vowels and diphthongs whose length is not apparent from spelling (the *dichrona* ‹α ι υ›, the 'long' diphthong ‹αυ›). As we shall see in the next paragraph, the atticist lexica – as most of the grammatical tradition in imperial times – had to deal with a writing system that only seldom included lectional signs: most of the entries that we may be tempted to understand as prescriptions on what accent or what breathing to *write* on a given word, must have originally aimed in the first place at prescribing what accent or breathing one should *pronounce* on the word in question. At the same time, some of the pronunciations prescribed for the *dichrona* could be reflected in writing by means of a quantity mark[2].

Skilled readers were supposed to identify the correct distribution of accents and breathings on texts that normally carried very few lectional signs, if any (see § 2). As we would expect in a system that does not employ diacritics consistently, the glosses in the lexica prescribe the position or type of the accent, or the pres-

---

[1] The definition may have only included accentuation originally, and then expanded to include vowel quantities and breathings – after Herodian προσῳδία came to incude virtually anything that could be written with a diacritic mark (Probert 2015, esp. 924–5, 927).

[2] Colomo (2017) has shown that the prose texts that include quantity marks are the ones aimed at a learned audience – this confirms that correct pronunciation of quantity was expected of the educated elites well into the imperial period. "[T]he papyri containing the highest number of quantity marks [...] come from the second and the third century AD, i.e. they are roughly contemporary with the activity of the Atticist lexicographers and the subsequent spread of their doctrines" (Colomo 2017: 115).

ence of an initial aspiration, either by employing technical terminology or by comparing and contrasting two or more words.

2 Lectures without lectional signs

In the delivery of an orator, the audience would prize the same qualities they prized in good reading – by whose imitation prospective orators would learn their art. School exercises of the 2nd century AD, the *progymnasmata* of Theon of Alexandria, regard reading as a central part of the training of the prospective orator, and make an explicit connection between the ability to read correctly (ἀνάγνωcιc) and to compose in the correct style (λέξιc):

> (24) ἡ δὲ ἀνάγνωcιc, ὡc τῶν πρεcβυτέρων τιc ἔφη, Ἀπολλώνιοc δοκεῖ μοι ὁ Ῥόδιοc, τροφὴ λέξεώc ἐcτι· τυπούμενοι γὰρ τὴν ψυχὴν ἀπὸ καλῶν παραδειγμάτων κάλλιcτα καὶ μιμηcόμεθα· τὴν δὲ ἀκρόαcιν τίc οὐκ ἂν ἀcμενίcειε, τὰ μετὰ πόνων τοῖc ἄλλοιc εἰργαcμένα ἑτοίμωc λαμβάνων;

> *anágnōsis* (reading aloud), as one of the older authorities said – I think it was Apollonius of Rhodes – is the nourishment of style; for we imitate most beautifully when our mind has been stamped by beautiful examples. And who would not take pleasure in *akróasis* (hearing a work read aloud), readily taking in what has been created by the toil of others?
> Theon of Alexandria, *Progymnasmata*, 61.28–62.1 Spengel[3]

Together with διαcτολή and ὑπόκριcιc, προcῳδία is one of the three components of reading according to the *Techne* (*Ars Grammatica*) attributed to Dionysius Thrax[4].

> (25) ἀνάγνωcίc ἐcτι ποιημάτων ἢ cυγγραμμάτων ἀδιάπτωτοc προφορά. ἀναγνωcτέον δὲ καθ' ὑπόκριcιν, κατὰ προcῳδίαν, κατὰ διαcτολήν. ἐκ μὲν γὰρ τῆc ὑποκρίcεωc τὴν ἀρετήν, ἐκ δὲ τῆc προcῳδίαc τὴν τέχνην, ἐκ δὲ τῆc διαcτολῆc τὸν περιεχόμενον νοῦν ὁρῶμεν· ἵνα τὴν μὲν τραγῳδίαν ἡρωϊκῶc ἀναγνῶμεν, τὴν δὲ κωμῳδίαν βιωτικῶc, τὰ δὲ ἐλεγεῖα λιγυρῶc, τὸ δὲ ἔποc εὐτόνωc, τὴν δὲ λυρικὴν ποίηcιν ἐμμελῶc, τοῦ δὲ οἴκτου ὑφειμένωc καὶ γοερῶc. τὰ γὰρ μὴ παρὰ τὴν τούτων γινόμενα παρατήρηcιν καὶ τὰc τῶν ποιητῶν ἀρετὰc καταρριπτεῖ καὶ τὰc ἕξειc τῶν ἀναγινωcκόντων καταγελάcτου παρίcτηcιν.

---

3 Transl. Kennedy 2003.
4 The *Techne* is quite likely a simplified reflection of Alexandrian grammatical doctrine as it was established in the first two centuries AD, especially in the work of Apollonius Dyscolus and Herodian; cf. Lallot 1998: 30–1, and also Morgan 1998: 154. On the dating of the *Techne* and its relation with ancient scholarship cf. Lallot 1998: 19–26 and 27–36 respectively.

> Reading is the impeccable pronunciation of poetry or prose. One needs to read according to delivery, προcῳδία, pauses. It is in the delivery that we can see the good qualities (of an author), in the προcῳδία the skill (of the reader), in the pauses the meaning that is contained (in the text): so that we may read tragedy in a heroic fashion, comedy in a lively one, elegy with a shrill tone, lyric poetry melodically, laments in a relaxed and wailing way. Whatever (reading style) that does not observe these (distinctions), ruins the good qualities of the poets, and makes the behaviour of the readers ridiculous.
>
> D. Thrax Ars gramm. 2.1–10 Lallot

Correct reading depends on three factors: delivery (ὑπόκριcιc)[5], word-division (διαcτολή, the pause between words), and προcῳδία: this is the trait that mostly reflects the reader's skill (τέχνη), when it is duly observed. The central role of προcῳδία goes back to the earliest doctrine included in the *Techne:* 'accurate reading, following the προcῳδία' (ἀνάγνωcιc ἐντριβὴc κατὰ προcῳδίαν, D. Thrax *Ars gramm.* 1.4 Lallot) is the first of the six elements that constitute grammar itself[6]. The adjective ἐντριβήc points to an 'elaborate' pronunciation, and κατὰ προcῳδίαν makes it clear that such an elaborate pronunciation is one that takes into account the differences between the quantitative rhythm, the three types of accent, and the breathing: all phonological traits that the Koine had lost by the imperial period[7].

Yet reading was based on texts that very rarely were equipped with lectional signs. Consistent marking of accents, breathings, or quantities was never the norm in the Roman period, and one must assume that most texts came without any lectional signs and word division. The average edition of a prose text in the

---

[5] The emphasis on delivery (ὑπόκριcιc) in accordance with the *ethos* of particular genres in passage n. 25 reflects rhetorical rather than grammatical tradition, cf. Aristot. *Rhet.* 1403b 20 ff. Note that the meaning of τόνοc must be different in Aristot. *Rhet.* 1403b 29, where it apparently refers to pitch (Allen 1987a: 116), and D. Thrax *Ars gramm.* 3 Lallot (cf. footnote 16 below), where it refers to the three types of accent. The definition of Aristotle refers to variations in pitch, but possibly not yet codified as acute, grave, or circumflex accentuation, and not necessarily defined as properties of a single accented vowel (they could be musical contours of whole phrases or sentences). The problem is thoroughly discussed by Vatri (2016, esp. pp. 377–83).

[6] The other components are (ii) the explanation of poetical tropes; (iii) the explanation of difficult words and topics; (iv) etymology; (v) morphological analysis (ἀναλογία); (vi) literary criticism; cf. the notes to this fragment in Lallot (1998: 69–82).

[7] Lallot 1998: 76–7; 'une diction 'travaillée', s'efforçant – mais avec quel succès, il est difficile de le dire – de retrouver, par delà de les transformations de la prononciation, le rhythme quantitatif et les fines nuances tonales qu'on savait avoir caractérisé la langue grecque des siècles archaïques et classiques' (Lallot 1998: 77).

2nd century AD would lack all prosodical marks⁸; in fact, the few texts that exhibit lectional signs are either editions of poetry, or learned, accurate editions of prose texts that can be linked with public performance and educated readers (cf. Colomo 2017)⁹; still in early Byzantine times one needed to make sure that accents were written in the copying of manuscripts¹⁰.

School teaching of Greek in Roman times aimed at enabling students to read texts with no word-division and very few or no lectional signs. The nature and the position of the accent, as well as the breathings and the quantities of the *dichrona*, were learnt at school, under the unifying label of προcῳδίαι, comprising χρόνοι, τόνοι, πνεύματα (quantity marks, accents, breathings).

The system of diacritical marks associated to προcῳδίαι was born with the aim of distinguishing ambiguous words ('γέγονε πρός τε διαcτολὴν τῆc ἀμφιβόλου λέξεωc' [Arc.] 211.9–10). προcῳδίαι tend to be consistently written throughout the text, mostly in school exercises (teachers may have supplied a number of them in the early stages of grammatical teaching)¹¹.

Again, Theon of Alexandria attests to the difficulties entailed by reading in the *Progymnasmata*:

> (26) γίνεται δὲ ἀcάφεια ἡ μὲν περὶ τὴν προφοράν, ἥν τινεc περὶ τὴν προcῳδίαν καλοῦcιν, ἡ δὲ περὶ τὸ ὄνομα, ἡ δὲ περὶ τὴν ὁμωνυμίαν, ἡ δὲ περὶ τὴν πολυωνυμίαν, ἥν cυνωνυμίαν ἕτεροι προcαγορεύουcιν, ἡ δὲ περὶ τὴν cύνταξιν, ἡ δὲ περὶ τὴν cύνθεcιν καὶ διαίρεcιν, ἡ δὲ περὶ πλεοναcμόν, ἡ δὲ περὶ ἔλλειψιν, ἡ δὲ περὶ τὴν μάχην. περὶ μὲν οὖν τὴν προφοράν ἐcτιν, ὅταν ἐν τῇ αὐτῇ τάξει κειμένων τινῶν λέξεων ὁμοίων, δυνατὸν ᾖ προφέρεcθαι διττῶc τὸ γεγραμμένον, οἷον θεράπαινα χρυcία μὴ φορείτω, εἰ δὲ μή, ΔΗΜΟCΙΑ ἔcτω. ἀμφιcβητοῦμεν γάρ, πότερον ἡ θεράπαινα δημοcία ἔcτω, ἢ τὰ χρυcία· δύναται γὰρ cυcτέλλεcθαι καὶ ἐκτείνεcθαι τὸ α.
>
> Some lack of clarity occurs from pronunciation, which certain authorities call "from prosody", some from the meaning of a word, some from homonymy, some from polyonymy,

---

8 Probert (2006: 18–21) discusses a passage in Galen (18(2).518.9–519.3), on the accentuation of γαῦcοc ~ γαυcόc, uncertain because readers in Galen's time only knew the word from books, and books did not bear accent marks.
9 One example is a sheet from a parchment codex of Demosthenes (Turner – Parsons 1987, n. 82 = P. Lit. Lond. 127), dating between second and the fourth century AD: the whole sheet has 72 lines (split in two columns), and despite its length only one accent and one *macron* can be read); a new fragment of the same codex does not contain any other accent or breathing marks (Perale 2010: 23).
10 Still in Byzantine times copying accents (and thus, expecting to find them in books) was not the rule: "[i]n the ninth century, the Stoudion Monastery imposed on a copyist the duty of copying punctuation (*PG* 99.1740: penalty prescribed εἰ μή ... παρατηρεῖται τά τε ἀντίcτοιχα καὶ τοὺc τόνουc καὶ τὰc cτιγμάc)" (Turner – Parsons 1987: 10 fn. 43).
11 Cribiore 2001: 189–92.

which others call synonymy, some from syntax, some from compounding and dividing words, some from pleonasm, some from ellipsis, some from inconsistency.

There is a problem from pronunciation whenever some similar words are used in the same order and it is possible to pronounce what has been written in two ways; for example, "Let a maid not wear gold ornaments, and if she does, *dēmosia estō* (let her/them be public property)." Here we are in doubt whether the maid is to become a public prostitute or the ornaments are to be confiscated, since it is possible for *dēmosia* to be pronounced with a short or long alpha.

Theon of Alexandria, *Progymnasmata*, 129.11–22 Spengel[12]

The ambiguity that depends on the length of the *alpha* has two implications: (a) that the length of the final vowel of δημοcια was not marked in the text, (b) that neither the accent was: otherwise its position (δημόcια ~ δημοcία) would have automatically signalled the length of the vowel. With no accent or quantity mark, δημοcια can either be a neuter plural agreeing with χρυcία, or a feminine singular agreeing with θεράπαινα.

We may wonder whether the reader of a sentence like Theon's example may have signalled the difference between δημόcιᾰ and δημοcίᾱ also by prolonging the final vowel. The position of the accent alone would be sufficient to make a distinction between the two terms[13]. Of course, for an audience who prized the rhythms of individual authors, vowel length was still crucial in the composition and delivery of refined speeches. If, as it seems, the distinction between short and long vowels had been lost in the speech of the greater part of the population, the educated speakers would restitute it artificially.

A similar passage earlier in the *Progymnasmata* is also based on texts without any reading marks:

(27) ἀcαφῆ δὲ τὴν ἑρμηνείαν ποιεῖ καὶ ἡ λεγομένη ἀμφιβολία πρὸς τῶν διαλεκτικῶν, παρὰ τὴν κοινὴν τοῦ ἀδιαιρέτου τε καὶ διῃρημένου, ὡς ἐν τῷ ΑΥΛΗΤΡΙC πεcοῦcα δημοcία ἔcτω· ἓν μὲν γάρ τί ἐcτι τὸ ὑφ' ἓν καὶ ἀδιαίρετον, αὐλητρὶc ἔcτω πεcοῦcα δημοcία, ἕτερον δὲ τὸ διῃρημένον, αὐλὴ τρὶc πεcοῦcα ἔcτω δημοcία. ἔτι δὲ καὶ ὅταν τι μόριον ἄδηλον ᾖ, μετὰ τίνοc cυντέτακται, οἷον ΟΥΚΕΝΤΑΥΡΟΙC ὁ Ἡρακλῆc μάχεται· cημαίνει γὰρ δύο, οὐχὶ κενταύροιc ὁ Ἡρακλῆc μάχεται, καὶ οὐχὶ ἐν ταύροιc ὁ Ἡρακλῆc μάχεται.

What is called "amphiboly" by the dialecticians makes the expression obscure because of the confusion between an undivided and divided word, as in the phrase "Let an *aulētris* ("flute-girl") that has fallen be 'public'". It means one thing when the word *aulētris* is taken as a whole and undivided, another when divided: "Let an *aulē tris* ("a hall thrice") fallen be public property." Furthermore, [the expression is ambiguous] when it is unclear what some part of a word belongs to; for example, Heracles fights *oukentaurois*. This has

---

12 Transl. Kennedy 2003.
13 Probert 2006: 20, fn. 9.

two meanings, that Heracles does not at all (*ouk^hi*) fight with the centaurs or that he fights not among (*ouk^hi en*) bulls.

Theon, *Progymnasmata* 81.30–82.7 Spengel[14]

Even without spacing between words, the ambiguity on which the whole passage rests would not be possible if accent marks and breathings were provided. Only the spellings without lectional marks αυλητρις and ουκενταυροις are truly ambiguous: if accents and breathings are written, the distinction between αὐλητρίς and αὐλήτρίς (or αὐλήτρίς), οὐκένταυροις and οὐκενταύροις becomes apparent[15].

When lectional marks are present, they may include not only accents and breathings, but also quantity marks – they provide the same sort of information that is found in the orthoepic prescriptions of the Atticist lexica. The fact that this information refers to elements of speech that were not normally represented in the spelling is an indirect proof that the Atticist prescriptions addressed facts of pronunciation, and not spelling, in the reading and delivery of texts.

Of all the προσῳδίαι, only the position of the accent is still a relevant phonological trait of Modern Greek: initial aspiration, distinctive vowel length, and the contrast between different accent types had been lost – with different chronology in different areas and sociolects of Greek – by the end of the Roman period. A hierarchy between different προσῳδίαι, whereby accents gain more prominence than breathings and quantities, is reflected in a scholion to a fragment of D. Thrax' *Techne* discussing the accent[16]: the scholiast[17] argues that breathings, quantities and other accidents (πάθη), are out of place in an introductory grammar handbook (εἰσαγωγικὴ τέχνη)[18]. The scholion dates to the 7th century AD; around the 2nd century AD, when the prescriptive Atticist lexica were composed, the different προσῳδίαι appear to be equally important: the lexica include glosses discussing initial aspirations, vowel quantities, and the position and the na-

---

14 Transl. Kennedy 2003.
15 Theon's exercise is similar to the exercises discussing ambiguity in the text of a law (see Atherton 1993: 194).
16 D. Thrax, *Ars gramm.* 3 Lallot: τόνος ἐστὶν ἀπήχησις φωνῆς ἐναρμονίου, † ἡ κατὰ ἀνάτασιν ἐν τῇ ὀξείᾳ, ἡ κατὰ ὁμαλισμὸν ἐν τῇ βαρείᾳ, ἡ κατὰ περίκλασιν ἐν τῇ περισπωμένῃ.
17 Stephanus, cf. Lallot 1998: 34.
18 Sch. in D. Thrac. *Art. Gramm.* (Stephan.), *GG* 1.3 176.19–23: σκοπὸν ἔχων ὁ τεχνικὸς εἰσαγωγικὴν γράφειν τέχνην ἀποφεύγει τῶν προσῳδιῶν τὰ δυσχερῆ, τουτέστι τὸ πνεῦμα, τὸν χρόνον καὶ τὰ πάθη· ἐπεὶ γὰρ ὁ περὶ τούτων λόγος πολὺς ἦν καὶ πολλῶν θεωρημάτων δεόμενος, ἦν δὲ αὕτη ἡ διδασκαλία πρὸς παῖδας ἀπρόσφορος, ἀναγκαίως καὶ αὐτὸς παρῆκεν. Cf. the commentary attributed to Melampos/Diomedes *GG* 1.3 22.16, which defines accent as the most necessary (ἀναγκαιότατος) of προσῳδίαι, Lallot 1998: 87.

ture of the accent. At the time when the lexica where composed, the educated speakers would also reproduce them in formal, spoken varieties of the language, as well as in reading: ἀναγιγνώσκειν occurs only twice in our corpus, and both times it refers to the position of the accent (→ ἁρπαγή, → ἀσφόδελος).

We have to expect the lexica themselves to have circulated without diacritical marks in the imperial period (cf. e.g. P. Amh. II 21, n. 14 in Wouters 1979, and our text n. (19) above). This strongly suggests that glosses concerning the quantities of vowels, or the position of the accent, or anything that modern conventions would signal in writing with a diacritical mark, have to do with the pronunciation of those words in the first place, and only secondarily with their spelling.

3 Lectional signs in inscriptions and papyri

The paucity of lectional signs in standard writing makes inscriptions not particularly useful to follow the distribution of the *dichrona*, as such documents normally do not include lectional signs to contrast e.g. ⟨ᾰ⟩ and ⟨ᾱ⟩ on the stone (for apostrophes, accents, breathings see Threatte 1980: 97–8).

The distribution of quantity marks on prose texts on papyrus is discussed in detail in Colomo (2017): some examples from Colomo's survey will be useful to illustrate the writing habits of papyri with quantity marks. Quantity marks on prose text on papyrus mostly confirm the distribution of quantities of Classical Greek, but there are also some incorrect attributions of quantity: P.Oxy. 4321, reads πρ]ᾰττειν (i 18) and πρᾰξειν (ii 54) (Colomo 2017: n. 1 (h) and (i)). At least in one case, their use signals that the writer is taking a stance against spellings that were popular in the imperial period, but did not belong to the standard. An instance is *PL* III/983, where we read πολῑταις (ii 5): the *longum* on the *iota* contrasts the forms in πολειτ-, very popular in literary papyri (Colomo 2017: n. 5). The same is true of the many instances of ⟨ῐ⟩, with a *breve:* the quantity mark signals that the writer did not mean to write ⟨ει⟩ there. Lectional marks are used in some cases to disambiguate homographs, as α]ποτῐν[ε]ι (< ἀποτίνω ~ ἀποτείνω, Colomo 2017 n. 4 (c)).

4 *Dichrona* in orthoepic prescriptions

In the previous chapter, we saw how variation involving a diphthong and a simple vowel, e.g. ⟨αι⟩ ~ ⟨ε⟩, ⟨ει⟩ ~ ⟨ι⟩, or ⟨ου⟩ ~ ⟨υ⟩, can be used as evidence for uncertainty in the distribution of vowel quantities. Yet, when it comes to the *dichrona* ⟨α ι υ⟩, quantity can be explicitly prescribed. Some times the terminology employed to prescribe length is completely unambiguous, e.g. when we find the adjectives μακρός/βραχύς 'long/short' or the verbs ἐκτείνειν/cυcτέλλειν 'lengthen/shorten'. In some fortunate cases, such terminology is employed for words whose accentuation is indifferent to quantity (Ael. D. φ 2 → φαρμακός) or for quantity and scansion too (Phryn. *Ecl.* 80 → πελαργός).

At the same time, however, quantity can also be prescribed indirectly, by the verbs περιcπᾶν, ὀξυτονεῖν and their derivatives: there are technical terms that prescribe accentuation, but at the same time they do give information on vowel quantity, as some accentuations depend on the length of the accented vowel, or the ones that follow it.

The entries dealing with the *dichrona* can be divided in six groups according to variables, i.e. whether also (or only) the accent is prescribed, in a manner that is telling of quantity (1–3), and whether the *dichronon* in question is in a metrically relevant position, that is to say, in a syllable whose quantity depends only on the quantity of the vowel (a – b). Schematising, we can group our entries (lemmatised as they are also in the second part of this book) in the following table:

Table 3

	A	I	Y	A	I	Y
	a			b		
1	ἀγνοία ἄρα* τριπλᾶ			μᾶζα		
2	ἄκρατον			χαμᾶζε		
3	ἀγυιᾶ ἀγοράζειν (?) ἀδολέcχηc ἀμφορέα ἀνεῖν ἅπαν ἀπέρατοc ἄρα* (βαδίζειν?) δένδρα ἱερεία	βοϊκόc κνημίc κυδώνιον ὄcτρια πνῖγοc	ἁλμυρόc ἀπαντικρύ βότρυc ξυρόν πάπυροc cτάχυc ψιμύθιον	ἀγοράζειν (?) πελαργόc	βαδίζειν	

---

* Two glosses discuss ἄρα: one, Philem. 354, only reads 'ἄρά γε μακρῶc', and for this reason is counted in row (3), the other, Heren. 34 mentions at once accent and quantity, and is therefore counted in row (1).

Table 3 *(Continued)*

A	I	Y	A	I	Y
μανόc					
μύcταξ					
νεαλέc					
τετρακέφαλοc					
ὑδαρέc					
φαρμακόc					

Entries (1) prescribing accent and quantity; (2) prescribing accent only (and therefore quantity); (3) prescribing only quantity; (a) in a metrically relevant position; (b) in a metrically irrelevant position.

Three entries in our corpus combine terminology referring to accent and quantity:

- Moer. ι 3 ἱερεία μακρῶc τὴν τελευταίαν καὶ ὀξυτόνωc τὴν παραλήγουcαν Ἀττικοί· ἱέρεια βραχέωc τὴν ἐcχάτην καὶ βαρυτόνωc τὴν παρατέλευτον Ἕλληνεc.
- Moer. μ 8 μᾶζαν προπεριcπωμένωc καὶ μακρῶc Ἀττικοί, βαρυτόνωc καὶ βραχέωc Ἕλληνεc.
- Moer. τ 22 τριπλᾶ τετραπλᾶ περιcπωμένωc καὶ μακρῶc Ἀττικοί· βραχέωc Ἕλληνεc[19].

The distinction between →ἆρα and ἄρα in the lexicon of Herennius Philo (Heren. 34) contrasts as 'κατὰ περιcπωμένην' and 'κατὰ cυcτολήν', i.e. 'with a circumflex (lit. syllable!)' and 'by abbreviation', showing how terminology referring to accent or to vowel quantity could actually be used interchangeably[20].

4.1 A

Some glosses prescribe, in addition to the quantity of ‹α›, also the type of its accent (Heren. 34, Philem. 354 →ἆρα, Moer. μ 8 →μᾶζα, the plurals of adjectives in

---

[19] We can compare this gloss with Phryn. fr. *367 →χρυcᾶ (a fragment from the *Suda*), that prescribes the Attic perispomenon, if it is implicitly condemning the same forms in τριπλά implied by Moeris τ 22, and not (only) the forms with diaeresis of Phryn. *Ecl.* 178 ἀργύρεα.

[20] Moer. α 6 →αἴτιαι (~ αἰτίαι) does not really imply a constrast between different quantities of ‹αι›; see the commentary to the entry.

-πλα like →τριπλᾶ, Moer. τ 22), or its position (Moer. ι 3 →ἱερεία; Ael. D. α 21 →ἀγνοία). The accent of →ἀγυιᾶ (Moer. α 13) is dependent on the quantity of the *alpha*, but the gloss does not mention it explicitly.

A smaller number of glosses is not related to accent at all: *Antiatt*. μ 37 →μύσταξ, Ael. D. φ 2 →φαρμακός, both concerned with the scansion of the suffix -ακ-, and Moer. υ 9 →ὑδαρές, rejecting a pronunciation not attested elsewhere in surviving Greek texts. A number of prescriptions on quantity depend on readings of metrical texts. Sometimes authors are explicitly mentioned, as is Pherecrates in Paus. α 118 →ἀνεῖν, in support of the attribution to Attic usage; or as examples of non-Attic usage, as is the case with Hipponax, quoted in Ael. D. φ 2 →φαρμακός, and Homer in Ael. D. α 155 →ἄπαν. Also Phryn. *PS* 89.6–7 →μανός, even if it does not quote directly any literary source, is likely to derive from readings of metrical texts. One gloss (Paus. ε 71 →τετρακέφαλος) possibly quotes a metrical inscription. Virtually all glosses that prescribe the quantity of a vowel in an open syllable can be linked to the scansion of metrical texts, even where none is directly quoted (as in Phryn. *PS* 36.5–12 →ἀδολέςχης and *PS* 37.8–9 →ἀπέρατος).

In some instances quantity distinguishes different inflections. There is a good number of glosses dealing with the accusative singular of nouns in -εύς (→ἀμφορέα, Moer. α 12, ι 4, ι 18, Philem. 355), whose scansion -εᾶ -εᾶς is typical of Attic, yet tended to be replaced by -εᾰ already in classical Attic. The same is true of neuter plurals in -πλα (Moer. τ 22 →τριπλᾶ) from adjectives -πλός, an analogical replacement of older contract adjectives in -πλόος.

Philem. 358 (→δένδρα· ἵνα μὴ ποιήςῃς μακρὸν τὸ α) does not use the typical terminology of the lexica when treating vowel quantity (μακρῶς ~ βραχέως, ςυςτέλλειν ~ ἐκτείνεςθαι).

All the entries above contrast words whose scansion depends on the quantity of the vowel involved. A much smaller group of glosses, however, prescribes quantities that are not metrically relevant. These are 'hidden quantities', i.e. quantities of vowels in closed syllables, which would be scanned as long even if their vowel were short. The most perspicuous case is →πελαργός (Phryn. *Ecl*. 80). Another entry (Moer. μ 8 →μᾶζα), involves also a change in the type of accent (see below, §§ 6 ff.), but still prescribes a long vowel in a position which is not metrically relevant in the standard scansion of Greek, and the same is possibly true of →χαμᾶζε (Ael. D. χ 3) and →ἀγοράζειν (Moer. α 139), if these glosses are not concerned exclusively with the accent[21].

---

[21] Aelius Dionysius only discusses the accent of χαμᾶζε, but of course the difference between χαμᾶζε and χαμάζε, the form that the gloss implies, is also in the quantity of the accented syl-

With the exception of πελαργός, all the other glosses involving hidden quantity deal with a *dichronon* followed by the letter *zeta*[22]: whether there is a relation between vowel quantity and the pronunciation of the sound represented by ⟨ζ⟩ is difficult to tell: nothing else in the lexica suggests that words containing ⟨ζ⟩ posed any problem for their correct pronunciation – see chap. V, § 5.

4.2 Ι

In two groups of glosses the quantity of ⟨ι⟩ is relevant for metrical scansion and for accentuation: one involves the suffix -ῐδ-/-ῑδ- (Phryn. *Ecl.* 142 →κνημίς) the other two the noun →πνῖγος (Moer. π 38, Phryn. *Ecl.* 77). Phrynichus' gloss on πνῖγος (*Ecl.* 77) may involve a hyperatticism: the lexicographer says that derivatives of the word have a long *iota*, but by doing so he is disregarding at least one noun, πνιγεύς, well attested in Attic comedy; and the passives of πνίγω formed on πνῐγ-η-, which only occur with a short root vowel.

The other glosses discuss ⟨ι⟩ in positions where its quantity is relevant for metrical scansion but indifferent for accentuation: these are →βοϊκός (Philem. 357), →ὄστρια (Moer. ο 32), and κυδώνιον μῆλον (*Antiatt.* κ 71). All these glosses may involve some variation in spelling, in particular between ⟨ι⟩ and ⟨ει⟩: even if none of them explicitly contrasts ⟨ι⟩ with ⟨ει⟩ in the shape they have reached us, there are reasons to believe that they may have originally referred to variant spellings with ⟨ει⟩ (βοεικόν, perhaps κυδώνειον) or ⟨ε⟩ (ὄστρε(ι)α). The increasing frequency of spellings with ⟨ει⟩ for /i:/ in Roman times would have stripped *iota* of its status as a *dichronon* if the habit of spelling ⟨ει⟩ every long /i:/ became standard. Some of the entries that contrast ⟨ει⟩ and ⟨ι⟩ may actually have to do with this more recent orthography, and it is possible that this was the case even with the three glosses mentioned above.

---

lable; Moeris explicitly say that the second *alpha* of ἀγοράζειν is long, but a parallel gloss of Herodianic descent lemmatises the aorist infinitive, ἀγοράσαι, in whose penultimate syllable a difference in quantity also entails a difference in accent type, and more importantly, results in a different scansion of the word.

[22] In addition to the ones with *alpha* listed above, we may only add Moer. β 15 →βαδίζειν, if as I believe it prescribes the quantity of the *iota*; for the reasons that make *iota* rather than *alpha* a better candidate for the vowel under discussion see the commentary to the gloss. However, if – by way of hypothesis – we imagine that the gloss prescribed the quantity of *alpha*, the gloss would fall in group (3), with the glosses that prescribe only quantity, in a metrical relevant position, with no information on the accent.

4.3 Y

No gloss involving ‹υ› contains explicit orthoepic prescriptions. In one instance the lexicographer is even surprisingly vague (Phryn. fr. *151 → ἁλμυρός 'τὰ πολλὰ ἐκτεταμένως', with a long vowel 'most times').

Many of the entries in this group have ‹υ› in an open or final syllable, that is to say, in a metrically relevant position (Philem. 355, Phryn. fr. *151 → ἁλμυρός, Moer. β 34 → βότρῡς and Moer. c 22 → στάχῡς, Moer. ξ 5 → ξυρόν, Moer. π 36 → πάπυρος, Moer. ψ 3 → ψιμύθιον). Some involve the accent as well (Philem. 355 → ἀπαντικρύ), and some have implications for the inflection as → βότρῡς, → στάχῡς (Moer. β 34 and c 22)[23]. Interestingly, Moeris and Philemon always ascribe the long vowel to the Ἀττικοί.

5 The attribution of long vowels to Attic

About three quarters of the glosses dealing with vowel quantity explicitly ascribe the long vowel to Attic. Sometimes Attic is said to have the short vowel, without further explanation (Philem. 394.10 R. → ἐβουλόμην, Phryn. *Ecl.* 241 → ὀπτάνιον, *Ecl.* 142 → κνημίς[24], Ael. D. ω 11 → ὦ τάν)[25]; in one the long vowel is said to be Ionic (Ael. D. φ 2 → φαρμακός) and nothing is said of the short, in three other cases the long vowel is stigmatised as an error (Phryn. *Ecl.* 346 → Διονυσεῖον, *Ecl.* 80 → πελαργός, *PS* 118.3–4 → υἱέος). The remaining two glosses are in the *Antiatticista* (μ 37 → μύσταξ, κ 71 → κυδώνιον μῆλον) and quote Attic playwrights, possibly to contrast other Atticist views supporting long vowels. One gloss by Moeris explicitly attributes the variant with a long vowel to the Ἕλληνες, and the variant with a short vowel to the speakers of Attic (Moer. υ 9 → ὑδαρές). Pausanias prescribes → ἅπᾱν (α 129) with no mention of the dialect it belongs to, but Aelius Dionysius (α 155) specifies that the form with a short vowel belongs to the Ionic dialect, whereas Attic has a long one.[26]

Such a strong tendency to ascribe long vowels to Attic confirms that it was perceived as having a more archaic phonology, in which distinctive vowel length

---

23 *Antiatt.* κ 71 → κυδώνιον is more likely to refer to the *iota* than to the *hypsilon*.
24 The *iota* of ῥαφανίδα, the fourth item in the gloss, is said to be either long or short.
25 A similar case could be γρυμέα – Phrynichus (*PS* 60.14) prescribes → γρυμεῖα, but notes that Old Comedy had γρυμέα (Diphilus fr. 128 K.–A.).
26 → ἆρα and ἄρα (Heren. 34), → δύω and δύο (Ael. D. δ 31) coexist, and the lexica do not prescribe one of the variants as the only correct Attic form (with the partial exemption of ἆρα, which at least Philemon 354 seems to prescribe with the long vowel only).

was preserved: almost none[27] of the prescribed long vowels has a special reason to be exclusively Attic, yet it seems that only speakers of good Attic would pronounce them. Many of the short vowels condemned by the lexicographers therefore can be explained as a contrast between isochronic Koine and a literary variety that used contrastive vowel quantities. The lexicographers supported their attribution of long vowels to Attic by metrical texts of the Attic canon in support of their recommended pronunciations. Further support could have come from the current pronunciation of speakers in Attica, a region that shows to have kept the original quantitative distinctions for longer; this resulted in a general labelling of variants with long vowels as 'Attic'.

A tendency to identify long vowels as Attic can be seen also in some ancient scholarship. Apollonius Dyscolus explains the long *alpha* of forms like ἀεί κλάω φανῶ ῥανῶ as the outcome of the suppression of an *iota* from Koine forms αἰεί κλαίω φαίνομαι ῥαίνω, because 'speakers of Attic are given to lengthening':

(28) ἀληθές ἐστίν, ὡς Ἀθηναῖοι ἐκτατικοί εἰςι τῶν φωνηέντων.

It is true, that the Athenians are fond of lengthening the vowels.

A.D. *Adv.* [*GG* 2.1.1] 187.20–1

(29) τὸ ἄρα πόρρω ἐκτέταται ὡς Ἀττικώτερον, ... ὅτι μᾶλλον μηκυντικοί εἰςι κατὰ τὰ φωνήεντα.

πόρρω has a long vowel, as it is rather Attic ... because they are rather fond of lengthening as far as the vowels are concerned.

A.D. *Adv.* [*GG* 2.1.1] 166.24–6

Also in this case the generalisation of vowel length may have gone too far: φᾶνῶ and ῥᾶνῶ are not attested anywhere in Greek literature[28].

---

27 With the partial exception of the synizesis in words like →ἀμφορέα, motivated on phonetic grounds, and typical of Attic and Ionic.
28 Modern editors correct to -φαίνω the only two instances of (ἀνα)φᾶνῶ in the manuscript tradition of Attic writers: (ϲε) φᾶνῶ, Ar. *Eq.* 300 codd. (Athenaeus 3.94c †φήϲω ϲετ†), corrected to φαίνω or φᾶνῶϲ ϲε (Porson), and ἀναφᾶνῶ, E. *Ba.* 528 codd. LP, corrected to ἀναφαίνω (Hermann). There are no other attestations of a future ῥαν- other than this passage (the aorist passive of ῥαίνω is ἐρράνθην, the long vowel is the regular outcome of ῥαν-ϲ- in the aorist active).

6 Accentuation

6.1 Accent types and accent changes

Ancient Greek accent has not survived on to Medieval and Modern Greek: whereas the latter varieties have a stress accent, for Ancient Greek a pitch accent can be reconstructed[29]: this is a suprasegmental trait based only on the relative height of the segments, not affecting their duration, and not affected by it[30]. Greek contrasted at least two pitch contours, one corresponding to the circumflex accent in writing, the other to the acute[31]. The accentuation written with the grave is only a context-conditioned variant of the pitch spelt with the acute[32].

The most apparent change in the transition from the ancient accent type to the modern one is the merger of the two pitch contours into one. The phonological contrast between different pitch contours was limited in ancient Greek: only on a final long vowel one could find either an acute or a circumflex, whereas on the penultimate the two contours are in complementary distribution, (the phenomenon known as *lex* cωτῆρα or 'law of the final trochee'), and on the antepenultimate only the acute was allowed[33].

The loss of distinctivity of the different intonational profiles is inextricably linked to vowel isochrony: when the distinction between long and short vowels is lost, the two intonational contours cannot be contrasted any more, and when

---

29 The accent of Classical Greek has been reconstructed as a pitch accent – what is phonologically identified as the accented syllable is a variation in pitch (the frequency of the accented segment): cf. Allen 1987a: 116ff.; Devine–Stephens 1994: 194–215; cf. also Probert 2001 and 2006: 55–7; on the interaction between pitch and stress in metrical composition see Nagy 2010: 384–5.
30 Pitch accents can mark accented syllables only by means of their higher or lower pitch, or contrast different pitch contours ('pitch differentiated stress', Devine – Stevens 1994: 206–8). Also stress accents can contrast different intensity contours (as the Danish *stød* does, Jakobson 1966: 96ff.). Ancient Greek, in that it contrasted the pitch contours of the acute and of the circumflex on long vowels and diphthongs, had therefore a 'pitch differentiated stress'.
31 The definition of Devine – Stephens (1985: 131) seems to me the most fitting: "the circumflex corresponds to high pitch on the first mora and low (or falling) pitch on the second, the acute to high pitch on the second mora with low pitch on the following vowel". We can add that the acute accent on a long vowel or diphthong does not need to be ascending from the first to the second mora. It is enough for it to not descend after the first mora.
32 "[a] lowered High tone" (Devine – Stephens 1991: 249).
33 Contrasts such as opt. λύcαι ~ inf. aor. λῦcαι or nom. plur. οἶκοι ~ loc. sing. οἴκοι depend on the different scansion of the final syllable, always scanned as either one or two morae when the prevocalic *sandhi* [ojV] had not been generalised (Kuryłowicz 1968: §§ 79–80; on the possile role of a circumflex accent contour in the preservation of these diphthongs see Lucidi 1966: 82ff.).

the accent type changed from pitch to stress, distinctive vowel length can easily be lost (cf. chap. III, §§ 3, 3.1). The two phonological changes are interdependent and the many attempts at establishing a relative chronology have not yielded definitive results. It is generally accepted that the change in accent type is a condition for isochrony[34], but whereas the beginning of both sound changes can be traced back to a period as early as the 3rd or 2nd century BC, for vowel quantity at least there is evidence that some varieties – among which Attic – had not lost it yet by the 2nd century AD.

The invention of accent signs in the 2nd century BC, traditionally attributed to Aristophanes of Byzantium, must point to the survival of the old pitch accent into Hellenistic times in at least some groups of speakers. The first clear examples of accentuative metre, implying a stress accent, come from Gregorius of Nazianzus (4th century AD, cf. Probert 2003: § 13–14). Of course, varieties of Greek that had a stress accent must have been spoken for some time before Gregorius of Nazianzus could think it acceptable to employ a stress-based verse to write theological poems. How long before Gregorius such varieties existed, and how widespread they were, however, is very difficult to say. The position of the accent seems to play a role in some Hellenistic quantitative poetry (see chap. III, § 3), which points to an early onset of the phenomenon.

As we shall see, Atticist lexicography prescribes more often the position of the accent than its type. Assuming that texts without lectional marks were equally open to interpretation as regarded the type of the accent as well as its position, we may expect to find approximately the same number of prescriptions concerning the type of the accent as we find prescriptions concerning its position.

The type of an accent is easily predictable once its position and the length of the accented vowel are known this may explain the disproportion between entries that prescribe the former and the ones prescribing the latter two. However, it is remarkable to see how it is nowhere apparent that the lexicographers had an interest in pointing out the difference in the pronunciation of the acute and the circumflex accents, and that most of their prescriptions (see next paragraph for the exceptions) can be easily read in a system that used a stress accent.

6.2 Accent prescriptions in the lexica

In the lexica, the nature of the accent can be deduced only from the employment of technical terms as περισπᾶν, ὀξυτονεῖν, βαρυτονεῖν and of their compounds

---

[34] Kretschmer 1890: 594, Allen 1987b, Devine – Stephens 1994: 215–23, Nagy 2000: 21.

and derivatives – all terms that describe at once the position and the nature of the accent; βαρύτονος / βαρυτονεῖν and derivatives only occasionally indicate the presence of the grave, but most often they only denote that the last syllable is not accented[35], and they are equally contrasted to terms that prescribe the acute or the circumflex accents.

Only a small group of entries discusses the opposition between acute and circumflex on the same vowel. The most common type contrasts different positions of the accent on the same word: the types of accent they contrast may be different, but only in that they obey the distribution laws of acute and circumflex. No gloss contains prescriptions on how to realise or keep distinct the two intonation contours: the only two glosses containing προφέρω prescribe the position of an acute (Ael. D. α 21 → ἀγνοία [...] ἐκτείνοντες προφέρονται τὴν τελευταίαν οἱ παλαιοὶ Ἀττικοὶ καὶ παροξύνοντες, Heren. 29 → ἀσφόδελος [...] ἐὰν μὲν ὀξυτόνως προενεγκώμεθα καθάπερ ἐν τῇ συνηθείᾳ [...]).

The table below divides the entries in the lexica in three groups, according to whether they make explicit mention of the accent position or type only, or both of them, and whether they also mention vowel quantity.

Table 4

	position, mentioned	type only	quantity, mentioned
type, mentioned	ἀγροῖκος ἄθρους αἴτιαι ἄκρατον ἀκταινοῦν ἀνίλλειν ἀτεχνῶς αὐτοχειρίᾳ ἀφοῦ ἐπιμέλου Θαλῆς ἱερεία (also quantity)	ἆ[36] νεώς τριπλᾶ χαμᾶζε χρυσᾶ	ἄρα γρῦ μᾶζαν νεώς ὦ τάν
position only	ἀληθές ἀποχρῇ ἁρπαγή ἀσφόδελος		ἀγνοία

---

35 Probert 2015: 940–1; not more generally the most recessive accentuation possible allowed by the law of the antepenultimate (Dickey 2007: 125–6).
36 Ael. D. α 1.

Table 4 *(Continued)*

	position, mentioned	type only	quantity, mentioned
	ἀχρεῖος		
	γέλοιος		
	γενέςθαι		
	δεξαμενή		
	διέτης		
	δόχμη		
	δύςερως		
	ἐπιτάδε		
	εὑρέ		
	ἰςότης		
	κάταντες		
	μάντεων		
	νεώς		
	ξυρεῖν		
	ὀπτάνιον		
	ὄφλειν		
	τητινόν		
	τιμώρια		
	τρίχα		
	φρούριον		
	(χαμᾶζε?)		

It is apparent that the entries contrasting an acute and a circumflex on the same syllable are a minority among in the number of entries discussing the accent. In some cases the entry prescribes the quantity of a vowel and the accent type at the same time (Moer. μ 8 → μᾶζα, τ 22 → τριπλᾶ), in the case of Ael. D. 1 α → ἄ and Philem. 358 → γρῦ possibly reflecting the doctrine that monosyllables ending in a *dichronon* are always perispomena[37]. Two entries, Heren. 34 → ἄρα and Ael. D. ω 11 → ὦ (τάν) contrast circumflex accentuation to short vowel quantity, basing on the principle that they are mutually exclusive. When the nature of the accent is not stated explicitly, it is always apparent from the context of the gloss (see commentaries to the individual entries; a partial exception may be Phryn. *PS* 27.13–17 → ἀφοῦ: the surviving text contrasts ἀφου – no indication of the accent type – with τὰ παροξύτονα ... ἄφου κτλ.: it is however unlikely that the non-paroxytone form should be ἀφού and not ἀφοῦ). Some glosses on the accent type (Moer. τ 22 → τριπλᾶ, Phryn. fr. *367 → χρυςᾶ, perhaps Moer. ν 1 → νεώς) may

---

[37] Cf. ps.-Arcadius (206.20–207.1) περιςπᾶται δὲ καὶ ὅςα ἔχει δίχρονον ἐκτεταμένον, ἄ, νῦν, γρῦ, κρῖ, ὁπότε ἐκτείνεται· ὁπότε δὲ ςυςτέλλεται, ὀξύνεται.

have aimed at distinguishing different inflection patterns by prescribing the accent type (a perispomenon τριπλᾶ needs to correspond to a nominative singular τριπλοῦc, not τριπλόc).

Three out of the five entries that prescribe the type of the accent involve word-final long vowels, the only context in which acute and circumflex could freely alternate in Greek. This could suggest that some speakers did still observe a distinction between the pitch contours associated to the acute and circumflex accent, and, if such lectional marks were only occasionally written, it is not impossible that one could have maintained a distinction between the two contours in speaking. However, the lexica do not provide any direct evidence of such a practice – we can only limit ourselves to observing that prescriptions on the type of accent are clearly subordinate to those on its position and on vowel quantity.

Be it as it may, the interest of the lexicographers in prescribing the position of the accent is clearly much better represented than any concerns about its type. When the lexica discuss the position of the accent, the underlying problem is normally of two kinds: either (1) there are two competing accentuations or (2) the lexicographer is discussing the accentuation of a rare (poetical, obsolescent) term[38].

As long as the spelling did not use accents consistently, only a prescription could tell the reader that in an Attic text a sequence ‹πονηρε› had to be accented πόνηρε and not πονηρέ, as it would be normal in the Koine[39], or that there are two possible accentuations for ‹αcφοδελοc›. In more than one case, the lexica use exactly the same strategy as P.Oxy. 1012 (text (19) above), an erudite work almost devoid of lectional marks: the position of the accent is prescribed by comparison with other words in Heren. 28, *de prop.* 13 →ἁρπαγή, Heren. 29 →ἀcφόδελοc, Phyrn. *Ecl.* 293 →δεξαμενή, Moer. ι 12 →ἰcότηc.

---

38 The systematic accentuation of every word, especially in prose texts, cannot be dated before the end of the 9th century AD (Probert 2003: § 23). The uncertainties on the accentuation of less common words are well exemplified by Galen (18(2).517–9) εἴτε δ' ὀξύνειν χρὴ τοὔνομα τὸ γαυcὸc εἴτε προπεριcπᾶν γαῦcοc ἄδηλον. οὐ γάρ ἐcτιν ἐν ἔθει τῷ τῶν Ἑλλήνων ἡ φωνή. κατὰ τὴν ἀναλογίαν ἔνιοι μὲν προπεριcπᾶcθαι κελεύουcιν αὐτὸ παραπληcίωc τῷ καῦcοc καὶ μαῦροc καὶ γαῦροc, ἔνιοι δὲ ὀξυτονεῖcθαι. [...] ἐπὶ τοῦτο γὰρ μόνον ἐπειράθην ῥεπόντων τῶν ἀναγινωcκόντων τὸ βιβλίον, ἄν τ' εἴπῃ τιc ἀξιῶν προπεριcπᾶν, ὡc ἂν ἐκεῖνοc ἐθελήcῃ καὶ cὺ φθέγγου, καὶ πάλιν ἂν ἑτέρῳ cυντύχῃc ὀξυτονεῖν ἐθέλοντι, καὶ αὐτὸc οὕτωc πρᾶττε καταφρονῶν καὶ τόνων καὶ ὀνομάτων [...].

39 The from πόνηροc discussed by the grammarians (e. g. [Arc.] 81.18–20 πόνηροc καὶ μόχθηροc [ἀεὶ] οἱ Ἀττικοὶ ἀντὶ τοῦ ὀξύνειν προπαροξύνουcιν, ὅταν τὸν ἐπίμονον καὶ ἐπὶ μόχθον cημαίνῃ) is an artificial creation: in Attic the proparoxytone accentuation is confined to the vocative πόνηρε (Probert 2006: 263, 327).

Some entries refer to specific texts (Phryn. *Ecl.* 293 → δεξαμενή and *PS* 39.12–15 → ἀκταινοῦν), in one case even to the accentuation of different manuscripts (if it is the actual words of Aelius Dionysius that we read at Ael. D. δ 30 → δόχμη, the gloss remarkably mentions 'the best editions' "ἐν ... τοῖς ἀκριβεστέροις ἀντιγράφοις"). Alexandrian scholarship was ultimately the source of the accentuation prescribed for classical Attic – the synonymical lexicon of Herennius uses Trypho's περὶ Ἀττικῆς προσῳδίας as a source (1st century BC, cf. Heren. 29 → ἀσφόδελος). Some glosses give information on rare or obsolescent words, whose accentuation must have become unclear – Paus. α 9, Phryn. fr. *48 → ἄγανος, Phryn. *PS* 114.14–16 → τητινός. Similarly, the two entries on → ἀσφόδελος ~ ἀσφοδελός (Ael. D. α 191, Heren. 29) point out the difference between a current and obsolescent word, differing only in the position of the accent. The position of the accent can also serve as a mark of different inflection types (Phryn. *PS* 39.12–15 → ἀκταινοῦν, *Philet.* 209 → ξυρεῖν, Moer. θ 4 → Θαλῆς, Ael. D. δ 23 → διέτης, πεντέτης, Phryn. *PS* 31.10–12 → ἀνίλλειν, ἐξίλλειν etc., similarly Moer. ε 32 → ἐπιμέλου).

Two regular outcomes of sound change are attested in more than one gloss. One is represented by Attic forms that had a more recent accentuation as the outcome of Vendryes' Law[40] (*Philet.* 241 → ἀχρεῖος, Moer. γ 4, Philem. 357, Ael. D. γ 4 → γέλοιος; cf. also Amm. 6 → ἀγροῖκος). The glosses that discuss them do not mention the chronological difference between a more recent and a more ancient Attic accentuation, as is the case in the tradition of other ancient scholarship transmitted in the scholia and in the grammatical treatises: they normally agree in identifying the outcomes of Vendryes' Law as Attic or later Attic[41].

The other sound change reflected in more than one gloss are the accent shifts in substantives in -ια: the lexicographers stigmatise the outcomes of the loss of syllabicity of ‹ι›, either resulting in accentuations on the following vowel (Phryn. *PS* 10.9–11 → αὐτοχεριᾷ, possibly Moer. υ 11 → ὑγεῖα) or on the preceding one (Moer. α 6 → αἴτιαι, τ 4 → τιμώρια); the cases involving -(ε)ιος are similar (*Philet.* 308 → φρούριον, and possibly also Moer. ι 3 → ἱερεία).

---

40 I.e. the change that transformed properispomena with a short antepenultimate syllable into proparoxytona, [⏑⏓⏑] > [⏒−⏑]. Vendryes' Law must have operated in the 4th century BC and affected in particular adjectives (Vendryes 1906; Probert 2003: § 317 and 2006: 88–9, with bibliography).
41 Probert (2004) discusses how the definitions of (older ~ later) Attic relate to the definition of Koine and the description of Homeric usage.

7 Breathings

7.1 Initial aspiration and psilosis in Greek

Initial aspiration was not a stable phoneme in many varieties of Greek. Some dialects, most notably Ionic and Lesbian, had already lost it even before the Classical period. One can therefore imagine that hypercorrections and misplacements of initial aspirations were likely to happen even before Hellenism, as a result of interference between different varieties of the language, and that they must have been common among Koine speakers. The loss of initial aspiration begun in the Hellenistic period: starting from the lower varieties, it was probably generalised during the Roman period[42].

Documentary texts of the 2nd century AD show uncertainty in the distribution of initial aspiration, suggesting that it had been lost among at least part of the population (cf. the texts in Horrocks 2010: 178–9). Attic inscriptions, on the other hand, are extremely regular in preserving initial aspiration – in fact, they are so regular that 'one could hesitate in attributing this lack to the conservatism of inscriptions in orthography' (Threatte 1980: 504). Once more, we are dealing with a sound change that was accomplished at very different times in different parts of the Greek speaking world.

In any case, the presence or absence of an initial aspiration remained apparent for longer in internal and external *sandhi*. It was possible to tell that a word began with an aspiration if it caused a preceding simple stop to turn into its aspirate counterpart when prefixed or following a word ending in a consonant. Attic inscriptions in the Ionian alphabet can only show this kind of alternation anyway. We can imagine therefore that the same speakers who were careful to turn, for instance, οὐκ to οὐχ before ἁμίς, would also say [ha'mis] in isolation.

7.2 Initial aspirations in the lexica

The technical terms to describe (or prescribe) initial aspiration in early Greek scholarship are ψιλοῦν and δασύνειν[43]. In addition to descriptive terminology, lexicographers and early scholars quite often show the presence of an initial as-

---

42 Allen 1987a: 50–1, Horrocks 2010: 171, Lundquist 2013.
43 Herodian must have treated initial aspirations in book 20 of the περὶ καθολικῆc προcῳδίαc, excerpts of which survive with the title περὶ πνευμάτων (cf. Dickey 2014, n. 42 and Dyck 1993: 779); Trypho (1st c. BC) wrote a treatise περὶ πνευμάτων (fragments have been edited by Valckenaer (1822: 188–215), cf. Dickey 2007: 84).

piration by observing the behaviour of a word in composition. We can see this procedure in the description of aspirated stops as the 'counterparts' of non-aspirated in the *Techne* attributed to Dionysius Thrax:

> (30) ἀντιςτοιχεῖ δὲ τὰ δαςέα τοῖς ψιλοῖς, τῷ μὲν π τὸ φ, οὕτως·
> Ἀλλά μοι εἴφ' ὅπη ἔςχες † ἰὼν εὐεργέα νῆα (Hom. *Od.* 9 279),
> τῷ δὲ κ τὸ χ·
> Αὐτίχ' ὁ μὲν χλαῖνάν † τε χιτῶνά τε ἔννυτ' Ὀδυςςεύς (Hom. *Od.* 5 229),
> τὸ δὲ θ τῷ τ·
> Ὣς ἔφαθ'· οἱ δ' ἄρα πάντες † ἀκὴν ἐγένοντο ςιωπῇ (Hom. *Il.* 3 95).

> The aspirated stops (δαςέα) correspond the simple ones (ψιλά)...
>
> D. Thrax, *Ars gramm.*, 6.25–30 Lallot

ps.-Arcadius mentions the rule according to which a simple stop turns into its aspirate counterpart when followed by a rough breathing:

> (31) ὅτι δαςυνομένου φωνήεντος ἐπιφερομένου, τὸ προηγούμενον ψιλὸν τρέπεται εἰς τὸ ἀντίςτοιχον δαςὺ· κατὰ ἡμῶν καθ' ἡμῶν. τὸ δὲ ἀνάπαλιν οὔ, εἰ μὴ κατὰ διάλεκτον τραπῇ· τὸ γὰρ ἀμπέχεςθαι Αἰολικόν ἐςτι.

> When an aspirated vowel follows, the preceding simple stop turns into the corresponding aspirate: κατὰ ἡμῶν καθ' ἡμῶν. the opposite does not happen, unless the word has undergone transformation according to a dialect: in fact, ἀμπέχεςθαι is Aeolic.
>
> [Arc.] 199.20–23[44]

Also the majority of entries in the lexica refers to initial aspiration (or lack thereof) by the technical terms δαςύνειν/ψιλοῦν and related forms[45], but in the same way as the *Ars* of Dionysius Thrax and ps.-Arcadius, the lexica prove the presence or the absence of an aspiration at word-beginning by means of derivatives or phrases in which a stop would immediately precede the word under discussion. This happens in Ael. D. α 98 (→ ἀμίς > κεῖνθ' ἀμίδες, ἅμαξα > καθημαξευμένα), Phryn. *PS* 23.1-2 (→ ἀνύειν > καθήνυςαν), where the principle is fully spelt out: 'δαςύνουςιν οἱ Ἀττικοί. καὶ δῆλον ἐκ τῆς ςυναλοιφῆς'. Similarly, the absence of an initial aspiration is made clear in Ael. D. α 150 (→ ἀνύειν > οὐκ ἀνύω, in Homer and the Koine, whereas Attic has an aspiration here), Ael. D. α 157 → ἀπηλιώτης, Phryn. *PS* 25.10–11 → ἀλοᾶν > ἀπαλοᾶν. A long entry in the

---

[44] = Herodian *GG* 3.1 547.10–12, cf. also Choeroboscus in *An. B.* 704.28.
[45] Ael. D. α 1, α 2 → ἅ, ἃ ἅ, α 46 → ἄθρους, α 47, Moer. α 11 → ἄθυρμα, Philem. 355 → ἅλις, Phryn. *PS* 25.10–11 → ἀλοᾶν, Ael. D. α 81 → ἀλύειν, Philem. 355 ἅλυςις, Ael. D. α 98 → ἀμίς, Ael. D. α 157 → ἀπηλιώτης, Ael. D. α 150, Moer. η 16, Phryn. *PS* 23.1-2 → ἀνύειν, Paus. α 154 → ἄρκυες, Ael. D. α 193, Amm. 86, Phryn. fr. †*274 → ἄττα, Ael. D. η 3 → ἦδος.

epitome of the *Praeparatio Sophistica* (Phryn. *PS* 25.16–25 →ἄπεφθοc) deals with exceptions to the rule, whereby a compound fails to show an aspirate consonant even when its second element does begin with an aspirate.

About half of the prescriptions prescribe 'unexpected' forms, i.e. initial aspirations where we would expect none, or psilotic forms of words that we know to begin with an aspiration in Attic. The table below shows the distribution of the prescribed forms (the listed words are my lemmata)

	Aspirated	**Unaspirated**
Expected forms	(ἄθρουc), ἁμίc, ἅμαξα, ἅττα, ἧδοc	ἀλοᾶν, ἀπηλιώτηc, ἄπεφθοc, ἄττα
Unexpected forms	ἄθυρμα, ἀνύειν, ἄρκυc (?)	ἅλιc, ἅλυcιc

Moeris' lexicon contrasts words with and without an initial aspiration only on three occasions (α 10 →ἁμίc, α 11 →ἄθυρμα, η 16 →ἀνύειν) and it consistently ascribes the rough breathing to Attic. On the other hand, the only two entries that single out Attic as being the psilotic dialect both come from Philemon's lexicon (→ἅλιc and →ἅλυcιc, Philem. 355). The lack of initial aspiration in is unexplained, and the reasons of its attribution to Attic very unclear – at least in the case of →ἅλιc we may have to deal with the misreading of a source.

On the other hand, there seems to be a tendency to hypercorrection, in favour of attributing initial aspiration to Attic. Both Aelius Dionysius (α 47) and Moeris (α 11) prescribe an Attic initial aspiration for →ἄθυρμα, which is otherwise not attested. In one instance, Attic speakers/writers are said to 'rejoice' in the initial aspiration (τῇ δαcείᾳ προcῳδίᾳ χαίρουcιν οἱ Ἀττικοί, Ael. D. α 98 →ἁμίc), just like they are said to rejoice in long vowels (cf. § 5 above). The reason for the prescription of an initial aspirate in Phryn. *PS* 23.1–2 →ἀνύειν are more complicated: the simple verb ἀνύ(τ)ειν is never attested with an initial aspiration, and the occurrences of its compound καθανύ(τ)ειν are problematic. The impression is that the verb had lost its initial aspiration (which is, however, etymological), and that it was reintroduced in the manuscripts only on the principle that wherever a form with initial aspiration was available, that should have been the authentic Attic reading. Like vowel length, also initial aspiration came to be regarded as a 'more Attic' feature, and therefore it was likely to be unduly extended to words which originally lacked it.

V Degemination

1 Degemination in Greek

Degemination, that is the reduction of long consonants (geminates) to simple ones (singletons), is a process that was never completed in all parts of the Greek speaking world. There are still dialects of Modern Greek that preserve geminates, most notably in Southern Italy and Cyprus (and in older times possibly also Asia Minor and the neighbouring areas). In the areas where geminates are lost, the process was possibly completed only in Byzantine times[1]. When it takes place, degemination in Greek always preserves all the traits of the original geminate, that is its place and type of articulation, including aspiration: compare – for instance – the outcome of the geminate in cικχαίνω /sikkʰáino:/ > MGk. cιχαίνομαι /siˈxenome/ [siˈçɛːnome] with the singleton in μάχη /mákʰeː₁/ > MGk. /ˈmaxi/ [ˈmaːçi][2]. The only trait that is lost is consonantal length[3].

Although the process of degemination was completed – where it was indeed completed – only in Byzantine times, the writing of geminates had not been always consistent in Ancient Greek. Especially in the Archaic period the writing of geminates is not the orthographical norm – this inconsistency in the notation of geminates should not suggest that gemination was being lost[4]: some among the most ancient alphabetical inscriptions are consistent in the notation of geminates[5]; geminates are consistently represented from the Classical period on; they count as two consonants in metrical texts. It is only from about the 3rd century BC onwards there are clear examples of confusion between singletons and

---

[1] Horrocks 2010: 274; the arrangement of lemmata κατ' ἀντιστοιχεῖαν of the *Suda* (cf. chap. II, § 1) treats double graphemes as singletons (cf. e.g. the sequence καλόπους, κάλλος, καλὸς κἀγαθός, *Su.* κ 249–251).

[2] The geminate /kkʰ/ is simplified to /kʰ/ and spirantised to /x/, which has a palatal allophone [ç] before a front mid or high vowel in Modern Greek.

[3] On degemination as a form of lenition see Kirchner 2000 and 2001, esp. 104ff., Lavoie 2001: 27, 167.

[4] As Teodorsson (1974: 302 fn. 357) seems to imply; his account is way more accurate when he states that "[t]he doubling of syngraphemes when corresponding to /C:/ was gradually established as an orthographic norm during a period of about 100 years, namely *ca.* 550–450 a.C." (1974: 231).

[5] καλλιστεφάνο on Nestor's Cup (8th century BC) *IGASMG* III 2 or ὠμφίννεω and Ψαμμήτιχος in Pedon's dedication, *Priene* 205*5; on the earliest examples of gemination in writing see Immerwahr 1990: 19 and 169.

geminates: the most uncontroversial kind of evidence for degemination are doubled letters replacing singletons in spellings such as ‹cτραττοc› for cτρατόc[6].

Preconsonantal gemination, that is the redoublement of the first consonant in a consonant cluster, is another common misspelling[7] that should not be taken as evidence of degemination. On the contrary, we need to consider it evidence that a contrast between geminates and singletons was still distinctive. The reason behind a spelling like ‹νυκκτει› for νυκτί is precisely that the writer identifies the stop at the beginning of the cluster as a geminate. The reason is that both the first element in a heterosyllabic consonant cluster and the onset of a geminate share the metrical property of realising a syllable coda[8]: if gemination were not a distinctive feature in the phonological system of the writer, such an identification would not be possible.

Also some instances of assimilation and dissimilation reflect the phonemic status of gemination. Especially in papyri dating between the 1st and 3rd centuries AD, clusters of a nasal preceding a stop are often replaced by a doubled stop (ἔνεκκ- for the aorist stem ἔνεγκ-, πρίκκιποc for πρίγκιποc, μεταλαββάνων, cυππεφωνημένηc, cf. Gignac 1976: 171–2[9]): for such assimilations to take place, geminates needed to be still present in the phonological system. Only geminates are sometimes turned into a cluster of nasal and stop (cάββατον > cάμβατον[10]): this must reflect the preservation of geminates rather than their disappearance, and that the sounds spelt by ‹ββ› and ‹β› were treated as different phonological entities (there are no comparable attempts at replacing ‹β› with ‹μβ›). The dissimilation can hardly be a reaction to the spirantisation /b/ > /β/[11], just like the spelling γλώντα of the *defixiones*[12] is hardly a reflection of a more accurate pro-

---

6 Horrocks 2010: 171; e.g. ‹νικοcτραττοc› in Attica *Agora* 17.347 (3rd/2nd century BC).
7 Cf. Threatte (1980: 527): "consonants forming the first element of a cluster are not infrequently doubled out of a confusion as to whether they go with the following syllable or the preceding".
8 Moreover, whereas in a language like English spellings with geminates may still have a bearing on the pronunciation, although they do not signal a geminate in the pronunciation (e.g. English *bitter* ~ *biter*), this is not the case with Greek, in which the outcomes of degemination are indistinguishable from the original singletons.
9 The very few instances of the assimilation in Attic inscriptions (e.g. *IG* II² 107.11 ξυββάλλεcθαι) are rather mistakes of the lapicide and not real signs of assimilation, cf. Threatte 1981: 637. Such misspellings must have been favoured by the prosodical equivalence of a consonant cluster and a geminate, and therefore can prove that spellings with a double consonant reflected geminates in the pronunciation.
10 Cf. Schwyzer 1934 and Biville 1990: 317–8 on the diffusion in of *sambaton* as the Latin rendition of Greek cάββατον.
11 "Besonders kann man Gemination der Media begreifen; sie stellte sich wohl ein aus der Tendenz der Schul- und Hochsprache, β als Verschlußlaut (*b*) zu wahren" (Schwyzer 1934: 232).
12 E.g. *IG* III app. 86.

nunciation, and certainly not an attempt a preventing the spirantisation of [t], which did never take place in Greek.

The phonological system of Greek did not employ gemination extensively: its low functional load may have favoured its loss[13]. In Attic, gemination is clearly seen for /pp⁽ʰ⁾ tt⁽ʰ⁾ kk⁽ʰ⁾ mm nn ll rr ss/, whereas the geminate voiced stops are particularly rare: some accounts of Attic phonology do not even discuss them[14]. Nevertheless they are common in other varieties of Greek: any dialect that uses κάτ (Att. κατά) has countless voiced geminates resulting from the assimilation of /tb td tg/ to /bb dd gg/ across word or morpheme boundaries[15]. In Attic, the geminated voiced velar stop [gg] must have been the standard realisation of /kg/, resulting from prefixation or *sandhi* (with ἐκ, e. g. ἐκγράφω, ἔκγονος[16]); yet a text search on Plato yields no results for ⟨ββ⟩ or ⟨δδ⟩[17]. Such geminates would be well integrated in the phonological system of the Koine, that already included voiceless and aspirate geminate stops, as it is apparent in the employment of the doubled letters ⟨ββ⟩ ⟨δδ⟩ in loanwords, e. g. the Molossian king's name Ἀρύββας, attested from the 4th century BC in Demosthenes (*Ol.* 1.13), and in a number of inscriptions from Attica and other areas of Greece[18]. By the end of Hellenism the letter ⟨ζ⟩ must have been pronounced as long voiced sibilant /zz/, but there are no prescriptions that address directly its pronunciation. There are, however, some that discuss the quantity of the immediately preceding vowel, suggesting that they were counteracting a degeminated pronunciation [z] (cf. § 5).

---

13 "Le rendement fonctionnel des géminées en opposition avec les consonnes faibles était tout a fait negligeable. L'opposition géminée: simple reste pour ainsi dire à l'écart du système phonologique du grec le plus ancien. [...] Il y avait [*scil.* in Greek] un processus d'affaiblissement des occlusives, mais la situation y était compliquée par l'existence des sourdes aspirées [...]. En outre, la fréquence des géminées en grec était bien inferieure à leur fréquence en latin vulgaire, et de même leur rendement fonctionnel. La distinction entre géminées et simples n'etait pas assez importante pour qu'il valût la peine de la maintenir comme en roman occidental" (Katičić 1959: 129, 131).
14 Lupaş 1972: 70–3, 133–4; the same picture in Teodorsson 1974: 43–4.
15 E. g. καδδῦσαι Hom. *Il.* 19.25, κάββαλε Hom. *Il.* 8.249, κάββαλλε, Alc. fr. 338.5.
16 Cf. Allen 1987a: 38–9 on the pronunciation of ⟨κγ⟩ as [gg].
17 Except for one instance of καββάλλω, yet in a Homeric quote (*Ion* 539c = Hom. *Il.* 12.206). All instances of ⟨κγ⟩ are in ἔκγονος, except one instance of ἐκγελάω (*R.* 473c).
18 In Attica: *IG* II² 226 (343/2 BC), II³ 441 (342 BC); Dodona: *SEG* 23.476 (4th/3rd c. BC); Thessaly: *SEG* 35.651 (100/50 BC).

2 Degemination in inscriptions and papyri

2.1 Degemination in Attic inscriptions of the archaic and classical periods

The data collected by Teodorsson for Attic between 400 and 340 BC[19] give a rough idea of how frequently geminates are misspelt in Classical Attic[20]. I summarised them in the following table, counting only the instances involving intervocalic singletons or geminates (the latter also across word boundaries, as in e.g. εἰc Cυκιωνίουc), and not considering redoublements of letters in consonant clusters or at the end of a word, unless followed by a vowel. The column marked C(C) counts the omissions (i.e. γραματέα for γραμματέα), and C{C} the irrational geminations (i.e. ἐππoίηcεν for ἐποίηcεν) of intervocalic consonants, within the same word and across word-boundaries:

Table 5

	C(C)	lexemes	inscriptions	C{C}	lexemes	inscriptions
λ(λ)	18	6[21]	17	16	12[22]	15
c(c)	8	8[23]	8	9	9	9
τ(τ)	36	9[24]	22	3	3	3
μ(μ)	9[25]	6[26]	9	2	2	2

---

19 Teodorsson 1974: 145–53, 1979: 67. Most works on geminates in Greek inscriptions do not make a distinction between prevocalic and intervocalic gemination (cf. e.g. Slavova 2004: 111–2).
20 A random search on some of the items in Teodorsson's list turned in more results than the ones listed in Teodorsson (1974). Any future research based on this data should verify them again on the digital databases that were not available at the time of Teodorsson's writing.
21 καλ- 10 times, χαιρυλλη 2x, Απολλοδωροc 2x.
22 καλόc and derivatives account for five instances of irrational gemination (κάλλοc may have exerted some pressure).
23 Three instances are omissions where a final *sigma* meets a word beginning with *sigma* and a vowel; two of such instances involve the preposition εἰc.
24 γλωτ(τ)α accounts for 20 of the instances of this omission, and it is especially common in *defixiones*; Θρᾷττα, τέτταρα and derivatives appear three times each, forms of πράττω, ἡττάομαι and of the name Cφήττιοc twice each.
25 Three omissions imply the assimilation of a final nasal to the following /m/ in external *sandhi*: the three inscriptions do write ⟨μ⟩ at the end of a word as a result of assimilation (e.g. the *defixio IG* III *app.* 68,b has τὸν δοῦλο(μ) Μέλανοc at line 15, but τὴμ Μέλανοc πάλ(λ)ακα at line 14: for some reason, Teodorsson does not include πάλ(λ)ακα in his list of omitted geminates.
26 Four instances are of γράμμα and derivatives.

Table 5 *(Continued)*

	C⟨C⟩	lexemes	inscriptions	C{C}	lexemes	inscriptions
π⟨π⟩	15	2[27]	15	1	1	1
ρ⟨ρ⟩	3	3	3	10 (5)[28]	4[29]	5
κ⟨κ⟩	3	1[30]	3[31]			
ν{ν}				5	5	5
ζ{ζ}				2	2	2
χ{χ}				1	1	1

If there really was some uncertainty in the perception of gemination in 4th century BC Attic, the distribution of irrational doubling should mirror that of irrational simplification. This however is the case only with ⟨λ⟩ and ⟨c⟩, and other singletons, especially ⟨τ⟩ and ⟨π⟩, are virtually never confused with their geminate counterparts: there is only one isolated case of ⟨χχ⟩, two of ⟨ζζ⟩, and the only other consonant that is irrationally geminate a substantial number of times is ⟨ν⟩.

Teodorsson's interpretation, that degemination had already taken place in the lower register of Attic, is not really supported by the data. Less polished texts – especially the *defixiones* and the horse price-tags[32] – are particularly inaccurate in the writing of geminates, but still, the general trend is to omit the doubling of a letter, not to spell simple consonants as geminates. The phonological system of Attic as it results from this analysis of the data does preserve the contrast between simple and geminated consonants.

Only in the cases of ⟨λ(λ)⟩ and ⟨c(c)⟩ the number of misspellings is high enough to suggest that the opposition between [l] ~ [ll] and [s] ~ [ss] was becoming weaker. The rarity of [ss] may have favoured its degemination in Attic. Most

---

[27] All instances but one are made by ἵππος, its derivatives and compounds (mostly proper nouns), the only other lexeme is cτυπ⟨π⟩εῖον.
[28] Five instances of ⟨ρρ⟩ occur at the beginning of a sentence, and seven at the beginning of a word. ⟨ρρ⟩ is the preferred spelling in compounds and augmented verbal froms, and was easily generalised to external *sandhi*, cf. Threatte 1980: 519.
[29] ῥυμός six times; three instances of Ἀρρι- at the beginning of personal names; all the other instances are of word-initial ⟨ρ⟩.
[30] ἐκκληcία accounts for all the omissions of ⟨κ⟩ in Teodorsson's corpus.
[31] All of them instances of ἐκ(κ)ληcία.
[32] Edited by Braun 1970.

instances of what is represented by ‹cc› in other dialects correspond the singleton [s] in Attic (μέcoc < *medʰ-i̯os, ὅcoc < * i̯od-i̯os, *d-s Att. ἠργάcαντο, Dor. ἠργάccαντο) or ‹ττ› (πλήττω < *pleh₂k-i̯ō)³³. There are few instances of original [ss], mostly in isolated lexemes, for the most part compounds with cύν like cuccίτιον and cύccημον, or compounds with δυc- (e.g. δυccεβήc)³⁴.

In Attic inscriptions, the earliest misspellings of singleton and geminate consonants involve ‹λ μ ν ρ c›³⁵. The misspellings never become so consistent to suggest that degemination had been fully accomplished in Classical Attic³⁶.

2.2 Degemination in Hellenistic inscriptions and papyri

From the 3ʳᵈ century BC Athenian inscriptions show again simplification of the geminates, this time along with a good number of instances of irrational gemination of simple stops. The variation ‹λ› ~ ‹λλ› is the only one which is attested so extensively that it actually suggests an early degemination of /ll/ in some varieties of Attic. It is also the first type of confusion between singletons and geminates to be attested in Attic inscriptions, followed by ‹ρ› ~ ‹ρρ›, and then ‹μ› ~ ‹μμ› and ‹ν› ~ ‹νν›³⁷: "[t]he frequency of λ{λ} and ρ{ρ} perhaps has phonetic significance", whereas the rest of the evidence can be dismissed as trivial errors³⁸. In this period, also simplifications of geminates in external *sandhi* are suggestive of ongoing degemination³⁹.

---

33 Threatte 1980: 514, Allen 1987a: 12–4.
34 Some of these terms may even be loanwords: cuccίτια are a typically Doric institution, cύccημον is not genuine Attic according to Phrynichus, *Ecl.* 394; Teodorsson (1974: 150, fn. 74) mistakenly includes ‹cuccεμαινοcθον› (cuccημαινούcθων, *IG* I³ 52, 434/3 BC) in the list of words with irrational gemination (cuccημαίνω may be rare, but is correctly formed and already attested in Demosthenes 35.15, 41.12, and it is certainly not a misspelling for *‹cuceμαινοcθον›)
35 Threatte 1980: 532.
36 Not even in Teodorsson's 'progressive' reconstruction of Attic phonology: "there was no point of time when the change [C:] > [C] can be said to have made a break-through in the population" (Teodorsson 1974: 302).
37 Threatte 1980: 514, 532. Cf. also Eckinger (1892: 104) "Bei keinem Consonanten ist der Wechsel von Gemination so häufig vie bei l, im Lateinischen sowohl wie im Griechischen". Lejeune (1972 §§ 144, 330) believes that nasals tend to spontaneous gemination. Early homophony of /mm nn/ and /m n/ seems to me a better explanation.
38 Threatte 1980: 534. Some consonants may indeed be more prone to degemination than others. It has been argued for instance that the intrinsic longer quantity of singleton sibilants made the distinction between /s/ and /ss/ weaker, and is ultimately the cause of its loss in languages that otherwise maintain geminates (Blevins 2004).
39 E.g. ἀνδρὸ cίμου = ἀνδρὸc c- *IG* II² 1534 B a-k 235, Schwyzer 1939: 230.

Attic may have been among the first dialects to undergo degemination. Lycian inscriptions, for instance, present most instances of degemination only in Roman times[40]. In both cases however, degeminations seems to have spread along the same lines: the first consonants to lose the gemination contrast are the continuants[41], whereas stops are affected only at a later stage; the same development can be traced in Hellenistic papyri[42]. Also the instances of irrational doubling of consonants[43] follow the same pattern: they are more frequent with continuants, and much rarer with stops[44], and their distribution in time is quite similar to the instances of simplification.

The simplification of the geminates was not completed in the transition from the Koine to the dialects of Modern Greek, as some modern dialects have mantained gemination as a distinctive phonological trait[45]. Dialects of Modern Greek that retain gemination as a distinctive feature not only maintained all the inherited geminates, but also extended gemination beyond its original boundaries[46].

As the process of degemination is not completed even in some dialects of Modern Greek, it is its starting point that is most interesting for us. If, by the 2nd century AD, degemination had started in some varieties of Greek, and perhaps was even well established, then the lexicographers were addressing their

---

40 The writing with a single letter is more common form the 1st century AD on in Lycian inscriptions. The most common instance involve ⟨c⟩c (more than 10 examples) followed by (λ)λ (7 examples) (ρ)ρ and (μ)μ (with 4 and 3 examples respectively – data from Hauser 1916: 65–8).
41 ⟨c⟩ for ⟨cc⟩ is the earliest attested and most frequent instance of reduction (Hauser 1916: 65–6).
42 "Was die Häufigkeit der Fälle betrifft, so stehen in erster Linie die Liquidae mit den Nasales, in zweiter Doppelsigma, in dritter Doppelmuta. .... Vereinfachung von Doppelmuta ist verhältnismäßig am seltensten" (Mayser 1923: 211 and 215). Schmoll (Mayser – Schmoll 1970: 185–94) omits these general remarks, but does not present much evidence contrasting Mayser's previous interpretation.
43 Cf. Hauser 1916: 67.
44 Mayser – Schmoll 1970: 193–4.
45 Horrocks 2010: 274. It is generally believed that varieties of Modern Greek with phonological geminates never underwent degemination (Thumb 1901: 20–1, 24, Dienstbach 1910: 98). Hermann (1923: 189) is sceptical, and Schmitt (1901: 71–3) denies the continuity between Ancient and Modern Greek geminates, although his argument in favour of secondary gemination as a result of stress is not convincing.
46 Following regular sound changes (e.g. assimilation of a nasal to a following fricative, κοχχύλι < κογχύλιον) or through analogy with inherited geminates (e.g. πολλύc form πολλοῦ). Some geminations seem irrational (e.g. Cypriot ποττέ for ποτέ). The case of Cypriot is interesting, in that it has preserved most geminates of ancient Greek, with the exception of [rr], which it has reduced to [r] – together with [kk] only in the word ἐκκληcία > [ekliˈʃa] – cf. Newton (1972: 90): ἐκκληcία shows early signs of degemination in Attic too, and the phenomenon seems here to confined this particular word.

prescriptions to a mixed audience, including speakers who would use geminates regularly, and speakers who would have to learn them.

Hermann (1923: 187–8) dates degemination to a time before the formation of the Koine. Of his 48 examples 31 are occurrences of the same words. ‹μ› for ‹μμ› is particularly frequent in the derivatives of γράφω γράμμα, γραμματεύς, γεγραμμένον, with 8 examples, followed by 7 instances of compound personal names[47] with ἴποϲ instead of ἵππος. ἄλλος and ἀλλά sum up for a total of 8 instances of single ‹λ› instead of the geminate.[48]

Also in Hermann's corpus [ll] > [l] is definitely the best attested simplification. Degemination is most frequent with [ll]. Spellings with ‹λ› instead of ‹λλ› account for a third (16 on 48) of the examples presented by Hermann (1923: 188), and they are predominantly constituted by ἄλλος and its derivatives, by κάλλος (mostly as part of compound personal names) and by the god name Ἀπόλλων. There is only one isolated instance of ἐπιτίλουϲα for ἐπιτίλλουϲα (*IG* XII 5.739 app. 14).

2.3 Degemination in papyri of the Roman period

The confusion between simple and geminate consonants in the examples collected by Gignac (1976: 155–62), confirms that /l/, /r/, /m/, and /s/ are the most frequent cases of variation. Whereas for the above consonants Gignac does not even list all the instances of variation, misspelling of geminate stops is much less frequent, and Gignac is able to list virtually in full all the variations in the papyri of his corpus. Uncertainty is often limited to specific words, like ἐκκληϲία, ϲάκκος, ἔλαττον/ἐλαττούμενοϲ (Gignac 1976: 160–2). There are very many instances of irrational gemination in the syllable coda (the type νυκκτεί (for νυκτί) *P.Strassb.* 216.6, AD 126/7; λεπτπτόν *P.Mich.* 245.22.23, AD 47): gemination may have been still a perceived phonological trait, if writers could equate the first element of heterosyllabic consonant clusters with the onset of a geminate (see § 2).

Further evidence that geminates were still distinctive for part of the population comes from spellings like -ττιος for post-vocalic -τιος in Roman names, e. g. Δομιττιανός. Such spellings continue to be attested on to the Roman and Byzantine period (Gignac 1976: 161, 255), and they suggest that the Latin redoublement of /t/ in the intervocalic cluster /tj/ was heard and recorded in writing. However

---

47 Λαβίτα in Hermann 1923: 188 is a misprint for Λαβίπ(π)α *IG* V,1 1277.
48 Thumb (1901: 23) is too cautious in dating the earliest stages of degemination to the imperial period.

in a very similar phonetic context, Attic inscriptions show variation between -ηττιος and -ητιος: the singleton is written instead of the geminate (Threatte 1980: 514). Again, the distribution of the variants suggests that we have to reckon with a very diverse number of coexisting varieties of Greek, some of which had undergone degemination, while some other still kept the original geminates.

3 Geminates in Greek loanwords in Latin

Latin normally preserves the geminates of Greek loanwords even if not always consistently (cf. It. *chiosa, canapa* < Lat. *glosa, canapa* not *glossa*, **cannapa[49]). Degemination in Latin did not take place at the same time as it did in Greek. Geminates are preserved in Latin of imperial times, whereas in Greek their notation can be rather irregular already in the 3rd century BC.

Moreover, not only degemination was not accomplished in all Romance languages (cf. Sardinian and central and southern Italian dialects), but it was also one of the last sound changes to take place in the transition from Latin to Romance[50], as it can be seen from the different outcomes of simple and geminate consonants in most daughter languages of Latin[51].

None of the loanwords quoted by Biville (1990) continues a Greek geminate with a simple Latin consonant, as one would expect if Greek had lost its geminates altogether. It is difficult to agree with Biville that "il règne, en latin comme en grec, une confusion certaine dans la notation des consonnes simples et des géminées; cette confusion a abouti à l'abolition des géminées anciennes en grec moderne et en roman"[52].

Early Greek loanwords in Latin often underwent radical reshaping, sometimes involving simplification of original geminates, e.g. *Acilles, Accheruns*, or gemination of simple consonants. Loanwords of Republican times are decidedly coherent in preserving Greek geminates (sometimes even introducing them where Greek had singletons, e.g. ἄκρατος, βάσιν, Ἀλκησιμάρχος, βασιλική = *ag-*

---

[49] Cf. Biville 1990: 250 fn. 114, 261 with fn. 154.
[50] The idea that Italian geminates are not inherited, and that all Latin geminates were lost in the transition to Romance (Biville 1990: 164, 175 fn. 79) is not supported by any evidence: for all we know Italian usually continues the geminates of Latin (cf. the outcomes of Lat. *mitto, appareo* etc.).
[51] E.g. lenitions: ROTAM > sp. *rueda*, fr. *roue* ma GUTTAM > sp. *gota*, fr. *gote*; fr. *pré* < PRATUM but *chat* < CATTUM (Väänänen 1982: 115), the different outcomes of /ll nn rr/ and /l n r/ in Ibero-romance.
[52] Biville 1990: 65.

*gratus, bassim, Alcessimarchus, bassilica*⁵³) this may depend on learned borrowing, perhaps based on knowledge of the Greek orthography, and maybe even on more accurate pronunciations of Greek that preserved gemination.

4 Geminates in Latin loanwords in Greek

Latin gemination is preserved virtually without exception in literary loanwords (e.g. the ones attested in Plutarch). Some loanwords which may have entered Greek via popular transmission are less consistent in preserving original geminates: some military terms, for instance, underwent simplification e.g. ἀπλικεύω < Lat. *applicari* and the reborrowing βαλίςτρα (but cf. βαλλιςτράριον)⁵⁴.

Some categories of nouns are particularly irregular. Some of their variability may even be associated to the formation of new geminates, in particular in clusters with [j]⁵⁵. The spelling of nouns in *-ilius* or *-inius* is most variable (there are many examples with Λικίν(ν)ιος between the 1ˢᵗ and the 2ⁿᵈ century AD). However, Greek may introduce geminates also in the absence of a glide, e.g. Οὐαλλέριος in Plutarch (*Mar.* 28.8, etc.), and in inscriptions, together with Οὐαλλέντ-⁵⁶. Such irrational geminations are parallel to the simplification affecting λ, μ, ς (e.g. Μάλιος⁵⁷, Plut. *Pomp.* 72 Πολίων, 54 Μεςάλας, Κόμοδος – although less common than Κόμμοδος –, Κάςιος, cf. Dittenberger 1872: 153). There are some examples of variation for stops too, and a good number of instances of ‹ττ› transcribing Latin /tj/, all dating between 1ˢᵗ and 2ⁿᵈ century AD⁵⁸. Such spellings can imply that the Greek could still distinguish between simple and geminate consonants, and write geminates when they heard them⁵⁹.

---

53 Biville 1990: 64. *Alcessimarchus* in Plautus *Cist.*, *Arg.* 11. *bassilica* and *bassim* are attested in inscriptions; the former is also condemned in the *Appendix Probi* (*GL* IV 199.9).
54 Cf. Viscidi 1944: 12–3, Adams 2003: 599–630. The spelling ἄγεςτα for *aggesta* may be due to the spelling conventions of Greek: [gg] would be the sound corresponding to ‹κγ›, but limited to compounds with ἐκ, whereas ‹γγ› would render Latin ‹ng›.
55 Cf. It. ['mɛddzo], ['vɛkkjo] < *MĔDJU, *VĔCLU < *medium, vet(u)lum*.
56 E.g. *TAM* V 916.5 and 1235 C 4, *Afrodisia* 662.
57 The spelling with a single ‹λ› is certainly the most common (it renders Lat. *Manlius* and not *Mallius*). Other names quoted by Dittenberger (1872: 154), Ὀφελίου, Μαρυλίνα, Μαρύλα, Γέλιος, are only rarely attested.
58 Δομίττιος *Thèbes à Syène* 227, Τιττιανός *CIG* 3990i, Phrygia (Eckinger 1892: 96–9).
59 Λούκκιος, several times in inscriptions of the 2ⁿᵈ and 3ʳᵈ centuries AD; cf. also Ϲενεκκας *IG* II² 2120, where [j] is not involved (Eckinger 1892: 102).

Also in this case, Greek spelling is most inconsistent with /ll/ and continuants in general. There are many examples of ⟨λ⟩ for Lat. ⟨ll⟩[60], as well as examples of ⟨λλυ⟩ for prevocalic Lat. ⟨li⟩ (κουρούλλιος in Argos and Sparta, *IG* IV 58 and V,1 533, AD 172–180); variations between ⟨ρ⟩ and ⟨ρρ⟩ are slightly later (2nd/3rd century AD, cf. Eckinger 1892: 108); and some cases, not dated, of ⟨νν⟩ for ⟨ν⟩ many of which trascribe prevocalic Lat. ⟨ni⟩[61].

5 The geminate ⟨ζ⟩

Three glosses involving hidden quantity (cf. chap. IV, § 4.1) deal with a vowel followed by ⟨ζ⟩: they are →μᾶζα (Moer. μ 8), →χαμᾶζε (Ael. D. χ 3), →ἀγοράζειν (Moer. α 139), and possibly →βαδίζειν (Moer. β 15); moreover, *Philet.* 230 →δανείζειν indirectly suggests that ⟨ειζω⟩ and ⟨ιζω⟩ were homophones.

It is difficult to tell whether there is a relation between vowel quantity and the pronunciation of ⟨ζ⟩. The letter must have denoted a geminate /zz/ by the late 4th century BC: the first example of intervocalic ⟨cζ⟩ for ⟨ζ⟩ appears in a decree of 321/0 BC[62] but the data from Attic inscriptions do not point to a specific date for its degemination to /z/[63], nor there is any clear evidence for compensatory lengthening of the vowel preceding it other than the entries quoted above.

There are no other glosses in the lexica dealing with intervocalic ⟨ζ⟩. Some entries – all coming from the lexica of Aelius Dionysius and Pausanias, and all through Eustathius as one of the testimonies (or the only one) – are transmitted with ⟨ζμ⟩ and ⟨ζβ⟩ instead of ⟨cμ⟩ ⟨cβ⟩, but without any mention of different pronunciations or spellings: for this reason they are not included in the second

---

[60] Eckinger 1892: 104–5. In the 5th century AD, the Roman grammarian Consentius would observe that *nam ecce Graeci subtiliter hunc sonum ecferunt. cum enim dicunt: ille mihi dixit, sic sonant duae primae syllabae quasi per unum l sermo iste consistat* (Consent. p. 16.8–10 Niedermann = *GL* Keil 5.394.25–27), cf. also Adams 2003: 433.

[61] [Δο]ννάτ[ου], *IG* XII,5 712.32/8/51/52, cf. Eckinger (1892: 112–3). Cf. also Cεπτούμμιος *IG* V,1 1174, 2nd c. AD (an inscription which is otherwise accurate in representing geminates – could this be an accurate representation in Greek of the Latin development /mj/ > /mmj/?).

[62]]φιcζεν *Hesperia* 6 (1937: 442, n. 1), Threatte 1980: 547.

[63] Allen 1987a: 58–9; cf. the spelling of intervocalic ⟨ζ⟩ as ⟨cζ⟩, Threatte 1980: 547. ⟨ζζ⟩ for ⟨ζ⟩ is a special case. It is extremely likely that the precursor of Mod. Greek /z/ ⟨ζ⟩ was a geminate voiced fricative /zz/: instances of double ⟨ζζ⟩ would then represent a true geminate. Yet ⟨ζζ⟩ replaces ⟨ζ⟩ just as frequently as it happens with other geminate consonants and their singleton counterparts. According to Teodorsson (1977: 252) ⟨ζ⟩ was a simple consonant /z/ already by the mid-3rd century BC; in his view geminates were lost also in the high variety of Attic by the end of the 3rd century BC (Teodorsson 1977: 245).

part of this book. They are ζμῆγμα (Ael. D. ζ 3), ζμικρόν (Ael. D. ζ 4), ζμινύη (Ael. D. ζ 5 and Paus. ζ 4), ζβεννυμενάων αἰγῶν (Paus. ζ 1), ζβέσαι (Paus. ζ 2), ζμῶδιξ, ζμῶξαι (both in Paus. ζ 5).

The voicing of the sibilant is already attested during Hellenism – the interchanges ‹cβ› ~ ‹ζβ› and ‹cμ› ~ ‹ζμ› are found in Attic inscriptions from the mid-4th century BC on (Threatte 1980: 547–9). These spellings were common enough to have gained an exemplary status in ancient Greek grammar: indeed, the interchange between *sigma* and *zeta* in this context is a well known problem of ancient ὀρθογραφία. When Sextus Empiricus discusses the three ways in which ὀρθογραφία is divided (quantity, quality, division), his definition of ποιότηc, quality, is exemplified precisely by this problem:

(32) ποιότητι δέ, ὅταν σκεπτώμεθα πότερον διὰ τοῦ ζ γραπτέον ἐcτὶ τὸ cμιλίον καὶ τὴν Cμύρναν ἢ διὰ τοῦ c.

Quality (ποιότηc), when we consider whether one should write cμιλίον and Cμύρνα with ‹ζ› or ‹c›.

SE *M.* 1.169

More evidence that the problem was one common enough to be turned into satire comes from Lucian: in the *Trial of the Consonants*, a distressed Sigma call the attention of the judges to his own patience:

(33) ὅτι δὲ ἀνεξίκακόν εἰμι γράμμα, μαρτυρεῖτέ μοι καὶ αὐτοὶ μηδέποτε ἐγκαλέcαντι τῷ Ζῆτα cμάραγδον ἀποcπάcαντι καὶ πᾶcαν ἀφελομένῳ Cμύρναν.

And you can witness by yourself that I am a letter that endures evil, as I never summoned for trial Zeta, even though he has dragged off emerald (cμάραγδοc) and took all Smyrna for himself.

Luc. *Iud. voc.* 9

Sextus himself makes fun of the discussion about spellings with *sigma* or *zeta* in his criticism of ὀρθογραφία (*M.* 1.173–5). A pseudo-Herodianic work, ζητούμενα τῶν μερῶν τοῦ λόγου[64], gives the orthographical rule in full:

(34) ζητεῖται, πῶc γραπτέον τὸ Cμύρνα. ἐπειδὴ τινὲc μετὰ το ζ γράφουcι αὐτό. ἕτεροι δὲ μετὰ τοῦ c. διπλοῦν γὰρ ὂν τὸ ζ, οὐκ ἐγχωρεῖ μετὰ τοῦ μ γράφεcθαι, διὰ τὸ μὴ δύναcθαι τρία cύμφωνα ἐν ἀρχῇ τίθεcθαι λέξεωc, εἰ μὴ μετὰ τοῦ ρ, ὃ ἔχει τινὰ οἰκειότητα πρὸc τὰ φωνήεντα.

---

[64] *Excerpta e Herodiano e cod. Paris. gr. 2552*, n. 9 in Dickey 2014, ed. Koch in Pierson – Koch 1830.

It is debated how one should write Cμύρνα. Because some people write it with the *zeta*. Others with the *sigma*. Since *zeta* is a double consonant, it does not allow to be written in combination with the *my*, beacuse it is not possible to have three consonants at the beginning of a words, unless if one of them is a *rho*, which has some similarity with the vowels.

[Hdn.] ζητ. τ. μερῶν p. 415 Koch[65]

This problem of ὀρθογραφία, however, is never addressed in our corpus. The definition of *zeta* as a double consonant serves the purpose of explaining why it cannot form a cluster with another consonant rather than it describes the phonetic that the grapheme ⟨ζ⟩ represents. The very existence of spellings like Ζμύρνα proves that it had lost real status of double consonant, /zd/ or whatever it may have been in the Classical period, and had become a voiced spirant /z/ whose geminate allophone [zz] would be confined to the intervocalic position. Since [zz] lacked a singleton counterpart, the grapheme that spelt it, ⟨ζ⟩ could be used to spell the voiced allophones of /s/, re-analysed as the short, preconsonantal allophones of /zz/.

6 Degemination in the Atticist lexica

There are nine word pairs contrasted because of gemination, and they make up for 16 entries. Table 6 arranges them according to whether the prescribed form has the singleton or the geminate, or the gloss only contrasts two words which differ because of a gemination contrast (two instances, λῆμα and γρυλίζειν); rows are arranged by the phonemes involved.

Table 6

phoneme	singleton	geminate	source
k	σάκος		Ael. D. c 4; Moer. c 32; Phryn. *Ecl.* 225
tt		κυνηγεττεῖν	Phryn. *PS* 84.1–2
r	ἀναριχᾶσθαι		Phryn. *PS* 32.1–4
m	νόμος		*Antiatt.* v 14
m ~ mm	λῆμα ~ λῆμμα		Heren. 109; Heren. *de propr.* 23; Moer. λ 8; *Philet.* 142
n	ἀποκτινύναι		Phryn. *PS* 51.12–13

---

65 Blank 1998: 199 (*ad* SE *M.* 1.169) quotes this passage as *Philetaerus* 415 Koch.

Table 6 *(Continued)*

phoneme	singleton	geminate	source
ll		ἀνίλλειν	Phryn. *Ecl.* 21; *PS* 31.10–12
		κυνοκέφαλλος	Phryn. *PS* 85.5–6
l ~ ll	γρυλίζειν ~	γρυλλίζειν	Phryn. *Ecl.* 72; *PS* 58.14–59.1

The number of examples is probably too low to draw any definite conclusions, but it looks like continuants are better represented than stops, and among them /l/ and /m/ are the most frequent, a distribution that matches well the data of inscriptions and papyri.

However, many of the lemmata showing degemination of a continuant do not prove much as far as the chronology and progress of degemination are concerned. There is no gloss that clearly contrasts a word with a variant which is the outcome of degemination. →κυνηγεττεῖν is an artificial formation created to explain a problem of morphology, and →cάκκος is an ancient variant of cάκος, too early to be the outcome of degemination. →ἀνίλλειν belongs to a group of competing formations, that have /l/ or /ll/ depending on their individual derivation type, →κυνοκέφαλλος hides in its spelling a metrical problem, the variants →νόμος and νούμμος are chronologically distant. The gemination in →ἀποκτινύναι depends on analogy, and →ἀναριχᾶσθαι had an unclear etymology that favoured confusion between ‹ρ› and ‹ρρ›.

Even though the atticist lexica do not provide conclusive evidence on the chronology of degemination, they surely attest to the attention that educated diction paid to the correct distribution of geminate consonants. Three entries, →ἀναριχᾶσθαι, →γρυλλίζειν/γρυλλιcμóc, and →λῆμμα, point clearly to actual uncertainty in the distribution of geminates. Only the first entry discusses variants of the same word, the other two contrast pairs of etymologically different lexical items. In these cases, degemination could have been a factor in blurring the differences between otherwise quite distinct words. The sounds involved are continuants, which show a slightly more marked tendency to simplification than stops, as we have seen above in this chapter. Two words are the object of overt prescriptions – γρυλλίζειν in Phrynichus' *Ecloga* (72), λῆμμα in Lucian's *Soloecista* (5) – and on this ground it is not unreasonable to think that also in Lucian's *Lexiphanes* (8.6) ἀναρριχᾶσθαι was the original reading, and its geminate the object of derision. It is clear from these prescriptions that there were instances in which gemination could be inappropriately used, and therefore that a distinction in speaking was made too (Phrynichus writes 'προφορά', and Lucian is reporting dialogues): note that Moeris explicitly writes that the *Hellenes* made no difference between λῆμα and λῆμμα (ἀδιαφόρως, Moer. λ 8 → λῆμα).

Most of the entries constrast near homophones; sometimes one of them has a much higher frequency (as is the case with λῆμα and λῆμμα), and it cannot be ruled out that the rarity of either term contributed to the confusion, regardless of whether the geminates were preserved. The lexicographers could contrast words basing on gemination, and insist on the correct spelling of the geminates, and the *Soloecista* clearly makes fun of a mistake made in pronunciation; this clearly suggest that the sophisticated speakers would have kept gemination alive in their speech, and that at least for some words there was actual confusion as to whether they had a geminate or a singleton.

VI Conclusions. Traits of atticising pronunciation

Straddling between orthography and orthoepy, the atticist lexica most times support a pronunciation based on spelling and on specific traits of the Attic dialect as preserved in Attica in the 2nd century AD.

The relevance of the Atticist prescriptions on pronunciation is twofold. On the one hand, it is this sort of scholarship that was integrated with orthography and continued in the orthographical tradition of Greek scholarship that survives into the Byzantine period. With a change in function, what was originally composed to prescribe pronunciation lived on as a source of orthographical information.

On the other hand, the lexica were originally composed in a cultural framework, the one outlined by Philostratus and Lucian, in which written texts had quite different orthographical standards form the ones we are used to when it came to accents, breathings and quantity marks, and which had very clear expectations about the pleasantness and accuracy of the pronunciation of individual speakers. Even some prescriptions that are surely orthographic must be opposing pronunciation habits that the learned considered inappropriate, and rejected, as usual, on the basis of the textual tradition of the Attic canon.

Attention to the correct distribution of vowel length is apparent in a great number of glosses. Inscriptions and papyri confirm that this trait was very unevenly preserved in the Greek speaking world, possibly starting already from Hellenism, and yet that Attica had maintained it until the beginning of the 2nd century AD. Attention to the correct distribution of vowel quantities in the lexica must be an attempt to preserve this distinction at a time when it was being lost even in Attica, and it is one of the most salient traits of the orthoepic prescriptions in the atticist lexica. The association of vowel length to specific spellings is also apparent in the glosses contrasting ‹ευ› and ‹υ›, when they equate the long vowel with the digraph and the short with the *dichronon*.

It is a tenable hypothesis that whoever adopted a conservative pronunciation of Attic Greek took literally all indications of spelling and translated them into habits of pronunciation, associating long quantities to all diphthongs and the letters ‹η› ‹ω›. Entries that also involve problems of spelling confirm that most of the changes in timbre leading to the Modern Greek system had taken place by the 2nd century AD, and that they were entirely acceptable even in the most accurate pronunciations. Two of the latest developments in the Greek vowel system, however, the monophthongisation of /oi/ to /y/ and the raising of ‹η› /e:₁/ to /i/, are not reflected in the lexica. The latter is attested consistently enough to support the view that ‹η› corresponded to [e:] in the pronunciation of the educated; the former is never addressed directly, but its presence in substandard pronunciations of Greek may have been the motive behind a very small number of entries dealing with the digraph ‹ου›.

A good number of entries deals with the position of the accent. These glosses either discuss the accentuation of difficult words, sometimes apparently basing on accented manuscripts or identify Attic forms: in particular various instances of non-Koine accentuations due to Vendryes' Law, an accent shift exclusive to Attic. Another group of glosses deals with accent shifts in words ending in -ια: they are probably contrasting an accent shift related to a recent reduction of disyllabic [ia(:)] to [ja(:)].

The pronunciation of the different types of accent is more difficult to infer form the glosses. Whereas there are many prescriptions on the quantity of the *dichrona*, a phonological trait that could be represented with a reading mark in writing, there is no clear indication that a distinction between intonation profiles originally associated with the acute and the circumflex accent were kept distinct in the pronunciation. This is not particularly surprising, given that the distinction between the two types of accent may have been lost particularly early, possibly already during Hellenism.

As we may expect, careful pronunciation of geminates was still associated to their representation in writing. Near homophones could be confused with one another, but the confusion does not seem to be systematic. Degemination and an artificial lengthening of the preceding vowel may explain the entries prescribing the quantities before ‹ζ›.

Hyperatticisms also make up of a small number of entries. More than once the lexica attribute to Attic forms that are never attested in surviving Classical Attic literature. They are particularly interesting in that they clearly appear to single out some phonological traits that must have been commonly perceived as particularly Attic: they all involve initial aspiration or one of the *dichrona*.

The entries that attribute an irrational rough breathing to Attic are only two, and both ascribe the forms with initial aspiration to Attic, Ael. D. α 47, Moer. α 11 →ἄθυρμα, Ael. D. α 81 →ἀλύειν. In neither case there is any evidence that the allegedly Attic forms actually existed, and the prescriptions resonate with the idea that speakers of Attic are fond of initial aspirations (τῇ δασείᾳ προσῳδίᾳ χαίρουσιν οἱ Ἀττικοί, Ael. D. α 98 →ἁμίς). Entries that attribute an irrational long vowel to Attic are five (involving only four lexical items): Philem. 355, Phryn. fr. *151 →ἁλμυρός, Phryn. *PS* 89.6–7 →μανός, Moer. ξ 5 →ξυρόν, Moer. ο 32 →ὄστρια. To these we may add further two entries, that support Attic variants with short vowels, *Antiatt.* μ 37 →μύσταξ (supporting μύστᾰκα, probably a reaction to a hyperattic μύστᾱκα) and Phryn. *PS* 118.3–4 and *Ecl.* 45 →υἱέος, contrasting a genitive υἱέως – in the *Ecloga* Phrynichus even calls ψευδαττικοί those who use the genitive in *omega*. Long vowels stand out as a feature that was easily associated with correct Attic pronunciation.

VII Lemmata and glosses

The entries from the Atticist lexica are lemmatised under the word that the Atticist recommend (in the nominative or infinitive when the inflected form itself is not the object of the prescription). Readers will be able to find all the relevant entries through the indexes at the end of this volume.

ἆ, ἃ ἅ

Ael. D. α 1 ἆ· ψιλούμενον καὶ περισπώμενον ἀντὶ τοῦ αἴθε λαμβάνεται. ⟨Καλλίμαχος (fr. 1.33 Pf.) 'ἃ πάντως ἵνα γῆρας'⟩,
Ael. D. α 2 ἃ ἅ· ἐπὶ τοῦ μεγάλου. ἔcτι δὲ καὶ cχετλιαcτικὸν ἐπιφώνημα. δαcυνθὲν δὲ γέλωτα δηλοῖ.

Although accent and initial aspiration are the topic of both glosses, neither is prescriptive, or marks a variant as Attic. Their value resides mostly in that they contribute to proving that there were indications on such matters in the lexicon of Aelius Dionysius.

Eustathius (1664.3, 1763.61, 855.21) refers to his source as οἱ παλαιοί (whom Erbse identifies with Aelius Dionysius). The lack of lectional signs motivates the description of the accentuation and initial aspiration of these words – neither entry, however, is prescriptive or Atticistic.

ἄγανος

Paus. α 9 (= Phryn. fr. *48 = Σ^b 248 = Phot. α 108) ἄγανον· τὸ κατεαγόc. ἡ πρώτη ὀξεῖα, καὶ τοῦτο τραγικώτερον τὸ ὄνομα.

Ael. D. α 15 (= Phryn. fr. *49 = Σ^b 249, ἀγανόν – βλέπειν = Phot. α 109) ἀγανόν· καλόν, ἡδύ. Ἀριστοφάνης Λυcιcτράτῃ (885–6)
   'ἐμοὶ γὰρ αὕτη καὶ νεωτέρα δοκεῖ
   πολλῷ γεγενῆcθαι καὶ ἀγανώτερον βλέπειν'.
Κρατῖνος Χείρωcιν (fr. 256 K.–A.[1])·
   '⟨ὡc⟩ μακάριοc ἦν ὁ πρὸ τοῦ βίου βροτοῖcιν
   πρὸc τὰ νῦν, ὃν εἶχον ἄνδρεc

---

[1] Text and metre of Cratinus' fragment are uncertain, cf. Kassel – Austin *ad loc.*

ἀγανόφρονες ἡδυλόγῳ σοφίᾳ
†βροτῶν† περισσοκαλλεῖς·
Σοφοκλῆς δὲ Ἐπὶ Ταινάρῳ (fr. 198b Radt) 'ἄγανον' ἔφη 'ξύλον' βαρυτόνως τὸ κατεαγὸς ἢ τὸ ἀπελέκητον.

We read the entry attributed to Aelius Dionysius in the version of the *Synagoge* transmitted in the codex Coislinianus 345, Σ^b, and partially in Photius: the text contrasts two words that can be distinguished only by the position of the accent: without accent marks αγανος would be the spelling for either ἄγανος or ἀγανός. The Atticist character of Ael. D. α 15 is apparent because of the sources quoted, Aristophanes and Cratinus. The wording of Pausianas α 9 strongly suggests that this gloss too derives from the same scholarship on Sophocles[2].

Earlier, non Atticistic scholarship, already discussed the accentuation of ἀγανός. Trypho derives the accentuation from a rule predicting that every adjective with three endings having an ‹α› in the penultimate syllable should be oxytone:

> τὰ εἰς ος τριγενῆ παραλήγοντα τῷ α καὶ ἔχοντα ἐν τῇ τρίτῃ ἀπὸ τέλους συλλαβῇ α ὀξύνεται· μαδαρός, πλαδαρός, ἀγανός· οὕτως οὖν καὶ ἀγαθός.

> The three-ending [adjectives] with an *alpha* in the penultimate [syllable] and an *alpha* in the antepenultimate syllable are oxytones: μαδαρός, πλαδαρός, ἀγανός: so likewise ἀγαθός.

Trypho fr. 16 von Velsen (= *Epimerismi Homerici* α 271 Dyck)

Neither word is very well attested: the only attestation of ἄγανος is the fragment of Sophocles that we know from the lexica, and it must have been a rare word by the lexicographers' time too[3]; also ἀγανός is a poetic word, but of Homeric descent: it is well attested in hexametric poetry, but less common in Attic. The scholia to the *Lysistrata* gloss ἀγανώτερος as ποθεινότερον, πρᾳότερον (sch. vet. *ad Lys.* 886 (R)). However, its presence in Aristophanes and Cratinus must have guaranteed the status of ἀγανός as good Attic in the eyes of Phrynichus[4].

---

[2] The two entries are not surprisingly conflated into a gloss of the synonymic-contrastive kind (cf. Bossi – Tosi 1980) in Eudemus (a source of the *Suda*, date uncertain), cod. Par. 2635 fol. 2b, 14–15 Niese ἄγανον· τὸ κατεαγὸς ξύλον. οἱ δὲ τὸ ἀπελέκητον. ἀγανόν· δὲ ὀξυτόνως τὸ καλὸν ἢ τὸ ἀγαθὸν ἢ τὸ ἱλαρόν.
[3] The nominative dual ‹Ϝαγανω› is attested in a Beotian inscription, the sacred inventory at Thespies, *IThesp* 38 (Taillardat – Roesch 1966: 76), cf. Drew-Bear 1972: 182.
[4] Hom. *Il.* 9.499–501 καὶ μὲν τοὺς θυέεσσι καὶ εὐχωλῇς ἀγανῇσι / λοιβῇ τε κνίσῃ τε παρατρωπῶσ' ἄνθρωποι / λισσόμενοι, ὅτε κέν τις ὑπερβῇ καὶ ἁμάρτῃ, quoted, but with slight variation and atticisation, by Plato (*R.* 364d–e: καὶ τοὺς μὲν θυσίαισι καὶ εὐχωλαῖς ἀγαναῖσιν κτλ.) the sol-

ἄγνοια

Ael. D. α 21 ἄγνοια καὶ ἀναιδεία καὶ πάντα τὰ τοιαῦτα ἐκτείνοντες προφέρονται τὴν τελευταίαν οἱ παλαιοὶ Ἀττικοὶ καὶ παροξύνοντες. Ἀριστοφάνης Δαιταλεῦσιν (fr. 238 K.-A.)· "ὦ παρανοία κἀναιδεία". μεταβάλλουσι δ' οἱ Ἴωνες τὸ τελευταῖον α ‹εἰς η›· "σοὶ γὰρ ἐγὼ καὶ ἔπειτα κατηφείη καὶ ὄνειδος" (Π. 16.498)· καὶ Ἀνακρέων (fr. 29a D.²)· "νεότης τε καὶ ὑγιείη". καὶ ἀναρροίη δὲ καὶ εὐπλοίη καὶ τὰ ὅμοια ἅπαντα παρὰ τοῖς Ἴωσιν ἐκ μακροῦ τοῦ α μετείληπται εἰς τὸ η.

This gloss discusses the long quantity of the final vowel in Attic, and the paroxytone accentuation that it entails. The same problem is discussed in Ael. D. ε 71 εὐκλεία καὶ τὰ ὅμοια· μακρὰ ἡ τελευταία καὶ παροξύνεται, ὥσπερ καὶ Ἐρατοσθένης ἐν ιβ Περὶ ⟨κωμῳδίας⟩ (fr. 47 Str.).

Abstracts in -εία are more common in Attic tragedy[5] (and in Thucydides as far as one can rely on the manuscript tradition: itacistic spellings obliterated the distribution of ‹εια› and ‹ια›). They are paralleled in the gloss by Ionic forms in -ίη (cf. ἀηδίη ~ ἀηδής) – a useful contrast to prove that the Attic *alpha*s are long vowels, in that they are reflected as *eta*s in Ionic[6].

Forms in -ιᾰ are attested in Aristophanes and in the Koine and tended to replace the older abstracts ending in a long vowel[7]. They are likely to have been the ones in actual usage[8]: the scholarship reflected in Hdn. περὶ ὀρθογραφίας (*GG* 3.2 453.4–23) attests to the variation between -ια and -εια: it contrasts the two suffixes basing on their spelling and accentuation, and defines the suffix -ίᾱ as 'ποιητικό(τερο)ν' (*GG* 3.2 453.13 and 20), possibly on the basis of its attestations in Attic theatre.

---

emn quality of the adjective is conspicuous in Aristophanes, *Lys.* 1109: δεινὴν ⟨μαλακήν⟩, ἀγαθὴν φαύλην, cεμνὴν ἀγανήν, πολύπειρον (in a similar context, cεμναὶ δ' αὐλῶν ἀγαναὶ φωναί, μολπά, Mnesimachus, fr. 4 K.–A. = Ath. 9.403d (ἄγαν αἱ mmss.: ἀγαναί Jacobs ap. Schweigh.)). The only other attestation of ἀγανός in Aristophanes is in *V.* 1467.
5 Cf. Kühner – Blass 126, 388; Chantraine 1933: 88, 91, and e.g. S. *Tr.* 350 ἀγνοία μ' ἔχει ||, whose long final vowel is metrically guaranteed.
6 This is a common τροπή, a dialectal transformation in the ancient theory of πάθη (cf. Lentz, *GG* 3.1 xcv).
7 They continue the inherited Indo-European forms in *-eh₂*, ancient collectives, as opposed to feminines in *-ih₂/*-i̯eh₂*.
8 Cassio 1977: 82.

ἀγοράζειν

Moer. α 139 ἀγοράζειν ἐκτείνοντες τὸ δεύτερον α Ἀττικοί· ἐν ἀγορᾷ διατρίβειν Ἕλληνες.

The length of the *alpha* may have been relevant in other stems of the verb, most notably the aorist, where the vowel is in an open syllable and its quantity is relevant for metre and accentuation: ἀγοράcαι is indeed the lemma in the similar entries of the *Philetaerus* (96) (and also *exc. Vind.* 7[9]) and the *Antiatticista* (α 26) – these entries (cf. Valente *ad Antiatt.* α 26) never mention the length of its *alpha*: the gloss in Moeris' lexicon is the only one that does – and without contrasting it with a different pronunciation of the *Hellenes*.

One might imagine that more scrupulous speakers resorted to lengthening the vowel in order to recreate the long quantity of the syllable originally closed by ‹ζ›: but we do know that other people would have just geminated the consonant, if we are to believe the *Soloecista*[10], when it satirises the inappropriate gemination of /m/ to /mm/ in →λῆμα.

ἀγροῖκος

Amm. 6 ἀγροῖκος καὶ ἄγροικος διαφέρει. προπερισπωμένως μὲν ὁ ἐν ἀγρῷ κατοικῶν, προπαροξυτόνως δὲ ὁ σκαιὸς τοὺς τρόπους.

The entry in Ammonius is not prescriptive, as it is normally the case with entries in synonymical lexica. Its interest, however, resides in its similarity with the atticist commentary preserved in P.Oxy. 1012 fr. 16, ll. 1–3 (text (19) above), which dates its doctrine to the 2nd century, and ascribes ἀγροῖκος to the Hellenes. The Attic form must therefore have been ἄγροικος (the relevant portion of the papyrus is missing), which is the form surviving in the text of Aristophanes.

Probert (2004: 287–8) discusses the very similar treatment of ἄχρειος: the proparoxytone, more recent form (it has undergone Vendryes' Law, cf. chap. IV, § 6.2), is identified as Attic. The discussion of ἄχρειος ~ ἀχρεῖος can in fact still be read in the surviving portion of P.Oxy. 1012 fr. 16, and it is coherent

---

9 Criscuolo prints ἀγορᾶcαι (possibly only a misprint?) in the anonymous comic quote a the end of the gloss (fr. com. adesp. 258 K.–A.).
10 Lucian, *Soloecista* 5, see →λῆμα.

with the discussion of ἀγροῖκος: the paroxytone is identified as the Attic form, the properispomenon as the form of the Hellenes.

ἀγυιᾶ

Moer. α 13 ἀγυιᾶ μακρῶς τὴν ἐπὶ τέλους Ἀττικοί· ἀγυιά Ἕλληνες βραχέως.

There are several interpretive problems underlying this gloss, despite its brevity. In the first place, the text of Moeris is uncertain. There is only an explicit reference to vowel quantity, but not to accentuation. The manuscripts have the readings ἄγυια (C) and ἀγυιᾶν (F) (Hansen does not say whether in the lemma or the in gloss). The reading of F is probably only a trivial corruption; but the reading in C resulted in some variation in the text that editors chose to print. Hudson has ἀγυιέᾱ Ἀ. ~ ἀγυιέᾰ Ἕ., Pierson ἀγυιᾶς Ἀ. ~ ἀγυιάς Ἕ..

Both readings imply some intervention on the text of Moeris. The most important bearings on its interpretation is that both end up implying a contrast between the accusatives of ἀγυιεύς (singular or plural, respectively). Hudson's text places the entry in the group of those dealing with the length of ‹α› in the accusative of nouns in -εύς (cf. Moer. α 12 → ἀμφορέα, the gloss immediately preceding this one). Hudson and Pierson are probably right in reading the lemma and its gloss as accusative plurals. The alternative, to read them as nominative singulars of ἀγυιά, is faced with the difficulty of explaining a nominative ἀγυιᾶ.

Ancient scholarship on Attic literature was familiar with the set phrase κνισᾶν ἀγυιάς, in which ἀγυιάς is most times understood as a synonym of ὁδούς, but other times is equated to the Hermae, or statues of gods, or the gods themselves. The *scholia vetera* to Aristophanes *Eq.* 1320 (VEΓΘΜ) also explain ἀγυιάς in the phrase κνισᾶν ἀγυιάς as ἀγυιαίους θεούς, and in the scholia to Lucian the explanation is the even more general (κνισᾶν ἀγυιάς] ἀντὶ τοῦ θύειν (ΒΔ) | θυμιᾶν (ΓV)).

κνισᾶν ἀγυιάς is found in Demosthenes' *Against Meidias* (D. 21.51), and is the object of an entry in Harpocration's lexicon of the ten Attic orators. The explanation in Harpocration recommends the perispomenon ἀγυιᾶς = ἀγυιέας over ἀγυιάς = ὁδούς. If the gloss is related to what we read in Harpocration then the constrast may have been ἀγυιᾶς, acc. pl. of ἀγυιεύς, and ἀγυιάς, acc. pl. of ἄγυια:

χόρους ἱστάναι κατὰ τὰ πάτρια καὶ κνισᾶν ἀγυιας καὶ στεφανηφορεῖν (D. 21.51)· ἔνιοι μὲν ὀξύνουσι θηλυκῶς χρώμενοι, οἷον τὰς ὁδούς· βέλτιον δὲ περισπᾶν ὡς ἀπὸ τοῦ ἀγυιέας. καθὰ καὶ Στειριᾶς καὶ Μηλιᾶς καὶ τὰ παραπλήσια λέγουσιν ἐν συναλοιφῇ. Ἀριστοφάνης

ἐν Ὄρνισι (Av. 1233)· μηλοσφαγεῖν τε [καὶ] βουθύτοις ἐπ' ἐσχάραις κνισᾶν τ' ἀγυιᾶς.
Harp. α 22 Keaney[11]

Humbert – Gernet (1959) print ἀγυιᾶς in D. 21.51 with explicit reference to Harpocration's gloss. They argue that the confusion between the acute and the circumflex depends on ἀγυιάς found in both oracles (the first in hexametres) quoted immediately after the passage in question in the oration. ἀγυιᾶς, accusative plural of ἀγυιεύς, a votive pillar or altar at the entrance a house (πρὸ τῶν θυρῶν)[12], may fit the context just as well as ἀγυιάς (= ὁδούς) as the object of κνισᾶν. The scholia to Demosthenes 21.51 traslate ἀγυιάς as ὁδούς, but mention that for some the term denoted the Hermae[13].

Even the lines of the *Birds* (Ar. *Av.* 1233) that Harpocration quotes in support of his view are not free from ambiguity. In fact, they are only one more occurrence of the same set phrase, κνισᾶν ἀγυιάς, that we find elsewhere. Whether the expected object of κνισάω should be the 'streets' or the 'altars' seems to depend largely on the opinion of the individual scholars or commentators: Harpocration's view for instance is continued in the *Synagoge* and the *Suda*, and found a strong supporter in Photius[14].

It is clear that Harpocration uses the feminine only as a term of comparison, and on the other hand he does not mention the quantity of the final vowel of the feminine: nothing tells us that he regarded this as an exception to the rule that first-declension accusative plurals end in -ᾱς, and that an oxytone ἀγυιά should behave just like μητρυιά, which has an acute and a long vowel in all direct cases of the three numbers.

However, the gloss as it stands in Harpocration and successive scholarship does not mention or involve quantity at all, but only the accent of ἀγυιας, and its interpretation as the accusative plural of ἀγυιεύς or ἀγυιά. It is different form the entry in the lexicon of Moeris, whose whole point is to make a distinction be-

---

11 = Harp. 7.8–9.2 Dindorf (1853).
12 And an epithet of Apollo, cf. Ar. *V.* 875 and *Th.* 489.
13 sch. D. 21 162 (VfTBcFj) Dilts κνισᾶν ἀγυιάς] κνίσης καὶ θυμάτων πληροῦν τὰς ὁδούς, οἱ δὲ ἀγυιάς φασι τοὺς Ἑρμᾶς, 159 [...] κνισᾶν μέντοι τὰς ἀγυιὰς τὸ θύειν τοῖς Ἑρμαῖς. ἀγυιὰς γὰρ τοὺς Ἑρμᾶς (ἐκάλουν) κατὰ στέρησιν διὰ τὸ μὴ χεῖρας ἔχειν μηδὲ πόδας. γυῖα δὲ τὰ μέλη [...].
14 Σ^b 200, *Su.* α 383, Photius α 277 Ἀγυιεύς· ὁ πρὸ τῶν αὐλείων θυρῶν κωνοειδὴς κίων, ἱερὸς Ἀπόλλωνος, καὶ αὐτὸς (ὁ) θεός. [...] καὶ τὸ "κνισᾶν Ἀγυιᾶς" (D. 21.51) τοὺς ἀγυιέας δηλοῖ συνηρημένως, οὐ τὰς ἀγυιὰς καὶ τὰς ὁδούς, and also α 279 Ἀγυιᾶς· ἔνιοι μὲν ὀξύνουσι θηλυκῶς χρώμενοι, οἷον τὰς ὁδούς· βέλτιον δὲ περισπᾶν, ὡς ἀπὸ τοῦ ἀγυιέας. ἀγυιεὺς δέ ἐστι κίων εἰς ὀξὺ λήγων, ὃν ἱστᾶσι πρὸ τῶν θυρῶν. ἰδίους δὲ αὐτούς φασιν εἶναι Ἀπόλλωνος, οἱ δὲ Διονύσου, οἱ δὲ ἀμφοῖν. ἔστιν οὖν τὸ ὁλόκληρον ἀγυιεύς, καὶ κατὰ τὴν αἰτιατικὴν ἀγυιέας, ἐν συναλιφῇ δὲ ἀγυιᾶς.

tween forms with a long and a short vowel. If also the accent were under discussion, Moeris would most likely have mentioned it explicitly (as is the case in Moer. μ 8 μᾶζα, τ 22 τριπλᾶ, τετραπλᾶ, ι 3 ἱερεία, where both quantity and accent are contrasted): only in a minority of instances the nature of the accent is implicit in the specification of the vowel length (e.g. Moer. π 38 →πνῖγος).

It is quite difficult to see ἀγυιᾶ as a perispomenon nominative singular, rather than as an accusative singular with hyphaeresis, like →εὐφυᾶ (Moer. ε 29): feminine oxytona in -ά normally end in [aː], and therefore an oxytone ἀγυιά would be expected to have [aː] and an oxytone accusative plural[15]. A nominative ἀγυιᾶ (similar to contracted nouns like μνᾶ) would be rather exceptional. Virtually no such formation based on ἄγυια is attested elsewhere: only the lexicon ascribed to Zonaras mentions a nominative ἀγυιᾶ[16], a formation that seems more likely to depend on a faulty interpretation of Moeris or a similar lexicon than on the real existence of such a nominative.

The form ἀγυιά attributed to the Ἕλληνες does not have the same accentuation as the Homeric term ἄγυια. The proparoxytone accentuation found in Homer is itself a relic, and it must have been prone to analogical levelling, as it is part of a paradigm including only oxytones and perispomena in the oblique cases of the singular and in most of the plural[17]. In fact, the oxytone feminine ἀγυιά is well attested since at least Xenophon (Cyr. 2.4.3[18]), and it did enjoy some popularity before it became obsolete[19], surviving only as a legal term most often found in the formula 'ἐν ἀγυιᾷ' – employed for the extension of documents by a notary.

Both forms in Moeris are much easier to understand as variants of the accusative plural of ἀγυιεύς. The expected outcome of hyphaeresis is ἀγυιᾶ in any va-

---

15 *Etymologicum Magnum* 14.25, that records first ἄγυια in the number of proparoxytona, and then as 'ἀναλογώτερον' to μητρυιά, which is exceptionally an oxytone, therefore implying ἀγυιά.
16 ἀγυιά. ῥύμη· ἄμφοδος παρὰ τὸ ἄγω τὸ πορεύομαι. τινὲς δὲ περισπῶσι τὸ ἀγυιᾶ ἐπ' εὐθείας (24.6–7 Tittmann); cf. also 20.14–26, where the accusative plural of ἀγυιεύς and of ἀγυιά are explicitly contrasted.
17 Scheller 1951: 134; cf. also Kuryłowicz 1968: 94 (§ 98), who implies a starting form *ἀγυῖα, possibly a non reduplicated perfect participle of ἄγω (Chantraine 1927: 45 and *DELG s.v*). Chantraine's etymology is difficult for the meaning (Szemerényi 1964: 206–9), and rejected by Beekes, who adds ἄγυια to the vast group of Pre-Greek loanwords (*EDG s.v.*). The antiquity of the oxytone accentuation of ἀγυιά is not entirely clear, and modern editions are not consistent in printing one or the other accentuation (Debrunner 1910: 10, cf. Pindar, *O*. 9.34, with ἄγυιαν in Snell-Maehler's text, but printed as oxytone in the scholia – which however do no mention the accentuation, and are therefore inconclusive).
18 Quoted also by Pollux (9.35), with no comment on the accentuation.
19 ἀγυιά/ἄγυια occurs several times in post-Ptolemaic papyri (Palmer 1946: 69; LSJ *s.v.* ἄγυια).

riety of Greek that had ἀγυιέᾰ and not – as Attic did – ἀγυιέᾱ. The contrast between these endings is the object of the gloss immediately preceding this one in Moeris' lexicon. If any value can be attached to the order of the glosses in Moeris (a lexicon which is alphabetised by the first letter only), then we may regard Moer. α 12–13 as a group of glosses dealing with the same problem, i.e. Attic ᾱ in third declension accusatives in -(ε)α (cf. Moer. α 12 → ἀμφορέα). One more gloss in this lexicon apparently deals with the same problem, Moer. ε 29 → εὐφυᾶ. It is interesting that ἀγυιᾶ and εὐφυᾶ survive only in one instance each in the surviving text of Aristophanes and both in the same play (*Th.* 489 and 968[20] respectively); and that moreover, out of the lexicographical and grammatical tradition, the accusative ἀγυιᾶ is attested in this form only at Ar. *Th.* 489: one wonders whether the two entries in Moeris stem from some earlier scholarship on the *Thesmophoriazusae*, now lost[21].

Attic accusatives in -ᾱ of the third declension had caught the eye of the Atticists: the long vowel is genuinely Attic, and it is therefore not surprising that the Atticist identified it as a trait to imitate.

ἀδολέcχηc

Phryn. *PS* 36.5–12 ἀδολεcχεῖν καὶ ἀδολέcχηc cημαίνει μὲν τὸ φιλοcοφεῖν περί τε φύcεωc καὶ ⟨τοῦ⟩ παντὸc διαλεcχαίνοντα. λεcχαίνειν δ' ἐcτὶ τὸ διαλέγεcθαι, καὶ λέcχαι οἱ τόποι, εἰc οὓc cυνιόντεc διημέρευον ⟨διαλογέμενοι⟩. λέγεται δὲ τὸ ἀδολεcχεῖν ἤτοι ἀπὸ τοῦ ἄδην καὶ τοῦ λεcχηνεύειν. ἀλλ' εἰ μὲν ἀπὸ τοῦ ἄδειν, προcγράφου τὸ ι ἐν τῷ ἀδολέcχηc. εἰ δὲ ἀπὸ τοῦ ἀηδοῦc, οὕτωc ⟨ἄνευ τοῦ ι⟩. οἱ γὰρ Ἴωνεc τὴν ἀηδίαν cυναλείφοντεc τριcυλλάβωc γράφουcιν, διὸ καὶ ἐξετάθη.

The prescription in this entry is very much of the orthographic kind, dealing with adscript *iota*. Modern discussions explain the long ⟨α⟩ of ἀδολέcχηc and its derivatives[22] as the result of ἀηδία contracting in ᾱδία[23]. The ancient explanation

---

20 εὐφυᾶ is a conjecture by Brunck, cf. → εὐφυᾶ.
21 The scholia do not address either problem directly: sch. Ar. *Th.* 489 (R) Ἀγυιεὺc οὕτω καλούμενοc Ἀπόλλων τετράγωνοc (it would certainly make clear that ἀγυιᾶ is no form of the feminine ἀγυιά, but does not make this point explicitly, and we cannot assume that it was written for that purpose). The scholion to *Th.* 968 does not mention any form of εὐφυήc.
22 The verb deriving from ἀδολέcχηc, ἀδολεcχέω follows the derivational pattern shared with masculines in -ηc (cf. κυνηγετέω). A back-formation from the verb explains the adjective ἀδόλεcχοc censored by the *Philetaerus* (179).

basing on ἄδην has been abandouned (note also that Phrynichus does not explain the change in breathing, a compound of ἄδην should have a rough one).

ἀδολέςχης and its derivatives are well attested in Attic prose, and in Aristophanes they always have a first long syllable (*Nu.* 1485 and 1480, ἀδολεςχία): the contrast with Ionic serves the purpose of explaining why Attic has a long ‹α›. It is worth noting that Phrynchus' remarks about the spelling with adscript *iota* are a truly orthographic prescription. The *iota* can serve the only purpose of signalling the long vowel, therefore implying that the 'long diphthong' ‹ᾳ›/‹αι› had already merged with [aː]. ἀδολέςχης is a Platonic word, common in prose through Hellenism and well attested in Atticising writers of the 2nd century AD (Dio Chrysostom, Aelius Aristides).

ἀείτης

Paus. α 30 ἀείτην· τὸν ἑταῖρον. Ἀρίςταρχος δὲ τὸν ἐρώμενον.

This gloss is not an orthoepic prescription, it rather belongs to the onomastic type (cf. Bossi – Tosi 1979–1980: 14). Interestingly, it attests a spelling with ‹ει› of a rare word with long [iː]. The word, however, is consistently written with ‹ι› in literary texts. The spelling with ‹ει› must have been acceptable for some in Eustathius' time (ὅτι δὲ ἄΐτης ὁ ἐρώμενος καὶ διὰ διφθόγγου γράφεται, οὐκ ἔςτιν ἀμφιβαλεῖν, Eust. 1574.21).

Theocritus (12.14) writes ἄίτης in a line that does not seem to have variants with the diphthong: the text shows both the spelling and the long quantity, and clearly handles ἄίτης as a rare word. Theocritus also is the only writer who ascribes the word to Thessalian (cf. Gow *ad loc*, and sch. Theoc. *arg. carm.* 12 = Alcman 34 *PMGF*). Elsewhere ἄίτης is found only in Dosiades, *Ara* 5, perhaps in a fragmentary choliamb ascribed to Cercidas (17.27, Powell 1925: 214, and in Lyco-

---

23 In general, modern etymologies do not explain the origin of ἀδολέςχης more convincingly than ancient explanations. Above all, the explanation of the second member of the compound is universally accepted, – (ο)λέςχης, from λέςχη. The two etymologies of ἀδολέςχης mentioned by Chantraine, *DELG*, essentially reproduce Phrynichus' one, the first in that it reconnects ἀδολέςχης to the adverb ἄδην, the other to the root of ἡδύς through a stage ἁϝαδο-, build on the zero ablaut grade plus the privative ἀ-. Chantraine does not mention the contracted form, but contracted forms of the adjective ἀηδής are quoted by Hesychius (α 1103 Latte ἀδής· ἀτερπής, α 1067 Latte, ἀδές ... ἀηδές), and are implied by interpretations as the one that Apollonius Sophista gives *ad* Hom. *Od.* 1 134 δείπνῳ ἀδήςειεν, glossed with ἀηδιςθείη (*Lexicon Homericum* 9.10–11 Bekker), and by Hesychius (α 1105 Latte) with ἀδημονήςειε καὶ ἀηδῶς διατεθείη.

phron (461), with a long first syllable. The *Synagoge* (Σ^b 409) ascribes the interpretation of ἀίτης as ἐρώμενον to an Aristophanes (identified as Aristophanes of Byzantium, fr. 408), not to Aristarchus as Pausanias does[24].

ἄθρους

Ael. D. α 46 ἄθρους· Ἀττικῶς δασύνεται οἷον ** (fr. com. ad. *200 K.–A.)·
  'ἄθρους ἐπελθὼν ὁ στρατηγός ⟨– ⌣ –⟩'
ἤγουν σὺν ὅλῳ τῷ στρατεύματι. καὶ Ἀριστοφάνης (fr. 642 K.–A.)·
  'ἑστῶτας ὥσπερ τοὺς ὀρεωκόμους ἄθρους'.
ὁ δὲ Ἀσκαλωνίτης ἀξιοῖ περισπᾶν ⟨αὐτὸ οὐκ⟩ ἀτόπως, ἐπεὶ ἡ διαίρεσίς ἐστιν ἀθρόος. ἡ δὲ χρῆσις παροξύνει.

While discussing the initial aspiration of ἀθρόος, Eustathius (1387.5) quotes the ῥητορικὰ λεξικά to account for a marginal Attic form of the contract adjective, showing an accent shift, and a change in meaning according to the presence or absence of the initial aspiration, that marks the difference between a privative prefix ἀ- and a sociative ἀ- (πρὸς διάφορον σημασία διαφόρως ἐπνευμάτιζον)[25]. Even though Aelius Dionysius does not discuss forms without the initial aspiration, its presence is associated with Attic; ps.-Arcadius ascribes the rough breathing to Attic[26], and associates a difference in meaning to the different accentuations, possibly reflecting the 2nd century doctrine of Herodian[27]. Moeris attributes the contracted form to Attic (α 33 ἄθρους Ἀττικοί· ἀθρόους Ἕλληνες), but later Atticist lexica present a more blurred picture (Oros B 5 ἀθρόους· καὶ ἄθρους λέγουσι δυσυλλάβως): in both instances the modern editors chose to print the smooth breathing.

In Attic this adjective occurs – in a minority of instances – as a paroxytone, despite originating from the contraction of ἀθρόος. The use of classical and post-

---

24 Cunningham *ad* Σ^b 409.
25 Differences between ἄθροος 'soundless' and ἄθρους 'gathered together' in *Epim. Hom.* α 100 Dyck, possibly datable to the 9th century AD.
26 [Arc.] 223.1–3: πᾶν φωνῆεν πρὸ δασέος καὶ τοῦ ρ ψιλοῦται·
ὀφρῦς ἀφρός ὄφρα. τὸ ἄθρους, ὅτε ἐπιτατικὸν
ἔχει τὸ α, δασύνεται παρὰ Ἀττικοῖς.
27 [Arc.] 46.12–13: τὸ δὲ ἀθρόος παροξύτονον τὸ ἅμα σημαίνει· τὸ δὲ προπαροξύτονον τὸ ἄφωνον. Hdn. Fr. 16 Hunger recommends ἀθρόος, paroxytone and with the initial aspiration (τὸ δὲ ἀθρόος παροξύνειν χρὴ καὶ δασύνειν τὸ α, ὅταν ἔμφασις εἴη τἀληθοῦς, καίπερ ἐναντιωμένων τῶν συμφώνων τῷ δασεῖ κτλ.).

classical authors varies between contracted and non contracted forms, and the contracted forms appear with or without retraction of the accent (on the variation see Kühner – Blass: 402). The *scholia vetera* to Aristophanes *Ach*. 26 (REΓ) signal the form as a proparoxytone with initial aspiration, a synonym of ὁμοῦ (as also reflected in Eust. 251.39); cf. Alpers *ad* Oros B 5 for further examples of ancient scholarship, with divergent opinions on the status of each form of the adjective.

ἄθυρμα

Ael. D. α 47 ἄθυρμα· δασέως Ἀττικοί, ψιλῶς Ἴωνες.
Moer. α 11 ἄθυρμα δασέως Ἀττικοί· ψιλῶς Ἕλληνες.

The word is not attested in literary texts with the rough breathing. The glosses of Aelius Dionysius and Moeris attest to a strand of Atticist scholarship that ascribed it to Attic[28]. They are isolated in 2nd century scholarship. The intrusive aspiration is a possible hyperatticism.

αἱματοπώτης

→ πῶμα

αἴτιαι

Moer. α 6 αἴτιαι ὡς ὅσιαι Ἀττικοὶ βαρυτόνως, αἰτίαι ὡς εὐδίαι Ἕλληνες παροξυτόνως.

As is usual in prescriptions on accents, the position of the accent is made clear by comparison. Moeris' gloss pairs the proparoxytones αἴτιαι and ὅσιαι, and the paroxytones αἰτίαι and εὐδίαι. The behaviour of the accent is independent of the quantity of the final diphthong ‹αι›, that had acquired the accentual properties of a short vowel alredy in prehistoric Greek.

---

[28] The entry could be an alteration of a different prescription, contrasting some doctrine like the one we read in Thom. Mag. 2.10 ἄθυρμα κρεῖττον ἢ παίγνιον. εὕρηται δὲ παρὰ Πλάτωνι καὶ ἀθυρμάτιον (Σακαλῆς 1977: 448–50).

The gloss echoes a Herodianic prescription about the accent of feminine paroxytone nominatives in -αι. We can read it in ps.-Arcadius' epitome of the περὶ καθολικῆς προςῳδίας. The epitome formulates a rule predicting that nominative plurals in αι have the same accentuation as the corresponding masculines, when there are any, and goes on to say that only Attic had some proparoxytone feminine plurals whose accentuation is independent from that of the masculine (in that there is no masculine corresponding form):

αἱ εἰς αι εὐθεῖαι παρεςχηματιςμέναι ἀρςενικοῖς ὁμοτονοῦςι ταῖς εὐθείαις τῶν ἰδίων ἀρςενικῶν· τύπτοντες τύπτουςαι, χαρίεντες χαρίεςςαι, ταχέες ταχεῖαι, εἰ καὶ μὴ τὸν αὐτὸν τόνον· ἐναντίοι ἐναντίαι, Βυζάντιοι Βυζάντιαι, ἥμεροι ἥμεραι (τὸ τριγενές, ἡμέραι δὲ τὸ μονογενές). οἱ δὲ Ἀθηναῖοι (προ)παροξύνουςί τινα μονογενῆ· ἥμεραι εὐπράξαι τιμώριαι αἴτιαι.

The nominatives in αι formed on the masculines have the accent on the same syllable as the corresponding masculines: τύπτοντες τύπτουςαι, χαρίεντες χαρίεςςαι, ταχέες ταχεῖαι, if not even also the same accentuation: ἐναντίοι ἐναντίαι, Βυζάντιοι Βυζάντιαι, ἥμεροι ἥμεραι (the three-ending [adjective], ἡμέραι the single-gendered [noun]). The Athenians have (pro)paroxytone accentuation for some single-gendered [nouns]: ἥμεραι εὐπράξαι τιμώριαι αἴτιαι.

[Arc.] 152.21–153.4

The paroxytones are defined as 'later Attic' and they exemplify a type of accentuation which is not to be followed: cf. e.g. sch. Il. 2.339b (A): ϲυνθεϲίαι τε: οὕτως ϲυνθεϲίαι τε ὡς θυϲίαι τε. ὅϲοι δὲ προπαροξύνουϲι, πταίουϲι· τῆς γὰρ μεταγενεςτέρας Ἀτθίδος ἡ τοιάδε ἀνάγνωϲις (cf. also sch. Il. 5.54 (A)).

Also Choeroboscus openly attributes this doctrine to Herodian[29], and discusses the anomalous nominative plurals that show accent retraction. Like the scholion to Hom. Il. 2.339 (A), he labels them as recent Attic forms (and includes three out of the four examples mentioned in ps.-Arcadius, including αἴτιαι[30]):

οἱ μέντοι Ἀθηναῖοι ἐπὶ ταύτης τῆς λέξεως, καὶ μάλιςτα οἱ νεώτεροι, προπαροξύνουςιν· πέντε γὰρ ἥμεραι καὶ δέκα ἥμεραι φαςὶ προπαροξυτόνως, ὡς ἀπαγγέλλουςιν οἱ περὶ Ἀττικῆς ςυνηθείας γράψαντες· οὐ μόνον δὲ ἐπὶ ταύτης τῆς λέξεως τοῦτο ποιοῦςιν, λέγω δὴ προπαροξύνουςιν, ἀλλὰ καὶ ἐπὶ τῶν παραληγομένων τῷ ι, οἷον εὐπράξαι τιμώριαι αἴτιαι

---

29 Ἰςτέον δὲ ὅτι ὁ Ἡρωδιανὸς ἐν τῇ Καθόλου οὕτω κανονίζει τὰς εἰς τὴν αι δίφθογγον ληγούςας εὐθείας τῶν πληθυντικῶν παρεςχηματιςμένας ἀρςενικοῖς· φηςὶ γὰρ ὅτι αἱ εἰς τὴν αι δίφθογγον λήγουςαι εὐθεῖαι τῶν πληθυντικῶν παρεςχηματιςμέναι ἀρςενικοῖς, ἐὰν μὲν ὦςιν ἀπὸ τῶν εἰς ος, τῷ τόνῳ τοῦ ἀρςενικοῦ ἀκολουθοῦςι, τουτέςτι τῆς εὐθείας τῶν πληθυντικῶν τοῦ ἰδίου ἀρςενικοῦ, οἷον ποικίλοι ποικίλαι, ἐναντίοι ἐναντίαι, ϲοφοί ϲοφαί, καλοί καλαί, λίθινοι λίθιναι, δρύϊνοι δρύϊναι, ἅγιοι ἅγιαι, τίμιοι τίμιαι, ὅςιοι ὅςιαι, Λύκιοι Λύκιαι τὸ τριγενές· Λυκίαι δὲ τὸ μονογενὲς πρὸς τὸ Λυκία· ἐὰν δὲ μὴ ὦςιν ἀπὸ τῶν εἰς ος, τοῖς ἑνικοῖς ἑαυτῶν ἀκολουθοῦςι κατὰ τὸν τόνον, GG 4.2 403.32–404.4.
30 The same forms are also mentioned in sch. E. Or. 261, →ἱερεία.

τραγῴδιαι ὀμίλιαι κωμῴδιαι· οὕτω γὰρ ἐπὶ τῶν μονογενῶν προπαροξυτόνως λέγουσιν οἱ Ἀθηναῖοι.

However, with regard to this word, the Athenians, and especially the younger generation, use proparoxytone accentuation: in fact they say πέντε ἥμεραι and δέκα ἥμεραι, with proparoxytone accentuation, as those who have written about Attic usage declare: and they do not do this only to this word (I mean, they accentuate it as a proparoxytone), but also to those whose penultimate syllable is *i*, like εὐπράξιαι τιμώριαι αἴτιαι τραγῴδιαι ὀμίλιαι κωμῴδιαι: in this way the Athenians speak (λέγουσιν) with proparoxytone accentuation as regards single-gendered [nouns].

Choerob., *GG* 4.2 403.16–23

Herodian may have been Choeroboscus' source for this passage too, and "οἱ περὶ Ἀττικῆς συνηθείας γράψαντες" the Hellenistic scholars whose works Herodian consulted, scholars who may have had some access to different varieties of Attic[31].

The obliteration of the Attic pronunciation may depend on its identification with 'later Attic' (see Probert 2004: 281–3). The accentuation prescribed by this gloss never became usual in the editions of Attic texts: the plural of αἰτία is regularly accented as a paroxytone, αἰτίαι, and only that of the adjective – the feminine counterpart of αἴτιοι – is proparoxytone (the distinction between noun and adjective however is clearly not the problem which is being discussed here).

The gloss as we read it in Moeris sounds like an oversimplification of the problems discussed in earlier scholarship. It belongs to the same branch of the tradition as ps.-Arcadius, that does not mention the distinction between older and recent Attic.

Cf. also Moer. τ 4 →τιμώρια.

αἰώρα

*Ael. D. α 59 αἰώρα· ἀγχόνη· καὶ ἐώρα διὰ τοῦ ε [ὅθεν καὶ μετέωρος]. Σοφοκλῆς (*OT* 1264)· "πλεκταῖς ἐώραις ἐμπεπλεγμένην".

The etymology of αἰώρα is uncertain. The word is usually attested with ‹αυ›[32]. A variant with ‹ε› implies a different scansion of the word, in addition to the reduc-

---

31 Probert (2004: 289), Tryphon according to von Velsen (1853).
32 The etymologies in *DELG* and *EDG* reconstruct an original diphthong. According to Chaintraine αἰώρα derives from a root *ayer-* via the verb αἰωρέω, which belongs with a group of words showing a "redoublement expressif Ϝαι-" (*DELG s.v.* 1 αἱρέω). Beekes (*EDG s.v.* αἰώρα) considers αἰώρα of uncertain etymology, and points out the unlikeliness of a derivation from *$h_2uōr$

tion to a simple vowel of the diphthong /ai/. In fact, the line of the *Oedipus Rex* quoted in the gloss needs to be amended if one wishes to keep the spelling αἰώρα with the regular scansion of the diphthong as a long syllable[33]. The spelling αἰώρα is the only one attested in classical prose (one metrical instance with a long first syllable guaranteed by the metre in *TrGF* II, *Adespota* 705b.6, possibly Hellenistic or later).

The attribution of the gloss to Aelius is dubious. Erbse reconstructed its text basing on the following lines of Eustathius: ὅτι δὲ ἡ ῥηθεῖϲα αἰώρα καὶ διὰ τοῦ ε ψιλοῦ ἔχει τὴν ἄρχουϲαν, ὡϲ δηλοῖ οὐ μόνον τὸ "πλεκταῖϲ ἑώραιϲ ἐμπεπλεγμένην", ἀλλὰ καὶ τὸ μετέωροϲ, ἕτεροι ἐπαγωνιζέϲθωϲαν. ὅτι δὲ καὶ κύριόν ἐϲτιν ὄνομα ἡ Αἰώρα γυναικὸϲ ἀπαγξαμένηϲ καὶ διὰ τί ἀπαγξαμένηϲ, τὸ τοῦ Παυϲανίου δηλοῖ λεξικόν (Eust. 614.24–8). The comparison with Pausanias in the following lines suggests that Aelius is the source of the passage.

It has been argued that Eustathius was in fact claiming here that the spelling with *epsilon* is authoritative, in spite of being otherwise unattested in classical writers. ἑώρα is the spelling found in the earliest manuscript transmitting the *Oedipus Rex*[34]. Chantraine (*DELG*, s.v. 1 ἀείρω) takes the reading ἑώραιϲ of Sophocles *OT* 1264 to reflect an early monophthongised pronunciation [eɔ́ːrais] or [eɔ́ːrɛːs] attesting to the pronunciation [ɛ(ː)] of ‹αι› in the 4th century BC.

A spelling with *epsilon* of the cognate verb αἰωρέω could be the original reading of Sophocles *OC* 1084, if we are right in correcting θεωρήϲαϲα of the manuscripts to ἑωρήϲαϲα with Wunder[35]. The line, in responsion with 1095, needs to begin with a short vowel, which excludes a form αἰωρήϲαϲα pronounced with the initial diphthong [ai] and could point to the introduction of forms beginning with a short [e]: this would be an instance of more recent phonology, implying the reduction of the diphthong to a simple, and short, vowel. However, there is a chance that the forms ἑώρα and ἑωρέω are actually earlier than their counterparts with a diphthong αἰώρα and αἰωρέω: ἑώρα could be a derivative of ἑωρέω, in its turn a present formed on a pluperfect *ἑώρεε < *ēor- < *ā(u̯)or- form the root *h₂u̯er- of αἴρω[36].

---

suggested in *DELG* (which implies three steps, all of them quite unlikely, i.e. the reduplication of *au̯ōr to *au̯au̯ōr, the dissimilation *au̯au̯ōr > *au̯ai̯ōr, and the continuation of prevocalic *au̯ai̯- as simple *ai̯-). It is disputed whether αἰωρέω is a secondary formation form the root *h₂uer- (cf. *LIV*, s.v.) or a deverbative from αἰώρα (*EDG*, s.v., which does not refer to the etymology in *LIV*).
33 Jebb (1893 [2004] *ad loc.*) explains the reading as a corruption of πλεκταῖϲιν αἰώραιϲιν.
34 The cod. Laurentianus XXIII 9, dating form the 9th or 10th century.
35 Wunder 1855; cf. the discussion in Jebb 1900 [2004], *ad loc.*, and Chantraine 1938.
36 *LIV* (s.v. *h₂uer*; Tichy 1983: 365–79): the αι depends on analogy with the present αἴρω.

Is it possible that Sophocles had actually written ἑώραιc with an *epsilon*? If so, he would have been using an archaism: in fact one may wonder whether ἑώρα was not a more common spelling than it appears to be today, if its occurrences that were not protected by metre have been obliterated in later manuscript tradition[37]. The spelling with ‹ε› seems to lie behind Byzantine scholarship on this line of the *Oedipus Rex*. The *scholion vetus* to *OT* 1264, written between the 10th and 14th century[38], reads 'ἑώρα λέγεται κρέμαcιc, ὕψωcιc, μέταρcιc'. The same spelling is to be found in the scholion to the same verse attributed to Maximus Planudes, 'δεδεμένην ἐν κεκλωcμέναιc κρεμάθραιc. ἑώρα διὰ τοῦ ε ψιλοῦ, ὅθεν καὶ μετέωρον' (Longo 1971), which repeats the notions attested in early byzantine lexica: three redactions of this gloss can be traced, and they appear together in the *Synagoge* (Σ ε 1097 ἑώρα, 1098 ἑωρηθήτω, 1099 ἑώρηcιc), with parallels, respectively, in the *Suda* (ε 1894, 1896, 1899), and in Photius (ε 2528, 2529, 2531). All the lexica list the word under the *epsilon*, where one would expect it if their compilers actually had in mind a word beginning with a simple vowel, and not the diphthong.

If ἑώρα and ἑωρέω are archaisms in Sophocles, and if the gloss is authentically Aelius' Dionysius work, the entry does not point to early itacism, i.e. in the 5th century BC, but rather to the fact that in the 2nd century a lexicographer like Aelius felt the need to disambiguate forms that were similar. A likely explanation is that ἑώρα and αἰώρα were homophonous in Aelius' time.

ἄκρατον

Moer. α 8 ἄκρατον βαρυτόνωc (Ἀττικοί)· ἀκρᾶτον περιcπωμένωc (Ἕλληνεc).

This gloss is unparalleled in the lexica, but is found in a longer version in the περὶ cολοικιcμοῦ ascribed to Herodian (310.11–15 Nauck)[39] "ὁμοίωc καὶ περὶ τόνουc βαρβαρίζουcιν οἱ λέγοντεc ἀκρᾶτον προπεριcπωμένωc· δεῖ γὰρ λέγειν ἄκρατόν ἐcτιν. ἡ γὰρ cτέρηcιc προτιθεμένη τῶν διcυλλάβων ὀνομάτων εἰc οc ληγόντων ἀναβιβάζει τὸν τόνον, οἷον ἄκακοc, ἄφθαρτοc· οὐκοῦν ἄκρατοc".

The prefixation with ἀ- could hardly have been a cause of confusion: it is a vital process in Greek, and the derivation should be unproblematic for most

---

[37] Tichy 1983: 356–64.
[38] Papageorgius 1888: v, xi.
[39] *Lexicon Vindobonense*, Nauck 1867 [rist. Hildesheim 1965].

speakers. The derivation of ἄκρατος from κεράννυμι is less straightforward than that of ἄκακος from κακός, yet this cannot be a reason good enough to make the position of the accent on ἄκρατος osbcure. Confusion may have originated with a suffix -ᾶτος, adaptation of Latin -ātus: the suffix is normally found after a fully recognisable stem, and almost always in Latin loanwords[40]. The first point is more problematic, as it implies that ἀκρᾶτος derives from something like a noun ἄκρα, rather than κεράννυμι (note that the verbal adjective *κρατός is not attested); the second, however, suggests that Greek ἄκρατος was borrowed into Latin[41] and re-entered some varieties of Greek with a Latin accentuation – most likely the Greek learnt by speakers whose first language was Latin.

ἀκταινοῦν

Phryn. *PS* 39.12–15 ἀκταινῶσαι ϲημαίνει μὲν τὸ ὑψῶϲαι καὶ ἐπᾶραι καὶ μετεωρίϲαι, εἴρηται δ' ἀπὸ τῆϲ ἀκτῆϲ, τοῦ φυτοῦ, ἀφ' οὗ τὰ ἀκόντια τέμνεται. καὶ ἐπεὶ τὰ ἀκόντια εἰϲ ὕψοϲ αἴρεται ἀφιέμενα, διὰ τοῦτο καὶ ἐπὶ παντὸϲ ὑψουμένου καὶ πηδῶντοϲ ἐτέθη τὸ ἀκταινῶσαι. Αἰϲχύλοϲ (*Eu.* 36) "οὐκ ἔτ' ἀκταίνω" φηϲί, βαρυτόνωϲ, οἷον οὐκ ἔτι ὀρθοῦν δύναμαι ἐμαυτήν. Πλάτων ⟨δὲ⟩ ἐν τῷ Φαίδωνι ὡϲ ἀπὸ περιϲπωμένου.

Since there are no traces of ἀκταινόω in the *Phaedon*, Meineke (and de Borries following him), corrected Phrynichus' text from ἐν τῷ Φαιδῶνι to ἐν τῷ Φάωνι (Plat.Com. fr. 303 K.–A.). However, ἀκταινόω is actually attested in Plato, in the *Laws* (672c, ἀκταινώςῃ), and the passage (and the verb) had drawn the attention of early commentators, as shown by a 2nd century glossary (P. Oxy. 2087, r. 22 "ακταινωϲαι Πλατ(ων) π(ερι) ψυχ(ηϲ) εξαραιωϲαι")[42]. The glossary at least on another occasion (ll. 42–4, *s.v.* αναρριχαϲθαι) quotes exactly the right author in question, but the wrong work. It is likely therefore that this gloss stemmed from the exegesis of Plato the philosopher, rather than the comic playwright (cf. Kassel – Austin *ad* Plat.Com. fr. 303).

The gloss contrasts the original ἀκταίνω and the innovative ἀκταινόω, therefore is mostly an indication of morphology. By contrasting the two accentua-

---

[40] These are the forms listed in Kretschmer–Locker (1944) ἀλυκᾶτος, βουκελλᾶτος, δικελλᾶτος, ἡρᾶτος, κομιτᾶτος, κονταρᾶτος, πιβρᾶτος, πιλλᾶτος, πλουμᾶτος, ῥουϲϲᾶτος, ϲκουτουλᾶτος, ταξᾶτος, τιρωνᾶτος, φάβατος (the accentuation of φάβατος seems suspect to me).
[41] Note that *acratophorum* is attested in Cicero, *Fin.* 3.15, and Varro, *R.* 1.8.5, and *Acratus/Aggratus* is attested as a personal noun several times (cf. *TLL* ss.vv.).
[42] Cf. Kassel – Austin *ad* Plat.Com. fr. 303.

tions, the gloss is actually contrasting two different formations, ἀκταίνω ~ ἀκται-νῶ, as is the case with *Philet.* 209 → ξυρεῖν).

Ἀλαείς

→ ἀλύειν

ἀληθές

Amm. 26 ἀληθὲς καὶ ἄληθες διαφέρει. ἀληθὲς μὲν γὰρ ὀξυτόνως τὸ ἐναντίον τῷ ψεύδει, ἄληθες δὲ προπαροξυτόνως τὸ κατ' ἐπερώτησιν λεγόμενον.

As usual with entries in the synonymic lexicon ascribed to Ammonius, the gloss is not prescriptive. But in the 2nd century AD, the learned commentary preserved in P.Oxy. 1012, fr. 16, ll. 3–14 (text (19), chap. I § 6.2) would contrast ἄληθες and ἀληθές, and define the proparoxytone as Attic, and the oxytone as the form of the *Hellenes*: the recessive accent on 'ἄληθες' 'really!', is a special accentuation that is found only in Attic, when the neuter of the adjective ἀληθής is used adverbially[43]. The doctrine is also attested in Apollonius Dyscolus,

> τὰ εἰς ας λήγοντα ὀξύνονται [...]. οὕτως ἔχει καὶ τὸ ἐντυπάς, ἑκάς, ἀνεκάς (ὅπερ Ἀττικοὶ οὐ δεόντως ἀναβιβάζουσιν, ὡς καὶ ἐν ἑτέροις ἐπιρρήμασι, χάριέν φασι καὶ ἄληθες, καθὼς δείκνυμεν [...]).

> The [adverbs] in *as* are oxytones [...]. This is the case also with ἐντυπάς, ἑκάς, ἀνεκάς (which the Attic writers pronounce retracting the accent, as is the case with other adverbs, and say χάριεν and ἄληθες [...]).
> A. D. *Adv.* [*GG* 2.1.1] 160.19–22

and it survives in later scholarship on Attic playwrights[44], possibly through Herodian, as reflected in the epitome of the by ps.-Arcadius:

> τὰ εἰς ες οὐδέτερα τῶν εἰς ης ὀξυτόνων ὁμοτονοῦσιν αὐτοῖς· εὐσεβής εὐσεβές, ἀληθής ἀληθές (καὶ ἄληθες παρ' Ἀττικοῖς τὸ ἐπίρρημα).

---

[43] Probert 2003: § 242.
[44] Sch. rec. Ar. *Pl.* 123 (123b (V), 123c (MHo), Tzetzae), sch. S. *OT* 350–3 (Thomae), cf. also Hdn. περὶ καθολικῆς προσῳδίας, *GG* 3.1 490.13–17, quoting Ar. *Nu.* 841 and *Ra.* 840.

The neuters in *es* from oxytones in *ēs* have the accent on the same syllables as them: εὐσεβής εὐσεβές, ἀληθής ἀληθές (and ἄληθες the adverb in Attic).

[Arc.] 134.24–6[45]

The adverb ἄληθες, however, does not seem to have survived in Atticist literature[46].

ἁλιέα

→ ἀμφορέα

ἅλις

Philem. 355 ἅλις ψιλοῦται.

The adverb is normally found with an initial aspiration – its absence is unexplained. Interestingly, the D-scholia to the Iliad gloss ἅλις with δαψιλῶς (*ad Il.* 1.137): one may wonder whether this isolated gloss in Philemon is based on some sort of corruption in a source reading αλις ⟨δα⟩ψιλως.

ἁλμυρός

Philem. 355 ἁλμυρὸν τὸ μυ μακρόν.
Phryn. fr. *151 ἁλμυρόν· τὰ πολλὰ ἐκτεταμένως. λέγουσι δὲ καὶ → ἁλυκός. Ἀριστοφάνης Λυσιστράτῃ (403) 'νὴ τὸν Ποσειδῶ τὸν ἁλυκόν, δίκαιά γε'. (Phot. α 1019).

Phrynichus' fragment describes rather than prescribes the pronunciation of ἁλμυρός with a long /y:/. It does not even state explicitly that ἁλμυρόν with a long penultimate syllable belongs to Attic. The iambic trimeter from the *Lysistrata* quoted by Phrynichus (fr. *151) requires ἁλῠκόν with a short penultimate syllable.

---

45 ≈ Hdn. περὶ καθολικῆς προσῳδίας *GG* 3.1 350.7–11, *511.14, περὶ ὀρθογραφίας *GG* 3.2 447.6.
46 Modern editions only preserve this accentuation in the text of some Christian authors, e.g. [Didymus Caecus, 3rd c. AD] *De Trinitate*, *PG* 39 868.53, Theodoretus [?, 4th/5th century AD], *Quaestiones et resp. ad orthodoxos* 7.26 Papadopoulos-Kerameus, etc.

The only occurrence of ἁλμυρός in surviving plays of Aristophanes is *Nu.* 567, where ἁλμυρᾶς is in responsion with ᾧ κόραι (l. 599): the second syllable in both cases realises an *anceps*[47]. However, Phrynichus may not have had this line of Aristophanes in mind when commenting on the vowel quantity of ἁλμυρός. At the end of another iambic trimeter, possibly spurious ([Ar.] fr. *131 K.–A.; *An. B.* 383 ἁλμυρίδες) εἰς Ἁλμυρίδας rests on a derivative Ἁλμῡρίς with long ῡ. Yet a gloss resting on that specific passage would quote Ἁλμῡρίς, not ἁλμυρός.

It is not very likely that ἁλμυρός had an inherited long vowel: both ἁλμυρός and ἁλυκός rest on the theme ἁλυ-[48] of a derivative of ἅλς, possibly *ἁλυρός[49], with a suffixal vowel is which is normally short. Only two adjectives in -ῡρο- are known, ἰσχυρός and ὀϊζυρός – and there are forms with ῠ of both – and the neuter nouns λάφῡρα, λέπῡρον, πίτῡρα[50]. In some instances the long vowel may depend on a denominative verb in -ῡρω < -υριω[51]. Bader (1974: 85–7) does not mark as short the ⟨υ⟩ of ἁλμυρός. The quantity of ⟨υ⟩ is variable in πλημῡρίς/πλημῠρίς, 'rise of the sea'[52]: the word is normally scanned πλημῡρίς in tragedy (LSJ s.v.), and it could have been the model for Ἁλμῡρίδας in [Ar.] fr. *131 K.–A.

If we have to trust the gloss in Philemon as we read it, it is probably generalising the long scansion of a *dichronon*, and therefore hyperatticising (cf. chap. IV, § 5).

---

[47] If the verse is cho + ia (Prato 1962: 76–7; Parker 1997: 194–6), then scansion as an 'aeolic dimeter' (Domingo 1975: 118) would call for a short syllable, ἁλμυρᾶς. Aristophanes however uses a similar the scheme [–⏑⏑–⏑–⏑–] in lyrical parts of the *Knights* (*Eq.* 551 ff., in responsion with ll. 581 ff.) and of the *Wasps* (*V.* 526 ff., in responsion with ll. 631 ff.), and in neither play the responsion is regular: Ar. *V.* 527 [–⏑⏑–⏑–⏑–] is in responsion with *V.* 632 [–⏑⏑––⏑⏑–], and – more remarkably – *Eq.* 552 [–⏑⏑–⏑–⏑–] is in responsion with *Eq.* 582 [–⏑⏑–––⏑–]. The metrical scheme in these choruses of the *Knights* and of the *Wasps* cannot therefore be an Aeolic dimeter: the syllables following the initial choriamb are treated exactly as a iambic *metron*, realised as a choriamb in *V.* 632 and with a long syllable as the first element in *Eq.* 582.
[48] "dont l'υ est obscur" Chantraine (*DELG* s.v. ἅλς).
[49] Schwyzer 1939: 482; de Lamberterie 1990: 595.
[50] Schwyzer 1939: 482 – according to Chantraine (1933: 233) the long vowels derives from themes in ῡ, from which the suffix -ῡρο- was created.
[51] On the quantity of -υ- in -υ-ρός see Schwyzer 1939: 482 fn. 11.
[52] Bader (1974: 86), Chantraine (1933: 97) πλημμυρίς – spelling of the manuscripts, cf. LSJ s.v. πλημυρίς.

ἀλοᾶν

Phryn. *PS* 25.10–11 ἀπαλοᾶν· διὰ τοῦ π γράφοντες οἱ Ἀττικοὶ δῆλον ποιοῦσιν, ὅτι καὶ τὴν ἅλω καὶ τὸ ἀλοᾶν ψιλοῦσιν. καὶ ἀλοάσουσι δὲ διὰ τοῦ α, ἀλλ' οὐχὶ διὰ τοῦ η. σημαίνει δὲ τὸ ἀλοᾶν καὶ τὸ ἐπιτρίβειν τύπτοντα· ἔνθεν καὶ πατραλοίας καὶ μητραλοίας, ὁ τὸν πατέρα καὶ τὴν μητέρα ἀλοῶν, ὅ ἐστι τύπτων καὶ ἐπιτρίβων.

Forms of this verb with a rough breathing are not attested elsewhere. The compound ἀπαλοάω is in Demosthenes (ἀπηλοημένος, 42.6). The cognate ἅλως, however, is transmitted with a rough breathing (*AP* 6.258, Galen 5.640, ἐφ' ἅλ-, and through Latin it survives as *halo* in English). The absence of initial aspiration is supported, as usual, by compound forms that do not turn a simple stop into its aspirate counterpart.

Phrynichus is also prescribing a form of the future stem that must have been marginal in Attic literature. The LSJ does not record it (but lists a number of futures in -η): the future stems in ἀλοη- (both active and passive), which Phrynichus rejects, must have been common only from the Hellenistic period on and are in fact the ones found in the LXX (*Is.* 41.15.2, *Je.* 5.17.5, *Jd.* 8.7.2). A reaction against the usage of Hellenistic and Christian authors may explain why Phrynichus prescribed a future ἀλοάσουσι.

The prescription is unparalleled. It is not clear why Phrynichus wanted to specify that the verb has a smooth breathing. Later scholarship, as seen in ps.-Arcadius' epitome of Herodian, expected vowels preceding a *lambda* to have a smooth breathing, and ἀλοάω would be no exception to the rule[53]. Phrynichus seems to follow this idea. The contrast with the aspirated form in Amm. 27 (ἀλοᾶν ~ ἀλοιᾶν) is an artificial distinction based on the attribution of initial aspiration.

ἀλύειν

Ael. D. α 81 ἀλύειν· ἔνιοι τὸ μὲν ἐπαίρεσθαι δασέως ἀξιοῦσι προφέρεσθαι οἷον (Hom. *Od.* 18.333)·

'ἦ ἀλύεις ὅτι Ἶρον ἐνίκησας;'
τὸ δὲ λυπεῖσθαι ψιλῶς (Hom. *Il.* 5.352)·
'ὣς ἔφαθ', ἡ δ' ἀλύουσ' ἀπεβήσατο'.

---

[53] [Arc.] 224.4–6: τὸ α πρὸ τοῦ λ ἑνὸς ἢ διςςοῦ ψιλοῦται, οἷον· ἄλλως. ὁμοίως καὶ τὸ ι· ἴλλειν, καὶ τὸ ω· ὤλλος. ςεςημείωται τὸ Ἕλλην Ἑλλάς.

Δίδυμος δὲ ἀμφότερα ψιλῶς· τὸ μὲν γὰρ ἀπὸ τοῦ ἀλεαίνεσθαί φησι, τὸ δὲ ἀπὸ τῆς ἄλης. Ἀττικώτερον δὲ τὸ ἀμφότερα δασέως· καὶ γὰρ τὸ ἀλεαίνεσθαι δασύνουσιν οἱ Ἀττικοὶ καὶ πάντα τὰ τοιαῦτα· ἀμίς ἄμαξα ἀμνός Ἀλαεῖς ἀνύειν ἀμῶς.

cf. also →ἀμίς, →ἀνύειν.

The scholarship reflected in Aelius' gloss accounts for the initial aspiration of ἀλύειν basing on its meaning (whether the verb is a synonym of ἐπαίρεσθαι or λυπεῖσθαι), a distinction that must have been controversial, as the second part of the gloss suggests: Aelius reports that according to Didymus neither form had an initial aspirate[54].

The gloss does not account for the aspiration of ἀλύειν in Attic on etymological grounds. The use of Ἀττικώτερον is similar to statements like the one in Apollonius Dyscolus on πρωπέρυςι and πόρρω (GG 2.1.1 166.24–6, cf. Phryn. PS 105.9–10 →πρωπέρυςι, and chap. IV, § 5). The gloss may reflect an hyperatticism, consisting in the extension of the aspiration to a word that originally did not have any. Cf. also Ael. D. α 98 →ἀμίς.

ἀλυκός

Moer. α 65 ἀλυκόν Ἀττικοί, ὡς Ἀριστοφάνης Λυςιςτράτῃ (403), ἀλικόν κοινόν.

The variance between ἀλυκός and ἀλικός does not suffice to prove their homophony. ἀλικός is a marginal form in classical Attic. ἀλυκός, the common spelling in Attic, has a -υ- very likely to have been introduced[55] by influence of other corradical formations (perhaps *ἀλυρός, cf. Phryn. fr. *151, Philem. 355 →ἀλμυρός). ἀλυκός and ἀλικός coexist in Roman papyri (Gignac 1976: 269), but ἀλικός is prevalent during Hellenism (Mayser – Schmoll 1970: 82, Lobeck 1820: 210). The spread of ἀλικός cannot prove in itself that ‹υ› was pronounced [i]. The gloss in Moeris aims at preserving a form that was increasingly rare after Hellenism, and a less obvious choice given the very high frequency of adjectives in -ικός.

ἄλυςις

Philem. 355 ἄλυςις Ἀττικοὶ ψιλοῦςιν.

---

54 The full quotation of Didymus is supplied on the basis of Photius α 1030 and Su. α 1428.
55 Lobeck 1820: 210.

With the exception of this gloss, a psilotic form ἅλυcιc is unexplained, unattested, and its prescription unparalleled in other ancient grammatical tradition. In fact, there is evidence for a prescription in the opposite sense: ps.-Arcadius[56] lists ἅλυcιc among the exceptions to the rule that prescribes the smooth breathing for all the words beginning with a privative *alpha*; following a folk etymology, ἅλυcιc, 'chain' would be a derivative of λύω. The origins of the initial aspiration in ἅλυcιc are not clear. If the word is a derivative of *u̯el-, i. e. a cognate of εἰλύω, it may owe its unexpected aspiration to a special evolution of inital *u̯-, possibly a confusion with initial *su̯-.[57]

ἅμαξα

→ ἀμίc

ἀμίc

Ael. D. α 98 ἀμίδα· δαcέωc. Εὔπολιc Αὐτολύκῳ (fr. 52 K.–A.)·
 'τί δῆτ' ἄν, εἰ μὴ τὴν ἀμίδα καθεῦδ' ἔχων',
καὶ ὁ Ἀριcτοφάνηc (fr. 653 K.–A.)·
 'κατεcκέδαcέ μου τὴν ἀμίδα κεχηνότοc'.
λέγουcι δὲ καὶ ἅμαξαν δαcέωc καὶ καθημαξευμένα καὶ ὅλωc τῇ δαcείᾳ προcῳδίᾳ χαίρουcιν οἱ Ἀττικοί. καὶ παρὰ Μενάνδρῳ [ὡc] λέγεται ἐν τῷ ⟨Νομο⟩θέτῃ (fr. 252 K.–A.) διὰ τοῦ θ ἡ cυναλοιφὴ αὕτη·
  'ἑκκαίδεκα
 κεῖνθ' ἀμίδεc.'
καὶ τὸ ἀμάξιον οὕτω λέγουcι θἀμάξιον, καὶ
  '⟨οὐκ⟩ ἀναβεβήκει πώποτε
 ἐφ' ἅμαξαν, ἀλλ' ἐφ' ἵππον.'
Νικόcτρατοc ἐν Παρακολυμβώcῃ (fr. 21 K.–A.).
Moer. α 10 ἅμαξαν δαcέωc ⟨Ἀττικοί⟩· ἅμαξαν ψιλῶc ⟨Ἕλληνεc⟩.
cf. also → ἀλύειν

---

56 [Arc.] 223.9–10 = Hdn. *GG* 3.1 539.13–14.
57 cf. *DELG* s.v. ἕλιξ. *EDG* too derives ἅλυcιc from *u̯el-, and similarly to *DELG* refers to ἕλιξ for its initial aspiration, which, differently form *DELG*, is considered to be a Pre-Greek loanword.

Eustathius (1387.9) quotes Aelius Dionysius (the source of the gloss is Photius, α 1197) in a context where the initial aspiration of the words under discussion is proved through comparison with derivatives showing an aspirated consonant as the result of composition or crasis – cυναλοιφή in the common terminology (ἄμαξα > καθημαξευμένα, τὸ ἀμάξιον > θἀμάξιον, a similar procedure in Paus. α 154 → ἄρκυες). This is a very convenient way of proving the presence of an initial aspiration even in the absence of a breathing mark[58]. The gloss of Aelius Dionysius contains a general statement about the fondness of the Attic speakers for initial aspiration. Whether these were Aelius' original words is hard to say (we could be reading Photius or Eustathius); the underlying assumption is anyway very close to the similar statements that Apollonius Dyscolus made about the fondness of Attic speakers for long vowels (cf. chap. IV, § 5), and it is confirmed by the overwhelming number of glosses prescribing as Attic the variants with initial aspiration (cf. chap. IV, § 7.2).

Cf. also Ael. D. α 157, Phryn. fr. *249 → ἀντήλιος.

ἀμνός

→ ἀλύειν

ἀμπίcχες, ἀμπίcχου

→ ἄπεφθος

ἀμφορέα

Moer. α 12 ἀμφορέα ἁλιέα μακρῶc Ἀττικοί· βραχέωc Ἕλληνες.
Moer. ι 4 ἱππέα ἁλιέα βασιλέα μακρῶc Ἀττικοί.
Moer. ι 18 ἱππέας μακρῶc Ἀττικοί· βραχέωc Ἕλληνες.
Philem. 355 Ἀτρέα, ὡς βασιλέα, τὸ α μακρόν.

The declension of nouns in -ευc is an important trait distinguishing Ionic-Attic from other Greek dialects. Only in Ionic-Attic the genitives and accusatives of

---

[58] On the inclusion of Menander in Aelius Dionysius' canon of Attic authors see Tribulato 2014, esp. p. 205 on Ael. D. α 98.

this paradigm have undergone synizesis[59], with the consequential lengthening of the desinential vowel.

In all Greek dialects but Ionic-Attic, substantives in -εύc would have a sequence of two short vowels in the genitives and accusatives of the singular – the kind gen. βαcιλέοc, acc. βαcιλέᾰ[60]. This sort of declension (which will eventually become common in Ionic too, Schwzyer 1939: 246) had been employed also in literary dialects and expanded into Attic literature as well. The endings -έᾱ and -έᾱc are common in the choral sections of Attic drama, which on the contrary tends to employ -έᾱ and -έᾱc in dialogue, scanned [⏑ –] or [–], with synizesis[61].

The accusatives -έᾱ -έᾱc were ascribed to Attic already in early scholarship, precisely because of the quantity of their final vowels, implying a ὑπερβιβαcμόc τοῦ χρόνου (a definition of synizesis similar to 'quantitative metathesis')[62]. No mention of quantity distribution is found in early scholarship on the genitives, possibly because their spelling (with ‹o› or ‹ω›) was unambiguous. In the terminology of the lexicographers the Attic genitive βαcιλέωc is different from Doric βαcιλέοc because one should be 'written with an ω' and the other 'with an o', not because one has a long vowel and the other a short one; the problem is discussed in Phryn. *PS* 118.3–4; *Ecl.* 45 →υἱέωc, a gloss that opposes two spellings by using the verb προφέρειν.

---

59 Schwyzer (1939: 245–6) and more in detail Méndez Dosuna 1993, who also defines the connection between the realisation as a glide of ‹υ› in nouns ending in -αιεύc and the preference for 'contract' endings -αιῶc -αιᾱ of the gen. and acc. singular. The seeming 'contraction' in all the forms like the genitive ἁλιῶc and the accusative ἁλιᾱ (form ἁλιεύc) is actually only the merger of the glide with the preceding [i], i.e. [halijâ:] vs [basilęâ:]. Inscriptions do write the ‹ε› after a consonant, but would show the 'contract' endings after ‹υ› (Threatte 1996: 233, 248). The chronological distribution of such spellings shows clearly that the tendency to contraction was exclusive to 5th / 4th century Attic, since after 300 BC inscriptions in and outside Attica show only the uncontracted, full spellings, the same that would be continued in the Koine.
60 Buck 1955: § 111.
61 La Roche 1897: 2. The metrical usage of both Attic accusatives in -έᾱ and non-Attic accusatives in -έᾱ is clearly only literary, and is quite artificial. The very concept of 'quantitative methatesis' relies on the artificial restitution of syllabicity to the glide (spelt ‹ε›) in the outcomes of synizesis -εωc and -εα (Cassio 1997: 194 fn. 18). In many of the instances collected by La Roche (1897) the ending -εα of the accusative singular can be scanned as a single long syllable, precisely in all the instances where La Roche (1897: 3–4) assumes that the scansion εᾱ is a soluted *longum* (e.g. S. *Aj.* 1293; E. *IA* 1341 (trim. troch.), etc. – cf. Baechle 2007: 110–1).
62 Cf. *EM* 190.6 and Choerob. *GG* 4.1 216.8–13 (= Hdn. *GG* 3.2 676.8–14), quoting E. *Andr.* 545, καὶ μὴν δέδορκα τόνδε Πήλεα πέλαc, where Πήλεα needs to scan [–⏑–]; cf. also Choerob. *GG* 4.1 252.10–30 (= Hdn. *GG* 3.2 625.14–34) on the 'ὑπερβιβαcμόc τοῦ χρόνου'.

The only plural is commented by Moeris (ι 18 ἱππέας). The theorerical framework is not different form the one used for the singulars. The gloss quotes the accusative plural in its usual classical Attic form, but does not mention the forms that were usual (in Attic and in the Koine) since the end of the 4th century BC ἱππῆς or ἱππεῖς[63]: it even ascribes to the Ἕλληνες a form ἱππέᾰς that must have been marginal in the Koine[64].

Moeris' prescription must have been directed to phonology rather than morphology. The question that these entries seek to answer is clearly how to pronounce an accusative in -εα(ς), rather than how to form one: for the plural at least, the obvious answer would be that Attic uses forms in -ης/-εις, but it was not that obvious what quantity should correspond to the *dichronon* of an accusative in -εα(ς).

ἀμῶς

→ ἀλύειν

ἀνάθημα

Moer. α 57 ἀνάθημα Ἀττικοί· ἀνάθεμα Ἕλληνες.
Philem. 354 ἀνάθημα· οὐκ ἀνάθεμα.
Heren. 6 ἀνάθημα ἀναθέματος διαφέρει. ἀνάθημα μὲν γάρ ἐστι, τὸ διὰ τοῦ η γραφόμενον, τὸ ἀνιερούμενόν τε καὶ ἀνατιθέμενον ‹ἐν› ἱερῷ τινι τόπῳ· ἀνάθεμα δέ, διὰ τοῦ ε ἐκφερόμενον, τὸ ὕβρεως ἐχόμενον καὶ ἀναθεματισμοῦ.
Moer. c 21 σύνθημα μετὰ τοῦ η Ἀττικοί· μετὰ δὲ τοῦ ε Ἕλληνες.
Phryn. *Ecl.* 420 εὕρημα χρὴ λέγειν διὰ τοῦ η, οὐχ εὕρεμα.
Philem. 393.22 R. εὑρέματα οὐκ εὕρηται.

The most likely reason for the variation is analogical levelling in the paradigm, in the case of roots whose paradigms could present either vowel, long or short[65]. The starting point are abstract nouns in -μα and -σις: during the Hellenistic pe-

---

63 On plurals in η/ει see Schwyzer 1939: 575, Threatte 1996: 247–8.
64 Mayser 1938: 29–30.
65 Mayser–Schmoll 1970: 48.

riod the two formations often became interchangeable⁶⁶, and often without rearranging the ablaut of the preceding stem, that would normally require the full grade before -μα, but not before -cιc. Therefore ἀνταπόδομα could be created basing on the short vowel of δόcιc δοτήρ δοτόc, θέμα was given the same vowel as θέcιc θετόc, and so on⁶⁷.

Moeris is right in stating that cύνθημα is the form of classical Attic (cf. e.g. ξύνθημα, Thuc. 4.112.1). cύνθεμα is attested for the first time in the scientific prose of the 3rd century BC (Philo Mechanicus, *Parasceuastica* 90.45, Bolus [Ps.-Democr.] *Physica et mystica* 2.49.6). The LXX has cύνθημα (*Jd*.(A) 12.6; 2 *Ma*. 8.23; 13.15) but also πρόcθεμα, ἔνθεμα, ἀφαίρεμα. Forms with a short vowel are habitual in the imperial period – cf. Apollodorus of Damascus, the mathematician Diophantus 3rd century AD) and Gregorius of Nazianzus (*PG* 37 col. 508.5 cύνθεμα cὸν νοέοντα λαλεῖ cιγώμενον ὕμνον, perhaps spurious). A similar levelling between nouns in -μα and nouns in -cιc explains the origin of εὕρεμα, a late but current form⁶⁸. Manuscripts tend to alternate between the two spellings⁶⁹.

ἀνάθεμα and ἄνθεμα (< ἀν(α)τίθημι) are the earliest attested derivatives in -εμα. In general, the first attestations of nouns in -μα with a short presuffixal vowel all seem to belong to Doric⁷⁰. ἄνθεμα for instance is attested in Epidauros, 4th century BC (*IG* IV²,1 121, ll. 7 and 59), Callimachus (*Ep*. 5.2), Theocritus (*Ep*. 13.2)⁷¹. Christian authors make a distinction between ἀνάθημα, 'votive offer', and ἀνάθεμα 'malediction'; the distinction is made already in the synonymical lexicon of Herennius (Heren. 6⁷²).

Paradigm levelling plays too big a role here to enable a reading of these glosses in pure phonetic terms, i.e. as evidence that the distinction between forms in -εμα and forms in -ημα was realised by contrasting /e/ and /eː/. None of the surviving entries employs any terminology that clearly refers to pronunciation (either vowel timbre or quantity): the only – partial – exception is the

---

66 Glaser 1894: 52, Schwyzer 1898: 48 and 1939: 523, Specht 1932: 50. θέμα and its compounds are overall more frequent that other nouns in -εμα replacing older -ημα (cf. Crönert 1903: 284–5, Mayser 1936: 54–61).
67 Blass – Debrunner – Funk 1961: § 109.3. On ἀνάcτεμα and διάcτεμα see Buresch 1892: 91–3, Schwyzer 1898: 49.
68 Lobeck 1820: 249, 445, Fraenkel 1910: 187 fn. 1.
69 Specht 1932: 50.
70 Specht 1932: 50–1.
71 Schmitt 1970: 101 fn. 7.
72 = Amm. *suppl*. 5, p. 156 Nickau; cf. also *Su*. α 1869, α 1878, Phot. α 1477.

lexicon of Herennius, opposing ἀνάθημα ... διὰ τοῦ η γραφόμενον ~ ἀνάθεμα ... διὰ τοῦ ε ἐκφερόμενον: ἐκφέρω however is not a technical term for pronunciation[73].

ἄναντεc

→ κάταντεc

ἀναπηρία

Phryn. *PS* 13.4–6 ἀναπηρία· διὰ τοῦ η τὴν τρίτην, οὐ διὰ τῆc ει διφθόγγου, ὡc οἱ ἀμαθεῖc, τὸ μὲν οὖν ἀνάπηροc καθωμίληται, τὸ ‹δ'› ἀναπηρία cπάνιον.
Antiatt. α 28 ἀναπειρίαν· Ἀριcτοφάνηc Πλούτῳ.

Although based on the rather common adjective ἀνάπηροc, the abstract noun ἀναπηρία is not well attested in surviving classical Attic literature. ἀναπηρία is used by Aristotle, but occurrences of ἀναπηρία in earlier Attic literature are based on later lexica only. The glosses on ἀναπηρία possibly stem from one single passage in Cratinus' *Pluti* (Pollux, *Onomasticon* 2.61 = Cratinus fr. 179 K.–A.) or Aristophanes (*Antiatt.* α 28 and *Suda* α 2014 = Ar. fr. 460 K.–A.).

The uncertainty between ἀναπηρία and ἀναπειρία allows for two interpretations: that Phrynichus' aim was to rebuke the pronunciation of the less educated speakers, whose idiolect had already merged ‹ει› and ‹η› into [i(:)], or to reject a more recent analogical formation ἀναπειρία (perhaps based on πείρα?). The latter is probably the most likely scenario: πηρός 'maimed', does not have a wide constellation of derivatives, and in Phyrnichus' perception ἀναπηρία too was an obscure word: the tiny group of words related to its root would be particularly reliable to paraetymology. ἀνάπηροc is commonly spelt ἀνάπειροc in the manuscripts (LSJ *s.v.* ἀνάπηροc).

Moreover, the contrast between ‹η› and [i(:)] sounds is not clearly represented in the lexica: in the 2nd century AD ‹ει› must certainly have represented a vowel [i(:)], whereas ‹η› had retained an [e] quality at least in the most educated varieties of the language (cf. chap. II, § 2.3.2).

---

[73] Cf. the opposition between ἐκφέρω and προφέρω in Amm. 293 λαλεῖν μὲν γάρ ἐcτι τὸ ἀτάκτωc ἐκφέρειν τὰ ὑποπίπτοντα ῥήματα, λέγειν δὲ τὸ τεταγμένωc προφέρεcθαι τὸν λόγον, διαλέγεcθαι δὲ τὸ ἀμείβεcθαι καὶ λόγον ἀντὶ λόγου ἀποδοῦναι πρὸc τὸν διαλεγόμενον κτλ.

ἀνάπλεως

Moer. α 67 ἀνάπλεων ⟨Ἀττικοί⟩· ἀνάπλεον (Ἕλληνες).
Ael. D. α 151 ἀξιόχρεων· ἐν τῷ ω λέγουςι καὶ λιπόνεων καὶ τὰ οὐδέτερα. οἱ γὰρ παλαιοὶ ὁμοίως. τὸ δὲ ἀξιόχρεον βάρβαρον.

The short ending is ancient in Ionic, and even if it implies a patent change of declension[74], analogical levelling explains it without difficulty (Schwyzer 1939: 246, 557–8). In the manuscripts, forms with synizesis (πλεῖος > πλέος > πλέως) are found even in authors who otherwise would not use 'Attic declension'.

In this gloss, Moeris is not necessarily pointing out that ⟨ο⟩ and ⟨ω⟩ have the same pronunciation. Rather than prescribing a pronunciation he is prescribing a declension pattern, trying to counteract the reduction of the Attic declension to the more common second declension pattern in -ος. The elimination of the Attic declension is habitual in the Koine, either as a continuation of non-Attic (Ionic?) forms or as the result of an internal process of regolarisation.

Forms with the long vowel were clearly identified as Attic, a doctrine that survived in the later grammatical tradition about this word: the *Etymologicum Magnum* quotes Choeroboscus, making a distinction between ἀνάπλεως, ἀξιόχρεως and neuters in -ον, precisely in that the former display 'Attic lengthening' (one of the πάθη according to his own phrasing): "τὸ ἀνάπλεων καὶ ἀξιόχρεων τῇ Ἀττικῇ ἐκτάσει ἔπαθον, ἀπὸ τοῦ ἀξιόχρεων καὶ ἀνάπλεων τῶν διὰ τοῦ ο. οὕτως ὁ Χοιροβοςκὸς εἰς τὸν τέταρτον κανόνα τῶν οὐδετέρων"[75].

ἀναριχᾶςθαι

Phryn. *PS* 32.1–4 ἀναριχᾶςθαι· πάνυ Ἀττικὴ ἡ φωνή. ςημαίνει δὲ τοῖς ποςὶ καὶ ταῖς χερςὶν ἀντεχόμενον ἀναβαίνειν, οἷον ἀνέρποντα. οἱ δὲ δύο ρρ γράφοντες ἁμαρτάνουςιν.

Phrynichus is explicitly addressing orthography here (γράφοντες). The variation in ἀνα(ρ)ριχᾶςθαι is typical of initial [r] in composition. Phrynichus seems to be recommending the 'less correct' form here, ἀναριχᾶςθαι with a single ρ[76]. Phry-

---

74 "eine Aporie der ionischen Grammatik", Bechtel, *GD* III: 143.
75 *EM* 116.17; cf. Choerob. in *GG* 4.1 347.35–348.2.
76 A similar gloss in a 2nd century AD lexicon on papyrus, P. Oxy. 2087.42–4 αναρριχαςθαι το ανελ[θειν] τοις ποςι [κ(αι) α]μα ταις χερ[ς]ι̣ α̣ν̣α̣β̣α̣[ινοντα]ς̣ Αριςτοτελ(ης) ζωων φυςε̣[ω]ς̣,

nichus' sources may be Aristophanes (Ar. *Pax* 70, ἀνηρριχᾶτο), whose manuscritps however only attest the spelling with a geminate (ἀνερρ- or ἀναρρ-, corrected to ἀνήρρ-, where the geminate is indifferent for scansion): the only textual problem there seems to be whether the augmented from of this verb has or has not an ‹ε›[77], i.e. whether it is prefixed with ἀνά[78], and whether the simple form is *ῥιχᾶσθαι or ἀρριχᾶσθαι[79].

The augmented forms of the verb are normally spelt ἀνηρρ-. The alternative ἠναρριχώμην is condemned by the *EM*, s.v. ἀναρριχᾶσθαι, which also attributes a present ἀριχῶμαι to Hipponax[80]. The verb is also attested in this variant in Arist. *HA* 624a (ἀριχώμεναι). Editors usually restore ‹ρρ› in both passages. A false etymology – originating with Herodian? (περὶ παθῶν *GG* 3.2 387.5–14) – in the scholion to Ar. *Pax* 70 links ἀναρριχᾶσθαι to the stem of ἀράχνη[81], which may have favoured the diffusion of ἀριχᾶσθαι with a single *rho*.

The spelling with ρρ is explicitly prescribed in later lexicography (*EM*, *Suda* and Photius). Ἀναρριχάομαι is one of the words that make up the ridiculous language of Lexiphanes in Lucian's satire (*Lex.* 8.6)[82], but Lucian does not make clear whether the choice of the from with a geminate contributes to the preposterousness of Lexiphanes' language.

Phrynichus' gloss too prescribes the seemingly non-Attic form with a single consonant, thereby supporting a derivation form ἀριχᾶσθαι, without the redoublement of initial *rho* that one would otherwise expect in composition. Although the gloss is of the orthographic kind, speakers would of course have the option of making the geminate sound, should they wish to make clear that they had chosen to use ἀνα-ρριχᾶσθαι. Maybe this is what Lexiphanes himself was doing, if Lucian actually meant to have him pronounce the variant with the dou-

---

with no remark on the geminate, and the attribution to the wrong work of Aristotle (ἀριχώμεναι is in *Hist. an.* 624a, not in *Nat. an.*) – cf. also ἀναρρίχησις, fr. 84 Rose.

77 Both readings of Ar. *Pax* 70 survive in *Su.* α 2049 and α 2313; ἀνηρριχᾶτο is restituted on the basis of Photius α 1641 and of *EM* s.v. ἀναρριχᾶσθαι.

78 Not even this reconstruction sheds light on the etymology of ἀναρριχᾶσθαι, notwithstanding the suggestions of Solmsen (1903: 132).

79 ἀρριχᾶσθαι would then be a back-formation, ἀνάρριχ- < ἀνά + ῥιχ- as if from ἀνά+ ἀρριχ- (Ehrlich 1912: 53).

80 fr. 150 Degani, who prints ἀρριχῶμαι.

81 γίνεται δὲ ἐκ τοῦ ἀράχνη ἀραχνιῶ, καὶ ἐν ὑπερβιβασμῷ ἀναρριχῶ (sch. Ar. *Pac.* 70f, Triclinius (Lh)).

82 The double ‹ρρ› is a correction of Arethas in the cod. Harleianus, the Vaticanus has the singleton; the future ἀναρριχησομένη is in Pollux (5.82) and the present ἀναρριχᾶσθαι in Hesychius α 4549 and α 4829.

ble *rho*, taking care to make a geminate sound clearly, just like the *Soloecista* when he said (mistakenly) →λῆμα.

ἀνεῖν

Paus. α 118 ἀνεῖν· ἐν ἐκτάcει ἔχει τὸ α· δηλοῖ δὲ τὸ πτίccειν.
Φερεκράτης (fr. 197 K.-A.)
    'νῦν δ' ἐπιχεῖcθαι τὰc κριθὰc δεῖ, πτίccειν, φρύγειν, ἀναβράττειν,
    ἀνεῖν, ἀλέcαι, μᾶξαι, ‹πέψαι›, τὸ τελευταῖον παραθεῖναι'.
καὶ ἐκ τοῦ πτίccειν καὶ ἀνεῖν ἡ πτιc[c]άνη.

The text of Pherecrates, in anapaests, requires two long syllables for the scansion of ἀνεῖν, a technical term denoting the rinsing of barley corns in water. A possible compound is ἀφᾱνέω, 'thrash, beat', because of a *varia lectio* ἀφανει in Aristoph. *Eq.* 394, that could be read either as ἀφαίνει (thus Ribbeck) as though from a compound of αἴνω, or ἀφανεῖ, from a compound of ἀνέω. Most editors however print ἀφαύει in Ar. *Eq.* 394, which is the reading of all manscripts except the Ravennas, and seems more fit for its literal meaning (ears of corn would rather be dried than washed, as opposed to the corns themselves) as well as for its metaphorical sense (the line of the *Knights* refers to the siege – and capture by starvation – of the Spartan aristocrats at Sphacteria (cf. Thuc. 4.8.8 and 41).

The text of Eustathius from which Erbse extracts the entry of Pausanias' lexicon also quotes Aristophanes: Παυcανίαc δὲ ἐν τῷ κατ' αὐτὸν ῥητορικῷ λεξικῷ οὐ διὰ διφθόγγου γράφων αἴνειν ἀλλὰ διὰ μόνου τοῦ α διχρόνου φηcίν· ἀνεῖν ‹ἐν› ἐκτάcει ἔχει τὸ α, δηλοῖ δὲ τὸ πτίccειν, ὡc Ἀριcτοφάνηc ἐν Εἰρήνῃ δηλοῖ (fr. 308 K.-A.). καὶ Φερεκράτηc δέ φηcι· νῦν – παραθεῖναι (Eust. 801.57).

The oscillation in the aspiration (Eustathius has both ἀνεῖν and ἀνεῖν) is addressed by Herodian as well (π. μον. λέξ. *GG* 3.2 930.28). Herodian quotes the form with a diphthong that Pausanias rejects (in the text of Eustathius but in Erbse's reconstruction), αἴνειν, still apparently referring to the same fragment of Pherecrates (he quotes the text as 'αἴνειν, πτίccειν', and explicitly defines αἴνειν as δαcυνόμενον καὶ βαρυνόμενον), and a form αἰνεῖν, with smooth breathing and final circumflex, which he says to be a denominative[83].

---

[83] For the etymology, with an original long [a:], see Solmsen 1901: 272-80.

The prescription uses a metrical text to prove the length of the *dichronon*. It does not discuss the initial aspiration[84].

ἀνίλλειν

Phryn. *PS* 31.10–12 ἀνίλλειν βιβλίον· οἱ μὲν ἄλλοι περισπῶσι τῆν λέξιν καὶ δι' ἑνὸς λ γράφουσιν. οἱ δὲ Ἀττικοὶ παροξύνουσι καὶ διὰ δύο λλ γράφουσιν. οὕτω καὶ τὸ ἐξίλλειν.
Phryn. *Ecl.* 21 ἀνειλεῖν βιβλίον διὰ τοῦ ἑτέρου λ κάκιστον, ἀλλὰ διὰ τῶν δύο, ἀνείλλειν.

It is unclear whether the text of the *PS* should read ἀνίλλειν and ἐξίλλειν, with ‹ι› and not ‹ει›. The entry in the *Ecloga* suggests ‹ει›, as does the manuscript tradition of Attic texts: the spellings of the *PS* could be due to a copyist's choice[85]. The entry of the *Ecloga* is also the only surviving attestation of the contract verb ἀνειλεῖν. The distinction between accent types in Phryn. *PS* 31.10–12 is a common way of distinguishing different inflections (cf. →ἀκταινοῦν): defining a verb as *perispomenon* is the usual way of saying that it is contract[86].

In the *PS* Phrynichus identifies the variant with the geminate with the uncontracted verb, and we can assume that he implied the same in the *Ecloga*. The prescribed Attic form had a geminate and was the uncontracted ἀνείλλω, and it was presumably competing with ἀνειλῶ. The contract verb, however, is never attested except in the grammatical tradition, where it normally glosses ἀνείλλω[87]. The spelling with the geminate or the singleton is uncertain in the manuscript tradition. Editors tend to introduce the geminate basing on Phyrinichus' prescription.

The variation, however, seems to be related to the formation of the verb itself. ἴλλειν and εἰλεῖν belong to a larger number of derivatives from the same root. LSJ lists them as a single entry, and lemmatises εἴλω, εἰλέω, εἰλέω,

---

[84] The initial aspiration in this word is controversial, but not directly discussed in our sources: Eustathius himself wrote a rough *and* a smooth breathing on ανειν, cf. van der Valk *ad* Eust. 801.24–58.
[85] Lobeck (1820: 29–30), Rutherford (1881: 89–90) is in favour of ‹ει›, and recalls the similar case the aorist of τίνω, ἔτεισα, normally spelt with ‹ει› in the Classical period, but then with in ‹ι› in the 2nd century AD.
[86] Dickey 2007: 128.
[87] Cf. the similar entries in Σ^b 1257 ἀνείλεται· ἀνειλεῖται, and in Timaeus *Lex. Plat.* α 46 ἀνείλ(λ)εται Valente.

εἴλλω, ἴλλω. The variants with the rough breathing are secondary (as proven by the compounds ὑπίλλω and κατίλλω), and those in -έω are later: εἰλέω is not found in Attic literature, nor in Homer[88] or Herodotus, in whose text it was introduced by the later manuscript tradition[89]. Later grammatical tradition established ἴλλω in the spelling[90].

Of the lemmata in the LSJ only εἴλλω/εἴλλω/ἴλλω have the meaning of 'wind, turn around', whereas the remaining formations mean 'enclose, press'[91]. The relations between the various spelllings are complicated by reciprocal analogical influences[92]. Phrynichus clearly considers the variants with the geminate to be the correct ones.

ἀντήλιος

→ ἀπηλιώτης

---

[88] In Homer, εἰλέω is guaranteed by metre against (ε)ἴλλω only in Il. 18.447 ἐείλεον and Od. 22.460 εἴλεον, (ε)ἴλλω is guaranteed at Il. 8.215, εἰλομένων (beginning of the line). Either reading is possible in Il. 2.294, 21.8, Od. 11.572, 12.210 (at the beginning of 12.210, εἰλεῖ ἐνὶ cπῆϊ, εἴλεεϊ ἐνὶ cπῆϊ is not metrical, εἶλε' ἐνὶ cπῆϊ impossible, but εἰλεῖ ἐνὶ cπῆϊ may have its second syllable shortened).
[89] Rutherford 1881: 89–90.
[90] "ἀνείλλεcθαι Suidas pro cυcτρέφεcθαι affert, cui posteriores vocalem praesonantem subtraxerunt, ut νείccομαι, νίccομαι, diphthongo ante consonam duplicatam obscurius subtinniente" Lobeck (1837: 30); cf. Zonaras 1249.5–13 Tittmann "οὐδέποτε δὲ γὰρ πρὸ τῶν δύο cc εὑρίcκεται δίφθογγον, οἷον φρίccω, ἀΐccω, πλὴν τοῦ κρείccων, καὶ τοῦ ῥήματος τοῦ ἐξ αὐτοῦ γινομένου. χωρὶc καὶ τοῦ γλαύccω, τὸ φωτίζω", similarly EM and Et.Gud. s.v. κρείccων. The gloss in Zonaras' lexicon aims at distinguishing the spellings with ‹ευ› and with ‹ι›.
[91] LSJ postulates an original meaning 'squeeze', but the verbs meaning 'close' seem to share a notion of 'ban' (cf. Tabulae Heracleenses (IG XIV 645 = Tavole greche di Eraclea) 1.152, ‹ἐγϝηληθιωντι›), whereas the sense 'turn, wring' would make εἴλλω/εἴλλω/ἴλλω similar to εἰλύω and Lat. volvo. In many cases the meanings are interchangeable, which makes the distinction between the two roots all the more difficult.
[92] Εἰλέω continues *u̯el-ne-ō and ἴλλω a reduplicated present *u̯i-u̯lō; on εἰλύω, Lat. volvo and Skr. vr̥ṇóti cf. Solmsen 1901: 232ff., Chantraine GH I 131 and Schwyzer 1939: 649; "à côté de εἰλέω existent des formes verbales médiocrement attestées εἴλλω, ἴλλω qui peuvent être dues à iotacisme ou à ἄλλω, lequel se rattache à εἰλέω 2 [...] il n'est pas sûr que les doublets rares -είλλω et ἴλλω soient autre chose que le résultat d'une confusion (graphique? ou plutôt étymologique?) avec εἰλέω 2." (DELG s.v. εἰλέω 1).

ἀνύειν

Ael. D. α 150[93] ἀνύτειν· οἱ Ἀττικοί, ὅπερ ἡμεῖς ἀνύειν. ἀνύειν δὲ τὸ σπεύδειν, δασείᾳ ⟨τ⟩ῇ πρώτῃ. Ὅμηρος δὲ τὸ ἀνύειν ὡς ἡμεῖς (Il. 4.56)· 'οὐκ ἀνύω φθονέουσα ...'
Moer. η 16 ἤνυσα δασέως Ἀττικοί· ψιλῶς δὲ Ἕλληνες.
Phryn. PS 23.1–2 ἀνύειν· δασύνουσιν οἱ Ἀττικοί. καὶ δῆλον ἐκ τῆς συναλοιφῆς. καθήνυσαν γάρ (S. El. 1451?).
→ ἀλύειν

The Homeric quote signals through the spelling οὐκ that ἀνύω does not begin with an aspiration: the text of Il. 4.56, even with no breathings or accents, would read ουχ ανυω if the verb began with an aspiration. The aspiration is attributed to Attic, as in most other glosses concerning initial aspiration[94].

The aspiration of the simple verb ἀνύω si attested only in the grammatical tradition (Hdn., περὶ καθολικῆς προσῳδίας, GG 3.1 541.20), and as a variant in manuscripts – the Ravennas is the only codex attesting the aspiration in Ar. Pl. 196, ταῦθ' ἀνύσηται. καθανύ(τ)ω is the only compound of ἀνύω that can show an aspiration (there are no attestations of compounds with μετά or ἀπό/ὑπό). Although etymological, and therefore a true archaism in Attic[95], the aspiration is never attested consistently in literary texts: καθανύσαι is an isolated reading in Xenophon HG 7.1.15 (Hsch.); but κατανύειν occurs in tragedy, and some manuscripts of Xenophon read κατανύτ- instead of κατανύθ- at Cyr. 8.6.17. The lemma in the lexicon of Moeris can refer either to ἀνύω or ἀνύτω: whether with or without an initial aspiration, only one aorist ἤνυσα corresponds to both verbs.

---

93 ≈ Σ^b 1544, cf. also Σ^b 1541 (δασέως).
94 Later scholarship too prescribes the aspiration, cf. Σ^b 1541 and 1544, Photius α 2164 and 2151, Su. α 2799.
95 ἀνύω goes back to the root *senH- of scr. sanóti. Outside of Attic, the initial aspiration is attested only in a Laconian gloss in Hesychius, κασάνεις· ἀνύεις, Λάκονες (κ 958 Latte), which points to an original καθ-αν(υ)ω, and in the Mycenean /a$_2$-nu-me-no/ (but Mycenean also attests a form /a-nu-to/). The late αὐθέντης suggests that speakers had preserved an internal aspiration in αὐτοέντης (a form attested in Sophocles), if the second member of the compound can be identified with a full grade agent noun formed on *senH. Cf. Beekes EDG s.v. ἄνυμι, αὐθέντης.

ἀνυπόδητος

Phryn. *Ecl.* 419 ἀνυπόδητος ἐρεῖς ἐν τῷ η· τὸ γὰρ ἐν τῷ ε ἁμάρτημα. καὶ γὰρ ὑποδήςαςθαι λέγεται, οὐ ὑποδέςαςθαι.
Phryn. *PS* 27.12 ἀνυπόδητος· διὰ τοῦ η, οὐ διὰ τοῦ ε.
Philet. 149 ἀνυπόδητος, οὐχὶ ἀνυπόδετος.[96]
Moer. α 63 ἀνυπόδητος Ἀττικοί· ἀνυπόδετος Ἕλληνες.
   Cf. *Antiatt.* α 118 ἀνυπόδετος· Ἐπίχαρμος Ὀδυςςεῖ (fr. 107 K.–A.).

As εὕρεμα εὕρηςις replaced εὕρημα εὕρεςις, so (ὑπό)δεςις replaces (ὑπό)δηςις, cf. →ἀνάθημα. With Phryn. *PS* 26.9–10 →ἀπέςβηςε, this is one of the few cases where the variation ‹η› ~‹ε› is explicitly specified by "διὰ τοῦ η, οὐ διὰ τοῦ ε".
   ἀνυπόδετος is 'an archaism common in Sicilian Doric and the Koiné'[97]. It is never found in Attic authors[98], yet many writers dating from the Hellenistic age onward use the adjective with ‹ε› in free variation with ἀνυπόδητος, and glosses condemning the variant with a short vowel are found in more than one lexicographer. Editors often correct ἀνυπόδετος to ἀνυπόδητος – the form continued, as a learned word, in Modern Greek ανυπόδητος.
   The earliest literary attestations of ἀνυπόδετος date to early Hellenism, if one can trust the indirect transmission of Aristotle, fr. 74 Rose, by Macrobius *Saturn.* 5.18.19, where the text has not only ἀνυπόδετος but also its denominal ἀνυποδετέω[99]. The *Antiatticista* (α 118) refers ἀνυπόδετος with ‹ε› to Epicharmus (107 K.–A.). The standard atticist prescription (with ‹η›) is continued virtually with no change in the *Synagoge* (Σ^b 1546) and in the *Suda* (α 2791)[100]. Pollux (2.199) attests ἀνυπόδητος and only forms with ‹η› (ὑπόδημα, ἀνυποδηςία).
   There are no attestations of ἀνυπόδετος in verse, and clearly forms with a long and with a short vowel are interchangeable in prose texts. It is therefore difficult to tell where ἀνυπόδετος has crept into texts which originally did not in-

---

[96] ~ οὐκ ἀνυπόδετος, *exc. Vind.* 16.
[97] Cassio 2012: 263. Forms in -δετος are the expected outcome of a zero grade verbal adjective from the root of δέω, *dh_1; the long vowel in -δητος is the result of analogy with verbs in -έω (Cassio 2012: 257), and is attested in Attic only: other dialects and the Koine had preserved δετός and its derivatives.
[98] Lobeck 1820: 445, Rutherford 1881: 501.
[99] In the immediately following century, the forms appears in Chrysippus (*Fragmenta logica et physica* 177.7 von Arnim) and in the 1st century AD in Musonius Rufus, *Dissertationum a Lucio digestarum reliquiae* 19.22 (Lutz 1947: 32–128).
[100] On Epicharmus, cf. also Oros A 10 a–b Alpers.

clude it, or if it is the occurrence of ἀνυπόδητος that depends on the atticising correction of more learned copyists.

Modern editions often alternate between ἀνυπόδετος and ἀνυπόδητος. In addition to the occurrences listed by Lobeck (1820: 445), among which there is [Lucian] *Asin.* 16.148 (yet cf. 43.182 ἀνυπόδητος), ἀνυπόδετος is in Plutarch *De fortuna* 98d (a reworked quotation of Plato, *Symp.* 203c–d, where the text has ἀνυπόδητος), Dio Cassius[101], Galen[102]. The intervention of modern editors is clear in the editions of Longus Sophista, in whose work the three occurrences of ἀνυπόδετος (1.4.2, 1.30.3, 2.23.1[103]) are printed with ⟨η⟩ with no indication in the apparatus by Schönberger (1989), whereas the more recent edition by Morgan (2004) has ⟨ε⟩[104]. Philostratus, *VA* 1.8.13, 6.11.241 has ἀνυποδηςία, but ἀνυπόδετος at 6.10.80 and in *Epistulae et dialexis* 1.18.7, 1.18.13, 1.37.5 without variants in Kayser's edition (*VA* 1870; *Ep.* 1871). The impression is that the norm of the grammarians is overall not right (Schmid 1887–1897: IV 341).

The gloss of the *Antiatticista* attests that ἀνυπόδετος might well be in use by the 5th century BC (in a non Attic author), but what may have made ἀνυπόδετος the goal of so much criticism could eventually be its frequency in the LXX, to which it owes its success in the writings of the Fathers of the Church during the following centuries, who use the phrase 'γυμνός τε καὶ ἀνυπόδετος' (LXX *Is.* 20.2–3; on the prophet Isaiah's ascension), even though editions of other texts tend to have the Attic forms ἀνυπόδητος, ἀνυποδηςία, cf. Clemens of Alexandria, who quotes: "Ἡσαΐας δέ, ἄλλος οὗτος προφήτης, 'γυμνός τε καὶ ἀνυπόδετος' ἦν" (*Paedagogus* 2.10bis.112.3.3), τίς δὲ σάκκον περιβέβληται γυμνὸς τὰ ἄλλα καὶ ἀνυπόδετος ὡς Ἡσαΐας (*Stromata* 3.6.53.5.3)[105]. Similarly, two out of the three instances of ἀνυπόδετος in Origen (*Contra Celsum* 7.7.24; *Philocalia* 26.4.17 = *Selecta in Psalmos* [*PG* 12] 1156.41) consist of the phrase 'γυμνός τε καὶ ἀνυπόδετος', whereas the spelling ἀνυπόδητος only appears out of that specific quote (*Contra Celsum* 4.39.30) – in a passage trasmitted without other variants. If this does not depend on a learned copyist, the choice of a more atticising spelling could be Origen's own. He would have preferred the spelling recommended by Atticists when not quoting from the Bible.

---

[101] In the epitome of Xiphilinus, S277.27, S322.1, yet elsewhere ἀνυπόδητος.
[102] *Adhortatio ad artes addiscendas* 13.9; *De usu partium* 3.4.4; *Thrasybulus siue utrum medicinae sit an gymnasticae hygieine* 5.889.3: no edition of Galen prints ἀνυπόδητος.
[103] In the biblical-sounding phrase ἡμίγυμνοι καὶ ἀνυπόδετοι (cf. LXX *Is.* 20.2–3).
[104] Morgan accepts the reading of the cod. *Florentinus* (F). Whoever epitomised the text of F, or whoever expanded the text of the *Venetus*, has anway kept the spelling ἀνυπόδετος, which is possibly what was in the archetype.
[105] Cf. also [Clemens Romanus] *Recognitiones* 9.22.5 Rehm – Paschke.

The mistake stigmatised by the grammarians concerns the formation of this word, from a stem with a short or with a long vowel and its stylistic connotation, one form being connected to the language of the Greek Bible and the other with Classical Attic. The two words may have been confused indipendently, not necessarily because they had the same pronunciation.

ἀξιόχρεως

→ ἀνάπλεως

ἅπαν

Ael. D. α 155 ἅπαν· οἱ μὲν Ἴωνες cυcτέλλουcι καὶ ὁ Ποιητὴς (Hom. *Il.* 20.156) 'τῶν δ' ἅπαν ἐπλήcθη πεδίον ...' οἱ δὲ Ἀττικοὶ ἐκτείνουcι τὴν ὑcτέραν καὶ τὸ 'παράπαν' ὁμοίως καὶ ἅπαντα τὰ τοιαῦτα.
Paus. α 129 ἅπαν· ὁ λόγος βραχύνειν ἀξιοῖ. τὰ γὰρ παραcχηματιζόμενα τοῖς εἰς ας οὐδέτερα βραχύνονται, οἷον μέλαν, τάλαν, ἅπαν.

The wording of Pausanias seemingly contradicts that of Aelius, at least as they have been edited by Erbse. Uncompound πᾶν has a long final vowel in Attic, probably the result of a levelling on the masculine πᾶc, where it is the regular outcome of a compensatory lengthening. In other Greek dialects, and as the first elements of compounds, πάν has a short vowel[106]. Apollonius Dyscolus also comments on ἅπᾰν when he discusses the quantity of the final *alpha* of adverbs in -αν: the rule he formulates is slightly different from that of Pausanias. Pausanias says that all neuters from masculine in -ας have a short *alpha* and end in -ᾰν, Apollonius that πᾶν has a long vowel in that it is a monosyllable, but since ἅπᾰν (and cύμπᾰν, πρόπᾰν) have two, then a short *alpha* is to be expected[107].

---

[106] Schwyzer 1939: 566; πᾰνῆμαρ in Oppian, *Halieutica* 4.178 results from the ancient interpretation of Hom. *Il.* 1.592, *Od.* 18.453 πᾶν ‹δ'› ἦμαρ (Schulze 1892: 173, fn. 1); the editors print πᾶν ἦμαρ.
[107] A.D. *Adv.* [*GG* 2.1.1] 158.26–159.9 ἀλλ' οὐδὲ τὸ πάμπαν ἄλογον ἂν εἴη διὰ τὴν cυcτολὴν τοῦ α· ἅπαντα γὰρ τὰ ἐξ ὀνομάτων μεταλαμβανόμενα εἰς ἐπιρρηματικὴν cύνταξιν, τὴν φωνὴν τοῦ ὀνόματος φυλάccει, ὡς ἔχει τὸ εὐρύ, τὸ ἀτρεκές, τὸ πυκνά, τὸ καλά, τὸ ἰδίᾳ, τὸ δημοσίᾳ, ἄλλα πάμπολλα. ᾧ λόγῳ οὐδὲ τὸ ⟨πάμπᾰν⟩ [πρόπαν] ὠλιγώρηται ⟨κατὰ τὸ πρόπαν⟩ ἢ cύμπᾰν· πάλιν γὰρ ἀπὸ ὀνοματικῆς cυντάξεως εἰς ἐπιρρηματικὴν ἐχώρηcεν. ἔcτι τὸ πᾶν, ⟨ὅπερ⟩ μονοcύλλαβον

In Apollonius' account, the final vowel of ἄπᾶν is short in that the word is not a monosyllable. ἄπᾶν has generally a short second syllable. The quantity is surely attested in at least an anapaestic tetrameter of Aristophanes, *Pl.* 493: βούλευμα καλὸν καὶ γενναῖον καὶ χρήcιμον εἰc ἅπαν ἔργον[108]. Yet ἄπᾶν becomes more common in later poetry, cf. e. g. Theocritus, 2.56 ἔμφυc ὡc λιμνᾶτιc ἅπαν ἐκ βδέλλα πέπωκαc, 22.86 βάλλετο δ' ἀκτίνεccιν ἅπαν Ἀμυκοιο πρόcωπον. There is no known model such forms seem to imitate.

ἀπαντικρύ

Philem. 355 ἀπαντικρὺ μακρὸν τὸ κρυ.

In Homer ἀντικρύ occurs only twice with a final short syllable (*Il.* 5.130 = 819, θεοῖc ἀντικρὺ μάχεcθαι). This may be the earliest form of the adverb on etymological grounds: if ἀντικρύ is related to κάρα or κρούω[109], in either case ablaut would not justify a long ῦ[110]. The scholion (A) to this line possibly reflects Herodianic doctrine, prescribing the long quantity for oxytone ἀντικρύ: ὀξύνεται καὶ ἐκτείνεται. ὅταν δὲ ἔχῃ τὸ c, cυcτέλλεται καὶ βαρύνεται. τὸ δὲ αἴτιον ἐν τῷ Περὶ ἐπιρρήματος ἐροῦμεν[111].

ἀπέδραν

Phryn. *PS* 16.6–12 ἀπέδραμεν· τετραcυλλάβωc, καὶ ἀπέδρατε καὶ ἀπέδραν, βραχείαc τῆc τοῦ ἀπέδραν ἐcχάτηc cυλλαβῆc. ἀλλὰ καὶ τὸ ἑνικὸν πρῶτον πρόcωπον

μὲν ὂν ἐν ἐκτάcει τοῦ α ἐcτίν, ὑπὲρ μίαν δὲ cυλλαβὴν καθεcτηκόc, εἴτε καὶ κατὰ cύνθεcιν εἴτε καὶ κατ' ἐντέλειαν τοῦ ἐλλείποντοc α, ἐν cυcτολῇ, cύμπᾶν, πρόπᾶν, ἅπᾶν· ὅπερ ἀνεδέδεκτο καὶ τὸ ἐπίρρημα ἐν τῷ πάμπᾶν.

[108] It is possible to scan the final syllable as long in *Ach.* 998 (καὶ περὶ τὸ χωρίον ἐλᾷδαc ἅπαν ἐν κύκλῳ) if one follows Bentley's reading καὶ περὶ τὸ χωρίον ἅπαν ἐλᾷδαc κύκλῳ.

[109] Eustathius 1323.16 and 527.9, and so Kretschmer (1913: 356), who adds it to the number of adverbs studied by Brugmann (1910: 233–78, ἅλιc, μόγιc, μόλιc, χωρίc): according to Brugmann these were originally masculine nominative singulars. If ἀντικρύ derives actually from the same root as ἀντικρούω, the final sibilant of its variant ἀντικρύc may not be the morphological relic of a nominative but belong to the root (cf. aor. ἐκρούcθην). Were this the case, ἀντικρύ should be understood as a secondary form, modelled on variations such as εὐθύc ~ εὐθύ.

[110] The long vowel seems to have received cirumflex accentuation in Byzantine times: ἀντικρῦ is in Gregorius Lacapenus (13th/14th c. AD), *Ep.* 23.n.16–19.

[111] Hdn. *GG* 3.2 846.24 = 48.17 (cf. also 19.30).

ἀπέδραν, ἐκτεταμένου τοῦ ἐπὶ τέλους α, καὶ ἀπέδρας καὶ ἀπέδρα. οὐχ ὡς οἱ ῥήτορες ἀπεδράσαμεν. τὸ δὲ ἀπέδραν τινὲς τῶν ῥητόρων διὰ τοῦ ω εἶπον, ἀπέδρων. ἀλλ' ἄμεινον διὰ τοῦ α. ὁμοίως καὶ ἐξέδραν.
Moer. α 80 ἀπέδραν Ἀττικοί· ἀπέδρων Ἕλληνες.
Philet. 103 ἀπέδραν ἐγώ, οὐχὶ ἀπέδρων, τὸ πρῶτον πρόσωπον. καὶ ἀπέδραμεν ἡμεῖς τὸ πληθυντικόν. καὶ Ἀριστοφάνης·

δεῦρο δ' ἂν οὐκ ἀπέδραμεν,

ἐν τοῖς Ταγηνισταῖς (fr. 519 K.–A.[112]). καὶ ἀπέδραν ἐκεῖνοι ἀκολούθως τὸ πληθυντικὸν τὸ τρίτον, ἀντὶ τοῦ ἀπέδρασαν.

cf. Oros A 11
a ἀπέδραν καὶ ἀπέδρα χρὴ λέγειν, οὐχὶ ἀπέδρασα καὶ ἀπέδρασεν·
ἔλυσα ἐμαυτόν, εἶτ' ἀπέδραν μόνος
(Men. fr. 173 K.–A.) καὶ Πλάτων (*Prot.* 310c)· ὁ γάρ τοι παῖς με ὁ Σάτυρος ἀπέδρα.
b ἀπέδρα καὶ τὸ πρῶτον πρόσωπον ἀπέδραν.
τί οὐκ ἐπανεχώρησα δεῦρο κἀπέδραν;
Φερεκράτης Ἰπνῷ (fr. 65 K.–A.). Μένανδρος Θετταλ( ) (fr. 173 K.–A.)·
εἶτ' ἀπέδραν μόνος.

The verb ἀποδιδράσκω is still used in the imperial period[113], and – differently form what the Atticists claim – the 3rd persons of the plural in -σαν are already attested in Thucydides (1.128.5) and Xenophon (*HG* 1.1.10 +); the plural ἀπέδραν however is found at least once in a lyric passage of Attic tragedy (Sophocles *Aj.* 167)[114].

The glosses on ἀπέδραν (and ἀπέδραμεν) address two different problems: whether the verb forms a sigmatic aorist, and whether it has a form ἀπέδρων at all (Moeris ascribes it to the Hellenes, the *Philetaerus* condemns it). The atticist lexicographers unanimously recommend the root aorist ἀπέδραν, supporting their choice with passages from an unusually varied range of Attic authors, comprising prose (Plato), Old and New Comedy (Pherecrates, Menander).

---

112 Anapaests, the metre guarantees ἀπέδράμεν.
113 Cf. e.g. Plutarch *Alc.* 3.1 γέγραπται, ὅτι παῖς ὢν ἐκ τῆς οἰκίας ἀπέδρα πρὸς Δημοκράτην τινὰ τῶν ἐραστῶν, *Cam.* 23.7 ἀπέδρασαν. Moeris' remarks on the meaning of ἀποδράω διαδράω (Moer. δ 3 διέδρα διαφέρειν καὶ ἀπέδρα τοῦτο δοκεῖν· διέδρα φυλακήν, ἀπέδρα δέ, ὅταν ἀφύλακτος ᾖ) suggest that the verb was still in use by the end of the 2nd century AD.
114 Forms of the aorist in -ν instead of -σαν are sometimes found in tragedy, cf. Sideras 1971: 105–6.

The only suriving attestation of the 3rd person plural *ἀπέδρᾶν is in Sophocles, *Aj.* 167, at line-end[115]. The distinction between the 1st person of the singular and the 3rd of the plural in Phryn. *PS* 16.6–12 can only be realised through a distincion in pronunciation between ἀπέδρᾱν and ἀπέδρᾰν, basing on the different quantity of the final vowel.

The sigmatic aorist is clearly a more recent formation. From a root *$dreh_2$-[116] the reconstructed root aorist is *e-$dreh_2$-$m̥$ in the 1st person sing., and *e-$dr̥h_2$-ent for the 3rd person plural, from which, respectively, *$édrān$ and *$édrănt$ > ἔδρᾱν ~ ἔδρᾰν[117]. Sigmatic aorists form the same root could easily have been created from a 3rd person plural formed with a suffix -cαν, as is schematised below:

	1st p.s.	3rd p.pl.
Proto-IE	*e-$dreh_2$-$m̥$	*e-drh_2-ent
	ἀπέδρᾶν	ἀπέδρᾶν
III p.pl. × -cαν	ἀπέδρᾶν	ἀπέδρᾶcαν
reanalysis as aor. in -cα-	ἀπέδρᾱcα	ἀπέδρᾶcαν

Sigmatic aorists of ἀποδιδράcκω like ἀπέδραcαν are found in a number of authors form Hellenism on (but starting already with Thucydides and Xenophon, as we have seen above[118]). The existence of a sigmatic aorist ἀπέδραcα must have favoured the creation of a present ἀποδράω[119], from which one could derive the imperfect ἀπέδρων quoted by Moeris and the *Philetaerus* (if it can be under-

---

115 The verse of the *Ajax*'s parodos consists of anapaests in series of different lengths, each closed by a *longum*. Line 167 is the first anapaest in one such series, concluding with three anapaests and one *longum*, l. 171 ciγῇ πτήξειαν ἄφωνοι [-- -- ⏑⏑- -]. This is an archaic sort of parodos, also employed by Aeschylus in the *Persians*, the *Supplicants* and *Agamemnon* (Pearson 1912: 66, Finglass 2011: 175–7). Thomas Magister is the only grammatical source that quotes these lines of Sophocles (Thom. Mag. 14.1–9) ἀποδράς, οὐκ ἀποδράcαc. ὡcαύτωc ἀπέδραν, καὶ ἐπὶ πρώτου τῶν ἑνικῶν καὶ ἐπὶ τρίτου τῶν πληθυντικῶν, οὐκ ἀπέδρων. Cοφοκλῆc ἐν Αἴαντι· "ἀλλ' ὅτε γὰρ τὸ cὸν ὄμμ' ἀπέδραν". [Ra εἰ καὶ ἐcφαλμένον ἀπέδρων εὕρηται. ἀπὸ γὰρ τοῦ ἀποδράω, ἀποδρῶ εἰc παρατατικὸν κανονίζεται. τὸ δὲ ἀποδράc, ἀπὸ τοῦ ἀπόδρημι εἰc δεύτερον ἀόριcτον· ὅθεν ἐcτὶ καὶ τὸ ἀποδραίην καὶ τὸ ἀποδρᾶναι, ὡc cταίην καὶ cτῆναι.]. A scholion to this line defines the form 'Calchidean', ἀπέδραcαν, ἐξέφυγον. Χαλκηδαϊκὸν λέγεται, sch. S. *Aj.* 167a (G^{sl}). The present optative ἀποδρῴη – implying a present ἀποδράω, as the imperfect ἀπέδρων does – is a *varia lectio* in Arist. *Oec.* 1353a.
116 *LIV* s.v. 1. *$dreh_2$-; cf. also Harðarson (1993: 181) only on the aorist participle ἀποδράc. DELG, s.v. διδράcκω: "[l]e thème de ἔδρᾱν [...] est issu d'une racine *der- d'où *dr-$eə_2$".
117 On the formation see Harðarson (1993: 43–5).
118 On the distribution of the textual variants see Lobeck 1820: 737–8.
119 *DGE* quotes ἀποδραcθεῖν as the passive aorist (?) of ἀποδράω, attested once in Themistius *Or.* 7.91a (4th c. AD), but the text is dubious. The verb is attested in Byzantine literature (*LBG s.v.*).

stood as an imperfect): the form is attested only once in the LXX (*Ju.* 11.16), and the earliest attestation thereafter is in Libanius (*Decl.* 26.1.11).

A very similar scenario involves the only attestation of the first person plural ἀπεδράσαμεν. This form, that Phyrnichus condemns and ascribes to the ῥήτορες, surivives only in Origen, who writes καὶ τοῦτον ἡμεῖς οἱ ἀπὸ τῆς ἐκκλησίας οὐχ ὑπερβαίνομεν, ἀλλὰ καὶ ἀπεδράσαμεν μὲν τὰς Ἰουδαίων μυθολογίας (*Contra Celsum* 2.6.5–7). Origen was active soon after the period in which the Atticists lexica were composed, and the *Contra Celsum* was with all likeliness composed just before the mid-3rd century AD.[120] It is striking that the only attestation of ἀπεδράσαμεν should be so close in time with the lexicographers that condemned it, and precisely in Christian literature, a genre that was soon to convert to the linguistic conservatorism that Atticism supported, but that in its beginnings adopted forms that literary varieties of Koine (and – even more so – atticising Greek) would avoid[121].

ἀπέρατος

Phryn. *PS* 37.8–9 ἀπέρατον ἐκτείνουσι τὸ α. λέγεται δὲ καὶ ἀπέραντον μετὰ τοῦ ν.

Both ἀπέρᾱτος and ἀπέραντος are compound from verbal adjectives in *-tos* deriving from a root *per, common to the adverb πέρα and the noun πεῖραρ (*DELG* s.v. πεῖραρ, *LIV* s.v. *per). The formations process however is different: ἀπέρατος comes from the theme of περάω 'drive through', in turn derived form the adverb πέρᾱ 'beyond' (*DELG* s.v. πέρᾱ), whereas ἀπέραντος is derived form the stem of περαίνω 'finish, complete', akin to πεῖραρ/πέρας, πέρατος[122].

ἀπέρατος is a *varia lectio* for ἀπέραντος in a couple of cases, and precisely in Aristophanes, *Nu.* 3, and Plato, *Theet.* 147c[123]. The scholion to Ar. *Nu.* 3 supports ἀπέρατος[124]. The metre allows for either a long or a short vowel in the penulti-

---

120 Borret 1967: 15.
121 Wifstrand 1967, Fabricius 1967. The first person of the aorist in -ησα occurs about 50 times in Demosthenes, yet virtually never in Aristotle (if not as part of quotations, e.g. *Rhet.* 1413b).
122 περαίνω from a nasal nominal theme **per-ṃ̄*, originally alternating with **per-ṃ̆* in the direct cases, the form continued in the nom./acc./voc. singular πεῖραρ (Rix 1992: 126–7).
123 ἀπέρατον is found instead of ἀπέραντον in the manuscripts of the anonimous author of a commentary on papyrus to the *Theaetetus* (Diels – Schubart 1905), who – not surprisingly – does not say anything about its scansion.
124 Sch. vet. Ar. *Nu.* 3 (RVEΘN) οἱ δὲ "ἀπέραντον" μετὰ τοῦ ν γράφοντες ἁμαρτάνουσιν.

mate syllable of the word[125]: the meaning would favour ἀπέρατος 'boundless', rather than ἀπέρᾱτος 'not to be crossed / passed', and the scholiast seems to be of the same opinion. In classical Attic literature ἀπέρᾱτος is at home in tragedy, but is never attested in prose[126]. The term enjoyed new popularity form the first centuries AD. It is found in Philo Judaeus (*De fuga et inventione*, 57), in Lucian (*Verae Historiae* 2.30) and Plutarch (*Pyrrh.* 2.4, *Mor.* 326e).

After all, at least in surviving Greek literature, the only occurrence of ἀπέρατος guaranteed by metre is in Aeschylus (*Supp.* 1049). One cannot draw definitive conclusions on such a small number of occurrences, but if Phrynichus did not read much more than what is available to us today, he may have drawn his information on ἀπέρατος form Aeschylus indeed, and may have attributed to the word a penultimate long vowel on the basis of that attestation.

ἀπέcβηcε

Phryn. *PS* 26.9–10 ἀπέcβηcε πῦρ· ὁμοίωc καὶ λύχνον. διὰ τοῦ η, οὐ διὰ τοῦ ε.

Phrynichus' gloss in its present state is problematic, as it seems to prescribe the post-classical aorist of (ἀπο)cβέννυμι, while rejecting the form that is actually attested in Classical Attic, (ἀπ)έcβεcα[127]. It contains diverse material. The second half could be a later addition to a gloss that originally only pointed out the classical usage of ἀποcβέννυμι, possibly echoing Aristophanes (*V.* 255; *Pl.* 668).

There are no attested nominal formations with a long vowel from (ἀπο)cβέννυμι, but only the types cβέcιc, cβεcτήρ, cβεcτήριοc. A root aorist ἔcβη[128] (well attested from Herodotus onwards) can easily be the starting point for a sigmatic aorist in -ηc-, as it is the case with ἔcτη : ἔcτηcα. The long vowel in the perfect active ἔcβηκα and in the future ἀποcβήcομαι must depend on ἔcβη. Interestingly, Modern Greek continues cβέννυμι in cβήνω, a present likely to be a back forma-

---

[125] ἀπέραντον. οὐδέποθ' ἡμέρα γενήcεται; – ἀπέρᾱτον implies the resolution of the first *longum* instead than of the initial *indifferens*, as ἀπέραντον/ἀπέρᾱτον requires.

[126] ἀπέρᾱτον is attested twice in Aeschylus – *Supp.* 1049 (ll. 1047–9: ὅ τί τοι μόρcιμόν ἐcτιν, τὸ γένοιτ' ἄν. / Διὸc οὐ παρβατόc ἐcτιν / μεγάλα φρὴν ἀπέρατοc) and *Pr.* 1078 (ll. 1076–9 εἰδυῖαι γὰρ / κοὐκ ἐξαίφνηc οὐδὲ λαθραίωc / εἰc ἀπέρατον δίκτυον ἄτηc / ἐμπλεχθήcεcθ' ὑπ' ἀνοίαc).

[127] On the root and its numerous formations see *LIV* s.v. **(s)gʷesh₂-*. The reconstructed laryngeal implies that the older aorist of cβήννυμι is ἔcβη < **esbē(h)at* < **e-sgʷesh₂-t*, and that the sigmatic ἔcβεc(c)α is a later Greek innovation. Forms of cβήννυμι in Greek generalise a stem cβηc-/cβεc- with no traces of **h₂*.

[128] From **sgʷēs-t* according to Ruijgh (2004: 61, *pace LIV* s.v. **(s)gʷesh₂-*) , "an intransitive root verb with phonetic lengthening of *e* in monosyllables (Ruijgh 1996: 359)".

tion from the post-classical aorist ἔcβηcα, the form prescribed in the *Praeparatio Sophistica*. The gloss is compatible with a pronunciation of both vowels as mid-front [e] ~ [eː], but does not use any technical terms that unmistakably point to a distinction in vowel timbre or quantity.

ἄπεφθοc

Phryn. *PS* 25.16–25 ἄπεφθον· διὰ τοῦ π μὲν ἐκφέρουcιν, ὅμωc ⟨δὲ⟩ δαcύνουcι τὸ ἑφθόν. ἡ δὲ αἰτία, ὅτι τραχὺ ἔδοξεν αὐτοῖc πρὸ τοῦ φ καὶ τοῦ θ, τῶν δαcέων, ἔτι τὸ φ παρενθεῖναι. οὕτω καὶ τὸ ἀπηδέc ἔχει, καὶ τὸ ἀντήλιον καὶ τὸ ἀπηλιώτηc καὶ τὸ ἀπηθεῖν. ὅθεν καὶ ἔπτυcχλοι, ⟨ὃ⟩ ὤφειλε διὰ τοῦ φ καὶ ⟨τοῦ⟩ θ. καὶ γὰρ τὸ ὕcχλοc δαcύνεται. ἔcτι δὲ τῶν ὑποδημάτων, ὅθεν οἱ ἱμάντεc ἐξάπτονται πρὸc τὸ cυνέχειν τὸν πόδα. ἡ δὲ ἔπτυcχλοc εἶδόc ἐcτιν ὑποδήματοc. καὶ τὸ ἀπηχία διὰ τοῦ π. cημαίνει δὲ μῖcοc καὶ ἔχθραν, οἷον ἡ ἀπηχοῦcα καὶ ἀπᾴδουcα δι' ἀναρμοcτίαν. ⟨ὅμοιον⟩ καὶ τὸ ἀμπίcχου καὶ ἀμπίcχεc.

Cf. also →ἀπηλιώτηc.

In this gloss, Phrynichus discusses a group of words which has the seemingly irregularity of escaping the rule of composition (cυναλοιφή, cf. above chap. IV § 7.2, according to which the initial aspiration of uncompound forms yields an aspirate stop in composition). Most of the forms under discussion are derivatives of words which clearly began with an aspirate. ἄπεφθοc is the compound of ἑφθόc, the verbal adjective of ἕψω, ἀντήλιον and ἀπηλιώτηc are connected to ἥλιοc. Phrynichus uses ἐκφέρω, rather than the more usual προφέρω, as a generic term to denote pronunciation[129].

In one or two instances the aspiration of the simple forms corresponding to the derivatives discussed here is debated in other Atticist lexicography. Ael. D. η 4 and Paus. η 3 had opposite views on the initial aspiration of →ἧδοc. In considering ἀπηδέc an exception just like ἄπεφθοc, Phrynichus takes sides with Ael. D η 4, who prescribes the rough breathing for ἧδοc.

The simple verb corresponding to ἀπηθεῖν is ἠθέω, whose initial aspiration is not discussed in surviving ancient scholarship. A scholion to Apollonius Rhodius 1.1294 seems to attest that Herodian prescribed an initial aspiration for its

---

[129] LSJ s.v. ἐκφέρω II.9.b: cf. Ath. 3.94f (cυαγόνα) διὰ τοῦ υ cτοιχείου ἐκφέροντεc, D.H. *Comp.* 15 ὅταν μακρῶc ἐκφέρηται, Archyt. 1 τὸ γὰρ αὐτὸ πνεῦμα διὰ μὲν τῷ μακρῷ τόπῳ ἀcθενὲc ἐκφέρεται, διὰ δὲ τῷ μείονοc cφοδρόν, Str. 9.5.17 τὴν δ' Ἰθώμην ὁμωνύμωc τῇ Μεccηνιακῇ λεγομένην οὔ φαcι δεῖν οὕτωc ἐκφέρειν, ἀλλὰ τὴν πρώτην cυλλαβὴν ἀφαιρεῖν.

derivative ἠθμός[130]. The first part of the scholion, however, where the scholiast explicitly references the twentieth book of Herodian's περὶ καθολικῆς προσῳδίας, reports the rule according to which disyllabic neuters in -ος beginning with a long vowel have an initial aspiration: despite being mentioned in the following lines of the same scholion, ἠθμός is a masculine. It is therefore surprising that Herodian should have mentioned it in the same context as the neuters, and the remarks on ἠθμός are more likely to be an addition on part of the scholiast than of Herodian. A sixth-century BC inscription from Sigeon[131], a dedication written twice, first in Ionic and then in Attic, seemingly attests the initial aspiration through the spelling hεθμον in the Attic version of the dedication. One may wonder whether the form with the initial aspiration was a genuinely Attic form (the reconstructed root of ἠθμός and ἠθέω is *seh_1-[132]: an initial aspiration would need to be explained as an exception to Grassmann's Law). Yet there is no trace of such a prescription in the surviving Atticist lexica[133].

The idea that ὕσχλος could conceal a psilotic form (Aeolic ὕσκλος according to Lobeck 1837: 34), which had entered the Koine cannot be proven, and there is no etymology of the word[134].

The case of ἀπηχία is not as clear. The word derives from non-aspirated ἦχος, which moreover fulfills the condition that every vowel preceding a χ should have a smooth breathing, πᾶν φωνῆεν πρὸ τοῦ χ ψιλοῦται (Herodian, GG 3.1 537.13 = [Arc.] 222.15–17).

ἀμπίσχω is usual in Attic and in all classical Greek literature, as is ἀμπέχω. The forms are the result of genuine dissimilation of /p^h ... k^h/ to /p ... k^h/, not an Aeolism. The idea that the absence of an aspiration is Aeolic, or rather, that is it an Aeolic τροπή that explains the non aspirated form of the preverb, is already ascribed to Herodian (GG 3.1 547.10–12 = [Arc.] 199.20–23, explained as the opposite, 'τὸ ἀνάπαλιν' of the rule that triggers an aspirate in the cluster of a stop and a rough breathing). The forms with ‹φ› are either simple reanalyses of the verb, restoring the the preverb ἀμφί with its aspirate (only found twice in the Ionic

---

130 sch. Ap. Rh. 1.1294: Ἡρωδιανὸς ἐν τῷ κ' φησίν (GG 3.1 537.10–12), ὅτι τὰ εἰς ος λήγοντα οὐδέτερα δισύλλαβα, ἀρχόμενα ἀπὸ φύσει μακρᾶς, ψιλοῦται· αἶσχος ἦθος εὖρος εἶδος. οὕτως οὖν καὶ τὸ ἦδος. τὸ δὲ ἠθμὸς δασύνεται καίτοι τὸ η ἔχον πρὸ τοῦ θ τῇ ἐννοίᾳ, τοῦ ἥσω μέλλοντος δασυνομένου (Hdn. GG 3.1 543.23–24).
131 SEG 38.1254.
132 Beekes EDG s.v. ἠθέω.
133 Clay (1968) fully discusses the whole question: the idea that 'the question of hēthmós or ēthmós was more a matter of orthography than of pronunciation' (Clay 1968: 16) should be corrected: the problem was whether to pronounce an [h] at the beginning of a word that most people would just write HΘMOC.
134 Pre-Greek according to Beekes, EDG, s.v. ὕσχλος.

medical writings of Aretaeus, 2nd c. AD), or the neologism ἀμφίσκω, occurring in the prose of Christian writers (Origen, Didymus Caecus)[135]. The entry survives in later lexica, glossed with ἐνδύειν (Hsch. α 4111, *Su.* α 1767).

ἀπηδές

→ ἄπεφθος

ἀπηθεῖν

→ ἄπεφθος

ἀπηλιώτης

Ael. D. α 157 ἀπηλιώτης· ἐν τῷ π καὶ ἀντήλιος καὶ πάντα τὰ ὅμοια ψιλῶς, καὶ ἡ ἔπηλις ἔςτι παρὰ Ποςειδίππῳ (fr. 42 K.–A.).
Phryn. fr. *249 ἀπηλιώτης ⟨ὁ ἄνεμος⟩· ἐν τῷ π. καὶ ἀντήλιος καὶ πάντα τὰ ὅμοια ψιλῶς. καὶ ἡ ἐπηλίς ἐςτι παρὰ Ποςειδίππῳ (fr. 42 K.–A.)[136].
  Cf. also → ἄπεφθος.

Aelius Dionysius is quoted by Eustathius (1562.36) while discussing psilotic Ionic forms (e.g. ἐπίςτιον, Hom. *Od.* 6.265). Some of them, among which ἀντήλιος, had made their way into Attic literature, hence their discussion in the lexicon. The forms with the aspirated consonants, despite being the expected ones in Attic, are not found before Theopompus (*Hist.* 367 ἀνθήλιος) and Theophrastus (*HP* 9.20.3, ἔφηλις). A strand of scholarship was able to trace the unaspirated forms to Attic authors of the classical canon – Eustathius also quotes Sophocles (fr. 1046 Radt) in support of the genuine Attic nature of ἔπηλις[137]. The entry is more concerned with the aspiration of the consonants in composition than with that of the initial vowels in the uncompound forms ἥλιος and ἧλος.

---

135 Origenes *Cels.* 3.41.14, 6.15.17, Didymus Caecus, *Fragm. in Psalmos* 187.16.
136 ≈ Σ^b 1779 (ἐν τῷ η). On the accentuation, ἔπηλις, cf. Herodian *GG* 3.1 91.9. Cf. Ael.D. α 157, ε 48, Oros B 30 Alpers.
137 On the accentuation, ἔπηλις, not ἐπηλίς, see [Arc.] 33.18–20 (= Hdn. *GG* 3.1 91.8–9).

ἀπηχία

→ ἄπεφθος

ἀποκτινύναι

Phryn. PS 51.12–13 ἀποκτινύναι· δι' ἑνὸς ν. οἱ δὲ διὰ δυοῖν γράφοντες ἁμαρτάνουσιν.

Morphology rather than phonology, i.e. the confusion between [nn] and [n], may be the primary concern of this entry. Even though among geminates the opposition between [nn] and [n] is among the earliest to be lost, the oscillations in the spelling of ἀποκτί(ν)νυμι are most likely due to analogical reshaping of the present stem.

The fluctuation in the writing of the geminate is common in several late Greek formations, as τίν(ν)ω, χών(ν)υμι (or χωννύω). These were reshapings basing on verbs that had a geminate as the outcome of a cluster *sn, as for instance ζώννυμι, whose stem ζωc- is visible in the noun ζωcτήρ. As these forms show a [nn] resulting from *sn[138], and have a sigmatic aorist, more verbs adjusted to the proportion ἔζωcα : ζώννυμι, and resulted in the new pairs as ἔχωcα : χώννυμι. The geminate becomes quite normal in later Greek, but the process of its extension to the present is very old[139].

ἀποχρῆ

Moer. α 9 ἀποχρῆ περιcπωμένωc ⟨Ἀττικοί⟩· ἀπόχρη βαρυτόνωc ⟨Ἕλληνεc⟩.

---

[138] Wackernagel 1916: 78–80 (esp. fn. 2, pp. 79 ff.), Gignac 1981: 281–2; on χώννυμι/χωννύω cf. also Veitch 1887 s.v. χόω. Wackernagel defines the geminate of verbs like ζώννυμι 'unphonetisch' (1916: 78); rather than being a later treatment of sn, the geminate outcome could depend on a tendency to preserve the morpheme boundary (Rix 1992: 79).

[139] Cassio (1993: 198–202) shows that the new formations with a geminate are as old as the 8th century BC, and that they tend to replace older formation with a singleton. Overall, new formations with a nasal tend to replace contracted presents in Modern Greek, cf. χέω ~ Mod.Gk. χύνω; all verbs in -όω are replaced by verbs in -ώνω, continuing the same vocalism as the aorist in -ωcα. The gemination is preserved as -ννω in the Cypriot dialect of Modern Greek, if it is the outcome of – ννύω < -ννυμι (Thumb 1901: 21); standard Mod. Gk. has the singleton.

A perispomenon ἀποχρῆ is not found in Attic texts as we know them, where the accentuation is always ἀπόχρη (cf. e.g. Plato, *R.* 380c; Isocrates *Antid.* 85; 270; *Philip.* 28), an accentuation resulting from a false etymology, that considers the verb a compound of χρή. The perispomenon belongs to a verb ἀπο-χράω, and its etymological spelling should be ἀποχρῇ. Photius too (α 2721 ἀπόχρη· ἐξαρκεῖ) uses the paroxytone form. ps.-Arcadius provides an etymological account of the different accentuations (ἀπόχρη from χρή, ἀποχρῇ from χρῇ, [Arc.] 198.3 = Hdn. π. καθ. πρ. *GG* 3.1 468.2).

A form ἀποχρῇ is restored by Elmsley in Ar. *Av.* 1603, against the reading of the manuscripts, which has ἀπόχρη[140]. ἀπόχρη is by far the best attested form: besides Elmsley's conjecture at Ar. *Av.* 1603, there is apparently only one instance of ἀποχρῆ in a classical author (Aeschines, *In Ctesiph.* 215). ἀπόχρῃ with a subscript *iota* can be read in Hippocrates, *De Visu* 4.4. All the other instances belong to either Christian authors (Nicetas Seides (twice), Michael Gabras (twice), Johannes Chortasmenus, Photius *Bibl.* 241, 333b.30) or to ancient scholarship ([Arc.] 198.3 quoted above, *Et.Gen.* α 1577, *EM* 128.9, and this gloss by Moeris).

ἆρα

Philem. 354 ἆρά γε μακρῶc.
Heren. 34 ἆρα καὶ ἆρα διαφέρει. ὁ μὲν γὰρ κατὰ περιcπωμένην λεγόμενοc cύνδεcμοc ἀπορη(μα)τικόc ἐcτιν, ὅτε διαποροῦντεc λέγομεν· 'ἆρά γε πῶc ἕξει τὸ πρᾶγμα;'. ὁ δὲ κατὰ cυcτολὴν cυλλογιcτικόc· '(εἰ ἡμέρα ἐcτί, φῶc ἐcτιν)· ἀλλὰ μὴν ἡμέρα ἐcτίν. (φῶc ἄρα ἐcτίν)'. 'εἰ τοῦτο cυμφέρει ποιεῖν, ποιητέον ἡμῖν ἄρα ἐcτίν.'[141]

As the entry of Herennius Philo shows, ἄρα and ἆρα differ both for the quantity of their first vowel and for its accentuation. ἄρα is a connecting particle, ἆρα an interrogative one: only in poetry ἄρα can replace ἆρα, clearly for metrical convenience (Denniston 1954: 44). Philemon is more clearly interested in the vowel's quantity, even if he does not state anything that may allow any specific consideration on the gloss.

---

[140] A reading accepted by Dunbar (1995; cf. commentary *ad loc.*) and Wilson (2007) in their editions of Aristophanes.
[141] Ammonius' text is almost identical to Herennius (Amm. 74): ἆρα καὶ ἄρα διαφέρει. ὁ μὲν γὰρ κατὰ περιcπαcμὸν λεγόμενοc cύνδεcμον ἀπορηματικόc ἐcτιν, ὅτε ἀποροῦντεc λέγομεν· 'ἆρα τέλοc ἕξει τὸ πρᾶγμα;'. ὁ δὲ κατὰ cυcτολὴν cυλλογιcτικόc· 'εἰ ἡμέρα ἐcτί, φῶc ἐcτιν· ἀλλὰ μὴν ἡμέρα ἐcτίν. φῶc ἄρα ἐcτίν'. 'εἰ τοῦτο cυμφέρει ποιεῖν, ποιητέον ἡμῖν ἄρα ἐcτίν.'

ἄρκυες

Paus. α 154 ἄρκυες· λίνα περιτιθέμενα θηρίοις, ἀπὸ τῶν ἑρκῶν. Ἀττικοὶ δασέως, (ὡς) ἀρκυωρὸς ὁ τῶν ἀρκύων φύλαξ, ἀφ' οὗ ἀρκυωρεῖν, ὅ ἐςτι φυλάςςειν. Εὔπολις (fr. 339 K.-A.)·
'cὺ δὲ τὰ καλώδια ταῦθ' ἀρκυώρει'.

As it is the case with Ael. D. α 157 →ἀπηλιώτης and α 98 →ἀμίς, ἅμαξα, here too the lexicographer quotes an Attic text that shows the presence of initial aspiration through its influence on the final consonant of a preceding (elided) word.

Eupolis' fragment is the only surviving occurrence of ἀρκυωρέω after a stop: there is no other evidence of the initial aspiration. The uncompound ἄρκυς is never attested with an initial aspiration: there are very few surviving occurrences of the word after a stop, and none showing the expected aspirate stop as a result of *sandhi*. They are also not very early: the earliest dates to the 2nd/3rd century AD, and is in the *Cynegetica* (4.412) of Oppian of Apamea. Some strands of ancient scholarship comment on the initial aspiration of ἄρκυς, linking it to ἁρπάζω and/or εἴργω (*Et.Gen.* α 1189, *Et.Gud.* α 199.1, ε 531.2, *EM* 144.9).

ἁρπαγή

Ael. D. α 175 ἁρπαγή· ὀξυτόνως ἡ διαρπαγή. ἡ δὲ ἁρπάγη βαρυτόνως τὸ ςκεῦος, ᾧ τοὺς κάδους ἀνάγουςιν ἐκ τῶν φρεάτων.
Heren. 28 ἁρπαγή καὶ ἁρπάγη διαφέρει παρὰ τοῖς Ἀττικοῖς, ὥς φηςι Τρύφων ἐν τρίτῳ Περὶ Ἀττικῆς προςῳδίας (fr. 12 von Velsen). ἐὰν μὲν γὰρ ὀξυτόνως προενέγκωμεθα καθάπερ ἐν τῇ ςυνηθείᾳ, τὴν αἰφνίδιον καὶ μετὰ [βίας] ἀφαίρεςιν δηλώςει· ἐὰν δὲ βαρυτόνως ἁρπάγην ὡς Ἀνάφην, ἐν ᾗ ἐκ τῶν φρεάτων τοὺς κάδους ἐξαίρουςιν. καὶ παρὰ Μενάνδρῳ (fr. 421 K.-A.)[142] ἀναγινώςκομεν·
"ποτήριον, τράπεζαν, ἁρπάγην, †δεύτερον† κάδον".
καὶ ἐν τῇ Ὑδροχόῳ (fr. 158 K.-A.)[143]·
"τὸν παῖδα δ' οὐ †δίδομεν,
ἀλλ' ἁρπάγην, ἣν αὐτὸ[ς] κατεςκεύαςεν"
καὶ Ἀριστοφάνης ἐν Νιόβῳ (fr. 296 K.-A.)

---

[142] = fr. 657 Koerte, Kassel and Austin leave out δεύτερον.
[143] Nickau (Amm. 73) ascribes the fragment of Menander to the *Eniochus* (and so also Kassel – Austin). A reading ἁρπαγή is still possible, if not preferable, as already suggested by Valckenaer and printed by Meineke and Körte (see Kassel – Austin *ad loc.*).

Heren. *de propr.* 13 ἁρπάγην ὡς Ἀνάφην, ἐν ᾗ ἐκ τῶν φρεάτων τοὺς κάδους ἐξαιροῦσιν.

Photius (α 2853) states explicitly that the accent retrocedes so that one term can become a noun (i. e. a concrete noun): "ἵνα ὀνοματικὸν γένηται". Just like the retraction of the accent can derive a noun from an adjective, Photius gives an interperation of ἁρπάγη as the concrete noun corresponding to the abstract ἁρπαγή.

Herennius' source, Trypho, introduces a chronological distinction between παλαιοὶ Ἀττικοί and the συνήθεια, absent in ps.-Arcadius: τὸ δὲ ἁρπαγή ὀξύνεται, διότι ἀπὸ τοῦ ἁρπάζω. τὸ δὲ ἁρπάγη (σιδήριόν τι) βαρυνόμενον, ἀπὸ τοῦ ἅρπαγος ([Arc.] 116.16–18), in the text of Herennius as printed by Palmieri (but present in the text of Ammonius[144]). It seems to me that the difference between older and more recent Attic here is that the older dialect distinguished between ἁρπάγη and ἁρπαγή that is absent in the Koine (which only employs ἁρπαγή). On the other hand the lack of chronological distinction in ps.-Arcadius could also mean that ἁρπάγη and ἁρπαγή were still distinct in the Koine: Modern Greek continues both (cf. Probert 2004: 289 fn. 22).

But the συνήθεια is only quoted for ἁρπαγή – as if at some point ἁρπάγη had dropped out of use, or had become at any rate a obscure term. ἁρπάγη is a technical term of Athenian daily life, as Herennius and the quote from Menander suggest, and ἁρπαγή a word that most people would still use in the 2nd century AD – Herennius refers it to the συνήθεια: the difference in meaning between ἁρπάγη and ἁρπαγή suggests that they belonged to different levels of the language, and that ἁρπάγη was at some point a word rare enough that its accentutation could not be guessed without specific indications, like the ones we reconstruct for Aelius Dionysius and Herennius / Ammonius.

ἁρπάγη is not very well attested in classical Attic literature. Its distribution in surviving literary texts suggests that the word may have gone out of use during Hellenism. In addition to the fragments of Menander quoted above, it only occurs once in Euripides, *Cycl.* 33 (with a different meaning, 'rake'). The next author to use the word is Philo Mechanicus, and then Dio Cassius. Both writers

---

[144] Nickau prints almost the same text as Amm. 73 ἁρπαγὴ καὶ ἁρπάγη διαφέρει παρὰ τοῖς παλαιοῖς Ἀττικοῖς, ὥς φησι Τρύφων ἐν τῷ τρίτῳ Περὶ Ἀττικῆς προσῳδίας (fr. 12 von Velsen). ἐὰν μὲν γὰρ ὀξυτόνως προενεγκώμεθα καθάπερ ἐν τῇ συνηθείᾳ, τὴν αἰφνίδιον καὶ μετὰ βίας ἀφαίρεσιν δηλώσει· ἐὰν δὲ βαρυτόνως ἁρπάγην ὡς Ἀνάφην, ἐν ᾗ ἐκ τῶν φρεάτων τοὺς κάδους ἐξαιρουσιν. καὶ παρὰ Μενάνδρῳ ἀναγινώσκομεν· "ποτήριον, τράπεζαν, ἁρπάγην, †δεύτερον† κάδον". καὶ ἐν Ἡνιόχῳ (fr. 158 K.–A.)· "τὸν †παῖδα δ' οὐ δίδομεν† / ἀλλ' ἁρπάγην αὐτῷ κατασκευάζομεν".

use ἁρπάγη with the technical meaning of 'grappling hook', much closer to the Modern Greek meaning of the word, and different from the meaning that ἁρπάγη has in Menander. The meaning of ἁρπάγη as a part of water-fetching devices was known to Pollux and Pausanias[145].

ἄρχων

Phryn. *PS* 47.15 ἄρχων· τὴν κλητικὴν διὰ τοῦ ω Ἀττικοί.

Kühner – Blass mention ἄρχον in the group of those consonant stems whose vocative has a different ending from the nominative (ἄνα, γύναι, γέρον ~ nom. ἄναξ, γυνή, γέρων), basing only on this gloss of the *Praeparatio Sophistica*, and conjecturing that Phrynichus was rejecting a vocative *ἄρχον: there are no other known instances of the vocative in Greek[146].

The reason why a vocative ἄρχον with a short vowel would arise must be a hypercorrection basing on morphology: ἄρχων would be inflected as γέρων ~ voc. γέρον, the only noun in -*nt* keeping the original distinction between nominative and vocative (e. g. Vedic voc. bṛhán, nom. bṛhā́n). Like all prescriptions involving ‹o› ~ ‹ω›, spelling and pronunciation may be involved at the same time – in this specific case, moreover, the confusion between ἄρχον and ἄρχων could arise because some speakers created an analogical vocative ἄρχον. To do so also in speaking, of course, they must have observed a disctinction (in quantity most likely), between the sounds spelt ‹o› and ‹ω›.

ἀςμενώτεροc

Phryn. *PS* 18.10 ἀςμενώτεροc· διὰ τοῦ ω. τὸ δὲ ἐπίρρημα ἀςμεναίτατα.

The gloss (τὸ δὲ ἐπίρρημα ἀςμεναίτατα) opposes the use of the comparative ἀςμεναίτεροc – one should use instead ἀςμενώτεροc. As the comparison with

---

[145] Pollux 6.88 κρεάγραν, ἣν καὶ ἁρπάγην ἐκάλουν καὶ λύκον καὶ ἐξαυςτῆρα, 10.31 μέρη δὲ τροχαλίας τονία τοπεῖα ἀξόνια. τῷ δὲ προςδεῖ καὶ ἁρπάγης καὶ κρεάγρας καὶ λύκου· οὕτω γὰρ ἐκάλουν τὰ ςκεύη οἷς τοὺς ἐκπεςόντας τῶν κάδων ἐκ τῶν φρεάτων ἀνέςπων· ὅτι γὰρ καὶ κρεάγραν καλοῦςι τὴν ἁρπάγην, δηλοῖ ἐν Ἐκκληςιαζούςαις (1037) Ἀριςτοφάνης λέγων 'τί δῆτα κρεάγρας τοῖς κάδοις ὠνοίμεθ' ἄν;', 10.98 ἐκ δὲ τῶν ςκευῶν καὶ ἐτνήρυςις καὶ ζωμήρυςις, καὶ κρεάγρα καὶ ἁρπάγη καὶ λύκος καὶ ἐξαυςτήρ, Paus. κ 42 κρεάγρα· ** καλεῖται δὲ καὶ ἁρπάγη καὶ λύκος.
[146] Kühner – Blass 416, Schwyzer 1939: 565.

the current form of the superlative adverb suggests, the contrast here must be between the adjective ἀςμενώτεροc and the adverb ἀςμεναίτατα, rather than between ἀςμενώτεροc and **ἀςμενότεροc[147].

ἀςφόδελοc

Ael. D. α 191 ἀςφόδελοc προπαροξυτόνωc ἀναγνωcτέον· "οὐδ' ὅcον ἐν μαλάχῃ τε καὶ ἀcφοδέλῳ μέγ' ὄνειαρ" (Hes. Op. 41)· τὸν δὲ τόπον, ἐν ᾧ φύεται, ὀξυτονητέον, ὡc καὶ παρ' Ὁμήρῳ (Od. 11.539)· "κατ' ἀcφοδελὸν λειμῶνα".
Heren. 29 ἀcφόδελοc καὶ ἀcφοδελόc κατὰ τὸν ὀξὺν τόνον διαφέρει ⟨παρὰ⟩ τοῖc Ἀττικοῖc· ἄλλοι τε καὶ Τρύφων (fr. 14 von Velsen) ἐν τῷ δευτέρῳ Περὶ Ἀττικῆc προcῳδίαc· τὸ βαρυτονούμενον γὰρ τὸ φυτὸν παρὰ τοῖc παλαιοῖc, [ὀ]ξυτονούμενον δὲ τὸν τόπον, ἐν ᾧ ὁ ἀcφόδελοc γίνεται· αὐτόc δέ τι ὁ Τρύφων προκρίνει ὁμοτόνωc τῷ φυτῷ καὶ τὸν τόπον ἐκφέρειν· πολλάκιc ⟨γάρ⟩, φηcίν, τοῖc περιεχομένοιc τὰ περιέχοντα ὁμοτόνωc λέγεται. καὶ cκόροδα γὰρ αὐτὰ λέγομεν καὶ τὸν τόπον ἔνθα cυμβέβηκε ταῦτα πιπράcκεcθαι· ὁμοίωc κρόκον αὐτὸ τὸ ἄνθοc καὶ τὸν τόπο[ν] ἐν ᾧ φύεται[148].

The distinction between ἀcφόδελοc, the flower, and ἀcφοδελόc, 'rich in asphodels' depends only on the position of the accent. The adjective is comparatively rare, as it occurs only five times, and only in Homer[149].

Herennius somehow identifies Attic and Homer. Readings of Homer could have had the oxytone adjective, when they followed the doctrine reflected in Ael. D. and Herennius (which may go back to Herodian, cf. [Arc.] 62.3–4). The oxytone accentuation of the adjective supported by Herennius Philo (and Herodian), but contrasted by Trypho (Probert 2006: 47, quoting P.Ryl.[150] I 53, fol. 92ʳ, whose spelling αcφόδελον disregards Herodian's doctrine altogether).

---

[147] ἀcμεναίτατα is one of the unadapted Greek words used by Cicero (e. g. ad Att. 13.22.1 "te autem ἀcμεναίτατα intexo, faciamque id crebrius"); ἀcμενέcτατα is corrected in ἀcμεναίτατα in Pl. R. 329c; Dio Cassius uses ἀcμεναίτατα (Hist. Rom. 36.45.2), but Clemens Alexandrinus ἀcμενέcτατα (Paed. 2.10, 95.1).
[148] Amm. 81 ἀcφόδελοc καὶ ἀcφοδελόc διαφέρει. προπαροξυτόνωc μὲν γὰρ τὸ φυτόν· ὀξυτόνωc δ' ὁ τόποc "κατ' ἀcφοδελὸν λειμῶνα" (Od. 11.539, 573, 24.13).
[149] As part of the formula quoted by Aelius Dionysius, κατ' ἀcφοδελὸν λειμῶνα (three times in the Odyssey – 11.539, 573, 24.13), and slightly varied as ἐc ἀcφοδελὸν λειμῶνα in h.Merc. 221 and 344.
[150] A. S. Hunt et al., Catalogue of the Greek Papyri in the John Rylands Library, Manchester (Manchester 1911–52).

The adjective ἀσφοδελός seems to be a back-formation from the noun ἀσφόδελος[151]. The distinction between the two forms is weak, as the noun is rather common, but the adjective is rare and used exclusively in Homer. Aelius' gloss is clearly a prescription (προπαροξυτόνως ἀναγνωστέον ... ὀξυτονητέον), even though it does not formulate the relation between accentuation and meaning as a rule (but cf. Photius α 2853, and → ἁρπαγή). Except for Herennius' entry, there is no evidence that ἀσφόδελος was used by the Atticists.

ἀτεχνῶς

Philet. 243 ἀτεχνῶς· οὕτω λέγουσιν οἱ Ἀττικοὶ περισπωμένως· σημαίνει τὸ ἁπλῶς. τὸ δὲ ἀτέχνως βαρυτόνως λεγόμενον τὸ ἄνευ τέχνης σημαίνει.

The two adverbs ἀτεχνῶς and ἀτέχνως come from two different adjectives, ἄτεχνος and ἀτεχνής (both derivatives of τέχνη)[152]. If no accent sign was written, the correct accentuation could be understood only on the basis of the meaning[153].

Ἀτρέα

Philem. 355 Ἀτρέα, ὡς βασιλέα, τὸ α μακρόν.

→ ἀμφορέα

ἄττα

Ael. D. α 193 ἄττα· σημαίνει μὲν ἡ φωνὴ τὸ τινά, ὁπότε ψιλοῦται, ἢ καὶ τὸ ὀλίγα ἢ παραπλήσιον· ὁπότε δὲ δασύνεται, τὸ ἅτινα, ὅπερ οἱ Ἴωνες ἅσσα λέγουσιν· σημαίνει δὲ καὶ τὸ ἅπερ ἄν, ὡς Δημοσθένης δηλοῖ ἐν τῷ ⟨Περὶ⟩ τῆς παραπρεσβεί-

---

[151] According to the inherited alternation between recessive accentuation of nouns ~ oxytone adjectives, cf. δόλιχος ~ δολιχός, ved. *kr̥ṣṇá-* ~ *kŕ̥ṣṇa-*, Schwyzer 1939: 420, Probert 2006: 236–7.
[152] Adjectives in -ής, originally derivatives of sigmatic nouns in *-es-/-os*, had become productive in Greek and could be derived even from non-sigmatic nouns, cf. Meißner 2006: 160 ff.
[153] The (synonymic) gloss is trasmitted by Ammonius as well, Amm. 84 ἀτέχνως καὶ ἀτεχνῶς διαφέρει. τὸ μὲν γὰρ παροξύτονον σημαίνει τὸ χωρὶς τέχνης καὶ ἀμαθῶς· τὸ δὲ περισπώμενον τίθεται ἀντὶ τοῦ ἁπλῶς καὶ ἀδόλως καὶ καθάπαξ καὶ καθόλου, ἄντικρυς.

ας (19.304)· 'ὁ δὲ πρεσβεύων Αἰσχίνης οὑτοσί· ἐλθὼν ⟨δ'⟩ [πῶς μὲν καὶ] ἄττα ⟨μέν⟩ ποτε διελέχθη ⟨καὶ ἐδημηγόρησεν, αὐτὸς ἂν εἰδείη⟩'. ἐνίοτε δὲ καὶ ὡς παρέλκον ἐστί, ὡς ἐν Χείρωνι Φερεκράτης (fr. 161 K.-A.)· 'τοῖς δέκα ταλάντοις προστιθείς', ἔφη, 'ἄλλ' ἄττα πεντήκοντα'.
   Ἀριστοφάνης Νεφέλαις (630)·
      'ὅστις σκαλαθυρμάτι' ἄττα μικρὰ μανθάνων'.
   παραλαμβάνει δὲ καὶ τὸ πότε ἢ τὸ ἰσοδυναμοῦν τούτῳ καὶ τὸ πηνίκα (cf. Eratosth. fr. 22 Str.) ⟨Χιωνίδης (Aristophanes, fr. 617 K.-A.)⟩·
      'πυθοῦ χελιδὼν πηνίκ' ἄττα φαίνεται'
   καὶ πάλιν (Ar. fr. 618 K.-A.)·
      'ὁπηνίκ' ἄτθ' ὑμεῖς κοπιᾶτ' ὀρχούμενοι'.
Phryn. fr. †*274 = Σ^b 2372 αττα· σημαίνει μὲν ἡ φωνὴ τὸ τινά, ὁπότε ψιλοῦται. ἢ καὶ τὸ ὀλίγα ἢ παραπλησίον. ὁπότε δὲ δασύνεται, τὸ ἅτινα, ὅπερ οἱ Ἴωνες ἅσσα λέγουσιν. σημαίνει δὲ καὶ τὸ ἅπερ ἄν. ἐνίοτε δὲ καὶ τὸ πότε καὶ τὸ ὅμοιον καὶ τὸ πηνίκα. Δημοσθένης δὲ ἐν τῷ παραπρεσβείας (19.304) ἐπὶ τοῦ ὅσα ἔλαβε τὴν λέξιν. τῶν δὲ κωμικῶν τις τὸ ἄττα ἐπὶ ἀριθμοῦ ἔταξεν (Pherecr. fr. 161.2 K.-A.), ἕτερος δὲ ἐπὶ χρόνου (Ar. fr. 617 K.-A.).
   cf. Amm. 86 ἄττα ψιλούμενον καὶ δασυνόμενον διαφέρει. Ψιλούμενον μὲν γὰρ σημαίνει τὸ 'τινά', δασυνόμενον δὲ τὸ 'ἅτινα'.

The gloss, in the wording that Erbse reconstructed for Aelius Dionysius (and the longer version of Σ^b 2372, tentatively attributed to Phrynichus by de Borries, as fr. †*274), does not prescribe the initial breathing as Attic, but only points out its function as the trait that differentiates the direct cases of the neuter plural of τίς/τις from the plural of ὅστις (in this sense, a reduced form of the gloss appears in Ammonius' lexicon).

αὐτοχειρίᾳ

Phryn. *PS* 10.9-11 αὐτοχειρίᾳ πεποίηται ἐπιρρηματικῶς. σημαίνει δὲ ταῖς αὐτοῦ χερσί. πρὸ μιᾶς ὁ τόνος. οἶδα δέ τινας οὐκ ἀδόξους περισπῶντας τὴν τελευταίαν, οὐχ ὑγιῶς.

The innovative pronunciation αὐτοχειριᾷ can be understood as the result of the loss of syllabicity of [i], yielding an accent shift on the following vowel (the phenomenon has been studied in detail by Scheller 1951). The popular pronunciation of some terms had made its way in to the standard and could find support at least in part of the ancient scholarship (Scheller 1951: 136).

It is noteworthy that in this gloss Phrynichus defines the speakers whose pronunciation he rebuts 'οὐκ ἄδοξοι' 'not obscure' (or even 'not disreputable'), and not ἀμαθεῖς 'ignorant' as he does on other occasions – the οὐκ ἄδοξοι could be a group ancient scholars (Scheller 1951: 130). The same lemma, but with different glosses, appears in the *Philetaerus* (193, quoting Strattis) and its *excerptum Vindoboniense* (*exc. Vind.* 31): in both cases the entry describes the meaning of the adverb, without mentioning the position or nature of the accent. Cf. also Ael. D. π 9 πανςτρατιᾷ· οὕτω λέγει καὶ Θουκυδίδης καὶ οἱ ἄλλοι and Ammonius (449) ςτρατεία ἐκτεταμένως τὸ πρᾶγμα, ςτρατιὰ δὲ ςυνεςταλμένως τὸ τῶν ςτρατιωτῶν πλῆθος. ἐναλλάςςει δὲ πολλάκις ἐν τῇ χρήςει, which associates to the accent shift a difference in quantity of the penultimate vowel.

ἀφοῦ

Phryn. *PS* 27.13–17 ἀφοῦ οἷον ἀπαλλάγηθι καὶ μὴ ἔχου. ὁ τόνος ἐπὶ τέλους. καὶ ἀφέςθαι τὸ ἀπαρέμφατον, ὅμοιον τῷ θοῦ, θέςθαι. τὰ γὰρ παροξύτονα τὸ ἄφου, ὡς τὸ πρόου καὶ μέθου καὶ ὕφου (ἐπὶ τοῦ δευτέρου προςώπου ἑνικοῦ τοῦ παρεληλυθότος τίθεται).

Imperatives of compounds form monosyllabic verbs (as in this case the root aorist of ἵημι) can have an accent on the preverb, as the result of the original enclitic nature of the verb, or they can retain the accent on the verb itself[154]. De Borries integrates the gloss with ἐπὶ τοῦ δευτέρου προςώπου ἑνικοῦ τοῦ παρεληλυθότος τίθεται, understanding the recessive ἄφου πρόου μέθου ὕφου as forms of the aorist (παρεληλυθώς). These forms, however, are never attested as past tenses. Aorist imperatives accented on the final vowel were exceptional, and an archaism of Attic that the manuscript tradition does not consistently preserve. The uncertainty between recessive and progressive accentuation of the aorist imperative must have been a concern by the time of the Atticists, as at least two more glosses attest (Moer. ε 32 → ἐπιμέλου, *Philet.* 227 → εὑρέ).

ἀχρεῖος

Philet. 241 ἀχρεῖος παρὰ τοῖς Ἀττικοῖς βαρυτόνως.

---

[154] Schwyzer 1939: 390–1 and 799.

The gloss points to an Attic pronunciation ἄχρειος, an instance of Vendryes' Law, signalled in the gloss by βαρυτόνως – a similar view is expressed in a scholion to Homer *Il.* 2.269[155], and in the 3rd century rhetorical work preserved in P.Oxy. 1012 (cf. above chap. I, § 6.2, ex. (19)). The *De accentibus* attributed to Arcadius defines both accentuations as Attic. The passage in question, possibly corrupt, reads:

> πᾶν εἰς ον ἐπιθετικὸν οὐδέτερον, παρεσχηματισμένον τοῖς εἰς ος λέγουσιν ἀρσενικοῖς, τούτοις φυλάττει τὸν τόνον, φιλόσοφος, φιλόσοφον, ἀχρεῖος, ἀχρεῖον, καὶ ἀττικῶς, ἄχρειως ἄχρειων.

> Every neuter of an adjective ending in ον, formed on the mascines ending in ος, keeps the accent that it has [in the masculine], φιλόσοφος, φιλόσοφον, ἀχρεῖος, ἀχρεῖον and in Attic ἄχρειως ἄχρειων.

[Arc.] 134.7–10

if ἄχρειως ἄχρειων are misspellings for ἄχρειος and ἄχρειον, here the grammarian ascribes to Attic the paroxytones, as *Philet.* 241 and sch. *Il.* 2.269a¹ (A) do. However, elsewhere in the *De accentibus* ἀχρεῖος is defined as the actual Attic form:

> ἄχρειος (τὸ κοινόν, ἀχρεῖος δὲ τὸ Ἀττικόν, ὡς ἀστεῖος).

> ἄχρειος (in the Koine (κοινόν), ἀχρεῖος in Attic, like ἀστεῖος).

[Arc.] 99.25–100.1

According to Probert (2004: 287) the two interpretations are only seemingly conflicting: one of them refers to 'ancient' Attic, and the other to recent Attic, two stages separated by the completion of the process known as Vendryes' Law: ἀχρεῖος is only more ancient than ἄχρειος, and both forms can claim a place in genuine Attic. Moreover, some forms that had undergone the law were current in the Koine (Probert 2004: 290), a distribution that may have engendered confusion as to the dialectal distribution of forms with or without retraction of the accent.

Modern editors always treat ἀχρειος as a properispomenon ἀχρεῖος. The prosodical scheme α.χρει.ος, the necessary condition for Vendryes' Law, is attested already in the 5th century BC – cf. e.g. Euripides, *Med.* 299 δοξεῖς ἀχρεῖον κοὐ

---

[155] sch. *Il.* 2.269a¹ (A) ἀχρεῖον {ἰδών}· Διονύσιος καὶ Τυραννίων τὴν πρώτην ὀξύνουσιν, ὥσπερ καὶ παρὰ τοῖς Ἀττικοῖς, καὶ ἀναλόγως· παρὰ γὰρ τὸ χρεία τὸ κατὰ στέρησιν ἄχρειος, ὡς μοῦσα ἄμουσος. ἡ μέντοι παρὰ τῷ ποιητῇ ἀνάγνωσις, ἀφορμῆς ἐχομένη τῆς κατὰ τὴν συνεκδρομήν, (προ)περιεσπάσθη. Cf. Probert 2004: 287.

σοφὸς πεφυκέναι, [Aeschylus] *Pr.* 363 καὶ νῦν ἀχρεῖον καὶ παράορον δέμας, yet the more archaic accentuation on the penultimate is kept in modern editions. The proparoxytone ἄχρειοι is found once in Aristotle, *APr.* 44b – in whose text however the properispomenon ἀχρεῖος is the regular spelling.

ἄχρειος did not only belong to more recent Attic, but was also the current form of the adjective in the Koine. The gloss in the *Philetaerus* opposes recent Attic and Koine on one side and more ancient Attic and Homer on the other. The same attribution pattern is true of →γέλοιος (cf. Moer. γ 4) ἀχρεῖος and γελοῖος are the only words glossed in the lexica that are also affected by Vendryes' Law. The pair γέλοιος ~ γελοῖος however also involves a semantic specialisation of the terms, disregarded in Moeris' gloss (contrast Ael. D. γ 4, Philem. 357, Amm. 119).

The lexicographers therefore seem to identify as genuinely Attic the form that is most remote form the Koine. The gloss in the *Philetaerus* is much shorter than the remarks in ps.-Arcadius: it only ascribes the properispomenon ἀχρεῖος to the Koine, the same accentuation that has become normal in the conventions of byzantine manuscripts, regardless of author and genre.

βαδίζειν

Moer. β 15 βᾱδίζειν μακρῶς Ἀττικοί· βραχέως Ἕλληνες.

Hansen prints βᾱδίζειν in his edition of Moeris, but the choice is difficult to support. The only evidence in its support is Arist. *Poet.* 1458b[156], where Aristotle quotes two lines of an otherwise unknown Euclides, both requiring forcible adjustment to the metre by various artificial lengthenings. The first one, Ἐπιχάρην εἶδον Μαραθῶνάδε βαδίζοντα, can be scanned as an hexameter if the first syllable of both Ἐπιχάρην and βαδίζοντα is scanned as long. Aristotle can hardly be source of Moeris' gloss. As it is the case with other fragments of Attic comedy in the Atticist lexica, if the Euclides in question was really an Attic playwright, Moeris could have known him through some Hellenistic treatise. But the glosses referring to βαδίζειν explicitly mention the ‹υ› and do not quote Euclides or Aristotle. Hansen's interpretation therefore does not rest on any sound evidence that the vowel in question was ‹α›.

---

[156] Arist. *Poet.* 1458b: ὥστε οὐκ ὀρθῶς ψέγουσιν οἱ ἐπιτιμῶντες τῷ τοιούτῳ τρόπῳ τῆς διαλέκτου καὶ διακωμῳδοῦντες τὸν ποιητήν, οἷον Εὐκλείδης ὁ ἀρχαῖος, ὡς ῥᾴδιον ὂν ποιεῖν εἴ τις δώσει ἐκτείνειν ἐφ' ὁπόσον βούλεται, ἰαμβοποιήσας ἐν αὐτῇ τῇ λέξει 'Ἐπιχάρην εἶδον Μαραθῶνάδε βαδίζοντα'.

Later grammatical tradition clearly identifies the problematic vowel with the *iota*: cf. [Hdn.] *de loc. prav., An. Ox.* 3 260.3–9:

ἁμαρτάνουσι οἱ λέγοντες ἐκτεταμένως βαδίζειν, δέον λέγειν συνεσταλμένως βαδίζειν, καὶ ἐβάδιζον, λόγῳ τοιούτῳ· τριῶν ὄντων διπλῶν ζ, ξ, ψ, καὶ τριῶν διχρόνων, α, ι, υ, πᾶν δίχρονον, διπλοῦ ἐπιφερομένου, ςυςτέλλεται, μάλιστα δὲ τοῦ ζ ἐπιφερομένου, οἷον φροντίζω, αὐγάζω, κουφίζω, ἀκοντίζω· οὕτως ἄρα καὶ βαδίζω, ἐβάδιζον, συνεσταλμένως, ὡς καὶ φροντίζω, ἐφρόντιζον[157].

A fragment attributed to Oros reflects a more flexible doctrine (both quantities are acceptable for the ‹ι› of βαδίζειν): διὰ τοῦτο βαδίσω καὶ βαδιῶ, ἀμφότερα δόκιμα, ἐπεὶ καὶ αὐτὸ τὸ ἐνεστηκὸς ἑκατέρως λέγεται, καὶ ἐκτεινομένου καὶ ςυςτελλομένου τοῦ ἐν τῇ μέςῃ ςυλλαβῇ[158].

It is difficult to tell whether βαδίζειν had been chosen as an exemplary case, to show the long quantity of the ending -ίζω: originally the length of the penultimate syllable was caused by the consonant ‹ζ› and not by the vowel. Educated speakers were taught that verbs in -ίζω and in -άζω had a penultimate long syllable: a pronunciation [i:zo:] would therefore be a hypercorrection, showing the more recent simplified consonant and making up for the prescribed length of the penultimate syllable by lengthening an originally short vowel[159]. A spelling βα-

---

[157] Cf. also *EM* 737.25 τὰ εἰς -ζω λήγοντα ῥήματα κοινολεκτούμενα οὐδέποτε ἔχει το α ἐν τῇ παραληγούςῃ μακρόν φύσει, and Dindorf in *ThGL* II 14d s.v. βᾰδίζω. The forgerer (see chap. I, § 5.5) of Osann's Philemon must have understood the atticist doctrine as prescribing [i:] and writes βαδίζειν (Osann 1821: 282).

[158] The whole passage – in Photius' wording, although quite later than the atticist lexica discussed in this book, is interesting for the connection it makes between correct pronunciation, public speaking, and Athenian identity:

θεριῶ καὶ κομιῶ καὶ ποριῶ καὶ ὁριῶ καὶ πάντα τὰ εἰς ζω βαρύτονα καὶ ὑπὲρ δύο ςυλλαβὰς βραχυνόμενον τὸ ι ἔχοντα, ἐν τῷ μέλλοντι ἄνευ τοῦ ς ἐκφέρουςιν Ἀττικοί· τὰ γοῦν ὁριστικὰ καὶ ἀπαρέμφατα· τὰ δ' ὑποτακτικὰ οὐδαμῶς· ςολοικιςμὸς γὰρ τὸ ἐὰν θεριῶ καὶ ἐὰν κομιῶ. ἐφ' ὧν δὲ τὸ ι ἐκτείνεται καὶ cὺν τῷ ς ὁ μέλλων λέγεται χρόνος καὶ ἐκτεινομένης τῆς παρεςχάτης ςυλλαβῆς, οἷον δανείζω, δανείςω, οὐκέτι τὸ δὲ δανειῶ βάρβαρον οὕτως, ὥστε καὶ τοὺς Ἀθηναίους φασὶν ἀθρόους εἰς ἐκκληςίαν ςυναθροιςθέντας ἐπὶ τῶν διαδόχων, ἐπειδὴ εἰς ἀπορίαν καθεστήκεςαν χρημάτων, ἔπειτά τις αὐτοῖς τῶν πλουσίων ὑπιςχνεῖτο ἀργύριον, οὕτω πως λέγων, ὅτι ἐγὼ ὑμῖν δανειῶ, θορυβεῖν καὶ οὐκ ἀνέχεςθαι λέγοντος διὰ τὸν βαρβαριςμὸν καὶ οὐδὲ λαβεῖν τὸ ἀργύριον ἐθέλειν· ἕως αἰσθόμενος ὁ μέτοικος, ἢ καὶ ὑποβαλόντος αὐτῷ τινος ἔφη, δανείσω ὑμῖν τοῦτο τὸ ἀργύριον· τότε δ' ἐπαινέςαι καὶ λαβεῖν. διὰ τοῦτο βαδίσω καὶ βαδιῶ, ἀμφότερα δόκιμα, ἐπεὶ καὶ αὐτὸ τὸ ἐνεστηκὸς ἑκατέρως λέγεται, καὶ ἐκτεινομένου καὶ ςυςτελλομένου τοῦ ἐν τῇ μέςῃ ςυλλαβῇ· οὐκέτι δὲ ἀγορῶ οὐδὲ κολῶ· οὐδὲ γὰρ ὅλως τῷ ι παραλήγει (Phot. θ 117 = *Su.* θ 242 = Oros B 79).

[159] It is unlikely that aorists of contract verbs in -άω/έω had an influence here. The first instances of confusion like ἐχάριcα for ἐχάρηcα date between the 4th and the 6th century AD (cf. Gignac 1981: 296), a time when isochrony was the norm everywhere. The very variation between ‹η› and

δείζοντας is attested in an inscription dating to the beginning of the 3ʳᵈ century (*IG* II² 1078.27; *ca.* AD 220). Even at the time of the inscription, ‹ευ› for short [i] is quite rare (although it does occasionally occur in inscriptions dating to the previous century, cf. chap. III, § 5.4): therefore it is likely that it was meant as an 'accurate' spelling for /iː/.

No other original geminate triggered a compensatory lengthening when it was reduced to a single consonant, and it is therefore hard to believe that this should have been the case exclusively with /zz/[160]. However, this particular geminate has the special qualities of being the only one written with a single consonant, and the only one that is not contrasted with a singleton: the pronunciation with a long vowel can therefore be explained as an attempt at rendering in speaking a quantity that was not apparent in the spelling. Cf. *Philet.* 230 → δανείζειν, possibly involving the same confusion, resulting form the homophony of ‹ιζω› ‹ειζω› (certainly implied, although at a later stage in the passage of Photius quoted in footnote 529 above, Phot. θ 117).

βιβλία

Moer. β 10 βιβλία διὰ τοῦ ι, ὡς Πλάτων, Ἀττικοί· βυβλία, ὡς Δημοσθένης, κοινόν. Ael. D. β 19 βύβλινον καὶ βίβλινον· διχῶς.

Spellings with ‹υ› are the most ancient, and may reflect an original semitic back vowel[161]. The ‹ι› of βίβλος and its derivatives must be the outcome of an old dissimilation: the first attestations of this word group in Attic inscriptions are already spelt with ‹ι›[162]. The variant βύβλος becomes more common during Hellenism (in Attica during the 1ˢᵗ century BC[163]) but is only occasionally attested in Roman times, when the Attic form βίβλος is again predominant[164].

‹ι› is always indifferent to the quantity of ‹ι›: this implies that both -ησω and -ισω where pronounced [iso] by the time they could interchange.

160 There are good structural reasons why /zz/ should be reduced to /z/ at an earlier stage than most consonants, as – whatever was the sound spelt by ‹ζ› – it lacked a single counterpart. The pronuciation [zd] was marginal enough to allow Aristotle (*Metaph.* 993a) to state as soon as the 4ᵗʰ century BC that ‹ζ› could spell a single consonant (cf. Hinge 2006: 94 fn. 3); cf. also the increasing use of ‹ζ› for the allophone [z] of /s/ (from the half of the 4th century BC in Attica, Threatte 1980: 547), cf. chap. V, § 5.
161 Kretschmer 1930: 252 fn. 4, Rosół 2013: 167.
162 *IG* I³ 475, fr. VIII, col. VI, 19.
163 Meisterhans – Schwyzer 1900: 28; Mayser – Schmoll 1970: 80.
164 Gignac 1976: 268.

Moeris' chronological distinction does reflect the distribution of the two spellings in Attic texts. The gloss, however, does not necessarily imply the merger of /y/ with /i/: the coexistence of both variants in the texts of the Atticist canon was already a sufficient ground for confusion.

βοϊκόc

Philem. 357 βοϊκόν· τὸ ι μακρόν.

Philemon was probably trying to defend a spelling βοεικόc, yet, while prescribing the pronunciation with [i:] he adopts a spelling with simple ‹ι›. A similar prescription can be found in Apollonius Dyscolus, κτητικῶν τῶν εἰc κοc ληγόντων ἡ παρεδρεύουcα βραχεῖά ἐcτιν, ἀλλὰ κεραμεικόc τέ φαcι καὶ βοεικόc (*GG* 2.1.1 166.28–9), and is attributed to Herodian by Choeroboscus (*An. Ox.* 2 183.31–33) βοϊκὰ ζεύγη: ι ἡ παράδοcιc· Ἡρωδιανὸc δὲ δίφθογγον αὐτῷ ἔταξεν ἐν τῷ περὶ ὀρθογραφίαc· ὁ δὲ λόγοc οὐ cυγχωρεῖ. βοεικόν has a metrically guaranteed long vowel in Aristophanes (fr. 111.1 K.–A.). The manuscripts transmitting this fragment (Stobaeus 4.14.2 p. 371 H.; codd. SMA) have βοϊκόν[165]: βοεικόν is a conjecture by Dindorf, based on Thuc. 4.128.4, and Xenophon, *An.* 7.5.2 and 7.5.4, where the best manuscripts have ‹ει›. Inscriptions, however, only attest βόειοc in Attica[166].

All these prescriptions only confirm that ‹ει› was an extremely common spelling for long /i:/, to the point that the prescription of the long vowel could sometimes equal the prescription of a spelling with the digraph.

βότρυc

Moer. β 34 βότρυc μακρὸν Ἀττικοί· βραχέωc Ἕλληνεc.
Moer. c 22 cτάχυc μακρῶc (Ἀττικοί)· βραχέωc Ἕλληνεc.

βότρῠc and cτάχῠc, the forms ascribed to the Hellenes, can be only be nominative singulars. Only about forty-five barytones in -ῠ- are attested in Greek, and there is evidence for the quantity of the suffixal vowel for only about a third

---

[165] βοϊκόν MA, βοῖκον S; cf. Kassel – Austin *ad loc.*
[166] In Attic inscriptions: β[οειον integrated in *IG* I³ 392 (*ca.* 420 BC), βοειοτομίαν *IG* II² 1590a (mid-4th c. BC), βόειου *SEG* 47.196 A/B (1st c. BC). Elsewhere both βόειοc and βοικόc are attested.

of them. In addition to βότρυc and cτάχυc, there are at least three more nouns for which variants with long vowel are attested: γένῡc (E. *El.* 1215), χέλῡc (Hom. *h.Merc.* 33), νέκῡc (Hom. *passim*). There is only one instance of the nom. sg. cτάχῡc, Euripides *HF* 4–5 ἔνθ' ὁ γηγενής / cπαρτῶν cτάχυc ἔβλαcτεν, ὧν γένουc Ἄρηc. As for βότρῡc, the gloss in Moeris β 34 is the only information we have on the quantity of the *hypsilon*, the nominative singular βότρῡc is never attested with a metrically guaranteed long vowel[167].

Euripides may ultimately be the source of some Atticist doctrine referring to the nominative singulars in -υc that had a long vowel in Attic. The attribution of a long vowel to βότρυc could rest on some lost attestation of the word in metre, or to the generalisation of a principle that this *dichronon* was long in Attic[168]. It certainly was in the plural, about which Herodian may have written, if it is his doctrine that we read in ps.-Arcadius' epitome: πᾶν δίχρονον ἐκ κράcεωc ὂν ἐκτείνεται· Θέτι ἱρεύc ἴρηξ οἱ νέκυc οἱ βότρυc ῥῦcθαι εὐφυᾶ εὐκλεᾶ ([Arc.] 222.3–5).

Whatever the relation between Moer. β 34 and Herodian may be, the entries in Moeris could also have the accessory function of establishing the inflection of cτάχυc and βότρυc. If a nominative singular in -ῡc is prescribed, the expected genitive singular is βότρυοc, and the accusative plural βότρυαc or βότρῡc. This is the inflection commonly attested in Attic writers, the commonest accusative plural being of the type βότρῡc: βότρυc itself provides the paradigm for this declension in Theodosius' *Canones* (*GG* 4.1 13.12–18).

The declension of βότρῠc, cτάχῠc can be the same as βότρῡc, cτάχῡc, but also as ablauting *u*-stems (e.g. πρέcβυc, πρέcβεωc), and form e.g. a gen. sg. βότρεωc, cτάχεωc[169]. Such forms are virtually not attested. However, there is at least one isolated example of a nom. pl. βότρειc dating to the 3rd century AD, in Christian literature: ἡ μὲν γὰρ πνευματικὴ ἄμπελοc ἦν ὁ cωτήρ, κλήματα δὲ καὶ cτελέχη εἰcὶν αὐτοῦ οἱ ἅγιοι οἱ εἰc αὐτὸν πιcτεύοντεc· βότρειc δὲ αὐτοῦ οἱ μάρτυρεc (Hippolytus, *De benedictionibus Isaaci et Jacobi* 98.8), and the personal

---

167 Gunnerson (1905: 37). The accusative plural βότρῡc is metrically guaranteed in Ar. fr. 581.1 (cf. also Ar. fr. 332.10 K.–A., but at line-end, where the quantity of its final vowel is indifferent).
168 A similar generalisation could explain Eustathius' comment on κάχρυc (αἱ δὲ τοιαῦται κριθαὶ καὶ κάχρυc διcυλλάβωc καὶ ἐκτεταμένωc ἐλέγοντο κατὰ Αἴλιον Διονύcιον θηλυκῶc, Eust. 1835.43), if it is not referred to the nom./acc. pl.; a nom. sing. is never attested, and the information on quantity is not included by Erbse in the text of Aelius Dionysius (κ 17).
169 On the original ablaut see Rix 1992: 148, on forms retaining -ῠ- Gunnerson 1905: 36–42. Nouns in short ῠ are often subject to analogical remodelling on the themes in ῡ, and the two original types are sometimes difficult to distinguish (Chantraine 1933: 118, Schwyzer 1939: 462 fn. 3, 463). On the nom./acc. pl. in -ῡc see Meyer 1896: § 355; Gunnerson 1905: 39, Threatte 1996: 217–220 (the inverse analogical levelling, i.e. the nominative replacing the accusative, is more common, cf. Schwyzer 1939: 563, Rix 1992: 155).

name Cτάχυc has a dative in -ει in the 4th century *Acta Philippi* (rec. e cod. Xenophont. 32, *passim*). At a much later date, some grammatical tradition must have been considered this inflection acceptable: cf. *EM* 431.5 Gaisford ἐπικατακλίνει δὲ τοὺς cτάχυας τοῖς cτάχεcιν[170].

It very unlikely that Moeris is contrasting forms of the plural with forms of the singular, without saying so, and unreasonale that the forms with short vowels of the Hellenes may be accusative plurals. However, Ammonius' synonymical lexicon has a similar entry on cτάχυc, that contrasts the two numbers basing on vowel quantity (Amm. 435 cτάχυc βραχέως τὸ ἑνικόν, ἐκτεταμένως τὸ πληθυντικόν).

βύβλινοc

Ael. D. β 19 βύβλινον καὶ βίβλινον· διχῶc.

→ βιβλία

γέλοιοc

Moer. γ 4 γέλοιον βαρυτόνως Ἀττικοί· γελοῖον προπεριcπωμένως Ἕλληνες.
  Cf. also:
Philem. 357 γελοῖοc· γέλοιοc ὁ ἄπειροc.
Ael. D. γ 4 γέλοιοc· ὁ καταγέλαcτος προπαροξυτόνως· προπεριcπωμένως δὲ γελοῖοc ὁ γελωτοποιόc.
Amm. 119 γέλοιοc καὶ γελοῖοc διαφέρει. γέλοιοc μὲν ὁ καταγέλαcτος, γελοῖοc δὲ ὁ γελωτοποιόc.

γέλοιοc is a more recent accentuation of γελοῖοc, resulting from the accent shift known as Vendryes' Law, and therefore exclusive to Attic. As is the case with *Philet.* 241 → ἀχρεῖοc, Moeris identifies as Attic the accentuation resulting from the accent shift.

The gloss reflects only one strand of Atticism. The pronunciation attributed to Attic, in particular if labelled as more recent, was not necessarily the recommended one: cf. *EM* 224.40–4 "οἱ μεταγενέcτεροι τῶν Ἀττικῶν τὸ γελοῖοc καὶ

---

[170] And in the 12th century AD Michael Glycas writes cτάχειc (*Versus in carcere scripti*, 321).

ὁμοῖος προπαροξύνουσι· οὐκ εὖ". The doctrine reflected in these passages may go back to Herodian (Probert 2004: 284–5).

The distincton between the meanings of γέλοιος and γελοῖος is probably artificial[171]. The source of Ael. D. γ 4 is the same as Ael. D. α 175 → ἁρπαγή, a passage of Eustathius (906.50) discussing various pairs of barytone and oxytone words, homophones except for the position of the accent, and quoting Iohannes Philoponus in support of the oxytone accentuation γελοιός[172]. The oxytone is otherwise not attested, and it may result from the mechanical (and artificial) application of this correspondence between barytones and oxytones (cf. Ael. D. α 191, Heren. 29 → ἀσφόδελος ~ ἀσφοδελός).

γενέσθαι

Philet. 252 γενέσθαι, λαβέσθαι παροξυτόνως μᾶλλον προ{c}ενεκτέον.

The accentuation of thematic aorist infinitives does not seem to have been controversial in antiquity. It is unclear why γενέσθαι and λαβέσθαι should 'rather' (μᾶλλον) be pronounced as paroxytones. They of course – like all strong aorist infinitives – had the same ending as recessive present infinitives. The paroxytone accentuation is not prescribed as being Attic. The entry may be an abridgement of some extended, general discussion on the accentuation of infinitives, similar to the scholarship on the accent of infinitives transmitted in Choeroboscus, *GG* 4.2 226.12–17[173]. There is nothing that suggests that there was any uncertainty regarding their accentuation, at least when their stem is clearly that of the aorist[174].

I wonder whether παροξυτόνως μᾶλλον προενεκτέον is a better reading here. The reading προσενεκτέον printed by Dain may have to be corrected to προ-

---

[171] A strand of scholarship, possibly Herodianic, explicitly says that the meaning does not change, e.g. sch. Ar. *Ra.* 6 (VE) γέλοιον Ἀττικῶς, γελοῖον δὲ κοινόν. ἡ δὲ σημασία ἡ αὐτή, and also later lexicography (*EM* 224.43, *Et.Gud.* γ 303. *Su.* γ 118 and 119) make the same distinction as Eustathius.

[172] The couple in Iohannes Philoponus is always γέλοιος ~ γελοῖος, and the meanings are reversed: γελοῖος· ὁ καταγέλαστος προπερισπᾶται, γέλοιος δὲ ὁ γελωτοποιὸς προπαροξύνεται (γ 6 (ACE), 7 (D), Daly 1983).

[173] Possibly going back to Herodian? Lentz edits the text of Choeroboscus as Hdn. *GG* 3.1 466.4–467.6.

[174] An example of more controversial instances, involving a decision regarding the verbal stem (whether it is an aorist or a present) is sch. *Il.* 16.827 (A) = Tyrannion fr. 42 Haas, discussed in Probert 2006: 28–9.

ἐνεκτέον. Phrases like βαρυτόνως προφέρειν have the same force as βαρύνειν in the grammatical tradition of the time (e.g. P.Oxy. 1012 fr. 16.15–16, 3ʳᵈ c. AD, αχρειον |με[ν β]αρυτονως προφερομενοι, our text (19)). There is only one other attestation of προσφέρω in a similar sense in our corpus, again in the *Philetaerus* (230 →δανείζειν), and also there I am not convinced that προσφέρω makes sense. I could only find one more instance of προσφέρω in a much later prescription, διὰ διςςοῦ c προσφερόμενα... προσφερόμενον (Theognost. *Canones*, *An. Ox.* 2 408.2–3)[175].

γήϊνος

Phryn. *Ecl.* 69 γήϊνον λεκτέον διὰ τοῦ η, ἀλλ' οὐχὶ διὰ τοῦ ε, γέϊνον.

Phrynichus does oppose ⟨η⟩ and ⟨ε⟩ in this gloss, but it is impossible to decide here whether the opposition between γήϊνος and γέϊνος consists in vowel quality, quantity or it only involves the spelling. γέϊνος is at least marginally attested in Greek[176]. The adjective γεϊκός attests that it was possible to shorten ⟨η⟩ to ⟨ε⟩ (and not to ⟨α⟩) where a suffixal vowel met the stem of γῆ. The adjective survives, of all extant Greek literature, only in Heron of Alexandria, a fact that strongly suggests that this is a technical term of Hellenistic scientific prose.

γρῦ

Philem. 358 γρῦ, τὸν ὑπὸ τοῖς ὄνυξι ῥύπον, περιςπωμένως.

This gloss could stem form the same Herodianic material we find in ps.-Arcadius, that establishes a correspondence between long *dichrona* in monosyllables and circumflex accentuation:

> περιςπᾶται δὲ καὶ ὅςα ἔχει δίχρονον ἐκτεταμένον, ἄ, νῦν, γρῦ, κρῖ, ὁπότε ἐκτείνεται· ὁπότε δὲ cυcτέλλεται, ὀξύνεται.

---

175 An isolated instance in Herodian (*GG* 3.2 800.4) is a mere misprint: the source passage (Choerob. *GG* 4.2 137.22) has προηνέχθη, and Lentz himself prints again the same text elsewhere, without adding the *sigma* (*GG* 3.2 360.17).
176 *pace* Lobeck 1820: 97 ("nusquam locorum vidi"): cf. *Papyri Magicae* 13.8 Preseindanz; Latte prints γέϊνα it in the explanation of Hesychius γ 487 γεγηνῶν (but γήϊνα Cyrillus, *gloss. in Proverbiis*, cf. Latte *ad loc.*).

It is a perispomenon also every [monosyllable] that has a long *dichronon*, ἇ, νῦν, γρῦ, κρῖ, when they are long, when they are shortened, they are oxytones.

[Arc.] 206.20–207.1

γρυλίζειν

Phryn. *PS* 58.14–59.1 γρυλίζειν καὶ γρυλιcμὸc ἐπὶ τῆc τῶν χοίρων φωνῆc. δι' ἑνὸc λ, καὶ οὐ διὰ δυοῖν. γρύλλοc δὲ διὰ τῶν δυοῖν λλ ὀρχήματοc εἶδόc ἐcτιν. ἡ μὲν οὖν ὄρχηcιc ὑπὸ τῶν Αἰγυπτίων γρυλλιcμὸc καλεῖται, γρύλλοc δὲ ὁ ὀρχούμενοc. ὑῶν μὲν οὖν ἡ φωνὴ γρυλιcμόc.
Phryn. *Ecl.* 72 γρυλίζειν διττὴν ἔχει ἁμαρτίαν, ἕν τε τῇ προφορᾷ καὶ τῷ cημαινομένῳ· ἐν μὲν τῇ προφορᾷ διὰ τῶν δύο λλ, ἐν τῷ cημαινομένῳ ὅτι παρὰ τοῖc ἀρχαίοιc τὸ γρυλίζειν ἐcτὶ τιθέμενον ἐπὶ μὲν τῆc τῶν ὑῶν φωνῆc, οἱ δὲ νῦν τάττουcι ἐπὶ τῶν φορτικῶc καὶ ἀcχημόνωc ὀρχουμένων. ἐρεῖc οὖν γρυλίζειν καὶ γρυλιcμόc, οὐ γρυλλιcμόc.

The themes γρυλλ- and γρυλ- are not mere variants of one and the same lexeme, but two different items, whose meanings and etymology are unrelated.

γρύλλοc and γρυλλιcμόc are the names of a kind of dance (γρύλλοc can also be a name for dancer only)[177]. There is no etymological relation with γρῦλοc, 'swine', a derivative of the onomatopoeic γρῦ, 'grunt'[178]: the family of γρύλλοc has consistenly a geminate, and an accentuation that implies a short vowel.

Apart from Phrynichus, *PS* 58, γρύλλοc seems to be attested only as a loanword in Pliny, *HN* 35.114[179], where *grylli* is transmitted without variants – with *Gryllus* shortly before (a word that gives all the impression of being an *ad hoc* back-formation aiming at explaining *grylli*). The geminate must have been pronounced in Latin in Pliny's time, but its presence in Latin is best explained as a faithful representation of Greek spelling in a learned loanword.

Both variants, γρυλίζω and γρυλλίζω, are attested in the manuscript tradition of Aristophanes at *Ach.* 746 (but A γρύλλ-) and *Pl.* 307 (RA γρύλλ-), and then in later writers (Dio Chrysostom, 7.74, Procopius, *Historia Arcana* 17). The *scholia vetera* to Ar. *Ach.* 746 (ΕΓΓ³) gloss the verb with 'χοίρων φωνὴν μιμ-

---

177 *DELG* s.v. γρυλλιcμόc: "ces termes sont caractérisés par Phryn. comme "égyptiens", ce qui veut dire hellénistiques"; cf. also Latte 1915: 385, fn. 1 [= *KS* 622, fn. 27] and 1955: 190.
178 *DELG* s.v. γρῦ.
179 A popular treatment of Lat. *gryllus*, with /y/ > /u/ is one of the possible explanations of Italian *grullo*, cf. *DELI* s.v. *grullo*.

ἤcεcθε': the gloss in Phrynichus could reflect an uncertainty on the reading of these lines in Aristophanes that was already current in the 2nd century AD[180].

γρυλιcμόc is in Aristotle, *Historia Animalium* 535b. In Pollux' *Onomasticon* (5.87), γρυλλιcμόc is the reading of two manuscripts (AB; Bekker (1846) and Bethe (1900) print γρυλιcμόc: cf. Bethe *ad loc.*). γρύλλοc, printed by Bethe a few paragraphs above (5.47, personal name – of Xenophon's father), is written with the singleton in a whole branch (FS) of the manuscript tradition of the *Onomasticon*. In neither place does Pollux make any comment on the spelling of γρύλλοc or γρυλιcμόc.

The confusion between γρύλλοc and γρῦλοc is interesting in relation to degemination more than the cases of →cάκκοc and →κυνηγεττεῖν. In this case degemination – together with isochrony – would cause two otherwise unrelated lexemes to sound exactly the same, and this seems to be precisely what worries Phrynichus in the *Praeparatio Sophistica*. In a world without accent marks in written texts, it was in the first place the number of *lambda*s in the spelling that could disambiguate between the two words.

In the formulation of the *Ecloga* the prescription is even more remarkable. γρυλλίζω with the sense of γρυλίζω is 'a double mistake (διττὴν ἔχει ἁμαρτίαν)', on account of the confusion of the meanings, and in pronunciaton (ἐν τῇ προφορᾷ). Here Phrynichus is clearly addressing a pronunciation of γρυλιcμόc with [ll]. Yet in the 2nd century AD there is clear evidence for degemination in Attic, and in particular of [ll][181].

Therefore the pronunciation (προφορά) that Phrynichus condemns could have had a real existence, and must have been widespread among the public to whom Phrynichus addressed the *Ecloga*, prospective public speakers / orators of the Antonine age. The pronunciation [ɣrylliz'mos] of γρυλιcμόc stigmatised in *Ecl.* 72 is a hypercorrection.

γρυμεῖα

Phryn. *PS* 60.14 γρυμεῖα· ἣν οἱ πολλοὶ γρύτην καλοῦcιν. Δίφιλοc (fr. 128 K.–A.) ἄνευ τοῦ ι γρυμέαν. ἔcτι δὲ παρ' Ἀθηναίοιc πήρα τιc γρυμέα καλουμένη, ἐν ᾗ

---

[180] Geldhart – Hall (1906²-1907) print λλ at *Ach.* 746 but λ at *Pl.* 307, Wilson (2007) now has forms with the singleton in both places.
[181] Note also φυλλα γυναικων = φῦλα γυναικῶν in an epigram of Eumenia in Phrygia (*SGO* II 16/06/02, l. 3: and the beginning of the same line καλλοcύνᾳ spelt correctly), precisely the sort of uncertainty implied by Amm. 506 φύλλον καὶ φῦλον διαφέρει. φύλλον μὲν γὰρ τὸ πέταλον δένδρου, φῦλον δὲ τὸ γένοc.

παντοῖα cκεύη ἐcτίν. Cαπφὼ δὲ γρύτην[182] καλεῖ τὴν μύρων καὶ γυναικείων τινῶν θήκην.
Philet. 208 γρυμέαν οἱ Ἀττικοὶ τὴν γρύτην τῶν cκευῶν.
  Cf. also:
Phryn. *Ecl.* 202 γρύτη· καὶ τοῦτο τῶν παραπεποιημένων· τὸ γὰρ τοιοῦτον ἅπαν γρυμέαν cυμβέβηκε καλεῖcθαι.
Pollux 10.160 (S) καὶ γρυμέα δὲ ἀγγεῖόν τι εἰc ἀπόθεcιν, ὃ ἔνιοι πήραν νομίζουcιν.

The entry in the *Praeparatio Sophistica* is the only one in the Atticist lexica that mentions the spelling with *iota* (the same reading appears elsewhere only in the *Et.Gud.* γ 323.25). The phrase 'ἄνευ τοῦ ι' makes more sense if the spellings that are being contrasted here are ‹ει› and ‹ε›. The word occurs in a number of variants in the manuscript tradition of the lexica that contain it. Two manuscripts (VQ) of the *Philetaerus* (208) have γρυμίαν (Dain prints γρυμέαν in the text); one (d) of the *Ecloga* (202, γρύτη) has γρυμαῖα, as does cod. F of Pollux' *Onomasticon*. γρυμέα, the reading in the rest of the manuscript tradition of the *Ecloga*, is the word that Phrynichus uses to gloss γρύτη, following the Attic usage he discusses in *PS* 60.14.

The entry belongs to the small group of entries contrasting ‹ει› with ‹ε›, not ‹ι› and it suggest that there was a tendency to replace /e/ before back vowels with /iː/. Cf. chap. II, § 2.1.2.

δανείζειν

Philet. 230 τῶν δὲ διὰ τοῦ -ίζω ῥημάτων τῶν ὑπὲρ δύο cυλλαβὰc τοὺc μέλλονταc κατὰ περιγραφὴν τοῦ ζ λέγουcιν οἱ Ἀττικοί· οἷον κομίζω κομιῶ, κιθαρίζω κιθαριῶ, λακωνίζω λακωνιῶ. πρόκειται 'ὑπὲρ δύο cυλλαβὰc' διὰ τὸ πρίζω, κτίζω· 'διὰ τοῦ -ίζω' δέ, διὰ τὸ κατάζω, πελάζω καὶ τῶν ὁμοίων· ταῦτα γὰρ ὁμοίωc ἡμῖν προcφέρονται. ἀπὸ μέντοι τοῦ δανείζω, οὐκέτι δανείω λέγουcιν, οὐδὲ δανειοῦμαι, ἀλλὰ δανείcω καὶ δανείcομαι.

We are not told whether the difference between δανείζω and the other verbs in -ίζω consists only of their spelling or involves their pronunciation as well. The entry addresses the spelling rather than the pronunciation of δανείζω: the *Philetaerus* does not mention the possible change in quantity, which elsewhere (e.g. Phryn. *Ecl.* 346 →Διονυcεῖον, Phryn. *Ecl.* 241 →ὀπτάνιον) functions as a marker

---

[182] Sappho, fr. 179 Lobel-Page, γρύτα.

of the distinction between spellings with ‹υ› and with ‹ευ›. The only other entry involving verbs in -ιζω, Moer. β 15 →βαδίζειν, reflects concerns on the quantity of the *iota* before *zeta* that are found elsewhere in the grammatical tradition (see discussion above, with Phot. θ 117, fn. 529 above); perhaps no distinction was made in the pronunciation of ‹ειζω› and ‹ιζω›, especially if vowel length was used to compensate for degemination of [zz] (cf. Moer. α 139 →ἀγοράζειν).

δένδρα

Philem. 358 δένδρον, ὡς ῥόδον, οὐ δένδρα· ἵνα μὴ ποιήςῃς μακρὸν τὸ α.

Philemon's gloss seems to address an othewise never attested form δένδρᾱ, seemingly a variant of the neuter plural δένδρᾰ or δένδρεᾰ[183]. Similar plurals belong to contracted nouns and adjective, as χρυςᾶ, ὀςτᾶ, yet they have a different accentuation. Only Attic has contracted plurals of neuters in -s, like τέρᾱ, γέρᾱ[184]: these are rather uncommon forms, but so far the only possible model for the long -ᾱ of δένδρᾱ. It is difficult to believe, however, that the small group of neuters in -ας may have had an influence on a noun belonging to the thematic declension.

δένδρεα, δένδρεον is well attested since Homer: Eustathius discusses Homeric δένδρεα together with forms with synizesis (δενδρε͡ῳ (*Il.* 3.15 etc.), cf. also δενδρε͡ων (*Od.* 19.520)), possibly basing on Aelius Dionysius (δ 6). In these cases the spellings δένδρῳ and δένδρων have not been recorded in the spelling, which preserved the usual Ionic forms as though from δένδρεον, although the verses were probably composed by a rhapsode who used the Attic form δένδρον[185]. In Homer δένδρεα always realises a dactyl – in some positions a scansion with synizesis may have been possible.

Attic playwrights use a contracted nom./acc./voc. pl. δένδρη, and δένδρεα in lyric parts[186]. Attic δένδρη received attention in the grammatical tradition on third-declension neuter nouns in -ος alternating with second-declension

---

[183] Since δένδρᾱ is compared to singular forms (δένδρον, ῥόδον), it could be understood as a feminine: in this case its final -ᾱ would be much more comfortable in the paradigm. But a feminine *ἡ δένδρᾱ is never attested.
[184] γέρᾱ comes from γέρας-α, i.e. from the contraction of identical vowels; the plural γέρεα is not attested (and in Attic, neuters in -ας would not form such plurals – cf. Shipp 1972: 61–2).
[185] Wackernagel 1916: 109–10.
[186] Euripides, fr. 782 (transmitted with δένδρεα); δένδρη fr. 223.123 (papyrus); 484.5 ([D. Hal.] *Rh.* 9, περὶ ἐςχηματιςμένων β' 11, p. 345.21 Usener-Radermacher).

nouns in -ov that we read in *Epimerismi* μ 64 and Eustathius (1433.48). With Athenaeus, these are the sources of Pherecrates fr. 137 K.–A.[187] One of the sources, the *Epimerismi*, reads actually δένδρα in the only manuscript that transmits this entry. If this somehow reflects the ancient layouts of editions of Attic playwrights, then some corrupt text, or doctrine based on it, could be the source of the obscure gloss in Philemon. δένδρη is metrically guaranteed in Pherecreates fr. 137.9: anyone reading δένδρα there could imagine that Attic used a plural δένδρᾶ.

δεξαμενή

Phryn. *Ecl.* 293 δεξαμενή φαϲι Πλάτωνα (*Criti.* 117b) ἐπὶ τῆϲ κολυμβήθραϲ εἰρηκέναι, ἐγὼ δὲ οὔ φημι· ἀλλὰ δεξαμένη τῷ τόνῳ εἶπεν ὡϲ ποιουμένη. χρὴ οὖν καὶ ἡμᾶϲ κολυμβήθραν λέγειν.

Phyrnichus claims that δεξαμενή is not the legitimate Attic form for 'pool' (on the meaning in Attic cf. Lobeck 1820: 322), and that the educated should say κολυμβήθρα – this word is attested in Plato (*R.* 453d), yet so is also δεξαμενή (*Tim.* 53a).[188] With the meaning 'cistern' κολυμβήθρα is first attested in the LXX (4 *Ki.* 18.17).

Changing the accentuation removes the difficult δεξαμενάϲ, and replaces it with the participle of δείκνυμι, δεξαμένη. The passage in question (Pl. *Criti.* 117 a–b) reads: περιϲτήϲαντεϲ οἰκοδομήϲειϲ καὶ δένδρων φυτεύϲειϲ πρεπούϲαϲ ὕδαϲι, δεξαμεναϲ τε αὖ τὰϲ μὲν ὑπαιθρίουϲ, τὰϲ δὲ χειμερινὰϲ τοῖϲ θερμοῖϲ λουτροῖϲ ὑποϲτέγουϲ περιτιθέντεϲ[189].

διέτηϲ

Ael. D. δ 23 διέτηϲ, τριέτηϲ, πεντέτηϲ καὶ πάντα τὰ ὅμοια βαρύνουϲιν Ἀττικοὶ προφέροντεϲ τῷ τόνῳ ὡϲ εὐεργέτηϲ.

---

187 Misquoted as Aristophanes in the *Epimerismi*, see Dyck *ad loc.*, Lentz *ad* Hdn. *GG* 3.2 204.7.
188 Cf. Chandler 1881: 199, and Rutherford 1881: 369 for instances of δεξαμενή in Herodotus as well as in Plato.
189 *Antiatt.* δ 33 {δε}δεξαμένη· Ἡρόδοτοϲ ϛ′ (6.119.3). Perhaps we should read δεξαμενή here, defending the word that Phrynichus condemns. Cf. Valente 2015a *ad loc.*

Herodian (*GG* 3.1 419.3–8) makes a distinction between Attic accentuation and the Koine but includes adjectives in -έτης in the paradigm of adjectives in -ης, prescribing a vocative masculine singular in -ες, whereas Choeroboscus (*GG* 4.1 167.37–168.10) remarks that forms with recessive accentuation have the same inflexion as first declension masculine nouns in -ης/-ας.

Pollux (1.54–55) makes a distinction between adjectives counting years, from διέτης to δεκαέτης, ascribing the oxytone accentuation to them when they refer to an extent of time, and the paroxytone when they refer to age (ἐπί παιδίου καὶ φυτοῦ καὶ οἴνου, 1.54). The difference in accentuation is explicitly prescribed[190]. The same difference is to be found in the synonymical lexica of Herennius and Ammonius[191].

Διονυςεῖον

Phryn. *Ecl.* 346 Διονυςεῖον· ἀπαίδευτον οὕτω λέγειν, δέον βραχύνειν τὴν ςι ςυλλαβήν· οἱ γὰρ ἐκτείνοντες παρὰ τὴν Ἀττικῶν διάλεκτον λέγουςιν. χρὴ οὖν Ἀριςτοφάνει ἀκολουθοῦντας λέγειν· ἐν γὰρ τῷ Γήρᾳ (fr. 130 K.–A.) φηςίν·

'τίς ἂν φράςειε, ποῦ 'ςτι τὸ Διονύςιον;
ὅπου τὰ μορμολυκεῖα προςκρεμάννυνται'.

The terminology employed here is ambiguous. The shortening of the syllable in question is signalled by the interchange of the spellings with ‹ει› and ‹ι›. The diphthong is clearly used to mark the long syllable as opposed to the short one, which has the simple vowel, and no difference in timbre is implied.

The spellings ‹ειος› and ‹ιος› were a common object of discussion in ancient orthography (e. g. the περὶ ποςότητος in *An. Ox.* 2 283–330). Nous and adjectives in -ιος (-ια, -ιον) are easily distinguished from derivatives in -ειος by the quantity

---

190 Poll. 1.54: ἡμίετες καὶ ἡμιέτης χρόνος, καὶ διέτης δὲ καὶ τριέτης, καὶ μέχρι δεκαέτους, ἐπὶ μὲν χρόνου παροξυνόντων, ἐπὶ δὲ παιδίου καὶ φυτοῦ καὶ οἴνου καὶ τῶν τοιούτων ὀξυνόντων'. More indications on the accent of numerals follow: ἐνοςκαίδεκα ἐτῶν καὶ δυοκαίδεκα ... τὸν ςύνδεςμον ὀξύνοντας (1.55).
191 Heren. 172 τρίετες βαρυτόνως καὶ τριετές ὀξυτόνως διαφέρει Πτολεμαῖος ὁ Ἀςκαλωνίτης (p. 61 Baege). βαρυτονούμενον μέν ἐςτιν ἐπὶ χρόνου· δι' οὗ καὶ ὁ Ὅμηρός φηςιν (*Od.* 2.106, 24.141)· "ὡς τρίετες μὲν ἔληθε δόλῳ". ἐὰν (δὲ) ὀξυτονῆται "τριετές", ὡς εὐφυές, "τὸ παιδίον". Amm. 477 τρίετες βαρυτόνως καὶ τριετές ὀξυτόνως διαφέρει, φηςὶ Πτολεμαῖος ὁ Ἀςκαλωνίτης (p. 61 Baege). ἐὰν μὲν γὰρ βαρυτονήςωμεν, ἔςται ἐπὶ χρόνου· διὸ καὶ ὁ ποιητής φηςιν (*Od.* 2.106, 24.141)· "ὡς τρίετες μὲν ἔληθε δόλῳ". ἐὰν δὲ ὀξυτονήςωμεν "τριετές" ὡς "εὐφυές", ἔςται ἐπὶ ἡλικίας οἷον "τριετές τὸ παιδίον" ὅθεν καὶ "ἑξέτε' ἀδμήτην" (*Il.* 23.266, 655). καὶ χρῆν ἀναγινώςκειν ὡς ἀξιοῖ ὁ Ἀςκαλωνίτης.

of the suffixal ‹ι›, which is always short. That the recommended form should be written with ‹ι› is made clear by a similar prescription in a treatise attributed to Herodian ([Hdn.] περὶ τῶν ζητουμένων κτλ.) ὅσα ἐπὶ γενικῆς ὀνόματα περισπᾶται, ταῦτα καὶ τοπικῶς cχηματιζόμενα περισπᾶται· ἐπεὶ οὖν Ἀcκληπιὸc Ἀcκληπιοῦ, Διόνυcοc δὲ Διονύcου, καὶ Θεcεὺc Θηcέωc, ἐπεὶ οὐ περιcπᾶται, διὰ τοῦτο οὐκ ἐροῦμεν Θηcεῖον, οὐδὲ Διονυcεῖον, ἀλλὰ Διονύcιον καὶ Θήcειον (An. Ox. 3 252.13–16).

It is remarkable that Phrynichus condemns the variants with a long penultimate syllable. The prescription suggests that speakers would replace the expected [ios] (or perhaps [jos]) with [iːos], a kind of hypercorrection that implies the preservation of length as a distinctive feature in the pronunciation of some speakers.

δόχμη

Ael. D. δ 30 δόχμη· τὸ τετραδάκτυλον. Ἀρίcταρχοc δὲ ὀξύνει, ὡc καὶ Ἀριcτοφάνηc ἐν τῷ[192] (fr. 959 K.–A.)· "οὔ τοι δ' ἀφεcτήκαcι πλεῖν ἢ δύο δοχμά." ἐν μέντοι τοῖc ἀκριβεcτέροιc ἀντιγράφοιc ὀξεῖα ἐπίκειται τῇ πρώτῃ cυλλαβῇ κατὰ τὸ λόχμη, λόγχη, ὄχνη, ὄγχνη.

According to Chantraine (DELG, s.v. δοχμόc) the expected accentuation of this noun, a derivative of δέχομαι, should be δόχμη, as a substantivised noun form the adjective δοχμόc[193]. The explicit mention of written sources is remarkable (ἐν ... τοῖc ἀκριβεcτέροιc ἀντιγράφοιc): if it can be traced back to Aelius' original work, it must point to accurate editons of Attic drama, including accent marks.

δύcερωc

Philet. 253 δύcερωc, φιλόγελωc, χρυcόκερωc προπαροξυτονοῦντεc οἱ Ἀττικοὶ λέγουcιν.

---

[192] The title of the play is missing. Eust. 1291.44 instead of ὡc καὶ Ἀριcτοφάνηc ἐν τῷ writes ὡc δηλοῖ καὶ ὁ κωμικόc, where, according to Kassel and Austin (ad Ar. fr. 959) Aristophanes needs to be understood as the comic poet par excellence.

[193] One of the few primary adjectives formed with -μο-, a suffix normally employed for deverbal nouns (e.g. cτέλλω > cτολμόc), cf. Probert 2006: 239.

Readers of the lexica would be warned that despite the long final vowel they should refrain from placing an accent on the antepenultimate. Texts lacking accent marks would have been misleading, and less proficient readers may have been tempted to read (or accentuate in writing) *φιλογέλως etc., only because they saw a long final vowel.

Forms like these show that the rule of the antepenultimate is the only law of Greek accentuation that had never been broken (Lucidi ([1950] 1966: 86, and similarly Schwyzer 1939: 392) – the accent cannot recede any further than that, but in some forms not even a long vowel can prevent it form moving away from the word end. Lucidi ([1950] 1966: 86 n. 20) maintains (against Grammont 1948: 399) that accentuations as πόλεως cannot be explained simply by postulating that ‹ε› was pronunced as a glide, and therefore can be considered a true trisyllabic word, with the accent on the antepenultimate and a long vowel in the final syllable, i.e. πό.λε.ως. Lucidi's point of view is perhaps too rigid and leaves out some necessary considerations for the understanding of the history the accentuation of these words. The phonology and accentuation of πόλεως and other words with the so-called 'quantity metathesis' depend on the syllabicity of the vowel spelt with ‹ε›, and in particular on its pronunciation as a glide as part of a synizesis. On the other hand, compounds displaying at the same time a long final vowel and the accent on the antepenultimate attest to a phenomenon not necessarily linked to the synizesis of -εως and similar endings.

In the first place, the accentuation of δύσερως, φιλόγελως, χρυσόκερως, βαθύγηρως etc. shows that maintaining the position of the accent in exocentric compounds (*bahuvrīhi*), with recessive accentuation on the antepenultimate as a norm (and as opposed to endocentric verbal compounds, normally paroxytona with the accent on the verbal root) was preferred to keeping the accentual limitations imposed by the last vowel[194]. The reason for this must have been in the priority given to morphology instead of phonology: a clearly recognisable *bahuvrīhi* accentuation, not subject to the law of limitation (remarkably, not the limitation to the antepenultimate, but only the limitation regarding the final vowel is disregarded).

The treatment of such compounds can certainly be compared with that of nouns like πόλεως, with synizesis in the last syllable. Forms like πόλεως had beyond doubt an influence within their own paradigm (πόλεων) and could take advantage of a scansion with diaeresis (πόλεως [⏑⏑–]) a possibility that the poets deployed and perhaps even alive in spoken Greek. Yet, to see in πό.λε.ως the model for the accentuation of φιλόγελως etc. would mean to understand as

---

194 cf. Lucidi [1950] 1966: 77.

the outcomes of one phonetical phenomenon items that reached the same prosody via two different paths, phonological change in the case of πόλεωc and a morphological restriction in the case of φιλόγελωc[195].

The Attic nature of these adjectives is clear in ps.-Arcadius' epitome, and the notion may therefore be traced back to Herodian and Greek scholarship of the imperial period:

> τὰ εἰc ωc cύνθετα πολυcύλλαβα ἀπὸ τῶν εἰc ωc παροξύνεται· ἔρωc χρυcέρωc, ἱδρώc λυcίδρωc. τὸ δὲ δύcερωc καὶ φιλόγελωc καὶ τὰ τοιαῦτα Ἀττικὰ ὄντα προπαροξύνονται.
>
> Polysyllabic compounds in ωc from [words] in ωc are paroxytones: ἔρωc χρυcέρωc, ἱδρώc λυcίδρωc. δύcερωc and φιλόγελωc and the like are Attic and therefore proparoxytone.
> [Arc.] 107.12–15

These adjectives do not only receive an unusual accentuation, which is explained as Attic in ps.-Arcadius and the *Philetaerus:* they also occasionally follow the Attic declension. This did not escape the Atticists' notice: see e. g. Moer. φ 12 φιλόγελῳ Ἀττικοί· φιλογέλωτες Ἕλληνες, and forms following the Attic declension are indeed found in later authors, atticising (Philostratus *VS* 513, 519) and not (acc. sg. φιλόγελω, Origen, *Hom. in Job (fragm. in Catenis)* 379.25 Pitra, Libanius, *Decl.* 29.1.12.5). However, they are not especially well attested in classical Attic writers; the earliest attestation is the acc. pl. φιλόγελωc (instead of φιλογέλωτας) in a passage of Athenaeus quoting Theophrastus (fr. 124 = Ath. 6.261d).

δύω

Ael. D. δ 31 δύο διὰ τοῦ ο καὶ δύω κατὰ ἔκταcιν Ἀττικοὶ λέγουcιν ἑκατέρωc, 'δυοῖν' δὲ ἐπὶ γενικῆc καὶ δοτικῆc, τὸ δὲ δυεῖν cπάνιον παρὰ τοῖc παλαιοῖc, ⟨cυνηθὴc δὲ τοῖc⟩ νεωτέροιc· ἔcτι δὲ ὅμωc παρὰ Θουκιδίδῃ (8.101.1) ('δυεῖν ἡμέ-

---

[195] ἀξιόχρεωc and λιπόνεωc, quoted by Ael. D. (α 151 ἀξιόχρεων· ἐν τῷ ω λέγουcι καὶ λιπόνεων καὶ τὰ οὐδέτερα. οἱ γὰρ παλαιοὶ ὁμοίωc. τὸ δὲ ἀξιόχρεον βάρβαρον), pose a similar problem, even though in this case attraction toward the thematic declension – οc is the main issue. Cf. also Philem. 358 δύcερωc, ὡc Μενέλεωc (possibly interpolated in Moer. δ 2 δύcεργοc ὡc ἄμουcοc καὶ δύcερωc λέγουcιν ὡc Μενέλεωc (cod. F)), where a form with actual synizesis is used to explain the phonology of the compound δύcερωc. These glosses show clearly that the lexicographers did not make a distiction between forms with or without synizesis: they were perhaps adopting a pronunciation πόλεωc and similar forms with diaeresis, or just basing their discussion entirely on the written sources. In this case these glosses should not be regarded as orthoepic at all.

ραιν'). λέγουσι δὲ καὶ 'τῶν δύο' καὶ 'τοῖς δύο'. τὸ δὲ 'δυσὶ' βάρβαρον καὶ κατὰ χρῆσιν Ἀττικὴν καὶ κατὰ λόγον γραμματικόν. Ὅμηρος δὲ ἐπὶ μὲν ὀρθῆς καὶ γενικῆς ‹καὶ δοτικῆς› καὶ αἰτιατικῆς 'δύο' λέγει, ἐπὶ δὲ κλητικῆς κατὰ ἔκτασιν 'δύω'.

The uninflected form δύο is ancient in Greek, and already attested in Homer (thence Aelius Dionysius' gloss). 'δύω κατὰ ἔκτασιν' implies a notion that represents δύο as the original form from which δύω can be derived through lengthening, according to principles of ancient pathology.

This is one of the cases where it is difficult to decide whether the gloss is an orthoepic prescription. The difference in length could be just a way to make a distinction between the letters (o) μικρόν ~ (ω) μέγα.

ἐβουλόμην

Philem. 394.10 R. ἐβουλόμην· οὐκ ἠβουλόμην.
Moer. η 5 ἤμελλον ἠβουλόμην ἠδυνάμην ηὐξάμην διὰ τοῦ η· διὰ τοῦ ε Ἕλληνες.
Moer. η 22 ἠδύνω ἠπίστω Ἀττικοί· ἐδύνασο ἐπίστασο Ἕλληνες.

The aorists and imperfects ἠβουλόμην ἤμελλον ἠδυνάμην start replacing the older ἐβουλόμην ἔμελλον ἐδυνάμην during the classical period[196].

μέλλω is the earliest of the three verbs to have the augment ἠ- (Hes. *Th.* 478 ὁππότ' ἄρ' ὁπλότατον παίδων ἤμελλε τεκέσθαι). Its augmented forms in ἠ- are attested also in Theognis and Aristophanes[197]. δύναμαι follows next, with at least one occurrence in Aeschylus[198]. Augmented ἠβουλ- from βούλομαι is not found before the 4th century BC.

Grammarians and lexicographers ascribe forms in ἐ- or in ἠ- indifferently to one or the other dialect, without any reason for their attributions. Moeris' glosses attribute the Ἀττικοί all the augmented forms in ‹η›, be ‹η› the augment proper, or the lengthening of an initial vowel (ηὐξάμην, ἠπιστάμην), and so do a number of passages in Lentz' Herodian[199]. Philemo is in this respect more accurate than Moeris, and reflects the state of affairs of Classical Attic, which does employ

---

[196] Augmented forms in ἐ- of these three verbs are the exception in Ptolemaic papyri (Mayser 1938: 93).
[197] Cf. Debrunner 1954: 102, with more examples for Hesiod.
[198] A. *Pr.* 206.
[199] Cf. Debrunner 1954: 103.

ἠβουλόμην before the 4th century BC[200]. The change is commonly ascribed to the influx of the forms ἔθελον ἤθελον, of θέλω and its paralled form ἐθέλω. The latter is the usual one in Classical Attic, whereas θέλω is normal in Ionic prose, and Ionic and Aeolic poetry[201].

Later in time, augmented forms in ἠ- are attested more frequently than those in ἐ-. The displacement of earlier augmented forms in ἠ- by ἐ- is not necessarily evidence of the confusion between /e/ and /e:/ (Mayser 1938: 93–4), but could depend on the generalisation of the augment in ἠ- as an allomorph of the augment in ἐ-.[202]

Neither Philemo's gloss, nor Moeris', nor any other source is clear enough to draw any conclusion on the pronunciation of this augment. In the whole *corpus* of lexicographers examined here there are no verbs which are not already attested in Classical Attic with ἠ-: since the reason for the augments in ἠ- in Classical Attic is morphological and not phonological, it is unlikely that these glosses are evidence for the confusion of /e/ and /e:/. The goal of these glosses is to determine which forms belong to Classical Attic. The trend seems to favour as genuinely Attic the augment in ἐ-, even though more recent Attic literature had also forms in ἠ- (as for instance Menander).

The picture is much more confusing in Moeris, who ascribes to Attic all the forms in ἠ-, including the imperfect ἠβουλόμην, thus contradicting Philemo (394.10 R.). The two glosses of Moeris dealing with these augments combine different linguistic problems. The imperfects ἠβουλόμην ἤμελλον ἠδυνάμην, genuinely Attic, are all postclassic and likely to have been stgimatised by stricter Atticists: they occur in Ptolemaic papyri and in Menander, who at least in Phrynichus is more often quoted as an example of what to avoid, rather than a model of good Attic.

For these reasons, the wording of Moeris is quite surprising, as it inverts the expected attribution, ascribing to Attic the forms that other lexicography would condemn. This could be a consequence of the process of epitomisation, if the lexicon we read is indeed an epitome. Another hypothesis is that the entry general-

---

[200] οὐκ ἠβούλετο, E. *Hel.* 752 is not guaranteed by metre, the elided form 'βουλόμην of Ar. *Ra.* 1147 is likely to come from ἐβουλόμην, as no other instance of βούλομαι is augmented in ἠ- elsewhere in Aristophanes.

[201] Debrunner 1954. The alphabetical *Epimerismi* in *An. Ox.* 2 ascribe to Ionic all the forms with the syllabic augment ἠ-, ἤμελλον, ἠδυνάμην, ἤθελον, in a system of transformations according to the dialect (πάθη/τροπαί) aimed at deriving the pluperfect ᾔδη form the aorist εἶδα (εἶδον) (*An. Ox.* 2 374.32–375.13).

[202] The generalisation of the augment ἠ- in some verbs suggests that it actually spread as an allomorph of ἐ- (Dieterich 1898: 212).

ises vowel length, attributing the long vowels to Attic. The identification of long vowels with Attic may explain why, in addition to ἠβουλόμην, ἤμελλον, and ἠδυνάμην Moeris ascribes to the Ἀττικοί also ηὐξάμην, ἦκασα, and ἠπίστω (η 5, 20, and 22), forms that have no particular Attic status[203]. In many cases forms in ἠ- are restored by modern editors, following the teachings of ancient scholarship: ἦκασα is restored in Sophocles, *El.* 662, but attested in the manuscripts of Aristophanes, *Nu.* 350. The imperfect of ἐπίσταμαι, ἠπιστάμην is usual in Attic prose (Schwyzer 1939: 668).

ἔγγεια

Philet. 200 ἔγγεια δανείσματα οἱ Ἀττικοί· ἔγγεα δὲ οἱ Ἴωνες. καὶ ἐπὶ τῶν κτημάτων ὁμοίως οἱ Ἴωνες ἔγγεα.

The attribution of ἔγγεα to Ionic is obscure[204]. However, the spelling of this word had been an object of discussion in ancient orthography, possibly also in Herodian's lost περὶ ὀρθογραφίας. Yet the orthographical problems that ἔγγεια comports in extant orthographical scholarship concern the spelling with ‹ει› as opposed to single ‹ι›, not the contrast in timbre implied by the gloss in the *Philetaerus*, which is – in this respect – isolated.

Later, pseudo-Herodianic scholarship, transmits reflections of Herodianic doctrine on derivatives of γῆ, discussing the variation ‹ει› ~ ‹ι›, and can be found for instance in the pseudo-Herodianic *Epimerismi*

> διφθογγίζονται ... καὶ τὰ ἀπὸ τοῦ γαῖα συγκείμενα· οἷον· εὔγειος· ἐπίγειος· μεσόγειος· πρόσγειος· καὶ ἔγγειος, ὁ πρὸς τὴν γῆν νεύων· ἔγγιον δὲ, τὸ πλησίον, ἰῶτα.
>
> Also the compounds from γαῖα have a diphthong: like εὔγειος, ἐπίγειος, μεσόγειος, πρόσγειος, and ἔγγειος, he who bends forward to the earth: but ἔγγιον, 'near', with ‹ι›.
>
> [Hdn.] *Partitiones* 172.8–10 Boissonade

and in Choeroboscus[205]

---

[203] ηὐξάμην and ἦκασα have an old augment. In fact, Attic shortened it to εὐ-, εἰ- at a rather early stage (Schwyzer 1939: 655). Verbs in αι- / ει- were particularly likely to avoid the older augment ἠ- (‹ευ› for ‹ηυ› is common in Attic inscriptions since the second half of the 4th century BC, Threatte 1980: 381; 1996: 482).
[204] But →ἐωθώς, another form that caught the attention of the Atticists for this same variation, i.e. ‹ευ› ~ ‹ε› before a vowel, is indeed Ionic in its form with ‹εω›.
[205] Lentz edited this material as Hdn. *GG* 3.2 440.15–18 and 495.17–18.

ἀνώγειοσ· πάντα τὰ παρὰ τὸ γέα διὰ τῆς ει διφθόγγου γράφεται· οἷον, βαθύγειοσ· ἔγγειοσ· μεςόγειοσ· κατώγειοσ· ὑπέργειοσ· οὕτως οὖν καὶ ἀνώγειος διὰ διφθόγγου.

ἀνώγειος: all the derivatives of γέα are written with the diphthong ‹ει›: like βαθύγειος, ἔγγειος, μεςόγειος, κατώγειος, ὑπέργειος: therefore also ἀνώγειος [is written] with a diphthong.

Choerob. περὶ ὀρθογραφίας, *An. Ox.* 2 174.32–4

ἔγγειοσ· διὰ τῆς ει διφθόγγου· τὰ γὰρ παρὰ τὸ γέα ὄντα διὰ τῆς ει διφθόγγου γράφεται· οἷον, ἀνώγειοσ· βαθύγειοσ· εὔγειοσ· μεςόγειοσ· κατώγειοσ· ὑπέργειοσ· οὕτως καὶ ἔγγειοσ διὰ τῆς ει διφθόγγου.

ἔγγειος: with the diphthong ‹ει›: for the derivatives of γέα are written with the diphthong ‹ει›, like βαθύγειος, εὔγειος, μεςόγειος, κατώγειος, ὑπέργειος: likewise also ἔγγειος with the diphthong ‹ει›.

ibid. 214.5–8

... χωρὶς τῶν παρὰ τὸ γαῖα συγκειμένων, ἅτινα γράφονται διὰ τῆς ει διφθόγγου, οἷον εὔγειος, μεςόγειος, ἐπίγειος, πρόςγειος, ἔγγειος, ὁ πρὸς τὴν γῆν κλίνων· ἔγγιον δὲ τὸ πλησίον, ι.

...except the compounds of γαῖα, which are written with the diphthong ‹ει›, like εὔγειος, μεςόγειος, ἐπίγειος, πρόςγειος, ἔγγειος, he who inclines toward the earth: but ἔγγιον, 'near', with ‹ι›.

Choerob. *Empimerismi in Psalmos*, 5.20–23 Gaisford

The homophony of ἔγγιον and ἔγγειον is also implied by an entry in Phrynichus' *Ecloga*:

ἔγγιον ἐπὶ τοῦ ἐγγύτερον μὴ λέγε, ἀλλ' ἐγγύτερον· ἐπὶ δὲ τοῦ ἐν τῇ γῇ, οἷον "ἔγγειον κτῆμα", εἴ τις χρῷτο, ἄριστα ἂν χρήσαιτο, ὡς καὶ Δημοσθένης ([Dem.] 34.24) "ἔγγειον τόκον" λέγει.

Do not say ἔγγιον for ἐγγύτερον, but [say] ἐγγύτερον: as regards the one [that is said] about the earth, as 'land possession (ἔγγειον κτῆμα)', should one use it, they would use it very well, like also Demosthenes says ἔγγειον τόκον.

Phryn. *Ecl.* 264

The equivalence between ἔγγιον and ἔγγειον may also imply a pronunciation [iː] of both ‹ει› and ‹ι›, that preserved the long quantity of both vowels, if Phrynichus adopted for comparatives in -ίων a strict doctrine that attributes a long /iː/ to all Attic forms, the same doctrine that Herodian attributes to Aristophanes of Byzantium, quoting καλλίων, ἡδίων, βελτίων, γλυκίων, κακίων[206]. The *Antiatticista* (η

---

[206] περὶ διχρόνων *An. Ox.* 3 291.9–12 = *GG* 3.2 13.14–7, Ar. Byz. fr. 347. Tosi (1997: 172–4) discusses

5 ἥδιον) contrasts the same view, quoting an example from Alexis (fr. 158 K.-A.) where the comparative was possibly scanned ἥδῐον (as it is certainly the case in another line of Alexis, fr. 25.6 K.-A., at the end of a trimeter[207]).

The gloss as we read it in the *Philetaerus* is an instance of normalisation of prevocalic ‹ε› to ‹ει›; other instances of the same contrast point to scholarship on variants with *epsilon* of words with *epsilon iota* attested in metrical texts (cf. chap. II, § 2.1.2).

Ἐλαία

Paus. ε 31 Ἐλαία· Αἰολὶς πόλις, Ἐλέα δὲ ἐν Ἰταλίᾳ.

Eustathius (1944.9) discusses the spellings Ἐλαία/Ἐλέα commenting Homer *Od.* 23.190, θάμνος ἔφυ τανύφυλλος ἐλαίης ἕρκεος ἐντός. The passages quotes Aelius Dionysius as well "ἦν δέ, φησι, καὶ Ἐλαία πόλις ἐν Ἰταλίᾳ (Ael. D. ε 30)· ἐν μέντοι ἑτέρῳ ῥητορικῷ λεξικῷ γράφει, ὅτι Ἐλαία Αἰολὶς πόλις, Ἐλέα δὲ ἐν Ἰταλίᾳ (Paus. ε 31)· καὶ ζητητέον ποία γραφὴ ἀκριβεστέρα ἐστίν", which goes on to quote Strabo (13.1.68 Meineke) in support of the spelling Ἐλαία for the city of Aeolia.

By the time of Eustathius it is no wonder that ‹αι› and ‹ε› sounded the same. The entry he was reading in Pausanias contrasted Ἐλαία and Ἐλέα – different names for different cities, but perhaps in Pausanias' time similar enough in pronunciation to be confused, if not altogether homophones. Isochrony in this case may have been favoured by a contextual shortening in prevocalic position.

We cannot be sure of the entry's original wording, and it is impossible to determine how explicitly it addressed, if it did, a confusion arisen after the merger of /ai/ and /e/. In Pausanias' time too ‹αι› and ‹ε› had identical timbre: the open question is whether the different quantities they implied were referred to in any way in Pausanias' lexicon.

---

the gloss in detail, and rejects the interpretation of Arnott, who wants to read ἴδιον, in part on the assumption that "the Atticists were not concerned with prosody" (1989: 347). Cf. also Valente 2015a *ad Antiatt.* η 5.

207 On the very few other examples of comparatives in -ίων in comedy and tragedy (doubtful and even fewer examples), cf. Diggle 1981: 29–30.

ἔπηλις

→ ἀπηλιώτης

ἐπιμέλου

Moer. ε 32 ἐπιμέλου παροξυτόνως Ἀττικοί, περισπωμένως Ἕλληνες.

ἐπιμέλου can be the indicative imperative middle of ἐπιμέλομαι, a variant of ἐπιμελέομαι. ἐπιμέλομαι, even if less and less common after the 4th century BC[208], survived in poetry (an unaugmented aorist μελόμην is attested in an Attic funerary epigram dating to the end of the 2nd century AD (*IG* II² 7447.12). ἐπιμελοῦ is the expected present imperative from ἐπιμελέομαι, the common form in Attic writers. The paroxytone ἐπιμέλου is transmitted in a γνώμη μονόστιχος of Menander (Men. *Mon.* 848). Editors disagree on the accentuation: Jaekel prints ἐπιμέλου, Meineke has ἐπιμελοῦ (*FCG* IV 1.551). Moeris may have attributed the less common form to the Attic dialect, more on account of its exceptionality than of its status of genuine Attic form (Σακαλῆς 1977: 460–2).

ἐπιτάδε

Philet. 254 ἐπιτάδε καὶ ἐπέκεινα, βαρυτόνως οἱ Ἀττικοί.

The prescription about ἐπέκεινα is quite easy to understand: a text written in *scriptio continua* without reading marks could be read indifferently as ἐπ' ἐκεῖνα or ἐπέκεινα. Knowing that in the text of an Attic author the form to be expected has a recessive accent, the use of βαρυτόνως here is easy to understand.

The same does not apply as easily to ἐπιτάδε (a form attested in the manuscripts, cf. LSJ *s.v.*). One may expect βαρυτόνως there to imply a form ἐπίταδε: not necessarily because of the meaning of βαρυτόνως, that can describe anything which is not accented on the last syllable, but because there is no oxytone competing with ἐπιτάδε. Modern editors choose either accentuation. Perhaps one should print ἐπίταδε here too – if the competing accentuation was ἐπιτάδε, then βαρυτόνως would be a better description of the accentuation in ἐπίταδε.

---

[208] Both verbs are attested in Attic inscriptions, ἐπιμελέομαι being by far the most common (Threatte 1996: 513–4).

ἔπτυσχλοι

→ ἄπεφθος

εὐκλεία

Ael. D. ε 71 εὐκλεία καὶ τὰ ὅμοια· μακρὰ ἡ τελευταία καὶ παροξύνεται, ὥσπερ καὶ Ἐρατοσθένης ἐν ιβ Περὶ ⟨κωμῳδίας⟩ (fr. 47 Str.).

→ ἀγνοία

εὑρέ

Philet. 227 εὑρέ ὀξυτόνως· τὸ δὲ λέγε βαρυτόνως, ὅτι ἐπὶ μὲν τοῦ εὑρέ μακρὰ ἡ πρώτη, ἕπεται δὲ βραχεῖα. τὰ δὲ τοιαῦτα ὀξύνεται· εἰπέ, εὑρέ· ἀλλὰ καὶ τὸ ἐλθέ διὰ τὴν θέσει μακράν· τὸ δὲ λέγε καὶ γράφε βραχείας ἔχει τὰς δύο· λέγε, γράφε. τὸ δὲ λαβέ παρὰ τοῖς Ἀττικοῖς παραλόγως ὀξύνεται.

Five aorist imperatives have oxytone accentuation in Attic, the four imperatives listed in this gloss and ἰδέ. The accentuation is inherited from Indo-European.

The *Philetaerus* explains the accentuation through a rule predicting that second aorist imperatives with a heavy first syllable will have an accented second: hence λαβέ has the same accentuation as an exception to the rule, παραλόγως. The rule does actually represent how thematic aorist imperatives are accented: all of them originally had an accented thematic vowel, but only some of them were preserved: εἰπέ, εὑρέ, ἐλθέ, and only in Attic ἰδέ and λαβέ The manuscript tradition does not preserve all of them consistently (according to some ancient scholarship, whose doctrine did not prevail, Attic also had paroxytone πιέ, φαγέ)[209]. Cf. also *Philet.* 251 → πυθοῦ.

εὕρεμα

→ ἀνάθημα

---

209 Cf. Schwyzer 1939: 799, Vendryes 1945: 125, Bally 1945: 101.

εὐφυᾶ

Moer. ε 29 εὐφυᾶ ⟨Ἀττικοί⟩· εὐφυῆ ⟨Ἕλληνες⟩.

The lemma is attested in the 5th-century AD lexicon of Cyrillus ((g) ευφ 3 = Σ ε 1012 εὐφυᾶ· καλὴν φύcιν ἔχοντα) and in Gregorius of Corinth – the quotation in Gregorius is revealing of the nature of the problem:

> καὶ τὰc εἰc α καθαρὸν ληγούcαc αἰτιατικὰc ἀρcενικάc, τὰc ἀπὸ τῶν εἰc ευc εὐθειῶν γινο-μέναc, διὰ τοῦ η προφέρεcθαι[210], Εὐρυcθέα Εὐρυcθῆ, Τυδέα Τυδῆ. Ἀττικῶν δὲ καὶ ἀντὶ τοῦ εὐφυῆ, ὑγιῆ, εὐφυᾶ, ὑγιᾶ λέγειν. καὶ ἀντὶ τοῦ Εὐβοέα, Πειραιέα, Εὔβοᾶ καὶ Πειραιᾶ λέγειν.

> Also the masculine accusative plurals ending in pure *alpha*, the ones deriving form nominatives in -ευc, are pronounced with *eta*, Εὐρυcθέα Εὐρυcθῆ, Τυδέα Τυδῆ. It is typical of the Attic [speakers[211]] to say εὐφυᾶ, ὑγιᾶ instead of εὐφυῆ, ὑγιῆ. And instead of Εὐβοέα, Πειραιέα, to say Εὔβοᾶ and Πειραιᾶ.
>
> Gregorius of Corinth, περὶ Ἀτθίδοc LXXXVIII–XC

Accusatives in -ᾶ like the ones in this excerpt can be explained as having undergone synizesis in a first stage, with a lengthening of the desinential vowel (εὐφυέᾶ), and then hyphaeresis, leading to a simplification to ὑγιᾶ, εὐφυᾶ. In turn, analogy with other nouns in -ηc tended to restore forms in η[212]. Classical Attic regularly attests the first stage of the development (e.g. ὑγιέᾶ). ὑγιᾶ, εὐφυᾶ, are fourth-century variants, possibly less common than the forms in ⟨η⟩[213].

The text of Aristophanes, *Th.* 968 is εὐφυῆ in ms. R, which Brunck[214] corrected to εὐφυᾶ, a correction that Austin – Olson (2004) and Wilson (2007) accept (without reference to any of the ancient lexica). The gloss in Moeris may be evidence that editions of Aristophanes (or other authors of the Attic canon) read εὐφυᾶ already in the imperial period.

---

210 Note the use of προφέρομαι in combination with a spelling prescription (cf. chap. I § 6).
211 Or 'writers': being a substantivised adjective, οἱ Ἀττικοί is unfortunately ambiguous. I supply [speakers] in my translations, but both interpretation, 'speakers' and 'writers' are always possible.
212 Simplification of the vowel sequence by hyphaeresis is more likely than proximity with ⟨υ⟩, and most cases of oscillation between ⟨υᾶ⟩ and ⟨υη⟩ affect α < εα (Schwyzer 1939: 189).
213 Kühner – Blass 443–4. The spelling εὐφυᾶ is found in *IG* II² 1612.35 (356/5 BC). Cf. Threatte 1996: 174, 298.
214 R.F.P. Brunck, *Aristophanis Comoediae*, Argentorati 1783.

ἑωθώς

Ael. D. ε 85 ἑωθώς· χωρὶς τοῦ ι Ἄρχιππος (fr. 55 K.-A.) καὶ Ἀραρὼς (fr. 16 K.-A.) ἔωθας καὶ Θουκιδίδης (8.69.2, 8.97.1) ἑώθεσαν.

There does not seem to be a chronological distinction between ἑωθώς and εἰωθώς. Both forms were in current usage at the same time[215], as their co-existence in literary Attic shows. The gloss is written as if to defend forms without ‹ι› as genuinely Attic. The perfect ἔωθα is widespread in Ionic (ἔωθα is the usual form in Herodotus[216]). Attic inscriptions show εἴωθα until the imperial period[217]. It is interesting that a form ἑώθαμεν should appear in the hyperatticising language of Lucian's *Lexiphanes* (14), where it could be a Ionic form mistaken to be Attic: the only other attestation of the same form is in Herodotus, 4.134.3, and Lucian is probably aware of its dialectal connotations[218].

Prevocalic [e:] as in εἰωθώς had already been raised to [i(:)] by the time Aelius Dionysius composed his lexicon (chap. II, § 2.1.2, chap. III, § 5.5), and glosses dealing with ‹ει› suggest that the digraph corresponded to [i] or [i:] – the distinction in length relying exclusively on how keen the speaker would be in retaining it. The gloss is not openly prescriptive, and it is therefore impossible to use it as evidence of a special pronunciation. If the speaker decided to follow a pronunciation based on spelling, the competing spellings with ἑωθ- or εἰωθ- must have been pronounced with [e] and [i(:)] respectively.

ἦδος

Ael. D. η 3 ἦδος· τὸ ὄξος, δασύνουσιν οἱ Ἀττικοί.

Eustathius (1417.21-3) mentions explicitly that Aelius Dionysius said the Attic word to have a rough breathing. The gloss is extracted from a lengthy passage

---

[215] Perfects with a redoublement ἐ- are attested in Homer (*Il.* 8.408 = 422 αἰεὶ γάρ μοι ἔωθεν ἐνικλᾶν ὅττι κεν εἴπω), where they alternate with the forms in εἰ- attested also in Attic (εἴωθα, εἰωθώς).
[216] The reduction of prevocalic [ei] to [e] is not attested in Ionic: in order to explain Homeric ἔωθα one needs to assume a simplification *sμ- > *μ in the root, rather than attributing the reduction of the diphthong to the following vowel (but cf. Peters 1980: 87 fn. 40).
[217] *Arch. Deltion* 33 (1978), *Chronika* 55 n. 1 l. 9, *ca.* AD 150.
[218] While imitating Ionic, he uses a pluperfect ἑώθεε (*De Syria Dea* 35), which, at least in surviving Greek literature, is only attested in Herodotus (1.11.1, 184, 4.134.2, 6.107.2).

of Eustathius' commentary on the Odyssey (1417.15–24), where he discusses the initial aspiration of a number of words that he derives from ἥδω. Pausanias (η 4 = Eust. 1417.23) mentions a form ἦδος, glossed as τὸ ὄφελος καὶ τὸ ὄξος, but – as Eustathius explicitly remarks – the lexicographer provided no information on the initial aspiration (οὐδέν τι περὶ πνεύματος ἔφη). The scholarship that ascribed a smooth breathing to ἦδος is attributed to Herodian (*GG* 3.2 904.23–4), and explains the lack of aspiration in this word as an Aeolic trait.

ἡδύνω

→ἐβουλόμην

ἠθάς

Ael. D. ε 10 ἐθάς· φίλος, cυνήθηc. τινὲc δὲ καὶ ἠθάc.

The passage of Eustathius from which this gloss is derived is a commentary on ἔται (Hom. *Od.* 4.16):

> δῆλον δὲ καὶ ὅτι ἀπὸ τοῦ ἔθους, οὐ μόνον ὁ ἑταῖροc καὶ ὁ ἔτηc, ἀλλὰ φανερῶc καὶ ὁ ἐθάc. ὃν τινὲc, καὶ ἠθάδα λέγουcιν ὥc φηcιν Αἴλιοc Διονύcιοc. ὅτι δὲ ψιλοῦται τὸ ἔτηc, κάλλιον ἐν τῇ Ἰλιάδι γέγραπται.
>
> It is also clear from ἔθοc, not only 'companion' and 'clansman', but apparently also 'familiar', ἐθάc. Which some people also call ἠθάc, as Aelius Dionysius says. That ἔτηc has a smooth breathing is discussed more in detail in [my commentary to] the Iliad.
>
> Eust. 1480.11–13

Eustathius seems to imply that the less common form is ἠθάc. Yet ἐθάc is found only in Thucydides, among all Attic writers. The sense of Aelius Dionysius' quotation is probably that ἠθάc is actually attested in good Attic writing. The two forms are attested in later lexicography[219], and the root from which they derive, *(s)u̯eh₁dʰ-[220], forms derivatives with a short vowel (ἔθοc, ἐθίζω) and with a long one (ἦθοc, ἠθεῖοc)[221].

---

219 Σ ε 73 ἐθάδαc, η 43 ἠθάδαc.
220 *su̯edʰ* IEW 883, s.v. ἐωθώc.

ἤμελλον

→ ἐβουλόμην

ἡμίσεια

Phryn. *PS* 73.4–6 ἡμίσεας καὶ ἡμίσεις ἄμφω μὲν Ἀττικά. Ἀττικώτερον δὲ τὸ ἡμίσεας. ἡμίσειαν σὺν τῷ ι. ἥμισυ–ἡμίσεως–ἡμίσεα, ἀλλ' οὐχὶ ἡμίση.

The inflected forms of ἥμισυ are attested in a number of spellings in Egyptian papyri[222], although none of the usual ones matches those listed by Phrynichus. The genitive ἡμίσεως is "presumably an orthographic variation of the regular ending -εος" (Gignac 1981: 129), and it is a *varia lectio* in Thucydides (2.78.2, 4.83.6)[223]. The accusative plural ἡμίσεις, a form apparently remodelled on the declension of nouns in -εύς, is normally found in Attic writers (e.g. Thuc. 4.42.4, Pl. *Tht.* 154c): the *Praeparatio Sophistica* however prescribes an acc. pl. masc. ἡμίσεας, and warns against the neuter pl. ἡμίση, a form that must have not been totally unknown to Attic, if at least at some point in the fourth century BC it could find its way into an official inscription[224].

The *iota* is expected in the feminine of this adjective, in which it is etymological, but not in the masculine or neuter, whose inflected forms have normally a prevocalic *epsilon*. Yet the feminine ἡμίσεα is well attested in Attic inscriptions, where it is actually more frequent than ἡμίσεια[225].

Speakers willing to follow this prescription would also associate a pronunciation [heːˈmisiːa] to the spelling ἡμίσεια, if they wished to give any phonetical reality to their choices in spelling, realising ‹ει› as a long vowel.

---

221 The most ancient derivatives of *$(s)ueh_1d^h$ have the long vowel; ἔθος must be a back-formation based on compounds like συνήθης, that had been reinterpreted as lengthened in composition – Wackernagel's *Dehnungsgesetz*, cf. Meißner (2006: 76–8).
222 The neuter ἥμισυ can even be uninflected or follow the second declension and it is attested as ἥμυσον, ἥμεσον, ἥμισον (Gignac 1981: 128–9).
223 ἡμίσεως is the norm in later writers, e.g. Dioscorides Medicus, LSJ s.v. ἥμισυς.
224 *IG* II² 1678, l. 23, dated before 315 BC.
225 The spelling without *iota* ἡμίσεα appears at least 18 times in 10 inscriptions dating between the second half of the fourth and the early third century BC, whereas ἡμίσεια is only found four times in two inscriptions (*IG* II² 1241 (300/299); *Agora* XIX, L 4a (leases of private land, 363/2)).

ἠμωδία

Moer. η 17 ἠμωδίαν ἐπὶ τῶν ὀδόντων διὰ τοῦ η Ἀττικοί· αἱμωδίαν Ἕλληνες.

Moeris is the only lexicon which inlcudes ἠμωδία, and with Hesychius (η 566) and Thomas Magister (173.8), the only source of the term ἠμωδία itself. If ἠμωδία is related to αἱμωδία by sound change, this would be a rather isolated instance where the form showing a more recent vocalism is that of the *Attikoi* and not the one of the *Hellenes*.

The spelling ἠμωδία is problematic, at least if compared with the more common αἱμωδία. There are no known attestations of ἠμωδία in Attic literature, or in fact anywhere out of the lexica quoted above. On the other hand, there is a number of glosses referring to the verb αἱμωδέω. It is possible that the spelling in Moeris is a by-product of glosses containing augmented forms of αἱμωδέω (like ἡμώδεις in Cratinus, fr. 41 K.–A.)[226] or αἱμωδιάω, whose infinitive αἱμωδιᾶν or imperfect ἡμωδία (as in Timocles, fr. 11.9 K.–A.), may have originated the wrong readings αἱμωδίαν and ἠμωδία.

The contrast between ἠμωδία and αἱμωδία implies that ‹αι› and ‹η› were both an [e] vowel at the time when Moeris' lexicon was written, and therefore that in the pronunciation of the Atticists, ‹η› was not confused with ‹ι› (cf. chap. II, §§ 2.2.2, 2.3.2, chap. III § 4.2).

ἤνυστρον

Phryn. *Ecl.* 133 ἤνυστρον λέγε, μὴ ἔνυστρον.
Phryn. *Ecl.* 414 {ἔνυστρον μὴ λέγε, ἀλλὰ ἤνυστρον, ὅτι καὶ ἀρχαῖον.}
Moer. η 12 ἤνυστρα Ἀττικοί· χορδαὶ ἢ αἱ κοιλίαι τῶν βοῶν Ἕλληνες.
   cf. also Pollux 2.204, ἤνυστρον.

The glosses contrast *eta* and *epsilon* but do not mention their different quantities. It is particularly difficult to reconstruct the history of a technical term poorly attested either in literary works or in documents. The later form seems to be

---

[226] One entry in Phryinichus' *Praeparatio Sophistica* deals with this problem (*PS* 14.3 αἱμῳδεῖν Ἀττικώτερον. λέγεται δὲ καὶ αἱμωδιᾶν). Photius (b, z) α 629, the source of Cratinus' fragment, quotes him to support the idea that αἱμωδέω is the real Attic form, and not the more common αἱμωδιᾶν. Hesychius has two glosses on αἱμωδιᾶν (α 1970 αἱμωδιᾶν· τὸ τοὺς ὀδόντας ναρκᾶν ἀπὸ ὁράσεως ἢ ἀκούσματος, η 567 ἡμωδίασαν· ἐνάρκησαν. αἱμωδίασαν) but also one on ἠμωδία, quite similar to Moeris (Moer. η 17 ~ Hsch. η 566 ἠμωδίαν· αἱμωδίαν).

ἔνυστρον, as Phrynichus' gloss suggests. The etymology of the word is not entirely clear either, but points to ἤνυστρον as the more ancient form. ἔνυστρον could be the result of analogical levelling on forms prefixed with ἐν, or perhaps with ἔντερα[227]. ἤνυστρον, the earliest attested of the two forms, is found in Ar. *Eq.* 356, and later a number of times in Aristotle, and it is also the only form that Pollux mentions in the *Onomasticon* (2.204). ἤνυστρον is also common in more recent times (it is found in Alexis, Aelian, Philo), yet in the LXX it alternates with ἔνυστρον (ἔν. *Deut.* 18.3; ἤν. *Mal.* 2.3); only ἔνυστρον is attested in Flavius Josephus (*Ant. Jud.* 4.74.3) and, in the 4th century AD, in Basilius of Caesarea (*Hom. in Hexaemer.* 9.5.21). Its occurrence in Aristophanes must have won ἤνυστρον the label 'ἀρχαῖον'[228].

Θαλῆς

Moer. θ 4 Θαλῆς περισπωμένως Ἀττικοί, βαρυτόνως Ἕλληνες.

The position of the accent contributed to the distinction between the two different inflections of this personal name. A spelling Θαλης could correspond to Θαλῆς (gen. Θαλοῦς), the most common inflection in Attic, or Θάλης (gen. Θάλητος), well attested in Attic literature only after Aristotle. The point is made clear in the scholion to Ar. *Nu.* 180 (RV): "διχῶς δὲ τοὔνομα ἐκφωνητέον· βαρυτόνως μὲν Θάλης, Θάλητος, ἔτι δὲ καὶ περισπωμένως Θαλῆς, ὡς Ἑρμῆς"[229]. The prescription focuses on the only form in either paradigm that could be pronounced in two different ways.

θεῶσαι

Antiatt. θ 20 θεώσειν καὶ θεῶσαι· κατ' ἔνδειαν τοῦ ι, τὸ περιενεγκεῖν θεῖον καὶ καθῆραι. Ἀραρὼς Καμπυλίωνι (fr. 12 K.–A.).

---

[227] DÈLG, *s.v.*, EDG *s.v.* ἤνυστρον.
[228] The gloss is possibly to be attributed to a copyist (the glosses 412–424 of the *Ecloga* are considered to be a later addition, cf. Fischer 1974: 29–31).
[229] The accentuation of Θάλης is discussed in relation to the position of the accent and the inflection, in Choeroboscus *GG* 4.1 153.27 ff. (=Hdn. *GG* 3.2 683.1–12), *Suda* θ 18, Thomas Magister, 176.8, and the scholia vetera to Homer, sch. *Il.* 15.302b2 (T).

The *Antiatticista* quotes Attic comedy in support of forms with a more recent phonology (prevocalic ‹ευ› is simplified to ‹ε›). περιθεωςάτωςαν needs to be restored in Menander (*Phasma* 55, cf. Austin 2012 *ad loc.*). See *Antiatt.* θ 13 → Θηςέῳ.

Θηςέῳ

Antiatt. θ 13 Θηςέῳ· ἀντὶ τοῦ Θηςείῳ. Φερεκράτης Δουλοδιδαςκάλῳ (fr. 46 K.–A.).

The *Antiatticista* contradicts the doctrine that nouns in -ευς always form derivatives in -ειος, showing that genuine Attic authors also used forms without a diphthong. Choeroboscus continues the Atticist doctrine in the περὶ ὀρθογραφίας (*An. Ox.* 2 219.10–17), boldly stating that derivatives from nouns in -εύς are always written with ‹ευ›, and adding the exception that (Θηςεῖον) λέγεται δὲ καὶ Θηςίον (219.17) – possibly a corruption of Θήςεον[230].

The *Etymologicum Genuinum* preserves a fuller wording of this exception, complete with a full quotation of Pherecrates and pointing out that the spelling has ‹ε›: εὕρηται δὲ διὰ τοῦ ε ψιλοῦ 'Κάλλαιςχρον ἐν τῷ Θηςέῳ καθήμενον' (*Et.Gen.* AB, Miller 1868: 159).

Attic inscriptions attest Θήςεον already in the second half of the fourth century BC[231], therefore granting authority to the spelling of the *Etymologicum genuinum*. However, a few instances of ‹Θηςια› for Θηςεῖα (the festival) are attested in the 2nd century AD[232]. The competing pronunciations must have been [iː] and [e], the former popular with those who generalised [iː] before non-front vowels, following the Atticist doctrine (but possibly hyperatticising), the latter widespread since the fourth century BC at least, considered less authoritative by some, but defended by the Atticists who based on a wider canon of comic playwrights.

---

[230] Dindorf, *ThGL* IV 381a, and 380d on the accent, discussed also in [Hdn.] *de loc. prav., An. Ox.* 3 252.12–17, together with that of → Διονυςεῖον.
[231] Threatte 1980: 315.
[232] Threatte 1980: 206, 417 (*IG* II² 2038, AD 125, 2208, AD 212/3 or later, Θηςίῳ is integrated in *SEG* 33: 134).

ἱερεία

Moer. ι 3 ἱερεία μακρῶς τὴν τελευταίαν καὶ ὀξυτόνως τὴν παραλήγουσαν Ἀττικοί· ἱέρεια βραχέως τὴν ἐσχάτην καὶ βαρυτόνως τὴν παρατέλευτον Ἕλληνες.

The entry in Moeris contradicts the Herodianic doctrine that prescribes a proparoxytone feminine in -ειᾰ (τὰ εἰς εια ἀπὸ τῶν εἰς ευς προπαροξύνεται· βασιλεύς βασίλεια, ἱερεύς ἱέρεια, [Arc.] 109.9)[233]. The long vowel that Moeris prescribes in the penultimate syllable is extremely rare in the text of Attic playwrights. Interestingly, its only authority of being a genuine Attic form seems to derive from New Comedy. It can be read, guaranteed by the metre, only twice in Menander (*Syc.* 242, 258), once in a comic papyrus of the 3rd century BC (fr. com. ad. 1032.5 K.–A.), and once in Lycophron, *Alex.* 991[234]. In all cases the metre guarantees the long quantity of ‹ει›, but not that of the final syllable. Editors consider it short, and accent ἱέρειαν.

Feminines in -ίᾱ and in -ιᾰ coexisted at some point in Attic. Attic and Ionic tend to replace the motion suffix -ιᾰ with -ίᾱ[235], in particular in derivatives of -ης adjectives. So forms like ἀλήθεια, contrasting the Ionic forms ἀληθείη, and the poetical εὐκλείᾱ, ὑγιείᾱ in Aeschylus *Th.* 685 and Aristophanes *Av.* 604 respectively[236]. Such forms did not become part of the Koine and must have been soon identified as peculiar to Attic. Feminines of nouns in -ευς are regularly derived with -ιᾰ (βασιλεύς > βασίλεια, reduced to βασίλεα in some varieties). The couple ἱερεία ~ ἱέρεια must have been created along the same lines, and the variant with a long final vowel identified as Attic just like εὐκλείᾱ, ὑγιείᾱ and the like.

The length of the final syllable is also not particularly well attested in Attic playwrights. It is guaranteed in Euripides *Ba.* 1114, πρώτη δὲ μήτηρ ἦρξεν ἱερέα φόνου. If we accept the reading of the manuscripts, ἱερεία (which is not impossible for the metre, as the syllable realises the *indifferens* in the last iamb), this may be the only instance of ἱερεία in Attic literature that confirms Moeris' prescription. It is however an isolated example in Euripides, whose remaining

---

[233] Cf. also [Hdn.] περὶ τῶν ζητουμένων κτλ, *An. Ox.* 3 254.8, constrasting the accentuation of ἱερεία, 'sacrifice, festival' and ἱέρεια 'priestess'.
[234] ἱερείαι also appears once in a corrupt line of Posidippus (fr. 28.21 K.–A. = Ath. 9.376e ἵερειαι (A)), but the reading and the scansion are uncertain: Kassel and Austin print ἱερέαι.
[235] The functional distinction between the two suffixes could be ancient (Solmsen 1909: 248–53): the identical inflection of the two suffixes in the oblique cases favoured the interpretation of abstracts in -ίᾱ as concrete nouns in -(ι)ᾰ.
[236] Chantraine 1933: 78–90, esp. pp. 86ff.

text consistenly requires ἱερέα. The length of the final vowel is never guaranteed by the metre – modern editors print ἱερέα, which is also the spelling commonly found in Attic inscriptions (Threatte 1976: 315), and happens to be the spelling of the papyrus transmitting Euripides fr. 370 Kannicht (l. 97, πόλει προθύειν ἱερέαν κεκλημένην).

The spelling of ἱερεία is also discussed in the scholia to E. *Or.* 261 (γοργῶπες, ἐνέρων ἱέρεαι, δειναί θεαί), where the manuscripts and the scholia are divided between ἱέριαι, ἱέρειαι, ἱερίαι (the editors print ἱερέαι), and one must either read ἱερεαι or scan a short ‹ει› in ἱερειαι[237]. The *scholia vetera* to this line of the *Orestes* prescribe the same recessive accentuation for ἱέριαι as for αἴτιαι and τιμώριαι: ἱέρ[ε]ιαι δειναί θοαί· τὸ ἱέριαι προπαροξύνουcιν ὡc τὸ τιμώριαι καὶ αἴτιαι (sch. E. *Or.* 261 (MTB) Schwarz / (mbc) Diggle).

The comparison with nouns in -ιᾱ suggests that the scholiast to the *Orestes* read ἱέριαι in the text, the spelling – but not the accentuation – that Triclinius will explicitly prescribe, centuries later[238]. On the accentuation of these plurals see Moer. α 6 →αἴτιαι.

ἱκετεία

Phryn. *PS* 77.1–2 ἱκετεία. διὰ τοῦ τ, οὐ διὰ τοῦ c. ἱκεcίουc μέν⟨τοι⟩ λιτὰc καὶ λόγουc ἱκεcίουc.
Phryn. *Ecl.* 52 ἱκεcία καὶ τοῦτο ἀδόκιμον, ἱκετεία δὲ λέγε.

By opposing ἱκεcία and ἱκετεία only in that one has a ‹τ› and the other a ‹c›, without any explicit prescription on their pronunciation, Phrynichus ignores at the same time the length and the timbre of the vowels spelt by ‹ει› and ‹ι›. Both isochrony and the merger of prevocalic /eː$_{1,2}$/ with /iː/ need to be accomplished in order for ἱκεcία and ἱκετεία to rhyme. One may assume that the same distincton in length that Phrynichus explicitly prescribes for μαγειρεῖον and →ὀπτάνιον (*Ecl.* 241), and is found in the *Antiatticista* (κ 71 →κυδώνιον μῆλον) was also true for the pair ἱκεcία ~ ἱκετεία.

---

237 Cf. Kühner – Blass 388 for this scansion and the attestations of variants in -ιᾱ in Attic literature.
238 Triclinius prescribes the spelling with *iota*, but not the proparoxytone accentuation: τὸ ἱέρειαι ἱερίαι χρὴ γράφειν Ἰωνικῶc, ἵν' ἔχῃ πρὸc τὸ μέτρον ὀρθῶc. τὰ γὰρ διὰ τοῦ εια προπαροξύτονα Ἰωνικῶc οἱ ποιηταὶ παροξύτονα ποιοῦντεc διὰ τοῦ ια γράφουcι, τὸ αὐθάδεια αὐθαδία λέγοντεc, καὶ τὸ εὐcέβεια εὐcεβία, καὶ τὰ τοιαῦτα, ὃ καὶ ἐξετάζων εὑρήcειc (sch. E. *Or.* 261 I Dindorf / T^{t3} Diggle), and sch. E. *IT* 39 T^2 (Diggle *ad loc.*).

It is apparent from a number of other glosses that the distribution of the two suffixes was not always clear (see chap. III, § 5.4). The same uncertainty is reflected in later scholarship, see for instance a passage transmitted in the orthographic treaties attributed to Choeroboscus, a passage reflecting a doctrine similar to the one we read in Phrynichus[239]:

> τὰ ἀπὸ ἀρσενικῶν ἐχόντων τὸ τ διὰ τοῦ ια γινόμενα καὶ τρέποντα τὸ τ εἰс c διὰ τοῦ ι γράφεται οἶον ἄλουτος ἀλουсία, ἀθάνατος ἀθανασία, ὑπηρέτης ὑπηρεсία.
>
> Derivatives of masculines in ‹τ› formed with ‹ια› and turning the ‹τ› to ‹c› are written with the *iota*, like ἄλουτος ἀλουсία, ἀθάνατος ἀθανασία, ὑπηρέτης ὑπηρεсία.
>
> Choerob. *An. Ox.* 2 269.23

ἱππέα

Moer. ι 4 ἱππέα ἁλιέα βασιλέα μακρῶс Ἀττικοί.

→ ἀμφορέα

ἱππέας

Moer. ι 18 ἱππέαс μακρῶс Ἀττικοί· βραχέωс Ἕλληνες.

→ ἀμφορέα

ἰсότης

Moer. ι 12 ἰсότης ὡс ἀρότης Ἀττικοί, ἰсοτήс ὡс βραβευτής Ἕλληνες.

The comparison ἰсοτής ὡс βραβευτής clearly points only to the position of the accent, as the two words do not share the same inflection. The gloss contrasts the remarks of ps.-Arcadius (and so possibly of Herodian) on the accentuation of feminine nouns in -της:

---

[239] Lentz prints these lines as part of [Hdn.] περὶ ὀρθογραφίας, *GG* 3.2 453.1–3.

τὰ εἰς της πολυσύλλαβα θηλυκὰ βαρύνονται· λογιότης λευκότης ποιότης. cεcημείωται ταχυτής βραδυτής ἁδροτής· καὶ τὰ παρ' Ἀθηναίοις ὀξύτονα· τραχυτής κουφοτής· τὸ μέντοι ποτής καὶ ἐcθής διcύλλαβα. τὸ δὲ νημερτής ἐπίθετον.

Feminine polysyllables in της are barytones: λογιότης λευκότης ποιότης. ταχυτής βραδυτής ἁδροτής are exceptions: and also the ones that are oxytones in the Attic writers: τραχυτής κουφοτής: however, ποτής and ἐcθής are disyllables. And νημερτής is an adjective.
[Arc.] 30.1–4

Whether this is genuinely Attic or not, the oxytone accentuation existed for some words (a very limited number, that does not include ἰcοτής), it is indeed ancient in a number of cases, and it had been discussed by Herodian[240]. The gloss as we read it in Moeris is surprisingly contradictory of what we know from the remaining grammatical tradition, that does never report an oxytone accentuation ἰcοτής. It is quite isolated in attributing to the Hellenes an accentuation that, if it was ever even real, must have been very much archaic. In this specific instance ἰcοτής would be the term that retained the more ancient accentuation, and therefore the form current among the Ἕλληνες is the relic of a more ancient state of affairs (as it is the case with Vendryes' Law, which affected only Attic, cf. *Philet.* 241 → ἀχρεῖος and Moer. γ 4, Philem. 357, Ael. D. γ 4, Amm. 119 → γέλοιος).

The gloss is echoed much later by Thomas Magister:

ἰcότης, οὐκ ἰcοτής ὡς βραδυτής καὶ ταχυτής. ἐπὶ δὲ ἀρcενικοῦ Ἀττικοὶ μὲν ἰcώτης λέγουcιν ὡς ἀρότης, οἱ δὲ ἁπλῶς ἰcωτής ὡς βραβευτής.

ἰcότης, not ἰcοτής like βραδυτής and ταχυτής. In the masculine the Attic [speakers] say ἰcώτης like ἀρότης, yet others simply ἰcωτής like βραβευτής.
Thom. Mag. 185.11

This gloss may be a Byzantine refutation of what we read in Moeris, or at least offer an explanation of the puzzling attribution of ἰcοτής to the Hellenes: the transmission of the entry may have been corrupt at a very early stage, and the accentuation in question was originally that of ἰcωτής, ἰcωτοῦ (a very poorly attested word, however). First-declension masculine nouns in -της are normally oxytone when they have a penultimate long syllable and denote the agent of an action (and in this case they normally are also deverbatives, like ἰcωτής < ἰcόω), but there are instances of variation, generally also implying some varia-

---

[240] It is quite likely that Hellenistic grammarians knew the oxytone, archaic accentuation from live recitations of Homer, which had kept the archaic accentuation (Lehrs 1882: 257–8, Probert 2006: 44). On Herodian's discussion of the accent of δηϊοτής etc. see Probert 2006: 38–45; the passage from the περὶ μονήρους λέξεως quoted by Hansen ad Moer. ι 12 (*GG* 3.2 945.23) only discusses the derivation of feminines in -της, -τητος, not their accentuation.

tion in meaning²⁴¹. This could have been the case with the masculine ἰcωτήc: the noun does not seem to have survived in any Greek literature (which it makes it even more likely that some sort of corruption is responsible for the entry in Moeris as we read it today); or Thomas Magister is using ἰcωτήc as a nonce-formation to clarify a behaviour of the accent that was more common in masculines -τηc than in abstract feminines in -τηc.

καρίc

→ κνημίc

κατάγειοc

Phryn. *PS* 81.11 κατάγειον· οὐχὶ κατάγαιον διὰ τῆc αι διφθόγγου.

In the Egyptian papyri, κατάγαιοc is more frequent than κατάγειοc during all the Roman and Byzantine periods (Gignac 1976: 260–1, the same is true for ἔγγαιοc²⁴²). Compounds of γῆ in -γειοc, -γαιοc, -γεωc, -γεοc, are all interchangeable forms in Greek manuscripts²⁴³. Their correct spelling was debated in ancient orthography, although the fragments that survive only contrast the variants with ⟨ευ⟩ or ⟨υ⟩, → ἔγγεια.

Manuscripts of Herodotus have κατάγαιοc, but the normal Attic spelling is κατάγειοc²⁴⁴. The prescription could have to do primarily with word-formation, and speakers may have associated two different prounciations to the two different spellings. From the treatment of other words in -ειοc in the lexica (cf. chap. II, § 2.1.2) one would expect [i:os] as the pronunciation of the last two syllables of κατάγειοc.

---

241 Probert 2003: §§ 170–2.
242 ⟨αυ⟩ is a common spelling for prevocalic ει in Egyptian papyri, cf. Ἀπελλείου for Ἀπελλαίου (AD 182), cεcημαίωμαι for cεcημείωμαι (AD 140), γλυκελείαc for γλυκελαίαc (6ᵗʰ century AD), τέλαιον for τέλειον (AD 324), see Gignac 1976: 260.
243 *DELG* s.v. γῆ.
244 Hdt. 2.150.3, 3.97.2, etc.; X. *An.* 4.5.25; Pl. *R.* 514a, 532b, *Prt.* 320e. LSJ and *DELG* s.v. κατάγειοc, and Gignac (1976: 260) ascribe κατάγαιον to the Ionic dialect.

κάταντες

Moer. κ 6 κάταντες τὴν πρώτην ὀξυτόνως Ἀττικοί, τὴν τελευταίαν ὀξέως Ἕλληνες.
Philet. 245 ἄναντες καὶ κάταντες βαρυτόνως μᾶλλον.

These glosses mirror accentual prescriptions that are also found in the grammatical tradition[245]. We can read them in ps.-Arcadius

> τὰ παρὰ τὸ αντης οὐδέτερα προπαροξύνονται· κατάντης κάταντες, προςάντης πρόςαντες, ἀνάντης ἄναντες καὶ τὰ ὅμοια.
>
> Neuters from [nouns in] -αντης are proparoxytones: κατάντης κάταντες, προςάντης πρόςαντες ἀνάντης ἄναντες and the like.
>
> [Arc.] 135.19–21[246]

With few exceptions, the accent of paroxytone adjectives in -ης shifts on the penultimate in the vocative singular of the masculine, and in the direct cases of the neuter singular if they end in -ες[247]. Glosses like these attest to the spreading of fixed accents in Koine paradigms, replacing the recessive vocative accentuation that was usual in classical Attic.

κεχρίςθαι

Phryn. *PS* 80.3–7 κεχρίςθαι ςκορπίῳ ἀντὶ τοῦ πεπλῆχθαι ὑπὸ ςκορπίου, καὶ ςὺν τῇ προθέςει ἐγκεχρίςθαι. διαφέρει τῇ γραφῇ τὸ κεχρίςθαι τὸ πεπλῆχθαί τε καὶ ὑπ' ἐλαίου κεχρεῖςθαι. τὸ μὲν γὰρ ὑπ' ἐλαίου διὰ τῆς ει διφθόγγου. τὸ δὲ κεχρίςθαι, τὸ ςημαῖνον τὸ πεπλῆχθαι, διὰ τοῦ ι πανταχοῦ.

The root vowel of χρίω 'anoint' is [iː] throughout the paradigm, even though its etymology is not clear[248]. The verb is usually spelt with ‹ι›, not ‹ει›; forms of χρίω with a short root vowel are exceptional and late (LSJ, *EDG s.v.*). Phrynichus does not point out that the spelling with ‹ι› may entail a short vowel, and does not contrast the two verbs because of the quantity of they root vowel; hence the editor's choice to print κεχρίςθαι and not κεχρῖςθαι would be motivated only on the

---

245 Σ α 499 = Σ^b 1158 ἄναντες· ἀνωφερές (ἄνεντες Β).
246 = Herodian *GG* 3.1 418.19–21, cf. also *GG* 3.1 350.28.
247 Probert 2003: § 120.
248 *DELG* and *GEW*, s.v. χρίω.

assumption that spellings with simple ‹ι› always indicate a short vowel. The hypothesis is not untenable (in fact, this equation of ‹ι› and short /i/ does happen in other cases, cf. chap. III, § 5.4), but there is nothing that motivates it in this specific instance. As in Phrynichus' time ‹ει› was pronounced [i:], the lexicographer must be introducing an artificial distinction between two homophones, attributing to each one a different spelling[249].

The gloss confirms that the digraph ει was a simple, front high-vowel even in the pronunciation of the Atticists. The length of the vowel is not specified, but we may infer that it was long. In Phrynichus' account the only difference between κεχρίcθαι and κεχρεῖcθαι is their spelling, and not their pronunciation.

κλῇcαι

Ael. D. κ 29 κλῇcαι οἱ ἀρχαῖοι λέγουcι, οὐ κλεῖcαι, καὶ κλῇδα. οὕτω καὶ οἱ τραγικοὶ καὶ Θουκιδίδηc[250].

Inscriptions of the Roman period attest to a revival of the more archaic spelling of κληίζομαι, in a time when the diphthong [ε:i], was normally written ‹ει› and not ‹ηι›[251]. There are however at least four instances of κληίζομαι, all dating to the 2nd or the 3rd century AD, all of them in metrical inscriptions[252]. One of these is provided with a diaeresis mark on the stone (κληΐζεται, *IG* II² 10826.6, 3rd century AD), and requires ‹ηι› to be scanned as two syllables. An artificial pronunciation with the diphthong /ε:i/, or with the simple long vowel spelt ‹η›, could correspond to the spelling ‹κληι›/‹κλη›. It is difficult to infer from the manuscript tradition how frequently was the *iota* actually spelt; κλῇδεc is a variant for κλεῖδεc in one of the versions of Pollux' *Onomasticon* (κλεῖδεc [καὶ κλῇδεc] 1.77 (B)).

---

249 Lobeck 1837: 415, Dindorf, *ThGL* VIII 1690d–1a; similar distinctions in *EM* 814.40; *Suda* χ 466 χρείειν· τύπτειν.
250 E. *Med.* 661 κλῇδα; Thuc. 2.4.3 ἔκλῃcε.
251 Cf. above, chap. II, § 5.
252 *IG* II² 5006.3 (age of Hadrian); 3575.2 (post AD 124/5); 10118.3 (2nd century AD); 10826. 6 (3rd c. AD).

κνημίς

Phryn. *Ecl.* 142 κνημίδα, πινακίδα, καρίδα· βραχέως τούτων τὴν παρατέλευτον. τὴν μέντοι ῥαφανίδα ἐκτείνουσι καὶ cυcτέλλουcι.

Herodian had discussed at length the accentuation of nouns in -ιδ- in the περὶ διχρόνων:

> τὰ εἰc ιc λήγοντα βαρύτονα ἀεὶ cυcτέλλει τὸ ι, εἰ μὴ cύνθετα ὑπάρχοι ἐξ ἁπλῶν ἐκτεινόντων τὸ ι, κόνις, δῆρις, μάντις, ὄρχις, ὄφις, λάτρις, ὄρνις, Ἀριστοκλῆς δὲ ἐν τῷ περὶ διαλέκτων φηςὶν Ἀττικοὺς ἐκτείνειν. προcέθηκα δὲ εἰ μὴ cύνθετα εἴη ἐξ ἁπλῶν ἐκτεινόντων τὸ ι διὰ τὸ κνημίc εὐκνήμιc, ψηφίc μελαμψήφριc καὶ ὅcα τοιαῦτα. Τὰ μέντοι ὀξύτονα θηλυκὰ εἰc ιc λήγοντα μὴ καθαρεύοντα μεμελέτηκε καὶ ἐκτείνεcθαι καὶ cυcτέλλεcθαι. τοῖc μὲν οὖν cυcτέλλουcι τὸ ι ἀδιάφορος ἡ πρὸ τέλουc εἴτε μακρὰ εἴη εἴτε βραχεῖα, βολίc, ῥανίc, αἰγίc, μηλίc, Δωρίc· τοῖc δὲ ἐκτείνουcι τὸ ι, καὶ μάλιcτα ἐπὶ διcυλλάβων, ἡ πρὸ τέλουc μακρὰ ὑπῆρχεν ἤτοι φύcει ἢ θέcει, κηκίc, κηλίc, νηcίc, κρηνίc, ψηφίc, cφραγίc, ἀψίc, βαλβίc, φαρκίc. τὸ μέντοι καρίc καὶ ῥιπίc ἡ μὲν κοινὴ cυνήθεια ἐκτείνει, ἡ δὲ τῶν Ἀθηναίων διάλεκτος cυcτέλλει. διcύλλαβα δὲ παρεθέμην, ἐπεὶ ὁρᾶται τριcύλλαβα βραχεῖα παραληγόμενα καὶ κατὰ τὴν cυνήθη χρῆcιν καὶ κατὰ τὴν τῶν Ἰώνων ἐκτείνοντα τὸ ι· κατὰ δὲ τοὺς Ἀττικοὺς cυcτέλλονται. πλοκαμίc, κεραμίc, καλαμίc, βλεφαρίc, ῥαφανίc· τὸ δὲ ἀγαθίc ἀεὶ cυcτελλομένωc· οὕτω δὲ καὶ ἡ τρυφαλίc cυcτέλλεται. καὶ ἐπίcταcιν ἔχει τὸ κληῖc ἐκτεινόμενον καὶ καθαρεῦον· τὰ δὲ λοιπὰ πάντα cυcτέλλονται, Λαῒc, Ναῒc, Θηcηῒc, δμωῒc, ἡρωῒc, Μινωῒc.

All non-oxytones ending in *is* always have a short *i*, unless they happen to be compounds of simple nouns ending in *īs*: κόνις, δῆρις, μάντις, ὄρχις, ὄφις, λάτρις, ὄρνις (Aristocles in his *On Dialects* says that the Attic lengthen the *iota* in these words). I added 'if they are not compounds simple nouns ending in *īs*' because of κνημίc εὐκνήμιc, ψηφίc μελαμψήφριc and the like. Yet feminine oxytones in impure *is* [i. e. not preceded by a vowel] customarily have either long or short *i*. Those with a short *i* may have a penultimate that is either long or short, βολίc, ῥανίc, αἰγίc, μηλίc, Δωρίc; those with a long *ī*, especially if disyllables, have a long penultimate syllable either by nature or position, κηκίc, κηλίc, νηcίc, κρηνίc, ψηφίc, cφραγίc, ἀψίc, βαλβίc, φαρκίc. Yet the common usage lengthens καρίc and ῥιπίc, whereas the Attic dialect shortens them. I added 'disyllables' since trisyllables with a short penultimate have been observed to have a long *i* both in common usage and in the Ionic dialect: in Attic they have a short *i*. πλοκαμίc, κεραμίc, καλαμίc, βλεφαρίc, ῥαφανίc: but ἀγαθίc always has a short *i*, and so also τρυφαλίc does. κληῖc too is problematic, in that it ends with a long vowel, preceded by another: all other words of this kind have a short *i*, Λαῒc, Ναῒc, Θηcηῒc, δμωῒc, ἡρωῒc, Μινωῒc.

Hdn. GG 3.2 18.14–32

Phrynichus' prescription is contradictory[253]. It partly coincides with Herodian: Herodian and Phrynichus agree on καρίc, said to have a short vowel in Attic,

---

[253] "[T]he passage is either corrupt or contains an erroneus statement" (Rutherford 1881: 255).

and partially on ῥαφανίс, which Herodian say to have a short vowel in Attic, yet according to Phrynichus it alternates between the two quantities. Herodian's rule would also predict πινακίс, although the word is not one of the examples of the περὶ διχρόνων.

It is unclear why Phrynichus also lists κνημίс, never attested with a short [i] in Attic (and also, in open contradiction with Herodian's rule). On ῥαφανίс, Phrynichus may be more accurate than Herodian: the long [iː] is metrically guaranteed in Attic (cf. e.g. Aristophanes *Nu.* 981, 1083; *Pl.* 544).

Also Athenaeus discusses the quantity of the suffixal vowel of καρίс (Ath. 3.105d–106e). He begins with an example from Archestratus, καρῖδ' εὐμεγέθη λήψῃ (105e = fr. 26.2 Olson – Sens). He then goes on to say 'ἐκτεταμένως δ' εἴρηκε καρῖδα Ἀραρὼс' (3.105e) and introduces a list of counterexamples, all instances of καρίс with a long [iː] in Attic comic playwrights[254], to conclude with 'сυνεсταλμένωс δ' εἴρηκεν Εὔπολιс' (3.106b), and quote Eup. frr. 2 and 120 K.–A. (= 32 Telò), where the metre guarantees the short vowel. Athenaeus formulates a rule quite similar to Herodian's, namely that nouns with long penultimate have a long vowel in the suffix: ταθείсηс δὲ τῆс παρατελευταίαс ἐτάθη καὶ τὸ τέλος, καὶ ὁμοίωс λέγεται τῷ ψηφὶс καὶ κρηπὶс [καὶ τευθίс] (Ath. 3.106c).

Phrynichus' gloss may be corrupt to some extent[255]. However, it is clear that the quantity of the *dichronon* in the suffix -ιδ- was debated[256]. Interestingly, there is no mention of the accent type, despite the quantity of the *iota* is relevant here. Trisyllables in -ῑδ- probably entered the Koine as Ionisms[257], and must have been perceived as non-Attic (e.g. πλοκαμίс, in Theocritus' *Hylas* (13) 7, within a mixture of epic and Doric elements, and cf. Homer εὐπλοκαμίс).

κυδώνιον

Antiatt. κ 71 κυδώνιον μῆλον· βραχέωс. Φιλήμων Ἰατρῷ (fr. 36 K.–A.).

---

[254] Anaxandr. frr. 23, 28, 38, Arar. fr. 8.2–4, Eub. frr. 78, 110, Ophel. frr. 1, 2 K.–A.
[255] Fischer corrects κνημῖδα of Phrynichus' manuscripts in κνημίδα. The manuscript tradition of ῥαφανίδα is split in two branches (ῥαφίδα Ub, ῥαφανίδα Bc). Rutherford does not even comment on the entry (other than "[t]he passage is either corrupt or contains an erroneus statement" (Rutherford 1881: 255)).
[256] Homeric epithets may favour one or the other suffix depending on how convenient they are for the metre, cf. e.g. εὐπλοκαμῖс ~ γλαυκῶπῑс, Chantraine 1933: 346–7. On the origin of -*id* from the motion suffix *-ieh_2/-ih_2 cf. Chantraine *GH* I, 208 (βοῶπῑс); Ruijgh 1985: § 3, p. 113; 1988: 462 [= Ruijgh *SM* II: 327].
[257] Schmidt 1968: 61, fn. 56a.

The short vowel implied by the gloss may be ⟨υ⟩, yet if the lemmatised phrase was taken from a iambic trimeter, the only possible scansion would be κυδωνῖον μῆλον, with ⟨υ⟩ realising an *anceps*. μῆλον needs to have been part of the original quote, as κυδώνιον μῆλον is the standard definition of quinces in ancient Greek (and thence in Latin (MALA) *CŬTŌNIA, as attested in Italian *mela cotogna*).

The short vowel in κυδώνιον μῆλον could be the *iota*, rather than the *hypsilon:* in this case the gloss of the *Antatticista* would be one more instance in which the lexica try to distinguish between the suffixes -ιος and -ειος (Phryn. *Ecl.* 346 → Διονυσεῖον and *Ecl.* 241 → ὀπτάνιον, and chap. III, § 5.4).

κυνηγεττεῖν

Phryn. *PS* 84.1–2 κυνηγεττεῖν· διὰ δυοῖν ττ λέγουσιν.

The gloss does not contrast κυνηγεττεῖν and κυνηγετεῖν: the circumflex is not on the codex, which reads κυνηγέττειν, and writes the acute on the *epsilon* (cod. Coislinianus 345, f. 57v). The verb is therefore the expected Attic variant of κυνηγέσσω, with the expected ⟨ττ⟩. The accentuation κυνηγεττεῖν chosen by the editors (De Borries and Bekker, *An. B.* 48.30), if it is not a trivial mistake[258], may depend on understanding the verb as the variant with a geminate of κυνηγετεῖν, the reading of Aristophanes, *Eq.* 1382[259].

Phrynichus may have read a text that actually employed κυνηγέττειν, with ττ granted by the metre, perhaps comedy anapaests (Maas 1973: 44 [=1912: 1075]; in Ar. *Eq.* 1382 ττ or τ would not make a difference for the metre). The present κυνηγέττειν is only attested in this gloss of the *Praeparatio Sophistica* and, in the form κυνηγέσσειν, in Theognostus, *Canones* (*An. Ox.* 2 143.19–20), where it appears together with πυρέσσω, ἐρέσσω, ἀηθέσσω in a list of verbs in -έσσω that Theognostus prescribes to be written with ⟨ε⟩.

κυνοκέφαλλος

Phryn. *PS* 85.5–6 κυνοκέφαλλος· διὰ τῶν δυοῖν λλ Ἀττικοί.

---

258 As already remarked by Lobeck (1837: 438) "κυνηγεττεῖν [...] quo pro κυνηγέττειν scribi vult".
259 Incorrectly quoted as l. 382 in Phryn. *PS* 84.

Cf. Paus. ε 71 Ἑρμῆς τετρακέφαλος· ἐν Κεραμεικῷ Τελεσιδάρχου ἔργον, ᾧ ἐπεγέγραπτο[260]·

'Ἑρμῆ τετρακέφᾱλε, καλὸν Τελεσαρχίδου ἔργον
πάνθ' ὁράᾳς ... '
ἡ δὲ τετρὰς ἱερὰ τοῦ θεοῦ.

κυνοκέφαλλος with ⟨λλ⟩ is attested only in this gloss by Phrynichus and in Photius[261]. The only occurrence of the compound in Aristophanes (*Eq.* 416) is spelt κυνοκεφάλῳ in the manuscripts, at the end of a iambic tetrameter, where the metre requires a long penultimate syllable. Bergk and Dindorf corrected the text to κυνοκεφάλλῳ basing on the glosses of Phynichus and Photius. The doubling ascribed to Aristophanes remains unexplained. There is no historical ground for κεφαλή to have a geminate.

In addition to the Aristophanic instance just mentioned, there are three more occurrences of compounds in -κέφαλος that need to be scanned -κέφᾱλος in surviving Greek literature. One is preserved by Eustathius, who quotes an hexameter from an epigram, presumably inscribed on the basis of a herm in the Kerameikos, in a passage that Erbse attributes to the lexicon of Pausanias (Eust. 1353.8 = Paus. ε 71). The first line of the epigram, Ἑρμῆ τετρακέφᾱλε καλὸν Τελεσαρχίδου ἔργον, does indeed require the penultimate syllable of τετρακέφαλε to scan long. Another instance is in Hesiod, *Th.* 287, Χρυσάωρ δ' ἔτεκε τρικέφαλον Γηρυονῆα[262]. This line too requires a long penultimate in τρικέφαλον (Χρῡσάωρ δ' ἔτεκε τ'ρικέφᾱλον Γηρυονῆα). As there is no trace of a geminate in the manuscript tradition of the text transmitting τετρακέφαλος, lengthening of the vowel in the penultimate syllable might have been the customary way of realising the metrical lengthening in this word, rather than the gemination of the consonant, as in κυνοκέφαλλος. The third instance is preserved by Athenaeus, who quotes a fragment of Eubulus, attesting a metrically guaranteed ἀμφικέφᾱλος (Eub. 106.10 K.–A. = Ath. 10.450a).

All these occurences of compounds in -κέφαλος suggest a metrical lengthening of the penultimate vowel – perhaps alive in epic recitations, as the line in Hesiod suggests –, and it is surprising that Phrynichus, and Photius after him,

---

[260] *Inscr. gr. metr.* n. 188 Preg. (Erbse).
[261] Phot. κ 1216: κυνοκέφα(λ)λος· ἐν τοῖς δύο λλ λέγουσι· οὕτως Ἀριστοφάνης.
[262] Referred to by the scholion to Ar. *Eq.* 416, even though the scholiast's attention does not focus on the abnormal scansion of τρικέφαλον or κυνοκεφάλῳ, but on the meaning of the compound in Aristophanes.

should prescribe a pronunciation with the geminate[263]. The very short prescription of the *PS* could attest to gemination as a way of realising a metrical lengthening, certainly uncommon if not altogether unparalleled, or a deliberate deformation of the monster's name, perhaps not exclusive to Attic. For other seemingly artificial lengthenings see also Philem. 358 → δένδρα and Moer. β 15 → βαδίζειν.

λαγώς

Philet. 89 λαγώς διὰ τοῦ ω μεγάλου ὁ χερσαῖος παρὰ τοῖς Ἀττικοῖς· λαγὸς δὲ ὁ θαλάσσιος[264]. φασὶ δὲ τοῦτον καὶ ἰὸν ἔχειν, ὅθεν καὶ τοὺς πονηροὺς ὁ Κρατῖνος (fr. 466 K.–A.) 'λαγοὺς' καλεῖ[265].
Phryn. Ecl. 156 λαγὼς ὁ Ἀττικός, διὰ δὲ τοῦ ο ὁ Ἴων λαγός· τὸ λαγωὸς δὲ οὐκ ἔστιν.

The gloss contrasts two terms with different meanings and spellings: λαγώς 'hare' and λαγός, a mollusc. Both forms are found in Attic literature, and they are originally variants of the same noun (cf. *DELG s.v.* λαγώς). The form λαγός is marginal in Attic, but attested Ionic poetry[266] and may have been introduced in Attic as the name of the animal only[267], whereas in Ionic it covers all the meanings of Attic λαγώς. The need to specify the spelling of λαγώς/λαγός may derive from the confusion between long and short vowels. The lexicographers focus on

---

263 "[T]he grammarians' statement that the λλ was specially Attic is unlikely: the forms with ᾱ or λλ were Epic (see Rzach on *Theog.* 287) and grotesque, used mainly in the epithets of monsters, as here" (Neil 1901: 64); cf. also Sommerstein 1981: 166 "The metre requires the penultimate vowel of the Greek word to be irregularly pronounced long [...]; this licence is derived from Hesiod who uses it several times (*Theogony* 287, 312; fr. 62 Rzach = 153 Merkelbach – West) in epithets for monstrous creatures like Geryon and Cerberus, and there may be an insinuation here that Paphlagon is a monster comparable to these". A plausible model for the gemination is the group of adjectives in -αλλος (e.g. compounds of μάλλος or θάλλος), a group that is however much smaller than the group of adjectives in -αλος. The contamination with φάλλος seems gratuitous in the line of the *Knights*, and even more so in the hexametres.
264 The mmss. have ἀστικός instead of θαλάσσιος, a correction by Cohn, basing on Hsch. λ 69 "λαγώς· ὁ χερσαῖος, λαγὸς δὲ ὁ θαλάσσιος καὶ ποτάμιος".
265 Cf. also *exc. Vind.* 4, ὅτι λαγώς ὁ χερσαῖος· λαγωὸς δὲ κοινῶς, the spelling λαγωός is exceptional.
266 λαγός is attested in Amipsias fr. 17 K.–A. and in Epicharmus (fr. 53 K.–A.), a parody of Ananius (fr. 5.5 West; cf. Epich. fr. 51 K.–A.), whose surviving fragments mostly deal with fish.
267 A fragment of Sophocles (fr. 111 Radt, satyric) too preserves λαγός, in a context that suggests it refers to the mollusc.

the spelling and possibly the pronunciation of the word, but do not discuss the problems posed by the inflection of this word: some speakers inflected it following the third declension (acc. sing. λαγώ, cf. Lucian, *Soloecista* 3). A change of inflection, from the exceptional Attic declension to the more regular group of masculines of the second declension, may have favoured the spread of non-Attic λαγóc.

λῆμα

Moer. λ 8 λῆμμα διὰ δύο μ τὸ θάρcοc, διὰ δὲ τοῦ ἑνὸc τὸ λαμβανόμενον. ἀδιαφόρωc Ἕλληνεc.
Philet. 142 διαφέρει λῆμα καὶ λῆμμα: τὸ μὲν γὰρ δι' ἑνὸc μ τὴν παράcταcιc τῆc ψυχῆc cημαίνει, τὸ δὲ διὰ τῶν δύο τὸ λαμβανόμενον[268].

λῆμμα and λῆμα are etymologically unrelated[269]. Moeris states clearly that the words are interchangeable in the speech of the Ἕλληνεc (Moer. λ 8 'ἀδιαφόρωc Ἕλληνεc'). A passage of the *Soloecista* makes fun of what could be hypercorrect gemination of λῆμα to λῆμμα (*Soloec.* 5 "εἰπόντοc δέ τινοc, Λῆμμα πάρεcτιν αὐτῷ, διὰ τῶν δύο μ, Οὐκοῦν, ἔφη, λήψεται, εἰ λῆμμα αὐτῷ πάρεcτιν")[270].

---

[268] Cf. also Heren. 109 λῆμμα μέν ἐcτι διὰ β΄ μμ τὸ κέρδοc, λῆμα δὲ δι' ἑνὸc μ ἡ ἀνδρεία, Heren. *de propr.* 23 λῆμα ἡ ἀνδρεία, λῆμμα τὸ κέρδοc, Amm. 299 λῆμα καὶ λῆμμα διαφέρει. λῆμα μὲν γὰρ ἐcτι δι' ἑνὸc μ τὸ παράcτημα τῆc ψυχῆc, λῆμμα δὲ διὰ δύο μμ τὸ λαμβανόμενον.
[269] The stem of λῶ – whence λῆμα (cf. Chantraine 1933: 93) – is reconstructed as *$l\bar{e}i$- (*IEW* 665) or as *$ul\bar{e}$ < *$uleh_1$- (*LIV* s.v. *$uleh_1$-; cf. also *DELG* s.v. λῶ), whilst λῆμμα is a deverbal of λαμβάνω, with a generalistion of the Greek vocalism λαβ/λᾱβ (*$slag^u$/$slāg^u$, < *$sleh_2g^u$, cf. *LIV* s.v. with fn. 1). Λῆμα is mostly used by Pindar and the Attic tragedians, in prose it is used a few times by Herodotus, and then it is seen again in Hellenistic and later prose. Generally λῆμμα has the menaning of 'prey, receit, income' and develops (in Hellenistic times?) the technical meaning (in logic) of 'premiss'. In Hesychius λῆμα and λῆμμα are confounded (perhaps only as a result of a copying error) in the entry λ 870 λῆμμα: θράcοc δύναμιc, τόλμα, ἀξίωμα, κέρδοc, φρόνημα ἢ δῶρον. The *Suda* (λ 441) makes a distinction between the spelling with the singleton or the geminate.
[270] For arguments in favour of the authenticity of the *Soloecista* see McLeod 1956: 106–10 and Bompaire 1998: 233–5. The *Soloecista* may be authentic and late, showing an "interest in the minutiae of *current usage* among the *learned Athenian clique*" (MacLeod 1956: 106), a scenario entailing the imitation of a live usage (in writing and/or in speaking) and an élite of literates who were active in Athens. Lucian may have composed the dialogue in Athens, and since many of the usages condemned in the *Solecista* can be found in classical Attic, the *Soloecista* needs to be criticising the usages of Lucian's contemporaries. Against the attribution to Lucian cf. Hall, *Lucian's Satire*, 1981: 298–307.

Degemination [mm] > [m] may be a reason for the homophony; it is also possible, however, that among some speakers there was genuine confusion between two nearly homophones one of them (λῆμα) was quite less common than the other. The confusion is probably ancient: an inscription of Pergamum writes λῆμμα in a context where λῆμα would be expected[271].

λητουργεῖν

Moer. λ 25 λητουργεῖν διὰ τοῦ η Ἀττικοί· διὰ δὲ τῆς ει διφθόγγου Ἕλληνες. λήϊτον γὰρ τὸ δημόσιον.

Moeris' lexicon quotes λητουργεῖν (and λητουργός, the other variant in the manuscript tradition of this gloss) as though spelt with simple ‹η›. This spelling is not found in literary texts, but is common in inscriptions[272]. There are no glosses contrasting ‹η› and ‹ει›: ‹η› here must be taken as representing a variant spelling for ‹ηυ›[273]. If Moeris contrasts two different spellings for the same pronunciation this gloss would suggest that ‹η› corresponded to a long /i:/ just like ‹ει› did. The other two instances of a contrast between ‹ει› and ‹η› do not point to a confusion between the two sounds (cf. chap. II, § 2.3.2).

λιπόνεως

→ ἀνάπλεως

---

[271] Müller 1989; *SGO* I n. 06/02/05. The reading λῆμμα makes worse sense than λῆμ{μ}α: accepting the latter reading, the geminate would be a misspelling. The mistake that Lucian satirises in the 2nd century AD would therefore have an attestation in the 3rd century BC.
[272] *Magnesia* 2 (197/6 BC); *Priene* 211 (2nd c. BC), 214 (2nd c. BC?), *Teos* 59 (303 BC), Pergamum (*IvP* I 40, *ca.* 250 BC).
[273] The lexicon of Ammonius contrasts λητουργεῖν and λιτουργεῖν: Amm. 300 λητουργεῖν διὰ τοῦ η καὶ λιτουργεῖν διὰ τοῦ ι διαφέρει, φησὶ Δίδυμος (p. 180 Schmidt) ἐν Ὑπομνήματι δευτέρας Ἰλιάδος. τὸ μὲν γὰρ λητουργεῖν τὸ τῷ δήμῳ ὑπηρετεῖν, λῆτον γάρ φασι τὸ δημόσιον· "λήϊτον ἀμφεπένοντο" (fr. adesp.). τὸ δὲ λιτουργεῖν κακὰ λέγειν.

μᾶζα

Moer. μ 8 μᾶζαν προπερισπωμένως καὶ μακρῶς Ἀττικοί, βαρυτόνως καὶ βραχέως Ἕλληνες.

The accent of μᾶζα depends entirely on the length of the first *alpha:* speakers would know that the *alpha* of the ending is a short one on the basis of inflection, not only of accentuation (only nouns with a final -ᾰ would have a genitive in -ης).

The accentuative problem was already clear to the scholiasts of Aristophanes (sch. Ar. *Pac.* 1g (RV) τὸ δὲ μᾶζα περισπαστέον, τουτέστι τροφήν), even though most scholia are concerned with the meaning of this word rather than its accentuation[274].

There may be a relation between the pronunciation of the ‹ζ› and the quantity of the vowel preceding it. A small number of entries in the Atticist lexica deals with the quantity of the vowel preceding *zeta*[275]. The accentuation μᾶζα is the only one found in Greek literature, and not only in Attic (the circumflex is the standard accentuation for Archilochus), and the most obscure fact in Moeris' gloss is indeed the form he attributes to the Ἕλληνες.

Even though there are virtually no attestations of the spelling with an acute ‹μάζα›[276], this is the form on which Latin *massa* rests: if Latin had borrowed a form with a long vowel, /ss/ would be reduced to /s/, as in e.g. *caussa > causa*[277]. Latin *massa* is one of the instances where the source of a Greek loanword is not Attic, but a different dialect (cf. e.g. Lat. *machīna* < non-Attic μᾱχᾰνά ~ Attic μηχανή) or the Koine: e.g. *schĕma* (Plautus, *Amphitruo*, 117) is not Attic σχῆμα but a cognate form of what Hesychius (c 2976) reports as σχέμα· σχῆμα Ἀχαιοί[278]. The variant μάδδα is attested in the Megarian's speech in Aristophanes (*Ach.* 732). Modern editors print μᾶδδα, but the acute may be original, and signal a short vowel there[279]. If this were the case, μάδδα would be the only attestation of the short vowel in this word, albeit with the consonantism of Megarian Doric.

---

274 Cf. sch. Ar. *Pac.* 1f (RVLh): μᾶζαν] μᾶζα κυρίως ἡ τροφὴ ἡ ἀπὸ γάλακτος καὶ σίτου· παρὰ τὸ μάττεσθαι.
275 →χαμᾶζε (Ael. D. χ 3), →ἀγοράζειν (Moer. α 139), and possibly →βαδίζειν (Moer. β 15), cf. chap. V, § 5.
276 But cf. μάζα in sch. *Nu.* 507a (EN) μελιτοῦτταν μάζαν †τῷ† μέλιτι συμπεφυρμένην.
277 Cf. Leumann 1977: 184–5, Meiser 1998: 125.
278 Leumann 1959: 173.
279 Colvin 1999: 133, 165.

The etymology of μᾶζα is not clear enough to shed any light on Moeris' gloss: μᾶζα is much more likely to be Indo-European (cf. *EDG s.v.*) than a borrowing from a Semitic language – Hebrew has *maṣṣāh*[280]. If it is a loanword from Greek, Hebrew *maṣṣāh* may be evidence in favour of a short root wovel, and the pronunciation of ‹ζ› as geminate, just like Latin *massa*.

μανός

Phryn. *PS* 89.6–7 μανόν· τὸ ἀραιὸν οὕτω λέγουσιν ‹οἱ› Ἀθηναῖοι τὴν πρώτην cυλλαβὴν ἐκτείνοντεc.

The atticist lexicon of Oros (A 62 Alpers) quotes the comic playwright Teleclides (fr. 23 K.–A., consisting exclusively of μανός) in support of a scansion μᾶνός, opposing Phrynichus, and supports it further with an example of μᾶν- in the adverb μᾶνάκις, attested in a iambic trimeter of Plato Comicus (fr. 178 K.–A. καὶ ταῦτα μανάκις μυριάκις τῆς ἡμέρας).

The gloss of the *Praeparatio Sophistica* does not find support in the known verse literature, whereas the one of Oros has a precursor in Herodian[281]. One of the most ancient fragments of the περὶ καθολικῆς προςῳδίας[282] gives a better definition of the problem:

> τῷ ἐπιρρήματι μανάκις cυcτέλλειν ἄξιόν ἐcτιν ὡc καὶ Ἐπαφρόδιτοc ἐν α′ περὶ cτοιχείων καὶ Διονύcιοc. κέχρηται δ' αὐτῷ Πλάτων ἐν Cυρφάκι· καὶ ταῦτα μανάκις, μυριάκις τῆς ἡμέρας. παρὰ μέντοι Ἐμπεδοκλεῖ ἐν β′ Καθαρμῶν ἐcτιν εὑρέcθαι ἐκτεταμένον τὸ α, ὡc δῆλον κἀκ τῆς παραγωγῆς cυ‹γ›κριτ‹ικ›ῆc· μανότεροc γὰρ ἔφη ὡc τρανότεροc. [...] παρ' Ἐπιχάρμῳ οὔτε πυκινὰc οὔτε μανάc κτλ.[283]

---

280 Assmann 1908. Griffith (2007: 86) tries to bring new evidence in support of Semitic cognates of *maṣṣāh*, but his revival of Assmann's hypothesis is not convincing, cf. the objections in Rosół (2013: 67–8) and Batisti (2014: 159–64).
281 Oros' gloss may come from his Κατὰ Φρυνίχου, possibly composed in the first half of the 5th century AD, and heavily relying on the works of Herodian (Alpers 1981: 6–7).
282 The first hand – that can be dated to the 10th century AD – of the palimpsest *Vindob. Hist. gr.*, cf. Hunger 1967.
283 Hunger (1967: 26. Cf. also περὶ διχρόνων (*GG* 3.2 13.33–5 = *An. Ox.* 3 292.3–6) Τὰ εἰc νοc λήγοντα διcύλλαβα ὀξύτονα καθαρεύοντος τοῦ ν, εἰ ἔχοιεν ἐν τῇ πρὸ τέλους τὸ α, ἐκτεταμένον αὐτὸ ἔχουcι, δανόc ὁ ξηρόc, τρανόc [τανόc Cramer, *An. Ox.* 3 292.5], μανόc. τοῦτο δὲ παρὰ τοῖc Ἀττικοῖc cυcτέλλεται.

It is appropriate for the adverb μανάκις to have a short vowel, as also Epaphroditus says in the first book *On the elements*, and Dionysius too. Plato used it in the *Surphax*: 'καὶ ταῦτα μανάκις, μυριάκις τῆς ἡμέρας'. In Empedocles, in the second book of the *Katharmoi* it can be found with a lengthened *alpha*, as it is clear also form the derivation of the comparative – for he said μανότερος like τρανότερος. [...] In Epicharmus 'οὔτε πυκινὰς οὔτε μανάς' etc.

Herodian frr. 9 and 28 Hunger

The variant with a long root vowel, μᾱνός, is preserved in the surviving fragments of Empedocles and of Epicharmus: Emp. fr. 75.1 D.-K. "τῶν δ' ὅς' ἔσω μὲν πυκνά, τὰ δ' ἔκτοθι μανὰ πέπηγε"; Epich. fr. 185 K.-A. "οὔτε πυκινὰς οὔτε μανάς", likely to be its parody[284]. Neither author writes in Attic, and the only two attestations of μανός in Attic authors (Telecl. fr. 23 and Plat. Com. fr. 178 K.-A.) point to a short [a].

The dialectal distribution of μᾱνός and μᾰνός is easily explained if the adjective derives from a form *manu̯-os. A gloss by Hesychius seems to prove the existence of a formation in -u from the root of μανός: μανύ· μικρόν Ἀθαμᾶνες (Hsch. μ 250 Latte; *DELG* s.v. μανός).

In this case, the long vowel of μᾱνός is the regular outcome of a compensatory lengthening. Although μανός is not attested in Homer (either with a long or with a short *alpha*), one would expect to find a form with compensatory lengthening following the loss of [w] in Homeric diction. Such a Homeric form would not be out of place in the hexametres of Empedocles. In Epicharmus, μᾱνός may be part of the parodic imitation of epic (as in the dialect of Syracuse the expected form would have been μᾰνός).

The *Praeparatio Sophistica* seems to ignore the real distribution of the forms of μᾱνός. The confusion may depend on an error in the epitomising process, but one cannot rule out that Phrynichus here was simply mistaken. The lexicographer did not necessarily read the texts first-hand (Alpers 1981: 104), and could have handled carelessly a lexicon or a treatise similar to the fragment of Herodian: his interest seems to be semantical in the first place, with a focus on the meaning of μανός rather than on its pronunciation.

μᾱνός, with a long root vowel resulting from compensatory lengthening would belong comfortably to Ionic. Phrynichus' prescription can be easily explained as a hyperatticism, proving that vowel length was artificially preserved in the pronunciation of the educated. [maːˈnos], current in Hellenistic Koine, was now obsolete, and had been replaced by [maˈnos] – and Phrynichus may have

---

[284] West 1968: 199–200, K.-A. *ad loc*. Epicharmus' fragment is extracted from passages of Herodian's Καθολικὴ προςῳδία (fr. 28.1 Hunger 1967) not included in Lentz's edition, quoting a fragment of Empedocles not included in Diels – Kranz's edition, cf. Lasserre 1969: 80–3.

identified forms with a long vowel as Attic, on the only basis that speakers of Attic are μηκυντικοί κατὰ τὰ φωνήεντα (cf. A.D. *Adv.* [*GG* 2.1.1] 166.24–6).

μάντεων

Moer. μ 12 μάντεων τὴν πρώτην ὀξυτόνως Ἀττικοί, τὴν δευτέραν ὀξυτόνως Ἕλληνες.

μαντέων is the genitive plural of μάντις: the accentuation μαντέων ascribed to the Ἕλληνες is never attested but in Moeris, nor continued in any variety of Modern Greek. It may depend on an analogical extension to the Koine of the accentuation μαντίων that is found in all the dialects other than Attic, which inflect nom. μάντις, gen. μάντιος[285].

The accentuation of this forms was probably discussed by Herodian and is reflected in part of later scholarship, beginning with this gloss of Moeris, and going down to Theodosius and Iohannes Philoponus. These passages give a fuller account of the prescription in Moeris, and possibly preserve more of the original context to which it originally belonged:

> τὸ πόλεων λέξεων καὶ τὰ ὅμοια τοίνυν ὀφείλει πρὸ μιᾶς ἔχειν τὸν τόνον, Ἀμμώνιος δέ φησιν αὐτὰ παρὰ Ἀττικοῖς προπαροξύνεσθαι.
>
> πόλεων λέξεων and the like ought to have the accent on the penultimate, but Ammonius says that these words are proparoxytones among the Attic [speakers].
>
> Theodos. *GG* 4.1 41.14–16

> αἱ εἰς -ες ὑπὲρ δύο συλλαβὰς εὐθεῖαι παροξύνουσι τὰς γενικάς· Αἴαντες Αἰάντων, ἑβδομάδες ἑβδομάδων, εὐσεβέες εὐσεβέων, σταχύες σταχύων, ὀσφύες ὀσφύων. ἔδει οὖν καὶ τὸ πόλεων, μάντεων [πελέκεων] καὶ τὰ τοιούτοις παραπλήσια πρὸ μιᾶς ἔχειν τὸν τόνον, ἀλλ' Ἀττικοὺς φασι προπαροξύνειν ταῦτα ἅπερ ἐστίν ἀπὸ τῶν εἰς -ις εὐθειῶν καὶ ἔτι δύο ἀπὸ τῶν εἰς -υς, τό τε πήχεων καὶ πελέκεων. σεσημείωται πάλιν γυναικῶν καὶ θυγατρῶν περισπώμενα.
>
> Nominatives in -ες with more than two syllables have paroxytone genitives: Αἴαντες Αἰάντων, ἑβδομάδες ἑβδομάδων, εὐσεβέες εὐσεβέων, σταχύες σταχύων, ὀσφύες ὀσφύων. Also πόλεων, μάντεων, [πελέκεων] and the words akin to these ought to have the accent on the penultimate, but they say that the Attic [speakers] accentuate them as proparoxytones in

---

[285] Schwyzer 1939: 572, fn. 9; the genitive plural of πῆχυς is accented πηχέων in Herodotus, and it most often written πηχων (πηχῶν) in Egyptian papyri (Mayser 1938: 25, Gignac 1981: 81), a form that the Atticists explicitly condemn (Phryn. *Ecl.* 217, Philem. 395, *Philet.* 317; cf. Probert 2008: 278 fn. 22).

that they come from nominatives in -ιc and two more form those in -υc, πήχεων and πελέκεων. Again, γυναικῶν and θυγατρῶν are exceptions, being perispomena.

Jo. Alex. 80 Xenis

As it is clear form the passage in Iohannes Philoponus, μάντεων was discussed in the context of the accentuation of forms like πόλεων. Herodian may have quoted Attic πόλεων, μάντεων and the like, as irregular forms, exceptions to a rule prescribing paroxytone genitive plurals, according to which we should expect *πολέων, μαντέων.

Moeris' gloss is the only one that actually attests one of these paroxytone genitive plurals, and attributes it to the Hellenes. Among the scholarship on this problem of accentuation, Moeris is also the earliest source and the one chronologically closest to Herodian.

Herodian, or in any case the pre-Atticistic sources of this scholarship, may simply have noted that Attic had an irregular accentuation. Atticists like Moeris contributed to establishing the Attic anomaly as the rule (Probert 2008: 277–8). The process may be seen as a shift in the meaning of 'Attic', form the neutral label of a specific variety to a synonym of 'correct' as Probert (2008) argues in full detail for this and other passages of ancient scholarship.

On this specific point, however, I think another explanation is also possible, although we are probably venturing in too speculative grounds: is it possible that μαντέων in Moeris is only a nonce-formation, substantiating with an example the expected (but in fact never attested) accentuation of the genitive plural of nouns in -ιc? Besides μαντέων in Moeris, there are no other attestations in the Koine of such an accentuation: we only infer it from statements like the ones in Theodosius and Iohannes Philoponus, who however only say that the expected accentuation of the genitive plurals of πόλιc and μάντιc 'ought to be' paroxytone (but by their time it was not heard or read anywhere). If this were the case, we would be dealing with an instance of *Hellenes* being used as a synonym of 'wrong', or perhaps 'expected/regular (but also just hypothetical)'.

μιαρόc

Phryn. *Ecl.* 280 ψίεθοc, μιερόc, ὕελοc· ἁμαρτάνουcιν οἱ διὰ τοῦ ε λέγοντεc, ἀδόκιμον γάρ. καὶ Κόριννα (fr. 36 Page) "τὸν ὑάλινον πόδα θήcειc".
Moer. c 17 cίαλον ἐν τῷ α καὶ οὐδετέρωc Ἀττικοί· cίελον ἐν τῷ ε καὶ ἀρcενικῶc Ἕλληνεc.
Phryn. *PS* 118.15–16 ὑάλινα καὶ ὕαλοc διὰ τοῦ α, οὐ διὰ τοῦ ε.

Ael. D. υ 1 ὕαλος· διὰ τοῦ α, οὐχὶ ὕελος, καὶ θηλυκῶς ἡ ὕαλος, καὶ ὑάλινον. Ἀριστοφάνης Ἀχαρνεῦσιν (74)·
"ἐξ ὑαλίνων ποτηρίων καὶ χρυσίδων".
Moer. υ 1 ὕαλος ἐν τῷ α Ἀττικοί· ἐν τῷ ε Ἕλληνες.
Moer. φ 15 φιάλη Ἀττικοὶ διὰ τοῦ α· διὰ τοῦ ε Ἕλληνες.
Philet. 81 φιάλη διὰ τοῦ α καὶ θηλυκῶς· εἴρηται ἀπὸ τοῦ πιεῖν ἅλις ἐξ αὐτῆς.
Moer. ψ 1 ψίαθος ἐν τῷ α Ἀττικοί· διὰ τοῦ ε Ἕλληνες.
cf. also Ael. D. ξ 2 → ξυάλη, and Philet. 182 (~ exc. Vind. 26) τὰς ῥᾶγας θηλυκῶς οἱ Ἀττικοί, οὐχὶ τοὺς ῥῶγας. ὁμοίως τὴν βῶλον, καὶ τὴν πύελον, καὶ τὴν ὕελον, καὶ τὴν φιάλην, καὶ τὴν λίθον (μάλιστα ἐπὶ τῆς σφραγῖδος).

Atticist lexica present a number of glosses contrasting Attic ‹α› with Koine ‹ε›, and a smaller number of glosses contrasting the opposite distribution (Phryn. Ecl. 281, Philet. 78 → πύελος). Words of either group that have survived in Modern Greek normally attest ‹α›, either when the lexica prescribe ‹α›, as is the case with ὕαλος, continued in Mod. Gk. γιαλί, or Mod. Gk. σάλιο < σιάλιον < σίαλον, or when they prescribe ‹ε›, as is the case with μυαλός, which has replaced the recommended Attic form μυελός (see → πύελος)[286].

The variation can be explained on purely phonological grounds, even if individual cases may require special explanations[287]. The suffixes - ερός / -ελός may have influenced the vocalism of some forms. With the exception of μιαρός, deriving from the same root as μιαίνω, none of these forms has an etymology that explains their vocalism. In some cases it is possible that the variation depends on different renderings of loanwords in Greek.

μιερός
μιερός is well attested since the Hellenistic period[288] as well as its compounds μιεροθύτης, μιερωσύνη (Trapp et all. LBG 1024). μιερός could result from a hypercorrection based on the idea that μιαρός is the outcome of a dissimilation process from [je] to [ja] (Wackernagel 1909: 336–7).

σίαλον
σίαλον is attested with ‹α› in Attic (Pherecr. fr. 75 K.–A., X. Mem. 1.2.54). σίελος is so well attested in the corpus Hippocraticum that there is a chance that the Hellenistic forms continue older Ionic ones (Schwyzer 1939: 243). σίαλον seems to be

---

286 Schwyzer 1898: 37, Thumb 1901: 75–6, Crönert 1903: 102, Hauser 1916: 22; the two vocalisms alternate in the NT, Blass – Debrunner – Funk 1961: § 29.2.
287 Schwyzer 1898: 36–7; 1939: 243.
288 Call. Hec. fr. 260.61; PGL, s.v. μιερός, 870; cf. Lobeck 1820: 343.

a lesser attested variant in Byzantine Greek (*PGL*, 1233), and the learned varieties of Modern Greek adopt the follow Hippocrates in adopting cίελος, whereas the current word for saliva, cάλιο, continues cίαλον.

ὔαλος, ὐάλινος
The etymology of ὔαλος is unknown, and the word may be a borrowed technical term. Like cίελον, it could be originally Ionic[289]. Atticist lexica list ὔαλος for two reasons: to specify its gender[290] (feminine in Attic, but masculine in the Koine); and to contrast the more recent form ὔελος. ὔελος is the only spelling found in Theophrastus; Attic literature has forms with ‹α› (e. g. Aristophanes, *Ach*. 74 and *Nu*. 768, where the scholia prescribe the *alpha*[291]), forms in ‹ε› are found in Aristotle and Theophrastus, perhaps as Koineisms.

The *Philetaerus* mentions the Koine form ὔελος in one gloss (*Philet*. 182): τὰς ῥᾶγας θηλυκῶς οἱ Ἀττικοί, οὐχὶ τοὺς ῥῶγας. ὁμοίως τὴν βῶλον, καὶ τὴν πύελον, καὶ τὴν ὔελον, καὶ τὴν φιάλην, καὶ τὴν λίθον (μάλιστα ἐπὶ τῆς cφραγῖδος). The lexicon seems to list the Koine form as if it were genuinely Attic, but trivial textual corruption (‹ε› for ‹α›) cannot be ruled out. ὔελος and ὔαλος keep alternating in Byzantine times. Lampe (*PGL* 1422) quotes ὑαλοψός, yet with a variant ὑελεψός, and a number of compounds of either ὔαλος or ὔελος are listed in Sophocles' lexicon (Sophocles 1888).

Phrynichus' quotation of Corinna is surprising. Together with Sappho and Epicharmus, quoted only three times in total[292], this is the only reference to a non-Attic author in Phrynichus. Yet, whereas Sappho and Epicharmus are quoted in support of the attribution of a form to Aeolic or Doric respectively, here Corinna is quoted as if in support of the attribution to Attic.

φιάλη
The form φιέλη[293] is not attested in literary texts[294]. The form is known only from Moeris' lexicon and the *Philetaerus*, but is sporadically attested in inscriptions

---

[289] Schwyzer 1939: 243.
[290] It seems that the spelling of this noun was not regular in Attica either: "nomen ὔαλος et ὔελος nullo discrimine ab Atticis usurpatum", Sallier in *ThGL* VIII 9a *s.v.* ὔαλος.
[291] sch. Ar. *Nu.* 768c (E).
[292] Epich. fr. 18 K.–A. (Phryn. *Ecl.* 43), fr. 209 K.–A. (Phryn. *Ecl.* 79); Sapph. fr. 189 L.-P. (Phryn. *Ecl.* 272). Phryn. *Ecl.* 43 is also the only gloss that does not label the language of Epicharmus as 'Doric': the other two glosses refer openly to Δωριεῖς and Αἰολεῖς.
[293] Elsewhere too the author of the *Philetaerus* seems to consider [a] the normal vowel in this word, cf. *Philet.* 182 Τὰς ῥᾶγας θηλυκῶς οἱ Ἀττικοί, οὐχὶ τοὺς ῥῶγας. Ὁμοίως τὴν βῶλον, καὶ τὴν πύελον, καὶ τὴν ὔελον, καὶ τὴν φιάλην, καὶ τὴν λίθον (μάλιστα ἐπὶ τῆς cφραγῖδος).
[294] Neither *PGL* or Sophocles 1888 have φιέλη.

(and as early as linear B tablets, cf. *pi-je-ra₃*[295]) and especially in Asia Minor, during the Hellenistic and imperial periods[296].

ψίαθος

The etymology of ψίαθος is unknown; this too may be a loanword. It appears an ‹α› in lexical gloss of Moeris, as the term of the *Hellenes*[297]. The spelling with ‹ε› is not attested in inscriptions or later literature: Lampe has ψιαθίδιον and ψιάθιον, *PGL* 1542, but no form with ‹ε›; Sophocles (1888) only records ψιαθώδης[298]. ψάθα and its derivatives attested in Christian times are continuations of the variants with ‹α›[299].

μόλυβδος

Ael. D. μ 24 μόλυβδος· διὰ τοῦ υ καὶ δ ⟨Ἀττικοί⟩.
Moer. μ 6 μόλυβδος Ἀττικοί· μόλιβος Ἕλληνες (VF) | μόλυβος (C).

The many variants of the word for 'lead', are ancient and they coexisted since the word was borrowed into Greek[300]. Therefore the variation must be ancient and indipendent from the merger of [y] with [i]. The common classical Attic form is μόλυβδος, the variant which also the lexica support: in Attic inscriptions μόλιβ(δ)ος is not attested. μόλυβδος and μόλιβδος alternate in the textual transmission of classical authors; the form attributed to the Hellenes by the manuscripts VF of Moeris lexicon is the best attested: however, μόλυβδος, μόλιβος, and μόλυβδος coexist in papyri[301].

μυελός

→ πύελος

---

[295] PY Ta 709.1, Bennett – Olivier 1973: 231.
[296] Schwyzer 1898: 36; *BCH* XVI 431 ff., n. 61₃, MDAI(A) XV 267 ff., 20₁₆.
[297] Moer. χ 18, χαμεύνιον Ἀττικοί· ψίαθος Ἕλληνες.
[298] From the sch. Ar. *Ach.* 72 (R); cf. also Ar. *Ra.* 567 ψιάθους and the sch. *ad loc.* (VΘ).
[299] The cluster [sj] was reduced to [s], cf. Scheller 1951: 107–10, 118–20.
[300] Possibly from Anatolian, *EDG s.v.* μόλυβδος.
[301] Mayser – Schmoll 1970: 82, Gignac 1976: 271.

μύσταξ

Antiatt. μ 37 μύστακα· βραχέως. Εὔβουλος Τιτθῇ (fr. 112 K.-A.)

μύσταξ belongs to the small group of nouns in -ᾰκ-[302]. The possibilty of forming pejoratives in -ᾰκ- was vital and employed mostly in the language of comedy. Ephemeral formations as πάσσᾱκι from πάσσᾱξ (Ar. *Ach.* 763), and Δημᾱκίδιον (*Eq.* 823), from δῆμᾱξ attest to the productivity of the suffix with the long vowel[303]. Hyperatticising pronunciations, generalising long vowels even where they are not to be expected, may explain the reaction of the *Antiatticista*; the quote of the *Antiatticista* may also point to the existence of a prescription to the contrary, i.e. that all nouns in -αξ had a long /aː/, an incorrect generalisation but likely to happen if one bases mostly on the language of comedy. The short vowel is also attested in Strattis fr. 65 K.-A. (anapaests, μύστᾰκα guaranteed by metre), Antiphan. fr. 46.4 K.-A. βύστᾰκας (end of trimeter, cf. Phot. β 318 βύσταξ· ὁ ὑφ' ἡμῶν μύσταξ).

νεαλές

Phryn. *PS* 90.9-13 νεαλές· παρὰ τὸ ἀλές, ὃ σημαίνει τὸ ἀθρόον, τὸ νεωστὶ γεγενημένον καὶ συνενηνεγμένον. τὸ γὰρ συνελθεῖν καὶ συναλισθῆναι ταὐτόν. ⟨ὁ δὲ⟩ Ἀριστοφάνης ⟨ἐν Λημνίαις (fr. 378 K.-A.) διὰ μακροῦ τοῦ α⟩ τὸ νεαλής ⟨τέθεικεν ἐπὶ τοῦ νέου καὶ ἀκμάζοντος⟩.

The entry is not prescriptive. The remarks on the quantity of ⟨α⟩ (etymologically long, cf. *EDG* s.v.) appear in Photius (ν 67), but the manuscript of the *PS* reads only Ἀριστοφάνης τὸ νεαλές[304]. The word was still in use in the 2nd century AD, and there was some debate on its etymology and correct usage, depending on whether the second part of the word was considered to derive from ἁλίσκομαι or ἅλς (it probably derives from neither, but from the same root as Lat. *alere*), cf. e.g. Galen 12.808.5 δὲ νεαλὴς [τῦρος] τουτέστιν ὁ νεωστὶ τοὺς ἅλας προσειληφώς[305].

---

[302] Chantraine 1933: 377-80.
[303] Cf. Peppler 1902: 42-4, Chantraine 1933: 380-2.
[304] -ὴς de Borries, but -ές on the ms., f. 58v. On the attribution to Phrynichus see Lobeck 1820: 375.
[305] Cf. *EDG* s.v., Lobeck 1820: 375 and Amm. 332.

νεώς

Moer. ν 1 νεώς τὴν εὐθεῖαν ἑνικῶς καὶ ὀξυτόνως Ἀττικοί, ναός Ἕλληνες.

The need to specify the nature and position of the accent with ὀξυτόνως (as opposed to more general prescriptions such as ὁ τόνος ἐπὶ τέλους, Phryn. *PS* 27.13–17, → ἀφοῦ) does not necessarily mean that Moeris is contrasting different pitch contours, or that he had in mind *νεῶς or *νέως. Despite ναός and νεώς are two diachronically related variants, we may consider the gloss as actually contrasting two different lexical items: according to the practice of the time, the προςῳδία of νεώς is described with the technical term ὀξυτόνως.

νῆςτις

Phryn. *Ecl.* 298 νήςτης βάρβαρον, τὸ δὲ ἀρχαῖον νῆςτις διὰ τοῦ ι.
Moer. ν 12 νῆςτις Ἀττικοί· νήςτης Ἕλληνες.
Phryn. *PS* 91.5–6 νῆςτις διὰ τοῦ ι, οὐχὶ διὰ τοῦ η. καὶ τὸ πληθυντικὸν νήςτιδες καὶ νήςτεις.

νῆςτις is Classical Attic for 'fasting', and is used both as masculine and as a feminine, and both as a substantive and as a noun. The masculine noun ὁ νήςτης, -ου is a later formation and is condemned by grammarians (cf. [Hdn.] *de loc. prav.*, *An. Ox.* 3 248.20–26[306]); it is however common in Galen and later authors. The entries in the Atticist lexica are concerned with the distinction between the noun/adjective νῆςτις and the noun νήςτης[307]. It is unclear whether a similarity in sound could have made the confusion between the two words more likely[308].

νόμος

Antiatt. ν 14 νόμο{υ}ς· τὸ νόμιςμα, οὕς οἱ Ἰταλικοὶ νούμ(μ)ους καλοῦςιν.

---

[306] On the treatise and its attribution see Dickey 2014: 333–4; Argyle (1989) attributes the work to Cornelianus.
[307] Pollux only mentions νῆςτις (2.209, νήςτεως 210, with no indiction or mention of νήςτης).
[308] My view (Vessella 2012: 263) that in Attic inscriptions the variation between ‹η› and ‹ι› is more frequent in the suffix -(τ)ης is not correct and misrepresents the data collected in Threatte (1980: 166): three sepulchral monuments show feminines of ethnics in -ης instead of expected -ις (Threatte 1980: 165), and the use of νήςτης for νῆςτις may be a similar case.

The reading of the lemma and its gloss is uncertain. Valente adopts the normalised Greek spelling νόμοc for the lemma, and νούμμουc for the word current among the *Italikoí* – νούμμ- is the spelling we find in Pollux when he quotes Epicharmus (fr. 134 K.–A.) in a line that, however, requires the word to be scanned with a short first syllable, although ⟨μμ⟩ is the spelling in the manuscript tradition of the *Onomasticon*[309].

Ancient Latin scholarship regards *nummus* as a loanword from Greek[310], and, conversely, some Greek scholarship considers it to be a genuinely Latin word[311]. The term is probably a loanword, as is often the case with currency names and other units of measurement, e.g. Gr. λίτρα and Lat. *libra*. The early attestation in Epicharmus makes it unlikely that the word is a borrowing from Latin; but either νόμοc or νόμιμοc are good candidates to have been borrowed into Latin from Greek[312]; the later Greek spelling νούμμοc would in turn be a re-borrowing from Latin[313].

Rather than degemination, the reason for spellings with a single ⟨μ⟩ could be paraetymology with Greek νόμοc. The shape of the gloss in the *Antiatticista* suggests that the lexicographer was only supporting the literary status of νόμοc as a currency unit, rather than contrasting two variants. There is no particular reason to believe that we are facing a case of degemination as early as the fifth century BC, if νόμοc is the actual form of the word as Epicharmus and Sophron employed it.

---

309 Pollux 9.80, 9.87 (= Aristot. frr. 589 and 590 Rose, Epicharmus fr. 134 and Sophron fr. 161 K.–A.). The manuscripts of Pollux have νοῦμμουc in the fragment of Epicharmus, but the metre requires a short first syllable (i.e. νόμ-), which could be the original reading of the lemma in the *Antiatt.* v 15; cf. Valente *ad Antiatt.* v 14. νόμων in Sophron fr. 161 is a conjectural reading, cf. Kassel – Austin, *ad loc*. On the definition of the Tarentine currency as Ἰταλικὸc νόμοc see Head 1911: 53–69, esp. p. 54.
310 Varro *L.* 5.173 "id [scil. nummi] ab Siculis"; Festus *Fr. e cod. Farn.* 176.35–177.1 Lindsay "nummum ex Graeco nomismate existimant dict⟨um⟩", cf. *DELL* s.v. *nummus*.
311 The *Suda* suggests a Latin etymology for νουμμίον (α 4126), from the name of the king Numa, which appears as Νουμμᾶc at α 4126, but as Νουμᾶc at ν 515, making the status of the geminate in this word difficult to understand. There is some variability in the transmission of the word with or without the geminate (cf. Hsch. χ 107 Cunningham – Hansen).
312 *DELL* s.v. *nummus*.
313 Willi 2008: 142.

ξῆναι

Phryn. fr. *341 ξῆναι ὁ ἀόριστος ἀπὸ τοῦ ξαίνω, οὐκ ἔχει τὸ ι, ὥσπερ οὐδὲ τὸ θερμῆναι, ἱῆναι, ϲημῆναι.

The text of this fragment is found in a lexicon dealing with subscript *iota* (Rabe 1892). I. de Borries attributed it only tentatively to the *PS*, and only on the ground of similarities with another entry of the epitome:

> ϲημῆναι καὶ ἐϲήμηνα ἐρεῖϲ ἀντὶ τοῦ ϲημᾶναι καὶ ἐϲήμανα. ὡϲαύτωϲ φῆναι καὶ ἀποφῆναι καὶ προφῆναϲ, καὶ ἐθέρμηνα καὶ θερμήναϲ, καὶ ἐτεκτήνατο τεκτήναϲθαι, καὶ ἐμήνατο μήναϲθαι καὶ ἐκμῆναι. καὶ διὰ τοῦ ρ ἐχθῆραϲ καὶ ἐκάθηραϲ. καὶ διὰ τοῦ λ ἔϲφηλα καὶ ϲφῆλαϲ.

> You shall say ϲημῆναι and ἐϲήμηνα instead of ϲημᾶναι and ἐϲήμανα. Likewise, φῆναι and ἀποφῆναι and προφῆναϲ, and ἐθέρμηνα and θερμήναϲ, and ἐτεκτήνατο τεκτήναϲθαι and ἐμήνατο μήναϲθαι and ἐκμῆναι. And with a ‹ρ› ἐχθῆραϲ and ἐκάθηραϲ. And with a ‹λ› ἔϲφηλα and ϲφῆλαϲ.
> Phryn. *PS* 108.10–15

Similar remarks are found in

> ϲημᾶναι ἐϲήμαναν καὶ θερμᾶναι ἐθέρμαναν καὶ καθᾶραι ἐκάθαραν· καὶ ταῦτα παρὰ τὴν ἀρχαίαν χρῆϲιν διὰ τοῦ α· λέγομεν δὲ διὰ τοῦ η ϲημῆναι, καθῆραι, θερμῆναι.

> ϲημᾶναι ἐϲήμαναν and θερμᾶναι ἐθέρμαναν and καθᾶραι ἐκάθαραν: and also those against the ancient usage [are found] with ‹α›: but we say, with ‹η› ϲημῆναι, καθῆραι, θερμῆναι.
> Phryn. *Ecl.* 15

> Phryn. *Ecl.* 17 ἐφλέγμανε, φλεγμᾶναι· διὰ τοῦ η καὶ ταῦτα λέγεται.

and

> Moeris ε 5 ἐρρύπηνα ἐκάθηρα Ἀττικοί· ἐρρύπανα ἐκάθαρα λέγουϲιν Ἕλληνεϲ.

The gloss of the *Praeparatio Sophistica* is possibly only evidence that ‹η› and ‹η› had the same pronunciation. Yet aorists of verbs in -αίνω were a concern to Atticists, as the entries in the lexica of Phynichus and Moeris show. The glosses focus on the derivation of the aorist stem: verbs in -αίνω form an aorist stem in -ᾱν- that yields -ην- in Attic, unless it follows ‹α›,‹ι›, or ‹ρ›. The entries in the Atticist lexica were meant to prescribe older, classical formations rather than an archaising pronunciation.

In post-Classical Greek, aorists in -ᾰν- started to replace those in -ην-, in all verbs, independently form the root consonant[314]. In addition to the widespread presence of ‹α› in the other tenses (e.g. cημανῶ, cεcήμαγκα, ἐcημάνθην), the merger of ‹αι› into a simple /ε:/ vowel may have made the necessity of a distinction more urgent, if ‹αι› and ‹η› sounded similar enough to be confused with each other. Cf. →αἱμωδία.

ξυάλη

Ael. D. ξ 2 ξυήλην· ἣν ξυάλην λέγομεν. Ξενοφῶν Κύρου Ἀναβάcει (4.7.15)· "εἶχον δὲ θώρακας λινοῦς μέχρι τοῦ ἤτρου, ἀντὶ δὲ τῶν πτερύγων cπάρτα πυκνὰ ἐcτραμμένα. εἶχον δὲ καὶ κράνη καὶ παρὰ τὴν ζώνην μαχαίριον ὅcον ξυήλη(ν) Λακωνική(ν)", ἣν Ἀττικοὶ κνῆcτιν [Λάκωνες δὲ ξυήλην λέγουcι μόνον. "ἐπὶ δ' αἴγειον κνῆ τυρόν / κνῆcτι χαλκείῃ" (Hom. Il. 11.639-40) οἱ μὲν οὖν Ἀττικοὶ ⟨λέγουcιν, ὡς καὶ⟩ τὸ ῥῆμα [οὕτως λέγουcιν] (fr. com. ad. 519 K.-A.)· "κἀπικνῆν κἀπεcθίειν", οἱ δὲ Λάκωνες τοὔνομα ⟨μόνον⟩ ξυήλην, ὡς καὶ Ξενοφῶν φηcιν ἐν τῇ τετάρτῃ τῆς Ἀναβάcεως (X. An. 4.8.25), ὅτι Δρακόντιος ἔφυγεν ἐκ Σπάρτης παῖς ἔτι ὢν ἀποκτείνας ξυήλῃ Λακωνικῇ παῖδα. διὰ τοῦτο δὲ καὶ τὸ κνεῖν οἱ Δωριεῖς ξύειν λέγουcιν ὡς καὶ Cώφρων (fr. 147 K.-A.)· "αἴ τις τὸν ξύοντα ἀντιξύει", καὶ πάλιν (ibid.)· "ὁ χοραγὸς ξύεται".

The variation between ξυάλη and ξυήλη resembles the case of →μιαρός and of the other variations between ‹α› ~ ‹ε› following /i/ or /y/. But whereas the group of μιαρός ~ μιερός includes different formations, and seems to be undergoing a process of lexical or phonetic change that yields only forms in ‹α›, in this case it is likely that we are faced with two different derivatives of ξύω, formed with similar suffixes[315].

The gloss of Aelius, the *Suda*, and Hesychius all mention ξυάλη as the current Koine form (ἣν ξυάλην λέγομεν, Ael. D. ξ 2, *Su*. ξ 91, ξυήλη· ξυάλη Hsch. ξ 92), and Herodian mentions ξυάλη as part of a list of words in -άλη[316]. Aelius is explaining a non-Attic word that he could read in Xenophon, mentioning almost in passing that ξυάλη was the common form at his time (if these are not Eustathius' words). We are not told that ξυάλη is Classical Attic – and there are not any

---

[314] Schwyzer 1939: 189, 754; Gignac 1981: 263–5 (esp. 263 fn. 2 on the diffusion of α in the aorist in post-Classical Greek), Rutherford 1881: 76–78 on -ανα and -ηνα forms in Attic.
[315] *DELG* and *EDG* s.v. ξύω, 768; on verbal derivatives in -ηλο- and in -αλο- see Chantraine 1933: 242, 244.
[316] π. μον. λέξ. *GG* 3.2 944.14, see also π. καθ. πρ. *GG* 3.1 320.27.

other attestations of either word in surviving Attic literature: outside of grammars and lexica, we are only left with ξυήλη in Xenophon, and Aelius' passing remark that there was a more common form ξυάλη.

ξυρεῖν

Philet. 209 ξυρεῖν περισπωμένως· καὶ ξυρήσω ὁ μέλλων, ὡς ἀπὸ τοῦ νοῶ, νοήσω.

The distinction is between ξυρέω and ξύρω: this explains the use of νοέω as a model. In a similar fashion, Phrynichus too uses the position of the accent to distinguish the inflection of a contract verb from that of a non-contract verb in *PS* 39.12–15 → ἀκταινοῦν. Some forms of the present stem of ξυρῶ may have posed a problem for loud reading, as they are ambiguous when written without accent marks (ξυρω, ξυρεις, ξυρουσι, ξυρων, ξυρειν, etc.). The prescription involves also the morphology of the verb as ξύρω and ξυρέω form different the future (and aorist) stems, ξῡρ- and ξυρης- respectively.

Lucian used at least twice the non-contract verb ξύρω: in the *Pseudologista* (27), where he seems to use the verb in an otherwise Attic context, and in the *de Syria Dea* (6, 53, 55), where the verb is part of the Ionic diction of the work (cf. also Hp. *Morb.* 3.1, Ionic)[317]. ξύρω/ξυρέω continues in Modern Greek as ξυρίζομαι, which possibly owes its suffix -ιζ- to a confusion with an active aorist of ξυρέω[318]: it proves that the form continued in Greek is the one that the *Philetaerus* prescribes.

On accent type used to distinguish different conjugations see → ἀκταινοῦν.

ξυρόν

Moer. ξ 5 ξυρόν μακρῶς Ἀττικοί· βραχέως Ἕλληνες.

The gloss in the lexicon of Moeris is a generalisation of the more nuanced doctrine reflected and Photius (ξ 79 ξυρόν ἐκτεταμένως τὰ πολλὰ λέγουσιν). The

---

[317] In later Greek, ξύρω is found at least once in Tzetzes (*Hist. var. chil.* 9.231 ξύρας – Dindorf in *ThGL* VI 1691d s.v. ξύρομαι).
[318] An aorist ἐξύρησα /eˈksyrisa/ and then /eˈksirisa/ is a homophone of **ἐξύρισα, the expected aorist of /ksiˈrizo/ ξυρίζω.

noun ξυρός (or ξυρόν), 'razor', has an inherited short root vowel[319], and is often attested with a short vowel in Attic comedy.

In the surviving text of Aristophanes the word occurs twice in a position that allows for a long scansion of the *hypsilon* – only because it realises the first syllable of an iamb. One of them is in a surviving comedy[320], but the other survives only in the *Onomasticon* of Pollux[321].

Moeris is generalising a false assumption, resulting in a hyperatticism. A long ‹υ› in ξυρός would not disrupt the metre, but would be unacceptable in most other contexts. Only pedantic readers of Aristophanes (or of the *Onomasticon*) could have introduced a long *hypsilon* in the noun: Moeris, and those who shared the lexicographer's view, perceived the long vowel to be more Attic, thus falling in line with the general assumption that long vowels were a particularly Attic phonological trait (chap. IV, § 5).

οἰνοπώτης

→πῶμα

ὀπτάνιον

Phryn. *Ecl.* 241 μαγειρεῖον· τὸ μὲν μάγειρος δόκιμον, τὸ δὲ μαγειρεῖον οὐκέτι. ἀντὶ δὲ τούτου ὀπτάνιον λέγουσι, τῆς μὲν δευτέρας συλλαβῆς ὀξυτονουμένης, τῆς δὲ τρίτης βραχυνομένης.

While it states openly that the third syllable of ὀπτάνιον[322] is short, this gloss implicitly contrasts it with μαγειρεῖον: yet it does not mention in the least that the contrast between the two syllables is not only in length, but also in spelling. Just by stating that the vowel of ὀπτάνιον is short, Phrynichus tells his readers that its spelling is ‹ι› and not ‹ει›. The text of the *Onomasticon* (Poll. 1.80) reads ὀπτα-

---

319 *EWAia*, I 292; a noun with an instrumental suffix *-tlo-, *ksnoṷ-eh₂-tlo- is represented by sscr. kṣṇotra-, and Lat. *novācula* (cf. *DELL*, s.v.).
320 The other is Ar. *Eccl.* 65 κἄγωγε· τὸ ξυρὸν δέ γ' ἐκ τῆς οἰκίας.
321 Pollux (7.95 (ABCFS)) is the only source for the first words of the fragment (Ar. fr. 332 K.–A.), which begins with ξυρόν. Aelian may have had the same passage in mind when he wrote 'τῶν δὲ Ἀττικῶν γυναικῶν τὴν τρυφὴν Ἀριστοφάνης λεγέτω' (*VH* 1.18).
322 Cf. Diggle 2004 on Theophr. *Char.* 20.9 μάγειρος εὖ τὸ ὄψον σκευάζων.

νεῖον τὸ καλούμενον μαγειρεῖον, with no explicit mention of the length or accentuation of either word.

This is further evidence that by this time *epsilon-iota* corresponded to a long simple vowel, and that, for at least some speakers, the digraph corresponded to the same vowel, irrespective of context (whether it preceded a consonant or a vowel).

ὄστρια

Moer. o 32 ὄστρια διὰ τοῦ ι μακροῦ Ἀττικοί· ὄστρεα Ἕλληνες.

The form attributed to the Ἕλληνες, ὄστρεα, is well attested in classical Attic prose[323], even though other traditions, reflected in Athenaeus, point out that ὄστρειον is the only ancient spelling. Athenaeus claims that ὄστρεια is the only ancient spelling (ὄστρεια δὲ μόνως οὕτως ἔλεγον οἱ ἀρχαῖοι, Ath. 3.92e–f), and quotes metrically guaranteed instances of ὄστρεια in Cratinus (fr. 8.1 K.–A.) and Epicharmus (fr. 40.3 K.–A.)[324]. He also read ὄστρεα in Plato, and misquotes *R.* 611d as containing an instance of ὄστρεια, to show that Plato used both forms[325].

If the aim of the gloss was to support the authority of the more ancient Attic form, preserved – as it is apparent in the quotations of Athenaeus – in Attic comedy, Moeris is thinking of the wrong spelling, once again confirming that the (learned) pronunciation of ‹ει› was /iː/ in all contexts, also before non-front vowels. The gloss explicitly prescribes a spelling with *iota*, to be pronounced as a long vowel – the definition 'ι μακρόν' rules out that the *iota* is a trivial mistake for ‹ει› in the manuscript tradition. The recommended form ὄστρῑα could therefore be some form of hypercorrection, adopting the less usual ‹ι› to spell the long vowel.

---

[323] E. g. Plato *R.* 611d (which Athenaeus quotes as having ὄστρεια); *Crat.* 424d; *Phaedr.* 250c; *Tim.* 92b; and cf. οστρεα in P.Oxy. 2660, a Latin glossary in the Greek alphabet dating to the 1st/2nd c. AD.

[324] Cf. also Alexis fr. 115 K.–A., where the metre guarantees ὄστρεια. Just before mentioning the problem of the spelling ὄστρεα ~ ὄστρεια Athenaeus (3.92d) quotes, without comments on the spelling, hexameters in which either form is guaranteed (Nicander of Colophon, fr. 83 Schneider, ὄστρεα, Archestratus, fr. 7 Olson – Sens, ὄστρεια).

[325] ὀστρείῳ is indeed in Plato (*R.* 420c), and is the reading of the worse manuscripts of Plato, *Phlb.* 21c, where the rest of the tradition has ὀστρείνων or ὀστρεΐνῶν.

Latin *ostrĕum* (or, more commonly, *ostrĕa*) presupposes ὄcτρεα, the form of the *Hellenes*. As in the case of *massa* < Gr. *μάζα (→ μᾶζα) Latin has borrowed the word in a form different from the one that the lexicographers attribute to Attic. But, whereas in the case of μᾶζα the form of Latin and the *Hellenes* is the worse attested in the pair, in this case it is the form attributed to Attic that was becoming marginalised – as Athenaeus shows with regard to Plato, even Attic prose normally read ὄcτρεα.

ὄφλειν

Ael. D. ο 44 ὄφλειν καὶ ῥόφειν· τὰc πρώταc cυλλαβὰc τῶν τοιούτων οἱ Ἀττικοὶ ὀξύνουcιν.

The present ὄφλειν is attested only in later Greek, and in the same period as the lexica (Dio Chrysostom 31.143 and 153); in the manuscripts, forms of the aorist ὀφλεῖν (from ὀφλιcκάνω), are often accented as if belonging to the present tense of ὄφλειν.

Hippocrates uses ῥόμμα, ῥοπτόc instead of ῥόφημα, ῥοφητόc, all derivatives of ῥόφειν and not of ῥοφεῖν; yet the usual Ionic form of the verb is the contract ῥυφέω[326]. Modern Greek ρουφάω continues the non-Attic form (ῥοφ)έω[327], which must be the stigmatised form here: as with →ἀκταινοῦν and →ξυρεῖν, the lexicographer prescribes the position of the accent to identify the conjugation of the verb.

πάπυροc

Moer. π 36 πάπυροc μακρῶc Ἀττικοί· βραχέωc Ἕλληνεc.

There is no known etymology for πάπυροc[328]. Metrical compositions attest the variable quantity of the penultimate syllable, e.g. *Anacreontea*, 32.4–5 West "ὁ

---

[326] Thus also Ael. D. ρ 12 ῥόφειν ‹Ἀττικῶc›, ῥυφεῖν Ἰακῶc Ἱππῶναξ (fr. 175 Dg.).
[327] The stem of Modern Greek ρουφάω can come either from ῥοφ- or ῥυφ- (cf. κωδών > κουδούνι and κυλίω > κυλάω > τcουλάω).
[328] The term must be Egyptian. The phonological similarity with the quasi-synonym and competing form βύβλοc, the form recommmended by Phrynichus (*Ecl.* 270) does not clarify the etymology, and des not take into account the different meanings of the nouns: πάπυροc is the plant or the writing material deriving from it, βύβλοc a papyrus scroll.

δ' "Έρως χιτῶνα δήσας ὑπὲρ αὐχένος παπύρῳ", and some the short, e. g. Antipater *AP* 6.249.2 "σχοίνῳ καὶ λεπτῇ σφιγγομένην παπύρῳ". Latin *papȳrus* matches the form that Moeris ascribes to Attic (as opposed to the cases of *massa* and *ostrea*, reflecting the Hellenistic forms, cf. →μᾶζα, →ὄστρια).

πελαργός

Phryn. *Ecl.* 80 πελαργός· οἱ ἀμαθεῖς ἐκτείνουσι τὸ α, δέον συστέλλειν· Πελαργὸς γὰρ οὐδὲν ἄλλο ἢ Ἐρετριακῶς Πελασγός.

This entry is one clearest examples of the existence of an Atticist pronunciation. The length of the *alpha* in πελαργός is not signalled by the accent, which falls invariably on the last syllable, nor does it show in metrical composition, as it is in a closed syllable.

The paraetymology that identifies in πελαργός a derivative of Πελασγός bases on the dialect of Eretria. The derivation it suggests is incorrect: only intervocalic[s] had turned to [r] in the dialect of Eretria (and of its colony Oropos) by the 5th century BC (Buck 1955: 143); Eretrian still displayed this local trait after the spreading of the Koine[329].

This is not the only instance in which Phrynichus quotes a dialect, but this is one of the few instances in which the dialect is not literary. However, there is a possible literary source for this information, namely Plato, who mentions the trait in the *Cratylus* (434c "[Cω.] Οἶσθα οὖν ὅτι ἐπὶ τῷ αὐτῷ ἡμεῖς μέν φαμεν 'σκληρότης', Ἐρετριῆς δὲ 'σκληροτήρ';"). Phrynichus may have had this passage in mind, or some other similar source that identified the correspondence /r ~ s/ as one of the *pathe* of the Eretrian dialect[330].

The long vowel may depend on popular etymology, that connected the word to the adjective ἀργός: the adjective, coming from ἀ-εργός[331], has actually a long

---

[329] "Der Dialekt muß der κοινή lange wiederstanden haben, denn die namenform Λυρανίας begegnet auf den Grabsteinen *IG* VII 276, 277, 285 [end of 4th c. BC], die um hundert Jahre jünger sind als der ἱερὸς νόμος [*IG* XII,9 189]" (Bechtel, *GD* III: 84): the forms attesting the change at this later date are however mostly anthroponymics.

[330] On the rhotacism of Eretria, affecting /s/ between vowels and before /d, g/, see Bechtel, *GD* III: 83–5 (§ 32). Final /s/ does not seem to be affected by rhotacism in Eretrian (the only known exception, ὅπως ἄν (yielding ὅπωρ ἄν) must be considered a single phonological word, cf. Buck 1955: §§ 60.3 and 97a).

[331] ἀργός is treated elsewhere in the *Ecloga* (Phryn. *Ecl.* 76), but without mention of the quantity.

[aː]. Educated speakers would have been aware of the vowel quantity, and reflected it in pronunciation. The pronunciation of the ἀμαθεῖc addressed by Phrynichus is hypercorrect, and proves that vowel length was artificially used by some speakers in Phrynichus' time.

πένταχα

Phryn. *PS* 114.10 τρίχα, τέτραχα, πένταχα βαρυτόνωc.

ThGL VI 735a, *s.v.* πενταχῆ, mentions πενταχά together with πένταχα as a rare (and ancient) variant of the adverb, attested only once in Homer, *Il.* 12.87. The model for such adverbs in -χα is possibly δίχα (*DELG s.v.* δίc), whose many derivatives have in most instances an accent after the ‹χ› (διχάθεν, διχάc, διχῆ, διχοῦ). It is possible that the diffusion of the oxytone adverbs favoured an accentuation *τριχά, *τετραχά, *πενταχά, which the Atticists were trying to contrast.

πινακίc

→ κνημίc

πνῖγοc

Moer. π 38 πνῖγοc μακρῶc Ἀττικοί· βραχέωc Ἕλληνεc.
Phryn. *Ecl.* 77 πνῖγοc· ἁμαρτάνουcιν οἱ βραχύνοντεc τὸ ι· ἐκτείνουcι γὰρ τοὔνομα καὶ τὰ ἀπ' αὐτοῦ {πνιγερὰ καλύβη} (Thuc. 2.52.2).

The length of the first syllble of πνῖγοc is metrically guaranteed in Aristophanes (*Av.* 1091, πνίγουc, holospondaic anapaests). Lobeck in *ThGL*, *s.v.* πνῖγοc, lists various instances of the paroxytone πνίγοc in later authors. In the 2nd century AD ‹ει› is virtually the standard spelling for [iː] in a number of texts whose orthography would otherwise be classical. This habit could have favoured the opposite error, and precisely to ascribe to a short quantity the simple vowel ‹ι›, resulting in a complementary distribution of vowel and quantities, εῖ ~ ῐ.

The final words of the gloss are probably a later addition[332]: however, the fact that they shoud be quoting a prose author regarding a matter of vowel quantity is remarkable. If they belong to the original text by Phrynichus, or if the insertion can at least be dated early in the textual transmission of the *Ecloga* (the words are present in all the manscripts transmitting this entry), then the last part of the gloss must have been conceived as an aid to the accurate pronunciation of *dichrona* in prose texts.

Most derivatives of πνῖγοc have a long /i:/, including πνιγηρός (πνῑγηράν is indeed guaranteed by metre in Ar. *Ra.* 122), but this is not true of them all, as Phrynichus claims instead. One of them, πνῐγεύc, is even well attested with a short first syllable in Aristophanes (*Nu.* 96, end of a trimeter[333]) and πνῐγόειc and πνῐξ, gen. πνῐγόc (possibly none of them Attic, cf. LSJ *ss.vv.*). The verb has a short [i] in the aorist and future passive, ἐπνῐ́γην, πνιγῆναι.

Whereas Phrynichus may have conceived the definition 'καὶ τὰ ἀπ 'αὐτοῦ' as limited to the nominal derivatives of πνῖγοc, thus excluding verbal forms with πνῐγ-, he is still overlooking the fact that some nominal derivatives of πνῖγοc do have a short vowel, and are even attested in Attic comedy, i.e., they are also genuinely Attic. The gloss sounds like a oversimplified generalisation of the long quantity to the whole group of derivatives of πνῖγοc, and could be one more instance of hyperatticism.

πρωπέρυcι

Phryn. *PS* 105.9–10 πρωπέρυcι· διὰ τοῦ ω λέγουcιν οἱ Ἀθηναῖοι, ὥcπερ τὸ πρωτόλειοc.

In surviving Greek literature, πρωπέρυcι is only a conjecture in a fragment of Pherecrates (196 K.–A.[334]) whose reading πρὸ πέρυcι may be a corruption of πρωπέρυcι, the form that woud fit the metre (the manuscripts have προπέρυcι or πρὸ πέρυcι, cf. Kassel – Austin *ad loc*).

---

332 Lobeck 1820: 107.
333 Cf. also Ar. *Av.* 1001 κατὰ π'νιγέα μάλιcτα. προcθείc οὖν ἐγώ [⏑–⏑(⏑)–,⏑–⏑||–,––⏑–], for the synizesis of -εα cf. → ἀμφορέα, for π'ν cf. *Ra.* 1016. It is true that most instances of initial πν- in Aristophanes do 'make position' (e. g. *Ra.* 122, *Pax* 525 etc.). A syllabication κατὰ 'πνιγέα results in a scansion κατὰ π'νιγέα μάλιcτα. [⏑⏑– ⏑–,⏑–⏑|||], but I wonder whether this is sufficient ground to disregard altogether the unequivocal πνῐγεύc of Ar. *Nu.* 96.
334 Transmitted by Zonaras, 1745.10 – 11 Tittmann = Oros A 79 Alpers.

Apollonius Dyscolus discusses πρωπέρυσι together with πόρρω³³⁵ (*GG* 2.1.1 166.24-6: "τὸ ἄρα πόρρω ἐκτέταται ὡς Ἀττικώτερον, καθὸ καὶ τὸ προπέρυσι πρωπέρυσί φασι', καὶ ὅτι μᾶλλον μηκυντικοί εἰσι κατὰ τὰ φωνήεντα"). Even though in all Greek dialects πρω- was associated with a number of adverbs denoting anteriority (πρωΐ, πρώην), Apollonius' passage is interesting in that it establishes once more a connection between long vowels and Attic. The form πρω- is an ancient variant of what surfaces in Greek as πρό, and it is well attested in other Indo-European languages³³⁶: the formation of πρωπέρυσι with πρω- had always been possible. The adverb with a long vowel in the first member, πρωπέρυσι, should not be considered the corruption of προπέρυσι depending on isochrony, but rather a competing formation. Isochrony could have favoured the confusion with προπέρυσι. The care put by the lexicographers in distinguishing προπέρυσι and πρωπέρυσι is evidence of how weak the opposition between different vowel quantities was.

πύελος

Phryn. *Ecl.* 281 πύελος διὰ τοῦ ε καὶ μυελὸς ῥητέον.
Phryn. *PS* 103.14 πύελος· (διὰ τοῦ ε, οὐ διὰ τοῦ α,) ἐν ᾧ ἐλούοντο, οἱ ἀρχαῖοι.
Philet. 78 πύελος διὰ τοῦ ε καὶ θηλυκῶς· ἔλεγον δὲ οὕτως καὶ τὰς ἐν τοῖς βαλανείοις ἐν αἷς λουόμεθα.

The confusion between [e] and [a] after a front vowel (or glide) is attested for a whole group of items (→μιαρός), and Atticist lexica are not consistent in prescribing forms with ‹α› or ‹ε›. As is the case with other words containing ‹υε› or ‹ιε›, πύαλος with ‹α› is first attested during Hellenism, alongside with with the (older?) forms in ‹ε›, which it does not entirely replace³³⁷.

πύελος and μυελός are the only two items for which the Atticists prescribe an ‹ε› in Attic. The vowel [e] may belong to a suffix *-elo- attached to the root of

---

335 The lemma πόρρω in the *Philetaerus* (26, πόρρω καὶ πρόσω ἀμφοτέρως) reads πόρρω καὶ πώρρω ἀμφοτέρως in Pierson's edition (Pierson 1830: 396). A form with ‹ω› may have been in use, as an inscription of the imperial age from Pergamum attests (*Inscr. Perg.* 245 A 7; Crönert 1903: 20). On the other hand, the spelling πώρρω for πόρρω may depend on confusion with the final ‹ω› in writing.
336 Cf. e. g. Lat. *prōgeniēs*, Ved. *prā-tár-*, Chantraine *DELG* ss.vv. πρό, 938, πρώην, 944; *IEW* 813-4.
337 Thumb 1901: 75-6, and above chap. II § 6. Forms in ‹α› eventually replace those in ‹ε›, if they survive in the usage. In Modern Greek, πύελος survives only as a learned term in anatomy (the major calyx of the kidneys).

πλύνω, yielding πλυ-ελοc > πύελοc 'bath tub' by dissimilation, if πύελοc is not Pre-Greek (as μύελοc probably is)[338].

Whatever its etymology, the word is attested with ‹ε› in Classical Attic. πύελοc is normal in Aristophanes and is found in fifth-century Attic inscriptions, cf. e.g. *IG* I³ 426.149 (414 BC). πύαλοc and its derivative πυαλίc are attested several times in Hellenistic inscriptions of Asia Minor, together with πύελοc[339]; πυαλίc is the normal derivative of πύελοc in Lycia (LSJ s.v.), and it appears a number of times carved on sarcophagi, where it is spelt ποιαλ(ε)ίc[340]. πυαλίτηc, a throw of the dice, possibly a derivative of πύαλοc, is attested already in Eubulus[341].

The gloss of the *Philetaerus*, by stating 'διὰ τοῦ ε', implies that the form to be avoided is πύαλοc. Phrynichus (*PS* 103.14) apparently recommends the same spelling (hence de Borries' integration). The Atticists recommended πύελον, as is implicit elsewhere in the text of the *Philetaerus* (*Philet.* 182): τὰc ῥᾶγαc θηλυκῶc οἱ Ἀττικοί, οὐχὶ τοὺc ῥῶγαc. ὁμοίωc τὴν βῶλον, καὶ τὴν πύελον, καὶ τὴν ὕελον[342], καὶ τὴν φιάλην, καὶ τὴν λίθον (μάλιcτα ἐπὶ τῆc cφραγῖδοc)[343].

μυελόc too – if not Pre-Greek – owes the [e] a suffix *-elo-*[344]. There are no epigraphical attestations of μυαλόc. The vocalism of Modern Greek μυαλό is indireclty attested already during Hellenism in the denominative μυαλόω (LXX *Ps.* 65.15; Sophocles 1888, *s.v.*), but epigraphically not earlier that the 4th century AD, in the adjective ἀμύαλοc[345] the derivative ἐκμυαλίζομαι (Cos, *SEG* 47.1291, 4th century AD). The lexica attest to the diffusion of μυαλόc, but the variant seems to have been successfully kept out of literary Greek.

---

338 *EDG* ss.vv., cf. Chantraine, *DELG* s.v. πύελοc (< πλύνω). The feminine gender is anomalous, since normally derivatives in *-elo-* are masculine (Chantraine 1933: 244).
339 Schwyzer 1898: 37; Mihalov 1943: 7.
340 Hauser 1916: 22, 37.
341 Eubulus fr. 57.4 K.–A. (= Pollux 7.205, quoted to show the variety of names for throws in dice games); Redard (1949: 48) links πυαλίτηc to πύελοc, without further comment.
342 ὕελον, a form otherwise condemned by the Atticists (→μιαρόc), is possibly a trivial copying mistake for ὕαλον.
343 Cf. *exc. Vind.* 26 τὴν πύελον: the excerpta continue entry 182, with information on the gender of πύελοc, but not entry 72, on vowel timbre – however, 78 is a partially a repetition of the same information on gender.
344 *DELG* s.v. μύω, Pre-Greek according to Beekes *EDG*, s.v. μύελοc.
345 ἀμυ]άλουc in a *defixio* with crude orthography, Audollent 1904, 162.19 (and ἀμειαλουc, 168.A31)

πυθοῦ

Philet. 251 πυθοῦ, λαβοῦ· οὕτως οἱ Ἀττικοὶ περισπῶσι.

This entry (and the following in the *Philetaerus*, 252 →γενέσθαι) reflects Herodianic doctrine on the accentuation of thematic aorists, continued also in the epitome of the περὶ καθολικῆς προσῳδίας by ps.-Arcadius:

> πᾶν προστακτικὸν ὑπὲρ μίαν συλλαβὴν ὁμοιοκατάληκτον τῷ οἰκείῳ ὁριστικῷ καὶ ὁμότονόν ἐστιν αὐτῷ· ἔτυπτε τύπτε, ἐνόει νόει, ἐβόα βόα, ἐτύπτου τύπτου. τὸ δὲ λαβοῦ καὶ πιθοῦ παρὰ Ἀττικοῖς περισπᾶται. ἔτι καὶ τὸ ἐλθέ καὶ εἰπέ καὶ εὑρέ ὀξύνουσι.

> Every imperative longer than one syllable that has the same ending as the corresponding indicative has also the same accentuation [as the indicative]: ἔτυπτε τύπτε, ἐνόει νόει, ἐβόα βόα, ἐτύπτου τύπτου. λαβοῦ and πιθοῦ are perispomena among the Attic. Moreover they also accentuate ἐλθέ and εἰπέ and εὑρέ as oxytones.
>
> [Arc.] 196.14-19

The wording of ps.-Arcadius is suspicious. It defines a rule that polysyllabic imperatives share the same endings and the same accentuation as the corresponding indicatives, and then presents as an exception – exclusive to Attic – two specific aorist imperatives, λαβοῦ and πιθοῦ[346].

The same view is reflected in a scholion to Aristophanes:

> τὸ "πιθοῦ" περισπᾶται· ἔστι γὰρ δεύτερος ἀόριστος, ὡς καὶ ἡ γραφὴ δηλοῖ καὶ τὸ μέτρον βούλεται. τοῦτο δὲ οἱ Ἀττικοὶ περισπῶσι, καὶ ἡ χρῆσις ἠκολούθησε τῇ διαλέκτῳ· ἡ γὰρ ἀναλογία βαρύνει, ὥς φησιν Ἀπολλώνιος.

> πιθοῦ is perispomenon: it is a second aorist, as the spelling shows and the meter requires. The Attic [speakers] accent it as a perispomenon, and the usage followed the dialect: it is barytone by analogy, as Apollonius says.
>
> sch. in Ar. *Pl.* 103b (V)

Later scholarship tends to generalise this view. Choeroboscus for instance quotes Herodian once only to claim that ἴδου and ἀφίκου are exceptions to the general

---

346 Hdn. *GG* 3.1 464.5 (πιθοῦ), which Lentz reconstructed from Choerob. *GG* 4.2 246.3 ff., actually reads πυθοῦ (246.12). With the scholion to Ar. *Pl.* 103b (V), ps.-Arcadius 196.14–19 is the only passage discussing πιθοῦ and not πυθοῦ. However, the fact that πιθοῦ is an uncommon aorist of πείθομαι and is attested in Aristophanes suggest that earlier scholarship originated on this form rather than πυθοῦ.

rule that aorists of the thematic aorists are usually perispomena[347]. This doctrine is roughly the same that informs modern descriptions of the accentuation of such imperatives (e. g. Vendryes 1945: 126, Probert 2003: § 83, all perispomena except ἴδου).

Choeroboscus (echoing Theodosius, GG 4.1 67.16–18), however, also repeats the same doctrine of ps.-Arcadius, quoting Herodian again (ὁ τεχνικός), to say that the perispomena are Attic, and that they are exceptions to the rule that aorist imperatives share the same accentuation of their indicative counterparts[348].

These imperatives did have a different accentuation in dialects other than Attic, and perhaps even in the Koine, in which regular forms like λάβου must have coexisted with forms like λάβε (~ Att. λαβέ, cf. Probert 2006: 76, discussing [Arc.] 170.16–17 τὸ δὲ λάβε καὶ ἴδε παρ' ἡμῖν μὲν βαρύνονται, παρὰ δὲ Ἀττικοῖς ὀξύνονται). This is also the scenario described by the scholiast to Ar. Pl. 103, who attributes it to Apollonius (Dyscolus? or perhaps a mistake for Herodian?), and possibly only in relation to the one aorist in question, πιθοῦ. The need to specify that it is an aorist is to do primarily with the fact that this form is uncommon (πείθομαι regularly forms a first aorist ἐπεισάμην).

Texts written in literary varieties that do not show the Attic contraction in ‹ου› also have the non-Attic recessive accentuation we expect: ἔλευ Hes. Th. 549, πύθευ Hdt. 3.68.4, ἀμβάλευ Theoc. 10.22 (cf. Chandler 1881: § 783 for more examples). Some of these forms are even attested in the textual tradition of Attic authors: τράπου Ar. Ra. 1248, ἀφίκου Eq. 584, ἐνέγκου S. El. 178, OC 470, ἴκου E. Or. 1230, IA 1626, S. OC 1495.

If we take the words of Theodosius and Choeroboscus (GG 4.1 67.16–18 and 4.2 255.16–25) literally, then these are Koineisms that have replaced the authentic Attic forms, and modern editors should print perispomena throughout[349]. How-

---

347 Choerob. GG 4.2 140.20–31: δεῖ δὲ γινώσκειν ὅτι τὸ προστακτικὸν τοῦ ἰδόμην, λέγω δὴ τὸ ἴδου, βαρύνεται· καὶ ξένον οὐδέν, εἴ γε καὶ τοῦτο βαρύνεται, τῶν προστακτικῶν τοῦ δευτέρου μέσου ἀορίστου ἔθος ἐχόντων περισπᾶσθαι, οἷον τυποῦ λαβοῦ νυγοῦ πυθοῦ· λέγει γὰρ ὁ Ἡρωδιανός, ὅτι τὰ προστακτικὰ τοῦ δευτέρου μέσου ἀορίστου οὐ πάντα περισπῶνται, καὶ παρατίθεται τὸ ἀφίκου βαρυνόμενον καὶ τὸ ἴδου. λέγουσι δέ τινες, ὅτι διὰ τοῦτο οὐ περισπᾶται τὸ ἴδου προστακτικόν, ἵνα μὴ συνεμπέσῃ τῷ ἰδού δεικτικῷ ἐπιρρήματι· οὗτοι δὲ οὐκ ἀκριβῶς λέγουσιν· εἰ γὰρ καὶ τῇ φωνῇ συνέπιπτον, ἀλλ' οὖν τῷ τόνῳ διεστέλλοντο· τὸ γὰρ ἰδού τὸ δεικτικὸν ἐπίρρημα ὀξύνεται, τὸ δὲ ἰδοῦ τὸ προστακτικὸν περισπᾶσθαι εἶχεν, ὁμοίως τῷ τυποῦ λαβοῦ νυγοῦ.
348 Choerob. GG 4.2 255.16–25, and esp. 24–5: τὰ προστακτικὰ τοῦ δευτέρου μέσου ἀορίστου, ὥς φησιν ὁ τεχνικός, παραλόγως οἱ Ἀττικοὶ περισπῶσιν, οἷον τυποῦ γενοῦ νυγοῦ πυθοῦ λαβοῦ. Cf. also Choerob. GG 4.2 140.24–6, quoting Herodian in support of paroxytone ἴδου and ἀφίκου, and 246.10–12 (the Athenians have perispomenon accentuation).
349 Göttling, 1835: 54–5.

ever, two more scenarios are possible: (a) in Attic almost all verbs had perispomenon accentuation, but there were some exceptions: we are reading 'traces of an older, more regular accentuation'[350], that was still in use for some verbs in Attic (note that according to Choeroboscus, *GG* 4.2 140.25–26, Herodian considered ἀφίκου good Attic); (b) that perispomenon accentuation was only typical of some verbs, even in Attic, just like oxytone accentuation is only proper of a handful of active thematic aorist imperatives: we owe the systematic perispomenon accentuation to a generalisation of a principle that considered Attic forms to be correct, and was subsequently applied to all texts (where ‹ου› was written – and this is why non-Attic forms in ‹ευ› or ‹εο› have retained the inherited recessive accentuation).

It is clear however, that at some point whoever wanted to sound Attic would have pronounced at least the middle aorists prescribed by the earliest grammatical tradition as perispomena. It would not be surprising if at an early stage those were only λαβοῦ and πιθοῦ (πυθοῦ?), and that then the number extended, as the identification of 'exceptionally Attic' > 'Attic' > 'correct Greek' progressed over time[351].

πῶμα

Philem. 393.32 R. ἔκπωμα· τὴν μέσην μακρὰν ποιητέον.
Ael. D. α 53 αἱματοπώτης· οἱ Ἀττικοὶ μηκύνοντες τὸ ο προφέρουσιν τὴν λέξιν, ὥσπερ καὶ τὸ οἰνοπώτης καὶ ὑδροπώτης, ἐπεὶ καὶ τὸ πόμα οἱ μὲν ἄλλοι διὰ βραχέος τοῦ ο γράφουσιν, Ἀττικοὶ δὲ ἐπεκτείνοντες.
Moer. υ 12 ὑδροπωτεῖν ἐν τῷ ω Ἀττικοί· ἐν τῷ ο Ἕλληνες[352].

The root of πίνω can form derivatives either in -πο- or in -πω-[353]. Forms with a short radical vowel like πόμα/ἔκπομα are well attested since the Archaic age (Pindar *N.* 3.79; Hdt. 3.23.1; then Call. fr. 178.20; several instances in the *Anthologia Palatina*[354]), and are common in later prose. However, they do not belong to Classical Attic, which employs πῶμα. The spreading of πόμα may have been fav-

---

350 Chandler 1862: § 784.
351 On Attic as an exception to the rules of Koine, cf. Moeris μ 12 →μαντέων, and on the progression from 'Attic' to 'correct' see Probert 2008.
352 Amm. 399 πόμα καὶ πῶμα διχῶς λέγουσι τὸ ἁπλοῦν {διὰ τοῦ ο *omitt. Nickau*}· ἐν δὲ συνθέτοις μόνον διὰ τοῦ ω μεγάλου, οἷον γαλακτοπωτεῖν καὶ ὑδροπωτεῖν.
353 πω- is the *e* grade of the root *peh_3-, from which πίνω.
354 *AP* 9.142; 313; 327; 356; 364; 770; 11.403; 12.50; 16.89; 333.

oured by the other derivative πόcιc (cf. above →εὕρεμα, →ἀνυπόδητος), even though the normal forms in classical Attic have ‹ω›.

The distribution of derivatives in -ποτης/-πώτης is more complex. Either form is attested in the text of Aristophanes, who uses αἱματοπώτης (*Eq.* 198, 208), but also φιλοπότης (*V.* 79), and Attic comedy too attests both forms of the root, with a short and with a long vowel (ὑδατοπότης Phrynichus Com. Fr. 74.2 K.–A., but ὑδατοπωτῶν Cratinus, fr. 319 K.–A.[355]).

Morphology, rather than phonology, explains why both forms exist. The purpose of the gloss could have been to prescribe the right spelling as well as to associate the pronunciation [o] or [oː] to this class of derivatives. Forms with a long vowel are clearly the ones favoured by the Atticists. This may be one more instance where Attic is regarded as a variety of Greek particularly found of long vowels (forcing the data, as actually Attic authors attest both quantities).

ῥαφανίς

→κνημίς

ῥοίδιον

Phryn. *Ecl.* 224 ῥοΐδιον διαιροῦντες λέγουσιν οἱ ἀμαθεῖς· ἡμεῖς δὲ ῥοίδιον.
Phryn. *Ecl.* (q) 223 ῥοΐδιόν τινες ἀμαθῶς διῃρημένως λέγουσιν· ἡμεῖς δὲ ῥοίδιον.

The gloss discusses the position of the accent, but it may also involve the timbre of ‹οι›. The difference between the contrasted forms would be rather subtle if the diphthong were pronounced [oi], but way more detectable if ῥοΐδιον was pronounced [ro'idion] and ῥοίδιον ['ry(ː)dion]. The pronunciation that Phrynichus recommends has not survived: the modern Greek descendant of this word, ρόδι /'roði/, suggests a pronunciation with diaeresis and a retraction of the accent, ῥόΐδι(ο)ν. Such pronunciation is incompatible with the rules of classical accentuation and not attested in our sources, but it can be derived rather unproblematically from the condemned form with a diaeresis, through the loss of the final vowel that is typical of nouns in -ιος / -ιον (ῥοΐδιον > ῥοΐδιν > ῥόΐδιν)[356].

---

[355] The mss. read ὑδατοποτῶν, impossible for the metre (cf. K.–A. *ad loc.*).
[356] Horrocks 2010: 175.

cάκκοc

Ael. D. c 4 cάκοc οἱ Ἀττικοὶ λέγουcι διὰ ἑνὸc κ.
Moer. c 32 cάκοc Ἀττικοί· cάκκοc διὰ δύο κκ Ἕλληνεc.
Phryn. Ecl. 225 cάκκοc Δωριεῖc διὰ τῶν δύο κκ, Ἀττικοὶ δι' ἑνόc.

cάκ(κ)οc, 'coarse cloth of hair; sack, bag', is one of those words that show "genuine hesitation between a simplex and a geminate consonant"[357]. The noun is a semitic loanword (cf. Akkadian *šaqqu*, Hebrew *šaq*[358]), possibly borrowed from Phoenician. The earliest attestations of cάκκοc in literature come from Ionia, and they have the geminate: cάκκοc is metrically guaranteed in Hipponax, fr. 57 W. = 59 Dg.; in prose is it found in Herodotus[359] and Ctesias[360]. Both the variant with the geminate, cάκκοc, and its derivatives have the greatest diffusion in postclassical Greek[361]. The oscillation between cάκκοc and cάκοc could depend on the borrowing process[362].

There is no confusion in the lexica between the masculine cά(κ)κοc, 'bag', and the neuter cάκοc[363], the Homeric shield, although the entry of Aelius Dionysius survives precisely because Eustathius points out twice in his commentary to the Iliad that the Athenians call cάκοc – with the singleton – what in Eustathius'

---

[357] Threatte 1980: 517. One can read both spellings e.g. in *IG* II² 1672, 329/8 BC (cακ- ll. 73, 74, 108, but cακκῶν l. 198). Cf. also a sarcophagus found in Korykos in Cilicia (*MAMA* III 470; Laminger–Pascher 1973: 33; 1974: 14), with both cακκᾶ and cακᾶ.
[358] *DELG*, *EDG* s.v. cάκκοc.
[359] Hdt. 4.23.3 cακκέουcι, 'they filter (through cloth)', and 9.80.2 (cάκκουc). The latter passage is transmitted with a variant reading cάκοc in the cod. Laurentianus Conv. Soppr. 207. The neuter cάκοc, 'shield', is transmitted without variants in Hdt. 1.52.1; Hdt. 4.23.3 cακκέουcι is the source of *Antiatt.* c 11 cακκέουcι, possibly via Aelius Dionysius (c 3 cακέουcι) – one of the entries suggesting that the *Antiatticista* made use of Aelius' lexicon (Erbse 1950: 70; Valente 2015a: 21 fn. 132, 39).
[360] *FGrHist* F 15 and F 45 h, cάκκον masculine.
[361] Lobeck 1820: 257, points out the Attic geminate in the Demosthenic corpus, cακχυφάντηc, Κατὰ Ὀλυμπιοδώρου βλαβῆc ([D.] 48) 12.4 and 13.4. Rutherford (1881: 323) suggests to correct it to cαχυφάντηc, basing on the usage of Aristophanes and on the Atticist prescriptions. Yet cακχυφάντηc is attested in an Attic law of 401/0 BC, *IG* II² 2403.5 (part of *IG* II² 10, cf. *SEG* 21.218, 24.75 and Threatte 1980: 517).
[362] Masson 1967: 25; see now Rosół (2013: 84–5), who does not comment on the variable ‹κκ› ~ ‹κ›.
[363] The Homeric cάκοc has no etymological relation with cάκ(κ)οc 'sack'. On the Homeric word see Mayrhofer (*EWAiA* I 684), Jamison (1986: 169–70) on Sanskrit *tvacas- .

time is commonly referred to as cάκκοc[364], whose meaning is – however – the same with the current word cάκκοc. The lexicographers clearly aim at pointing out that ὁ cάκκοc, 'the bag' has a variant ὁ cάκοc in Attic.

There are three instances of cάκοc and four of cάκκοc In Aristophanes[365]: three times out of four the spelling is metrically guaranteed. The form cάκοc with a singleton is guaranteed by metre in *Ach.* 822 (in fact, Triclinius signals it in his scholion[366]) and *Eccl.* 502. The double stop is guaranteed by metre in *Ach.* 745, in a line of the Megarian. The scholia signal that the word has a double *kappa* in that line (sch. vet. Ar. *Ach.* 745 EΓ³).

Knowledge of this specific occurrence of cάκκοc in the *Acharnians* could be the reason why Phrynichus ascribes cάκκοc to Doric: note also that the very next line could be source of two prescriptions in Phrynichus, *Ecl.* 72 and *PS* 58.14–59.1 → γρυλίζειν. Except from this line of the *Acharnians*, there are no instances of the word in literary Doric. The reading cάκκουc in *Lys.* 1209 is less certain[367]: only Geldart and Hall print it (and Blaydes 1880) but not Coulon nor Wilson. The metre does not support any variant, as the first syllable of cάκ(κ)ουc realises an *indifferens* in the line[368].

Phrynichus could have read a text of the *Lysistrata* in which cάκουc appeared with a single ‹κ› – which seems likely, since the geminate there is a scarcely attested textual variant. This may have been one more reason to ascribe the variant with a single consonant to Doric and the geminate to Attic.

The lexicographers ascribe to Attic the form cάκοc without the geminate, even if it is the less frequent spelling, and cάκκοc has become the standard orthography of the word. Gemination does not seem to be used as a special mark of genuine Attic, at least with this lexical item. cάκκοc and cάκοc are both literary spellings, and it is not possible to gather any evidence of degemination on the only basis of the prescription.

---

[364] Eust. 940.16–19 ἰcτέον δὲ ὅτι οὐ μόνον τὸ πολεμικὸν cκεῦοc, ἀλλὰ καὶ ὁ κοινὸc λεγόμενοc cάκκοc δι' ἑνὸc κάππα προεφέρετο παρὰ Ἀθηναίοιc, καθά φηcι Αἴλιοc Διονύcιοc (the source of Ael. D.'s entry); still in Eustathius' time, one could parody a Homeric line by replacing cάκοc with cάκκοc (Eust. 588.12, on Hom. *Il.* 5.619). The entry continues in the *Suda* as a remark on the Homeric shield, *Su.* c 40: καὶ cάκοc, ἀρcενικόν, δι' ἑνόc κ.
[365] cάκοc in *Ach.* 822, *Eccl.* 502., *Lys.* 1209; cάκκοc in *Ach.* 745.
[366] sch. Ar. *Ach.* 822 (Tr) cάκον] cάκοc δι'ἑνὸc διὰ τὸν μέτρον, ἐν ἑτέρῳ διὰ δύο.
[367] Rutherford (1881: 323) does not mention this line of the *Lysistrata*.
[368] Ar. *Lys.* 1209 is in responsion with l. 1064 (that realises the same *indifferens* with a short syllable). The lines are part of an antistrophe (ll. 1203–15; the strophe is in ll. 1058–71).

cίαλον

→ μιαρός

cτάχυc

→ βότρυς

cύνθημα

→ ἀνάθημα

τητινόc

Phryn. *PS* 114.14–16 τητινόν τὸ ἐπέτειον. τῆτες γὰρ τὸ ἐπ' ἔτος. Ἀττικώτερον ⟨οὖν⟩ τὸ τητινόν, εἴρηται μέντοι καὶ ἐπέτειον. τῷ δὲ τόνῳ, ὡς ἐαρινόν, ὀξυτόνως.

The consonantism of τητινόc points to a genuine Attic origin of the word[369] (and possibly made it all the more evident to the Atticists). The uncertainties on the accentuation may depend on the rarity of the word, whose very meaning would have suggested the right accent to the speakers, as it belongs to a rather large group of adjectives of time in -ινόc, of which ἐαρινόc that Phrynichus quotes is only an example.

The derivation is clear in the *Epimerismi Homerici*, where τητινόc appears in a list of adjectives of time (ἐχθεcινόc πρωϊνόc περυcινόc ὀψινόc καὶ παρὰ τὸ τῆτες ἐπίρρημα τητινόc παρὰ Ἀττικοῖc, ὡc ἅδην ἀδινόc, π 144 Dyck). The same comparison is used to describe the position of the accent.

The rarity of τητινόc is confirmed by its near absence form all the texts available to us; one of the few instances is in Lucian, and indeed it is the pedantic main character of the *Lexiphanes* who employs it (Luc. *Lex.* 1.2).

---

[369] The adverb comes from a compound of *$\underline{u}et$-es/os* (Ion.-Att. ἔτος) *$\underline{k}i\bar{a}$-$\underline{u}etes$*, whose first element *$\underline{k}i\bar{a}$-* has been extracted from *$\underline{k}i\bar{a}meron$* (where it results from the combination of a morpheme *$\underline{k}i$* with the theme of Homeric ἦμαρ). Depending on the dialect, the outcome of *$\underline{k}i$-* is either τ or c (e.g. Attic τῆτες, Ionic cῆτες, Doric cᾶτες). Cf. *EDG, DELG* s.v. τῆτες.

τιμώρια

Moer. τ 4 τιμώρια Ἀττικοί, παροξυτόνως Ἕλληνες.

The entry is exceptional in that it lemmatises the singular τιμώρια, and not the plural, which is a standard example in the discussion of nominative feminine plurals that show a retraction of the accent in (more recent) Attic (see Moer. α 6 →αἴτιαι). The accentuation τιμώρια entails either that the length of the final vowel was disregarded, or that τιμώρια was scanned with synizesis, τι.μω.ριᾶ.

So far, this is an isolated instance this accent shift affecting the singular. The Modern Greek Italian *timóña* /ti'mɔɲa/ would be the only continuant of this accentuation, if the position of the accent has not been influenced by Latin[370], and if the entry in Moeris does not result from some brutal simplification of a prescription on the plural τιμώριαι.

τριπλᾶ

Moer. τ 22 τριπλᾶ τετραπλᾶ περισπωμένως καὶ μακρῶς Ἀττικοί· βραχέως Ἕλληνες.

The adjectives with a long vowel that Moeris ascribes to Attic are likely to result from analogical levelling of uncontracted adjectives; isochrony may have played no role here. τετραπλοῦς is never attested if not in later Greek. The adverb τετραπλῆ is already in Homer, but it can derive either from an adjective in -όος or in -ος[371]; forms in -όος may be the more ancient[372].

The direct cases of the neuter plural (-πλά ~ -πλᾶ) are among the few points of the declension where the distinction between the adjective in -οος and the adjective in -ος relies exclusively on accent and quantity. Only the accent would distinguish the two formations in the nom./voc. sg. of the feminine (-πλή ~ -πλῆ); whereas the nom./voc. pl. masculine and feminine (-πλοῖ, -πλαῖ ~ -πλοί, -πλαί) may have been different for the quantity as well as for the accent. Cf. also Phryn. fr. *367 →ἁπλᾶ.

---

[370] Scheller 1951: 125.
[371] On the formation cf. Schwyzer – Debrunner 1950: 163.
[372] Schwyzer 1939: 598 "(Umgebildet?) ἁπλόος usw. zu πλοῦς"; cf. *DELG s.v.* ἁπλόος.

ὑάλινος

→μιαρός

ὕαλος

→μιαρός

ὑδαρές

Moer. υ 9 ὑδαρές βραχέως τὸ α Ἀττικοί· μακρῶς Ἕλληνες.

Moeris ascribes to the Ἕλληνες a pronunciation which is not attested elsewhere. Schwyzer (1898: 96) considers this one of the instances in which ancient scholarship attests pronunciations typical of the Koine (cf. →πάπυρος).

One would expect a composition theme ὑδᾰρ- or ὑδᾰτ- from the stem of ὕδωρ, but not ὑδᾱρ-. This is one of the few entries that attributes the short quantity to the Attic speakers (cf. →υἱέος). It supports anyway the idea that vowel quantity was a tell-tale trait in the identification of different varieties of Greek.

ὑδροπωτεῖν

→πῶμα

ὑδροπώτης

→πῶμα

ὑγίεια

Moer. υ 11 ὑγίεια Ἀττικοί, ὑγεῖα Ἕλληνες.

ὑγεῖα is frequently attested in Attic inscriptions since the late 2nd century BC[373], and by the 2nd century AD ὑγίεια is only a residual spelling in Egypt[374]. If the Atticists consistently attributed a pronunciation [iː] to ‹ει›, the pronunciations associated to the different spellings ὑγίεια and ὑγεῖα would have been nearly or altogether indistinguishable: the only difference is that the older spelling results in one more syllable. This is exactly how the question is put in later scholarship:

> ἔτι πλημμελοῦσιν οἱ λέγοντες ὑγεία τρισυλλάβως, δέον ὑγίεια τετρασυλλάβως· μόνως γὰρ οὕτως οἱ ἀρχαιοὶ εἰρήκασιν· ὡς ἐν τῇ κωμῳδίᾳ 'αὗται γὰρ ἐπιθυμοῦσιν ὑγιείας τυχεῖν' (fr. com. ad. 256 K.-A.)
>
> And they also err, those who say ὑγεία as three syllables, whereas one should [say] ὑγίεια as four syllables: for the ancient only said like this; as in comedy 'αὗται γὰρ ἐπιθυμοῦσιν ὑγιείας τυχεῖν'.
>
> [Hdn.] de loc. prav., An. Ox. 3 251.13–16

υἱέος

Phryn. *PS* 118.3–4 υἱέος· (Thuc. 1.13.6) ἁμαρτάνουσιν οἱ διὰ τοῦ ω τὴν γενικὴν προφέροντες, ὡς Πηλέως.
Phryn. *Ecl.* 45 υἱέως οἱ ψευδαττικοί φασιν οἰόμενοι ὅμοιον εἶναι τῷ Θησέως καὶ τῷ Πηλέως.

The inherited genitive of υἱύς is υἱέος < -eu̯-os, showing the ablauting -eu̯- form of the suffix -u-, generalised from the full-grade cases in the paradigm (e.g. nom. plur. υἱέες)[375]. υἱέος is the only form of the genitive of υἱύς found in Egyptian papyri (Gignac 1981: 101). The nominative υἱύς itself is extremely less frequent than υἱός[376]. The variation results form analogical levelling, likening βασιλεῖς :

---

[373] LSJ s.v. ὑγίεια. The classical Attic spelling is ὑγίεια, regularly scanning [⏑⏑–⏑], cf. e.g. Ar. *Av.* 603–4, E. *Or.* 235 etc. The word had probably undergone an early reduction to /hy'giːa/ for reasons of its own (the vowel cluster, or the influence of the adjective/personal name ὑγιεινός), see Threatte 1980: 416–7.
[374] Gignac 1976: 296–7. In Egyptian papyri of Roman times ὑγιής, ὑγίεια, ὑγιαίνειν are often spelt without ‹ι› or ‹γ›, indirect evidence that the stop spelt by ‹γ› was spirantised and palatalised to [j] or [ʝ] (Gignac 1976: 71).
[375] Gunnerson 1905: 34; Schwyzer 1939: 573–4.
[376] Gignac 1981: 101 with fn. 1.

υἱεῖς = βαcιλέωc : υἱέωc, as Phrynichus states in the *Ecloga*. υἱέωc is very rare in the the manuscript tradition of Attic prose witers[377].

The label ψευδαττικοί suggests that this was a hypercorrection of those who wished to use the less regular inflection of υἱόc, and the technical term 'προφέροντεc' in the *PS* may suggest a flaw in the pronunciation, rather than just in spelling. The trait that reveals the ignorance of the ψευδαττικοί is, once more, a misplaced vowel quantity. Cf. →ὑδαρέc.

φαρμακόc

Ael. D. φ 2 φαρμακόc· τὸ κάθαρμα, βραχέωc. οἱ δὲ Ἴωνεc ἐκτείνοντεc λέγουcι φαρμᾶκόν. οὗτοι γὰρ διὰ τὴν τῶν βαρβάρων παροίκηcιν ἐλυμήναντο τῆc διαλέκτου τὸ πάτριον, τὰ μέτρα, τοὺc χρόνουc. δηλοῖ καὶ Ἱππῶναξ.

The same gloss appears, with a different accent, in Photius (φ 64) οἱ δὲ Ἴωνεc ἐκτείνοντεc λέγουcι φαρμᾶκον. Choliambs proving the scansion φαρμᾶκόν are quoted by Tzetzes as well. In those verses φαρμακόc is oxytone, and at least in four instances it is surely to be scanned with a long penultimate[378]. The same syllable is short in Hippon. fr. 48.4 Degani.

Another fragment of Hipponax, 147 Dg. χελιδόνων φάρμακον, transmitted by the *Suda* (χ 188) may not be the end of a scazon, as φάρμακον there follows a syllable that is surely long, whereas normally the last *metron* of this kind of verse would be preceded by a short syllable. Only a scansion φάρμᾰκον would fit a iamb. The *Suda* treats φάρμακον as a proparoxytone. The fragment could have been altered in its transmission[379].

Some speakers may have adopted a pronunciation with a long vowel, possible in some dialects but not belonging to Attic. The idea that a long vowel is inherently Attic could have triggered Phrynichus' reaction: there may be indeed a long vowel in φαρμᾶκόc, but it is Ionic, not Attic.

---

[377] Modern editors print consistently υἱέοc. Cf. Rutherford 1881: 142 for instances of υἱέωc in the manuscript tradition of Attic prose witers (Thuc. 1.13.6 and scholion), Plato *R.* 378a, 378d, *Lg.* 687d; Xenophon *HG* 4.1.40; [D.] 43.40, 73, 77 and 40.23 (a correction by Reiske).
[378] Hipponax fr. 6.2, 27, 28.2, 29.2, 30.2, 107.49 Degani. The penultimate syllable of φαρμακόc occurs in a indifferent position in fr. 43 Dg.
[379] And so do the manuscripts of Photius' lexicon (cf. Theodoridis *ad loc.*); cτέφανοc is quite likely a false scansion in Athenaeus 3.49e = Hipponax fr. 62 Degani, cτέφανον εἶχον κοκκυμήλων καὶ μίνθηc. The verse is probably only missing a syllable (‹καὶ› cτέφανον Gaisford, cτέφανον ‹μὲν› Liebel, cf. Degani 1983 and West *IEG, ad loc.*).

φιάλη

→ μιαρός

φιλόγελως

→ δύcερωc

φρούριον

Philet. 308 τὸ φρούριον τρίτην ἀπὸ τέλουc ἔχει τὴν ὀξεῖαν.

Neuters in -ιον (for the most part diminutives) are generally paroxytona if the syllable preceding the suffix is long[380], so φρούριον belongs to the small group of the exceptions to the rule. Two passages of ps.-Arcadius mention the accent of φρουριον: 137.10–11 τὸ δὲ φρούριον προπαροξύνεται· οὐ γὰρ ὑποκοριστικόν, and 138.3–5 τὰ διὰ τοῦ ιον τριcύλλαβα ἔχοντα δίφθογγον ἐν τῇ ἀρχούcῃ προπαροξύνεται, μὴ ὄντα ὑποκοριστικά· φρούριον παίγνιον ποίμνιον. As is the case with most glosses concerning the accent, its nature and position need to be described in full for the reader to understand the prescription.

χαμᾶζε

Ael. D. χ 3 χαμᾶζε ἀεὶ (προ)περιcπᾶται, τὸ δὲ χαμᾶθεν ὡc ἐπὶ πλεῖcτον.

The mention of frequency (ὡc ἐπὶ πλεῖcτον, 'most of the times') is surprising in prescriptions. The formation of χαμᾶθεν is not obscure in itself: the adverb belongs to a rather common type. The original accent was probably *χαμᾶθεν (Lejeune 1939: 96; 1940: 232)[381]. The paroxytone accentuation is seldom found in modern editions: Lucian, *Ind.* 9.21; A.D. *Adv.* [*GG* 2.1.1] 187.20, the scholion to Ar. *V.* 249 quotes χαμᾶθεν in the line, but does not comment. The editors of

---

[380] Bally 1945: 63–4.
[381] Starting from an adverb χαμά, of the same kind as πύκα, κάρτα, cῖγα (Benveniste 1935: 89–90).

the *Wasps* have χαμᾶθεν: the long vowel is required by the metre, as in Cratinus fr. 328 K.–A.

Similar hints at the existence of a variant χαμάζε are in ps.-Arcadius (208.11–13): καὶ τὰ εἰς αι δίφθογγον ὀξύνεται· χαμαί βαβαί. τὸ δὲ εἴθε καὶ αἴθε παροξύνεται. τὸ χαμάζε δὲ προπερισπώμενον εὗρον, ἀλλ' ἡ συνήθεια παροξύνει[382] – and Migne adopts χαμάζε in the text of Gregorius of Nazianzus, *Carmina Moralia* (*PG* 37) I 675.

The two accentuations imply a decision on the length of the accented vowel, that – given the short vowel in the last syllable – must be short if accented with an acute (and necessarily long if accented with a circumflex). The difference in the type of accent could be realised also as a difference in vowel quantity.

χρέως

Phryn. *Ecl.* 371 χρέως· Ἀττικῶς ἂν φαίνοιο καὶ ἐπιμελής, εἰ διὰ τοῦ ω μεγάλου χρέως λέγεις. σὺ μέντοι τῇ σεαυτοῦ πολυμαθίᾳ τὸν Ἀριστοφάνην διὰ τοῦ ο ἐδείκνυες τὸ χρέος ἐν ταῖς {ἑτέραις} Νεφέλαις (*Nu.* 30) εἰπόντα

'ἀτὰρ τί χρέος ἔβα με μετὰ τὸν Πασίαν;'

ἔοικε δὲ παρῳδικῶς εἰρηκέναι, διόπερ οὐ χρηστέον αὐτῷ.

Ael. D. χ 17 χρέως· Ἀττικοί, χρέος Ἴωνες. ⟨οὕτ⟩ως Πλάτων καὶ Δημοσθένης (*passim*). λέγουσι δὲ καὶ χρέος. καὶ τοῦτο μὲν διαφέρουσαν ἔχει γενικὴν 'τοῦ χρέους' [γάρ], τὸ δὲ χρέως τὴν αὐτὴν ⟨'τοῦ χρέως'⟩. τὰ σύνθετα δὲ μᾶλλον διὰ τοῦ ω, ὑπέρχρεως, ἀξιόχρεως.

Moer. χ 7 χρέως Ἀττικοί· χρέος Ἕλληνες.

Philet. 146 Τὸ χρέως καὶ τὸ χρέος, ἀμφοτέρως.

Ἀτὰρ τί χρέος ἔβα με μετὰ τὸν Πασίαν;

Ἀριστοφάνης ἐν Νεφέλαις (l. 30)

Philem. 396.26 R. χρέως τὸ δάνειον, οὐδὲ εἷς ἐρεῖ χρέος.

The Attic shape of this noun is regularly χρέως. Even though there is no sure etymology of the word[383], the comparison with the epic forms χρέος, χρεῖος and the root noun χρή points to synizesis as the starting point of χρέως, a neuter in – *os*

---

[382] Herodian, περὶ μονήρους λέξεως (*GG* 3.2 951.29) χαμᾶζε. οὐδὲν εἰς ζε λῆγον ἐπίρρημα τῷ α παραληγόμενον προπερισπᾶται, ἀλλὰ μόνον τὸ χαμᾶζε, παραιτοῦμαι δὲ τοὺς προπερισπῶντας τὸ θύραζε.

[383] *EDG* and *DELG*, s.v.

following the 'Attic declension' (cf. gen. sing. χρέως[384], plur. χρέᾱ in Ar. *Nu.* 39, 443). The variants that the Atticists rejected compete with χρέως in that they are more regular in their morphology and are supported by literary prestige: χρέος is found in Homer (along with the more common χρεῖος)[385], and Attic tragedy employs the form too. The verse quoted by Aristophanes is certainly parodic[386], as Phrynichus – but not the *Philetaerus*[387]– remarks, and the very use of χρέος is part of the parody. The two instances of χρέος in the surviving text of Menander (*Dysc.* 472, *Heros* 36) support the idea that χρέος was the form spreading during Hellenism (χρέως would have been metrically acceptable in both lines).

In the alternance between χρέος and χρέως, homophony is not the only factor at play: the falling into disuse of Attic declension must have favoured χρέος on χρέως. The Attic spelling χρέως however is still attested in papyri dating to the 4th century AD (Gignac 1981: 67[388]; Crönert 1903: 167 fn. 3), and, as the gloss of the *Ecloga* suggests, the distinction between χρέος and χρέως was still a mark of prestige in the speech of the educated.

χρυσᾶ

Phryn. fr. *367 χρυσᾶ· τὸ ἁπλᾶ καὶ διπλᾶ καὶ πολλαπλᾶ καὶ πάντα τὰ τοιαῦτα περισπῶσιν οἱ Ἀττικοί, ἀργυρᾶ, χρυσᾶ, καὶ κεραμεᾶ ἀπὸ τοῦ κεραμεοῦν, καὶ φοινικᾶ ἀπὸ τοῦ φοινικοῦν. (≈ *Su.* α 3221 = *An. Bach.* 122.8–11 = Σ[b] 1799, φοινικιᾶ ἀπὸ τοῦ φοινικιοῦν).

The gloss, extracted from the *Suda* (α 3221) includes heterogeneous atticistic material (cf. Σ[b] 1799), and touches on two different problems.

One is the accent type and its position in ἀργυρᾶ, χρυσᾶ, contrasted with the uncontracted and recessive ἀργύρεα, χρύσεα (Ionic forms acconding to Phrynichus, *Ecl.* 178 ἀργύρεα); the other is only the accent type of ἁπλᾶ or διπλᾶ,

---

[384] In [D.] 48 18.4; χρέους the manuscripts of Lysias 17.5; χρέος in the manuscripts of other Attic texts (e. g. Pl. *Plt.* 267a, *Lg.* 958b). This may be a trivial error of the copyists (Rutherford 1881: 482).

[385] Chantraine *GH* I: 70, Shipp 1972: 29–30.

[386] The parody builds on the Doric ἔβα and Πασίας, and plays on the phrase 'τί χρέος;' 'what is the matter', and Attic χρέως 'debit'. Aristophanes is parodying Euripides (Rutherford 1881: 48; van Leeuwen 1897 *ad loc.*), fr. 1011 Kannicht (Degani 1990: 121; Sommerstein 1991: 160).

[387] This gloss, compared to Phryn. *Ecl.* 231 together with *Philet.* 121, is conclusive evidence for Argyle (1989) the author of the *Philetaerus* is the dedicatee of the *Ecloga*, Cornelianus.

[388] The genitive, χρέως in the Attic declension, is never met if not in the form without synizesis χρέους, Gignac 1981: 67 and fn. 4.

that are not paralleled by trisyllabic **ἄπλεα, **δίπλεα, and could only be contrasted to ἁπλόc, διπλόc. The material of this gloss is found separately in other glosses, which supports the idea that this fragment of Phrynichus results form the conflation of originally independent material. Cf. the discussion of Phrynichus, *Ecl.* 178 ἀργύρεα and Moeris τ 22 →τριπλᾶ.

χρυcόκερωc

→δύcερωc

ψίαθοc

→μιαρόc

ψιμύθιον

Moer. ψ 3 ψιμύθιον διὰ τοῦ υ καὶ μακρῶc Ἀττικοί.

The gloss involves at once vowel quality and quantity. ψιμύθιον is attested with the variants ψίμυθοc, ψιμίθιον, ψιμούθιον; the variants with ‹ι› or ‹ου› are not attested in literary works, in which the usual spelling is ψιμύθιον, with either a long or a short ‹υ›. On the other hand, ψιμίθιον is the normal spelling in papyri since the Ptolemaic period: there the forms with ‹υ› are only sporadically attested (Mayser – Schmoll 1970: 82; Gignac 1976: 269). The word could be a loanword from Egyptian, variously adapted to Greek phonology[389].

The form ψιμύθιον prescribed by Moeris is actually the one found in Attic comedy (Ar. *Eccl.* 878, 929, 1072, *Pl.* 1064, fr. 332.4 K.–A., Amips. fr. 3 K.–A.) and at least in these instances ψιμύθιον is always at the end of the trimeter[390].

---

[389] Schwyzer 1939: 329; Chantraine (*DELG* s.v. ψίμυθοc) deems the etymology impossible to prove, Pre-Greek according to Beekes, *EDG*, s.v. ψίμυθοc.
[390] From this it follows that the quantity of the first syllable is not determined in Attic. This does not help our understanding of the late spellings ψιμμύθιον, ψημύθιον – cf. LSJ s.v. ψιμύθιον.

ψίμῦθος is attested with a short ῠ in an epigram attributed to Lucian (*AP* 11.408)[391], supporting the reality of the variant condemned by Moeris.

ψύα

Phryn. *Ecl.* 268 ψύα· οἱ μὲν ἁπλῶς ἁμαρτάνοντες διὰ τοῦ υ, οἱ δὲ διπλῇ ἁμαρτάνοντες ψοία· ἔστι δὲ καὶ τὸ ὄνομα πολὺ κίβδηλον. νεφρὸν οὖν λέγε.

Phrynichus disapproves of the term in the first place, even if used in what he considers to be its purest form, ψύα. In this respect, this is a synonymical gloss. ψύα and ψοία could represent two different stages in the history of a single word, if ψύα results from the monophthongisation of ψοία – the spelling of the latter in the *Ecloga* is uncertain too, the manuscripts read ψοά, ψοῖα, ψοιά. If Phrynichus wanted to write 'διὰ τοῦ υ' and gave no indication of the accent, it seems reasonable that the spellings he meant to contrast were actually ψύα and ψοία.

The quantity of the first vowel is attested as either short or long. In metrical texts, ψύα could be a corruption of ψοία. I could only find one certain instance of such a scansion, in the *Nosti*, fr. 11.2 ψύας ἔγχεϊ νύξε, the beginning of an hexameter. The word survives in one fragment of Attic New Comedy, Euphro (fr. 7 K.-A.) λοβός τίς ἐστι καὶ ψύαι καλούμεναι, an iambic trimeter with no resolutions, in which ψύαι can only be scanned [⏑–]. Current editorial practice, however, always treats the *hypsilon* as a short vowel (e.g. plural ψύαι, not *ψῦαι).

Both fragments come from Athenaeus (9.399a–c), who makes no explicit mention of the spelling or scansion of the word. What we read depends largely on the combination of choices of modern editors with the variability of the texts as they were available in the 2nd century AD. For instance, in the passage of Athenaeus that transmits both the fragment of the *Nosti* and that of Euphron, modern editors print constantly ψύα throughout. This may well be what Athenaeus had intended to write, and he, as Phryichus clearly states, must have preferred the spelling ψύα. But modern editions of Hippocrates have ψόα preponderantly, and only on one occasion editors print forms with ‹υ› (*Morb. Sacr.* 3.10 ψυήν, in Ionic). Athenaeus may have chosen to write forms in ‹υ› rather than ‹ου› following the same principles that guided Phrynichus. One wonders then whether ψύα is a later spelling in the *Nosti* and in Euphron, as transmitted by Athenaeus:

---

[391] Cf. Baldwin 1975: 331; some manuscripts ascribe the epigram to Lucillius (1st century AD). ψίμῦθος is also in *AP* 11.374, 6th century AD.

the two texts may have read originally ψοία and ψόα³⁹². Such an emendation in the *Nosti* would also solve the metrical problem posed by an otherwise unattested ψῦα, with a long first vowel.

This gloss of the *Ecloga* is the earliest surviving attestation of the uncertainty between the two spellings of the word, and the only one that explicity prescribes one of the two variants. ps.-Arcadius 118.11–15 mentions ψύα and ψοία as variants of ψύη, without further commentary; later lexicography vacillates between the two spellings: Hesychius has ψ 228 ψόα (also possibly at ψ 227), 262 ψυῖα, the *Suda* had both ψοία (ψ 142) and ψύα (ψ 145), Photius lemmatises ψόα (655.17 Porson, ψόας· ἢ ψοίας, ἢ ὅπη χρὴ καλεῖν, παρ' οὐδενὶ Ἀττικῶν εὗρον· οἱ δὲ παλαιοὶ γυμνασταὶ ἀλώπεκα προσαγορεύουσιν). The compiler of the *Suda* clearly thinks of the various spellings as being equivalent in the gloss to νότιος (ν 508). The lexica are not consistent in writing one form or the other, even though they seem to prefer ψόα in the explanations of the lemmata.

The various spellings of the word seem to coexist in Greek (cf. *EDG s.v.* ψόαι³⁹³), especially in later imperial times. ψόα can be explained as the outcome of ψοία through the reduction of prevocalic /oi/; it would support the view that older texts – like the *Nosti* and New Comedy – contained indeed ψοία rather than ψύα. The spelling ψόα seems to be normal in the *corpus Hippocraticum* and the LXX, all texts that certainly were not part of Phrynichus' canon. ψόα is also the spelling attested in Pollux (2.185, ψόαι³⁹⁴): as is usual in the *Onomasticon*, however, the spelling and the pronunciation of the word are left unexplained.

By recommending ψύα Phrynichus is recommending at the same time a more recent form, that depends on the monophthonigisation of /oi/, and possibly a textual variant that had crept into the text of some authors of his Attic canon. The variant with ⟨υ⟩ had already a place the in earliest examples of Atticist lexicography, one century before Phrynichus: Irenaeus (fr. 3, Reitzenstein 1896: 383) mentions ψύη as the Alexandrian form, and suggests an etymology from ψαύειν, and explanation in support of the spelling with *hypsilon* that survives in later literature (Meletius, *De natura homini, An. Ox.* 3 92.11).

Even if it is more likely that ψοία is the more ancient form, by Phrynichus' time ψοία and ψύα must have been interchangeable spellings; they corresponded to one and the same pronunciation /'psya/ in the idiolect of some speakers, but not the most educated. To Phrynichus, speakers who pronounced /'pso(j)a/

---

392 On prevocalic ⟨ου⟩ scanned as a short vowel word-internally cf. Arnott 2001.
393 Chantraine, *DELG s.v.* ψόαι, considers ψοία a reverse spelling for ψύα. This explanation clashes with Hellenistic ψόα, a form that must have arisen from /'psoja/, not /'psy(:)a/.
394 With the variants φύες A and ψοιαί FS.

must have sounded like they were hypercorrecting from /ˈpsya/, and moreover as if they were adopting a form that does not belong to Attic (which has νέφρον), but to the technical language of medicine, which on other occasions he was eager to mark as model of bad Greek.

ᾤδηκεν

Phryn. *Ecl.* 124 ᾤδηκεν, ᾠκοδόμηκεν διὰ τοῦ ω ἄριστα ἐρεῖς, ἀλλ'οὐ διὰ τῆς οι, οἴδηκεν, οἰκοδόμηκεν.
Moer. ω 2 ᾠδηκώς Ἀττικοί· οἰδηκώς Ἕλληνες.

The difference in pronunciation between presents in ‹οι› and their augmented/reduplicated tenses in ‹ωι› could only become greater if the present began with /y/ and not /oi/ anymore. When the change /oi/ > /y/ was accomplished, augmented tenses in /y(ː)/ instead of /ɔː(i)/ would become the most logical derivation. This is probably reflected in their spelling, that would retain the ‹οι› in all tenses[395].

ὦ τάν

Ael. D. ω 11 ὦ οὗτος, ὦ τάλαν καὶ ὦ μέλε· ταῦτα παρὰ τοῖς νεωτέροις ὑπὸ μόνων λέγεται γυναικῶν, παρὰ δὲ τοῖς παλαιοῖς καὶ ὑπ' ἀνδρῶν. πολλάκις δὲ καὶ ἐπὶ πλήθους φασὶ τὸ "ὦ τάν", ὡς παρὰ Νικοφῶντι (fr. 30 K.-A.). οἱ γὰρ Ἀττικοὶ τὴν πρώτην συλλαβὴν περισπῶσιν, τὴν δὲ δευτέραν βραχύνουσιν. καὶ βέλτιον· ἀδύνατον γὰρ εὑρεθῆναι μίαν λέξιν δύο ἔχουσαν περισπωμένας. Δίδυμος δὲ (p. 403, fr. 10 Schm.) τὸ πλῆρες εἶναί φησιν "ὦ ἐτάν" ἀγνοῶν, ὡς ἄρα τοῦ ἔτης ἡ κλητική ἐστιν ἔτα καὶ †Δωρικῶς ἔταν†.

The meaning of ὦ τάν 'oh my friend' may suggest that this is a form of ἔτης (vocative ἔτα): this is the interpretation we find in the *scholia vetera* to Plato[396]:

---

[395] It has been suggested that the scribes of the NT have changed ‹οι›, the more common Hellenistic spelling, to ‹ωι›, because of prescriptions like this one in the *Ecloga* (Elliott 1980: 9). In the NT verbs with ‹οι› are the less consistent in keeping the temporal augment of classical Attic, and in particular οἰκοδομεῖν seems to be often unaugmented (Gignac 1981: 239, Blass – Debrunner – Rehkopf 1975: § 67).
[396] Cf. Szemerényi 1987: 576–8 (Doric vocative of ἐτάϝων = ἔτης, 'kinsman'), Dickey 1996: 160; cf. Willi 2003: 233 (perhaps allegro form of τάλαν, as Kretschmer 1909: 58). A Doric etymology is

ὦ τάν (sic B: ὦ τᾶν TW). ὦ οὗτος, ὦ τάλαν, καὶ ὦ μέλε. ταῦτα παρὰ τοῖς νεωτέροις ὑπὸ μόνων λέγεται γυναικῶν, παρὰ δὲ τοῖς παλαιοῖς καὶ ὑπ' ἀνδρῶν. πολλάκις δὲ καὶ ἐπὶ πλήθους φασὶ τὸ ὦ τάν, ὡς παρὰ †Κτησιφῶντι. οἱ γὰρ Ἀττικοὶ τὴν πρώτην συλλαβὴν περισπῶσιν, τὴν δὲ δευτέραν βραχύνουσιν. καὶ βέλτιον· ἀδύνατον γὰρ εὑρεθῆναι μίαν λέξιν δύο ἔχουσαν περισπωμένας. Δίδυμος δὲ τὸ πλῆρες εἶναί φησιν ὦ ἔταν, ἀγνοῶν ὡς †ἀπὸ τοῦ ἔτης ἡ κλητική ἐστιν ἔτα, καὶ Δωρικῶς ἔταν.

ὦ τάν. ὦ οὗτος, ὦ τάλαν, and ὦ μέλε These words among the younger generation are only said by the women, but among the ancient also by men. And many times they say ὦ τάν referring to a group of people, as is the case in †Ctesiphon. In fact the Attic [speakers] accentuate the first syllable with a circumflex, and shorten the second. And it is better like this: in fact it is impossible to find one word that has two syllables with a circumflex. Didymos says that the full form is ἔταν, ignoring that †from ἔτης the vocative is ἔτα, and in Doric ἔταν.

sch. Pl. *Ap.* 25c (= sch. Pl. *Ep.* 319e)

The lexicographer (i.e. the source of the scholion) was clearly trying to reconcile the notions that ὦταν is a single word, that is has a circumflex on the first vowel, but also that is formed form τᾶν which was apparently known to have a long vowel (and a circumflex). The problem is apparent in the corrections of the very manuscripts transmitting this doctrine (cf. Valente to Tim. *Lex.* ω 7). The prescription is already in Apollonius Dyscolus:

τὰ εἰς αν λήγοντα ἐπιρρήματα ἐν μακρῷ ἐστὶ τῷ α, τάσει δὲ βαρείᾳ, ὡς ἔχει τὸ λίαν, ἄγαν, πέραν ... ἀλλ' οὐδὲ τὸ πάμπαν ἄλογον ἂν εἴη διὰ τὴν συστολὴν τοῦ α· ἅπαντα γὰρ τὰ ἐξ ὀνομάτων μεταλαμβανόμενα εἰς ἐπιρρηματικὴν σύνταξιν, τὴν φωνὴν τοῦ ὀνόματος φυλάσσει ... ὁ αὐτὸς λόγος παρακουλουθήσει, ὡς ἕνεκά γε τοῦ τύπου, καὶ ἐπὶ τοῦ ὠτᾶν, τὴν μὲν μακρότητα τοῦ α φυλάξαντος[397], οὐ μὴν τὴν τάσιν. καὶ κατ' ἄλλον δὲ λόγον ἐπιστάσεως ἔτυχε, καθὸ διτονεῖ.

Adverbs ending in αν have a long α, and they are barytones, like λίαν, ἄγαν, πέραν. And πάμπαν ought not be considered an exception because of the short α: because anything that is changed from nouns into an adverbial combination keeps the sound (φωνή) of the noun ... the same reasonment will follow, as far as regards the formation, also for ὠτᾶν, which retains the long quantity of the α, but not the accent. And for another reason it has received attention, in that is has a double accent.

A.D. *Adv.* [*GG* 2.1.1] 158.21–2, 26–159.1, 10–12

---

also discussed by A.D., *Adv.* [*GG* 2.1.1] 159.26–160.17, following the idea – that Apollonius traces to Didymus, and was refuted by Trypho (159.13, 15) – that ὠτᾶν is a contraction of ὦ ἐτάν, ἐτάν being a vocative of ἔτης (cf. also Schneider's commentary in *GG* 2.1.2 175–6).

[397] τοῦ τόνου, ⟨οὐ⟩ | φυλάξαν *GG* 2.1.1 159, I print the text as corrected by Schneider in his commentary *ad loc.* (*GG* 2.1.2 176).

The short vowel is entirely artificial, prescribed to justify the accentuation of uni-verbed ὤταν, which Apollonius treats as an adverb, and subsequently as one word, with the prosodical problems that it entails. Of course, it was apparent from metrical texts that the ‹α› was long (cf. e. g. Ar. *Eq.* 1036 etc.). If the pronunciation had any linguistic reality, it would become one more instance in which the a short – and not a long – vowel is a mark of good Attic (cf. Moer. υ 9 →ὑδαρέc).

VIII Concordances and indexes

Phonological traits involved in Atticist prescriptions

The following table includes all the entries discussed in the second part of this book. Next to each entry, an abbreviation signals the phonological trait that the entry involves, irrespectively of whether it is merely implied or openly addressed in the wording of the entry. For a list of technical terms see the next table.

The phonological traits are abbreviated as follows:

A:p Position of the accent (42 items[1] on a total of 180);
A:t Accent type (25 items);
B   Intial aspiration (breathing) (21 items);
G   Degemination (11 items);
T   Vowel timbre (43 items);
Q:d Vowel quantity: *dichrona* (45 items);
Q:s Vowel quantity: different spellings (36 items).

An asterisk in the last column marks possible hyperatticisms.

	A:p	A:t	B	G	T	Q:d	Q:s	Hyp.
ἄ, ἆ ἄ		A:t	B					
ἄγανος	A:p							
ἀγνοία	A:p					Q:d		
ἀγοράζειν				G		Q:d		
ἀγροῖκος	A:p	A:t						
ἀγυιᾶ		A:t				Q:d		
ἀδολέσχης					T	Q:d		
ἀείτης					T		Q:s	
ἄθρους	A:p	A:t	B					
ἄθυρμα			B					*
αἱματοπώτης							Q:s	
αἴτιαι	A:p	A:t						
αἰώρα					T			
ἄκρατον	A:p	A:t						

---

[1] Items include all the word(s) for which the entry prescribes a pronunciation or a spelling, not only the lemmata.

ἀκταινοῦν	A:p	A:t				
ἀληθές	A:p					
ἁλμυρός					Q:d	*
ἁλίεα					Q:d	
ἅλις			B			
ἁλοᾶν			B			
ἀλύειν			B			*
ἁλυκός				T		
ἄλυςις			B			
ἅμαξα			B			
ἀμίς			B			
ἀμπίςχες			B			
ἀμφορέα					Q:d	
ἀνάθημα					Q:s	
ἄναντες	A:p					
ἀναπηρία				T		
ἀνάπλεως					Q:s	
ἀναριχᾶςθαι			G			
ἀνεῖν					Q:d	
ἀνίλλειν	A:p	A:t	G	T		
ἀπηλιώτης			B			
ἀνύειν			B			
ἀνυπόδητος				T	Q:s	
ἀξιόχρεως					Q:s	
ἅπαν					Q:d	
ἀπαντικρύ					Q:d	
ἀπέδραν					Q:d	
ἀπέρατος					Q:d	
ἀπέςβηςε					Q:s	
ἄπεφθος			B			
ἀπηδές			B			

ἀπηθεῖν		B			
ἀπηλιώτης		B			
ἀπηχία		B			
ἀποκτινύναι				Q:d	
ἀποχρῆ	A:p	A:t			
ἆρα		A:t		Q:d	
ἄρκυες		B			
ἁρπαγή	A:p				
ἄρχων				Q:s	
ἀςμενώτερος				Q:s	
ἀςφόδελος	A:p				
ἄττα		B			
ἀτεχνῶς	A:p	A:t			
Ἀτρέα				Q:d	
αὐτοχειρίᾳ	A:p	A:t			
ἀφοῦ	A:p	A:t			
ἀχρεῖος	A:p				
βαδίζειν			?	Q:d	
βύβλινος			T		
βιβλία			T		
βοϊκός				Q:d	
βότρυς				Q:d	
γέλοιος	A:p	A:t			
γενέςθαι	A:p				
γήινος				Q:d	
γρῦ		A:t			
γρυλίζειν			G		
γρυμεῖα			T	Q:s	*
δανείζειν			T	Q:s	
δένδρα					
δεξαμενή	A:p				

διέτης	A:p				
Διονυσεῖον			T	Q:s	
δόχμη	A:p				
δύcερως	A:p				
δύω				Q:s	
ἐβουλόμην				Q:s	
ἔγγεια			T	Q:s	
Ἐλαία			T		
ἐπιτάδε	A:p				
ἐπιμέλου	A:p	A:t			
ἔπτυσχλοι			B		
εὔκλεια	A:p			Q:d	
εὑρέ	A:p				
εὕρεμα				Q:s	
εὐφυᾶ			T		
ἑωθώς			T		
ἦδος			B		
ἡδύνω				Q:s	
ἠθάς				Q:s	
ἤμελλον				Q:s	
ἡμίcειαν			T		
ἡμῳδία			T		
ἤνυστρον				Q:s	
Θαλῆς	A:p	A:t			
θεῶcαι			T		*
Θηcέῳ			T		*
ἱερεία	A:p	A:t		Q:d	
ἱκετεία				Q:s	
ἱππέα				Q:d	
ἱππέας				Q:d	
ἰσότης	A:p				

καρίς				Q:d	
κατάγειος			T		
κάταντες	A:p				
κεχρίσθαι			T	Q:d	
κλῆσαι			T		
κνημίς				Q:d	
κυδώνιον				Q:d	
κυνηγεττεῖν		G			
κυνοκέφαλλος		G		Q:d	
λαγώς					Q:s
λῆμα		G			
λητουργεῖν			T		
λιπόνεως					Q:s
μᾶζα	A:t	G		Q:d	
μανός				Q:d	*
μάντεων	A:p				
μιαρός			T		
μόλυβδος			T		
μυελός			T		
μύσταξ				Q:d	*
νεαλές				Q:d	
νεώς	A:p	A:t			
νῆστις			T		Q:s
νόμος		G			
ξῆναι			T		
ξυάλη			T		
ξυρεῖν	A:p				
ξυρόν				Q:d	*
οἰνοπώτης					Q:s
ὀπτάνιον	A:p		T		Q:s
ὄστρια			T		Q:s	*

ὄφλειν	A:p	A:t			
πάπυρος			Q:d		
πελαργός			Q:d		*
πένταχα	A:p				
πινακίς			Q:d		
πνῖγος			Q:d		*
πῶμα				Q:s	*
πυθοῦ	A:p				
πρωπέρυσι				Q:s	
πύελος		T			
ῥαφανίς			Q:d		
ῥοίδιον	A:p	T			
cάκκος		G			
cίαλον		T			
cτάχυc			Q:d		
cύνθημα				Q:s	
τητινόc	A:p				
τιμώρια	A:p				
τριπλᾶ		A:t	Q:d		
ὑάλινον		T			
ὕαλοc		T			
ὑδαρέc			Q:d		
ὑδροπωτεῖν				Q:s	
ὑδροπώτηc				Q:s	
ὑγίεια		T			
υἱέοc				Q:s	*
φαρμακόc			Q:d		
φιάλη		T			
φιλόγελωc	A:p				
φρούριον	A:p				
χαμᾶζε	A:p	A:t	Q:d		

χρέως				Q:s
χρυcᾶ	A:t			
χρυcόκερως	A:p			
ψίαθος			T	
ψιμύθιον			T	Q:d
ψύα			T	
ᾤδηκεν			T	Q:s
ὦ τάν	A:p	A:t		Q:s

Technical terms employed in the glosses

The columns in the following table list technical terms by groups (e.g. βαρύτονος, βαρυτόνως, βαρυτονεῖν are all listed in one column). In each column:
- verbs are listed in the present infinitive active (including participles, but not adjectives in -τέος or adverbs in -μένως);
- noun/adjectives in the nominative (gender unchanged);
- adverbs are unchanged.

Technical terms listed in the same row are not also necessary found in the same lexica, if the lemma in the table refers to more that one entry. Readers who wish to check the particular usage of one lexicon should refer to the commentary to the individual entries, where the full text of the lexica is reported.

	spelling prescriptions	ἀναγιγνώσκειν	βαρύτονος	βραχύς	γράφειν	δασύς	ἐκτείνειν	ἐκφέρειν
ἄ, ἄ ἄ						δασύνειν		
ἄγανος								
ἄγνοία							ἐκτείνειν	
ἀγοράζειν							ἐκτείνειν	
ἀγροῖκος								
ἀγυιά				βραχέως				
ἀδολέςχης					γράφειν, προςγράφειν		ἐκτείνειν	
ἄθρους						δασύνειν		
ἄθυρμα						δασέως		
αἱματοπώτης				βραχύς				ἐπεκτείν
αἴτιαι			βαρυτόνως					
αἰώρα	διά							
ἄκρατον			βαρυτόνως					
ἀκταινοῦν			βαρυτόνως					
ἀληθές								
ἀλιέα				βραχέως				
ἄλις								
ἀλμυρός							ἐκτεταμένως	
ἀλοᾶν	διά				γράφειν			
ἀλύειν						δασέως, δασύνειν		
ἄλυςις								
ἄμαξα						δασεία, δασέως		
ἀμίς						δασεία, δασέως		
ἀμπίςχες	διά					δασύνειν		ἐκφέρει
ἀμφορέα				βραχέως				
ἄναντες			βαρυτόνως					
ἀναπηρία	διά							
ἀνάπλεων	ἐν							
ἀναριχᾶςθαι	δυο				γράφειν			
ἀνεῖν							ἔκταςις	
ἀνίλλειν	διά							
ἀντήλιος	ἐν							
ἀνύειν						δασεία, δασέως		
ἀνυπόδητος	διά, ἐν							
ἀξιόχρεως	ἐν							
ἅπαν				βραχύνειν			ἐκτείνειν	
ἀπαντικρύ								
ἀπέδραν	διά			βραχεία			ἐκτείνειν	
ἀπέρατος							ἐκτείνειν	
ἀπέςβηςε	διά							
ἄπεφθος	διά					δασύνειν		ἐκφέρει

ειν	μακρός	ὀξύς	περισπᾶν	ποιεῖν	προφέρειν	συναλείφειν	συστέλλειν	τόνος	ψιλός
			περισπᾶν						ψιλοῦν
		ὀξεῖα							
	μακρόν	παροξύνειν			προφέρειν				
		προπαροξυτόνως προπερισπᾶν							
	μακρῶς								
						συναλείφειν			
		παροξύνειν	περισπᾶν						
									ψιλῶς
μηκύνειν									
		παροξυτόνως							
			περισπωμένως						
			περισπᾶν						
		ὀξυτόνως, προπαροξυτόνως							
	μακρῶς								
									ψιλοῦν
	μακρόν								
									ψιλοῦν
					προφέρειν				ψιλῶς
									ψιλοῦν
						συναλοιφή			ψιλῶς
						συναλοιφή			ψιλῶς
	μακρόν, μακρῶς								
		παροξύνειν	περισπᾶν						
									ψιλῶς
						συναλοιφή			ψιλῶς
							συστέλλειν		
	μακρόν								

	spelling prescriptions	ἀναγιγνώcκειν	βαρύτονοc	βραχύc	γράφειν	δαcύc	ἐκτείνειν	ἐκφέρειν
ἀπηδέc	διά					δαcύνειν		ἐκφέρειν
ἀπηθεῖν	διά					δαcύνειν		ἐκφέρειν
ἀπηλιώτηc	διά, ἐν					δαcύνειν		ἐκφέρειν
ἀπηχία	διά					δαcύνειν		ἐκφέρειν
ἀποκτινύναι	διά							
ἀποχρῆ			βαρυτόνωc					
ἆρα								
ἄρκυεc						δαcέωc		
ἁρπαγή		ἀναγινώcκειν	βαρυτόνωc					
ἄρχων	διά							
ἀcμενώτεροc	διά							
ἀcφόδελοc		ἀναγνωcτέον	βαρυτονεῖν					
ἀτεχνῶc			βαρυτόνωc					
Ἀτρέα								
ἄττα						δαcύνειν		
αὐτοχειρίᾳ								
ἀφοῦ								
ἀχρεῖοc			βαρυτόνωc					
βαδίζειν				βραχέωc				
βιβλία	διά							
βοϊκόc								
βότρυc				βραχέωc				
βύβλινοc	διχῶc							
γέλοιοc			βαρυτόνωc					
γενέcθαι								
γήινοc	διά							
γρῦ								
γρυλίζειν	εἷc, δύω							
γρυμεῖα	ἄνευ							
δανείζειν								
δένδρα								
δεξαμενή								
διέτηc			βαρύνουcιν					
Διονυcεῖον				βραχύνειν			ἐκτείνειν	
δόχμη								
δύcερωc								
δύω							ἔκταcιc	
ἐβουλόμην	διά							
ἔκπωμα								
ἔπηλιc	ἐν							
ἐπιμέλου								
ἐπιτάδε			βαρυτόνωc					
ἔπτυcχλοι								ἐκφέρει

	μακρός	ὀξύς	περισπᾶν	ποιεῖν	προφέρειν	συναλείφειν	συστέλλειν	τόνος	ψιλός
									ψιλῶς
			περισπωμένως						
ν	μακρῶς		περισπᾶν				συστολήν		
		ὀξυτόνως			προφέρειν				
		ὀξὺς, ὀξυτονεῖν, ὀξυτονητέον, προπαροξυτόνως						τόνος, ὁμοτόνως	
μακρόν, μακρῶς			περισπωμένως						
									ψιλοῦν
			περισπᾶν					τόνος	
		παροξύτονον						τόνος	
μακρῶς									
μακρόν									
μακρόν									
		προπαροξυτόνως	προπερισπω- μένως						
		παροξυτόνως			πρό{ς} ἐνεκτέον(?)				
ον									
			περισπωμένως						
					προφορά				
μακρόν				ποιεῖν					
								τόνος	
					προφέρειν			τόνος	
√		ὀξεῖα, ὀξύνειν							
√		προπαροξυτονεῖν							
√									
μακρά									
									ψιλῶς
		παροξυτόνως	περισπωμένως						

	spelling prescriptions	ἀναγιγνώσκειν	βαρύτονος	βραχύς	γράφειν	δασύς	ἐκτείνειν	ἐκφέρε•
εὔκλεία								
εὑρέ			βαρυτόνως	βραχεία				
εὕρημα	διά							
ἑωθώς	χωρίς							
ἧδος						δασύνειν		
ἠδυνόμην	διά							
ἤμελλον	διά							
ἡμίςεια	cύν							
ἡμωδία	διά							
ἤνυστρον								
Θαλῆς			βαρυτόνως					
θεῶςαι	ἐνδεία							
ἱερεία			βαρυτόνως	βραχέως				
ἱκετεία	διά							
ἱππέα				βραχέως				
ἱππέας				βραχέως				
ἰςότης								
καρίδα				βραχέως				
κατάγειος	διά							
κάταντες			βαρυτόνως					
κεχρίςθαι	διά				γραφή			
κλῆςαι								
κνημίς				βραχέως				
κυδώνιον				βραχέως				
κυνηγεττεῖν	διά							
κυνοκέφαλλος	διά							
λαγώς	διά							
λῆμα	διά							
λητουργεῖν	διά							
λιπόνεως								
μᾶζα			βαρυτόνως	βραχέως				
μανός							ἐκτείνειν	
μάντεων								
μιαρός	διά							
μόλυβδος	διά							
μυελός	διά							
μύςταξ				βραχέως				
νεαλές								
νεώς								
νῆςτις	διά							
ξῆναι	οὐκ ἔχειν							
ξυήλη								
ξυρεῖν								
ξυρόν				βραχέως				

	μακρός	ὀξύς	περισπᾶν	ποιεῖν	προφέρειν	συναλείφειν	συστέλλειν	τόνος	ψιλός
ιν									
	μακρά	παροξύνειν							
	μακρά	ὀξύνειν, ὀξυτόνως							
ιν									
			περισπωμένως						
	μακρῶc	ὀξυτόνως							
ιν									
	μακρόν, μακρῶc								
	μακρόν, μακρῶc								
		ὀξέως, ὀξυτόνως							
ιν									
ιν									
	μακρῶc		προπερισπω- μένως						
ιν									
		ὀξυτόνως							
ον									
	μακροῦ								
		ὀξυτόνως							
ιν									
			περισπωμένως						
	μακρῶc								

	spelling prescriptions	ἀναγιγνώσκειν	βαρύτονος	βραχύς	γράφειν	δασύς	ἐκτείνειν	ἐκφέρειν
οἰνοπώτης				βραχύς				ἐπεκτείν
ὀπάνιον				βραχύνειν				
ὄστρια	διά							
ὄφλειν								
πάπυρος				βραχέως				
πελαργός							ἐκτείνειν	
πένταχα			βαρυτόνως					
πινακίς				βραχέως				
πνῖγος				βραχέως, βραχύνειν			ἐκτείνειν	
πῶμα	διά, ἐν			βραχύς			ἐπεκτείνειν	
πρωπέρυσι	διά							
πύελος	διά							
πυθοῦ								
ῥαφανίς							ἐκτείνειν	
ῥοίδιον								
σάκκος	διά							
σίαλος	ἐν							
στάχυς				βραχέως				
σύνθημα	μετά							
τετρακέφαλος	διά							
τητινός								
τιμώρια								
τριπλᾶ				βραχέως				
ὑάλινος	διά							
ὕαλος	διά, ἐν							
ὑδαρές				βραχέως				
ὑδροπώτης				βραχύς				ἐπεκτείν
ὑδρωτεῖν	ἐν							
υἱέος	διά							
φαρμακός							ἐκτείνειν	
φιάλη	διά							
φιλόγελως								
φρούριον								
χαμᾶζε								
χρέως	διά							
χρυσᾶ								
χρυσόκερως								
ψίαθος	διά, ἐν							
ψιμύθιον	διά							
ψύα	διά							
ᾤδηκεν	διά							
ὦ τάν				βραχύνειν				

Technical terms employed in the glosses — 277

	μακρός	ὀξύς	περισπᾶν	ποιεῖν	προφέρειν	συναλείφειν	συστέλλειν	τόνος	ψιλός
	μηκύνειν								
		ὀξυτονεῖν							
	μακρόν								
		ὀξύνειν							
	μακρῶς								
							συστέλλειν		
	μακρῶς								
	μακράν, μηκύνω			ποιητέον					
			περισπᾶν						
							συστέλλειν		
	μακρόν, μακρῶς								
		ὀξυτόνως							
		παροξυτόνως							
	μακρῶς		περισπωμένως						
	μακρῶς μηκύνειν								
					προφέρειν				
		προπαροξυτονεῖν							
		ὀξεῖα							
			προπερισπᾶν						
			περισπᾶν						
		προπαροξυτονεῖν							
	μακρῶς								
			περισπᾶν						

IX Abbreviations and bibliography

1 Abbreviations; Atticist lexica

Atticist lexica are quoted according to the abbreviations of the list below. Where the editors did not number the glosses, the page and line numbers are given (with the exception of Philem[on], followed only by the page number when quoted from Cohn's edition). Whenever a comparison with editions other than the ones listed below has been necessary, these are quoted according to the general bibliography at the end of the volume. All other abbreviations are listed alphabetically in the general bibliography.

Ael. D.	*Aelii Dionysii Atticistae fragmenta*, ed. H. Erbse, in *Untersuchungen zu der Attizistischen Lexica* [Abhandlungen der Dt. Akad. d. Wiss. zu Berlin, Phil.-Hist. Kl. 1949, 2], Berlin [1949] 1950: pp. 95–151.
Amm.	*Ammonii qui dicitur liber De adfinium vocabulorum differentia*, ed. K. Nickau, Leipzig 1966.
Antiatt.	The Antiatticist, ed. S. Valente, Berlin – New York 2015 [= Valente 2015a].
exc. Vind.	*Excerpta ex ⟨Herodiani Technici⟩ Philetaero Vindoboniensia*, ed. U. Criscuolo 1972: 153–6.
Heren.	Herennius Philo, *De diversis verborum significationibus*, ed. V. Palmieri, Neaples 1988.
Heren. *De propr.*	Herennius Philo, *De propria dictione*, in Palmieri 1988, pp. 238–42.
Moer.	*Das attizistische Lexikon des Moeris*, ed. D.U. Hansen, Berlin – New York 1998.
Paus.	*Pausaniae Atticistae fragmenta*, ed. H. Erbse, in *Untersuchungen zu der Attizistischen Lexica* [Abhandlungen der Dt. Akad. d. Wiss. zu Berlin, Phil.-Hist. Kl. 1949, 2], Berlin [1949] 1950: pp 152–221.
Philem.	L. Cohn, "Der Atticist Philemon", *Philologus* [NF] 11 (1898): 353–67.
Philem. R.	Philemon, in R. Reitzenstein, *Geschichte der griechischen Etymologika*, Leipzig 1896: 392–6.
Philet.	*Le Philétaeros attribué a Hérodien*, ed. A. Dain, Paris 1954.
Phryn. *Ecl.*	*Die Ekloge des Phrynichos*, ed. E. Fischer, Berlin – New York 1974.
Phryn. *PS*	*Phrynichi sophistae Praeparatio sophistica*, ed. I. de Borries, Leipzig 1911.
Phryn. fr.	*Phrynichi sophistae fragmenta*, in Phryn. *PS* [= de Borries 1911], pp. 130–180.

Inscriptions are quoted according to the abbreviations of the Packhard Humanities Institute's on-line *Searchable Greek Inscriptions* project[1]. Greek and Roman are abbreviated according to the conventions of LSJ and the *Oxford Latin Dictionary* respectively. Where possible and relevant (in particular in the case of the scholia), the sigla of the manuscripts are quoted in brackets after the scholion number. All other abbreviations are listed in the bibliography in alphabetical order (Greek letters follow their Latin counterparts in transliteration).

---

[1] http://epigraphy.packhum.org/biblio#b3.

2 Bibliography

Adams, J. N., Janse, M., Swain, S. (eds.) 2002. *Bilingualism in Ancient Society. Language Contact and the Written Text*, Oxford.
Adams, J. N. 2003. *Bilingualism and the Latin Language*, Cambridge.
Adams, J. N. 2007. *The Regional Diversification of Latin*, Cambridge.
Adrados, F.R., Gangutia, E., Lopez Facal, J., Serrano Aybar, C. 1977. *Introducción a la lexicografía griega*, Madrid.
Allen, W. S. 1968¹. *Vox Graeca. A Guide to the Pronunciation of Classical Greek*, Cambridge.
Allen, W. S. 1973. *Accent and Rhythm*, Cambridge.
Allen, W. S. 1987a. *Vox Graeca. A Guide to the Pronunciation of Classical Greek*, 3rd ed., Cambridge.
Allen, W. S. 1987b. "*The Development of the Attic Vowel System: Conspiracy or Catastrophe?*", *Minos* N.S. 20–22 [Studies in Mycenaean and Classical Greek Presented to J. Chadwick]: 21–32.
Alpers, K. 1981. *Das attizistische Lexikon des Oros*, Berlin – New York.
Alpers, K. 1990. "Griechische Lexicographie in Antike and Mittelalter", in H.-A. Koch, A. Krup-Ebert (eds.), *Welt der Information: Wissen und Wissenvermittlung in Geschichte und Gegenwart*, Stuttgart.
Alpers, K. 1998. "Lexicographica minora", pp. 93–108 in Ch.-F. Collatz *et al.* (eds.) 1998, *Dissertatiunculae criticae. Festschrift für G. Ch. Hansen*, Würzburg.
An. B. = I. Bekker 1814–1821, *Anecdota Graeca*, Berlin.
An. Bach. = L. Bachmann 1828, *Anecdota Graeca*, Leipzig [repr. Hildesheim 1965].
Anderson, G. 1993. *The Second Sophistic: a Cultural Phenomenon in the Roman Empire*, London – New York.
An. Ox. = J. A. Cramer 1835–1837. *Anecdota Graeca e codicibus manuscriptis bibliothecarum Oxoniensium*, 4 vols., Oxford [repr. Amsterdam 1963].
Argyle, S. 1989. "A New Greek Grammarian", *CQ* 39: 524–35.
Arnott, W. G. 1989. "A Note on the Antiatticist (98.17 Bekker)", *Hermes* 117: 374–6.
Arnott, W. G. 2001. "Some Orthographical Problems in the Papyri of Later Comedy I: πο(ι)εῖν (along with Compounds and Congeners)", *ZPE* 134: 43–51.
Arrighetti, G. 1987. *Poeti, eruditi e biografi: momenti della riflessione dei Greci sulla letteratura*, Pisa.
Arrighetti, G. – M. Tulli 2006. *Esegesi letteraria e riflessione sulla lingua*, Pisa.
Assmann, E. 1908. "Zur Vorgeschichte von Kreta", *Philologus* 67: 161–201.
Atherton, C. 1993. *The Stoics on Ambiguity*, Cambridge.
Audollent, A. 1904. *Defixionum tabellae quotquot innotuerunt*, Paris.
Austin, C. 2012. *Menander. Eleven Plays*, Cambridge.
Bader, F. 1974. *Les suffixes grecs en – m*, Paris.
Baechle, N. 2007. *Metrical Constraint and the Interpretation of Style in Tragic Trimeter*, Lanham – Boulder – New York – Toronto – Plymouth.
Baldwin, B. 1975. "The Epigrams of Lucian", *Phoenix* 29: 311–35.
Bakker, E. J. 2010. *A Companion to the Ancient Greek Language*, Malden, MA – Oxford.
Barber, P. 2015. "Comparative Adjectives in Herodian", *Mnemosyne* 68: 234–53.
Bartoněk, A. 1966. *Development of the Long Vowel System in Ancient Greek Dialects*, Brno.
Batisti, R. 2014. *Ricerche sull'allungamento di compenso in greco antico*, [PhD diss.], Bologna.

Bechtel, *GD* = F. Bechtel, 1921–1924. *Die griechischen Dialekte*, 3 voll., Berlin.
Beck, R. 1973. "Length and monophthongization in Gothic", *IF* 78: 113–40.
Beck, J.-W. 1993. *Terentianus Maurus*, De Syllabis, Göttingen.
Beekes, R. S. P. et al. 1992. *Rekonstruktion und Relative Chronologie. Akten der VIII. Fachtagung der Indogermanischen Gesellschaft*, Innsbruck.
Bennett E. L. – J.-P. Olivier 1973. *The Pylos Tablets Transcribed*. Part I, Text and Notes, Rome.
Benveniste, É. 1935². *Origines de la formation des noms en indo-européen*, Paris.
Bergk, Th. 1872⁴. *Poetae Lyrici Graeci*, Leipzig.
Bethe, E. 1900. *Pollucis Onomasticon, libri I–V*, Leipzig [repr. Stuttgart 1966].
Bethe, E. 1931. *Pollucis Onomasticon, libri VI–X*, Leipzig [repr. Stuttgart 1967].
Biville, F. 1990. *Les emprunts du latin au grec. Approche phonétique, I, Introduction et consonantisme*, Louvain – Paris.
Biville, F. 1995. *Les emprunts du latin au grec. Approche phonétique, II, Vocalisme et conclusions*, Louvain – Paris.
Blass, F. 1888³. *Über die Aussprache des Griechischen*, Berlin.
Blass F. – A. Debrunner – R. W. Funk 1961. *A Greek Grammar of the New Testament and Other Early Christian Literature*, Cambridge.
Blass, F. – A. Debrunner – F. Rehkopf 1976. *Grammatik des neutestamentlichen Griechisch*, Göttingen.
Blaydes, F. 1880. *Aristophanis Lysistrata*, Halle.
Blevins, J. 2004. "Klamath sibilant degemination: implications of a recent sound change", *International Journal of American Linguistics* 70: 279–89.
Boissonade, J.F. 1819. *Herodiani partitiones*, London [repr. Amsterdam 1963].
Bompaire, J. 1958. *Lucien écrivain. Imitation et creation*, Paris.
Bompaire, J. 1998. *Lucien. Œuvres* II: opuscules 11–20, Paris.
Borret, M. 1967. *Origène. Contre Celse*, vol. I, Paris.
Bossi, F. – R. Tosi 1979–80. "Strutture lessicografiche greche", *BIFG* 5: 7–20.
Bowersock, G. W. 1969. *Greek Sophists in the Roman Empire*, Oxford.
Bowersock, G. W. (ed.) 1974. *Approaches to the Second Sophistic*, University Park, PA.
Bowie, E. 1982. "The importance of the sophists", *Yale Classical Studies* 27: 29–59.
Bowie, E. 2011. "Men from Mytilene", pp. 181–95 in Schmitz – Wiater (eds.) 2011.
Brandt, P. 1888. *Parodorum epicorum graecorum et Archestrati reliquiae*, Leipzig.
Braun, K. 1970. "Der Dipylon-Brunnen B₁", *MDAI(A)* 85: 129–269.
Brixhe, C. 1976. *Le dialecte grec de Pamphilie: documents et grammaire*, Paris.
Brixhe, C. 1987². *Essai sur le grec anatolien au debut de notre ère*, Nancy.
Brixhe, C. 1993. *La koiné grecque antique: I. Une langue introuvable?*, Nancy.
Browning, R. 1983². *Medieval and Modern Greek*, Cambridge.
Brugmann, K. 1910. "Adverbia aus dem mask. nom. sing. prädikativer Adjektiva", *IF* 27: 233–78.
Bubeník, V. 1983. *The Phonological Interpretation of Ancient Greek: A Pandialectal Analysis*, Toronto.
Bubeník, V. 1989. *Hellenistic and Roman Greece as a Sociolinguistic Area*, Amsterdam – Philadelphia.
Buck, C. D. 1955. *The Greek Dialects*, Chicago.
Bühler, W. 1972. "Zur Überlieferung des Lexikon des Ammonius", *Hermes* 100: 531–55.
Buresch, K. 1892. "Kritischer Brief über die falschen Sibyllinen", *Philologus* 51: 84–112.

Cassio, A. C. 1977. *Aristofane. Banchettanti* (Δαιταλῆς), *i frammenti*, Pisa.
Cassio, A. C. 1993. "La più antica iscrizione greca di Cuma e τίν(ν)υμαι in Omero", *Die Sprache* 35 [1991–1993]: 187–207.
Cassio, A. C. 1997. "Futuri dorici, dialetto di Siracusa e testo dei lirici greci", *AION (fil)* 19: 187–214 (= A. C. Cassio (ed.), *Katà Diálekton*. Atti del III Colloquio Internazionale di Dialettologia Greca).
Cassio, A. C. 1998. "La lingua greca come lingua univerale", pp. 991–1013 in Settis (ed.) 1998.
Castellani, A. 1973. *I più antichi testi italiani*, Bologna.
Castellani, A. 1992. "Ritorno all'Anonimo Romano", *Studi Linguistici Italiani* 18: 238–50.
Cavenaile, R. 1958. *Corpus papyrorum Latinarum*, Wiesbaden.
CEG = P.A. Hansen 1983. *Carmina Epigraphica Graeca*, Berlin – New York.
Chadwick, J. 1992. "The Thessalian Accent", *Glotta* 70: 2–14.
Champlin, E. 1980. *Fronto and Antonine Rome*, Cambridge, MA – London.
Chandler, H. W. 1881. *A practical introduction to Greek accentuation*, Oxford [repr. New Rochelle, NY, 1983].
Chantraine, P. 1927. *Histoire du parfait grec*, Paris.
Chantraine, P. 1933. *La formation des noms en grec ancien*, Paris [repr. 1979].
Chantraine, P. 1938. "First Examples of the Change of -αι to -ε in Greek", *The Link* 1: 7–10.
Chantraine, P. 1945. *Morphologie historique du grec*, Paris.
Chantraine, P. 1954. "À propos de l'adverbe ionien λείως, λέως", *Glotta* 33: 25–36.
Chantraine, P. *GH* = *Grammaire Homérique*, I: *Phonétique et morphologie* 1973^5, Paris.
Christidis, A. F. 2007. *A History of Ancient Greek. From the Beginnings to Late Antiquity*, Cambridge.
Clay, D. 1968. "The Aspiration of *ēthmós*", *Glotta* 46: 15–8.
Cohn, L. 1888a. "Unedirte Fragmente aus der atticistischen Litteratur", *RhM* 43: 405–18.
Cohn, L. 1888b. "Konstantin Paleokappa und Jakob Diassorinos", pp. 123–43 in *Philologische Anhandlungen Martin Hertz zum siebzigsten Geburtstage von ehemaligen Schülern dargebracht*, Berlin.
Cohn, L. 1898. "Der Atticist Philemon", *Philologus* NF 11: 353–67.
Collitz, H. – F. Bechtel 1884–1915. *Sammlung der Griechischen Dialekt-inschriften (SGDI)*, Göttingen.
Colomo, D. 2017. *Quantity Marks in Greek Prose Texts on Papyrus*, pp. 97–125 in G. Nocchi Macedo – M. C. Scappaticcio (eds.) 2017. *Signes dans les textes, textes sur les signes*, Liège.
Connolly, J. 2001. *Problems of the Past in Imperial Greek Education*, pp. 339–72 in Too (ed.) 2001.
Consani, C. 1993. "La koiné et les dialectes grecs dans la documentation linguistique et la réflexion métalinguistique des premiers siècles de notre ère", pp. 23–39 in Brixhe 1993.
Consani C. – L. Mucciante (eds.) 2001. *Norma e variazione nel diasistema greco*, Alessandria.
Corradi, M. 2006. *Protagora e l'ὀρθοέπεια nel* Cratilo *di Platone*, pp. 47–63 in Arrighetti – Tulli 2006.
Costas, P. S. 1936. *An Outline of the History of the Greek Language, with Particular Emphasis on the Koine and Subsequent Periods*, Chicago.

Cribiore, R. 2001. *Gymnastics of the mind: Greek education in Hellenistic and Roman Egypt*, Princeton.
Criscuolo, U. 1972. "Per la tradizione bizantina dei lessici atticisti", *Bollettino della badia greca di Grottaferrata*, NS 26: 143–56.
Crönert, W. 1903. *Memoria graeca Herculanensis cum titulis Aegypti papyrorum codicum denique testimoniis comparati.*, Leipzig [repr. 1963 Hildesheim].
Cunningham, I. C. 2003. *Synagoge. Cuvαγωγὴ λέξεων χρηcίμων*, Berlin – New York.
Dain, A. 1930. "La transcription des mots latins en grec dans les gloses nomiques", *Revue des Études Latines* 8: 92–113.
Dain, A. 1954. *Le Philétaeros attribué a Hérodien*, Paris.
Daly, L. W. 1983. *Iohannes Philoponus. De vocabulis quae diversum significatum exhibuint secundum differentiam accentus*, Philadelphia.
de Borries, J. 1911. *Phrynichi Sophistae Praeparatio Sophistica*, Leipzig.
de Lamberterie, Ch. 1990. *Les adjectives grecs en -uc*, Louvain-la-neuve.
De Lollis, C. 1885. "Dei raddoppiamenti postonici", *Studj di filologia romanza* 1: 407–24.
Debrunner, A. 1907. "Zu den konsonantischen *jo*-Präsentien im Griechischen", *IF* 21: 13–98; 201–76.
Debrunner, A. 1910. Rev. of Boisacq, *Dictionnaire étymologique de la langue grecque*, *Göttingische gelehrte Anzeigen* 172/2: 1–18.
Debrunner, A. 1932. "Bericht über die Literatur zur nachklassischen Griechisch aus den Jahren 1907–1929, I. Teil", *BJB [Jahresberichte über die Fortschritte der klassischenaltertumswissenschaft]* 236: 115–239.
Debrunner, A. 1933. "Bericht über die Literatur zur nachklassischen Griechisch aus den Jahren 1907–1929, II. Teil", *BJB [Jahresberichte über die Fortschritte der klassischenaltertumswissenschaft]* 240: 1–25.
Debrunner, A. 1954. "Das augment ἠ-", pp. 85–110 in [AAVV], 1954, *Festschrift für Friedrich Zucker zum 70. Geburtstage*, Berlin.
Debrunner, A. – O. Hoffmann 1953–1954. *Geschichte der griechischen Sprache*, vol 1 (1953), vol. 2 (1954), Berlin.
Degani, E. [H.] 1983. *Hipponax. Testimonia et Fragmenta*, Leipzig.
Degani, E. 1990. "Appunti per una nuova traduzione delle "Nuvole" di Aristofane", *Eikasmos* 1: 119–45.
Degani, E. 1995. "La lessicografia", in G. Cambiano *et all.* (eds.), *Lo spazio letterario della Grecia Antica*, II, *La ricezione del testo*, Rome, 505–27.
DELG = P. Chantraine 2009. *Dictionnaire étymologique de la langue grecque (nouv. éd.)*, Paris.
DELL = A. Ernout – A. Meillet 1959[4], *Dictionnaire étymologique de la langue latine. Histoire des mots*, Paris.
Denniston, J.D. 1954[2]. *The Greek Particles*, Oxford.
Devine, A. M. – L. D. Stephens 1985. "Stress in Greek?", *TAPhA* 115: 125–52.
Devine, A. M. – L. D. Stephens 1991. "The Phonetics of Ancient Greek Accent", *TAPhA* 121: 229–86.
Devine A. M. – L. D. Stephens 1994. *The Prosody of Greek Speech*, New York – Oxford.
Dewing, H. 1910. "The Origins of the Accent Prose Rhythm in Greek", *AJPh* 31: 312–28.
DGE = F. R. Adrados *et al.* 1980 – …, *Diccionario griego-español* , Madrid.
Dickey, E. 1996. *Greek Forms of Address*, Oxford.

Dickey, E. 2007. *Ancient Greek Scholarship*, New York – Oxford.
Dickey, E. 2012a. "Latin Loanwords in Greek: A Preliminary Analysis", pp. 57–70 in M. Leiwo, H. Halla-aho, M. Vierros (eds.) 2012, *Variation and Change in Greek and Latin*, Helsinki.
Dickey, E. 2012b. *The colloquia of the Hermeneumata Pseudodositheana*, Cambridge.
Dickey, E. 2014. "A Catalogue of Works Attributed to the Grammarian Herodian", *Classical Philology* 109: 325–45.
Dickey, E. 2015. "Teaching Latin to Greek speakers in antiquity", pp. 30–51 in E. P. Archibald, W. Brockliss, J. Gnoza (eds.) 2015, *Learning Latin and Greek from Antiquity to the Present* [*Yale Classical Studies* 37], Cambridge.
Diels, H. – W. Schubart 1905. *Anonymer Kommentar zu Platons Theaetet (Papyrus 9782) nebst drei bruchstucken philosophischen Inhalts (pap. n. 8; p. 9766. 9569)* [*Berliner Klassikertexte* II], Berlin.
Dienstbach, Ae. 1910. *De titulorum Priensis sonis*, Marburg.
Dieterich, K. 1898. *Untersuchungen zur Geschichte der griechischen Sprache von der hellenistischen Zeit bis zum 10. Jahrhundert n. Chr.*, Leipzig.
Diggle, J. 1981. *Studies in the text of Euripides*, Oxford.
Diggle, J. 2004. *Theophrastus, Characters*, Cambridge.
Dihle, A. 1954. "Die Anfänge der griechischen akzentuierenden Verskunst", *Hermes* 82: 182–99.
Dihle, A. 1989. *Die griechische und lateinische Literatur der Kaiserzeit. Von August bis Iustinian*, Munich.
Dittenberger, W. 1872. "Römische Namen in griechischen Inschriften und Literaturwerken", *Hermes* 6: 129–55; 281–313.
Domingo, E. 1975. *La responsión estrófica en Aristofanes*, Salamanca.
Douglas, A. E. 1956. "Cicero, Quintilian, and the Canon of Ten Attic Orators", *Mnemosyne* 9: 30–40.
Drerup, E. 1929. "Das Akzentuationprobleme im Greichischen", *Neophilologus* 14: 291–301.
Drettas, G. 1997. *Aspects pontiques*, Paris.
Drew-Bear, Th. 1972. "Some Greek Words. Part II", *Glotta* 50: 182–228.
Dunbar, N. 1995. *Aristophanes. Birds*, Oxford.
Dunst, G. 1973. "Aristomenes-Uhren in Samos", *Chiron* 3: 119–22.
Dyck, A. R. "Aelius Herodian: Recent Studies and Perspectives for Future Research", *ANRW* II 34.1: 772–94.
EAGLL = G. K. Giannakis et all. (eds.) 2013. *Encyclopedia of Ancient Greek Language and Linguistics*, Leiden – Boston.
Eckinger, Th. 1892. *Die Orthographie lateinischer Wörter in griechischen Inschriften*, Munich.
EDG = Beekes, R. S. P. 2010. *Etymological Dictionary of Greek*, with the assistance of L. van Beek, Leiden – Boston.
Ehrlich, H. 1912. *Untersuchungen zur griechischen Betonung*, Berlin.
Elliott, J. K. 1980. "Temporal Augment in Verbs with Initial Diphthong in the Greek New Testament", *Novum Testamentum*, 22: 1–11.
Erbì, M. 2006. "P.Oxy. 1012 come testo d'erudizione", pp. 127–57 in Arrighetti – Tulli 2006.
Erbse, H. 1950. *Untersuchungen zu den Attizistischen Lexica*, [*ADAW* Phil.-hist. Kl., Jg. 1949, nr. 2], Berlin.
Esposito, E. 2009. "Fragments of Greek lexicography in the papyri", *Trends in Classics* 1.2: 255–97.

EWAia= M. Mayrhofer, 1992. *Etymologisches Wörterbuch des Altindoarischen*, Heidelberg.
Fabricius, C. 1967. "Der Sprachliche Klassizismus der griechischen Kirchenväter", *Jahrbuch für Antike und Christientum* 10: 187–99.
Fewster, P. "Bilingualism in Roman Egypt", pp. 220–45 in Adams – Janse – Swain 2002.
Fischer, E. 1974. *Die Ekloge des Phrynichos*, Berlin – New York.
Foy, K. A. Ph. H. 1879. *Lautsystem der griechischen Vulgärsprache*, Leipzig.
Fraenkel, E. 1906. *Griechische Denominativa in ihrer geschichtlichen Entwicklung und Verbreitung*, Göttingen.
Fraenkel, E. 1910. *Geschichte der griechischen Nomina agentis auf -τήρ, -τωρ, -της (-τ-). Erster Teil*, Strassburg.
Fraenkel, E. 1912. *Geschichte der griechischen Nomina agentis auf -τήρ, -τωρ, -της (-τ-). Zweiter Teil*, Strassburg.
Friedrich, J. 1960^2. *Hethitisches Elementarbuch*, vol. 1, Heidelberg.
Gaisford, T. 1842. *Georgii Choerobosci epimerismi in Psalmos*, Oxford.
Garde, P. 1972. *Introduzione ad una teoria dell'accento* [transl. by G. R. Cardona], Rome.
Geldart W. M. – F. W. Hall 1906^2 – 1907. *Aristophanis Comoediae*, vol. 1 (1906^2), vol. 2 (1907), Oxford.
GEW = Frisk, H. 1970. *Griechisches etymologisches Wörterbuch*, Heidelberg.
GG = *Grammatici Graeci* (Leipzig 1867–1910), quoted as per the 1965 reprint (Hildesheim): 1.3: *Scholia in Dionysii Thracis Artem grammaticam*, ed. A. Hilgard 1901; 2.1.1: *Apollonii Dyscoli quae supersunt: Apollonii scripta minora*, ed. R. Schneider 1878; 2.1.2: *Apollonii Dyscoli quae supersunt: Commentarium criticum et exegeticum in Apollonii scripta minora*, R. Schneider 1902; 3.1: *Herodiani technici reliquiae*, ed. A. Lentz, 1867; 3.2: *Herodiani technici reliquiae*, ed. A. Lentz, 1868–70; 4.1: *Theodosii Alexandrini canones, Georgii Choerobosci scholia, Sophronii Patriarchae Alexandrini excerpta*, ed. A. Hilgard 1889; 4.2: *Theodosii Alexandrini canones, Georgii Choerobosci scholia, Sophronii Patriarchae Alexandrini excerpta*, ed. A. Hilgard 1894.
Gignac, F. Th. 1976. *A Grammar of the Greek Papyri of the Roman and Byzantine Period*, vol.1: *Phonology*, Milan.
Gignac, F. Th. 1981. *A Grammar of the Greek Papyri of the Roman and Byzantine Period*, vol.2: *Morphology*, Milan.
Glaser, O. 1894. *De ratione quae intercedit inter sermonem Polybii et eum qui in titulis saec. III, II, I apparet*, Giessen.
Goldhill, S. 2001a (ed.). *Being Greek under Rome. Cultural Identity, the Second Sophistic and the Development of Empire*, Cambridge.
Goldhill, S. 2001b. *Rhetoric and the Second Sophistic*, pp. 228–41 in Gunderson 2001.
Grammont, M. 1933. *Traité de phonétique*, Paris.
Grammont, M. 1948. *Phonétique du grec ancien*, Lyon.
Grenfell, B. P. 1896. *An Alexandrinian Erotic Fragment and Other Greek Papyri, Chiefly Ptolemaic*, Oxford.
Grenfell, B. P. – A. S. Hunt, 1897. *New Classical Fragments and Other Greek and Latin Papyri*, Oxford.
Griffith, R. D. 2007. "Μᾶζα, 'Barley-Cake'", *Glotta* 83: 83–8.
Grossardt, P. 2006. *Einführung, Übersetzung und Kommentar zum* Heroikos *von Flavius Philostrat*, Basel.

Guillén, L. R.-N. 2005. *Aelian and Atticism. Critical Notes on the text of* De Natura Animalium, *Classical Quarterly* 55: 455–62.
Gunderson, E. 2001. *The Cambridge Companion to Ancient Rhetoric*, Cambridge.
Gunnerson, W. C. 1905. *History of u- Stems in Greek*, Chicago.
Hansen, D. U. 1998. *Das attizistische Lexikon des Moeris*, Berlin – New York.
Harðarson, J. A. 1993. *Studien zum Urindogermanischen Wurzelaorist und dessen Vertretung im Indoiranischen und Griechischen*, Innsbruck.
Hatzidakis, G. N. 1892. *Einleitung in die neugriechische Grammatik*, Leipzig.
Hatzidakis, G. N. 1895. "Neugriechische Miszellen", *KZ* 33: 105–24.
Hatzidakis, G. N. 1896–1897. "Zur Synizesis im Neugriechischen", *KZ* 34: 108–25.
Hauser, K. 1916. *Grammatik der griechischen Inschriften Lykiens*, Basel.
Head, B. V. 1911². *Historia Numorum. A Manual of Greek Numismatics*, London.
Hermann, E. 1923. *Die Silbenbildung im Grechischen und in den andern indogermanischen Sprachen* [*KZ Ergänzungsheft* 2], Göttingen.
Hermann, G. 1812. *Draconis Stratonicensis liber de metris poeticis*, Leipzig.
Hiller von Gaertingen, F. 1906. *Inschriften von Priene*, unter Mitwirkung von C. Fredrich, H. von Prott, H. Schrader, Th. Wiegand und H. Winnefeld, Berlin.
Hinge, G. 2006. *Die Sprache Alkmans: Textgeschichte und Sprachgeschichte*, Wiesbaden.
Holwerda, D. 1977. *Scholia Vetera in Nubes* [= *Prolegomena de Comoedia. Scholia in Acharnenses, Equites, Nubes*, Fasc. III 1], Groningen.
Horrocks, G. 2010. *Greek: A History of the Language and its Speakers*, Chichester – Malden, MA.
Humbert, J. – L. Gernet, 1959. *Démosthène, Plaidoyers politiques* II, Paris.
Hunger, H. 1967. "Palimpsestfragmente aus Herodians Καθολικὴ προςῳδία, Buch 5–7, Cod. Vindob. Hist. gr. 10", *Jahrbuch der Österreichischen Byzantinistischen Gesellschaft* 16: 1–33.
Hunger, H. 1978. *Die Hochsprachliche Literatur der Byzantiner*, 2 vols., Munich.
Hunter, R. L. 1983. *A Study of Daphnis & Chloe*, Cambridge.
Hutchinson, G. O. 2015. "Appian the Artist: Rhythmic Prose and its literary implications", *CQ* 65: 788–806.
IEW = J. Pokorny, 1989². *Indogermanisches Etymologisches Wörterbuch*, 2 vols., Bern.
IG I³ = *Inscriptiones Atticae Euclidis anno anteriores, editio tertia, fasciculus I. Decreta et tabulae magistratum*, ed. D. Lewis, Berlin – New York 1981.
IG II² = *Inscriptiones Atticae Euclidis anno posteriores. Pars prima decreta continens, fasciculus alter, decreta anno 229/8 posteriora, accedunt leges sacrae*, ed. I. Kirchner, Berlin 1916.
Immerwahr, H. R. 1990. *Attic Script. A Survey*, Oxford.
Jakobson, R. 1931. "Die Betonung und ihre Rolle in dem Wort- und Syntagmaphonologie", pp. 117–36 in *Selected Writings* I, The Hague 1962.
James, P. 2008. "Atticistic Pronunciation in the Second Sophistic", paper read at the 139th APA annual meeting, Chicago 2008.
Jannacone, S. 1951. "Sur l'hypercorrection en grec [médievale et moderne]", *Neophilologus* 35: 151–61.
Jannaris, A. N. 1903. "The true meaning of the κοινή", *CR* [NS] 12: 93–6.
Janse, M. 2002. "Aspects of Bilingualism in the History of the Greek Language", pp. 332–90 in Adams – Janse – Swain 2002.

Jebb, R. C. 1893. *Oedipus Tyrannus*, Cambridge [repr. London 2004].
Jebb, R. C. 1900. *Oedipus Coloneus*, Cambridge [repr. London 2004].
Jones, C. P. 2007. "Three new letters of the Emperor Hadrian", *ZPE* 161: 145–56.
K.–A. = Kassel, R. – C. Austin, 1983–2001. *Poetae Comici Graeci*, Berlin – New York.
Kaibel, G. 1896. *Sophokles Elektra*, Leipzig.
Kapsomenos, S. G. 1953. "Das Griechische in Ägypten", *MusHelv* 10: 248–63.
Kapsomenos, S. G. 1972–1973. "Γλωccοϊcτορικὰ cχολία εἰc χωρία ἑλληνικῶν παπύρων ἐξ Αἰγύπτου", *Ἀθηνᾶ* 73–74: 551–74.
Kaster, R. 1988. *Guardians of the Language: The Grammarian and the Language in Late Antiquity*, Berkeley.
Katičić, R. 1959. "Le sort des consonnes géminées en grec", *ZAnt* 9: 129–32.
Keil, B. 1908. "Über Kleinasiatische Grabinschriften", *Hermes* 43: 522–77.
Kennedy, G. A. 2003. *Progymnasmata. Greek Textbooks of Prose Composition and Rhetoric*, Atlanta.
Kim, L. 2010. *The Literary Heritage as Language: Atticism and the Second Sophistic*, pp. 468–82 in Bakker 2010.
Kirchner, R. 2000. "Geminate inalterability and lenition", *Language* 76: 509–45.
Kirchner, R. 2001. *An Effort Based Approach to Consonant Lenition*, New York.
Knight, C. M. 1919. "The Change from the Ancient to the Modern Greek Accent", *The Journal of Philology* 35: 51–71.
Kramer, J. 1995. "κράβατος, κραβάτιον und Verwandtes in den Papyri", *Archiv für Papyrusforschung* 41: 205–16.
Kretschmer, P. 1890. "Der Übergang von der musikalischen zur ekspiratorischen Betonung im Griechischen", *KZ* 30: 591–600.
Kretschmer, P. 1899. "Zur griechischen Lautlehre", *KZ* 35: 603–8.
Kretschmer, P. 1901. *Die Entstehung der Koine* [Sitzungsberichte der Wiener Akademie, Phil.-Hist. Cl. 143, X Abhandlung].
Kretschmer, P. 1909. "Zur Geschichte der griechischen Dialekte", *Glotta* 1: 9–59.
Kretschmer, P. 1913. "Literaturbericht für das Jahr 1910", *Glotta* 4: 310–57.
Kretschmer, P. 1925, "Ersatz von Doppelmedia durch Doppeltenuis", *Glotta* 14: 31–3.
Kretschmer, P. 1930. "Altindisch *amba*", *KZ* 57: 251–5.
Kretschmer, P. 1932. "Literaturbericht für das Jahr 1929", *Glotta* 20: 218–56.
Kretschmer P. – E. Locker, 1944. *Rückläufiges Wörterbuch der griechischen Sprache*, Göttingen.
Kühner-Blass = R. Kühner, *Ausführliche Grammatik der griechischen Sprache, 1. Teil. Elementar- und Formenlehre*, in neuer Bearbeitung besorgt von Dr. Friedrich Blass. 1890–92, Hannover.
Kuryłowicz, J. 1968. *Indogermanische Grammatik, Band II, Akzent · Ablaut*, Heidelberg.
La Roche, J. 1897. "Zur griechischen und lateinischen Prosodie und Metrik", *Wiener Studien* 19: 1–14.
Lahiri, A. – T. Riad – H. Jacobs 1999. "Diachronic Prosody", pp. 335–422 in van der Hulst 1999.
Lallot, J. 1998[2]. *La grammaire de Denys le Thrace*, Paris.
Laminger-Pascher, G. 1973. *Index Grammaticus zu den griechischen Inschriften Kilikiens und Isauriens* I, Vienna.

Laminger-Pascher, G. 1974. *Index Grammaticus zu den griechischen Inschriften Kilikiens und Isauriens* II, Vienna.
Lasserre, F. 1969. "Trois nouvelles citations poetiques", *MusHelv* 26: 80–7.
Latte, K. 1915. "Zur Zeitbestimmung des Antiatticista", *Hermes* 50: 373–94 (= KS 612–30).
Latte, K. 1955. "Zur griechischen Wortforschung II", *Glotta* 34: 190–202.
Latte, K. 1968. *Kleine Schriften zu Religion, Recht, Literatur und Sprache der Griechen und Römer*. Hrsg. von O. Gigon, W. Buchwald und W. Kunkel, Munich.
Lavoie, L. M. 2001. *Consonant Strength. Phonological Patterns and Phonetic Manifestations*, New York – London.
LBG = E. Trapp *et all.* 1997 – , *Lexikon zur byzantinischen Gräzität: besonders des 9.- 12. Jahrhunderts*, Vienna.
Le Bas P. – W.H. Waddington, 1847–73. *Voyage archéologique en Grèce et Asie-Mineure*, 8 vols., Paris.
Lehrs, K. 1873. *Die Pindarscholien, eine kritische Untersuchung zur philologischen Quellenkunde. Nebst einem Anhange über den Heyschius Milesius und den falschen Philemon*, Leipzig.
Lehrs, K. 1882[3]. *De Aristarchi studiis Homericis*, Leipzig.
Lejeune, M. 1939. *Les adverbes grecques en -θεν*, Bordeaux.
Lejeune, M. 1940. "Sur l'accentuation attique de χαμᾶζε", *REA* 42: 227–33.
Lejeune, M. 1972. *Phonétique historique du mycénien et du grec ancien*, Paris.
Leumann, M. 1959. *Kleine Schriften*, Zürich – Stuttgart.
Leumann, M. 1977. *Lateinische Laut- und Formenlehre*, Munich.
LIV = H. Rix 2001. *Lexicon der indogermanischen Verben*, unter Leitung von H. Rix, Wiesbaden.
Lobeck, Ch. A. 1820. *Phrynichi Eclogae Nominum et Verborum Atticorum*, Leipzig.
Lobeck, Ch. A. 1837. *Paralipomena grammaticae graecae*, Leipzig.
Lobeck, Ch. A. 1843. *Pathologiae sermonis Graeci prolegomena*, Leipzig.
Longo, O. 1971. *Scholia Byzantina in Sophoclis Oedipum tyrannum*, Padua.
Lucidi, M. 1966. "L'origine del trisillabismo in greco", pp. 77–102 in *Saggi linguistici* [ed. W. Belardi = *AION* sez. linguistica, Quaderni IV], Neaples.
Lundquist, J. 2013. *Psilosis*, in *EAGLL*.
Lutz, C. E. 1947. *Musonius Rufus "The Roman Socrates"*, New Haven.
Maas, P. 1912. "Zu den neuen Klassikertexten der Oxyrh.-Pap. (vol. IX)", *Berliner philol. Wochenschr.* 32: 1075–77 [= Maas 1973: 44–7].
Maas, P. 1962. *Greek Metre* [Engl. transl. H. Lloyd-Jones], Oxford.
Maas, P. 1973. *Kleine Schriften*, Munich.
MacLeod, M. D. 1956. "Ἄν with the future in Lucian and the *Soloecist*", *CQ* 50: 102–11.
Mahlow, G. H. 1926. *Neue Wege durch die griechische Sprache und Dichtung*, Berlin.
Maidhof, A. 1912. *Zur Begriffbestimmung der Koine, besonders auf Grund des Attizisten Moeris* (= pp. 277–373 in von Schanz 1912), Würzburg.
Marek, Ch. 1993. *Stadt, Ära und Territorium in Pontus-Bithynia und Nord-Galatia*, Tübingen.
Marrou, H.-I. 1965[6]. *Histoire de l'éducation dans l'antiquité*, Paris.
Martinet, A. 1977[2]. *Elementi di linguistica generale* [*Éléments de linguistique générale*, 1969[4], transl. G. C. Lepschy], Rome–Bari.

Matthaios, S. 2013. "Pollux' Onomastikon im Kontext der attizistischen Lexikographie. Gruppen 'anonymer Sprecher' und ihre Stellung in der Sprachgeschichte und Stilistik", pp. 67–140 in Mauduit 2013.

Matthaios, S. 2015. "Zur Typologie des Publikums in der Zweiten Sophistik nach dem Zeugnis der Attizisten: ‚Zeigenossige' Sprechergruppen im *Onomasticon* des Pollux", pp. 286–313 in M. Tziatzi *et al.* 2015.

Matthaios S. – F. Montanari – A. Rengakos (eds.) 2008. *Ancient Scholarship and Grammar. Archetypes, Concepts and Contexts*, Berlin – New York.

Mauduit, Ch. 2013. *L'Onomasticon de Pollux: aspects culturels, rhétoriques et lexicographiques*, Lyon.

Mayser, E. 1923. *Grammatik der griechischen Papyri. I. Laut- und Wortlehre*, Berlin – Leipzig.

Mayser, E. 1926. *Grammatik der griechischen Papyri. II. Satzlehre. Analytischer Teil. Erste Hälfte*, Berlin – Leipzig.

Mayser, E. 1936. *Grammatik der griechischen Papyri aus der Ptolemäerzeit. I. Laut- und Wortlehre, III. Stammbildung*, Berlin – Leipzig.

Mayser, E. 1938. *Grammatik der griechischen Papyri aus der Ptolemäerzeit. I. Laut- und Wortlehre, II. Flexionslehre*, Berlin – Leipzig.

Mayser, E. – H. Schmoll 1970. *Grammatik der griechischen Papyri. I. Laut- und Wortlehre, I. Teil Einleitung und Lautlehre*, zweite auflage, bearbeitet von Hans Schmoll, Berlin und Leipzig.

McNelis, Ch. 2007. *Grammarians and Rhetoricians*, pp. 285–96 in Dominik, W. – J. Hall (eds.) 2007, *A Companion to Roman Rhetoric*, Malden, MA.

Meier-Brügger, M. 1992. "Relative Chronologie: Schlüsse aus dem griechischen Akzent", pp. 283–89 in Beekes *et al.* 1992.

Meißner, T. 2006. *S-stems Nouns and Adjektives in Greek and Proto-Indo-European*, Oxford.

Méndez Dosuna, J. V. 1988. "La evolución del diptongo οι en beocio", *Emerita*, 56: 25–35.

Méndez Dosuna, J. V. 1992. "⟨ΕΙ⟩ por ⟨Ε⟩ ante vocal en griego, el valor del signo ⟨h⟩ en Tespias y otras cuestiones", *Veleia* 8–9 [1991–1992]: 309–30.

Méndez Dosuna, J. V. 1993. "Metátesis de cantidad en jónico-ático y heracleota", *Emerita* 61: 95–134.

Méndez Dosuna, J. V. 2002. "Deconstructing 'height dissimilation' in Modern Greek", *Journal of Greek Linguistics* 3: 83–114.

Meyer, G. 1896³. *Griechische Grammatik*, Leipzig.

Miller, E. 1868. *Mélanges de littérature grecque: contenant un grand nombre de textes inédits*, Paris.

Montanari, *et al.* 2015 = F. Montanari – S. Matthaios – A. Rengakos (eds.) 2015. *Brill's Companion to Ancient Greek Scholarship*, Leiden – Boston.

Morgan, J. R. 2004. *Daphnis et Chloe*, Oxford.

Morgan, T. 1998. *Literate Education in the Hellenistic and Roman World*, Cambridge.

Morgan, T. 2007. *Rhetoric and Education*, pp. 303–19 in Worthington 2007.

Müller, H. 1989. "Ein helleinstisches Weihepigram aus Pergamon", *Chiron* 19: 499–553.

Nachmanson, E. 1903. *Laute und Formen der magnetischen Inschriften*, Uppsala.

Nagy, G. 2000. "Reading Greek Poetry Aloud: Evidence from the Bacchylides Papyri", *QUCC* NS 64: 7–24.

Nagy, G. 2010. "Language and Meter", pp. 370–87 in Bakker 2010.

Naechster, M. 1908. *De Pollucis et Phrynichi controversiis*, Leipzig.

Neil, R. A. 1901. *The Knights of Aristophanes*, Cambridge.
Nickau, K. 1966. *Ammonii qui dicitur liber De adfinium vocabulorum differentia*, Leipzig.
Niese, B. 1922. "Excerpta ex Eudemi codice Parisino n. 2635", *Philologus* suppl. 15: 145–60.
N. Pauly = H. Cancik, H. Schneider (hrsg.), 1996–2003. *Der Neue Pauly, Enzyklopädie der Antike*, Stuttgart – Weimar.
OLD = P. G. W. Glare (ed.), 2012. *Oxford Latin Dictionary* (2nd ed.), Oxford.
Osann, F. 1821. *Philemonis Grammaticis quae supersunt, vulgatis et emedatiora et auctiora*, Berlin.
Palmer, L. R. 1946. *A Grammar of the Post-Ptolemaic Papyri*, London.
Palmieri, V. 1988. *Herennius Philo. De diversis verborum significationibus*, Neaples.
Papageorgius, P. N. 1888. *Scholia in Sophoclis tragoedias vetera*, Leipzig.
Parker, L. P. E. 1997. *The Songs of Aristophanes*, Oxford.
Pearson, A. C. 1912. *Sophocles. Ajax*, Cambridge.
Penney, J. H. W. (ed.) 2004. *Indo-European Perspectives: Studies in Honour of Anna Morpurgo Davies*, Oxford.
Peppler, C. W. 1902. *Comic Terminations in Aristophanes and in the Comic Fragments. Part I: Diminutives, Character Names, Patronymics*, Baltimore.
Perale, M. 2010. "Un nuovo frammento della 'membrana Grafiana' (P.Vindob. G 29775: Demostene, *Sulla falsa ambasceria*, 16, 18)", *ZPE* 172: 22–6.
Peters, M. 1980. *Untersuchungen zur Vertretung der indogermanische Laryngale im Griechischen*, Vienna.
Petrounias, F.B. 2007. "Development in pronunciation during the Hellenistic period", pp. 599–609 in Christidis 2007.
Pierson, J. – G. A. Koch 1830. *Moeris Atticista. Lexicon Atticum. Aelius Herodianus. Philetaerus*, Leipzig: Lauffer [repr. 1969 Hildesheim – New York].
PG = *Patrologiae cursus completus* [...]. *Series Graeca* [...], accurante J.-P. Migne, I–CLXI, Parisiis 1857–1866.
PGL = G. W. H. Lampe, 1961. *A Patristic Greek Lexicon*, Oxford.
PMG = D.L. Page, 1962. *Poetae Melici Graeci*, Oxford.
PMGF = M. Davis, 1991. *Poetarum Melicorum Graecum Fragmenta*, Oxford.
Powell, J. U. 1925. *Collectanea Alexandrina: reliquiae minores poetarum graecorum aetatis ptolemaicae 323–146 A.C. epicorum, elegiacorum, lyricorum, ethicorum. Cum epimetris et indice nominum*, Oxford.
Prato, C. 1962. *I canti di Aristofane*, Roma.
Probert, Ph. 2001. Rev. of Devine–Stephens 1994, *CR* NS 51: 87–8.
Probert, Ph. 2003. *A New Short Guide to Acentuation of Ancient Greek*, London.
Probert, Ph. 2004. "Accentuation in Old Attic, Later Attic and Attic", pp. 277–91 in Penney 2004.
Probert, Ph. 2006. *Ancient Greek Accentuation*, Oxford.
Probert, Ph. 2008. "Attic Irregularities: Their Reinterpretation in the Light of Atticism", pp. 269–90 in Matthaios – Montanari – Rengakos 2008.
Probert, Ph. 2015. "Ancient Theory of Prosody", pp. 923–48 in Montanari – Matthaios – Rengakos 2015.
Rabe, H. 1892. "Lexicon Messanense de iota ascripto", *RhM* 47: 404–13.
RE = *Paulys Real-Encyclopädie der classischen Altertumswissenschaft*, neue bearb. von G. Wissowa *et all.*, Stuttgart 1894–1978.

Redard, G. 1949. *Les noms grecs en -ΤΗΣ -ΤΙΣ*, Paris.
Rehm B. – F. Paschke 1965. *Die griechischen christlichen Schriftsteller [Pseudo-Clementina]*, II. *Rekognitionen, in Rufins Übersetzung*, [Die griechischen christlichen Schriftsteller der ersten Jahrhunderte; Bd. 42, 51], Berlin.
Reitzenstein, R. 1896. *Geschichte der griechischen Etymologika: ein Beitrag zur Geschichte der Philologie in Alexandria und Byzanz*, Leipzig.
Ritschl, F. 1832. *Thomae Magistri sive Theoduli monachi ecloga vocum Atticarum*, Halle 1832 [repr. Hildesheim 1970].
Rosół, R. 2013. *Frühe semitische Lehnwörter im Griechischen*, Frankfurt.
Rothe, S. 1989. *Kommentar zu ausgewälten Sophistenviten des Philostratos*, Heidelberg.
Ruijgh, C. J. 1978. Rev. of Teodorsson 1974, *Mnemosyne* 31: 79–89.
Ruijgh, C. J. 1980. Rev. of Chantraine, *DELG, tome IV-1 P-Y, Lingua* 51: 86–94.
Ruijgh, C. J. 1985. "Problèmes de philologie mycenènne", *Minos* 19: 105–67 [= *SM* II: 43–105].
Ruijgh C. J. 1988. *Observations sur les traitements des laryngales en grec préhistorique*, pp. 443–69 in *Die Laryngaltheorie*, Heidelberg 1988 [=*SM* II: 308–34].
Ruijgh C. J. 2001. "Le *Spectacle des lettres*, comédie de Callias (Athénée X 453c–455b)", *Mnemosyne* 54: 257–335.
Ruijgh, C. J. 2004. "The Stative Value of the *PIE* Verbal Suffix *-eh_1-", pp. 48–64 in Penney 2004.
Ruijgh, *SM* II = C. J. Ruijgh, 1996. *Scripta minora II*, Amsterdam.
Ruipérez, M. 1956. "Esquisse d'une histoire du vocalisme grec", *Word* 12: 67–81.
Rüsch, E. 1914. *Grammatik der delphischen Inschriften*, I Band. *Lautlehre*, Berlin.
Russell, D. 1983. *Greek Declamation*, Cambridge.
Rutherford, I. 1998. *Canons of Style in the Antonine Age*, Oxford.
Rutherford, W. G. 1881. *The New Phrynichos*, London [repr. Hildesheim 1968].
Scheller, M. 1951. *Die Oxytonierung der griechischen Substantiva auf -ιᾱ*, Zürich.
Schmid, W. 1887–1897. *Der Attizismus in seinen Hauptvertretern*, I-V, Stuttgard [repr. Hildesheim 1964].
Schmidt, V. 1968. *Sprachliche Untersuchungen zu Herondas*, Berlin.
Schmidt M. 1860. Ἐπιτομὴ τῆς καθολικῆς προσῳδίας Ἡρῳδιανοῦ, Jena 1860 [repr. Olms 1983].
Schmitt, J. 1901. rev. of Thumb 1901, *IF Anz.* 12: 68–81.
Schmitt, R. 1970. *Die Nominalbildung in den Dichtungen des Kallimachos von Kyrene*, Wiesbaden.
Schmitz, Th. A. – N. Wiater 2011, *The Struggle for Identity. Greeks and their past in the First Century BCE*, Stuttgart.
Schönberger, O. 1989, *Longos. Hirtengeschichten von Daphnis und Chloe*, 3rd ed., Berlin.
Schulze, W. 1892. *Quaestiones Epicae*, Gütersloh: Bertelsmann [repr. Hildesheim 1967].
Schwyzer [Schweizer], E. 1898. *Grammatik der pergamenischen Inschriften*, Berlin.
Schwyzer, E. 1900. "Die Vulgärsprache der attischen Fluchtafeln", *Neue Jahrbücher für das klassische Altertum* 5: 244–62.
Schwyzer, E. 1902. *Die Weltsprachen des Altertums in ihrer geschichtlichen Stellung*, Berlin.
Schwyzer, E. 1933–1934. "Dissimilatorische Geminateauflösung als Folge von Übersteigerung, zunächst im Neugriechischen und im Spätaltgriechischen", *KZ* 61: 222–52.

Schwyzer, E. 1939. *Griechische Grammatik*. Auf den Grudlage von Karl Brugmanns griechischer Grammatik, Erster Band, Munich.
Schwyzer, E. – A. Debrunner 1950. *Griechische Grammatik*. Auf den Grudlage von Karl Brugmanns griechischer Grammatik, Zweiter Band, Munich.
Serrano Aybar, C. 1977. "Historia de la lexicografía griega antigua y medieval", pp. 61–106 in Adrados *et al*. 1977.
Settis, S. (ed.) 1998. *I Greci. Storia Cultura Arte Civiltà*, Turin.
SGO = R. Merkelbach – J. Stauber. 1998–2004 *Steinepigramme aus dem griechischen Osten*, Munich – Leipzig.
Shipp, G. P. 1972². *Studies in the Language of Homer*, Cambridge.
Sideras, A. 1971. *Aeschylus Homericus. Untersuchungen zu den Homerismen der aischyleischen Sprache*, Göttingen.
Slavova, M. 2004. *Phonology of the Greek Inscriptions in Bulgaria*, Stuttgart.
Slater, W. J. 1977. rev. of Fischer 1974, *Gnomon* 49: 258–62.
Solmsen, F. 1901. *Untersuchungen zur griechischen Laut- und Verslehre*, Strassburg.
Solmsen, F. 1903. "Zwei verdunkelte Zusammensetzungen mit ἀν- = ἀνά-", *IF* 13 [1902–1903]: 132–42.
Solmsen, F. 1909. *Beiträge zur griechischen Wortforschung*, Strassburg.
Sommerstein, A. H. 1981. *Aristophanes: Knights*, Warminster.
Sommerstein, A. H. 1991³. *Aristophanes: Clouds*, Warminster.
Sophocles, E. A. 1888. *Greek Lexicon of the Roman and Byzantine Periods*, New York.
Specht, F. 1932. "Beiträge zur griechischen Grammatik", *KZ* 59: 31–131.
Strobel, C. 2005. "The Lexicograher of the Second Sophistic as Collector of Words, Quotations and Knowledge", pp. 131–57 in Piccione, R. M. – M. Perkams (eds.), *Selecta Colligere*, Alessandria 2003.
Strobel, C. 2009. "The Lexica of the Second Sophistic: Safeguarding Atticism", pp. 93–107 in A. Georgakopoulou – M. Silk, in *Standard Lanugage and Language Standards: Greek, Past and Present*, London.
Sturtevant, E. H. 1940². *Pronunciation of Greek and Latin*, Philadelphia.
Su. = *Suidae Lexicon*, ed. A. Adler, Leipzig, 1928–1938.
Supplementum Hellenisticum = H. Lloyd-Jones, P. Parsons 1983. *Supplementum Hellenisticum*, Berlin – New York.
Swain, S. 1996. *Hellenism and Empire. Language, Classicism and Power in the Greek World AD 50–250*, Oxford.
Szemerényi, O. J. L. 1964. *Syncope in Greek and Indo-European and the Nature of Indo-European Accent*, Neaples.
Szemerényi, O. J. L. 1987. "*Etyma Graeca* VI (33–34)", *Minos* 20–22: 569–80.
Σ (and Σᵇ) = *Synagoge*. Συναγωγὴ λέξεων χρηςίμων, ed. I. C. Cunningham, Berlin–New York 2003 [= Cunningham 2003].
Σακαλῆς, Δ. Θ. 1977. "Ἀνάττικα καὶ ψευδαττικά στὸν Ἀττικιστή Μοίρη", Δωδώνη 6: 441–70.
Taillardat, J. – P. Roesch 1966. "L'inventaire sacré de Thespies. L'alphabet attique en Béotie", *Revue de Philologie* 40: 70–87.
Taylor, D.J. (ed.) 1987. *The History of Linguistics in the Classical Period*, Amsterdam.
Telò, M. 2007. *Eupolidis* Demi, Florence.
Teodorsson, S.-T. 1974. *The Phonemic System of the Attic Dialect 400–340 BC*, Göteborg – Lund.

Teodorsson, S.-T. 1977. *The Phonology of Ptolemaic Koiné*, Lund.
Teodorsson, S.-T. 1978. *The Phonology of Attic in the Hellenistic Period*, Uppsala.
Teodorsson, S.-T. 1979. "Phonological Variation in Classical Attic and the Development of Koine", *Glotta* 57: 61–75.
Teodorsson, S.-T. (ed.) 1990. *Greek and Latin Studies in Memory of Cajus Fabricius*, Göteborg.
Theodoridis, Ch. 1976. *Die Fragmente des Grammatikers Philoxenos*, Berlin – New York.
Theodoridis, Ch. 1982–. *Photii Patriarchae Lexicon*, vol. I A–Δ (1982), vol. II E–M (1998), vol. III N–Φ (2012) Berlin – New York.
ThGL = C. B. Hase *et al.* (eds.), 1831–1865³. H. Stephanus, *Thesaurus Graecae Linguae* [...], 9 voll., Paris.
Thom. Mag. / Thomas Magister = Ritschl 1832.
Threatte, L. 1969. "A Second Look at the Dual Pronunciation of Eta", *TAPhA* 100: 587–91.
Threatte, L. 1977. "Unmetrical Spellings in Attic Inscriptions", *CSCA* 10: 169–94.
Threatte, L.1980. *The Grammar of Attic Inscriptions*, I, Phonology, Berlin – New York.
Threatte, L. 1982. "The Alleged Conservatism of Attic Epigraphical Documents: A Different View", *Hesperia Suppl. XIX:* 148–56.
Threatte, L. 1996. *The Grammar of Attic Inscriptions*, II, Morphology, Berlin – New York.
Threatte, L. 2007. *The Inscribed Schist Fragments from the Athens Academy Excavations*, Athens.
Thumb, A. 1900. "Die griechische Lehnwörter im Armenischen. Beiträge zur Geschichte der Κοινή und des Mittelgriechischen", *ByzZ* 9: 388–452.
Thumb, A. 1901. *Die griechische Sprache im Zeitalter des Hellenismus*, Strassburg.
Thumb, A. 1908. Rev. of Mayser, *Grammatik der griechischen Papyri* [Ia. ed. 1906]", *Archiv für Papyrusforschung* 4: 487–95.
Thumb – Scherer 1959. A. Thumb, *Handbuch der griechischen Dialekte*, II. Teil, zweite erweiterte Auflage von A. Scherer, Heidelberg.
Tichy, E. 1983. *Onomatopoetische Verbalbildungen des Griechischen*, Vienna.
Tittmann, J. A. H. 1808. *Iohannis Zonarae Lexicon*, Leipzig.
TLL = *Thesaurus Linguae Latinae*, online, 1900 – ...
Too, Y. L. – N. Livingstone (eds.), 1998. *Pedagogy and Power: Rhetorics of Classical Learning*, Cambridge.
Too, Y. L. (ed.), 2001. *Education in Greek and Roman Antiquity*, Leiden – Boston.
Tosi, R. 1997. "Osservazioni sul rapporto tra Aristofane di Bisanzio e l'Antiatticista", pp. 171–7 in P. d'Alessandro (ed.), ΜΟΥΣΑ. *Scritti in onore di Giuseppe Morelli*, Bologna.
Tosi, R. 2003. "Recenti acquisizioni sulle metodologie lessicografiche", pp. 149–56 in P. Volpe Cacciatore (a c. di) *L'erudizione scolastico-grammaticale a Bisanzio*, Atti della VII Giornata di Studi Bizantini, Neaples.
Tosi, R. 2013. *Onomastique et lexicographie: Pollux et Phrynichos*, pp. 141–6 in Mauduit 2013.
Tosi, R. 2015. "Typology of Lexicographical Works", pp. 622–36 in Montanari *et al.* 2015.
TrGF = B. Snell – R. Kannicht – S. L Radt, 1971–2004. *Tragicorum Graecorum fragmenta*, Göttingen.
Tribulato, O. 2014. "'Not even Menander would use this word!': Perceptions of Menander's Language in Greek Lexicography", pp. 199–214 in A. H. Sommerstein (ed.), 2014. *Menander in Contexts*, New York.

Turner – Parsons 1987 = Turner, E. G. *Greek manuscripts of the ancient world,* 2nd ed., edited by P.J. Parsons, London.
Tziatzi, M. et al. (eds.) 2015. *Lemmata. Beiträge zum Gedenken an Christos Theodoridis,* Berlin-Boston.
Usher, S. 2010. "Eurhythmia in Isocrates", *CQ* 60: 82–95.
Väänänen, V. 1982³. *Introduzione al latino volgare,* a c. di A. Limentani; trad. di A. Grandesso Silvestri, Bologna.
Valckenaer, L. C. 1739. *De adfinium vocabulorum differentia,* Leiden.
Valckenaer, L. C. 1822. *Ammonius: De differentia adfinium vocabulorum* (2nd ed. of Valckenaer 1739), Leipzig.
Valente, S. 2013. "Osservazioni su cυνήθεια e χρῆcιc nell'*Onomastico* di Polluce", pp. 145–63 in Mauduit 2013.
Valente, S. 2015a. *The Antiatticista,* Berlin – New York 2015.
Valente, S. 2015b. "Orthography", pp. 949–77 in Montanari et al. 2015.
Valiavitcharska, V. 2013. *Rhetoric and Rhythm in Byzantium: the Sound of Persuasion,* Cambridge – New York.
van der Hulst, H. (ed.) 1999. *Word Prosodic Systems in the Languages of Europe,* Berlin – New York.
van der Valk, M. 1955. "A Few Observations on the Atticistic Lexica", *Mnemosyne* [NS IV] 8: 207–18.
van Leeuwen, J. F. 1897. *Aristophanis Nubes,* Leiden.
van Velsen, A. 1853. *Tryphonis grammatici alexandrini Fragmenta* Berlin [repr. Amsterdam, 1965].
Vatri, A. 2016. "Between Song and Prose: the Meaning(s) of *Harmonia* in Aristotle's *Rhetoric* and *Poetics*", *Rhetorica* 34: 372–92.
Veitch, W. 1887. *Greek Verbs Irregular and Defective: Their Forms, Meaning and Quantity Embracing all the Tenses used by the Greek Writers, with References to the Passages in which they are found,* new ed., Oxford.
Vendryes, J. 1906. "L'accent de ἔγωγε et la loi des propérispomènes en attique", *MSL* 13 [1905–1906]: 218–24.
Vendryes, J. 1945². *Traité d'accentuation grecque,* Paris.
Versteegh, K. 1987. "Latinitas, Hellenismos, 'Arabiyya", pp. 251–74 in Taylor 1987.
Vessella, C. 2012. "Reconstructing Phonologies of Dead Languages: The Case of Greek ⟨η⟩", *RSO* 84 (2011): 257–71.
Viscidi, F. 1944. *I prestiti latini nel greco antico e bizantino,* Florence.
von Schanz, M., (ed.) 1912. *Beiträge zur historischen Syntax der griechischen Sprache, XX (= Festgabe für M. von Schanz),* Würzburg.
Wackernagel, J. 1909. "Attische Vorstufen des Itazismus", *IF* 25: 326–37, [= *KS* II: 1022–33].
Wackernagel, J. 1916. *Sprachliche Untersuchungen zu Homer,* Göttingen.
Wackernagel, J. *KS* = Wackernagel, Jacob, *Kleine Schriften,* 3 vols., Göttingen 1953 [=1969²] (vols. I, II), 1979 (vol. III).
West, M. L. 1968, "Notes on Two Newly-Discovered Fragments of Greek Authors", *Maia* 20: 195–205.
Wentzel, G. 1895. "Zu den Atticistischen Glossen in dem Lexicon des Photios", *Hermes* 30: 367–84.
Whitmarsh, T. 2001. *Greek Literature and the Roman Empire: The Politics of Imitation,* Oxford.

Whitmarsh, T. 2005. *The Second Sophistic* [Greece and Rome, New Surveys in the Classics, 35], Oxford.
Wifstrand, A. 1967 [1957]. *Die alte Kirche und die griechische Bildung* [= *Fornkyrkan och den grekiska bildningen*, trasl. R. Mautner 1967], Bern – Munich.
Willi, A. 2003. *The Languages of Aristophanes. Aspects of Linguistic Variation in Classical Greek*, Oxford.
Willi, A. 2008. *Sikelismos: Sprache, Literatur und Gesellschaft im griechischen Sizilien (8.–5. Jh. v. Chr.)*, Basel.
Wilson, N. G. 1997. *Aelian. Historical Miscellany*, Cambridge, MA – London.
Wilson, N. G. 2007. *Aristophanis Fabulae*, Oxford.
Winterbottom, M. 2011. "On Ancient Prose Rhythm: the Story of the Dichoreus", pp. 262–76 in D. Obbink and R. Rutherford, *Culture in Pieces. Essays on Ancient Texts in Honour of Peter Parsons*, Oxford.
Worthington, I. (ed.) 2007. *A Companion to Greek Rhetoric*, Malden, MA – Oxford.
Wright, W. C. 1921. *Philostratus and Eunapius. The Lives of the Sophists*, [Loeb Classical Library 134], Cambridge, MA – London.
Wunder, E. 1855. *Sophocles, with Annotations, Introduction, etc.*, London.
Xenis, G. 2015. *Iohannes Alexandrinus. Praecepta tonica*. Berlin – Munich – Boston.

Index locorum

Aelian		ς 15	29
VH		υ 1	63, 226
1.18	235	φ 2	89, 91, 93, 253
Aelius Dionysius		χ 3	34, 91, 114, 221, 254
α 1	97, 102, 122	χ 17	78, 255
α 2	102, 122	ω 11	93, 98, 260
α 15	122 f.	Aeschines	
α 21	91, 97, 124	*In Ctesiph.*	
α 46	102, 131	215	167
α 47	102 f., 120, 132	Aeschylus	
α 53	30, 32, 78 f., 245	*Eumenides*	
α *59	53, 80, 134	36	137
α 81	102, 120, 141	*Prometheus*	
α 98	102 f., 120, 142–4, 168	206	193
α 150	102, 154	363	176
α 151	78, 149, 192	1076–9	162
α 155	91, 93, 157	*Septem contra Th.*	
α 157	102, 165, 168	685	207
α 175	168, 182	*Supplices*	
α 191	100, 171, 182	1047–9	162
α 193	102, 172	Alcaeus	
β 19	60, 178	fr. 338.5	106
γ 4	100, 176, 181 f., 210	Alcman	
δ 6	187	fr. 34	130
δ 23	100, 188	Alexis	
δ 30	100, 190	fr. 25.6	197
δ 31	79, 93, 192	fr. 115	236
ε 10	79, 202	fr. 158	197
ε 30	197	Amipsias	
ε 48	165	fr. 3	257
ε 71	124, 199	fr. 17	218
ε 85	50, 201	Ammonius	
ζ 3–5	115	*De adfinium vocabulorum differentia*	
η 3	102, 202	6	31, 100, 125
η 4	163, 202	26	31, 138
κ 17	180	27	141
κ 29	62, 213	73	168 f.
μ 24	60, 228	74	167
ξ 2	226, 233	81	171
ο 44	237	84	172
π 9	174	86	173
ρ 12	237	119	176, 181, 210
ς 3	247	125	58
ς 4	116, 247	165	24

273	24, 58	v 14	117, 230 f.
293	148	v 15	231
299	58, 219	c 11	247
300	24, 58, 220	Antipater	
332	229	AP 6.249.2	see AP
399	245	Antiphanes	
435	181	fr. 46.4	229
436	23	AP	
449	80, 174	6	
477	189	249.2	238
506	185	258	141
521	63	9	
suppl.		77, 142, 313, 327, 356, 364, 770	245
5	147	11	
An. Ox.		374	258
περὶ τῆϲ αι διφθόγγου		403	245
An. Ox. 2 315–8	59	408	258
περὶ διχρόνων		436	7
An. Ox. 3 291.9–12	196	12	
περὶ ποϲότητοϲ		50	245
An. Ox. 2 283–330	59, 189	16	
An. B.		89, 333	245
383	140	Apollonius Dyscolus	
An. Bach.		*Adv.*	
122.8–11	256	GG 2.1.1 158.21–2, 158.26–159.1,	
Anacreon		10–12	261
fr. 29a	124	GG 2.1.1 158.26–159.9	157, 261
Anacreontea		GG 2.1.1 159.26–160.17	261
32.4–5	237	GG 2.1.1 160.19–22	138
Ananius		GG 2.1.1 166.24–6	94, 142, 224, 241
fr. 5.5	218	GG 2.1.1 166.28–9	179
Anaxandrides		GG 2.1.1 187.20	254
fr. 23, 28, 38	215	GG 2.1.1 187.20–1	94
Anon. Rhet. Spengel		Apollonius Sophista	
[I] 322.27–9	3	*Lexicon Homericum*	
Anthologia Graeca see AP		9.10–11	130
Anthologia Palatina see AP		Araros	
Antiatticista		fr. 8.2–4	215
α 26	125	fr. 12	205
α 28	57, 148	fr. 16	201
α 118	155	[Arcadius]	
δ 33	188	30.1–4	210
η 5	18, 197	33.18–20	165
θ 13	50, 206	46.12–13	131
θ 20	50, 205	62.3–4	171
κ 71	80, 92 f., 208, 215	81.18–20	99
μ 37	18, 91, 93, 120, 229	99.25–100.1	175

107.12–15	192	502	248
109.9	207	878, 929	257
116.16–18	169	1037	170
118.11–15	259	1072	257
134.7–10	175	*Equites*	
134.24–6	138 f.	198, 208	246
135.19–21	212	300	94
137.10–11, 138.3–5	254	356	205
152.21–153.4	133	416	217
170.16–17	244	551 ff.	140
196.14–19	242 f.	584	244
198.3	167	823	229
199.20–23	102, 165	1036	262
206.20–207.1	98, 184	1382	216
208.11–13	254	*Lysistrata*	
211.9–10	85	403	139
222.3–5	180	1109	124
222.15–17	164	1209	248
223.1–3	131	885–6	122
223.9–10	143	*Nubes*	
224.4–6	141	3	161
Archestratus		30	255
fr. 7	236	39	256
fr. 26.2	215	96	240
Archippus		350	195
fr. 55	201	443	256
[Aristides]		567	140
Ars Rhetorica		580	63
2.10.1	15	599	140
Aristophanes		630	173
Acharnenses		768	227
74	226 f.	841	138
732	221	872–3	50 f.
745	248	981, 1083	215
746	184 f.	1480, 1485	130
763	229	*Pax*	
822	248	70	150
998	158	525	240
Aves		*Plutus*	
603	252	307	184
604	207, 252	493	158
1001	240	544	215
1091	239	668	162
1233	127	1064	257
1603	167	*Ranae*	
Ecclesiazusae		122	240
65	235	567	228

840	138	Rhet.		
1016	240	1403b		84
1147	194	1413b		161
1248	244	fragmenta		
Thesmophoriazusae		fr. 74		155
489	127, 129	frr. 589, 590		231
968	129, 201	Athenaeus		
Vespae		3.49e		253
79	246	3.92d		236
255	162	3.92e-f		236
631ff.	140	3.94c		94
875	127	3.94f		163
1467	124	3.105d-106e		215
fragmenta		6.261d		192
fr. 111.1	179	9.376e		207
fr. 130	189	9.399a-c		258
fr. *131	140	9.403d		124
fr. 238	124	10.450a		217
fr. 296	168	Ausonius		
fr. 308	151	Technopaegnion		
fr. 332	235	14.3–4		56
fr. 332.4	257	Basilus of Caesarea		
fr. 332.10	180	Hom. In Hexaemer.		
fr. 378	229	9.5.21		205
fr. 460	148	Bolus		
fr. 519	159	Physica et mystica		
fr. 581.1	180	2.49.6		147
frr. 617, 618	173	Callimachus		
fr. 642	131	Ep. 5.2		147
fr. 653	143	fr. 1.33		122
fr. 959	190	fr. 178.20		245
Aristophanes Byzantinus		fr. 260.61		226
fr. 347	196	Cercidas		
fr. 408	131	17.27		130
Aristoteles		Choeroboscus		
APr.		An. B. 704.28		102
44b	176	An. Ox. 2		
HA		174.32–4		196
535b	185	183.31–33		179
624a	150	214.5–8		196
Metaph.		219.10–17		206
993a	178	269.23		209
Oec.		Epimerismi in Psalmos 5.20–23		196
1353a	160	GG 4.1		
Poet.		153.27ff.		205
1458b	176	167.37–168.10		189
		216.8–13		145

Index locorum — 299

252.10–30	145	Cyrillus		
347.35–348.2	149	ευφ 3		200
GG 4.2		Demosthenes and *corpus Demosthenicum*		
137.22	183	1.13		106
140.20–31	244	19.304		173
140.25–26	245	21.51		126 f.
226.12–17	182	35.15, 41.12		109
246.3 ff.	243	40.23		253
246.10–12	244	42.6		141
255.16–25	244	43.40, 43.73, 43.77		253
403.16–23	134	48.12, 13		247
403.32–404.4	133	48.18		256
Chrysippus		Didymus Caecus		
fr. 177.7	155	*Fragm. In Psalmos*		
Cicero		187.16		165
ad Att.		PG 39		
13.22.1	171	868.53		139
Fin.		Didymus Chalcenterus		
3.15	137	fr. 10		260
Clemens of Alexandria		Dio Cassius		
Paed.		*Hist. Rom.*		
2.10	171	36.45.2		171
2.10bis.112.3.3	156	Dio Cassius (Xiphilinus)		
95.1	171	S 277.27, S 322.1		156
Stromata		Dio Chrysostom		
3.6.53.5.3	156	7.74		184
[Clemens of Alexandria]		31.143, 31.153		237
Recognitiones 9.22.5	156	Diomedes		
Comica adespota		*comm. in D. Thrac.*		
fr. *200	131	GG 1.3 22.16		87
fr. 256	252	Dionysius Halicarnassensis		
fr. 258	125	*Comp.* 15		163
fr. 519	233	[Dionysius Halicarnassensis]		
fr. 1032.5	207	*Ars Rhetorica*		
Corinna		9, p. 345.21		187
fr. 36	225	Dionysius Thrax		
Cratinus		*Ars Grammatica (Techne)*		
fr. 41	204	1.4		84
fr. 179	148	2.1–10		83 f.
fr. 256	122	3		84, 87
fr. 319	246	6.25–30		102
fr. 328	255	Diphilus		
fr. 466	218	fr. 128		93, 185
Ctesias		Dosiades		
FGrHist		*Ara* 5		130
F 15, F 45 h	247	Empedocles		
		fr. 75.1		223

Epicharmus
- fr. 18 — 227
- fr. 40.3 — 236
- frr. 51, 53 — 218
- fr. 107 — 155
- fr. 134 — 231
- fr. 185 — 223
- fr. 209 — 227

Epimerismi Homerici
- An. Ox. 2 374.32–375.13 — 194

Epimerismi Homerici (Dyck)
- α 100 — 131
- α 271 — 123
- μ 64 — 188
- π 144 — 249

Eratosthenes
- fr. 22 — 173
- fr. 47 — 124, 199

Etymologicum Genuinum
- α 1189 — 168
- α 1577 — 167

Etymologicum Gudianum
- α 199.1 — 168
- γ 303 — 182
- γ 306.16 — 23
- γ 323.25 — 186
- ε 531.2 — 168

Etymologicum Magnum
- 116.17 — 149
- 128.9 — 167
- 144.9 — 168
- 190.6 — 145
- 224.40–4 — 181
- 227.52 — 23
- 431.5 — 181
- 737.25 — 177
- 814.40 — 213

Eubulus
- fr. 57.4 — 242
- fr. 78 — 215
- fr. 106.10 — 217
- fr. 110 — 215
- fr. 112 — 229

Eudemus
- cod. Par. 2635
  - fol. 2b, 14–15 — 123

Euphro
- fr. 7 — 258

Eupolis
- fr. 2 — 215
- fr. 52 — 143
- fr. 120 — 215
- fr. 339 — 168

Euripides
- *Andromache*
  - 545 — 145
- *Bacchae*
  - 528 — 94
  - 1114 — 207
- *Cyclops*
  - 33 — 169
- *Electra*
  - 1215 — 180
- *Hecuba*
  - 752 — 194
- *Hercules Furens*
  - 4–5 — 180
- *Iphigenia Aulidensis*
  - 1341 — 145
  - 1626 — 244
- *Medea*
  - 299 — 175
  - 661 — 213
- *Orestes*
  - 235 — 252
  - 1230 — 244
- *fragmenta*
  - fr. 223.123 — 187
  - fr. 370.97 — 208
  - frr. 484.5, 782 — 187
  - fr. 1011 — 256

Eustathius
- 251.39 — 132
- 527.9 — 158
- 588.12 — 248
- 614.24–8 — 135
- 801.57 — 151
- 855.21 — 122
- 906.50 — 182
- 940.16–19 — 248
- 1323.16 — 158
- 1353.8 — 217
- 1387.5 — 131

1387.9	144	172	189
1417.15–24	202	*De propria dictione*	
1433.48	188	13	99, 169
1480.11–13	202	23	116, 219
1562.36	165	Hermogenes	
1574.21	130	*Id.*	
1664.3, 1763.61	122	1.6	49
1835.43	180	1.6.247–248	65
1944.9	197	Herodian	

exc. Vind. see Philetaerus
Festus
  fr. e cod. Farn.

		fr. (Hunger)	
		9	222 f.
		16	131
176.35–177.1	231	28	222 f.

Flavius Josephus
  Ant. Jud. 4.74.3   205

Lexicon Vindobonense (Nauck)

		310.11–15	136

Flavius Philostratus *see* Philostratus
Galen

GG 3.1

3.4.4	156	91.8–9	165
5.640	141	320.27	233
5.889.3	156	350.7–11	139
12.808.5	229	350.28	212
18(2).517–9	99	365.12	66
18(2).518.9–519.3	85	418.19–21	212
		419.3–8	189

Adhortatio ad artes addiscendas

		464.5	243
13.9	156	466.4–467.6	182

Gregorius Corinthius

		468.2	167

περὶ Ἀτθίδος

		490.13–17	138
lxxxviii–xc	200	534.7	66

Gregorius Lacapenus

		537.13	164

Ep.

		539.13–14	143
23.n.16–19	158	541.20	154

Gregorius of Nazianzus

		547.10–12	102, 164

PG 36

GG 3.2

224	7	13.14	196

PG 37

		13.22–5	66
col. 508.5	147	13.33–5	222
Carm. mor. I 675	255	18.14–32	214
		19.30	158

Harpocration

α 22 (Keaney =7.8–9.2 Dindorf)	126 f.	48.17	158
		281.4–6	40

Herennius Philo

		360.17	183

De diversis verborum significationibus

		387.5–14	150
6	146 f.	440.15–18	195
28	99, 168	447.6	139
29	97, 99 f., 171, 182	453.1–3	209
34	89, 90, 93, 98, 167	453.4–23	124
107	24	495.17–18	195
109	116, 219		

625.14–34	145	α 4111	165
676.8–14	145	α 4549, 4829	150
683.1–12	205	γ 487	183
800.4	183	η 566	204
846.24	158	λ 870	219
904.23–4	202	μ 250	223
930.28	151	ξ 92	233
944.14	233	c 2976	221
945.23	210	χ 107	231
951.29	255	ψ 227, 228, 262	259

[Herodian]
de loc. prav. (= περὶ τῶν ζητουμένων κτλ.)

An. Ox. 3 248.20–26	230		
An. Ox. 3 251.13–16	252		
An. Ox. 3 252.12–17	206		
An. Ox. 3 252.13–16	190		
An. Ox. 3 254.8	207		
An. Ox. 3 260.3–9	177		

Epimerismi (Boissonade) = *Partitiones*

172.8–10	195

ζητούμενα τῶν μερῶν τοῦ λόγου (Koch)

p. 415	116

Hippocrates

De Visu 4.4	167
Morb. 3.1	234
Morb. Sacr. 3.10	258

Hippolytus

De benedictionibus Is. Et Jac. 98.8	180

Hipponax

frr. 6.2, 27, 28.2, 29.2, 30.2, 43	253
fr. 48.4	253
fr. 59	247
fr. 62	253
fr. 107.49	253
fr. 147	253
fr. 150	150
fr. 175	237

Herodotus

1.11.1	201
1.52.1	247
1.184	201
2.150.3	211
3.23.1	245
3.68.4	244
3.97.2	211
4.23.3	247
4.134.3	201
6.107.2	201
6.119.3	188
9.80.2	247

Hesiodus

Op.

41	171

Th.

287	217 f.
312	218
478	193
549	244
fr. 153 M.-W. (=62 Rz.)	218

Hesychius

α 1067, 1103, 1105	130
α 1970	204

Homer

h.Merc.

33	180
221, 344	171

Ilias

1.592	157
2.269	175
2.294	153
3.15	187
4.56	154
5.130, 819	158
5.352	141
5.619	248
8.215	153
8.249	106
8.408, 422	201
9.499–501	123
11.639–40	233
12.87	239
12.206	106
16.498	124
18.447	153

19.25	106	*Judicium vocalium*	
20.156	157	9	115
21.8	153	*Lexiphanes*	
23.266, 655	189	1.2	249
Odyssea		8.6	117, 150
2.106	189	14	201
6.265	165	*Pseudologista*	
11.539	171	1	11
11.572	153	27	234
11.573	171	*Soloecista*	
12.210	153	3	219
18.333	141	5	117, 125, 219
18.453	157	*Verae Historiae*	
19.520	187	2.30	162
22.460	153	[Lucian]	
23.190	197	*Asin.*	
24.13	171	16.148, 43.182	156
24.141	189	Lucillius	
Irenaeus		*AP* 11.374 see *AP*	
fr. 3	259	LXX	
Isocrates		*2 Ma.*	
Antid.		8.23, 13.15	147
85, 270	167	*Deut.*	
Philip.		18.3	205
28	167	*Is.*	
Johannes Alexandrinus see Johannes Philoponus		20.2–3	156
		41.15.2	141
Johannes Philoponus		*Jd.*	
De vocab. ... differentiam accentus		8.7.2	141
γ 6, 7	182	*JdA.*	
Praecepta tonica		12.6	147
fr. 80	224 f.	*Je.*	
Libanius		5.17.5	141
Decl.		*Ju.*	
26.1.11	161	11.16	161
29.1.12.5	192	*4 Ki.*	
Longus Sophista		18.17	188
1.4.2, 1.30.3, 2.23.1	156	*Mal.*	
Lucian		2.3	205
Adversus Indoctum		*Ps.*	
9.21	254	65.15	242
AP		Lycophron	
11.408, 11.436	see *AP*	*Alexandra*	
De Syria Dea		461	131
6	234	991	207
35	201	Lysias	
53, 55	234	17.5	256

Macrobius
   Saturn. 5.18.19   155
Martianus Capella
   3.235   56
Melampus
   comm. In D. Thrax see Diomedes
Meletius
   de nat. homini
      An. Ox. 3 92.11   259
Menander
   Dysc. 472   256
   Heros 36   256
   Mon. 848   198
   Phasma 55   206
   Syc. 242, 258   207
   fragmenta
   fr. 158   168f.
   fr. 173   159
   fr. 252   143
   fr. 421   168
Michael Glycas
   Versus in carcere scripti 321   181
Mnesimachus
   fr. 4   124
Moeris
   α 6   90, 100, 132, 250
   α 8   136
   α 9   166f.
   α 10   103, 143
   α 11   34, 102f., 120, 132
   α 12   91, 126, 129, 144
   α 13   91, 126
   α 33   131
   α 57   79, 146
   α 63   79, 155
   α 65   60, 142
   α 67   78, 149
   α 80   159
   α 139   91, 114, 125, 187, 221
   β 10   60, 178
   β 15   92, 114, 176, 187, 218, 221
   β 34   93, 179f.
   γ 4   34, 100, 176, 181, 210
   δ 2   192
   ε 5   232
   ε 15   53
   ε 29   128f., 200
   ε 32   100, 174, 198
   η 5   62, 79, 193, 195
   η 12   204
   η 16   102f., 154
   η 17   44, 53, 57, 204
   η 20   195
   η 22   79, 193, 195
   θ 4   100, 205
   ι 3   90f., 100, 128, 207
   ι 4   91, 144
   ι 12   99, 209f.
   ι 18   91, 144, 146
   κ 6   212
   λ 8   24, 117f., 219
   λ 25   26, 57, 62, 220
   μ 6   60, 228
   μ 8   90f., 98, 114, 128, 221
   μ 10   32
   μ 12   224, 245
   ν 1   98, 230
   ν 12   58, 75, 79, 230
   ξ 5   93, 120, 234
   ο 32   50, 81, 92, 120, 236
   π 36   64, 93, 128, 237
   ς 17   63, 225
   ς 21   79, 146
   ς 22   93, 179
   ς 32   116, 247
   τ 4   100, 250
   τ 22   90f., 98, 128, 250, 257
   υ 1   63, 226
   υ 9   91, 93, 251
   υ 11   100, 251
   υ 12   78, 245
   φ 12   192
   φ 15   63, 226
   χ 7   78, 255
   χ 18   228
   ψ 1   63, 226
   ψ 3   60, 93, 257
   ω 2   59, 62, 260
Musonius Rufus
   Diss. A Lucio dig. Reliquiae 19.22   155
Nicander of Colophon
   fr. 83   236
Nicophon
   fr. 30   260

Index locorum — 305

Nicostratus		fr. 197	151
fr. 21	143	Philemon	
Nosti		354	79, 89f., 93, 146, 167
fr. 11.2	258	355	26, 91, 93, 102f., 120, 139, 142, 144, 158
Ophelio			
frr. 1, 2	215	357	33f., 49, 81, 92, 100, 176, 179, 181, 210
Oppianus Anazarbensis		358	91, 98, 183, 187, 192, 218
Halieutica 4.178	157	395	224
Oppianus Apamensis		393.22 R.	79, 146
Cynegetica 4.412	168	393.32 R.	78, 245
Origen		394.10 R.	79, 93, 193f.
Contra Celsum		394.18, 394.34 R.	22
2.6.5–7	161	395.20 R.	21
3.41.14	165	396.26 R.	78, 255
4.39.30	156	Philemon Comicus	
6.15.17	165	fr. 36	215
7.7.24	156	*Philetaerus*	
Hom. In Job (fr. *In Catenis*)		26	241
379.25	192	78	59, 63, 226, 241
Philocalia		81	63, 226
26.4.17	156	89	78, 218
Oros		96	125
A 10 a-b	155	103	159
A 11	159	121	22, 256
A 62	222	142	24, 116, 219
A 79	240	146	22f., 78, 255
B 5	131	149	79, 155
B 30	165	179	129
B 79	177	182	226f., 242
Pausanias		193	174
α 9	100, 122f.	200	50, 195
α 30	49, 81, 130	208	186
α 118	91, 151	209	100, 138, 234
α 129	93, 157	227	174, 199
α 154	102, 144, 168	230	81, 114, 178, 183, 186
ε 31	53, 197	241	31, 100, 174f., 181, 210
ε 71	91, 217	243	172
ζ 1–2, 4–5	115	245	212
η 3	163	251	199
κ 42	170	252	28, 32, 182, 243
Pherecrates		253	190
fr. 46	206	254	198
fr. 65	159	308	100, 254
fr. 75	226	317	224
fr. 137	188	*exc. Vind.*	
fr. 161	173	4	218
fr. 196	78, 240	7	125

26	226, 242	β 318	229
31	174	ε 2528, 2529, 2531	136
Philo Judaeus		θ 117	177f., 187
De fuga et inv. 57	162	κ 1216	217
Philo Mechanicus		ν 67	229
Parasceuastica 90.45	147	ξ 79	234
Philostratus		φ 64	253
Epistulae et dialexeis		(ψ) 655.17 Porson	259
1.18.7, 1.18.13, 1.37.5	156	Phrynichus	
Heroicus		*Ecloga*	1, 79
4.5–6	9	15	53, 232
Vita Apollonii		17	232
1.7	6f.	21	117, 152
1.8.13, 6.10.80, 6.11.241	156	22	34
Vitae Sophistarum		41	28f.
489	10	43	227
513, 519	192	45	120, 145, 252
531	9	52	80, 208
553	8, 35	69	57, 183
567–8	14	72	32, 117, 184f., 248
585–590	24	76	238
592–594	24	77	92, 239
593§	19	79	227
594	4, 19, 31, 66	80	2, 26, 30, 89, 91, 93, 238
621	3f.	124	59, 62, 260
624	10, 35	133	79, 204
627–8	10	142	92f., 214
Photius		156	218
Bibliotheca		178	90, 256f.
149	14	197	22
157	20	202	186
158	13, 19	217	224
241	167	224	246
152–3	19	225	116, 247
333b.30	167	231	22f., 256
Lexicon		241	33f., 80, 93, 186, 208, 216, 235
α 108, 109	122	264	196
α 277, 279	127	268	60, 81, 258
α 629	204	270	237
α 1019	139	272	227
α 1030	142	280	63, 225
α 1197	144	281	59, 63, 226, 241
α 1477	147	293	99f., 188
α 1641	150	298	58, 75, 79, 230
α 2151, 2164	154	346	28, 80, 93, 186, 189, 216
α 2721	167	371	22f., 78, 255
α 2853	169, 172	384	26

Index locorum — 307

412–424	205	*fragmenta*	
414	79, 204	fr. *28	29
419	79, 155	fr. *48	100, 122
420	79, 146	fr. *49	122
Ecloga (fam. q)		fr. *151	93, 120, 139, 142
223	246	fr. *249	144, 165
Praeparatio Sophistica		fr. †*274	102, 173
1.1–6	29	fr. *341	53, 57, 232
1.4	30	fr. *367	90, 98, 250, 256
10.9–11	80, 100, 173	Phrynichus Comicus	
13.4–6	57, 148	fr. 74.2	246
14.3	204	Pindar	
16.6–12	158, 160	*N.* 3.79	245
18.1	170	*O.* 9.34	128
23.1–2	102f., 154	Plato	
25.10–11	102, 141	*Cratylus*	
25.16–25	103, 163	418b-d	43, 56
26.9–10	32, 57, 79, 155, 162	424d	236
27.12	57, 79, 155	434c	238
27.13–17	98, 174, 230	*Critias*	
31.10–12	100, 117, 152	117a-b	188
32.1–4	116, 149	*Ion*	
36.5–12	62, 91, 129	539c	106
37.8–9	91, 161	*Leges*	
39.12–15	100, 137, 234	672c	137
47.15	170	687d	253
51.12–13	116, 166	958b	256
58.14–59.1	117, 184, 248	*Phaedrus*	
60.14	50, 93, 185f.	244c-d	66
73.4–6	50, 203	250c	236
77.1–2	80, 208	*Philebus*	
80.3–7	49, 80, 212	21c	236
81.11	50, 53, 211	*Politicus*	
84.1–2	116, 216	267a	256
85.5–6	117, 216	*Protagoras*	
89.6–7	91, 120, 222	320e	211
90.9–13	229	*Respublica*	
91.5–6	58, 75, 79, 230	329c	171
103.14	241f.	364d-e	123
105.9–10	78, 142, 240	378a, d	253
108.10–15	53, 232	380c	167
114.10	239	420c	236
114.14–16	100, 249	453d	188
118.3–4	32, 64, 78, 93, 120, 145, 252	473c	106
118.15–16	63, 225	514a, 532b	211
128.9–10	63	611d	236

Symposium		9.35	128
203c–d	156	9.80, 9.87	231
Theaetetus		10.31, 10.98	170
147c	161	10.160	186
154c	203	Posidippus Comicus	
Timaeus		fr. 28.21	207
53a	188	fr. 42	165
92b	236	P.Oxy.	
Plato Comicus		1012	30–2, 80, 99, 125, 138, 175, 183
fr. 178	222 f.	1803	26, 32
fr. 303	137	Procopius	
Plautus		*Historia Arcana* 17	184
Amphitruo 117	221	περὶ τῆϲ αι διφθόγγου see An. Ox.	
Cistellaria, Arg. 11	113	περὶ διχρόνων see An. Ox.	
Pliny		περὶ ποϲότητοϲ see An. Ox.	
Naturalis Historia 35.114	184	Quintilian	
Plutarch		*Institutio Oratoria*	
Alc.		1.1.4–5	12
3.1	159	1.1.5	38
Cam.		1.1.13	12
23.7	159	1.5.6, 1.5.8, 1.5.10–13	11
Mar.		1.5.17	11, 27
28.8	113	1.5.32–33	27 f.
Mor.		Sappho	
98d	156	fr. 179	186
326e	162	fr. 189	227
Pomp.		Scholia in Aristophanis	
54, 72	113	*Acharnenses*	
Pyrrh.		26	132
2.4	162	72	228
Pollux		745	248
Onomasticon		746	184
1.54–55	189	822	248
1.77	213	*Equites*	
1.80	235	416	217
1.162	25	1320	126
2.61	148	*Lysistratam*	
2.185	259	886	123
2.199	155	*Nubes*	
2.204	204 f.	3	161
2.209, 2.210	230	180	205
3.78	25	507	221
5.47	185	768	227
5.82	150	*Pacem*	
6.88	170	1 f	221
7.95	235	1 g	221
7.205	242	70 f	150

618	29	1.118	34
Plutum		1.169	115
103	243 f.	1.169–170	33
123	138	1.173–5	115
Ranas		Sophocles	
6	182	*Ajax*	
567	228	167	159 f.
Thesmophoriazusas		1293	145
489	129	*Electra*	
Vespas		178	244
249	254	662	195
Scholia in D. Thracem		1451	154
GG 1.3 176.19–23	87	*Oedipus Coloneus*	
Scholia in Demosthenem		470	244
21		1084	135
162	127	1495	244
Scholia in Euripidis		*Oedipus Tyrannus*	
Iphigeniam Tauricam		1264	134 f.
39	208	*Trachiniae*	
Orestem		350	124
261	133, 208	*fragmenta*	
Scholia in Homeri *Iliadem*		fr. 111	218
1.137	139	fr. 198b	123
2.269	175	Sophron	
2.339, 5.54	133	fr. 147	233
15.302b2	205	fr. 161	231
16.827	182	Stobaeus	
Scholia in Platonis		4.14.2	179
Apologiam		Strabo	
25c	261	13.1.68	197
Epistulas		Strattis	
319e	261	fr. 65	229
Scholia in Sophoclis		*Suda*	
Ajacem		α 383	127
167	160	α 1428	142
Oedipum Tyrannum		α 1767	165
350–3	138	α 1869, 1878	147
1264	136	α 2014	148
Scholia in Theocritum		α 2049, α 2313	150
Arg. Carm.		α 2791	155
12	130	α 2799	154
Scholia in Thucydidem		α 3221	256
6.27.1	19	α 4126	231
Sextus Empiricus		γ 118, 119	182
Adversus Mathematicos		θ 18	205
1.115	43 f., 52, 56, 58, 79 f.	θ 242	177
1.117–8	51 f.	κ 249–251	104

λ 441	219	GG 4.1 67.16–18		244
ν 508	259	Theognostus		
ν 515	231	Canones		
ξ 91	233	An. Ox. 2 143.19–20		216
ο 835	14	An. Ox. 2 408.2–3		183
π 1951	24	Theon of Alexandria		
π 3038	27	Progymnasmata		
ϲ 40	248	61.28–62.1		83
χ 188	253	81.30–82.7		86f.
χ 466	213	129.11–22		85f.
ψ 142, 145	259	Theophrastus		
Synagoge see Σ, Σ^b		Char. 20.9		235
Σ		HP 9.20.3		165
α 499	212	fr. 124		192
ε 73	202	Theopompus		
ε 1012	200	Hist. 367		165
ε 1097–9	136	Thomas Magister		
η 43	202	2.10		132
Σ^b		14.1–9		160
200	127	176.8		205
248, 249	122	185.11		210
409	131	Thucydides		
1158	212	1.13.6		252f.
1257	152	1.128.5		159
1541, 1544	154	2.4.3		213
1546	155	2.52.2		239
1779	165	2.78.2		203
1799	256	4.8.8, 4.8.41		151
2372	173	4.42.4, 4.83.6		203
Teleclides		4.112.1		147
fr. 23	222f.	4.128.4		179
Terentianus Maurus		8.69.2, 8.97.1		201
De syllabis 450–2	56	8.101.1		192
Themistius		Timaeus		
Or. 7.91a	160	Lexicon Platonicum		
Theocritus		praef. 7–11		13
2.56	158	α 46		152
10.22	244	Timocles		
12.14	130	fr. 11.9		204
13.7	215	Tragica adespota		
22.86	158	fr. 705b.6		135
Ep. 13.2	147	Trypho		
Theodoretus		fr. 12		168f.
Quaestiones et resp. 7.26	139	fr. 14		171
Theodosius		fr. 16		123
GG 4.1 13.12–18	180	fr. 108		63
GG 4.1 41.14–16	224			

Tyrannion		*Cyropaedia*	
fr. 42	182	2.4.3	128
Tzetzes		*HG*	
Hist. 9.231	234	1.1.10	159
Varro		4.1.40	253
L. 5.173	231	7.1.15	154
R. 1.8.5	137	*Memorabilia*	
Xenophon		1.2.54	226
Anabasis		Zonaras (Tittmann)	
4.5.25	211	20.14–26, 24.6–7	128
4.7.15, 4.8.25	233	1249.5–13	153
7.5.2, 7.5.4	179	1745.10–11	240

Index of Authors

Aelian   10, 205, 235
Aelius Aristides   130
Antipater of Sidon   69, 238
Apollodorus of Damascus   147
Apollonius of Tyana   6f., 9
Aristophanes of Byzantium   3, 13, 17, 96, 131, 196
Aspasius of Ravenna   10

Callimachus   14, 147
Claudius Aristocles   14
Cornelianus   13, 20, 22f., 230, 256

Dio Chrysostom   130, 184, 237
Dionysius of Halicarnassus   13, 18, 27
Diophantus Mathematicus   147

Favorinus of Arelate   10

Gregorius of Nazianzus   7, 70, 96, 147, 255

Harpocration   14f., 126f.
Heraclides of Miletus   23
Herodes Atticus   4, 7f., 14

Irenaeus   15, 259

Johannes Chortasmenus   167
Julius Vestinus   14

Lexica Segueriana   17
Lucian   3, 7, 9, 11f., 115, 117, 119, 125f., 150, 156, 162, 201, 219f., 234, 249, 254, 258

Michael Gabras   167
Minucius Pacatus   see Irenaeus

Nicetas Seides   167

Oros   15

Pausanias of Caesarea   4–7, 19, 66
Philemon of Aexone   14
Philetas   13
Philo Judaeus   162
Polemon   9
Ptolemy of Ascalona   23f., 27

Quirinus of Nicomedia   3

Theophrastus   165, 192, 227
Timaeus   13, 152

Valerius Diodorus   14
Valerius Pollio   14

Index of Subjects

accent marks   32, 64, 82, 85, 87, 96, 123, 172, 185, 190 f., 234
Aeolic   27, 102, 140, 164, 194, 202, 227
artificial distinctions in meaning 182, 213 artificial formations 50, 99, 117, 262 artificial pronunciations 2, 34, 55, 60, 66, 86, 99, 117, 120, 141, 145, 176, 213, 218, 223, 239
Asianic   5
aspiration (initial)   6, 32, 34, 38, 64, 82 f., 87, 101–103, 120, 122, 131 f., 139, 141–4, 151 f., 154, 163–5, 168, 202
breathings   29, 31–3, 39, 57, 82, 84 f., 87 f., 101–3, 119 f., 130–2, 141, 143 f., 151 f., 154, 163–5, 168, 173, 201 f.
Christian literature   139, 141, 147, 156, 161, 165, 167, 180
dichrona, dichronon   33, 48, 64, 82, 85, 88 f., 92, 98, 119 f., 140, 146, 152, 180, 183 f., 215, 240
Doric   65, 109, 145, 147, 155, 215, 221, 227, 248 f., 256, 260 f.
Eretrian   2, 238
Fathers of the Church *see* Christian literature
hyperattic   92, 120, 132, 140, 142, 201, 206, 223, 229, 235, 240
hypercorrect, hypercorrection   101, 103, 170, 177, 185, 190, 219, 226, 236, 239, 253, 260,

Ionic   50, 67, 93 f., 101, 124, 130, 145, 149, 164 f., 187, 194 f., 201, 207, 211, 214, 218, 223, 226 f., 234, 237, 249, 253, 256, 258
koine   13, 18, 34 f., 40, 42–45, 51, 55, 68, 71, 84, 94, 99–102, 106, 110 f., 120, 124, 145 f., 149, 155, 161, 164, 169, 175 f., 189, 207, 212, 215, 221, 223–227, 233, 238, 244 f., 251
lectional marks/signs   32 f., 64, 82–5, 87 f., 96, 99, 122
monophthong/monophthongisation   42, 45, 50–52, 55, 58–60, 68, 71, 73, 75, 81, 119, 135, 258
orthoepy, orthoepic   27 f., 32 f., 87 f., 93, 119, 130, 192 f.
orthography/ὀρθογραφία   1, 28, 30, 32 f., 40, 44, 49, 54, 59, 64, 80 f., 92, 101, 104, 113, 115 f., 119, 129 f., 149 f., 164, 189, 192, 195, 203, 209, 211, 239, 242, 248
pitch   68, 70 f., 84, 95 f., 99, 230
quantity marks   62, 82, 85–8, 119
rhythm, rhythmical   3, 5, 31, 84, 86
stress   68–72, 95 f., 110
synizesis   47, 94, 145, 149, 187, 191 f., 200, 240, 250, 255 f.
Thessalian   69, 130
Vendryes' Law   100, 120, 125, 175 f., 181, 210

Index of lemmata and glosses

This index lists all terms discussed in the lexica, either as lemmata or in the the glosses. It also includes terms discussed in other ancient scholarship. Items whose initial aspiration or accent type/position are the object of discussion are intentionally printed without accents and/or breathings.

ἆ 97f., 102, 122, 183f.
ᾶ ᾶ 102, 122
ἄγανος 100, 122–4
ἀγνοία 89, 91, 97, 124
ἀγοράζειν 89, 91f., 114, 125 (ἀγορᾶcαι ~ ἀγορᾶcαι), 177 (ἀγορῶ), 187, 221
ἄγροικος 31, 97, 100, 125f.
ἄγυια 89, 91, 126–9
ἀγυιεύς see ἄγυια
ἀδολεcχεῖν, ἀδολέcχηc 62, 89, 91, 129f.
ἀδροτής 210
ἀείτης 49, 81, 130f.
αθροοc 131
αθυρμα 34, 102f., 120, 132
αἱματοπώτης 30, 79, 245f.
αἱμωδ-
   αἱμωδία 44, 53, 204
   αἱμωδέω/αἱμωδιάω 204
αινειν see (αφ)α(ι)νειν
ἄϊτης see ἀείτης
αἰτίαι 62, 90, 97, 100, 132–4, 208, 250
αἰώρα 53, 80, 134–6
ἄκρατον 89, 97, 136
ἀκταινοῦν 97, 100, 137f., 152, 234, 237
Αλαεις 142
ἀλεαίνεcθαι 142
ἀληθεc 31, 97, 138f.
ἁλιεύς 144f.
ἁλικόν 60, 142
ἅλις 102f., 139, 158
ἁλμυρ-
   ἁλμυρόc 89, 93, 120, 139f., 142
   Ἁλμυρίc 140
ἀλοᾶν 102f., 141
ἀλύειν 102, 120, 141f.
ἁλυκός 60, 139f., 142
ἅλυcις 102f., 142f.
ἅμαξα 102f., 142–4, 168
ἀμβάλευ 244

ἀμίc 101–3, 120, 142f., 168
ἀμνός 142
ἀμπίcχες 163
ἀμπίcχου 163
ἀμφορεύς 89, 91, 94, 126, 129, 144, 240
ἀμῶc 142
ἀνάθεμα / ἀνάθημα 79, 146–8, 155
ἀναιδεία 124
ἄναντες / ἀνάντης 212
ἀναπειρία / ἀναπηρία 148
ἀνάπλεον 149
ἀνάπλεως 78, 149
ἀναρ(ρ)ιχᾶcθαι see ἀρ(ρ)ιχᾶcθαι
Ἀνάφη 168f.
ἀνείλλειν 152f.
ανειν see (αφ)α(ι)νειν
ἀνίλλειν 97, 100, 117, 152
ἀντήλιος 163, 165
ἀνύειν 102f., 142, 154
   καθανύ(τ)ειν (κατ-) 103, 154
   καcάνεις 154
ἀνυπόδετος / ἀνυπόδητος 57, 79, 155f.
ἀνύτειν see ἀνύειν
ἀνώγειος 196
ἀξιόχρεος / ἀξιόχρεως 149, 192
ἀπαλοᾶν 102, 141
ἅπαν 89, 91, 93, 157f.
ἀπαντικρύ 89, 93, 158
ἀπέδρων see ἀποδιδράcκω
ἀπέρα(ν)τος
   ἀπέραντος 161f.
   ἀπέρατος 89, 91, 161f.
ἀπέcβηcε 32, 57, 79, 155, 162
ἄπεφθος 103, 163
ἀπηδές 163
ἀπηθεῖν 163
ἀπηλιώτης 102f., 163, 165, 168
ἀπηχία 163f.
ἁπλᾶ 250, 256

ἀποδιδράσκω 159–61
  ἀπέδρα 159
  ἀπέδραν (ἀπέδραμεν, ἀπέδρατε) 158–60
  ἀπέδρων 159 f.
  ἀποδρασθεῖν, ἀποδρῶ, ἀποδρῴη 160
ἀποκτινύναι 116 f., 166
ἀποχρη 97, 166 f.
ἀρ(ρ)ιχᾶσθαι 116 f., 137, 149 f.
ἄρα 89 f., 93, 97 f., 167
ἀργυρᾶ / ἀργύρεα 90, 256 f.
ἄρκυς 102 f., 144, 168
ἀρκυωρεῖν, ἀρκυωρός 168
ἁρπαγη 88, 97, 99, 168–70, 172, 182
ἄρχον / ἄρχων 170
ἀσμεναίτατα, -έστατα, -ώτερος 170 f.
ασσα, αττα 102 f., 172 f.
ἀσφοδελος 88, 97, 99 f., 172, 182
ἀτεχνως 97, 172
Ἀτρέα 26, 144
αὐτοχειριᾳ 80, 97, 100, 173
(ἀφ)α(ι)νειν
  αἴνω, ἀφαίνει, ἀφανεῖ, ἀφανέω 151
ἀφίκου 243–5
ἀφου 97 f., 174, 230
ἀχρειος 31, 98, 100, 125, 174–6, 181, 183, 210
ἀχρειως 175

βαδίζειν 89, 92, 114, 176 f., 187, 218, 221
  βαδιίζειν, βαδίcω, βαδιῶ 177
βαθύγειος 196
βασιλέα 26, 144, 207, 252 f.
βελτίων 196
βιβλ-
  βιβλίον 60 f., 178
  βίβλινος 178
βοεικός 92, 179
βόειος 179
βοϊκός 34, 49, 81, 89, 92, 179
βότρεις 180
βότρυς 89, 93, 179 f.
βραδυτής 210
βύβλινος 60, 178
βύσταξ 229

γεϊκός 183
γέινος 57, 183

γελοιος 34, 98, 100, 176, 181 f., 210
γενεσθαι 28, 32, 98, 182, 243
γενοῦ 244
γήινος 57, 183
γλυκίων 196
γρῦ 97 f., 183 f.
γρυλ(λ)ίζειν, γρυλ(λ)ιςμός 116 f., 184 f., 248
γρῦλ(λ)ος 184 f.
γρυμ-αῖα, -έα, -εῖα, -ίαν 50, 93, 185 f.
γρύτα, γρύτη 185 f.

δανείζειν 81, 114, 177 f., 183, 186
  δανείcω, δανειῶ 177
  δανειοῦμαι, δανείω 186
{δε}δεξαμένη see δεξαμενη
δένδρα (δένδρᾱ) 89, 91, 187 f., 218
δεξαμενη 98–100, 188–90 {δε}δεξαμένη 188
διετης 98, 100, 188 f.
Διονυcεῖον 28, 80, 93, 186, 189 f., 206, 216
διπλᾶ 256
δοχμη 98, 100, 190
δύο, δύω 79, 93, 192 f.
δύcερως 98, 190–2
δύω see δύο

ἐβουλόμην 79, 93, 193 f.
ἔγγε(ι)α 50, 195 f., 211
ἐθάς 202
εἰπέ 199, 243
εἰωθώς 50, 201
ἐκάθαρα/ἐκάθηρα 232
ἔκληcε 213
Ἐλαία 53, 197, 211
Ἐλέα 197
ἔλευ 244
ἐλθέ 199, 243
ἐνέγκου 244
ἔνυcτρον / ἤνυcτρον 79, 204 f.
ἐξέδραν 159, see also ἀποδιδράσκω
ἐξίλλειν 100, 152
ἔπηλις 165
ἐπίγειος 195 f.
ἐπιμέλου 97, 100, 174, 198
ἐπιτάδε 98, 198
ἔπτυσχλοι 163
ἐρρύπανα/ἐρρύπηνα 232

ἐτάс 260 f.
εὔγειοc 195 f.
εὔκλεία 124, 207
εὐπράξιαι 133 f.
εὑρέ 98, 174, 199, 243
εὕρεμα 146 f., 155, 246
εὕρημα 79, 146, 155
εὐφυ-ᾶ, -ῆ 128 f., 180, 200
ἔωθ-α, -αc, -εε, -εcαν 201
ἐωθώc 50, 195, 201
ἑώρα 134 – 6
ἑωρήcαcα 135

ἠβουλόμην 193 – 5
ἠδίων 196
ἦδοc 102 f., 163 f., 201 f.
ἠδυνάμην 79, 193 f.
ἠθάc 79, 202
ἦκαcα 47, 195
ἤμελλον 62, 79, 193 – 5
ἥμεραι 133 f.
ἡμίcεια 50, 203
ἥμιcυ, inflected forms 203
ἠμωδία 44, 53, 57, 204
ἠναρριχώμην 150, see also ἀρ(ρ)ιχᾶcθαι
ἠπίcτω 79, 193, 195
ηὐξάμην 62, 79, 193, 195

Θαληc 97, 100, 205
θέμα 147
θερμᾶναι/θερμῆναι 232
θεωρήcαcα 135
θεῶcαι / θεώcειν 50, 205
Θηcε(ι)ον
  Θηcέῳ 50
  Θηcεῖον 190, 206
  ‹θηcια› 206

ἴδε 199, 244
ἴδου 243 f.
ἱερ-έα, -εία, -ία
  ἱερεία 89 – 91, 97, 100, 128, 133, 207
  ἱέρεια, ἱρείαι 207
  ἱερέα 207 f.
  ἱέρεαι/ἱερέαι, ἱερία 208
ἰῆναι 232
ἱκεcία 80, 208

ἱκετεία 208
ἴλλειν 141, 152 f.
ἱππέα(c) 144, 146
ἴcοτηc 98 f., 209 f.
ἰcωτηc 210 f.

καθαίρω see ἐκάθηρα/ἐκάθηρα
καθανύcαι see ἀνύειν
κακίων 196
καλλίων 196
καρίc 214 f.
κacάνειc see ἀνύειν
κατά-γαιοc, -γειοc 53, 211
κάταντεc 98, 212
κατανύειν see ἀνύειν
κατώγειοc 196
κάχρυc 180
κεραμεᾶ 256
κεραμεικόc 179
κεχρ(ε)ιcθαι 212 f.
κληῖc 213 f.
κλῆcαι 62, 213
κνημίc 89, 92 f., 214 f.
κυδώνιον 80, 89, 92 f., 208, 215 f.
κυνηγέccειν 216
κυνηγετ(τ)ειν 116 f., 185, 216
κυνοκέφαλ(λ)οc 117, 216 f.
κωμῴδιαι 134

λαβε 199, 244
λαβου 243 – 5
λαβεcθαι 28, 32, 182
λαγω(ο)c 78, 218 f
λῆμ(μ)α 24, 116 – 8, 125, 219 f.
λειτουργ- (λη-, λη-) 24, 26, 47, 57 f., 62, 220
λέξεων 224
λιπόνεωc 78, 192

μαδδα 221 see also μαζα
μαζα 89 – 91, 97 f., 114, 128, 221 f., 237 f.
μανάκιc 222 f.
μανόc 90 f., 120, 222 f.
μανότεροc 222 f.
μάντεων 98, 224 f., 245
μέθου 174
μεcόγειοc 195 f.

Index of lemmata and glosses —— 317

(μεϲογεία τῆϲ Ἀττικῆϲ) 8, 10
μετέωροϲ 134–6
μιαρόϲ / μιερόϲ 63, 225 f., 233, 241 f.,
μόλιβοϲ 228
μόλυβ(δ)οϲ 60, 228
μυαλόϲ / μυελόϲ 63, 226, 241 f.
μύϲταξ 18, 90 f., 93, 120, 229

νεαλήϲ, -έϲ 90, 229
νεώϲ 97 f., 230
νῆϲτηϲ / νῆϲτιϲ 58, 75, 79, 230
νόμοϲ see νουμ(μ)ουϲ
νούμ(μ)ουϲ, νόμοϲ 116 f., 230 f.
νυγοῦ 244

ξῆναι 53, 232
ξυάλη / ξυήλη 79, 226, 233 f.,
ξυρειν 98, 100, 138, 234, 237
ξυρόν 89, 93, 120, 234 f.

οἰδεῖν (οἴδηκεν, -ώϲ/ᾠδηκεν -ώϲ) 59, 62, 260
οἰκοδομεῖν (οἰκο-/ᾠκοδόμηκεν) 59, 260
οἰνοπώτηϲ 245
ὁμίλιαι 134
ὀπτάνιον 33, 80, 93, 98, 186, 208, 216, 235
ὄϲτρε(ι)α, ὄϲτρια 50, 81, 89, 92, 120, 236–8
ὀφλειν 98, 237

πάμπαν 157 f., 261
πανῆμαρ 157
πάπυροϲ 64, 89, 93, 237, 251
πελαργόϲ 2, 26, 30, 89, 91–3, 238
πελέκεων 224
πενταχα 239
πεντετηϲ 100, 188
περιθεωϲάτωϲαν 206
πηρόϲ 148
πήχεων 224 f.
πιέ 199
πιθοῦ 243–5
πινακίϲ 215
πλοκαμίϲ 214 f.
πνιγερόϲ 239
πνιγεύϲ 92, 240
πνιγοϲ 89, 92, 128, 239 f.

πόλεων, -εωϲ 191 f., 224 f.
πολλαπλα 256
πόμα 30, 79, 245
πρόου 174
πρόπαν 157 f.
προϲάντηϲ 212
πρόϲγειοϲ 196
πρωπέρυϲι 78, 142, 240 f.
πύελοϲ 59, 63, 226–8, 241 f.
πύθευ 244
πυθοῦ 173, 199, 243–5
πῶμα 78 f., 245

ῥαφανίϲ 93, 214 f.
ῥοίδιον 246
ῥόμμα 237
ῥοπτόϲ 237
ῥόφειν 237
ῥυπαίνω see ἐρρύπανα/ἐρρύπηνα
ῥυφεῖν 237

ϲακ(χ)υφάντηϲ 247
ϲακκεῖν (ϲακκέουϲι) 247
ϲάκκοϲ 111, 117, 185, 247 f.
ϲάκοϲ 116 f., 247 f.
ϲημᾶναι / ϲημῆναι 232 f.
ϲίαλον / ϲίελοϲ 63, 225–7
ϲτάχειϲ, ϲτάχεϲιν see ϲτάχυϲ
ϲτάχυϲ 89, 93, 179–81, 224
  ϲτάχειϲ 180
  ϲτάχεϲιν 181
ϲτέφᾰνοϲ 253
ϲύμπαν 157 f.
ϲύνθεμα 147
ϲύνθημα 79, 146 f.
ϲχέμα 221

τάν 93, 97 f., 260 f.
ταχυτήϲ 210
τητινόϲ 98, 100, 249
τιμώρια, τιμώριαι 98, 100, 133 f., 208, 250
τραγῳδίαι 134
τράπου 244
τριετηϲ 188–9
τριπλα 89–91, 97–9, 128, 250, 257
τυποῦ 244

ὑάλινος 63, 225–7
ὕαλος 63, 225–7
ὑαλοψός 227
ὑγιᾶ 200
ὑγίεια 207, 251 f.
ὑγιῆ 200
ὑδαρές 90 f., 93, 251, 253
ὑδατοπότης 246
ὑδροπωτεῖν 246
ὑελεψός 227
ὕελος 63, 225–7
υἱέος 64, 78, 93, 120, 251–3
ὑπέργειος 196
ὑποδέςαςθαι 155
ὕφου 174

φαγέ 199
φαρμακός 89–91, 93, 253
φιάλη 63, 226 f., 242
φιλόγελως 190–2
φλεγμᾶναι 232
φοινικᾶ 256

φρούριον 98, 100, 254
φυλ(λ)ον 185

χαμᾶζε 34, 89, 91, 97 f., 114, 221, 254 f.
χαμᾶθεν 34, 254 f.
χρέος 255 f.
χρέως 78, 255 f.
χρυς(ε)α 90, 97 f., 187, 256
χρυσόκερως 190 f.

ψακάζειν / ψεκάζειν 63
ψάλια / ψέλια 63
ψημύθιον 257
ψίαθος 63, 226, 228
ψιαθώδης 228
ψίεθος 63, 225
ψιμίθιον, ψιμούθιον and variants 61, 257 f.
ψιμύθιον 60 f., 89, 93, 257 f.
ψο(ι)α, ψύα 60, 81, 258 f.
ψύα *see* ψο(ι)α

ὦλλος 141

Index of Greek technical terms and other notable words

ἀρχαῖος 26, 62, 184, 204f., 213, 230, 232, 236, 241, 252
Ἀθηναῖοι 8, 10, 94, 133f., 137, 177, 185, 210, 214, 222, 240, 248
ἀμαθής 2, 29f., 148, 174, 238f., 246
ἁμαρτάνειν 64, 78, 149, 161, 166, 177, 225, 239, 252, 258
ἁμάρτημα 155
ἁμαρτία 184f.
ἀναγιγνώσκειν 29, 88
ἀναγνωστέον 29, 83, 171f.
ἀνάγνωσις 83f., 133, 175
ἀπαίδευτος / -ευσία 7–9, 28, 189
ἀποψάλλειν 8
Ἀτθίς 8, 133
ἀττικίζειν 10
Ἀττικοί 21, 26, 28, 30f., 34, 44, 63f., 79, 90, 93, 97, 99, 102f., 120, 124–6, 131f., 136, 138, 141–4, 146, 149, 152, 154f., 157, 159, 166, 168–72, 174–9, 181f., 186, 188–90, 192f., 195, 198–201, 203–5, 209f., 212, 214, 216, 218, 220–2, 224–8, 230, 232–7, 239, 242–5, 247, 249–253, 255–7, 259–62
Ἀττικός, -ῶς 6f., 13, 94 (ἀττικώτερος), 131, 134, 142 (ἀττικώτερος), 149, 175, 181f., 189, 193, 203f. (ἀττικώτερος), 218, 237, 241 (ἀττικώτερος), 249(ἀττικώτερος), 255

βαρβαρίζειν / βάρβαρος 8, 11, 27, 136, 149, 177, 192f., 230, 253
βαρύνειν 151, 158, 169, 183, 188, 210, 243f.
βαρυτονεῖν / βαρύτονος, -ως 23, 29, 32, 90, 96f., 123, 132, 136f., 166, 168f., 171f., 174f., 177, 181, 183, 189, 198f., 205, 207, 212, 214, 221, 239
βαρύς (βαρεῖα) 87, 261
βέλτιον 126f., 260f.
βραχύνειν 28, 80, 157, 177, 189, 235, 239, 260f.

βραχύς -έως 4f., 18, 21, 28, 30, 66, 79, 89–91, 126, 144, 176, 179, 181, 199, 207, 209, 214f., 221, 229, 234, 237, 239, 250f., 253

γλῶττα 4, 6–8
γράφειν 29f., 79, 87, 115, 130, 141, 148f., 151f., 161, 166, 196f., 199, 208f., 245
γραφή 49, 212, 243

δασύνειν 101f., 122, 131, 142, 151, 154, 163f., 168, 172f., 201
δασύς, -έως 29, 102f., 120, 131f., 141–3, 151, 154, 163, 168
διφθογγίζειν / δίφθογγος 26, 59, 65, 80, 130, 133, 148, 151, 153, 179, 195f., 211f., 220, 254f.
δύο (of geminate consonants) 149, 152f., 166, 184, 216f., 219, 247f.

ἔκτασις 79, 149, 151, 158, 192f.
ἐκτατικός 94
ἐκτείνειν 2, 26, 28, 30 (ἐπεκτ-), 43, 52, 66, 79 (ἐπεκτ-), 80, 85, 89, 91, 93f., 97f., 124f., 129, 139, 157–9, 161, 174, 176f., 180f., 183, 189, 214f. (τείνω (ταθεῖσα, ἐτάθη), 215), 222, 234, 238f., 241, 245 (ἐπεκτ-), 253
ἐκφέρειν 28, 146, 148, 163, 171, 177
Ἕλληνες 13, 21, 26, 28, 31, 34, 44, 63f., 66, 90, 93, 99, 125, 126, 128, 131f., 136, 141, 143, 146, 149, 154f., 159, 166, 176, 179, 181, 192f., 198, 200, 204f., 207, 209, 210, 212, 219–21, 224–6, 228, 230, 232, 234, 236f., 239, 245, 247, 250f., 255, 260
ἑλληνίζειν 10
ἑλληνισμός 27
ἐπεκτείνειν see ἐκτείνειν

κίβδηλος 258
κοινός 21, 142, 175, 178, 182, 214, 218, 248

Λάκονες 154
λέγειν (in prescriptions)   13, 25 (ῥητέον), 28 f., 31, 34, 52, 126, 131, 134, 136, 137–9, 143, 146, 148 f., 155, 159, 161, 167, 171–5, 177, 180, 186, 188–90, 192 f., 196, 199 f., 202, 204, 206, 208, 213, 215–7, 220, 222, 225 f., 232–6, 240 f. (ῥητέον, 241), 245–9, 252 f., 255, 258
λέξις   29 f., 33, 64 f., 79, 83, 85, 115, 133, 152, 173, 176, 245, 260

μακρός, -ῶς   21, 26, 28, 34, 64–6, 79, 81, 89–91, 124, 126, 139, 144, 158, 163 f., 167, 172, 176 f., 179, 187, 199, 207, 209, 214, 221, 229, 234, 236 f., 239, 245, 250 f., 257, 261
μερισμός   33, 44
μεταγενέστερος   181

νεώτερος   133, 192, 260 f.

ὁμοτονεῖν / ὁμότονος, -ως   133, 138, 171, 243
ὀξυ(το)νεῖν   23, 29, 33, 89, 96, 98 f., 123, 126 f., 138, 158, 169, 171, 175, 183, 189 f., 199, 235, 237, 243 f., 255
ὀξύτονος, -ως   21, 32, 90, 97, 123, 138, 168 f., 189, 199, 207, 210, 212, 214, 222, 224, 230, 249
ὀξύς, -έως   87, 122, 171, 190, 254
ὀρθογραφία   33

παλαιοί   25, 66, 97, 122, 124, 149, 169, 171, 192, 259, 260 f.,
παροξυ(το)νεῖν   66, 97, 99, 124, 131, 152, 189, 192, 199, 224, 255
παροξύτονος, -ως   28, 32, 98, 131 f., 172, 174, 182, 198, 208, 250
περισπᾶν   21, 29, 87, 89 f., 96, 98, 122, 126–8, 131, 136 f., 152, 166 f., 172 f., 183, 190, 198, 205, 221, 224, 234, 243 f., 250, 260 f.

ποιότης   33, 44, 115, 210
ποσότης   33, 44 f., 49
προενεκτέον/προσενεκτέον   28, 32, 182 f.
προπαροξυ(το)νεῖν   66, 99, 133, 182, 190, 192, 207 f., 212, 224, 254
προπαροξύτονος, -ως   125, 131, 134, 138, 171 f., 181, 208
προπερισπᾶν   29, 34, 90, 99, 125, 136, 175, 181 f., 221, 255
προσενεκτέον see προενεκτέον
προσγράφειν   129
προσφέρειν   183, 186, see also προενεκτέον
προσῳδία   6, 28, 33, 38, 63 f., 66, 82–5, 87, 100 f., 103, 120, 133, 138 f., 143, 154, 168 f., 171, 222 f., 230, 243
προφέρειν   28–32, 51, 64, 78 f., 85, 97, 124, 141, 145, 148, 163, 183, 188, 200, 245, 248, 252 f., see also προενεκτέον
προφορά   28, 64, 83, 85, 117, 184 f.

συναλείφειν /συναλ(ο)ιφή   102, 126 f., 129, 143 f., 154, 163
συνήθεια   13, 21, 66, 97, 133 f., 168 f., 214, 255
συστέλλειν   2, 4 f., 28, 43, 52, 65 f., 79 f., 85, 89, 91, 98, 157 f., 174, 177, 183, 214 f., 222, 238

τείνω see ἐκτείνω
τάσις   261
τόνος   31, 87, 99, 133, 136, 171, 173–5, 188, 224, 230, 244, 249, 261

φωνή   6–11, 27, 65, 87, 99, 149, 157, 172 f., 184, 244, 261

χρῆσις   131, 193, 214, 232, 243

ψευδαττικοί   120, 252 f.
ψιλός, ψιλοῦν   101 f., 122, 131, 139, 141 f., 164, 172 f., 202

www.ingramcontent.com/pod-product-compliance
Lightning Source LLC
Chambersburg PA
CBHW030606230426
43661CB00053B/1865